1972

This book may be kept

ORIGINS OF ASTROLOGY

Jack Lindsay

ORIGINS OF
ASTROLOGY

BARNES & NOBLE, Inc.
NEW YORK
PUBLISHERS & BOOKSELLERS SINCE 1873

First published in Great Britain in 1971 by
Frederick Muller Ltd., Fleet Street, London, E.C.4
First published in the United States in 1971 by
Barnes & Noble, Inc.
New York, N.Y. 10003

ISBN: 389 04118 1

Printed and bound in Great Britain

Contents

Illustrations

To
Robert and Gunvor Leeson

Another world of power and light
revolving in darkness with no flaw:
our world reflected in the skies
in patterns of freedom and of fate:
we lifted up our stolen eyes
and lavished all our love and awe
on the giddy contradictory sight.

The earth was dwarfed by cliffs of space;
a slavish toy of starry kings
it hung below the regular rings,
the harmonies of circling law.
The wheeling heavens were contracted
to our small body's involved design;
we felt ourselves in turn extend
pneumatically from end to end;
the prickling stars were drops of sweat
on our huge bodies expanding still,
galactic, nebulous, compacted,
which nothing less than all could fill.

Exalted and crusht by what we saw
and the dire entanglement of things:
upon our back the enormous weight
of the whole curving universe,
but also the great upswinging wings
that bore us up against the storm
of matter bursting into form.
We sought with patient anxiety
and diagrams of eternity
to trace the promise and the threat,
to break or loosen the tightening curse.

This drama still is being enacted;
this conflict's not resolved as yet,
though the terms change. We still are far
from being able to realise
our simple kinship with a star.

Jack Lindsay

Author's Note

I have written this book as a companion-piece to go with my work on the Origins of Alchemy in Graeco-Roman Egypt. As such it is part of the larger series of books which I began with *Daily Life in Roman Egypt* and which seek to use the papyri as the basis for a picture of the culture of Egypt in Ptolemaic and Roman times. True, Egypt does not play such a large part here as it did in the story of Alchemy; Mesopotamia must be given the credit for founding astronomy and its fellow astrology. Still Graeco-Roman Egypt had enough to do with the following development for the work not to be wholly out of place in the series. I have at no point conceived the books to be strictly limited to events or developments in Egypt; I have more and more found that one must seek and be aware of the more ancient Egyptian roots of many elements in the Graeco-Roman scene; and I have felt all along that, while making Egypt the main theme, I could continually use it also for throwing light onto other areas of ancient culture. Thus one can begin to do something like justice to the abundant material which makes Graeco-Roman Egypt unique in ancient history.

J.L.

I

Babylonian Bases

Astrology arose in Babylonia, but it needed to fuse with Greek mathematics before it could make a decisive advance. The Babylonians created the basis on which the Greeks carried out their great astronomic researches, and so we must thoroughly understand what they did before we can estimate the Greek contribution. Any ancient society with a well-organised priesthood was likely to study the stars and accumulate astronomic data, both for religious reasons and through the need to work out calendaric systems which in turn had their religious basis. The Egyptians collected a certain amount of star-lore; and civilisations like the Incan, the Mayan, and the Mexican, which never emerged from a stone-age level, still had complex calendars with remarkable observations and computations behind them. But the Babylonians went further than any of these others. At first their results were crude; but at least by the Assyrian period we see a strong movement towards mathematical description, and by the last three centuries B.C. the priests had worked out a stable mathematical theory of lunar planetary motions.

To explain this advance, stress has often been laid on the clarity of the Babylonian sky. "The Egyptians and Babylonians," said Cicero, "reside in vast plains where no mountains obstruct their view of the entire hemisphere, and so they have applied themselves mainly to that kind of divination called astrology."[1] But the nearness to the desert also meant that sandstorms were common and blotted out the phenomena close to the horizon, with which the observers were most concerned. What they were looking for were the moments when the moon rose on the western skyline or set in the east, when the various planets rose and set; and "opposition" of a planet was defined, it seems, as rising or setting at sunrise or sunset respectively.[2] The landscape made only occultations and eclipses easy to note. Hence Ptolemaios later

1

remarked that lists of eclipses were to be had for a period of some 900 years (from about 747 B.C. in the reign of Nabonassar) while there was no such reliable material about planets.

The collection of observations about the stars, the weather, any sky-phenomena, was linked with the general search for omens and their interpretation. Before the invention of the Zodiac there were no horoscopes; there was only an omen-technique dealing with the sky and stars. But we must examine certain aspects of the whole attitude to omens and how they were treated, or we cannot grasp the general background of Babylonian sky-lore. Like all ancient peoples, the Babylonians felt that signs and omens lurked all around them; the unknown, the spirit world, was continually intruding and revealing itself in any event or phenomenon in the least out of the ordinary. Thus tables deal with omens such as scorpions in a house, various aspects of the sky and the weather, happenings in the city, bites of horses, asses, or other creatures, the birth of lions, smoke and fire coming from burnt offerings, the making of coffins, bird-flutterings, things occurring to the king as he drove his chariot, and the condition of his bow, dreams, the colours and deposits of rivers, foundations, walls and other parts of a house, events in the fields, the relations of man and wife, monstrous or odd births. "When a woman bears a child with small ears, the house will fall into ruin." Men noted the colour and condition of hair, water, the ears of a sick man, the behaviour of dogs.

When a yellow dog enters a palace, there will be destruction in its gates. When a piebald dog enters, that palace [the king] will make peace with its enemies. When a dog enters and someone kills it, the palace will enjoy an abundance of peace. When a dog enters and lies on a bed, no man will capture the palace. When a dog enters and lies on a throne, the palace will be in sore straits. When a dog enters a temple, the gods will show no mercy to the land. When a white dog enters, the temple's foundation will be established. When a black dog enters, its foundations will not be established.[3]

One omen tells of the results to a houseowner "if a pig is seen to enter his house with palmfibres in its mouth". Oddly, this tradition seems to have lingered on into Dickens' *Old Curiosity Shop,* where we hear of Mr Swiveller: "He also observed that while standing by the post at the street corner, he had observed a pig with a straw in his mouth issuing out of the tobacco-shop, from which appearance he argued that another fine week for ducks was approaching and that rain would certainly ensue."[4]

But the Babylonians linked their anxious scrutiny of the world with an intellectual curiosity, a search for comprehensive meanings, which in the end transformed omen-systems into science.

As an example of sky-omens we may take this, probably of the seventh century.

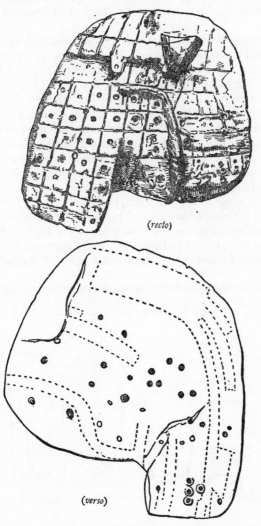

(recto)

(verso)

Fig. 1. Clay liver (in British Museum): both sides

When on the 1st of month Nisàn the rising sun appears red like a torch, white clouds rise from it and the wind blows from the east, then there will be a solar eclipse on the 28th or 29th day of the month, the king will die that very month, and his son will ascend the throne.[5]

Eclipses were considered as specially dangerous moments. From the archives of Nineveh we meet:

To my Lord the King of All Countries [Assurbanipal] from your servant Bel-u . . . May the gods Bel, Nabu, and Shamash bless your Majesty.

If an eclipse occurs but is not observed in the capital, such an eclipse is considered not to have happened. The capital means the city in which the king is staying. Now there were clouds everywhere; we thus do not know whether the eclipse occurred or not. The Lord of All Kings should write to Assur and to all cities such as Babylon, Nippur, Uruk, and Borsippa. Possibly it was observed in these cities . . . I have already written everything to your Majesty about the portent of an eclipse that happened in the months Adarru and Nisannu. And as to the apotropaic rites for the eclipse that are already performed, what harm can be done [even if there was none]? It is profitable to perform the rites. The King then should not send [the ritual experts] away.

The Great Gods who live in the city of your Majesty have covered up the sky and not shown the eclipse. That is what the King should know; that this eclipse has no relation to your Majesty or his Country. On this account the King should be happy. PS: If the stormgod Adad thunders in the month of Nisannu, the small-barley crop will lessen.[6]

The cities mentioned are clearly those with organised astronomers.

To the King, my Lord [Assurbanipal] your servant Adad-shumi-usur.

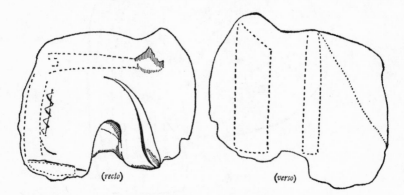

(recto)   *(verso)*

Fig. 2. Clay liver: Boghaz-Keui

Good health to your Majesty. May the gods Ashur, Sin, Shamash, Bel, Nabu, and Nergal bless your Majesty many times.

The Sun did not have an eclipse. It let [the computed event] go by. The planet Venus will reach the constellation Virgin; the heliacal rising of the planet Mercury is near; there will be hard rain and the stormgod Adad will thunder, your Majesty should know. Nobody has reminded [the King] of Arad-Gula, a servant of your Majesty; he is dying of a broken heart. It is in your Majesty's power to bestow grace [?]. Your Majesty is one who has granted mercy to many people.[7]

We should think it would be perilous for astrologers to give such definite predictions about deaths, as in the first excerpt; and the plea in the second report shows a confidence in their status and role. A third report—to Eserhaddon—shows how the kings consulted the astrologers on rather intimate matters. Here Eserhaddon has asked whether it was propitious for the crown-prince to come before him; and if the prince had twenty men as retinue, should they all come in or only the prince by himself?

I answer: They should appear together only in audience. It is excellent: this is the month of Abu and it has many favourable days. I am dancing with joy. It's an extremely propitious time for appearing in audience before your Majesty. Your Majesty will then be looked on by all the great gods. The shadow cast by your Majesty is favourable beyond anything.[8]

Nabu-ahhe-eriba wrote to the same king on a day of eclipse.

Good health to your Majesty. As this is a day of darkness, I did not send the customary blessings. The eclipse of the moon moved from the eastern quadrant and settled over the whole western quadrant of the moon. The planets Jupiter and Venus were visible during the eclipse until it cleared. This is propitious for your Majesty and evil for the Westland. Tomorrow I'll send your Majesty a tablet for dealing with the eclipses of the moon.[9]

The king inquired, "Is there anything in the sky that you have noted?" Balasi replied, "I am very watchful, and who am I that I would not have reported to the king if I had seen anything? But nothing has appeared above the horizon. I have observed nothing." An eclipse of which the king had spoken did not occur. Still, "this is the month to observe the sun. Twice we will watch it: on 26th month Arahshamnu and 26th month Kislimu." On the 27th he would again report. In a PS he added that the king "has abandoned me. I am deeply upset. I have no report to make."[10]

The same man in another letter mentioned that the king had written about an omen, apparently not from the stars, perhaps from a liver. "What is the meaning of: The King will come to nought together with his powerful officials?" Balasi explained, "Experts must be put to work. Predictions in omens depend on the month of the year. So one is not like another; they take their meanings from their contexts. [Here] the omen's prediction does not mean: He will come to nought. As for the recent earthquake, there is nothing to it." Still, the relevant ritual connected with the god Ea should be performed. "There were no earthquakes in the times of the King's Father, and even of his Grandfather, and I myself am too young to have experienced earthquakes. But

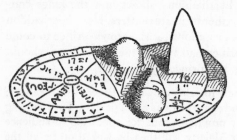

Fig. 3. Bronze liver from Placentia: tablet of intestinal patterns

this god [Ea] has given the King a warning. The King should pray to the god with uplifted hands and recite the [apotropaic] *namburbi*-ritual, and, I say, the evil will be averted."[11]

We have a letter from an observer Kuddurri to his brother Bel-rimanni. 'A cloud appeared just when I was observing [the moon]. Did the eclipse take place? Please send me an exact report. Find out what [prayers] are to be said. Write down your considered opinion. Send me an exact report as to the finances [?] of Zerutu."[12]

Behind the theory and practice of omens there was gathering a strong sense of the correspondences or connections within the universe, especially a link of heaven and earth. The earthly phenomena were in some sense a reflection or repetition of the heavenly ones. We can perhaps see an early expression of these ideas in the myth which tells of the universe being created out of the body of the primeval monster Tiamat. (She and Apsu were two kinds of primeval Water, merged into a single body.) Marduk, her defeater, divided the body into two parts, heaven and earth.[13] There are worldwide myths of creation as the separation of two primal parents; a sophisticated version appears in Egypt where Geb, the prostrate Earthgod, is separated by Shu, the Airgod, from Nut, the arching-over Sky-goddess. But the image of the two split halves suggests more an equivalence of heaven and earth than that of two separated figures. Again the *ziqqarat* as a mount or tower, binding heaven and earth, and providing a way of ascent, belongs to a worldwide series of world-poles, mounts, or trees, and has close affinities with the pyramid of Egypt. But it has been argued

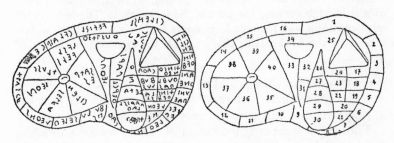

Fig. 4. Bronze liver from Placentia with inscriptions and their order

that the *ziqqarat* early developed a far richer complex of correspondence-ideas than the pyramid did, and that already Sumerian thought showed a well-ordered synthesis between heavenly and earthly things. The temple at *ziqqarat*-top brought out this point, being a link between heaven and earth, gods and men. For the *ziqqarat* was the embodiment of the bustling life of the city, not a single ruler's power-lust, as the pyramid was.[14]

Something of all this appears in the account of how Gudea, ruler of Lagash, steward or *ensi* of the god Ningursu, was told in a dream to build a temple. He saw a gigantic man with a divine crown, winged like a big bird, his body tailing off in a floodwave; to his right and left lay lions. This giant gave Gudea orders. Then day broke on the horizon. A woman appeared and razed a building plot; in her hand was a gold stylus and a clay-tablet on which were set down the constellations of the stars, which she studied. Then came a warrior with a tablet of lapis-lazuli, on which he sketched a building's plan. Awakening, Gudea went to a smaller town where the goddess Nabshe, skilled in dream-interpretation, had her shrine. She told him the winged man was Ningursu; the Daylight was Gudea's personal god, who would be active all over the world and bring success to the trade-expeditions sent for materials; the Goddess was determining the star under which it would be propitious to start the work; the Plan was that of the temple:[15]

The sun that rose for you out of the horizon is your god Ningishzida; like the sun he rose for you out of the horizon. The maiden who made . . . on the head held a tablet-reed of shining silver in the hand, placed a star-tablet on the knee, takes counsel with it—this is surely my sister Nidaba, to build the house in accordance with the holy stars, she had called you. Next a hero—he crooked the arm, held a lapis-lazuli block— this is Nindub drawing the plan of the house on it. The holy basket planted before you, the holy brickmould set straight, the brick of fate placed on the brickmould; this is surely the enduring brickwork of Eninnu.

Here then we have the link of an enterprise with a star-moment; and though we must not press the point, we can say that the earthly structure imitates a heavenly counterpart.

Further, we meet early the notion of correspondences invading spells and incantations. A man warding off sorcery from his body cries, "I am Heaven and you cannot touch me; I am Earth, you cannot bewitch me." Another apotropaic spell identifies each part of the body with a deity:

Enlil is my Head, my Face is the Day.
Urash, peerless god, is the protecting spirit that guides my way.
My Neck is the Necklace of the goddess Ninlil.
My two Arms are the sickle of the Moon in the west.
My Fingers, Tamarisk, bone of the gods of heaven.
They ward from my body the embrace of all sorceries.
The gods Lugal-edinna and Latarak are my Breast and Knees.
Muhra, my everwandering Feet.[16]

These are only momentary unions, brought about by the spell; but the system of thought is nonetheless instructive. Also, in texts from the Kassite era (second half of the second millennium B.C.) as well as from Assyrian and Seleukid times, we find objects such as minerals or plants identified with various gods. "Copper is Ea. Lead is Ninmah . . . The cypress is Adad . . . The god

Sakkut in midst of the ponds. The god Silakku in the ruins. The god Equrum in the leg-muscles." And so on.[17]

For long the most important way of finding and reading omens was by scrutiny of the entrails of sacrificed animals, especially the liver; and since the whole approach to the problem of grasping and understanding phenomena was strongly coloured by the liver-examinations, we need to look in some detail at the method

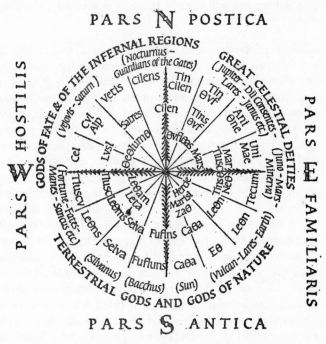

Fig. 5. The Etruscan division of the sacred place or *templum*

and theory. In general the *haruspex* (to use the Roman name for the Etruscan entrails-diviner) analysed his findings in terms of a set of strict categories; the presence, or absence, of certain factors; the situation, right, left, high, low; the state, good, bad, dry, moist; the dimension, normal, abnormal, large, small; the position, upright, bent, and so on; the colour, clear, dark, black, red, yellow-green, white; the number, single, double, triple. Bent over the liver, lung, or intestine, he took care to note any fortuitous mark.[18]

Thus, in a treatise on liver-scrutiny we read:

Length [of observed element]: Success. Mobility: success. Freedom: success. Going-right: enemy defeat. Abundance: renown. Protuberance: renown. Point: victory. Thickness: force. Amplitude: valour. Bigness: rivalry. Attachment: firm seat . . .
    If the Presence, long, reaches the Road: the Prince will succeed in the undertaken campaign. If the intestinal convolutions are mobile: success. If the Bitter [biliary vesicle] is pierced from right to left, and its cutting[?] is free: you will succeed against the adversary who's reared against you.

The Akkadian has the same word for *succeed* and *reach*. Such effects reinforced the conviction of interpreting the omen aright; the augural link here, however, lay in the notion of length. No rigid formulas were used. There was a given aspect, but no necessary deduction that applied in all cases. Signs could not be interpreted *a priori*; the generalisation had to come to life in the particular application. And findings could be upset. "With three, the matter changes." That is, two signs might confirm one another, yet a third could demolish or transform the portent.[19] Still, there was devised a list of ten to twenty major signs, the favourable or unfavourable value of which was memorised. If the favourable dominated, the god had said yes to the inquiry; if the unfavourable, no. If the answer was no, one had to give up or try a new consultation, a counter-examination to find how far the god would relent. A fresh approach was tried also if the favourable signs were dubious or not decisive. Already in Old-Babylonian texts we meet a systematic development of omens in cases where the constant (the normal state of the *azygos*, the third lobe of a lamb's lung) enclosed a variable (say, the abnormal presence of a fourth lobe and this lobe's disposition). The anomaly symbolised and announced a social disequilibrium, a conflict among the central powers.[20]
    An Assyrian treatise lists as proper subjects for entrails-observation: "the welfare of a king, arms, a military expedition, a city's capture, a sick man's health, raining of the heavens, accomplishment of wishes." Another list allows a wider range, accepting the concern for "signs favouring the practice of medicine, the fate of patients, childbirth", but adds the usual public issues of "going on a march, capture of a city, audience of a messenger, accomplishment of wishes". The medical element is strong. We

may assume the patients to be of the highest class, who could afford a consultation, but several times is mentioned the meaning of signs when they are found "in the sacrifice of a subject".[21] This phrase means something different from the sacrifice for a great man, a *kabtu*. So the social level of the consulter was one of the many distinctions the diviner had to keep in mind.[22]

Careful note, we saw, was made of any chance-marks, called Desires, anywhere on the biliary vesicle, the Bitter. "If on the right of the middle of the Bitter, is found a Desire, the enemy will take by assault a frontier town; as for the lot of arms, the enemy will be superior." So on, for a Desire on the right of the base, the head, and for desires of a dark colour in the same three places. One on the right of the middle meant that "a priestess has had intercourse with a clerk and does not please her god". Then we get a series for marks on the left. We notice that marks on the right predict a gain for the enemy, those on the left a gain for the consulter. Thus, a mark on the left of the Bitter's head meant "the enemy will demand [literally, desire] a frontier-town, but as for the lot of arms, you will defeat the enemy army"; but a mark on its right meant a defeat by the enemy in the same situation. When the Desire was darkish, the change was linked with a change in the field of reference, which became religious, then political. The information given by the omens did not always refer to the future; it might unveil or put right something hidden or misunderstood.[23]

Sometimes the priest wrote the questions, *tamit*, on a tablet before the sacrifice. The *tamit* were formulas in which the questioner's name had been left blank. A god was invoked: "God Shamash Great Lord reply in all truth to what I ask." (Shamash was the sungod.) Then came the question, with a final formula: "Your Great Divinity knows that: Is it decided in your August Divine Will? Will it be heard?" A clause at times demanded that the diviner, *baru*, commit no error in performing the rite. Most of the texts of this type which we possess deal with matters of State. Another type was that concerned with collecting signs noted during the liver-examination; after each sign came the corresponding presage, always general enough to be easily adapted to fresh cases. What the *baru* sought were analogies, and generally they made up an antithesis—the contrary presage being given with the contrary sign.[24] This type we have already glanced at; but some further examples of both types will help:

If the liver surface surrounds the Bitter in its circumference [if the vesicle does not go past the liver's limits]: oracle of Sargon by virtue of which he marched against Elam, conquered the Elamites by encircling them and cutting off their line of supply.

How the conclusion there is worked out is not hard to see. Again:

Oracle of Sargon who as a result of this presage dominated by arms the whole area of the land of Sabaru that had attacked him.

If the head of the Bitter encloses the lymphatic gland [covers it up] and is surrounded by Weapons: presage of Urumush, the King whom his courtiers killed by striking him with their seals.[25]

The seals at that time were large and heavy. Again we see how a presaging image is developed from the state of the liver: the gland covered by the appearance known as Weapons represents the king surrounded by his murderers.[26]

Fig. 6. Terracotta of Humbaba (Louvre); schematised representation of the face (B.M. terracotta)

We have the catalogue of two collections of liver-texts from Assurbanipal's library with their lists of anomalies and presages.

There is a Place, the Road is double. That on the right crosses that on the left. The enemy will rage with his weapons against those of the prince. . . . A Finger is placed on the right side of the Place: ruin of the army or of the sanctuary.

The left part of the Bitter is closed: your foot crushes the enemy. The lower face of the liver bears lesions on the right: lesion of the head, change of plan of campaign.

And so on. At last we come to the question asked by the king.

He is warring with Nabu-bel-shimati of the Confines of the Sea.

Has he assembled the archers in Elam? Will he go? The warriors, the troops of Assurbanipal, King of Assyria, the Akkadians or the Chaldeans or the Ahlamu who have embraced Assurbanipal's feet, the creation of your hands will they go to give combat, battle, massacre? Will they engage him in pitched battle? Not favourable.

[*Ezib* formula:] Let him go and hold himself in the territory of Elam or in that of his own land. Let him be the cause of fear and of succour. Let him not penetrate into the territory. . . . Asur-dan-in-sharri, reporter of the consultation. The ceremony was carried out in the New Palace (4th Nisan).[27]

Certain priests, for whom the presages were favourable, were chosen.[28]

The collection *Baratu* sets out the full system in ten chapters: (1) the parts of the victim other than the liver, lung, intestines, for instance, the spine, flanks, reins; (2) intestines, especially the spinal colon; (3) the line and zone of the liver, called the (Divine) Presence; (4) another hepatic groove, normally perpendicular to the preceding, called the Road; (5) the Stomachal Face of the liver, with its Crucible, its Fort, its Palace-door (probably the umbilical cut), its Peace (lymphatic vesicule), its Throne-foundation; (6) the Bitter or biliary vesicule, previously called the Shepherd, and which, with the Finger, was from the start the typical part of the sheep's liver; (8) the Weapons and other fortuitous marks; (9) the lung in its various sections; (10) the confrontation, the dialectic of the signs in their relations with one another and with outer circumstances. The *Baratu* was a large work to master; there were also texts of selections, manuals for use in cases of pressing need. And there must have been oral commentaries for learners as well.

Further there were systems of calculation that enabled the diviner to estimate the exact scope of his predictions; texts on the Signs of Contradiction that annulled or reversed other signs; and the Construction of the Bird, a manipulation that seems closely connected with hepatoscopy. Orientation as to left and right was important; and there was a long series of Twin Signs—signs that did not merely go together but combined. Some diviners even sought to study the general appearance and behaviour of a lamb before sacrifice in the hope of discovering there what the torn-out liver would reveal. Finally the gods themselves had to be brought in, so that they were drawn to aid the diviner and somehow be present in the divining process. Short prayers were made at every gesture. Archives show the occasions when the Sargonid kings of the seventh century B.C. consulted the stormgod Adad or the sungod Shamash.[29]

Fig. 7. Cylinder of Nuzi and Assyrian cylinder of tenth century B.C.: in the first, Ashtar, winged, appears in the scene of the antelope's death—note head of already-devoured antelope. The morning star is shown as the little globe on the lion's head

No doubt only a difference in tone or emphasis is to be traced between statements like "There will be epidemics in the country" and "There will be such epidemics that neighbour will not dare to enter a neighbouring house"—or "There will be a flood in the land" and "The stormgod will flood." Illness had come to be considered as not merely due to an attack by demons, but rather as a divine punishment for faults or sins; and so a sign that was rated as good for a healthy man was rated as bad for a sick one. The evil that the latter suffered was taken, it seems, as a preliminary sign, and a sign of contradiction at that. The diviners, we already have noted, were able to speak out where others would have kept silence; they could therefore announce reversals. "The bound will bind the binder." "The wealthy will become poor and the poor wealthy." "A throne will carry away a throne."[30] The paradoxical conciseness of such utterances was to have an important future in prophetic and apocalyptic literature, when, in the Hellenistic and Roman worlds, there were large numbers of people who dreamed passionately of a total social reversal; it was also to play its part in the formulations of astrology and alchemy.

Mesopotamian omen-methods spread over a wide area, as is shown by the finds of liver-representations and the like: in the Mari kingdom, in the Hittite archives, at Alalah, Megiddo (Ugaritic), Hazor, Gibeon. Copies of Babylonian presages have turned up, with or without liver-models, at Nuzi, Susa, Qatna. We also meet local adaptations, in Elam or among the Hittites. Texts discovered at Ugarit imitated Mesopotamian originals (astrologic and hemerologic) and closely followed the Babylonian calendar, though local forms also existed.[31] In Anatolia both the Babylonian type of entrails-scrutiny and divergent forms are found; imported and indigenous methods seem to go on side by side.[32]

The Assyro-Babylonians concentrated on the liver, *kabittu* (from root *kbt*, to be heavy), because they were impressed by its shape, weight, and amount of blood. The Hebrews made the heart and the reins the seat of emotions; the Babylonians looked to the heart, but even more to the liver. Their language abounded in

Fig. 8. Syrian cylinder seal (second millenium B.C.) with dawn-scene in its elaborated form. From left: lion-star menacing; the dog-headed creature ready to salute the sun; the god Ashtart; morning-star; griffin on twisted cloud; bulls of heat ready to change vegetation; fish-sign of Ashtart

metaphors such as "the liver burns" with irritation, "let his heart repose, his liver be at peace". The liver "carried" a man to such and such an action.[33] It was an organ that attracted attention at the cutting open of a victim's body—generally that of a sheep or goatkid. Monuments show the faithful taking a goat to be sacrificed. When it had been immolated and slashed open, the *baru* inspected the liver and adjacent parts. Then the liver was torn away, set on the *baru*'s flat palm, with the biliary vesicle shown and its cul-de-sac turned out.[34] The one clear representation of a liver-inspection is however Etruscan: on a sarcophagus-cover at Volterra we see the *haruspex* holding the liver in his hands.

The face at which the *baru* looked was divided in its lower part into three lobes. A horizontal furrow separated the lower from the upper part, in which was the *lobus caudatus*. On that lobe rose the *processus pyramidalis*—with the *processus papillaris* on the left.[35]

The clay-models show us clearly enough how the *baru* saw it all. A fine example in the British Museum is covered with compartments. On the upper face it is scribbled over with fine writing; on the lower there are lines following the contours of the areas to be examined. The *processus pyramidalis* stands up in pyramidal form. (The little round holes were probably made so that the oven-heat would not break up the clay; they are common on large examples.) On the recto we can make out statements about a siege, the defeat of an enemy army, and so on; on the verso seems a reference to lightning.[36]

Such models were often sent with reports. The word *tertum* designated both the act of taking the presage and the organs themselves or their representation in clay. So the king needed at hand at all times a diviner able to decipher both message and model. If by any chance there was no diviner at court, the correspondent would have to supply the lack. Mukan-nishun wrote to his king, who was absent from Mari: "The diviners have dealt with four lambs and I have had the Presages taken to my Lord. Let my Lord send me a complete report."[37] Bahdi-Lim wrote to Zimri-Lim, "For the troops' safety I have had presages taken, then in accordance with the favourable presages, I have sent the troops. Also I have had these presages to be taken to my Lord and I have sent a diviner to him." Iasmah-Addu sent to his brother the heart of a sacrificed beast, with model, at the same time as an

Fig. 9. Pre-Sargonid cylinder seal from N. Syria: Shor El, horned, orders his servant to kill the lion; door of eastern sky shown where sun comes out; above, moon and stars (end of night) with celestial serpent

interpreter.[38] An Assyrian Sargonid text even admitted, "The Prince lacked lambs for his consultations."[39] When we read of a portent or omen being sent, we may generally assume that a model is meant. For instance: "I have just now sent off a caravan to you," from Shubat-Enlil, "a caravan that brings an oracular response to Qatanum. This caravan you must not take possession of. The men must be allowed to take an omen and . . . write to Terqa that they are to be given ten days' provisions, so that they can reach Qatanum." No liver or heart would last ten days; the men must have been taking a model.[40]

There was certainly a direct relation between Etruscan and Assyrian divination. Take for instance the liver model of clay from Falerii. Here we see perpendicular incisions at the centre of the left lobe, exactly like the *manzazu* (the divine presence) and the *padanu* (the road): the fundamental elements of Babylonian heptascopy. If the Presence lacked, there was no omen. Cuneiform texts set out the four necessary parts: the Presence, the Road, the Bitter, and the Finger (*lobus caudatus*). Each of these get a chapter in the main treatise. All four appear in the Falerian example; but the Placentian model and the cover from Volterra show only the biliary and lymphatic vesicules. We may compare the two Megiddo livers, where already the *lobus caudatus* was shown, not as it actually was and as it was represented on most Mesopotamian models, but in the form of a pyramid. The only question is how the eastern ideas entered Etruria. Phoenicia, Syria, Lydia have been suggested as the sources; but no doubt the clue lies in whatever Anatolian area it was the Etruscans (or a section of them) emigrated from to Italy. Not that liver-omens were unknown to the early Greeks. Calchas in the *Iliad* used them; in the fifth century a priestess, Diotima of Mantinea, was called into Athens to carry out purificatory rites after the great plague; she was depicted holding a liver in her hand and must have used some sort of hepatoscopy to learn the will of the gods; such consultations were traditionally held before battles. However, the link of the Etruscan and Babylonian techniques is too close to be the result of vague general influences; its existence constitutes one of the strongest arguments for connecting with the East an early section of what became the Etruscan people.

We may pause to note how Babylonian terminology was imported into Greece, as we see from such sources as the glossary of Hesychios. We have the following similarities in technical

B

terms: for road, *Padanu, Keleuthos*; for signs of opposition, *Niphu, Antistates*; for twin-signs, UZU.MEŠ.MAŠ. TAB.BA.MEŠ, *Dioskouroi*; for the divine Presence, *Manzazu, Theos*; for river or canal, *Naru, Potamos*; for the great-gate, *Abullu, Pylē* and we may perhaps add for arm or weapon, *Kakku, Machaira*; for filament, *Qu, Desmon.* The Latin terms are less known, but we may note *fissum*, used both for a constituent part of the liver and for fortuitous signs: the Babylonian *pitru* had the same duality.

Fig. 10. Mesopotamian cylinder seal: Shamash rises above the mountains of the eastern horizon; door of heaven is opened with its two guards; cedars of the Forest of Cedars on mountains

A most interesting liver-model is the bronze one from Piacenza (Placentia), derived from the Mesopotamian tradition. The Etruscans had a strongly developed system of heaven-earth correspondences, with orientations and divisions of space given a fundamental importance. We can compare the names of the deities inscribed in the compartments dividing the Placentia liver and those of the deities inhabiting the various partitions of the Etruscan sky as set out by Plinius and Martianus Capella. In this system of spatial divisions we meet the notion of a consecrated place, the *templum* of the Latins, as identified with the heavens. (The place could be a sanctuary, a city, an acropolis, or even the liver of a victim.) Orientation was determined by the four cardinal points joined by two intersecting straight lines: the north-south line called the *cardo* (a word of pre-Latin origin) and the east-west line the *decumanus.* These terms come to us from Roman town-planning, camp-construction, and surveying, and were closely linked with Etrusco-Italic traditions of long standing. An observer placed at the meeting-point of the two lines, with his back to the North, had behind him the space south of the *decumanus*, which was therefore called the Posterior Part. The other half of the circle, facing him, was the Anterior Part. A further partition of space was made along the *cardo*; the eastern half, the Left Part or *familiaris*, was of good omen, while the western half, the Right or *hostilis*, was of ill omen. (The Babylonians too were much concerned with orientations. We find the rule: "What is of the right is mine, what is of the left is the enemy's.") The dome of heaven, thus oriented and quartered, was in turn subdivided into sixteen parts, in which were set the homes of various deities.

This plan appears in the outer ring of the liver with its sixteen compartments and in the inner compartments which seem, though not clearly, to correspond to them. The names of the deities on the liver are certainly similar to those given by Capella for the sixteen sky-regions. The identity is not complete; many centuries have intervened and the tradition has been in part lost or corrupted; the series has some breaks. But we can make out that the great deities, generally favourable, lay in the eastern sectors, especially north-east; the gods of earth and nature lay towards the south; the infernal ones and the gods of fate lay in the western regions, especially north-west, the most inauspicious direction of all. The position of sky-signs (thunder, birdflight, weather-portents) showed what god had brought the sign about and indicated its good or bad aspect. Meaning was further clarified by a complex body of doctrine dealing with a sign's characteristics: shape, colour, lighting-effects, and so on.

Thus the same system operated for sky-signs and for the signs thought to be found on a victim's liver. There was a close connection between the arts of the *fulguriator* and the *haruspex*, the diviner concerned with thunder and lightning, and the one analysing the entrails of victims. Similar rules of orientation and sky-division governed the interpretation of birdflight, as Umbrian sources (the Iguvine tablets) and Latin made clear. Here special stress was laid on the orientation of the observation-point, the augural *templum*.[41]

There can be no doubt then that behind Babylonian and Etruscan omen-practices there was a system of orientations which linked and equated heaven and earth, and the disciplines thus involved made possible the more complex constructions and sense of relationships in astronomy and astrology proper. It is important to realise that behind them in turn lay certain tribal systems which in some form or another can be traced all over the world. There was then nothing peculiar in the underlying ideas and schemes; the originality of the Mesopotamians lay in the use to which they put the tribal systems.

In those systems we find cosmogonic ideas fused with the lay-out of the camp. Thus, the Winnebago tribe of Wisconsin was divided into two exogamous phratries: Those-Above, with birds as clan-totems, and Those-Below, with land and sea-animals as clan-totems. The leading clan of Those-Above was the Thunder-bird, the clan of Peace; in its lodge the tribal chief presided and disputes were settled. The leading clan of Those-Below was the Bear, the clan of War. The dual division of the tribe was reflected in the arrangements of the camp when the men were on the warpath, and in the lay-out of the villages. The animal world was divided into five classes: empyrean, celestial, earthly, aquatic, and subaquatic. This classification, resting on the same principle as did the tribal organisation, was elaborated by the shamans or medicine-men in charge of tribal festivals. Again the Ponkas of the Missouri were a tribe with two moieties, four phratries, nine clans. The camp was circular, with entry generally on the west side. In the first quarter (left of entry) was the phratry of fire; behind it, in the second quarter, the phratry of wind; in the third quarter (right of entry), the phratry of water; behind it the phratry of earth. The Zunis of New Mexico had seven village-wards or phratries based on the four cardinal points, the zenith, nadir, and centre. The North was associated with wind, water, war, and yellow; the South with fire, summer, tillage, and red; the East with frost, autumn, magic, and white; the West with water, spring, peace, and blue. Each section, made up of three clans, was linked with three birds or beasts, except the Centre, which had a single clan and one creature (the macaw).

Among the Aztecs, who had a pictographic script and a solar calendar, we find such systems developed in more sophisticated ways. The year was of 18 months, each of 20 days, plus five additional days (with probably a sixth on leap-years). A month was divided into four pentads (five days), with the first days of each named after rabbit, house, flint, cane. The years were grouped in Knots, Bonds, and Eras: 13 years=1 knot, 4 knots=1 bond, 2 bonds=1 era. A cosmic cycle was made up of 4 eras; it ended in cataclysm and a new start emerged. The successive years in each knot were designated by the four signs mentioned above, in such a way that a given number coincided with a given sign (say Year 13 Flint) only once in 52 years. Further the rabbit was linked with North, black, winter, air; the flint with South, blue, summer, fire; the house with East, white autumn, earth; the cane with West, red, spring, water. To the cardinal points were added zenith and nadir; the universe was divided into three levels: the upper world of gods, the middle one of men, the lower one of the dead. An eternal war was fought out by light and dark, heat and cold, the rising and the setting sun; even the stars were divided into armies of the west and the east; and gladiatorial combats expressed this idea on earth, as also did the two great warrior orders.[42]

We see then that the basis of Babylonian thought about omens in cosmic divisions and correspondences had nothing unusual about it; the same basis can in turn be found in Egypt. What was unique was the extent to which the Mesopotamians, from Sumerian days on, kept on reaffirming and concentrating the inherited ideas on new levels, creating out of them a unified system, which was applied to omens in general and in particular to the victim's liver and to the sky-world with its various phenomena. The four-fold division which we have seen as characteristic of the tribal world was carried on in Babylonia as elsewhere. A poem shows that in the third millennium B.C. the Sumerians had divided the world into four regions. The area covered had become very wide, ranging from the Armenian highlands to the Persian Gulf, from the Iranian highlands to the Mediterranean. Thus the tribal scheme had expanded to deal with something truly like a world-area. On the other hand the astrologer Kritodemos tells us that Romulus divided Rome into four regions after the four elements.

One more aspect of the entrails-omen deserves attention. The Babylonians worked out complex pattern-systems for interpreting the convolutions of the intestines as well as the *templum* of the liver. The diviner examined a piece of determined length. Tablets show designs of the sinuous lines. They depict the typical forms which were likely to be encountered; and each design corresponded to a particular kind of prediction.[43] Further, out of the continuous curves of the entrails a face was composed, bearded and grimacing. On the back of one we read: "If the convolutions of the entrails resemble the head of Humbaba, it's the presage of Sargon, who became master of the land."[44] Humbaba (Humwawa in Sumerian) was a giant, guardian of the cedar-forests of the Amanus in North-West Syria, whom the hero Gilgamesh had to fight. The diviner, gazing into the confused whorls and spirals of the entrails, saw them running together to form the face of the elemental giant.[45]

Humbaba was an important demon, who may have been the prototype of the Greek Medusa. In the epic poem, the first and one of the greatest, he fastens on Gilgamesh a medusa-eye of death; in the Old-Babylonian version he owns *mulimmu*, a sort of devastating magical glint. He was also furnished with seven *pulhatu*, who strengthened him; they seem connected with snakes and so add a further medusa-aspect. On the seal of Shaushshatar,

Fig. II. Scenes of Dusk. Lion-star attacks bull of day, celestial eagle above. Note fish-symbol in the last example (gold cup of Ras Shamra; ivory pyxis, Tell Duweir, fourteenth century B.C.; seal of Ras Shamra)

King of Mitanni (about 1450 B.C.), we see in the top left-hand corner a figure that looks like a prototype of Mithras slaying the bull (as on Roman monuments). Mitannian gods included the Vedic figures Varuna and the Nasaya Twins; Varuna may be here on the left, while the Twins are the pair below wrestling with lions. In the centre a female sphinx rampant (probably a form of Ishtar, perhaps she of Nineveh) holds two lions. A lion forms the lower part of the sphinx-body: this beast seems in Syria an avatar of Ishtar, as in Anatolia it was the sacred creature of Kybele, while in Phoenicia the female lion-sphinx was an emblem of the goddess Ashtart; in any event here is the Lady of the Wildbeasts who appears often in archaic Greek art. In the top of the field is the hairy head of Humbaba.[46]

The killing of the giant is met in the Iron-Age art of North Syria, at Tell Halaf and Charchemish, and on two bronze bowls from Nimrud.[47] Here we see a pair of heroes (Gilgamesh and Enkidu, or a similar pair) forming a symmetrical group with Humbaba, whom they kill with swordblows on the head or neck. A terracotta shows the hero standing on the decapitated head, which is represented as a grinning mask. We also find the head depicted by itself, as a clay-mask in Babylonia, perhaps with apotropaic power. Versions of these grinning clay-masks were carried west to Phoenician colonies such as Tharros, Iviza and Carthage. They must have had some ritual use, perhaps as *oscilla* like those that the Roman vine-planters dedicated to Dionysos and hung on vines. They were also taken to Sparta, where they were found in some numbers in the shrine of Orthia.[48]

As we noted, Humbaba brings us close to one of the main sources of the legend of Perseus: but he also conjures up the gigantic figures who appeared in trance-visions of the Babylonian diviners, especially those induced by staring at bright surfaces. Such figures perhaps corresponded with the *shakkanakkhum* of a Mari liver-model, as they certainly did with the prince or king escorted by a host who came up at the uttering of a spell and who, after due preparations, answered questions.[49] We see that the diviner, staring into the entrails and beholding the face of Humbaba loom up, was in one sense the hero himself confronting the monster whom he defeated not with a *harpē* (a crooked sword) but with

Fig. 12. Scenes of Dawn and of Dusk, on two pastry-moulds of Mari (first half second millenium B.C.). The figure is Ashart, the passing animals represent the daily renewal of the forces

superior knowledge. He is a sort of Gilgamesh or Marduk confronting the forces of chaos and disaster, and reducing them to controllable proportions; by grasping the interconnections of the universe (divine or heavenly, and human or earthly) in a system of vital correspondences, he masters the tremendous pattern.

The Mesopotamians used the same mixture of imaginative reverie and systematic space-division in dealing with the sky as with the entrails of victims. There was nothing unusual in attaching a name to bright and impressive stars, or in grouping several together in some pattern. What was new was the extent to which an anxious and persistent imagination was brought to bear on the earthly or heavenly event. These peoples, says Cumont, "believed, in the complicated patterns of the stars, which gleamed in the night, they could recognise fantastic shapes, of polymorphous monsters, of strange objects of sacred animals, of imaginary personages—some of which still figure in our celestial maps". The powers thus revealed and given significant shapes could be friends or enemies. The stars in their movements, appearances and disappearances seemed to live a life and perhaps a death of their own, involved in obscure but critical combats, chasing one another, linked in battle and in marriage, fleeing and doubling in escape, returning, threatened by a dragon of darkness which could at times devour even the sun.[50]

We may take an example of the way in which such imaginings led to the formation of constellations with mythical characters. The planet Venus was considered by peoples of the ancient East to have the form of a luminous lion roaming the heavens from east to west. At dawn the lion was obliterated: put to death by emissaries of the great god El and cast down into the underworld. He was punished for his pride, his lustre, his height in the firmanent, which made him measure himself against El. This myth appears in the Old Testament in the tale of Lucifer flung down at El's orders by the archangel Michael, whose name means "Who is like El"?[51] At Ras Shamra, Venus as the morning-star was the god Ashtar, with his wife Ashtart as the lioness of evening. It had been imagined, from the third (perhaps even the fourth) millennium B.C., that the star-lion was killed in the west, became the evening-star, and passed under the earth to rise as the morning-star again. The heat of day was represented by a bull, the cool of night by an antelope or a hare. The star-lions devoured these creatures in turn or led them along. They were depicted in time in a mixed form, lions with human heads, or humans with lion heads: but at Ras Shamra they appeared as wholly human, though Ashtar holds in his arms a small lion.

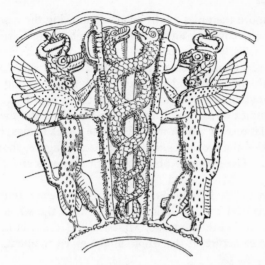

Fig. 13. Figures on a vase of Gudea: the twined snakes and staff between the dragons are sky-supports, distant ancestors of the snakes on the Greek caduceus

   The killing of the night-antelope by the lion-star was shown on Assyrian seals, with Ashtar as a human or as a lion, together with the star. In one case he stands on a lion, who has a small globe-star on his head; in another he appears as a man, wielding the *harpē* and grasping the antelope's hind leg, while the lion attacks from the front. A dagger from Byblos and a vessel from Tell Mardikh show a succession of scenes, the lion about to devour the antelope and himself killed by El's servitor. In these examples the lion is slaughtered ritually by a sword thrust up the anus. On the dagger we see also a Dog, companion of Ashtar and Ashtart, and a Fish, symbol of the goddess. On a Syro-Hittite seal (second millennium B.C.) is found a conglomeration of symbols: the lion-star threatening; a dogheaded creature preparing to salute the sun (an Egyptian motive); Ashtar, the morning-star; a griffin seated on a cloud (shown in twist form); the heat-bulls, one of whom is getting ready to charge against the vegetation; and the fish-symbol (in the same register as clouds and star). On a pre-Sargonic seal from North Syria we see Shor El, horned, who orders his servitor to

kill the lion-star; on the right, the horizon-door through which
the star will come; above, the moon and several stars indicating
the end of the night; and right across the top, the celestial
serpents.[52]

Many more examples might be cited, showing the way in which
these beliefs, covering an area from Egypt to the Caspian, were
depicted. Clearly the peoples who made up such images were
going to see them reflected and figured in the sky. In fact the
figure with the *harpē* and the scene of monster-slaying appeared
in the Babylonian sky-system and was taken over by the Greeks
in the complex of figures grouped round Perseus and the Monster
—constellations for which we still use the Greek names. Perseus in
myth carried the crooked *harpē* of the Ashtar-figure, showing how
directly the Greeks drew on the eastern accounts and patterns.[53]

To return to the Babylonian diviner: he somehow felt the blow
of the sacrificial knife to link the victim with the whole universe
in a sort of lightning-stroke, which made the victim's organs
reflect the structure of the whole at the given moment. The will

Fig. 14. Vase of Gudea's epoch: priests beating a great drum
(Louvre)

of the gods in the heavens was imprinted on the liver or entrails
in a comprehensive pattern. No doubt the diviner would not have
expressed things in quite such definite way; but he came near it
with his conception of the tutelary gods of his omens (under the
Assyrians), Shamash the Sun and Adad of the Storm. Shamash,

all-seeing, read the tablets through their envelopes and inscribed the answering message inside the lamb; the rite established the special relation of Sungod and victim, which created the omen-pattern. All the while indeed the intuition of a unitary process involving both heaven and earth was vitally present, and slowly it grew stronger, playing an essential part in the growth of astronomy-astrology.[54]

We can claim that, partly because of the pressure of these men's anxieties (in which must be included the sense of guilt at the blood-shedding of the sacrifice itself), they learned to scrutinise phenomena in a keen and sustained search for their meanings. The fact that there was a strong vein of fantasy in the thinking, in the concept of causation, does not lessen the fact that they thus evolved powerful intellectual forms for organising the material. Without the fantasies they would have had nowhere to begin, no guiding lines, no creative impulsion. The struggle to read the wills of the gods, the forms of fate, in liver-formations and in sky-phenomena or star-configurations, gave birth to subtle disciplines for dealing with the interconnections of things and of processes, for attempting to grapple with specific events or moments within a generalising system. We can thus note that at the heart of scientific origins there lay the urge to read and understand omens, to realise human destiny by working out the correspondences of man and nature. Without that urge there would have been no science.

As an example of the way in which liver-scrutiny and sky-observation merged we may take a text from the time of Nabonid, who sought to revive the prestige of Ur by appointing a royal priestess for the Moongod according to ancient precedent. The text starts with an eclipse of the moon in the morning watch during the month of Elul, which was taken to mean that the god wanted a priestess. To strengthen and refine the decision the king then turned to sacrifice and obtained another omen. The text here has a number of cross-references and subtleties: thus the word *erishtu* is used both of the omen-feature and the effects it will have, but with different ideograms in each case. The result is a pun of two homonyms in Akkadian, *ereshu* to desire and *erishu* to cultivate. As a parallel with the heavenly omen the two pustules (?) of the gall-bladder are found to be black, one lying over the other: thus referring to the eclipse and to the way in which the god will copulate with the priestess (on top of her)—an idea re-

Fig. 15. The demon Pazuzu (Assyrian bronze, Louvre): an apotropaic spell runs: "I am Pazuzu, son of Hanpu, king of the evil spirits of the air, who come from the mountains, violently, in a fury." Two scribes of Assyrian epoch, one writing on a tablet, one on a parchment

sumed in the final sign for *ereshu*, which suggests the meaning of cultivation. After this confirmation came the two more sacrifices regularly used to define the person who was to be appointed. Evidently the result was "perfect".[55]

We can now return to the question why it was the Mesopotamians who alone so richly developed the fundamental ideas about orientation and correspondences, which we have traced back to early tribal days. The answer must lie in their social and economic history, and has indeed already been suggested in the distinction drawn between *ziqqarat* and pyramid. Here in Mesopotamia were thriving towns with extensive mercantile and industrial activities; there were even certain democratic elements surviving in various degrees, at different times, from the old tribal assembly.[56] There was nothing like the immobility of Egyptian society with its centralised controls. (That immobility was not simple or absolute, but in comparison with the Mesopotamian situation we may speak of it.) At the same time there was a large and stable body of priesthoods able to build up records over the centuries, and these priesthoods were often linked effectively with the economic and political life of the cities. Further, the fact of the area's vulnerability to attack from many sides led to periodic disorders and disasters, with new starts made under new dynasties. There were thus many drastic changes and yet also certain elements of cohesion and stability in the social life. Increase the stability and we get something like the Egyptian world; increase the instability and we get a world in which nothing steady could develop. For millennia the Mesopotamians were able to make on the whole a fruitful combination of stability and instability. They sought to grasp the danger-points through their omen-systems with a theory of vital correspondences between man and nature. The political and magical virtues of those systems may have been illusory; but as a by-product the systems begot science, or rather they brought about the preconditions making science possible.

2

Babylonian Astronomy

For long Babylonian astronomy consisted of the simple accumu-
lation of data with various kinds of collation. Only with the
Assyrian period did mathematical forms of description intrude.
Then, during the last three centuries B.C., there came texts based
on a consistent theory of lunar and planetary motion. These late
texts were of high quality, comparable with Greek work of the
same years; mathematics was lodged firmly in the centre of
astronomical concepts.[1]

The calendar was lunar. When the new crescent was first
visible, the new month began. Hence in the Seleukid era the main
aim of astronomers in their lunar theory was to work out the
evening of this visibility. We know little of the ways in which their
position had been reached; but by now the method had matured
for the reckoning of ephemerides or almanacs. The watchers
wanted to find the exact moment of the conjunction; and most of
the almanacs were devised to answer this problem. The moment
of opposition (of the full moon) also had to be arrived at; but
this needed no new principle. Also the morning of the last visibility
before the conjunction had to be determined. Then, if the moon's
latitude was taken into account, much could be learned as to the
likelihood of an eclipse, and its size. So the watchers tried to work
out the first and last visibility, and to fix eclipses. They did well
in view of the rough mathematical means at hand. To be sure
about eclipses caused them much trouble as they were omitting
an essential part of the situation: parallax.[2]

A text, apparently of the Kassite era, and a few fragments of
the same kind, show something like a picture of the cosmos as
consisting of eight different spheres, starting with that of the
moon. However, this image, if it existed, seems to fade out and no
model of any kind can be distinguished as underlying later
astronomical work. But it is unlikely, in view of the correspondence

30

systems we have traced, that men did not have in mind some sort of model or chart of the skies, which would reflect the lay-out in the maps of the world that were beginning to be made. The same sort of question comes up in connection with other texts, probably of the same period, which show a division of the sky into three zones of twelve sectors each. Each zone has in it the names of constellations and planets, as well as numbers in simple arithmetical progressions. Here is perhaps the first sketch of a scheme that later became important for grasping and describing periodic phenomena, the Zigzag function. But at this point the numbers, simple and schematic, can be variously interpreted; and even if there was some sort of cosmic model at the back of men's minds, it was never effectively objectified and applied as was done by the Greeks.[3]

An early set of texts show the first known records of direct observation in Mesopotamia. Under Hammurapi, in the tablets of Ammisaduqa, we meet the appearances and disappearances of Venus. The records are doubtless connected with omen-systems in which the stars played the same sort of role as the markings and shapes of the sacrificial liver. If so, here is the start of astrology proper, leading on to the fullblown systems of judicial astrology (concerned with State-events and the like) and then on to personal and horoscopic applications.

The Old-Babylonian texts consist of the tablets dealing with Venus and two more works composed in the second millenium B.C.: one from Nippur and the so-called astrolabes, which are lists of 36 stars connected with the twelve months of the year. It is the astrolabes that show the start of a scientific attitude. They try to systematise the information built up about stars appearing at different seasons. Naturally they have their weaknesses; but the essential thing was the start, with all it implied, of new attitudes. Later texts, especially the two tablets of the series mulAPIN (mul means star) modified and improved the system, round about 700 B.C. These tablets summarise the astral knowledge of the period. The first tablet deals with the fixed stars arranged in Three Roads, the middle one being an equatorial belt of some 30° width. The second tablet deals with planets, moon, seasons, length of shadow, and related matters. The Roads or concentric zones consisted of: (1) the Road of Anu, god of the sky above the Pole, where the revolving stars never set; (2) the Road of Enlil, god of the atmosphere—what the Greeks were to call the ecliptic and later the zodiac; and (3) the Road of Ea, god of the deep, down in the celestial ocean. There were also perhaps a series of planispheres, on which were pictured the human and animal designs that came to represent the constellations, but this is uncertain. We see that the Babylonians had arrived at rationally-devised systems for dealing with elementary astronomic facts, though the descriptive method still dominated. About the same time came the systematic reports of observations made to the court. What the sky-phenomena meant had become the main question, though there was no clear distinction drawn between astronomical and meteorological aspects. Clouds and haloes were put in the same sort of category as eclipses; but already it was known that solar eclipses were possible only at the end of the month (new moon), lunar ones in the middle.

We cannot trace in detail the movement into mathematical theory, but it went on slowly in the years 700–500 B.C. Then it began to assert itself. Up to 480 B.C. the intercalations in the lunar calendar showed no regular system; but a century later the rule of seven intercalations in 19 years, at fixed intervals, seems to be in regular use and to provide the basis of all lunar calendars derived from Babylonia.

Intercalations tell us a lot about the levels reached. They imply a grasp of the relation of solar and lunar years: so many moon-months equalling so many solar years in a 19-year cycle—235 moon-months=19 solar years. Before this system was worked out, a year was made up at the end of either twelve or thirteen months, with the state of the harvest no doubt determining whether or not to insert the thirteenth. A more precise idea of the year appears in the cycle and we may assume that the comparison and connection of lunar and solar years was made possible by noting the moment of the summer solstice. Certainly such solstices were regularly computed, while winter solstices were merely added at equal intervals. The 19-year cycle was probably devised well before the Seleukid period, when more accurate methods had become possible.

By 300 B.C., at latest, mathematical astronomy was definitely consolidated. The 19-year cycle had probably come in some time after 450; the fourth century saw the invention of the zodiac; the constellations then used as signs had been known much earlier. It was solely for mathematical reasons that the watchers devised a great circle measuring the progress of sun and planets with

respect to exact 30°-long sections. Indeed the Zodiac was always
a mathematical abstraction used for calculations. Till the end of
the cuneiform period, actual positions were expressed by references to well-known bright stars. Side by side with the determination of positions by degrees and zodiacal signs, the more
primitive method was used in Greek horoscopes of the Roman
period.[4]

We can now look more closely at some of the Babylonian
methods. The first phenomena they sought to master were: (1)
the duration of day and night; (2) the rising and setting of the
moon; and (3) the appearance and disappearance of Venus. In
the Venus-computations (in a copy of the omen-series *Enuma
Anu Enlil*) the star is assumed to be visible for 8 months 5 days,
then unseen for 3 months, after which she reappears as the evening-
star—or during the 7 days when she shows up again as the
morning-star.[5] For computations of day and night we find two
systems. System A, the older (dated probably before 1000 B.C.),
gives the spring equinox as 15 of month XII, the longest day as
15 of III and its proportion to the shortest night as 2 to 1; the
year is divided into 12 months of 30 days each. System B (about
700) gives the spring equinox as 15 of month I; the longest day
is 15 of IV and the proportion of the longest day to the shortest
night is as 3 to 2, though sometimes both proportions are found in
the same text. The 3:2 proportion, closer to the facts, is not used
in computations. The months are now related to a division of the
Zodiac (not yet the later definite circle) into four parts, in each of
which the sun stays three months. Both A and B see the day-
duration waxing for two months, then waning for six, at a constant
rate. From the given proportions of the longest and shortest days,
the duration of any day or night can be reckoned. In the Seleukid
era more accurate rules came in. The constant rate was changed
monthly; near the equinoxes the increase was made faster than
near the solstices; the day-duration was related, not to the schematic year, but to the sun's position in the Zodiac. Along the same
lines the Babylonians devised methods for dealing with other
astronomic variables (such as the moon's latitude or its velocity),
and the Greeks took them over.

As for the moon's rising and setting, the oldest texts assume that
the night before a new moon the moon sets at sunset and is missing
for that night; then on till the fifteenth night the moon is progres-

sively later by a fifteenth-of-the-night in setting; on the fifteenth day she rises at sunset and sets at sunrise; after that she is progressively a fifteenth-of-the-night later in rising, so that on the thirtieth night she rises only with the sun.[6]

For what we called system A we have the fourteenth tablet of the great omen-series, two related texts, and a circular astrolabe.[7] In the last-named the outer ring has a series of numbers for each month: 3;20, 3;40, 4, 3;40, 3;20, 3, 2;40, 2;20, 2, 2;20, 2;40, 3. (The group 3;20 for instance means $3\frac{20}{60}$.) In the middle ring are numbers a half of those: in the inner ring, a quarter. The outer numbers stand for the duration of a daywatch: a third of the day expressed by means of the weight of water that has to be poured into a waterclock at the start of a watch.[8]

The same numbers, multiplied by four, occur in the first part of the fourteenth tablet of *Enuma Anu Enlil*, which deals with *tamartu*, visibility (of the moon.)[9] We find there is a rule: multiply the

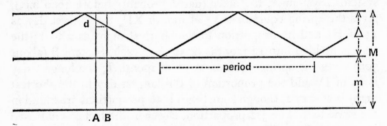

Fig. 16. Graph showing velocity of sun between conjunctions of the moon (with constant increase or decrease) with bounds of the function the maximum M and minimum *m*; the amplitude $\triangle$ =M—*m*; the aim being to determine the period of the function. A linear zigzag function of Neugebuaer's System B (after G. Huxley)

mana of the night-watch by four and you get the *tamartu* of the moon. (*Mana* is a water-measure: 18 *mana*=3 night-watches and 3 day-watches, so that the sum of 1 day-watch and 1 night-watch= 6 *mana*.)[10]

The fundamental unit of time-computations is the uš, 20 of which make 1 *mana*, while 1 uš=60 *gar*=4 minutes. To get the duration of a night-watch in uš we multiply the *mana* by 20. To move from 1 night-watch ($\frac{1}{3}$ of night) to one-fifteenth of the night, we divide by 5; but to multiply by 20 and divide by 5 means multiplying by 4; hence the use of 4 in the texts. They seek to compute a fifteenth of the night so as to find the *tamartu*: that fifteenth is the time of delaying in the moon's setting from the 15th to the 25th. This computation gives rise to an arithmetical progression; but for the last 5 days a geometrical one takes over.[11] In general, however, the older texts start with a simple scheme for the lengthening and shortening of days and nights, and another simple scheme for the rising and setting of the moon; and they work out the arithmetical results in a logical way.[12]

An ivory prism discovered at Nineveh shows that the Babylonians divided day and night into twelve equal parts. Herodotos tells us, "From the Babylonians the Greeks learned *polos* and *gnomon* and the twelve parts of the day." Seasonal hours occurred on the circular astrolabe, found by halving and again halving the three day-watches. These were, as in Greece and Rome, the popular units of time. Astronomers like Ptolemaios used equinoctial hours of equal length, and we have followed them today, and the Babylonian time-units of uš and *beru* (30 uš or 2 hours) were the only ones used in Babylonian texts of Persian and Seleukid times. But the older tests show the popular units, thus an eclipse-omen depends on the night-watch when it occurs. The prism was probably used for converting popular units into *beru* and uš and back again.[13]

Here are some of the texts about the moon or eclipses:

When the Moon reaches the Sun and with it fades out of sight . . . there will be truth in the land and the son will speak the truth with the father. On the 14th the god was seen with the god. . . . When the Moon and Sun are seen with one another on the 14th, then will be silence, the land will be satisfied, the gods intend Akkad for happiness. . . .

When the Moon does not wait for the Sun and disappears, then will be a raging of lions and wolves. . . . On the 15th it was seen with the Sun; afterwards in Tishritu the Moon will complete the day . . . [from Balasi]

With a normal start to the month—the crescent seen for the first time at evening and morning 1·4 days after conjunction—the full moon will fall on the night of the 14th: the average being 14·7 days. On the night of the 13th the moon is not yet full; at sunset she is seen already in the east. Setting before sunrise, she does not wait for the sun. Next night she is seen at sunset and has not set when the sun comes up; she then dims in the west: "the Moon was seen with the Sun". These events, being the usual thing, are favourable; but if she does not wait and the full moon comes later, not till the 15th is she seen with the sun. Now things are disorderly and so forebode trouble.

When the Moon is eclipsed, you shall observe exactly month, day, nightwatch, wind, course, and position of the stars in whose realm the eclipse takes place. You shall indicate the omens relative to its month, day, nightwatch, wind, course, and start . . .
On the 14th an eclipse will take place. It is evil for Elam and Amurru, lucky for the King my Lord. Let the King my Lord rest happy. It will be seen without Venus. To the King my Lord I say: There will be an eclipse. From Irashi-ilu, the King's servant.

If the whole moon was eclipsed the omen applied to all lands; if only a part, then each of the four sides was interpreted in relation to a different region.
By luck we can compare a Babylonian and a Greek record of the same event.

Babylonian. Year 7 Duzu 14 at night $1\frac{2}{3}$ *beru* after sunset an eclipse of the moon visible from start to finish, extending over the northern half of the disk.
Greek. In the 7th hour of Kambyses, in the night after the 17th Egyptian Phamenoth, an hour before midnight, a lunar eclipse was seen at Babylon, extending over half of the diameter from the North.[14]

Ptolemaios no doubt took his account from Hipparchos. But there is a difficulty. If we convert the $1\frac{2}{3}$ *beru* after sunset by means of correct (or more or less correct) tables into hours before midnight, we arrive at 10 hours 20 minutes—more than one and a half equinoctial (or one and three quarter seasonal) hours before midnight, not Ptolemaios' 1 hour. However, if we do the conversion by the prism's rough rules we get a different result. We learn that $\frac{5}{12}$ of the night in Duzu are just $1\frac{2}{3}$ *beru*. So a Babylonian astrologer would convert the time of his report into 5 seasonal hours after sunset or one hour before midnight. In this form the report reached Ptolemaios many centuries later, while the more precise statement remained in Babylonia till its tablet was brought to Europe.[15]
In Seleukid times two different systems (I and II) were used to compute the course of sun and moon. Dating of either is hard, but II may be the older. The texts seem to take I as the work of

Kidinnu (Kidenas in Greek) and II as that of Nabu-Rimanni (Nabourianos in Greek). All moon-tables have one column setting out daylight-duration, expressed in uš. Here both I and II derive the sun's position in the Zodiac (computed in the preceding column)—a big advance on the crude method of making duration depend merely on the month. Also a fair approximation was now achieved by taking the longest daylight duration as ⅗ of the whole day-and-night. The spring equinox was put by I on the Ram 8°; by II on the Ram 10°. Here I was nearer the facts, while II was nearer the ᵐᵘˡAPIN estimate of 15°.[16]

It has been argued that the 10° of II shows a date round 500 B.C. when the solstices were close to that point. However, the Babylonians were not precise in their placing of the solstices; even in Seleukid days they were ready to blink the fact that the seasons differ in length.[17] Both I and II divide the quarter of the Zodiac (between equinox and solstice) into three parts of 30° each, and assume that daylight increases or decreases at a differentrate in each of the three parts. They come fairly near to the facts. Their aim is to reduce the computed time of an eclipse to the time after sunset; and as the astronomic reckoning gives the time after midnight, they need to add half the night to get the sunset-relation.[18]

Now let us turn to the almanacs, which provide for years or even longer periods the positions of moon and planets at regular intervals.[19] A typical moon-almanac includes a column of dates and a list of numbers increasing or decreasing regularly from item to item. The dates deal with mean conjunctions of moon and sun; the numbers tell of the sun's monthly movements—its velocity from one conjunction to another. If we plot out the rise and fall, we get a regular series of points that yield a graph. Thus the astronomers worked out simple procedures for dealing with periodic phenomena. Those of a complex kind were taken to show the superimposition of a simpler pattern of functions; and for the elementary functions the computer used periodic step-functions (or linear zigzag functions). He had learned the use of arithmetical progressions to describe periodically variable quantities.[20]

In all this development we see the Babylonians struggling to find basic recurrent patterns or functions which could be used to reduce complexity to a manageable level. In turn the patterns or functions were felt to reveal a system or order at work in the universe. A new dimension of scientific understanding was opened up, of infinite potentialities. For the first time men had grasped the concept of periodicity with something like a full intellectual comprehension. They were thus able to reduce the multiplicity of phenomena to mathematical expressions and to predict what would happen in the future.[21] The importance of this step can hardly be exaggerated.

The almanacs fall into the two types which we discussed above in connection with computations of the course of sun and moon: I uses the linear zigzag function to explain variations in solar velocity and II takes the velocity to be constant on two complementary arcs of the ecliptic in a certain way—the sun thus seeming to move on alternately slow and fast arcs. Probably there had been considerable progress in Babylonian astronomy in a fairly short time, so that different methods came up. System I was an improvement over II, but was not necessarily later; II might have been devised as a reaction against the complications to which I led. Both systems were being used in the period 250 to 50 B.C. for which almanacs are preserved. (It is noteworthy that in planetary theory a still larger number of methods went on competing together.) No evidence exists to show that I and II had different provenances.[22]

Non-mathematical astronomic texts of the Seleukid period consists of Almanacs, Normal-Star Almanacs, Goal-Year Texts, and Diaries.[23] The Almanacs never mention Normal-Stars; but in N.S. Almanacs and Goal-Year Texts, when a planet passes a Normal-Star, the date and the planet's distance above or below the star is recorded. The diaries give more or less the same information about the Moon as well. In all these texts a zodiacal sign is mentioned only, (a) with a few main points about it, such as its first and last appearances, or in some of the genres, (b) at the entry of a planet into a zodiacal sign or its presence at the start of the month. In the three centuries before the Seleukid era, of the genres mentioned, we meet only Diaries, and these are rare. The earliest Diary, or perhaps we should call it a proto-Diary, is dated 567–566 B.C., and the first that seems to mention zodiacal signs is of 418–417. All Diaries use the Normal-Stars, and the fact that observations of position with regard to such stars went on after the invention of the Zodiac may be due to the inertia of custom or to the higher degree of accuracy they made possible. To realise the Zodiac's potentialities one had to be able to convert the longtitude of a Normal-Star to an expression involving a certain number of degrees inside a zodiacal sign. Hence, perhaps, the compiling of a catalogue of such stars.[24]

This catalogue, perhaps dated in the later Persian era or in Seleukid–Arsakid times, is a fragment dealing with Normal-Stars, a group scattered about the ecliptic belt. We meet among the names: the Loin (of the Lion?); Rear Foot of the Lion; Root of the Barley-Stalk and Bright Star of the Barley-Stalk (both connected with the Virgin); the Southern and the Northern Balance-Pan (both connected with the Balance).[25]

The columns of the almanacs deserve a glance. First came a column of dates (the year of the Seleukid era and the months in order). Next a column (found in System II only) dealing with lunar velocities, with time-degrees as units; it was used to estimate the variable length of the synodic month (with constancy of solar velocity assumed). Then a column dealing with solar velocity (System I): from it was derived a column with longitudes of sun and moon at conjunction or (for full moons) longitudes of the moon, the sun then being $180°$ away.[26] Two columns, with variants, gave the length of day and night according to solar longitude, tackling arithmetically the underlying issue, which is one of spherical trigonometry. Two more columns described variations of lunar velocity and the magnitude of eclipses. The next dealt with variations of lunar velocity. After that came the length of synodic months (solar velocity taken as constant, lunar as variable); then corrections of the preceding column on account of variable solar velocity.[27] Next the algebraic sum of the last two sets gave the length of the synodic month as it resulted from variability of moon and sun. Finally a column gave the dates and moments of all consecutive conjunctions referred to sunset. Thus the scholars had reached the first goal of lunar theory: to know the moments of conjunction and opposition in their relation to sunset or sunrise. The other sections of almanacs dealt with the key-issue: the determination of the evening of first visibility after conjunction, when the new crescent was visible.

We see the high degree of thoroughness with which the scribes worked in compiling their tables. In Systems A and B an important attempt was made to grasp underlying patterns and thus to simplify the mass of materials; but it was in the carrying-out of this kind of theoretical reduction that the weakness lay. However, in all new fields of knowledge it is the first step that is crucial; and the Babylonians made that first step.

We know the names of several court-astrologers of the seventh century B.C.: Asharidu, Bullutu, Balasi, Istar-shumerish, Nabuach-iriba, Nabupshumishku, Nergaleter. Nothing of the same sort is known of Egypt in the same period. The Uruk tablets usually end with a colophon mentioning both owner and scribe. The latter all belong to two families: those of Ekur-zakir and of Sin-leqe-unnini. The scribe is commonly cited as A son of B son of C descendant of N. We can thus work out the family trees, but do not know if we are dealing with real families or with guilds consisting of adopted members—though even if the connections are of guild-members, there would be a very strong tendency for son to follow in father's footsteps. The name of the ancestor often has after it a priestly title, which may apply either to the ancestor or to A, but most likely to the ancestor. Otherwise it is hard to explain why all members of Ekur's family were *mashmash* priests, all of Sin's, *kalu* priests. In one case, however, the ancestor is not qualified, but the scribe is a *kalu* priest of Anu.[28]

The scribe Anu (-abaputer) is called the scribe of Enuma-Anu-Enlil, a reference to the astrological series of that name; so he has been taken as an astrologer. In a few cases owner and scribe are the same person; one scribe is the owner's brother, another his son. We may note the composition of names with Bel, Nabu, Marduk. One text says, "He who worships Bel will protect it" (the tablet). Other texts mention Nanna, Shamash, Marduk. Nabu-iddin-akhi, writing out a list of stars with explanatory remarks, deposited the tablet as a votive offering in the temple of Ezida at Babylon.[29] The colophons often show an anxiety to invoke divine protection on the tablets, with an invocation on the tablet's upper edge as well as sometimes a brief account of the contents and even rules for working out certain parts of the ephemeris. The most complete invocation runs: "According to the command of Anu and Antu may whatever I do go well in my hands, may I be satisfied with its abundance" (from Uruk, year 61 of the Seleukid era). Other Uruk texts end with a prayer: "He who worships Anu and Antu shall not remove it by thievery. Whoever does carry it off, may Adad and Shala carry him off." Such curses suggest that the tablets were coveted by many persons.

Nabu-Rimmani, son of Balatu, known to Strabon, Plinius,

Vettius Valens, may have devised the older moon-system; Kidinnu, the later. The latter's name appears on a colophon in connection with the term *tersitu*, which may mean lunar tablet or system. Certainly both men played important parts in the development of later Babylonian astronomy in its secure establishment as a science.[30]

We learn some interesting things about the scribes and mathematicians from texts dealing with a room or building called the *bit mummu*. Esarhaddon states that at the start of his reign there were signs in heaven favourably ordering him to restore the images of the gods and reconstruct their sanctuaries. After prayers and prostrations he gathered the diviners, *mare baruti*, at the entrance of the *bit mummu* and there consulted the omens. As the signs were good, he brought carpenters, masons, metalworkers, engravers, and other skilled workers into the *bit mummu*, "the place of renewal or restoration", to restore and decorate the images, and to make ornaments for the sanctuaries. A Babylonian text, about the sixth century B.C., shows that the magical animation of the gods' statues also took place in the *bit mummu*; through this ritual the gods were said to be "born". A text from Assur, about 700 B.C., tells how wise craftsmen repaired the damaged statue of a god in the *bit mummu* and brought the god back to life by means of the ritual of mouthwashing and other ceremonies. A bull was also taken in and ritually killed, its skin then used as a small drum—an important instrument in the temples. Further, Narbonidus, on failing to find the old foundation-terrace, *temennu*, of Shamash's sanctuary, collected the elders of the city, the Babylonians, and the wise mathematicians who dwelt in the *bit mummu* and guarded the mystery of the great gods, and ordered them to find the terrace. A Middle-Assyrian contract mentions "a scribe of the [*bit*] *mummu*"; a medical document from Ashur calls up the curse of "Nabu who dwells in the [*bit*] *mummu*" against anyone who removes or hides a tablet; an incantation from Ashur similarly cites the curse of "Nabu and Nisaba, the patron of the *bit mummu*"; and a fragmentary text shows that Nabu's wife, Tashmetum, also dwelt in the place.

We see then both tablets and scribes (including mathematicians) are all closely connected with the *bit mummu*, which was the workshop of the temple and probably consisted of a complex of rooms. Nabu, Tashmetum, and Nisaba were all patron deities of the scribes; and the place was probably connected with Ea, creator of all things, of ordinances and ceremonies, "the god of wisdom, the creator of creation, the fashioner of all things", the god of oracles and incantations, patron of craftsmen and inventor of writing. A catalogue listing works and authors from the library of Ashurbanipal gives Ea as the first author; and in his powers and achievements he resembled both Ptah and Thoth in Egypt. The *bit mummu* was something of a divine or primeval workshop, where a microcosmic reflection of the original act of creation occurred; and the scribes, who included mathematician and astrologer, had a key-part there, since their deities guarded it.

How great was the prestige of the planets under the Assyrians is shown by the preamble of a treaty between Esarhaddon and the Median king Ramataia in 672 B.C.:

In the presence of the planets, Jupiter, Venus, Saturn, Mercury, Mars, Sirius, and in the presence of Assur, Anu, Enlil, Ea, Sin, Shamash, Adad, Marduk, Nabu, Nusku, Urash, Nirgal, Ninlil, Sheru'a, Belet-ilani Mistress of the Gods, Ishtar of Nineveh, Ishtar of Arbela, by all the gods in [the cities of] Assur, Nineveh, Kalah, Arbela, Kakzu, Harran, by all the Gods of Assyria, by all the Gods in Babylon, Borsippa, Nippur, by the gods of Sumer, all of them, by the Gods of the Lands, all of them; by the Gods of Heaven and Earth.

The planets come before all the ancient deities, even the Sun and the Moon. The treaty invokes a whole set of lurid curses on the transgressor of its clauses; the planets may be assumed to hold both scrutinising and punishing powers. In the text, however, it is the gods who are made the agents of justice. Assur is the one "who determines the fates"; Shamash the Sun is judge; Sin the Moon, "who illumines heaven and earth", inflicts leprosy and desolation; Adad, in charge "of the waters of heaven and earth", causes famine. But the planet Venus intrudes among these powerful gods. "Let Venus, most brilliant among the stars, cause your wives to lie in the bosoms of your enemies before your eyes, let your sons not inherit your house . . ."[31]

A textbook, *Appearances of the Planets, Behind You It Will Return,* was composed by Labashi, son of Bel-shar-ibni, in 577 B.C. "Appearance of the god Sin, 27 days the time will return." That is, the moon-cycle is 27 days. "Appearance of the goddess Dilbat, she will return 8 years behind you." That is Venus comes back to the same point every 9 years. But "four days you must subtract, you observe". The precise time is 8 years minus 4 days.

"Mercury [Salbatanu] returns 6 regular years behind you." Mercury is a particularly difficult planet, so Labashi remarks, "Its time you will ascertain, the time of its appearance you will observe." Mars has a cycle of 47 years minus 12 days; Saturn (Kaimanu), 59 years. But "day by day you will observe". As also with Sirius, "the Weapon of the Bow-Star", with its 27-year cycle.[32]

An almanac of 568 B.C. states, "On the 18th of the month, Dilbat was 2° 55′ above the King"—Regulus, the brightest star in the Lion constellation. "Night of the 8th, evening, Sin stood at 6° 15′ under the Balance of the North."[33] For 523 B.C. we find in tables: "Year VII [of Kambyses], Abu 22, the god Mulu-babbar entered before the face of Sherua." Jupiter set with the sun, west of the Virgin constellation. "Ululu 22, behind Sheru'a he makes his appearance." He rose heliacally with the sun, east of the Virgin. "Tebertu 27, before the face of the Balance he stands still"; reached his first turning-point, where he seemed stationary to the eye for four or more days. "Year VIII, Airu 4, in the place of Sherua he stands still," at this second turning-point. "Ululu 4, behind the Balance he enters" the Underworld; he set with the sun. "Year VIII, Simanu 10, the goddess Dilbat entered in the evening into the head of the Lion; Simanu 27, at morning she made her appearance in the place of the Crab." Venus disappeared as evening-star and 16 days later reappeared as morning-star; later she moved from her place in the Tail of the Fish as morning-star, to her position as evening-star in the Chariot. And we meet the eclipses. "Year VII, Duzu night of the 12th, $1\frac{2}{3}$ double hours after night came, Sin was eclipsed, the whole was established, the going-out of the disk went north."[34]

The standard order of the planets in Seleukid texts is Jupiter-Venus-Mercury-Saturn-Mars, whereas the Greek arrangements is Sun-Moon-Saturn-Jupiter-Mars-Venus-Mercury, except where the system depends on an horoscopic moment, on the positions of the bodies at that particular point and space of time. The Greek list is concerned with the relation of the bodies in space; the Babylonian has some other principle—perhaps the linking of Jupiter and Venus as beneficent, Saturn and Mars as malign, with Mercury doubtful: though we have no evidence of this view-point from the texts.[35]

On an astronomical tablet with observations of moon and planets for part of the years 273–272, there have been added notes on the price of grain, dates, etc., movements of the king and city-governors, the prevalence of sickness, and so on. A similar tablet for 232–231 has notes on current prices, the height of the water in the Euphrates, and other such matters.[36] Official reports seem to be regularly made, generally to the king. On the vernal equinox: "on 6 Nizan, the day and night were equal; the day was 6 *beru* [12 hours] and the night was 6 *beru*; may Nabu and Marduk be propitious to the King my Lord." On the Moon: "We kept watch and on the 19th day we saw the Moon. May Nabu and Marduk be propitious to the King my Lord." We find Nabu also writing to the king's son. Ishtar-nadin-apli reported lack of success with the Moon; he was chief of the astronomers of Arbela. "May Marduk and Ishtar of Arbela be propitious to the King my Lord. We kept watch on the 29th day. The sky was cloudy and we did not see the moon. Shabat 1." Mar-Ishtar stated that an expected eclipse of the sun did not take place and corrected a former report of an observation about Jupiter. Nabu-shum-iddina, chief of astronomers at Nineveh, wrote to the Chief Gardener, "May Nabu and Marduk be propitious to the Chief Gardener my Lord. We kept watch for the moon on the 14th day. The moon was eclipsed." The Gardener would be interested because of the belief in the moon's influence on plants.[37]

We noted how the fifth century B.C. saw the introduction of a cyclic system of intercalations. The basic unit was a lunation, the time between two conjunctions of sun and moon, about $29\frac{1}{2}$ days. The lunar month was thus made up of 29 to 30 days; twelve such months (354 days) were some 11 days less than the solar year; the gap became about 33 days after 3 years. So another lunar month had to be inserted to bring the system roughly back to the solar year. More accurate reckonings brought out the fact that 19 solar years has 235 lunar months: 12 years of 12 lunar months each and 7 intercalary lunar years of 13 months each. The result was fairly exact. Only after 310 Julian years the cyclically computed mean new-moons turn up one day too soon. On this basis the Seleukid calendars were worked out, as also the Jewish and Christian religious calendar for Easter. Meton, as we shall see, proposed the cyclic scheme at Athens, but failed to get it taken up.[38]

We must now glance at Babylonian mathematics, which based its number-system on 60—though only in definitely mathematical or astronomical contexts. For matters such as dates, measures of weight, areas, the Babylonians used a mixed system. A key-point of the sexagesimal system lay in its use of place-value notations without concern for the value of the ratio between consecutive units. There was also a decimal system; but in the end the sexagesimal one triumphed, and with it the place-value writing derived from the use of bigger and smaller signs.[39] (It has been argued that the whole development leading from the decimal to the sexagesimal system was already an accomplished fact when the Sumerian numerals were named.[40]) The decimal substratum could still be made out in numbers up to 60. The mathematical texts with their consistent use of a sexagesimal place-value notation created the basis for a mathematical astronomy, which spread to the Greeks, then to the Hindus. The latter contributed the final step: the use of place-value notation also for small decimal units. The Babylonian place-value method had great advantages over the Egyptian way of additive computation with unit fractions, and it was taken over for this reason by all Greek astronomers. Still, the sexagesimal system was not used by its inheritors as strictly as in cuneiform texts of the Seleukid era. Ptolemaios used its place-values only for fractions, not for integers; and so did the Arabs. For this reason our astronomers write integers decimally, but use sexagesimal minutes and seconds.

Babylonian mathematics come down mainly from two periods: (1) under the Hammurapi dynasty (1800–1600 B.C.) and (2) under the Seleukids (last three centuries B.C.). In the second period we find a zero sign in use, and tables, especially of reciprocals, were extensively computed, without any new principles being involved. Already by 1800 B.C. the system of tables was enough advanced to put the Babylonians ahead of all ancient computers.

Between 350 and 400 A.D. Theon Alexandrinus wrote pages of explanations in his commentaries to Ptolemy's sexagesimal computations in the *Almagest*. A scribe of the administration of an estate of a Babylonian temple 2000 years before Theon would have rightly wondered about so many words for such a simple technique. (Neugebauer.)[41]

Old-Babylonian tables deal with such matters as squares and square roots, cubes and cube roots, sums of squares and cubes required to solve special kinds of cubic equations, exponential functions for reckoning compound interest, and so on. Division by irregular numbers is rarely found. The scribes could, however, determine the diagonal of a square from its sides and thus knew Pythagoras' Theorem more than a thousand years before Pythagoras. But they made little use of geometrical ideas in their algebra, in which quadratic equations made up the main group.[42]

3

The First Horoscopes

During the fifth century B.C. there was a tendency to turn to astrological divination for the benefit of the individual. Behind this development there lay the fact that more precise computations had become possible, the invention of the zodiacal circle, and the weakening of astrology's political role under the Persians. Some sections of astrologers remained contemptuous of the petty applications. Strabon tells us that still in his period, the later first century B.C., "There are several classes [tribes] of Chaldean astronomers. Some have the name of Orchenoi, others of Borsipeneoi [citizens of Borsippa], and many others, as if divided into sects who disseminate different tenets on the same subjects. The *mathematikoi* mention some individuals among them, such as Kidenas, Nabourianos, and Soudines. Seleukos of Seleukeia is also a Chaldean and many other remarkable men." He adds, "A settlement is put apart for the local philosophers called Chaldeans, who are chiefly devoted to the study of *astronomia*. Some, not approved of by the rest, profess to understand genethliology or the casting of nativities."[1]

The earlier omen-predictions, we saw, were general or judicial, though individuals appeared in various aspects; e.g., a monstrous or peculiar birth (which however held a warning for the whole land). Personal predictions came up only when someone was caught in an ominous happening: a man digs a well, meets a snake, has a cleft chin, or finds his house infested with brown ants fighting black ones. Small details about a king, such as things that occur to his chariot, are not personal; for the king and his family symbolise the whole land. At some point however the personal aspect definitely detached itself from the public. Already in the latter half of the second millennium we have a Hittite version of a Babylonian omen-text which gives personal predictions according

to the month of a child's birth, a very crude precursor of the
horoscope. A similar Babylonian text exists.[2]

It has been argued that the personal horoscope must be the
work of the Greeks with their more democratic outlook, their
concern for the individual.[3] But though the Greeks finally took
over and developed the horoscope, they did not invent it. We must

The Babylonians did

Fig. 17. Assyrian bronze plaque of an exorcism (Louvre). Winged
monster at back looks over. Four registers: the great gods, the
winged disk of Assur, crescent of Sin, etc., with seven planets; next
seven monsters, then the earth-scene of the sick or dying man with
priests in fish-guise of Ea and genii; below, the underworld, the
goddess Lamashtu, etc.

recall that in the last Persian years Babylon was no longer a capital city with a clergy serving the king; the last Achaimenids did nothing to make it prosper. There had been seditions involving the Chaldean priests. The kings, no longer calling themselves Kings of Babylon, did not come to receive consecration from the hands of the god Marduk. But the priests, still well-endowed, carried on with their studies; they kept the annals of each reign and went on transcribing in cuneiform the old astrological texts and rules as well as religious, scientific, and literary texts. They reproduced the structure of old temples in the new ones. In such a situation it was natural they should to some extent direct the astrological techniques to lesser ends than their predecessors.[4]

As we saw, the preconditions of horoscopal astrology had arrived. What was now needed was the systematic working-out of the supposed qualities and influences of the planets and the zodiacal signs. Possibly a transitional stage appeared when predictions were based on a variety of combinations of the planets, seen or unseen, at the moment of birth.[5] The earliest horoscope seems securely dated 409 B.C., but even if the dating is incorrect we still have abundant evidence of priority for Babylonia, since there are four other texts from the third century. The 410 text runs:

Month Nisan night of 14th [?] . . . son of Shuma-usur, son of Shuma-iddina, descendant of Deke, was born. At that time the Moon was below the Horn of the Scorpion, Jupiter in the Fish, Venus in the Bull, Saturn in the Crab, Mars in the Twins. Mercury, which had set [for the last time] was [still] in[visible].

Month Nisan 1st [day following the 30th of previous month], [the new crescent having been visible for] 28 [uš] [the duration of the moon's visibility after sunrise on] the 14th was 4; 40 [uš]; the 27th was the day-when-the-moon-appeared-for-the-last-time. [Things] will be good for you. Month Du'uz year 12. . . .[6]

The terminology fits in with the very early Seleukid era, and the astronomical material suggests a date round 30 April 409. The Horns of the Scorpion are its Shears (corresponding to the Northern and Southern Pans of the Balance).

The next horoscope is probably for 4 April 263. The personal part reads:

. . . was born . . . love [?] . . . they made. He will be lacking in wealth. . . . His food will not suffice for his hunger[?]. The wealth he had in his youth [?] will not [stay]. His days will be long. His wife whom people

C

will seduce in his presence will . . . [or; his wife, in whose presence people will overpower him, will bring it about . . .] He will have . . .s and women. He will see profit. Between [among or along?] the roads upon wealth he will . . .[7]

The roads may refer to trading ventures. We see that phrases from the old omen- or curse-text are carried on (such as that about the wife), but the techniques are fully astral.

The third text, of 15 December 258, consists wholly of star-data; but that on Aristokrates, dated 3 June 235, tells us:

The Moon set its face from the middle towards the top. If from the middle towards the top it sets its face [there will be] destruction. Jupiter . . . in 180° the Archer. The place of Jupiter means [his life] will be regular, well, he will become rich, he will grow old. His days will be long. Venus in 4° the Bull. The place of Venus means: Wherever he may go, it will be favourable; he will have sons and daughters. Mercury in the Twins with the Sun. The place of Mercury means: the brave one will be first in rank, he will be more important than his brothers. . . .[8]

The subject here has a Greek name; he would no doubt be a citizen of one of the post-Alexander foundations.

The next two texts are of the night of 3 July 230 and of 1 March

Fig. 18. Archer on Assyrian boundary-stone; Archer in Dendera Round Zodiac

142 with no particular points.[9] The series show certain uniformi-ties. All begin with the year, month, and day of birth or conception; in the third the day is absent. Only one, that of 258, gives data for the conception-moment. The planetary order keeps to the standard Seleukid system; and the positions are given in terms of zodiacal signs, one text (for 235) adding the exact number of degrees inside the sign. The date of equinox or solstice nearest to the date of

birth or conception is added only in two texts. Only two give the predictions. There is no mention of the Horoskopos, the zodiacal sign or point rising at the birth-time, or of any of the other secondary positions used in Graeco-Roman astrology.[10]

A text which exemplifies the sort of transitional form mentioned above has passages like these:

If a child is born when the Moon has come forth, [then his life will be] bright, excellent, regular, and long. If a child is born when the Sun has come forth. .... If a child is born when Jupiter has come forth, [then his life will be] regular, well, he will become rich, he will grow old, his days will be long. If a child is born when Saturn has come forth, [then his life will be] dark, obscure, sick and constrained. . . .

But an eclipse makes his life "dark, obscure, not bright". Planetary positions are dealt with: ". . . of the portion of the Ram, in the midst of which the Sun and Moon pass by. I pointed them out to you."

The place of the Ram: death of his family. The place of the Bull: death in battle. The place of the Twins: death in prison. The place of the Crab: death in the ocean, longevity. The place of the Lion: he will grow old, he will be wealthy, secondly the capture of his personal enemy. The place of the Virgin: he will be rich, anger. . . .

The characters of the planets are already much like those they hold in later astrology. "If a child is born when Venus comes forth and Jupiter has set, his wife will be stronger than he." Also, though we are not shown the precise purpose, a sign of the Zodiac is divided into 12 equal parts, forming a micro-zodiac, to which are assigned the same names and sequences of those of the signs themselves. We see both the operation of the micro-macrocosmic idea and the ingenious methods of refinement and subdivisions which were to rule in horoscopic astrology.[11]

The text seems then to support strongly the Babylonian origin of the Greek system of *dodekatemoria* (twelfth-parts), by means of which the astrologer, taking (say) the latitude of the moon at a given moment, computed as astrologically valid the different longitudes. With the two different latitudes of the moon he could make twice as many predictions. The matter may be put also in this way: If we assume that a point A of a zodiacal sign is *sigma* degrees from the start of the sign, then with A is associated as its *dodekatemoron* a second point B which is 12 times *sigma* away from A.[12]

How the Zodiac was devised we have no detailed knowledge; but it certainly was the work of Babylonians. In their area alone existed the preconditions and the needs leading up to it. The Greeks used the zodiacal signs for two purposes. Firstly they built up systems, as explained by Aratos, to tell the time at night. Noting that approximately six signs came up in any one night, they saw that the time at which each rose was a 6th of the night (2 night hours) after the previous sign. So, by counting the risings, they could make out the numbers of hours passed since sunset. Aratos mentions a number of stars that rose at the same time as the signs, which could be used if the exact limits of a sign was not known or if clouds or mountains obscured a part of the sky. This

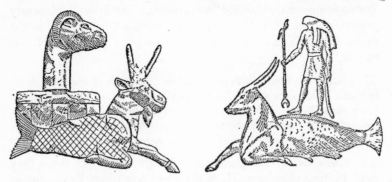

Fig. 19. Goatfish on boundary-stone and at Dendera

method arose in Babylonia and was connected with the division of night-and-day into 12 seasonal hours.[13] Secondly, the Greeks used zodiacal schemes in calendars: the division of the year into 12 artificial months representing the time taken by the sun in each sign. This system was already implied by 700 B.C. in mulAPIN. There are 12 signs because there are 12 months; the signs have to be equal in length in order to obtain months of equal duration; they were divided into 30 as each month was supposed to have 30 days.[14] Already in the so-called Astrolabe Lists (1100 B.C. or earlier) there was some correspondence noted between the months and constellations. The lists allotted every month three stars or constellations. But the system was imperfectly worked out and several constellations did not rise in the associated month. However, by 700 B.C. things were very different.[15]

The symbols have a long prehistory. In the twelfth century

B.C., on a *stēlē* of Nebuchadnezzar I, the Lightning-Bull of Adad and the Scorpion of Ishara appear on the bottom register, with Turtle and Lamp. The four emblems have been taken to stand for the seasons: Bull—Spring, Scorpion—Autumn, Turtle—Winter, Lamp—Summer. At the top of the relief, from left to right, we see a Serpent, the Star of Ishtar (goddess of fertility), the Crescent Moon with serpent-head above it; and on the right the solar sphere of Shamash. The motion of the Serpent shows a progression upwards and to the right.[16] The *Enuma Elish* states that Marduk "created stations for the great gods; the stars their likenesses, the signs of the zodiac, he set up. He determined the year, defined the divisions. For each of the twelve months he set up three constellations." This part of the epic cannot go back to the days of Hammurapi; it must be a revision made at a much later time. But it does seem likely that such constellations as the Bull and the Scorpion, easy to make out, were correlated roughly with spring and autumn equinoxes long before the Zodiac was invented.[17]

Take the Serpent in the Nebuchadnezzar *stēlē*. Among the many creatures gathered round the god or goddess of the planet Venus, as symbols or attributes, the serpents were among the

Fig. 20. Mesopotamian water-pouring god; Aquarius at Dendera

oldest.[18] They go back to the fourth millennium on Iranian stamps. They were still found on the pendants of Ras Shamra and on Egyptian *stēlai* of the New Kingdom, though reduced in size.[19] Ashtart had from one to four serpents; and these attendants were certainly linked with some constellation that could be imagined as serpentine.[20] In one representation the upper section depicts the heavens with the symbols of gods below; right at the top climbs a vast serpent beside Sun, Moon, and planet. Venus must traverse or come near this constellation, from which presages were drawn. Only in one early case (about 3000 B.C.) do we know of the serpent playing a mythical part; he was sent to kill the morning-star lion.[21] In a suggestive relief on a New Kingdom *stēlē* we see Ashtart (here called Qadeshet and described as Beloved-of-Ptah); she holds two serpents and two lotuses, standing on a lion, which is marked with a St-Andrew's-Cross as emblem of the planet Venus; six globes, symbolising six planets, surround her. She herself is the seventh planet, Venus, and probably the artist took the solar disk over her headgear to be another star-globe. She is offering immortality.[22] The general idea was in accord with Egyptian belief; for the Pyramid Texts have the celestial serpent, *Kbhwt*, who also gives the food of immortal life.

I am bound for the Field of Life, the abode of Re in the firmament, I have found the Celestial Serpent, the daughter of Anubis, who met me with these four *nmst*-jars of hers with which the heart of the great god was refreshed on that day of awakening, and she refreshes with them my heart for me for life; she cleanses me, she censes me.[23]

Kbhwt seems derived from *Kbhw*, firmament. Later we find the Greeks setting serpents in the constellations.

In mulAPIN the first tablet cites the "constellations in the path of the Moon" and names them thus in order:

The Hair-Brush [Pleiades]; the Bull of Anu [the Bull]; Anu's True Shepherd [Orion]; the Old Man [Perseus]; *gamlu* Sickle Sword or Harpē [Auriga]; the Great Twins [the Twins]; Al.Lul [Prokyon or Crab]; Lion or Lioness [Lion]; Furrow [Spica]; Balance [Balance]; Scorpion [Scorpion]; Archer(?) [Archer]; Goatfish [Capricorn]; Great Star or Giant(?) [Aquarius]; the Tails [Fishes]; the Great Swallow [Piscis S.W. with *epsilon pegasi*]; the Goddess Anunitum [Piscis N.E. with middle part of Andromeda]; Hireling [Ram].[24]

The text states that not only the Moon but also the Sun and other planets move in the moon path defined by these constellations.

All the constellations here given are of the zodiacal belt except
Orion, Pegasus, Auriga. These latter were perhaps added as
paranatellonta (companions or simultaneously rising stars) for
Ram and Bull. In astrological texts Perseus is said to rise with the
Ram, and Auriga and Orion with the Bull.[25] (In connection with
the patterns later taken by Perseus and his associated figures in
the Greek sky, it is of interest to note that, in the text cited above
as transitional to horoscopes proper, we find: "When the star
[which became *eta pegasi*] comes forth, [he will die] the death of
his fate. [When the constellations round *nu andromedae*] comes
forth, death [caused] by a snake . . . [When *beta per*] *sei* comes forth
death by a we [apon?]."")
    We cannot begin to realise how the preconditions for the
Zodiac developed in Babylonia when we note how the system of
36 stars arose. When the calendar was unified and names given
to the months, the scribes linked these names with the risings
of stars (long observed for practical reasons, for instance in
farming lore). The formula for what happened is given, as we
saw, in the *Epic of Creation*: "Marduk fixed three stars (or constellations) for each month of the year." We have three copies of
the list of these 36 stars; these are the "astrolabes", which the
scribes named *The Three Stars Each*. We find the stars set out in
three groups, twelve in each: those of the outer ring called the
Stars of Ea, those of the middle ring Stars of Anu, those of the
inner ring Stars of Enlil. Those of Anu were thought to stand
near the equator with those of Ea to their south, those of Enlil to
their north. One text (about 1000 B.C.) of Assur included a commentary on the stars' relative positions, their rising and setting,
their farming significance, their mythology. Two texts give 12
Stars of Elam, 12 of Akkad, 12 of Amurru; their basis must be
ancient, since these three names correspond to the political
situation in Old-Babylonian times. Such a division seems more
primitive than that according to zones parallel with the equator.
It may also represent the bringing together of three different
regional ideas as to which stars best indicated the seasons: perhaps
the work of scribes under Hammurapi with his unification of
local gods into one pantheon, of local calendars into a central
calendar, and his codification of the laws. Marduk appears twice
in this system, under different names, no doubt to assert his
importance. One of these stars, which occurs for the first time in
the two lists, is ^mul^*nibirum*:

The red star, which, when the stars of the night have finished, stays where the southwind comes from, halves the sky and stays there, is the god *nibiru*, Marduk. (Astrolabe B.)[26]

In [mul]APIN *nibiru* is identified with *sag.-me.gar* (Jupiter). The 36 heliacally-rising stars in that text represent a halfway-stage between the astrolabes and the Chaldean dekans described by Diodoros in the last century B.C.; for already among them we find eleven of the twelve zodiacal constellations (*suhurmašu*, Capricorn, is missing). These constellations now have no connection with the zones of Ea, Anu, and Enlil, but their link with the Zodiac is not yet established. Still, the second tablet of [mul]APIN shows the solar year divided into twelve months, during which the sun dwells in different parts of the sky: "From XII 1 till II 30 the sun is in the path of these of Anu: wind and storm," and so on. The scribes knew that the sun moves in an oblique circle, passing through the zodiacal constellations—the circle being divided by the zones of Ea, Anu, Enlil, into four equal sections, in each of which the sun stayed three months.

According to this zodiacal scheme, the equinoxes and solstices must be in the middle of the months I, IV, VII, and X. Now, this is just what [mul]APIN asserts, once in the first tablet and twice in the second. . . .

But to these twelve months there was as yet no corresponding twelve parts of the ecliptic, or at least the text does not mention them. Thus, the zodiacal scheme was imperfect; the solar year was divided into twelve parts, but the zodiac only into four parts. In order to establish a perfect correspondence, the four parts of the zodiac had further to be divided into three parts each, of equal length. . . .

This division was actually effected some time afterward. It gave rise to the twelve *zodiacal signs*. (Van Waerden.)

Later texts increase or decrease the number of stars and constellations. New star-groups were named to make planetary positions in the belt; more exact and names were given to single stars.[27] The list of zodiacal constellations, for reasons which we have examined, was limited to 12.[28] Older texts had begun the year with the Pleiades, but by [mul]APIN the first sign was the Ram. The signs at the outset (as in early Greek astronomy) were connected, not with the equinoxes, but with fixed stars, which were easy to find, while the equinoxes were not so easy to determine. Also the zodiacal signs were devised to coincide approximately with constellations from which they took their names and to fit in fairly well with the civil calendar. The equinoxes did not relate at all to such aims.[29]

On the other hand Greek geometrical astronomy had to concern itself with equinoxes and solstices, which determined the points at which the fundamental circles of the sphere intersected, and which were required for all computations and constructions. The Babylonians took for granted that the lengths of the astronomical seasons were equal, and so, satisfied with rough estimates for equinox and solstice, they did not discover precession.[30]

Much argument has gone on as to whether an observation-text dated from year 6 of Dareios II (420–419 B.C.) refers to the Zodiac proper. Many scholars have seen it as holding a clear reference to zodiacal signs, not merely to zodiacal constellations.

Nisanni. Jupiter and Venus at the beginning of the Twins, Mars in the Lion, Saturn in the Fish. 29th day: Mercury's evening setting in the Bull. *Addaru 2.* Jupiter at the beginning of the Crab, Venus in the Ram, Saturn, Mars and Mercury invisible.

Others have argued that the texts seem rather to mention planets as "behind" or "in front of" the alleged signs, and that the signs

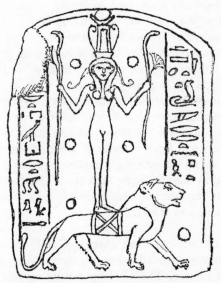

Fig. 21. Goddess Ashtart (here called Quadeshet) on a funerary *stèle* (Berlin Museum); she holds two snakes and two lotuses; the cross on the lion is a sign of the planet Venus; the six globes are the six planets, she herself the seventh (Venus)

may be in fact ecliptical constellations, not zodiacal. However, by this time the Zodiac must have been worked out.[31]

Diodoros tells us that the 12 stars in the Zodiac, with the 12 stars north and the 12 stars south of it, were all considered as gods by the Chaldeans, gods who controlled and oversaw all events in heaven and earth. The cuneiform texts show that the stars were indeed worshipped as gods; and three magical texts lay down the need to repeat the names of the zodiacal signs a number of times for certain results. Diodoros also says that these signs had 30 subordinate gods called Councillors. (There is perhaps a connection here with the dekans and the 30 brilliant stars of Ptolemaios.) Every ten days one of the Councillors, like a messenger, *angelos*, went down from on high to inform the overseers of the underworld of what was happening, while another left the lower world to go aloft. The earth was seen as shaped like a boat. Of the 24 stars to north and south of the Zodiac, the visible ones were concerned with the living, the unseen ones with the dead. The five planets (apart from the Sun and the Moon) were the Interpreters, who by their position, character, affinities, even colours, gave the clues to the secrets of the skies.[32]

The world-system thus had a strong correspondence with earthly politics. We meet an interlinking series of powers with Saturn in dominance (attributed to the Sun); one power can at times check another; at other times it joins with others in doing good or evil, without any hope of control or rejoinder from lesser beings. There is an imposing hierarchy with its functionaries, interpreters, judges, councillors, messengers, serving as intermediaries between the supreme gods and their empire of the world. The astrologer in one sense stood outside this system of uncontrollable powers and fates, a mere observer: in another sense he was right in its midst, gaining a sense of power by his fancied insights, the only human being who could rise to something like the level of the star-forces by his knowledge, his struggle to manipulate the mechanism of fate.

In the next chapter we shall discuss Greek contacts. For the moment we may go on with the emergence of Babylonian astrologers in Greek history. The Chaldeans were said to have warned Dareios III, "The Persian will fall to those whose arms he has copied"—that is, to the Greeks whose war-methods he had imitated. Here we clearly have a tale made up after the event to please the Greeks, whether the Chaldeans or the Greeks invented it.[33] The relations of Alexander the Great and the Chaldeans were soon good. He wanted the priestly caste on his side; they, who, as we saw, had no strong reasons to be loyal to the Persians, were ready to put their powers at his disposal. The texts often refer to them as mages, which had become a somewhat omnibus term for diviners and magicians.[34]

A popular tale showed Alexander circumventing the astrologers. When he was about 300 stades from Babylon, says Diodoros, "the so-called Chaldeans, who have the highest reputation for astrology, being accustomed to predict the future on the basis of age-old observations, chose from their midst the oldest and most experienced men. They knew through the prophecy [*manteia*] of the stars that the king's death would occur in Babylon, and instructed the delegates to reveal his danger to him and urge him not to enter the city at all, no matter from what direction. He might however escape the danger if he rebuilt the Tomb of Belos destroyed by the Persians and then approached the city on the planned route." He suspected, we are told, that they merely wanted to stop him from interfering with their activities in Babylon; so he changed his route and entered from the west. However, he left them unharmed, "having proved the falsity of the prophecy of the Chaldeans".[35] This tale provided a favourite theme for declamation in the class-rooms well into the Roman Empire. It seems invented to prove the superior rationality of the Greeks; but in fact the Chaldeans had the last word, since Alexander did die in Babylon, though later, in June 323.

He had favoured the Babylonian priests. He sacrificed in their city according to the rites they prescribed; and as he set out for India he ordered the restoration of Bel's temple. When he died, he left the priesthoods well-disposed. Despite Babylon's weakened position, he decided to make it the centre of his Asian provinces; no doubt he was thinking of the past and felt that the title of King of Babylon conferred on him in eastern eyes the right to a universal empire. He seems to have been impressed by the surviving luxury, the fine gardens, the whole ancient atmosphere of the place, and also perhaps by the triumphal reception he had received.[36]

His successors in the area had different ideas. Seleukos founded Seleukeia on the Tigris, using materials from Babylon and drawing on that city for inhabitants.[37] He and the other kings, like

Alexander, were offered many prophecies, several by astrologers. Thus, Antigonos at the outset of his struggles with Seleukos Nikanor was pleased when the latter fled to Ptolemy I, but the Chaldeans told him that Seleukos, if let slip, would gain all Asia and would kill him in battle. "Although Antigonos was accustomed," says Diodoros, "to despise prophecies of this sort on other occasions, now he was not a little troubled, as he was disturbed by the reputation of these men, who were thought to own a great deal of experience and to make the most exact observations from the stars." If the astrologers indeed intruded on this occasion, as they may well have done in their anxiety to impress the new rulers, Seleukos must have thought of them when he saw Antigonos' body on the battlefield in 301.[38]

He is said to have consulted astrologers when founding his Seleukeia. The Chaldeans could not but have been jealous of this foundation, which did in time bring about a complete desertion of the old metropolis.[39] When Seleukos asked for an auspicious hour on which to carry out the foundation-rites, they decided to trick him and gave him an unlucky hour for the cornerstone. But, roused by some impulse of enthusiasm, the workers began to build before the hour and thus saved the situation. Appian says, "The heralds tried to stop the workers but failed . . . Seleukos, troubled, again inquired of the mages about his city and they after gaining a promise of impunity, replied: That which is fated, King, neither man nor city can change; for there is a fate for cities as for men." This tale, which belongs to a type favouring astrologic claims, may have been made up to explain why the astrologers were unable to prevent the new town being built.[40]

For another city built by Seleukos, Antioch, we possess a much later horoscope; the foundation-date given is 22 May, 300 B.C. By the end of the Hellenistic era the casting of city-horoscopes was common, and is attested by Cicero and Ploutarch.[41] There have survived the birth-calculations of Constantinople, Alexandreia, Gaza, Caesarea, Neapolis (Palestine); but these were probably composed after the places were built. Hellenistic coins of Syrian cities and mints such as Alexandreia show planetary and zodiacal symbolism.[42]

The pattern of the story about Seleukeia appears in reverse in the story which grew up of Alexander's birth. The *Romance* tells us that as his mother Olympias was about to give birth, the astrologer Nektanebos stood by her, observing the heavenly bodies and from time to time begging her to hold back till an auspicious hour arrived. Not till he saw a certain splendour in the sky and knew that all the heavenly bodies were in a favourable position did he permit her to produce the child. When he said, "Queen, you will now give birth to a ruler of the world," the child fell to the ground, the earth quaked, lightnings flashed, thunders roared. We are told that Nektanebos used a tablet made of gold, silver, and acacia wood, to which were fitted three belts. On the outer belt was Zeus, with the 36 dekans about him; on the second the twelve signs of the Zodiac; on the third, the Sun and Moon. He set the tablet on a tripod, then emptied out on it from a small box models of the Seven Stars that were in the belts, and put into the middle belt 8 precious stones, which he arranged in the system of the planets at the birth-moment. Then he told the child's fortune from them.[43]

We also find tagged on to Alexander a tale of how he brought Nektanebos to death. When aged twelve, the prince, to prove the futility of a craft which could not forewarn its practitioner, pushed the old man (his real father in the *Romance*) off a wall. Here we meet a folk tale that turns up more than once in connection with astrologers.[44]

Later we shall deal with men like Soudines and Berosos, who played their part in the direct development of Greek astrology. Soudines was attached to Attalos I of Pergamon as adviser, for instance during his war against the Galatians (about 240 B.C.); he was a Chaldean prophet, *mantis*, and four hundred years later Vettius Valens was using his lunar tables.[45] However, we may note here that many scholars came out of the Mesopotamian area into the Greek world: Dionysios and Isidoros of Charax, geographers; Agathokles of Babylon, historian, and Apollodoros of Artemita, who wrote on the Parthians; Herodikos of Babylon, a grammarian. Such men were doubtless Greeks, but they had grown up in the Eastern environment. Under the Seleukids the scholars went on with their work in institutions at Borsippa, Uruk, Sippara.[46] After the loss of India in about 280 B.C. the Seleukids made Antioch their capital, and the Arsakid inheritors of the Achaimenid role were menacing the Chaldean area. About 140 B.C. the Parthian king took Babylon, which was regained by Antiochos VII of Syria, then lost again to Phraates. Mesopotamia was badly ravaged. Babylon, sacked and burned in 125, went steadily down, though the philhellene Parthians in 109 gave prizes at the Greek gymnasion there. A little later Zachalias of Babylon made a treaty with the Parthians, in which he attributed the fates of men to the influence of gems. The old schools at some towns like Uruk carried on, but the Parthians were not much interested.[47]

4

The Greeks and the East

There is no sign of astronomy proper in Homer or Hesiod; but
in the latter there is much folklore about weather with a certain
amount of practical star-knowledge. He is even said to have
written a poem *Astronomy*. Athenaios says, "And the author of
Astronomy, attributed indeed to Hesiod, always calls the Pleiades
the Peleiades: 'But mortals call them Peleiades.' And again: 'The
stormy Peleiades hide away.'"[1] A scholiast on Pindar cites some
lines that give the names of the Pleiades, and another on Aratos
cites other lines giving the names of the Hyades. Finally the
pseudo-Erathosthenes in his *Katasterisms* lets us know two of
the legends it retailed: how Kallisto became the Bear and Bootes
the Bearward, and how Orion was set in the stars. The poem
then was a collection of legends about persons who became
stars and would seem much later than Hesiod (about 700 B.C.).
However in *Works and Days* there are some authentically early
pieces of starlore. Three times he cites as basis of calculations the
solstices:

> Sixty days after the winter solstice is past
> Zeus completes the time of winter at last.
> The star Arktouros leaves the holy stream
> of Okean and first in the dusk shows his bright gleam . . .
> When the Pleiads, Atlas' daughters, rise up, begin
> your harvest; plough when they're setting once again . . .[2]

The Greeks, especially the farmers and sailors, had a clear enough
idea when certain prominent constellations rose and set, and they
made rough estimates of time based on the solstices. Precise
estimates were not available for at least three centuries more.
Still, the reckonings in the more or less contemporary Babylonian text, mulAPIN, of which the earliest copy is dated 687,
were even less exact than Hesiod.[3] But the systematic compilations

of Mesopotamia cannot in any way be compared with the simple rules of the farmers set down by Hesiod.

Cosmogonic speculations involving the heavenly bodies appeared with Ionian philosophy; but not until the fifth century can Greek mathematical astronomy be said to begin.[4] However, ideas and images from the East had been impacting well before that, even if they did not take firm root in the unprepared soil. Especially from late in the sixth century, when Asianic Greeks and Babylonians were both subjects of the Persians, we must expect something like a steady flow of informations, even if these were imperfect, haphazard, and often misunderstood.[5] Hesiod's world-picture is certainly much influenced by, or based on, the myths of the Near East, such as the Hittite stories of Kumarbi and Ullikummi. Here we need not try to estimate the extent of the borrowings, but we may note how early Greek cosmogonic thought bears many marks of the East. Thus, Pherekydes of Syros (sixth century) says that he taught himself by getting hold of the secret books of the Phoenicians; Philon of Byblos says that he was inspired by the Phoenicians in his account of the god he named Ophioneus (a snakegod) and the Ophionidai. The *Souda* calls his book the *Seven Recesses*, which may be linked with the Babylonian myth of the Descent of Ishtar into the Underworld through a series of Seven Gates. In an Ugaritic text, the goddess Anat visits the god El, who replies to her "in the Seven Chambers, inside the Eight Enclosures".[6] Pherekydes' Recesses, *antra* or *mychoi*, were sections or levels of the cosmos and were assigned to fire, vapour, water, and so on; the whole concept was close to Egyptian or Babylonian cosmic geography. The Recesses were also called abysses or gates, *bothroi* or *pylai*, and revealed the same sort of imagery as Plato's *chasma* of heaven and earth.[7]

As another example of the way that Eastern cosmic imagery was picked up by the Greeks, this time in a misunderstood form, we may take the account in Herodotos, repeated by Plinius, of griffin-gods, guardians of gold, who lived "near the Cavern from which comes the Northwind". A tablet of Ras Shamra tells of Ashtart entering "the Cavern of the House of Mlk". Mlk is the griffin-god, servitor of the goddess (the evening-star or Venus). In Ugaritic mythology the griffins live on the eastern borders of the world, at a place where the stars rise, so that it is natural for the evening-star to visit them. Representations show that in fact the griffin-cave was the rigid vault (*firmamentum*) of the sky. At times the griffins aided the star-lion to devour the antelopes of the night; in daylight they accompanied the Sun and the now-invisible Venus; they often took part in killing the bulls of day. At night they became guardians of the Plant or Tree of Life.[8]

We may note too in passing that *Works and Days* had its Sumerian prototypes, Farmers' Almanacs such as the text starting, "In days of old a Farmer instructed his son", which enables us to follow a full year's activities on the farm, from the inundation of the fields in May or June to the crops twelve months later, newly harvested, as they are winnowed and cleaned. This text is some thousands of years before Hesiod, but such calendars would most likely have gone on being compiled. A brief one dealing with farmwork is inscribed on a limestone plaque from Gezer, Palestine, dated about the second half of the tenth century B.C.[9]

We can briefly summarise the early developments among the Greeks as follows. Herakleitos stressed the idea of periodicity. Parmenides saw the universe as made up of concentric rings or bands of fire, and said it was Necessity that guided the heavens to hold the limits of the stars. Empedokles brought in a strong sense of cyclic and circular movements. The Pythagoreans did much to have the sphere accepted as the typical astronomical shape; to Empedokles' notions of circular movement they added the concept of a definite centre of rotation; they saw the stars as divine; and they introduced schemes of numerical and proportional relations as fundamental. The atomists Leukippos and Demokritos, carrying on the idea of the vortex from Empedokles, emphasised the notion of matter as made up of atoms of various geometrical shapes. At the same time practical knowledge of the stars was accumulating and to some extent being correlated with astronomic ideas, as shown by the development of the *parapegmata* or astronomical calendars: they were stone or wooden tablets, on which an almanac was engraved. Each day was originally represented by a hole beside that part of the text which gave the prognostication for its date; a moveable peg was stuck in and daily moved on. Fragments of four stone examples from Miletos and elsewhere have been found, the earliest of the second century B.C. The entry for a day was like this: "Day 26: summer solstice, Orion rises in the morning, a south wind blows." But they were known and used by the later fifth century; for Demokritos wrote a book *Parapegma*, and the calendar attached to the work of Geminos uses him as a source.

One good pointer as to astronomical information flowing in is to be found in the names adopted for zodiacal constellations, which the Greeks took over in the sixth century, if not even earlier, with little change. The Cretan sage-shaman Epimenides (about 600) is said to have mentioned Capricorn.[10] Then near the end of the sixth century Kleostratos, of Tenedos, an island near Troy, tried to determine the solstices by observing successive sunrises behind Mt. Ida; according to Plinius he also distinguished the zodiacal constellations. To him is further attributed an *oktaeteris* or eight-year lunar-solar cycle.[11] A similar cycle began under the Persians in 527. Kleostratos may have heard of the Eastern developments and tried to introduce them into Greece,[12] but it is very likely that he has had far more achievements listed under his name than was in fact the case. We have to be thoroughly sceptical of the tales told about early Greek thinkers. For instance there can be no basis for the accounts of Thales of Miletos in the sixth century predicting an eclipse of the sun. (It is not clear whether he was Milesian by birth or Phoenician; Herodotos calls him a Milesian of Phoenician descent.) Commentators have argued that he learned how to make his prediction from Babylonia; Herodotos merely says that he foretold the year of the eclipse. At this time the Babylonians could not themselves make reliable predictions of such events, which are not visible at regular intervals from any one point on the earth's surface. To foretell them presupposes accurate observations involving accurate time-measurements; even Hipparchos in the second century could not guarantee to be more correct than a quarter of a day in solstitial computations. Further, Thales' prediction would have meant the use of a fixed calendaric scheme and a knowledge of the solar year's length: neither of which factors existed in Greece till Meton and Euktemon.[13]

The solar eclipse in question is said to have ended a war between Lydians and Medes, who stopped fighting in dismay on the Halys River. Perhaps the eclipse did occur and had this effect, and then later the story about Thales was invented to glorify him, like the anecdote that he foresaw the fall of meteors. The suggestion that with the use of Babylonian materials he prophesied a lunar, not a solar, eclipse, has little to recommend it: more likely, garbled accounts of Babylonian powers of prediction had filtered through, and the Greeks wanted to show that they too had their prophets.[14]

The Babylonian tables for solar eclipses were computed like those for lunar eclipses, but with no extra column allowing for parallax for quantities depending on the sizes of bodies and their distance from the earth. So it was possible to say that a solar eclipse would not occur or that it might, but not that it would. This was the position in the last three centuries B.C.; before that there was even less likelihood of a correct prediction.[15] It has been suggested that Thales used an old lunar cycle of 18 years 11 days (233 moon-months) in which both lunar and solar eclipses repeated themselves in roughly the same positions, a cycle which he learned from the Babylonians,[16] but the latter did not themselves use such cycles to foretell solar eclipses, which they calculated from observations of the moon's latutide made shortly before the expected syzygies. In any event even today there is no cycle for solar eclipses visible at a given place.[17]

Greek writers, handed on by Plinius, said that Anaximandros discovered the obliqueness of the sun's circle. Others said that Oinopides found out "the engirdlement, *diazōsis*, of the Zodiac", or that he stole the idea of the oblique circle from Pythagoras. Certainly there was no idea in the sixth century that the sun and moon moved in oblique circles, though during the fifth century glimmerings of the Zodiac crept in. The Greek Zodiac was not the result of a slow long evolution, but was introduced all at once. Not till about 400 do we find a clear use of it by Euktemon and Eudoxos in calendars, and Eudoxos in his *Phainomena* used the division of the ecliptic into twelve equal signs.[18]

Once the idea of systematic investigation got through to the Greeks there was certainly large-scale borrowings from the East. What is obscure is the way that research was carried out and organised, how results were communicated, and so on. There was nothing like the priestly institutions of Mesopotamia or the Museum of later Alexandreia. We have already noted some of the points taken over, for example the methods for computing variables such as the moon's velocity or latitude. The rules for the moon's rising and setting that we examined reappear in nearly the same form in Plinius and Vettius Valens; they were linked with a Greek method of determining the time during the night by observing the rising of zodiacal signs.[19] As for the question of the moon's visibility, Vettius Valens again gives a table by which to reckon the setting of the moon on the 1st, 2nd, etc., to the 15th night of the month. The times are stated in seasonal hours and the daily retardation of the setting is just $\frac{4}{5}$ hours (one-fifteenth of the night) as in the Babylonian tables.[20] Plinius states that the daily delay in the moon's setting is *dodrans* and *semiuncia* ($\frac{3}{4}$ and $\frac{1}{24}$ hours). If $\frac{4}{5}$ is expressed as a multiple of the Roman *as* ($\frac{1}{12}$), we get 9 and $\frac{2}{5}$ *as*, to which Plinius' $9\frac{1}{2}$ is a near approximation. His rule thus derives from the same source as Valens' table.[21] The *Geponika* gives another table for dealing with the moon's rising and setting at night, and ascribes it to Zoroaster (to an Iranian or Eastern source); it has been shown that the table was computed by means of Plinius' rule. Further evidence for the Roman use of Babylonian methods for calculating astronomical matters is to be found in the Egyptian planetary texts dating from Augustus to Hadrian.[22]

Again, according to Xenophon, Sokrates told his pupils to learn astronomy only as far as was needed to tell the time from the stars at night: something that could be learned from hunters and sailors. Aratos in his poem shows us what the method was. One noted what part of the Zodiac rose at night, and then could work out how near one was to sunrise, "for with one of the signs Helios himself comes up". Aratos then added a list of stars rising or setting with the signs, the *paranatellonta*.[23] Later these had much importance in astrological calculations; originally they were merely used as aids in telling which signs were above or below the horizon. Aratos' material goes back to Eudoxos, who apparently made use of a wooden stellar sphere; but the astrologic *paranatellonta* were based, not only on the Greek constellations, but also on the Oriental or Barbaric Sphere.[24] Aratos' method implies the Babylonian system which held that six signs were always above the horizon and that each sign was of equal length. A scrutiny of his poem shows that he considered the equinoxes and solstices to lie in the middle of the Ram; he is here in accord with Eudoxos and mulAPIN. Further, the geographical latitude for which the *paranatellonta* of Eudoxos and Aratos were accurate was that of Babylon.[25]

If we consider the old method for calculating the time of the moon's rising and setting we find the logic depends on three assumptions:

(1) the moon's motion in latitude is negligible, (2) the moon moves in the Zodiac at a constant speed in such a way that it needs exactly 30 days to overtake the sun, and (3) equal parts of the Zodiac rise and set in equal times during the night. . . .

I do not know whether the Babylonians were conscious of all the steps of this reasoning. I only wanted to show that the method of the fourteenth tablet of the Great Omen-series and the method of Aratos belong to the same order of ideas, that there is a logical connection between them, and that may be deduced from the same fundmental hypothesis, *viz.*, that equal parts of the zodiac rise and set in equal times during the night. (Van Waerden)[26]

The Greeks were as interested as the Babylonians in simultane-ously rising and setting stars, and for the same reasons; they were drawing on the Babylonian tradition.[27]

They took over from that tradition the notion of time-division by twelves; but it is not quite correct to say, as Herodotos does, that they thus learned to divide the day into twelve. It was the 24-hour period that the Babylonians thus divided. But any mathematical division of the day did not come into use in Greece, even in scientific work, till the late fourth century. Only rough-and-ready terms were used to describe time of day: "early", "at full-market time", "before-market". Or the length of a man's shadow was noted: thus writes Aristophanes:

> All labour and toil to your slaves you'll leave,
> your business will come when the shadow at eve
> is tenfoot-long—and you'll scamper to dinner.[28]

The use of the *gnomon* to tell the time, except perhaps for noon, did not come till the latitude of the place of observation could be taken into account. And there again we touch an inheritance from Babylonia, where it was that scholars first devised the idea of expressing a site's latitude by means of the ratio of the longest and shortest day there.

The Babylonians used the *ziqpu* or pole, an upright split stick, to measure shadow-lengths. Originally this pole was used as a crude transit instrument to make out the north-south orientation of buildings, later to secure the altitude of stars. It was found that the shortest shadow was cast at noon on the summer solstice, the longest at the winter one. A table in ᵐᵘᶫAPIN gives the time at which the shadow of a stick of one cubit reaches the length of 1, 2, or 3 cubits, etc., for different seasons.[29] The assumptions in this table are: (1) the time after sunrise when the shadow is shortened to 1 cubit is 2 *beru* (4 hours) at summer solstice, 3 *beru* (6 hours) at winter solstice, and $2\frac{1}{2}$ *beru* at the equinoxes;

(2) the ratio of *gnomon*-length to shadow-length is proportional to the time after sunrise, so that, when the ratio is 1:2 or 1:3, the time is one-half or one-third of the time in which the ratio is 1:1. The resulting approximation is fairly good in summer, but fails badly in winter when the ratio of *ziqpu* to shadow reaches its highest noon-value long before the 3 *beru* have gone by, and never gets to the value 1:1.

The Babylonians made repeated observations and calculations in the attempt to determine an average. They thus learned that seasons are of unequal length. Their autumn came out only half an hour too short.[30] The use of the pole, linked with observation of the circumpolar stars, led to the idea of the celestial sphere revolving round the earth on the hinge of its axis. *Ziqpu* finally became the name for the theoretical point in the heavens (then close to alpha of the Dragon) round which the heavenly system was found to revolve. These ideas, embryonic among the Babylonians, were to prove very fruitful for the Greeks.[31]

However, the accurate determination of the solstices took a long time. Anaximandros (a Milesian thinker, about 550) is said to have set up a sundial in Sparta.[32] But again if we scrutinise the ancient authorities we see how strong was the tendency to keep on antedating discoveries. Diogenes Laertes merely says that Anaximandros was the first (in Greece) to discover and set up a *gnomon* (here a vertical marker throwing a shadow) of the sort "marking solstices and equinoxes". His phrase describes the *gnomon* without committing himself to a statement as to what Anaximandros did with it. Eusebios goes on to assert that Anaximandros was said to have made more than one *gnomon* so as to distinguish the dates and hours of solstices and (perhaps) equinoxes: the term he uses is *isomeria*, equal-days. The *Souda* then assures us that Anaximandros treated the whole matter on geometrical lines.[33] Modern writers have assumed that he calibrated the ground around his *gnomon* so as to arrive at the time of the day as well as the sun's position on the ecliptic and thus the year's season.[34] But this statement cannot be correct. The observation of *gnomon*-shadows will give only a very crude notion of the time of day unless the *gnomon* is placed so that its axis is parallel to that of the earth, that is, unless the latitude is known. Which in turn implies the clear concept of a spherical earth set in the middle of the celestial sphere. Otherwise the *gnomon* gives only the time of noon and of the solstice to within some five or six days.

Not until the fourth century B.C. did mathematicians deal with the problem of projections on a plane-surface.[35]

But there is more about the *gnomon* to be considered. It seems originally to have been stepped. In *II Kings* and *Isaiah* we hear of a prophet repeating to Hezekiah the message that in response to his prayer his life will be spared and he will live fifteen more years:

And this shall be a sign to you from the Lord that the Lord will do the thing that he has spoken. Behold, I will cause the shadow on the steps, which is gone down on the dial of Ahaz with the sun, to return backward ten steps. So the sun returned ten steps on the dial, on which it was gone down.[36]

Hezekiah was the son of Ahaz, King of Judah, who had appealed in 734 to Tiglath Pileser IV of Assyria (745–727 B.C.) for help against Pekah of Israel and Rezin of Damascus. Ahaz was subject to the Assyrians; he took the silver and gold from the Jerusalem Temple as a gift to Tiglath and made the high priest build a pagan altar there, modelled on one he had seen in Damascus. Perhaps Tiglath gave him the stepped *gnomon*.[37]

The stepped aspect is upheld by the Greek term. *Gnomon* means carpenter's square as well as dial-pointer; it is a geometrical as well as an arithmetical term—the number added to a figurative number to get the next number of the same figure (a step-concept).[38] The stepped *gnomon* in turn suggests the *ziqqarat*, the stepped mount that led up to heaven and may have had seven platforms (later identified with the seven planets). Seven was early a sacred number through its association with the moon. The *ziqqarat* consisted of superimposed cubes made of sundried or burnt brick. The Assyrians carried on the *ziqqarat*-tradition: Sargon II built one at Khorsabad and Nebuchadnezzar reconstructed one at Borsippa in the first quarter of the sixth century B.C. The Pythagoreans had their gnomic or odd numbers and may well have got their ideas from Babylon. Nikomachos of Gerasa in Judaea (about A.D. 100) stated that the "most perfect proportion", consisting of four terms and called "musical", were discovered by the Babylonians and brought by Pythagoras to Greece. This proportion, used by various early Pythagoreans and by Plato in the *Timaios*, is—

$$a : \frac{a+b}{2} = \frac{2ab}{a+b} : b$$

For instance 12:9 as 8:6. The two middle terms are the arithmetic and harmonic means between the extremes.³⁹ Philolaos is said to have called the cube a "geometric" harmony because it has 12 edges, 8 angles, 6 faces; and 8, in harmonics, is the mean between 12 and 6. His system had a close relation to Plato's in the *Timaios*, and it is noteworthy that Plato assigns the form of the cube to the element Earth. It seems likely that these ideas about the "most perfect proportion" and the cube came from Babylonia and entered Greek thought through the early Pythagoreans.

Thus, it is clear that the Babylonians had certain proportions in mind while constructing such large works, so important as cosmic symbols, as the *ziqqarats*; and we get a clue to what they were in a series of numbers (28, 17, 8, 5, 3) out of which the Jabirian alchemical corpus believed the universe to be constructed.⁴⁰ How far did that idea go back? Right to the age of early Pythagorean speculations on numbers, it seems. Take the Pythagorean *gnomon* as set schematically out in the square below:

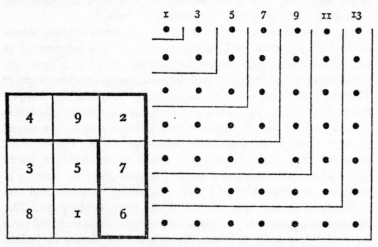

Fig. 22. Two Gnomon figures. Magic square assigned to Saturn and Lead; rectangular figure gained by lay-out of tiles, etc.
(Stapleton)

The *gnomon* consists of the five squares strongly outlined. The total of the five numbers is the *gnomon* 28; the others make up the series 8, 5, 3, 1 (17). Thus we find that the alchemical cosmic numbers are all in the Pythagorean *gnomon* and its magic square (alchemically assigned to Saturn and to Lead).⁴¹

The actual *ziqqarats* seem to have been constructed on the same general system, for instance, that at Borsippa, where we find the ratios 13:11:9:7. For a seven-stepped *ziqqarat* the areas of any face of each cube would be in proportion to the series of odd numbers 1, 3, 5, 7, 9, 11, 13. The sum of these numbers, 49, was the square of the sacred 7. And if we take the simple figures for the platforms, 1 to 7, we get a total of 28 or 4 × 7, the second perfect number. We can juggle with these numbers much further; but one point more may be made.[42] In a wall made of cubic bricks as in a floor made of square tiles, the Babylonians, with their keen eye for correspondences, could not but have noted that in every group of 4 bricks or tiles, one was partially enclosed by the other three; in every square group of 9, the former square of four was partially enclosed by another 5, and so on. The resulting figure, resembling in shape the carpenter's-square, was called *gnomon* in Greek; and the odd totals (3, 5, etc.) of the bricks or tiles needed to complete each new square group were called the *gnomic* numbers. Taking all these facts and conjectures together, we get a strong case for the derivation of the key-ideas of the Pythagoreans about numbers directly or indirectly from Babylonia. The *gnomon* appears as an aspect of the *ziqqarat*, and its connected numbers have a cosmic significance, which leads on to the cosmogonic schemes of Philolaos and Plato. Waterclocks were developed in both Babylonia and Egypt. In Egypt the quantity of water was measured from levels marked on the inside; in Babylonia the water escaping was weighed to the shekel—the talant represented a full day of twelve double-hours.[43]

The Greeks did not distinguish planets from fixed stars till the fifth century, and then only through Babylonian influence.[44] We are told that the Pythagoreans called the Pleiades the Lyre of the Muses and the planets the Hounds of Persephone. We do not know the date when they used these names, but they have an early ring. The term for the planets suggests that they were seen as ranging in the heavens to collect or harry souls. The term *planetes*, wanderer, for a planet, was well known to Plato, who in the *Timaios* expounds a considered planetary theory.

. . . With a view to the generation of Time, the Sun and Moon and five other stars bearing the name of planets came into existence for the preservation and determination of the numbers of Time. And when God had made the bodies of each of them he set them in the orbits along which the revolution of the Other was moving, seven orbits for the seven bodies. The Moon he set in the first circle round the Earth; and the Morning Star [Venus] and the Star described as Sacred to Hermes he set in those circles which move in an orbit equal to the Sun in velocity, but endowed with power that goes contrary to it. So it is that the Sun and the Star of Hermes and the Morning-Star regularly overtake one another and are overtaken by one another.[45]

The World-Soul, he has argued, combines within itself one Circle of the Same and Seven Circles of the Other; the Circle of the Same is that of the Fixed Stars. His system, whatever its weaknesses, is not that of a hesitant pioneer in astronomic fields; it clearly has a considerable development behind it. And yet the literature of the fifth century (for instance the drama) knows nothing of the distinction of planet and fixed-star. Plato's stress on Time suggests Iranian influence—perhaps via the Pythagoreans, perhaps in some more direct way.

Aristotle in his *Meteorology* uses both *planetes* and *planomenos* for planet, and *kyklos*, circle, for the zodiacal ring. In discussing comets he argues against the idea that they were due to the conjunction of two planets, and asserts that some fixed stars have tails. "For this we need not rely on the evidence of the Egyptians who state they have observed it; we also ourselves have done so. One of the stars in the thigh of the Dog has a tail, though a dim one." He goes on to say that Demokritos has declared that stars have been seen to appear at the dissolution of some comets. "This might, on his view, happen, not sometimes, but always. And further the Egyptians say there are conjunctions both of planet with planet, and of planets with fixed-stars [*aplaneis*, non-wandering], and we ourselves have observed the planet Zeus in conjunction with one of the stars in the Twins and hiding it completely, but no comet resulted."[46]

A passage in Simplikios repeats the statement by Eudemos that Anaximandros investigated planetary sizes and distances; but this claim can be disregarded.[47] The report by Diogenes Laertes, citing the edition of Demokritos' *Complete Works* by Thrasyllus, that that thinker wrote a book *On the Planets* is a different matter. Demokritos seems to have had a long life, which carried on well into the fourth century; he certainly knew Babylonian thought and the ideas of the Mages.[48] He may well have learned many ideas of Babylonian astronomy and have set them out in his works, without being in the position to give detailed mathematical expositions. The list of his books published by Thrasyllus, which may be taken to represent the findings of Alexandrian scholarship, has an impressive number of titles dealing with cosmological and astronomic matters:

The Great Diakosmos [Order of the Universe], which the School of Theophrastos attribute to Leukippos; *The Lesser Diakosmos; Kosmographe* [Description of the Universe]; *Causes of Celestial Phenomena; Causes of Phenomena on the Air; The Great Year or Astronomy, Calendar; Contention of the Waterclock [and Heaven]; Description of Heaven; Geography; Description of the Pole; Description of Light-Rays; On Images or on Foreknowledge of the Future.*[49]

Diogenes adds, "Some include as separate items in the list the following works taken from the Notes": *Of the Sacred Writings in Babylon; A Chaldean Treatise* . . . Under mathematical works we find *Ekpetesmata*, which may mean *Projection of an Armillary Sphere on a Plane*. We learn that the *Calendar* dealt with droughts, rains, winds, storms, according to the rising or setting of stars.

Diakosmos (*diakosmēsis*) is an interesting term. We are told by Aristotle and others (Diodoros, Ploutarch, Sextus Empiricus, Porphyrios) that it was the term used by Pythagoreans to define the Orderly Arrangement of the Universe.[50] Among the Stoics it was used to describe the new order arising after one of the periodic world-ends through fire. Perhaps by dealing with a Greater and a Lesser Order-System, or by coming with a treatise to supplement one by Leukippos, Demokritos was setting out the theory of Correspondences, of the Micro-Macrocosm. *The Great Year* may have been a table such as the bronze that Oinopides set up at Olympia; a later example shows that it predicted the movements of sun, moon, the planets, and gave weather-predictions. A cuneiform calendar of this type exists for 425 B.C. Censorinus, centuries later, reporting on these matters, has confused them, and it may even be that Demokritos first mooted the idea of the 19-year Cycle to the Greeks.[51]

His interest in atmospheric questions is witnessed by a passage from Cicero, which follows an account of observations of the Dogstar made in order to foretell "the character of the ensuing season".

Demokritos believed that the ancients had wisely enjoined the inspection of the entrails of animals which had been sacrificed, because by their condition and colour it is possible to determine the salubrity or pestilential state of the atmosphere, and sometimes even what is likely to be the fertility or sterility of the earth.[52]

This comment on entrails-scrutiny brings out the Babylonian colouration of his thought, just as his fascination with *eidola* connects him with the Mages.[53] There is every reason to look to him as the man who did most to popularise Babylonian and other Eastern ideas in the later fifth century and thus lead on to the more purely astronomic attempts to grapple with what could be learned from the Chaldeans. We must not regard him as a practised astronomer who could carry over Babylonian methods as Eudoxos did. Rather he was a great populariser, not without original insights and a bold grasp of the necessary lines on which scientific thought and research were to develop. Avidly interested in ideas and their applications, he was especially keen to learn what he could from the East, and to spread his gains among his fellow-Greeks. Whether he studied in Babylon itself, or picked up his information in various parts of the Greek world into which the Mages, *Magousaioi*, and other Eastern scholars and diviners had penetrated, does not matter.

Thrasyllus, with Alexandrian scholarship behind him, could not have been much in error in his list of attributions; and the works cited above must have covered a wide field of physical, astronomical, meteorological and related fields. What was in them, if not something along the lines I have outlined? Demokritos had the reputation of an encyclopaedic mind and continued to be held in the highest repute; his relation to the alchemic tradition, while raising many difficult problems, makes clear that he was looked on as an adventurous thinker breaking into many new territories. It is more than plausible, then, to consider him the main populariser of such things as the theory of the planets and the Zodiac in ways that diffused the general concepts and made it possible for more specialised scientists like Eudoxos to take up the detailed and mathematical applications. If this conjecture is at all correct, we may assign to him the role of naming many of the constellations or stars in the Greek sky, following Babylonian suggestions but drawing on Greek mythology for the names. Somehow or other during the fifth century, and presumably in the later part of it, this naming process went on. The surprising thing is the speed with which it was carried out and imposed on a world which had no scientific organisation of any kind, neither an ancient one of learned priesthoods like those of Babylonia and Egypt, nor a deliberately built-up one of a university-type such as the later Alexandrian Museum. Fifth-century

Greece was made up of a diverse set of political groups, each clinging to its own autonomies; whom else than Demokritos can we think of with anything like the authoritative position at this time to get a naming system widely accepted? The only figure that seems at all likely is Anaxagoras, but as far as we can judge he seems much more in the line of the old devisers of cosmological hypotheses, aware of certain trends in astronomy but ignorant of such matters as the planets, or the sun's obliquity of course. At least there is no sign of interest or knowledge in such aspects of astronomy in his fragments or the references to his work, though he knew well such matters as the celestial sphere or the moon's borrowing of her light.

It is perhaps significant that the architect Vitruvius (probably of the earlier Augustan years) ends his account of the constellations thus: "I have expounded in accordance with the principles of Democritus, the natural philosopher [*physicus*], the figures of the constellations which are shaped and formed in the firmament, and planned by nature and the divine spirit." This sentence seems to mean that the account is based on that of Demokritos; but it has been argued that the clause about Demokritos refers only to the words "planned by nature and the divine spirit".[54] Either grammatical interpretation is possible, but surely we should expect at the end of the long and eloquent exposition a tribute to its inspirer, not a brief aside on the question of the divine spirit. One of the Stoics, such as Poseidonios, would have been a more natural author to mention if that spirit was the main thing in Vitruvius' mind; not Demokritos, the atomist, whose materialism seems to have afflicted Plato so much that he makes no reference to him anywhere, not even in the *Timaios*.

This does not mean that the passage in Vitruvius is a direct translation from one of the works of Demokritos. It might come rather from someone like Aristarchos, Eratosthenes, Hipparchos or Poseidonios, or from a yet later source. A handbook based on such writers, like Geminos' *Introduction*, is more likely to be in the scope of Vitruvius' reading than the original text of Demokritos—though Geminos himself, of the last century B.C., might be too recent a source. If the source paid a tribute to Demokritos, Vitruvius would feel impelled to do the same. It was characteristic of ancient writers thus to imply or claim that they were using primary sources when in fact they were very far from them. That Vitruvius' source knows of the 360° division of the circle (first noted in the *Anaphorikos* of Hypsikles, probably earlier second century B.C.), is no disproof of these contentions. If we are to take at all literally a passage in Lucretius, Demokritos did know about the zodiacal signs:

> It's likely indeed the truth lies in the judgment,
> revered, of Democritus, that worthy man.
> The nearer the constellations hug the earth,
> the less they're borne along by heaven's vortex.
> Its force's velocity grows less, he says,
> the intensity dwindles in the lower parts,
> and the sun's left slowly behind with the rearward signs,
> for, lower than the burning signs, he moves.
> And even more the moon. The lower her path,
> the further she is from heaven, the nearer swinging
> to earth, the less she keeps up with the signs.

And so on. He seems citing from Demokritos, and the Zodiac plays an integral part in his argument. We can make out vaguely Demokritos' cosmic system from quotations and references. He took the sphere to be the most mobile shape and in his system of the universe he saw the moon as nearest to the earth, then the sun, then the planets (at different distances away), then the fixed stars; the sun and moon were composed of smooth round atoms, which were the constituents alike of fire, the soul substance, and mind (*nous*), and which he equated with the divine. Many of his ideas were close to those of Anaxagoras. If however we had his works, we might find that his views were fused with various Babylonian or magousaian elements.

A decisive point for the entry of Babylonian ideas into Athens appears in the attempt of Meton to introduce the 19-year Cycle into Athens.[55] He and Euktemon are the first firmly-based Greek astronomers, and the date to which we can attach them is 432 B.C. Meton must have been young at that time; for he is said to have feigned madness in order to escape service when the Sicilian Expedition was being prepared (about 415). This tale was however probably invented to suggest that he had prophetic knowledge through the stars of the coming disaster in Sicily. He was jeered at by Aristophanes in the *Clouds* and the *Birds*, though not mentioned by name:

> Will you then now believe in no gods but ours:
> this Chaos and the Clouds and the Tongue—these three?[56]

Phrynichos also satirised him in *The Solitary* (414 B.C.). We do not gain much confidence from the stories about him: that he had his attention drawn to the 19-year Cycle by Phaeinos, an astronomer who observed the solar tropics on Mt. Lykanettos. *Phaeinos* means "shining" and was an epithet of the Sun; it occurs in a

Fig. 23. Cockheaded man on Brading mosaic (Isle of Wight), with griffins and sky-temple (?)

line by Aratos discussing the 19-year Cycle: "The Nineteen Cycles of the Shining Sun". Phaeinos thus appears to be a personification of the Cycle, the Sun who stimulated Meton into his theory.[57]

The Babylonians seem to have used the 19-year Cycle consistently in calendars from about 380 B.C. The discussions about it in Greece, whether initiated by Demokritos or Meton, occurred at least fifty years before that; but it is clear that the question had long been raised in Babylonia where intercalation-rules had been linked with the observation of the heliacal risings of the Dogstar. A papyrus of the second century B.C. states that Euktemon gave the lengths of the astronomical seasons (starting from the summer solstice) as 90, 90, 92, 93 days respectively—the modern figures to the nearest whole days are 92, 89, 90, 94. Euktemon, then, knew of the non-uniformity of the sun's course round the earth. Here is proof that Pythagorean ideas of the spheres were bearing scientific fruit. In ways that we cannot trace, mathematics, observation, and general ideas were fusing.[58]

What is certain is that, in the last three or four of our decades of the fifth century, Greek attention was seriously drawn to Babylonian astronomy, and some of its certain general ideas, with a few particular applications, began to circulate and stir discussion. Further, the Pythagorean image of a spherical earth helped to stimulate the drawing of models and the kind of concepts soon to issue in Plato's *Timaios*, where it is stated that the Demiurge created Sun, Moon, and Planets so that men might grasp the notion of Time. Plato admits however that very little was known about the periods of the planets. The Sun and Moon bring about Night and Day, Month, Year and make their computation possible. But

of the other stars the revolutions have not yet been discovered by men, save for a few out of the many. So they have no names for them, nor do they compute and compare their relative measurements. As a result they are not as a rule aware that the Wanderings [*planai*] of these bodies, which are of wondrous complexity, constitute Time.[59]

The Circle of the Same, with the fixed-stars, has its own motion (that of the celestial equator moving "horizontally to the right", east to west), while the Circle of the Other represents the ecliptic, moving west and east, at an angle to the Same.

Oinopides of Chios, we noted, was another shadowy figure with whom the idea of the Zodiac was associated. Diodoros says he lived in Egypt and learned from the priests about the obliquity of the ecliptic; Ailian makes him the inventor of the 59-year Cycle for bringing lunar and solar years into harmony—while Censorinus makes Philolaos its author.[60] (He seems to have been a Pythagorean; and he had a strong sense of correspondences if we may trust the story that he held the Milky Way to be the sun's original course, from which it was frightened in horror at the spectacle of Thyestes' cannibalistic meal.[61]) Plato mentions him in the introductory picture of *The Lovers*, which gives us an invaluable description of the sort of arguments now going on:

I entered the Grammar School of the teacher Dionysios and saw there the young men who are considered the most handsome in appearance, who come from distinguished families, and their lovers. It happened that two of the youngsters were disputing, but about what, I didn't clearly overhear. They were arguing, however, it seemed, about Anaxagoras or Oinopides. At any rate they appeared to be drawing circles, and they were imitating certain inclinations with their arms, bending to it and taking it most seriously. Then I—for I was sitting by the lover of one of the pair—nudged him with my elbow and asked him whatever it was that had worked the youngsters up so much. I said, "Is it then something great and fine that has made them so zealous?" "Great and fine, indeed," he replied. "Why, these chaps are chattering about the heavenly bodies and indulging in a babble of philosophy."

The inclinations made by the young fellows were meant to depict the ecliptic and so on. They do not unfairly represent the way in which astronomic expositions were being made. About this time a simple rotating globe marked with the chief circles of the celestial sphere and a few constellations was probably being used; but angular distances were most likely still estimated merely by means of a hand stretched out in front of the eye. The persistence of the term *daktylos* (finger or finger's-breadth) in astronomic nomenclature to express the degrees of totality in an eclipse suggests the long use of such a simple method. Twelve *daktyloi* defined a total eclipse.

Someone—Demokritos, I have suggested, perhaps with some aid from Pythagoreans like Philolaos and Oinopides—had managed to fix the nomenclature of the Greek skies. We have seen how the names of some constellations were direct translations from Babylonian. Others, like Capricorn, were modifications—here of Goatfish. The name of the sign Virgin and the star Spica (*absin*) originally meant Furrow; but we find in it ^{mul}APIN as "the corn-ear of the goddess Shala", and a Seleukid text depicts a rather solid Virgin holding a corn-ear to represent *absin*. There is no reason to suspect Greek influence in the image. So Spica (corn-ear) and the Virgin are taken over from Babylon. For the Babylonian Balance the Greeks put the *Chēlai*, the Scorpion's Claws; but ^{mul}APIN already had the Scorpion's Horn as a synonym for the Balance, *zibanitu*. The Tails were closely connected with the Greek Fishes. The Zodiac at Dendera in Egypt and a Babylonian boundary-stone show a winged Centaur with bow; at Dendera the image stands for the Archer constellation while the archer on the stone may be an astral deity or a minor god who was transferred to the sky. The Goatfish, who is found at Dendera and on boundary-stones, was certainly thus transferred before 700 B.C., and no doubt the same fate was met by the Archer. As for Aquarius, we have Old-Babylonian representations of a water-pouring god very like the Waterman of Dendera. The Crab is more obscure, and we do not know why the Hired man turned

D

to the Ram. If he stood for a farmhand, then one of the flock took the place of the shepherd.[62] We also find the names of Babylonian constellations carried over into Greek: thus the Greeks called the Great Bear by a second name, *Amaxa*, Wagon (our Charles' Wain)—the Babylonians called it *Mar-gid-da*, the Long Wagon.

It is true that there are many exceptions to the rule that the Greeks borrowed the names and patterns of constellations from Babylonia; and the evidence from Dendera, for instance, since it belongs to the Roman period, is not conclusive as to the signs. Still, taken by and large, the number of similarities are too great to be accidental and, in the general perspective of the Greek debt to Mesopotamia, the link of the Greek zodiacal signs with the Chaldean may be taken as proved, even as regard the names.

A papyrus from Egypt has a few fragments of what seems an alphabetical glossary (late second or early third century A.D.); it gives us some idea of Mesopotamian terms known to scholars. The compiler shows interest in Skythia, Babylonia, and the region west of the Black Sea (with reference to a writer Glaukos); one passage shows a basis shared with the *Etymologicum Magnum* and Zonaras, another with Photios. Of Chaldean words we meet *mindoloessa, misai,* and *mithorg*. The last named is "a sort of *harmonia* among the Chaldeans"; *mindoloessa* is "an arrangement [*syntaxis*] of numbers"; *misai* deals with "the prognosis of the future" and seems connected with the Sumerian *me-zu,* to divine. (The papyrus also says that Mithras is to be identified with Prometheus.) In view of the shortness of the surviving text the proportion of Mesopotamian terms is high, but we do not know at what date, or by which writers, they were introduced.

We have already noted how certain patterns of struggle in the Babylonian sky (similar to those in Egypt centred round the Bull's Foreleg) seem carried over into the constellations of Perseus, Andromeda, the Monster and so on. A key-area for the Perseus group seems to be Cilicia, Pamphylia, and the regions around, where we find the Perseus cult strongly rooted as well as traditions of a storm-god with the *harpē* or crooked sword. The Babylonians had in their sky the Old Man, Shibu, and nearby the sickle-sword or *gamlu*. The Old Man may lie behind Perseus; for the hero Gilgamesh, who fought the elemental giant Humbaba, had as his original name Bilgamesh, in which *bilga* (or rather *bilaga*) means the Old or Ancient Man.[63] In making this point we are turning back to the Sumerian world, but there is no reason why some sort of Gilgamesh-associations should not cling round Shibu. An important point is that in the Cilician region there had grown up considerable settlements of mages or *magousaioi* who were carrying on a mixture of Babylonian and Iranian traditions and who played a big role in developing the Mithraic cult as known in the Roman Empire.

At last with the fourth century B.C. we reach a firm foundation for Greek developments. The man who made the decisive step was Eudoxos, of Knidos, where his observatory was still extant in the time of Strabon—no doubt a house-roof with perhaps a shed on it. Strabon also says that Eudoxos lived in Egypt thirteen years, and Seneca incorrectly states that it was there he got his knowledge of the planets. Aristotle must be nearer the mark in declaring that he made separate spheres for sun, moon, stars and planets.[64] Diogenes Laertes, who classifies him among the Pythagoreans, tells how, after being a pupil of Plato, he journeyed to Egypt, where he used letters of introduction to Nektanebos and was recommended to the priests.

There he remained one year and four months with his beard and eyebrows shaved, and there, some say, he wrote his *Oktaeteris*. Thence he went to Kyzikos and the Propontis, giving lectures; afterwards he went to the court of Mausolos. At length he returned to Athens, bringing a large number of pupils. Some declare that he did this to annoy Plato, who had originally passed him over. Others say that, when Plato gave a banquet, Eudoxos, owing to the numbers present, introduced the custom of arranging couches in a semicircle. Nikomachos, Aristotle's son, says that he declared Pleasure to be the Good.

He was received in his native city with great honour; the proof is the decree about him. But he also became famous throughout Greece, as legislator for his fellow-citizens, as we learn from Hermippos in Book IV of *On the Seven Sages*, and as the author of astronomical and geometrical treatises and other important works.

He had three daughters, Aktis, Philtis, and Delphis. Eratosthenes in his writings addressed to Baton says that he also composed *Dialogues of Dogs*. Others say that that work was written by Egyptians in their own tongue and that he translated it and published it in Greece. Chrysippos of Knidos, son of Erineus, attended his lectures on the gods, the cosmos and the phenomena of the heavens, while in medicine he was the pupil of Philistion the Sicilian.[65]

Tales of the visits by sages to Egypt or the East always need to

be treated with caution; but Eudoxos does seem to have travelled
to the Nile and also to Sicily. Favorinus says that, while in Egypt
with Chonouphis of Heliopolis, he had his cloak licked by the
sacred bull Apis, so that the priests prophesied he would be
famous but short-lived. Diogenes composed a poem on the occasion:

> At Memphis Eudoxos learned his fate was nigh
> from a Bull with beautiful horns, as men relate.
> How can a Bull use words? No words it spoke.
> No chattering tongue for Apis did Nature devise;
> but standing sideways there, it licked his cloak
> and plainly thus foretold: You soon will die.
> And so, soon after, on him came his fate
> when fifty-three times he'd seen the Pleiads rise.[66]

Perhaps the intention of the anecdote was to suggest that the
Egyptian forms of divination were superior to those of the star-
gazer. Cicero, however, stated that Eudoxos was opposed to
horoscopes. "Now let us consider the prodigies of the Chaldeans.
Eudoxos, a disciple of Plato, and, in the judgment of the greatest
men, the first astronomer of his time, formed the opinion, which
he put into writing, that no credence should be given to the produc-
tions of the Chaldeans, in their calculation of a man's life from the
day of his nativity." Eudoxos may have been referring to the use
of liver-omens or the like; Cicero was unaware that Chaldean in
earlier days meant much more than astrologer. But in view of
Eudoxos' own astral interests, it is extremely likely that he
referred to astrology. That he had a close link with Babylon is
suggested by material associated with his name, which shows
parallels with Mesopotamian omens of thunder, clouds, the
position of the moon's horns, and so on. Greek calendars of the
same type as the Babylonian are also related to him.[67]

We saw that the image of the earth's sphericity had stimulated
the ideas of a spherical sky and of the circular motion of its bodies.
Eudoxos proceeded to work out, not merely suggest or infer, a
mathematically and geometrically based model of the cosmos;
to give a systematic account of the heavens and to grasp the
interrelations of the various circles in the sphere, ecliptic, equator,
tropics, solstitial and equatorial colures.[68]

He discovered the properties of curves, says Apollodoros, who
wrote a *Chronography*. He sought to explain the retrogradations
and find the key in the idea that the motions of sun and moon

combined the uniform motions of two concentric spheres: one in fast daily rotation round the pole of the equator, the other turning slowly in the opposite direction about an inclined axis perpendicular to the ecliptic.[69] He followed the Babylonians in using a fixed Zodiac with twelve signs of equal length firmly linked with the fixed stars. His division differed only one or two degrees from the Babylonian one. Like mulAPIN he assumed that the equinoxes and solstices lay at 15° to the signs: which had been true in 1000 B.C. but was untrue in 300. He also adjusted his globe to a geographical latitude of 30°, corresponding to Babylonia or Phoenicia.[70] But it was not so much any particular doctrine which marks his importance. His greatness as the founder of something like a fully scientific astronomy lay in his grasp of the concept of the celestial sphere and of the need for quantifying the data and treating them mathematically. The new start he gave was intimately bound up with the new bases provided by Platonic thought, and in turn Plato was certainly much affected by him in his later phases. His work, though building on earlier Greek work and decisively continuing its conceptualising and generalising attitudes, was linked with the first full impact of Babylonian ideas and methods which the *Epinomis* recorded.

Much of the spreading of his doctrine was done by Aratos, who embodied it in a poem, *Phainomena*. Born at Soloi in Cilicia,

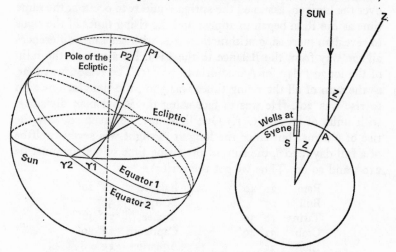

Fig. 24. The Precession of the Equinoxes discovered by Hipparchos; measurement of Earth's circumference as worked out by Eratosthenes

the latter visited Athens and then went to the Macedonian court where he composed his poem in the earlier part of the third century. It had an enduring vogue. The third century also saw the work of Aristarchos, Archimedes, and the Alexandrians, Timocharis, Aristyllos, and Eratosthenes. Apollonios worked on the geometry of epicycles and eccentrics, probably stimulated by the work previously done by Herakleides of Pontos on the revolutions of Mercury and Venus. (Herakleides argued that they went round the sun, not round the earth.)

Then in the second century B.C. Hipparchos made his comprehensive formulations, on which Ptolemaios in the second century A.D. built his work; he added more accurate details (such as the treatment of the moon's motions) and a complete theory for each of the five planets; and he seems to have discovered the precession of the equinoxes. Only in the second century do we have clear evidence for an acquaintance with the sexagesimal system of dividing the circle into 360 degrees.[71]

But despite all the mathematical, geometrical, and trigonometrical advances made by the Greeks, there was still a strong mark of Babylonian origins. Instead of turning to trigonometry, astronomers often felt it was easier to use the numerical approximations of the Babylonian tables. In his *Anaphorikos*, Hypsikles, concerned with reckoning when the zodiacal signs should rise over the horizon, assumed the spring equinox to occur at the same time as the Ram began to appear and the rising times of the signs to reveal an increasing arithmetic series, with the same differences all the way from the Balance to the Fish. He also took the ratio of the longest day for Alexandria to be 7:5. The reason was that, as the sum of all the rising times was 360°, the time for one sign to rise was 30°. (He was in fact using the Babylonian divisions, with units of UŠ and *Gar*.) One light-day, he assumed, saw the rise of 6 signs; but since the longest daylight was seven-twelfths of a full day (210°), the sum of the rising time of 6 signs must be 210°, and so on. Thus we get the series:

Ram	21° 40'	Balance	38° 20'
Bull	25°	Scorpion	35°
Twins	28° 30'	Archer	31° 40'
Crab	31° 40'	Capricorn	28° 20'
Lion	35°	Aquarius	25°
Virgin	38° 20'	Fish	21° 40'

And this list is only one of a set of similarly devised lists for different *klimata*. We find such lists by astrologic writers like Manilius, Vettius Valens, Firmicus Maternus, Kleomedes, Martianus Capella, Gerbert. Hypsikles and the first three of these used one system while the last three used another, in which the difference between the rising-times of Twins and Crab is twice as large as are the other differences. These two systems can in turn be shown to be connected with the systems A and B which we discussed in dealing with the Babylonian computation of daylight-durations.[72]

The trail of Babylonian survivals could be carried much further. Thus, Geminos about 70 B.C. cites the Babylonian value for the anomalistic month but his derivation is not quite right, through his merging of two methods.[73] We saw that the cuneiform texts have a doctrine similar to that of the Greek *dekatemoria*; but we may add here a further proof of this important derivation. Two tablets, which may date from the Persian period (as shown by their way of writing the zodiacal signs) embody the doctrine in the following form: take as given a place A in the Zodiac, n degrees inside a certain sign (n being a number between zero and 30). Another place B is linked with A, and is found thus: multiply n by 12 and add the result to the position A, counting multiples of 30° as so many zodiacal signs. For instance, let A be the Bull 6°, then $n=6$ and $12n=72=2$ signs $+12$. Adding this to A we get for B the position Crab 18°. In the Greek doctrine there is associated with every position A in a zodiacal sign another position called its *dodekatemorion* (12 degrees): the relation is exactly the same as in the Babylonian text. However, A and B are not related to sun and moon, but to any planet. One had to take into account not only the influence of a planet's being in A, but also the significance of the linked position B. An example of this sort of relation appears in the aspect of the trine or trinity. Assume that A is at the 10th degree of a sign, then B falls exactly $10.12=120°$ further ahead. Repeating this process we find a point C 120° ahead of B (240° ahead of A). The next step brings us back to A. So ABC form the aspect of the regular triangle so important in Graeco-Roman and medieval astrology.[74]

We must also note that despite the strictly logical development of Greek mathematics in one direction, as shown in the work of Eukleides, Archimedes, Apollonios and others, there was also another direction which maintained Egyptian and Babylonian procedures. Heron and Diophantes represent this second line.

The fact that, *e.g.*, Heron adds areas and line-segments can no longer be viewed as a novel sign of the rapid degeneration of the so-called Greek spirit, but simply reflects the algebraic or arithmetic tradition of Mesopotamia. On this more elementary level, the axiomatic school of mathematics has as little influence as it has today on surveying. Consequently, parts of Heron's writings, practically unchanged, survived the destruction of scientific mathematics in late antiquity. Whole sections from these works are found again, centuries later, in one of the first Arabian mathematical works, the famous algebra of al-Khwarimi [about A.D. 800 to 850]. (Neugebauer.)[75]

Looking back we may summarise certain points. Difficulties in comparing Babylonian astronomy with what developed in Greece centre on the bald nature of the Babylonian texts, the difference in their aims, the schematisation of their methods and the extent to which they are based on calculation rather than observation, and the question as to how the Greeks managed to learn from Babylonia. With regard to the aims, we may note that the Babylonians were concerned primarily with reading omens and improving the calendar, while the Greeks were attempting to relate astronomy to a general conception of the cosmos as a whole and to build up a mathematically-based scheme which would cover all the phenomena they could get at. So the Babylonians never arrived at a clear notion of the celestial sphere or of terrestrial latitude and longitude.[76]

As to the ways in which the Greeks might have learned much of Babylonian views and methods, we may generally rule out the direct studying of them by Greeks at the Mesopotamian centres before the time of Alexander the Great. It is barely possible that a man like Demokritos may have gone to Babylon and talked with the priests through a translator; and it is also possible that men like Berosos later brought much Babylonian lore westward. But we cannot effectively explain a flow of information along these lines. Rather we must look to the priestly bodies in Asia Minor who in varying degrees had absorbed the Babylonian disciplines, even if they did not do much in actual astronomic work. They would be mainly the mages or *magousaioi* who from early days of the Persian empire had been active as far as the Aegean and from whose positions Mithraism was to develop. We have tales linking Demokritos with such priests; and we may note the important fact that the home town of Eudoxos, Knidos, was under Persian domination in the sixth century and later part of the Delian League, while Anaxagoras had been a Persian subject before he went to Athens. This detail, together with his unorthodox opinions, helped to bring him under suspicion of Medism. From the Anatolian mages the Greeks would have gained many general ideas of the Babylonians, which would be highly stimulating and which, when added to their own mathematical trends, became fertile and led off in new directions. That this fertilisation did occur cannot be doubted: attempts to see Greek mathematical astronomy coming about in an autonomous way are against all probability and common sense.[77]

5

The World of the Stars

We can call astrologic any doctrine that sees the stars as controlling the lives and fortunes of men on earth; but the creed becomes precise only with a high degree of mathematical astronomy. Ancient astrology had a dual aspect, of hope and submission. On the one hand, it more and more saw the mechanism of star-movements as a fate determining all the events of universe, large and small; and yet, on the other hand, it sought to gain more definite and comprehensive knowledge of those movements as an escape from fate, as a means of dominating the world. In a sense this duality has dominated most scientific work so far: a conviction that knowledge is power and a method that assumes mechanistic determination. I have shown elsewhere how the alchemists sought to resolve this contradiction. In their own way too the astrologers attempted that resolution, though not so clearly or consistently as the alchemists. Dealing, as they thought, with the very stuff of destiny, they felt ever more acutely the contrasts between the determinism of cosmic law and the knowledge that should save men and give them the power to avert disaster.

At the earlier Babylonian phases the dilemma had not come out into the open. There was no strict and inclusive system of omens and star-divination. Men felt that strange and dangerous powers were all around them, liable to erupt into the normal courses of existence with death, disease, downfalls of all kinds; "If the temples hurt," runs a text on head-afflictions, "it is the hand of a ghost and it will attack."[1] But men also hoped to circumvent these powers by a mixture of abject submission and bold inquiry. The diviner, we saw, was in a sense the cosmic hero as he summoned up and confronted the elemental monster Humbaba in the convolutions of the entrails. If he learned what Humbaba was up to, he could give counsel adequate to the perilous occasion.

The Greeks had long had their many systems of divination and oracular responses; but they had nothing fully corresponding to the Babylonian methods and attitudes. For they lacked the kingship and the guilds of temple-priests. But with the breakdown of the free city from about 400 B.C., with the inability to find any federating or mediating units that could effectively carry democracy on into larger units, they had no choice but a reluctant acceptance of kingly systems. And with that breakdown they needed cultural and religious forms that could express the new dimensions. The city-gods, oracular Apollo, or the mystery-gods (at the stage they had then reached) could not meet the new needs. With Alexander the horizon became worldwide, and world-systems were required. With Plato a powerful and definite otherworldly bias entered Greek thought, a psychological split that was bound up with the division coming over men as individuals and as *politikoi*. The real world, the world of power, had broken away from individual life. Citizens, *idiōtai*, felt themselves more and more the puppets of distant forces on which they found it hard to focus.[2]

True, there were already mystery-religions like those of Eleusis where initiation, instead of opening for men the fullness of life on earth, had begun to appear more as a promise of blessedness after death; and the Orphic cults were gathering the emotions of the distressed and oppressed with similar promises. But it was with Plato, deeply disillusioned with Attic democracy, that the split entered Greek thought at its heart. And this turning to the otherworld was linked with a glorification of the stars as gods or the seats of gods, a superior world in which regularity of movement and complete embodiment of law were felt to contrast in an absolute way with the confused and distracted movements of earth.

We noted in Babylonian thought the sense of two worlds, heavenly and earthly, with complex correspondences between the two and with the heavenly more and more asserting itself as the realm of power and law, so that earth-life tended to become a reflection of the higher sphere. But here the union and opposition was not worked out with any philosophic rigour; there were all kinds of loose ends. It was left to Plato to do the rigorous working-out. It is not without significance, however, that in the Persian empire with its absolutism the idea of afterdeath-rewards for the obedient and faithful had been highly developed. In the Behistan inscriptions of Dareios as in the Daiva ones of Xerxes, life in another world was promised to the true worshipper of Ahura Mazda.[3]

There were inevitably many trends making the same way. The early Babylonians had no idea of a star-ascent by the righteous, since their only notion of an otherworld was a vague space of gloom like the Hebrew Sheol. But in Iran, as we have noted, there was a tradition of ascent into the eternal light of Ahura Mazda.[4] So it is probable that the Mages brought the idea of the star-ascent into the Chaldean area, where their world-outlook fused with that of Babylonian astrology. They further spread their cosmology in its new form in Anatolia, from which it reached Greece by various channels. In Ionia Herakleitos taught that souls were of the same nature as the *aither,* which thus was in some sort the soul of the cosmos.[5] Thales seems to have been the first to put much stress on evaporation, as something that nourished even "the very fire of the sun and stars".[6] Thus the idea of an ascent from the earth was brought in. Herakleitos says of the soul that it is "the vaporisation out of which everything else is derived". Areios Didymos interprets him as saying that souls, "as they rise up in vapour, become intellectually aware", and as holding the soul to be "a perceptive exhalation".[7] A Pythagorean catechism for minor brothers of the order asked, "What are the Isles of the Blessed?" and the answer was, "Sun and Moon."[8] (There was an interesting link of the notion of the moon as the home of the blessed with the Hesiodic myth of the race of gold. The Pythagoreans held that virtuous souls became *daimones* of that race, and Plato in the *Laws* used a political Pythagorean myth that made them the guardians of human affairs. These *daimones* also became those of the Moon.)

By 432 B.C. the idea of the soul's ascent to the stars had become strong enough to gain official recognition in the epitaph of the men fallen at Potidaia: "The *aither* received their souls, the earth their bodies."[9] Some sects, Orphic or Pythagorean, taught that souls went to live on the moon or shine in the constellations. A fifth-century inscription from Koumai states, 'No one not a Bacchic initiate has the right to lie here." It seems to mean that only the initiate's soul would be blessed in the afterlife.[10] Euripides in *Helen* writes:

> The mind of the dead
> does not live indeed, but into the immortal *aither*
> is driven and has immortal understanding.[11]

In his *Melanippe* he speaks of "the holy *Aither* the dwelling of Zeus". Aristophanes in the *Peace* mocks at the poet Ion:

"Is it true then, in the air, what people say,
    when a man dies, he's turned into a star?"
"Certainly." "Who's now a star up there?"
"Ion of Chios, who some time past composed
    the *Morning-Star*. When he went yonder, at once
    all called him the Morning-Star." "And who are those
    erratic stars that run about and blaze?"

The erratic stars seem to be, not planets or comets, but shooting-stars; and the passage ends with a joke: "They're certain of the rich stars coming home with lanterns." Note how the sky-ascent is linked with the shamanist idea of a possessed person (poet) transported aloft. Trygaios declares that he met dithyrambic poets (with their wild oracularly-obscure diction) flying about, wandering, collecting "certain ode-beginnings of men that float in air". Kinesias of the *Birds* is the type, and also Sokrates as astronomer in the *Clouds*.[12]

In considering the ultimate origins of star-observation and theories of the heavens, we may note further that the shamanist ritual-mime of sky-ascent has itself the background of initiation-experience. Among the Australian natives we find the tribal ancestors or heroes going up to the stars. Thus the Eucla tribe told how they had been much troubled by two huge birds of prey; two men attacked and killed the monsters, then went up and took their residence in the dark patches of the Milky Way, where they still live. The dual heroes were often linked with the Milky Way, which played an important part in initiation-rites. In such a rite or *bora* at Mount Milbirriman, seven fires were lighted round an oval ring; at the south end stood a native threatening a big clay figure of a crocodile with a spear. The seven fires represented the Pleiades, who were seen as seven young men dancing to a song sung by three young women in Orion's Belt. The clay-figure in the middle of the ring was a giant crocodile frequenting the dark river of the Milky Way; and the novices were told that this fiery monster would swallow them if they showed any weakness in passing through the rites. Such ritual imagery, given an intensely dramatic quality by the heightened consciousness of the initiation-moment with its fasting, drugs, and other forms of excitation, would be deeply imprinted on the minds of the initiates; it helps to explain legends like those of Perseus, Bellerophon, Orion, Horos, and others, with their link between monster-slaying and sky-ascent. The initiate staring at the sky could not fail to see strange designs and combinations among the stars, which in turn were related to the imagery of the passage-rite. Thus, to return to the Eucla, the sky-ascent was called *walyeyooroo*. During circumcision the

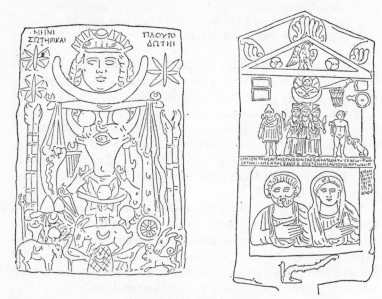

Fig. 25. Ex-voto to Men (B.M.); Phrygian funerary *stēlē* with Men and triple Hekate

novice had to keep his eyes fixed on the two spots where lived the killers of the gigantic birds. In another account the novices were left lying on the ground after circumcision till the Milky Way was visible. Then each lad was asked, "Can you see the two black spots?" When he saw them, he was let go back to the camp where the medicine-men (shamans) told him a form of the monster-killing and sky-ascending myth. The black spots were called Faraway-Men. A Budera (Root) man who had not taken part in the killing, when old, went up to the stars; but he is seen only when he walks across the moon (? eclipse or interlunary days) and then he is angry. Plato was said to have written the epigram:

Aster, once, as Morning-Star, light on the living you shed.
Now, dying, as Evening-Star you shine among the dead.

At Peiraios in the fourth century we meet the epitaph:

The moist *Aither* has the soul and the powerful mind
of Eurymachos; in this tomb his body was left behind.

At Larisa: "The soul is given to *Aither*, the body hidden in dust."
At Athens (probably fourth century) we read:

I, a godlike man, leave my body to Earth my Mother.
He's gone to the Band of the Blest, the Circle of *Aither*.

The soul is the *pneuma* of life, at Korkyra, Rhodes, Kyme. At
Arkesine, perhaps in the first century B.C., the dead girl is even
made to say:

Mother, don't weep. What use? Just reverence me.
An evening-star among the gods you see.[13]

Early Pythagorean ideas are hard to make out clearly, in themselves or in their origins. But certainly they owed much to various
Eastern sources. The Old-Babylonian text from Nippur dealt in
a few of its lines with star-distances; and at first these were taken
to be marvellously accurate. In fact they seem to use radial

Fig. 26. Reliefs with Mēn: from Athens with Pan; from Thorikos
riding a cock

distances and the numbers given are entirely speculative. What
they resemble is Pythagorean fantasies on the same subject. The
Pythagorean Harmony of the Spheres assumed that the distances
between the planetary spheres have the ratios of simple whole
numbers, and this kind of speculation was quite probably linked
with, and derived from, Babylonian cosmology and number-systems.
The early Pythagoreans were certainly much influenced by the
Mages or *magousaioi* of Asia Minor. They had a taboo against
killing or eating a white cock because, says Aristotle, the bird

was "consecrated to Mēn", who was a Phrygian god of the moon, presiding over the months; and Ailian says that at moonrise the cock is seized with ecstasy and leaps like a bacchanal. Aristoxenes on the same taboo says that the cock is both solar and lunar; and indeed in Asia Minor it was sacred to Mithras as well as Mēn. Coins of Trapezos in Pontos represent Mithras riding towards a high pedestal on which perches a cock surmounted by a star; many coins of Asia Minor depict Mēn with a cock at his feet; a terracotta shows a cock on his knees; a relief at Thorikos shows him riding a huge cock. The dawn-crow made the cock a solar creature as if he called up the Sun; Babrius records the tradition that he was also an hour-prophet or announcer, *hōromantis*, and much earlier the comic poet Kratinos had written "The Persian bird with full voice crows out every hour." The Mazdeans divided the day-and-night into five *gahs* (dawn to noon, noon to 3 hours, 3 hours to dusk, dusk to midnight, midnight to dawn), with the cock crying out in the fifth *gah* to arouse men. The cock, then, who seems to have come from Persia to the Greek area in the fifth century, had various time-roles in connection with sun and moon; and the Pythagorean taboo was certainly derived from the Mages. Plinius considered that cocks knew the stars and that they called out every three hours, the length of a military *vigilia*.

Plato in the *Timaios* brought to a head the Pythagorean trend to look on Order, expressed in Number, as something controlling earthly existence, and thus above it, not merely incarnated in it. We cannot judge with any certainty how far he went beyond the cosmic views of Philolaos, which he made much of and elaborated: but clearly here, as throughout much of his work, the split to which I referred was strongly asserting itself. He refers to Babylonian astrology, though he does not seem to know any horoscopic applications:

The choric dance of these same stars and their crossings, one with another, and the relative reversals and progressions of their orbits, and which of the gods meet in their conjunctions, and how many are in opposition, and behind which and at what times they severally pass before one another, and are hidden from our view, and again reappearing send upon men unable to calculate alarming portents of the things which will come to pass later on—to describe all this without an inspection of models [*mimemata*] of these movements would be labour in vain.[14]

He is assuming that the models cannot be constructed. But his summary reveals a considerable awareness of planetary astrology.

His development shows a growing insistence on astronomy and star-worship. In the *Republic* and the *Phaidros*, astronomy is subordinated to dialectic, but it comes strongly to the fore in the *Laws*, attached to a system of education which he desperately hopes will cure what he feels to be the rot in the Greek world. The *Epinomis* may have been put together by his editor Philip of Opous; but what it sets out is the logical next step after the *Laws*. It is integrally related to the corpus of Platonic works. The identification of the gods with the souls of the sun, moon, planets, and other heavenly bodies is what we expect after *Timaios* and the *Laws*.[15] In the Herculanean library of the proconsul Piso, patron of the Epicurean Philodemos, among the blackened rolls was a *History of the Academy*, which tells of an astronomer (probably Philip) and of a Chaldean who visited the aged Plato. Music played to calm the fever of the dying man, but a Thracian piper lost measure. Someone, perhaps the Chaldean, said that a barbarian was incapable of learning and keeping measure; the fever returned.[16] Whether this Chaldean really existed or came in as an allegorical figure, his presence was true to the actual situation of Plato in his later years. In using the legend of Er the Pamphilian in the *Republic* Plato seems to go out of his way to admit the debt he owes to Iranian and Babylonian ideas or images brought into the Greek world by visits of the Mages and by the tales of those who had spoken with them in Anatolia or further east.[17] It is significant that it is in the Er myth that he introduces the problem of Fate and its relation to the heavens.[18]

The science of Number, says the *Epinomis*, is a gift of the God Heaven. For it is the succession of day and night, the phases of the moon, the position of the stars in relation to one another, that teach us how to count, then how to compare number with number. And the science of Number itself brings us back to the heavens; for only through it do we have knowledge of good order, of heavenly gods. The contemplation of this good order constitutes true religion. We attain to true piety when we distinguish in nature the divine from the mortal, the regular course of divine beings, stars, from the movement without calculation, order, beauty, rhythm, harmony, of mortal beings.[19]

This theme pervades the work, repeated and drawn out into many variations: Wisdom, which is Piety, consists in the Science of the Stars or Astronomy. There could not be a more explicit statement that the old civic religion had failed; its gods with human faces have lost their spell.

In what concerns the gods, it is necessary to draw a more beautiful and correct image than has so far been done.

Now as for the gods, Zeus, Hera, and all the others, let them be arranged according to the same principle [genealogical classification] in whatever way one likes, and let the chosen order be strictly adhered to. But as for the Visible Gods [Stars]. . . .[20]

The civic gods are to be left as they are, out of respect for convention, not the least innovation regarding them is to be allowed. The serious cult, that of the spirit touched by philosophic issues, is solely that of the stars. The Invisible Gods, according to the author, are connected with the five regions of the cosmos corresponding to the five elements (*aither*, fire, air, water, earth); with the aid of each element the World-Soul fashions living beings in which one or other of the elements dominates. The beings inhabit the region constituted by their dominant element. Those of fire are the stars; those of *aither* and air are daimons, invisible intermediaries between the stars and men; those of water are semi-divine, sometimes seen, sometimes unseen; those of earth are men.[21]

The author is aware that he is borrowing the star-cult from the East. He says that Greece is the land best situated for favouring moral or human excellence, halfway between northern cold and southern heat. Still,

our climate, inferior in summer to that in the region over there [Egypt, Syria] has been much later in grasping the purpose [or contrivance, *katanoēma*] of these deities. But let us take it that whatever Greeks carry over from barbarians they finally turn into something nobler.

Here too the same thing must be borne in mind with regard to our present statements; that though it is hard to discover everything of this kind beyond dispute, there is hope, both strong and noble, that a truly nobler and juster cult will be paid by the Greeks to all these gods than is in the combined reputation and worship which came from barbarians: since Greeks have the advantage of their various education, their prophecies from Delphoi, and the whole system of worship under their laws. And let no Greek ever be apprehensive that as mortals we should never be concerned with divine affairs. . . .[22]

There is however no reference to star-divination. No doubt the author thought such matters trivial in comparison with the issue of directing all serious worship to the stars as gods and of striving to attain unity with them through contemplation. He says there are eight powers: sun, moon, fixed stars, and the five planets. And he asks for no hair-splitting as to whether some are gods, others not, and so on.

But let us all say and declare that they are brothers and share brotherly lots [*moirai*]; and let us give them all due honour—but not, while giving to one a year, to another a month, appoint to others neither a certain lot nor a certain time in which each travels through its particular orbit, completing the system which the divinest reason of all ordained to be visible. At all this, first, the man who is blest marvels. Then he feels a passion for understanding as much as is possible for mortal nature, believing that thus he will best and most happily pass through life, and at the end of his days will arrive at regions suitable for virtue [*aretē*] . . .[23]

This experience is defined as an initiation (into a mystery-cult), and as in the *Timaios* the star-movements are connected with Time. The correspondences of above and below are stressed, but no longer in a vital and organic way; only the abstractions of number or harmony on earth are of significance, not in themselves but as reflections of the superior order of the stars and as pointers to it.

Every diagram and system of number, and every combination of harmony, and the agreement of the revolution of the stars, must be made manifest as one through all to him who learns in the proper way, and will be made manifest if, as we say, a man learns aright by keeping his gaze on unity. For it will be manifest to us, as we reflect, that there is one bond naturally uniting all these things. But if one goes about in some other way, one must call on Fortune [Tyche] as we also put it.[24]

The rather obscure compression of the first sentence means that we must grow aware of a single unifying scheme of proportion that runs through geometrical figures and proportions, mathematical proportions, harmonic proportions (corresponding to square, line and cube, as he has previously shown), and the rotation of the stars. The comment on Fortune suggests a contempt for the use of Star-divination; the man who truly worships the stars does not need to inquire what fate they weave for him, he is lifted above the reach of fate in his communion.[25] By becoming one with the stars he becomes one with his own fate.

The development leading up to the *Epinomis* was linked with strong social conflicts which had their basis in the breakdown of the city-state and its democratic forms. In earlier times, Plato says, the Sun and Moon were thought to be "gods" in some loose sense by everyone—including Sokrates, says the *Apology*; the heavenly bodies, asserts the *Kratylos* (incorrectly), were the primitive gods of Greece. However this reverence was being broken down by mechanistic explanations and the general spirit of questioning expressed by the sophistic movement. As Athenian democracy went down, there was a tendency among common folk to see in any mockery or undermining of the traditional cults an aristocratic contempt of democracy itself or an impious egoism that would bring a disastrous retort from the gods. We see something of this attitude or mood in Aristophanes' *Clouds*. Much disquiet was roused by such things as the Club of *Kakodaimonistai* or Devilworshippers—a parody of the name *Agathodaimonistai* sometimes taken by respectable clubs—which deliberately met on Unlucky Days and generally derided religious custom and superstitious fears. The shocked upholders of convention told tales about the way most of the members died young and how the sole survivor, the poet Kinesias, lingered on with an agonising disease. This Kinesias, we may note, was a dithyrambist whose song-flights were a sort of sky-ascent. Aristophanes laughs at him in the *Birds*. "I wish to be furnished now with wings and fly up in the air, and from the clouds I'll get some new preludes snow-beaten tossed in air." "What, can one get preludes from the clouds?" "Indeed, yes, our profession depends upon them." Kinesias says he'll wander through the whole air, and sings, "You forms [*eidola*] of winged *aither*-skimming birds . . . ascending towards the southern part, or again bringing my body bear to Boreas, cutting the harbourless furrow of the *aither* . . ." In such a dithyrambic possessed poet we see a link with the sky-ascending shaman; but his claim to personal inspiration has now become an affront to established religion. About 432 B.C. disbelief in the supernatural and the teaching of astronomy could be used against a man in the lawcourts at Athens and the next thirty years saw a series of heresy trials: Anaxagoras, Diagoras, Sokrates, almost certainly the sophist Protagoras, and perhaps Euripides. In all the cases but the last the accused was found guilty; Sokrates was put to death, Anaxagoras was fined and banished, it seems, while Diagoras and probably Protagoras escaped by flight. There was even, if the tradition about Protagoras is true, a burning of books; and there must have been many more prosecutions than the famous ones. Anaxagoras had been accused of saying that the heavenly bodies were merely material; from fragments of his *Treatise of Nature* and references to his work we know that he considered these bodies to be stone (Sun) or earth (Moon) carried round in a rotatory motion.

Some of the pressure for the prosecution of men like Anaxagoras may have come from the professional diviners, who saw in the new rationalism a threat to their prestige and livelihood. Such a diviner, Diopeithes, proposed the decrees that set the prosecutions off; but he and his associates could not have succeeded without a wide popular prejudice against the scientists. *Meteorologia* was much disliked and disapproved of. Many persons denounced it as foolish and presumptuous, or as dangerous to religion, and it was generally associated with the unsettling sophists. Plato, then, feeling that the traditional city-cults had lost their power to keep men in order, set himself to rehabilitate the stars as divine beings; he felt that the stars, proved to be themselves eternally orderly and regular, supplied a superior basis for religion. Ploutarch in his *Life of Nikias*, dealing with the military disaster at Syracuse and its connection with a moon-eclipse, tells us:

The eclipse frightened Nikias very much, as well as the others who were ignorant or superstitious enough to mind such things. For though by this time even the masses had accepted the idea that an eclipse of the Sun towards the end of the month had something to do with the Moon, they could in no way conceive the effect of a full Moon suddenly becoming obscured and changed in colour. This they considered uncanny, a sign sent by God to announce some great calamity.

Anaxagoras, the first man who had the understanding and the courage to commit to writing an explanation of the phases of the moon, was but a recent authority and his book little esteemed. In fact it circulated in secret, was read by few, and was cautiously received. For in those days there was no tolerance for the natural philosophers, or "babblers about things in heaven", as they were called. They were charged with explaining away the divine and substituting irrational causes, blind forces, and the sway of necessity. So Protagoras was banished, Anaxagoras was jailed and it was all Perikles could do to get him out, and Sokrates, though he had nothing at all to do with the matter, was put to death for being a philosopher.

It was only much later, through the brilliant reputation of Plato, that the reproach was removed from astronomical studies and access to them opened up for all. This was on account of the respect in which his life was held and because he made natural laws subordinate to the authority of divine principles.

Ploutarch is no doubt exaggerating a bit, in order to enhance Plato's glory; Sokrates in the *Apology* refers to Anaxagoras' books as buyable in the marketplace for a drachma; and it is obviously quite incorrect to assume, as some historians have, that astronomy was ever actually forbidden at Athens. But it seems sure that such studies were in extreme disrepute. That the attitudes to them had become entangled with political issues does not disprove the point; rather it strengthens the argument. Anaxagoras suffered as a friend of Perikles; Sokrates as a friend of the aristocratic reactionaries. That is, the advocates of the new views were liable to be lumped with the anti-democrats and the underminers of the old ways (which were now being glamorised). This was precisely the sort of situation that was most likely to stir Plato with a sense of the failure of the traditional city-gods and the need for a reassertion of the aristocratic principle by directing the attention to the stars aloofly on high as the sole true gods who could never let a worshipper down.

Aristotle in his early years took over much of the cosmogonic mysticism of Plato's Academy. His *On Philosophy* shows him seeking to replace the theory of Ideas (*eide*) with astral theology; the proof of God within the spectacle of the starry heavens. His whole picture is close to the *Epinomis* except that he introduces the *aither* as the element of the heavens, and the eternity of the world.[26] As he matured, he moved to a much more pragmatic position, expressed in *On Heaven*, though some elements of the early phase persisted. Many of his views helped the star-worshipping or astrologic outlooks, for instance his stress on the sphere of the fixed-stars.[27] His geocentric system made it easier to argue that the stars controlled earthly affairs; his teleology and his acceptance of the prevalent ideas about comets also helped.[28] He was much concerned with the effect of one revolving sphere on another; in his picture of the cosmos he inserted a third sphere between any concentric set of two, endowing the first pair with motion equal to, but opposite in direction to, the inserted one. He thus neutralised the motion of the third sphere and cleared the field for the next enclosed sphere. By this procedure he obtained 55 spheres, which he seems to have considered as owning a physical reality—thus differing in attitude from Eudoxos and Kallippos.[29] It is also important that he furthered the notion of heaven-earth correspondences by seeing the eternal unchanging motion of the first heaven as symmetrical with the eternal fixed earth, and the continuous yet changing motion of the sun as symmetrical with the ceaseless changes in the sublunary region. To some extent he here appears as a halfway house between Plato and the Stoics. We may note that he also follows the *Epinomis* in emphasising the debt of Greek astronomy to the East.

His disciple Theophrastos, as cited by Proklos, stated that "his Chaldean contemporaries possessed an admirable theory" on the subject of signs. "This theory predicted every event, the life and death of every human being. It did not merely foresee general effects, as for example good and bad weather." This comment is not detailed enough for us to be sure that it refers to horoscopes; but it certainly makes sense best if we assume that it does.[30]

In the *Epinomis* and Aristotle's *On Philosophy* we see Eastern influences having an intense but narrow effect. The full stream came with the Stoics. Many of their leading thinkers were men born in areas of strong Semitic or Babylonian culture. After Alexander the Great and his successors, with their foundations and their hellenisation of so many eastern regions, we can no longer assert definitely that these men were Syrians or Babylonians by birth; but even if some or all of them were of Greek families, they grew up in towns where Greek and Syro-Babylonian elements were being merged.

Zenon from Kition in Cypros brought to Athens a deep belief in predestination, in the inexorable rule of law; for him mankind and the universe were bound together in the system of fate. Such attitudes had been stimulated by the astrologic discipline and in turn they stimulated it to further development. On the one hand we find a deeply-felt pantheism, reuniting man with Nature after the rupture of Platonism. Diogenes Laertios tells us that Zenon was the first to define the end of human existence as "life in accordance with nature". That meant virtuous living, "for virtue is the goal to which nature guides us". This view was repeated by Kleanthes in *On Pleasure*, by Poseidonios, by Hekaton in *On Ends*.

Living virtuously is equivalent to living in accordance with experience of the actual processes of nature, as Chrysippos says in Book I of *On Ends*. For our individual natures are part of the nature of the whole universe. And that is why the end may be defined as life in accordance with nature, or, in other words, in accordance with our own human nature as well as with that of the universe, a life in which we refrain from every action forbidden by the law common to all things, *i.e.* the right reason which pervades all things and is identical with this Zeus, Lord and Ruler of all that is. And this very thing constitutes the virtue of the happy man and the smooth current of life, when all actions promote the harmony of the spirit [daimon] dwelling in the individual man with the will of him who orders the universe. Diogenes then expressly declared the end to be to act with good reason in the selection of what is natural. Archedemos says the end is to live in the performance of all befitting actions.[31]

It must be recalled that *aretē* in such contexts has the sense of living as befits a man, as truly fulfills one's humanity. The depth of devotion to which the concept of *Aretē* could stir a man at this period is shown by the hymn of Aristotle, which anticipates the heroic note of the Christian martyr: "There is no Fate more enviable in Hellas than to endure for you devouring crushing pain."[32] And *logos* or right reason is not some externally imposed rule but the continually deepening consciousness of what makes a man. The Stoic feels that this struggle to become truly human implies a way of life that harmonises with the formative principles at work on the universe.

Chrysippos lays it down that all existence is brought into a unity by the penetration as it were of spirit [*pneuma*] through it all, whereby it is both drawn together and remains compact and the whole is harmonious with itself. (Alexandros of Aphrodisia.)[33]

The term *pneuma* as used by the Stoics has an essentially materialist quality; spirit is some sort of fine matter, a formative principle, not a force abstracted from matter and driving it from outside.

It was Poseidonios who popularised in religious interests the microcosm-macrocosm doctrine originating in Chaldean speculations. He held that "the world is administered according to Mind, since Mind permeates every part of it as soul does in us". Of Poseidonian origin is the statement of Macrobius—"The physicists had declared that the world is a great man and man a little world." Poseidonian influence in Philon has caused the same thought to appear frequently, *e.g.* "traverse the greatest and most perfect man, this world"; and "thus some have been bold enough to declare that the smallest animal in the world, man, is equal to the world on the ground that each man is composed of body and rational soul; hence analogically they make man a little world and the world a great man, and in this they are not far wrong." (Angus.)[34]

The Stoics were very aware of the close link of their world-outlook and the astral cults, astrology. Indeed we do not go too far if we define their philosophy as astrology raised to a new level by its fusion with Greek thought, which both brought out into the open the pantheist aspect of the correspondence-theory and made it fully conscious of the unitary principle of process that was implied, but also made explicit the contradictions in assuming a world of fate and then trying to control it by knowledge of its mechanism. Plato in his despairs had turned to the stars as providing a guiding or controlling force right off the earth; the Stoics sought to overcome the split between heaven and earth, fate and free will, systems of law and organic process. They varied in their attitudes towards astrology according to the way in which they individually approached the problem of freedom and necessity, but they were all deeply aware of the need to define their relations to the stars (that is, to cosmic process and law).

The evil person, they said, was the one who resisted the formative principle of nature, who stunted himself and thus obstructed the impulses and arguments of both nature and reason. So they felt they had resolved, emotionally if not intellectually, the conflict of fate and freedom. The harmony of nature and reason, realised by man, is freedom: a recognition of necessity that converts it into a happy acceptance, a rhythm of fulfilment, while the disharmony, masked as an assertion of free choice in its egoist wilfulness, is a cankered submission to the denied forces, which provide a nemesis of enslavement. Stobaios tells us:

It is the opinion of Zenon and the Stoic philosophers following him that there are two kinds of men; the good and the wicked. The class of the good never cease, all their lives, to act virtuously; that of the wicked to act in a vicious way. As a result the first attain the right end in all the actions to which they apply themselves, while the others miss that end. As the virtuous man bases himself on the experience he has of the necessity inherent in the events of his life in all the actions he performs, he acts well, conformably with prudence, temperance, and the other virtues. On the contrary the wicked man acts in a vicious manner.[35]

We shall glance later at some of the attitudes of individual Stoics towards astrology. Here we shall keep to matters more directly concerned with the impact and expansion of Babylonian astrology among the Greeks. A key-figure in the later direct flow of astrologic information from the East was Berosos, a priest of Bel Marduk at Babylon, who came west and settled at Kos, where there was a

well-established school of medicine. No doubt as a learned priest
of Babylon he was acquainted with much medical lore, including
the omens connected with various diseases; and the fact that he
chose Kos suggests the lack of centres of astronomical research
in the Greek area. Eudoxos does not seem to have founded any
school that carried on at a particular spot and there built up its
methods, library, archives and so on.[36]

Berosos wrote, about 280 B.C., a history of his homeland,
Babyloniaka (often wrongly called *Chaldaika*), dedicated to
Antiochos I, son of Seleukos Nikanor, which was treated seriously
by Plinius, Josephos, Alexandros Polyhistor, as well as by Christians like Tatian and Eusebios. We may disregard the story that
he was father of the Sibyl, except as a testimony to his fame as a
predictor. Plinius says that the Athenians honoured him with a
statue "on account of his divine prophecies". His *History*, a work
meant to propagandise the claims of Babylonian culture, covered
the whole past of his country, at least some 470 thousand years.
The first book told of Tiamat-Omorka who personified the chaos
of water and darkness, with the monsters of her following:
winged men with two faces or two sexes, satyrs and centaurs,
human-headed bulls, dog-headed fish, dogs with four bodies and
fish-tails. Their images were set in Bel's temple. (We may compare
the strange combinations that Empedokles puts at the start of the
evolutionary process, as if nature had to make all sorts of blunder-
ing experiments before she came on rational forms.) The demiurge
Bel was identified with Zeus, Ea with Kronos, Sandis with Herakles, Anaitis with Aphrodite. Bel's defeat of Omorka signified the
victory of light and order over darkness and chaos. The monsters
perished. Travelling over the fertile but deserted land, Bel cut
his own head and formed men and animals by mixing his blood
with the dust of the soil; thus were made creatures able to live
in the light.

Berosos based his tales on the archives of Babylon and Borsippa
where tablets recorded the revelations of the Fishman Oannes,
the inventor of letters, sciences, arts, and founder of laws, cities,
civilisation. He told how Bel created the sun, moon, and planets.
The Moon was not lit by the Sun, but was a spherical surface
half-luminous, half-dark. Eclipses occurred when it entered into
the shadow of the earth and its phases were produced by a rotatory
movement due to the Sun's action.[37] Berosos set out the doctrine
of the Great Year, each with its winter and summer. Summer,

bringing universal conflagration, came when all planets were in conjunction in the sign of the Crab; winter brought its universal flood when all were in Capricorn. Earthquakes and such calamities were caused by astral forces: when planets were in conjunction with the Sun or indeed in favourable aspect with it, especially in quadrature.[38]

Seneca gives a detailed account of the Berossan doctrine in these last matters. After mentioning the Conflagration and the Flood, he goes on:

I accept this theory; for so complete a ruin could not come from a single [cause or star]. And the opinion we hold about the Conflagration can in my opinion be transferred to the other disaster. Whether the cosmos is alive or mere matter [*animus, corpus*] with nature governing it like trees and crops, all that is to come about from birth to death is there enclosed in advance, as in a seed are enclosed all the characters of man. The foetus bears in itself the principle of the beard, of grey hairs, of the whole body, and the lineaments of the following phase are there in minute and hidden form. So the cosmos, at its origin. Similarly contained sun and moon and the circle of star-revolutions, and the animals not yet born, and also the system by which earthly things undergo change.[39]

He continues with a vision of world-cataclysm, drawing on Berosos or on some apocalyptic poem. In the days of flood-cataclysm the equilibrium of the elements will be broken:

The earth will begin to soften, to dissolve, to be diluted, and at last it will flow in a liquid form. New rivers will burst out under the mountains and shake them; soon they'll drip their way out quietly; everywhere the earth will give up the waters that it covers; springs will spurt from the mountain-tops. Thus the healthy flesh near a wound is corrupted; the parts near an ulcer grow ulcerated. To the extent that all the waters come together out of an earth in dissolution, that earth will be inundated, washed away, trickle, and then gush, the stones opening up all over the place will release more waters to jet into the seas and unite them into a single ocean. There will be no more Adriatic, no Sicilian Strait, no Charybdis or Scylla; a new sea will overrun everything, and the Ocean, today the boundary and girdle of the world, will occupy its centre. What then? Winter will extend its empire over the months of other seasons; no more summer; the stars that parch the earth will lose their powers of heat. How many names will be wiped out: the Caspian and the Red Sea, the gulfs of Ambracium and of Crete, the Bosphoros and the Black Sea; all distinction will go. What nature has made into separate parts will be confounded into a single mass. Towers, walls, temples, citadels will be unable to protect, to preserve the suppliants. The waves will overtake the fugitives and sweep them away from the highest points. East, west will send out waves that meet. A single day will eliminate the human race. Whatever the long indulgence of Fortune has left to flourish, whatever she raised above the rest, the realms of great nations, noble and well-adorned, she will destroy.

But after the universe's foundations have been destroyed, there will arise everything afresh "in pristine innocence when no teacher of evil survives". The cycle repeats itself. "Man, ignorant of any crime, will once again be given to the world, born under better auspices." But evil revives too and destroys the earthly paradise. "Vice needs no teacher, while Virtue is hard to learn."

This creed of world-end and renewal became an important part of Stoicism; it found many outlets in literature, of which the most striking was Virgil's Fourth Eclogue. It was the supreme expression of astrologic Fatalism; and yet, as we hear in the tones of Seneca's exposition, it somehow nourished an exultant hope. Partly, the thought of disaster coming on an ungrateful and corrupted world, alienated from nature, was gratifying; but even more the image of the returning golden-age was something that deeply appealed, despite the admission that it too in time must be undermined and polluted.

The idea of a world-disaster through some crucial act of dis-obedience or wickedness has very old roots; but the scheme of eternal cycles, each controlled and brought to its end by the positions of the stars, each lasting exactly the same length of time and involving an exact repetition of the previous cycle, could only come about after astronomy, with its astrologic interpretations and applications, had reached a high level of achievement. However we approach Stoicism we are forced to see it as the philosophy of astrologic fatalism; but that does not mean that it was a simple reflection of positions reached by the Chaldeans. Only when those positions had been brought into the Greek world and lifted to a new level of unified comprehension, could they emerge as Stoicism. The disciplines of Greek thought gave a new depth of consciousness, a new sense of the unity of relation-ships.

Looking back over the years we have been considering, with the rise of the belief in a starry otherworld, a strong effort to check astronomy as impious and dangerous when it came out into the open, and the Platonic justification of star-worship and astronomy,

we can make various social correlations. The Alexandrian textbook
of Geminos gives us important clues to the social emotions active
behind the wish to discredit the stars or to glorify them. The
planets in particular did not seem amenable to law or reason.

There underlies the whole science of astronomy the asumption that the
Sun, the Moon and the five Planets move at even speeds in perfect
circles in an opposite direction to the cosmos. It was the Pythagoreans,
the first to approach these questions, who laid the hypothesis of a
circular and uniform motion for the Sun, Moon, and Planets. Their
view was that, in regard to divine and eternal beings, a supposition of
such disorder as that these bodies should move now more quickly and
now more slowly, or should even stop, as in what are called the stations
of the planets, is inadmissible. Even in the human sphere such irregu-
larity is incompatible with the orderly procedure of a gentleman. And
even if the crude necessities of life often impose upon men occasions of
haste or loitering, it is not to be supposed that such occasions inhere in
the incorruptible nature of the stars. For this reason they defined their
problem as the explanation of the phenomena on the hypothesis of
circular and uniform motion.[40]

That is, a social emotion or prejudice dictated the terms on which
the geometrical and mathematical procedures should work, the
direction they should take. Plato puts the Pythagorean position
in different words:

A man who lived well would return home to a happy life on his native
star. One who failed would be reincarnated as a woman. If he persisted
in wrong-doing his next birth would be in the body of some animal
suitable to the evil propensities he had developed. There would be no
respite from this change from bad to worse until the soul allowed the
superior uniform motion of the stars to subdue the riotous and irrational
desires which had clung to it owing to its incorporation in a body made
of earth, water, air and fire.[41]

The movements of the stars are seen as a moral, psychological,
and social phenomenon, which the mathematics merely interpret.
Plato's contemporary Isokrates further illustrates the aspects of
their society against which the wealthy and powerful were react-
ing.[42] There was a large number of sturdy beggars or vagabonds,
and the same word is used for them as for planets by Sophokles,
Euripides, Isokrates himself; a tragedian writes of the *planētes*
of the sea, sea-wanderers. Isokrates had a project for enlisting the
dangerous rovers, drilling them, and sending them out against
the Persian Empire; he was forecasting the situation which was

soon to come about under Alexander the Great. "If we cannot
check the growing strength of these Vagabonds by providing them
with a satisfactory life, before we know where we are, they'll be
so numerous as to constitute as great a threat to Greeks as to the
barbarians." Hence the dire need felt to provide the gentlemen
with a universe which behaved in a gentlemanly way and did not
give a divine justification of the *planētes* of the earth and sea.

An indication of the spread of astrologic ideas is given by *The
Liar*, a comedy of Sosipatros, in which a cook claims a profound
scientific basis for his craft:

> We alone keep up the school of Sikon;
> he was the great teacher of all our art;
> he first taught us to scan the stars with judgment.
> Yes, the great Sikon. Next he made us architects;
> he opened up the paths of physical knowledge
> and after that taught us rules of military science:
> all these but prefaces to help us on
> to the pre-eminent godlike art of Cooking . . .
> In the first place a cook must have acquired
> the sublimer sciences; must know when, and why,
> the Stars rise up and set—when the Sun returns,
> bringing long days and short days to the earth,
> and in what zodiacal signs he stays
> from time to time. Men say all fish and meats,
> all herbs, we eat, have varying qualities
> at varying seasons of the revolving year . . .

We cannot date the play with any precision, but it no doubt
belonged to the third century B.C.[43]

6

Man as the Universe

About a generation after Berosos, Soudines was living at Pergamon. He was famed for his lunar tablets and was called a prophet. He must have been an astrologer, but like Berosos he was a man of wide interests. He wrote a commentary on Aratos' *Phainomena*; and Plinius cities him as an authority on the nature and properties of pearls and stones like onyx, crystals, amber, chrysophal, *astolos*. Like many later astrologers he must have been concerned with the relation of star-power to stones and plants.[1] He seems one of the first to use the pearl as symbol of soul.

The Berosan school at Kos probably dealt with hemerology as well as horoscopic astrology.[2] Two disciples who carried on from Berosos were Antipatros and Achinapolis. The second name may be an error for Athenodoros (a Stoic), but the three best manuscripts have the odd name, suggesting a barbarian. These men defended the notion that horoscopes should be concerned with the moment of conception as well as with that of birth. We know that by this time a similar position had appeared in Babylonia.[3]

Another pioneer, who seems a Greek, was Kritodemos. However, he too was said to draw directly on Babylonian sources; perhaps he followed Berosos. Vettius Valens blamed him for a cryptic style in the manner of other early writers; Firmicus Maternus puts him in a list of the founders of astrology with legendary figures like Hermes, Orpheus, Abraham, Petosiris and Nechepso. The problem of his work is not made easier by the fact that horoscopes attributed to him can be shown to originate some three centuries later than his period.[4] A treatise of his, *Horasis* (*Vision*), claimed to set out a double visionary message; we have a synopsis of it, which shows that later writers like Valens and Rhetorios knew it and borrowed from it. Another treatise, *Pinax*, is mentioned by Hephaistion.[5] In *Horasis*, using the tones of an hermetic prophet, he tells how he wandered long on sea and desert, till at last he arrived by the grace of the gods at a sheltered port and assured rest. He asks from the initiate a promise of silence confirmed by "the most terrible oaths".[6] He then reveals the truths that will ensure immortality. His fragments show signs of the Babylonian trinity: Sin, Shamash, Ishtar— Selene, Helios, Aphrodite.[7]

We may take Kritodemos as an example of how difficult it is to date these early astrologers with any precision. Valens often cites him and indeed seems to consider him as one of his most important sources apart from the traditional Petosiris and Nechepso; but there is not much about him in later authors.[8] Maternus, we saw, dutifully puts him among the great originators; Hephaistion cites him verbatim on stillborn children in what is conventional astrological doctrine. Theophilos in the eighth century ascribes to him, with Valens, Dorotheos and Timocharis, a method for counting latitudes: in which matter he is historically incorrect.

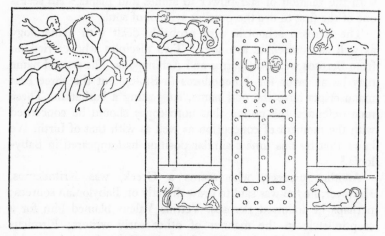

Fig. 27. Reliefs of a Tomb (Tlos, Asia Minor) showing Bellerophon on Pegasus (Mould, B.M.)

In seeking to put his date back, we come to Plinius, who cites him as an authority and names him with Berosos in regard to some fictitious Babylonian chronological schemes.[9] Valens blames him for obscurity and artificiality, but what we have ascribed to him is not particularly difficult. Valens, besides the references to the *Horasis*, quotes excerpts dealing with particular points of

astrologic doctrine and horoscopes with dates around A.D. 100,
which are not in any definite way different from the others he
gives.[10] Various suggestions have been made in explanation: that
there were two writers with the same name, that Kritodemos
wrote not long before Plinius, or that he was one of the very first
Greeks directly using Babylonian astrology. We may add the
possibility that writers after Plinius used parts of Kritodemos in
ways that confused them with their own work, and that Valens
drew on them uncritically. On the whole it seems likely that
Kritodemos was one of the pioneers.

We may say the same of Apollonios of Myndos, whose influential ideas on comets were said to have been taken from the
Babylonians.[11] Also of uncertain date was Epigenes of Byzantion,
who claimed to have studied under the Chaldeans. Seneca
declares:

Two men indeed, who claim to have studied under the Chaldeans,
Epigenes and Apollonios of Myndos, differ on this point: the latter, a
very skilled observer of nature, says that the Chaldeans count the
comets among the planets and know their courses; Epigenes on the
contrary says that the Chaldeans know nothing of comets and take them
to be bodies which are enflamed by a whirlwind turned in violently
upon itself.

Let us first, if you agree, consider this opinion and refute it. According
to Epigenes, Saturn is of all the planets the one with the greatest
influence on the movements of heavenly bodies. When it weighs on the
neighbourings signs of Mars or passes near to the Moon or finds itself in
conjunction with the Sun, its cold and stormy nature condenses the air
and at several points conglomerates it. Then if the sun's rays meet it,
thunder sounds, lightning gleams. . . .[12]

We need not follow him into his exposition of the different elements
in thunder and lightning. Epigenes is certainly following Babylonian tradition in stressing Saturn. Similarly, one of the points
that show clearly the close Babylonian inspiration of the *Epinomis*
is this treatment of Saturn:

And now [after Sun, Moon, Venus, Mercury] there remain three stars,
of which one is distinguished from the others by its slowness, and some
speak of it under the name of Saturn [Kronos]; the next after it in
slowness is to be cited as Jupiter; and the next after this as Mars, which
has the ruddiest hue of all.[13]

The two best manuscripts here give Helios or Sun in place of
E

Kronos, and thus make Kronos the planet of the Sun, as in
Babylonian astrology. These readings cannot be the result of
accident; they prove that the *Epinomis* was drawing directly on
Chaldean sources. The link was probably Eudoxos. As this is
an important point linking Plato with Babylonia we may pursue
it further. Simplikios, dealing with Saturn's 30-year period, adds
that "the ancients used to call" that planet "the star of the Sun".
Didoros tells us that the ancients here cited were the Chaldeans;
and cuneiform texts confirm his statement. We find the connection
made in the writings of many other authors, in the Epitome of
Eratosthenes, Hyginus, the scholiast on Germanicus, Servius on
Aeneid i 729, Damaskios, Eusebios. Nonnos tells us in a long
apostrophe to the Sun:

> Starclad Herakles fire-lord universe-prince,
> O Helios longshadowed shepherd of human life . . .
> Nurse of wise birth you bring forth the threefold image
> of the motherless Moon . . .
> Belos on the Euphrates, called Ammon in Libya,
> by the Nile you are Apis, Arabian Kronos, Assyrian Zeus . . .
> Be you Kronos or Phaethon of many names or Mithras
> the Sun of Babylon, in Hellas Delphic Apollo . . .
> Be you pain-quelling Paieon or patterned Aither . . .

Simplikios probably added his comment on Kronos because the
planetary periods used by Eudoxos were borrowed from Babylonia.

Some scholars have taken Epigenes as a disciple of Berosos and
a date around 200 has been suggested. He may have been a main
source for Varro as well as being used by Plinius and Censorinus
(*On the Birthday*); the Stoic Poseidonios may have helped to
spread his ideas.[14] Another shadowy yet important figure is
Teukros of Babylon (presumably of Seleukeia on the Tigris),
whom we know only by much later citations.[15] But difficult as are
the problems raised by Berosos and his successors, we can safely
assume that it was they who, after Eudoxos, brought in further
information from the East in something like an organised way.
After the start made by Eudoxos it is impossible to believe that
there were not intellectual circles in the Greek areas which would
do their utmost to learn more of the Chaldean science, make
contact with Babylon, or draw in Eastern scholars who had something new to tell. But the process by which the Chaldean lore

was brought in and built up into the coherent system of Hellenistic astrology is largely veiled from us. Thus, we do not know the stages by which the year-by-year almanacs were developed into tables based on mean motions.[16] We can say in general that two directions appeared: one leading on to Ptolemaios' *Almagest* with

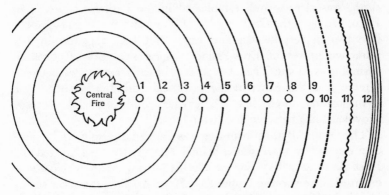

Fig. 28. Scheme of Philolaos: Central Fire, Anti-Earth (1), Earth (2), Moon (3), Sun (4), Venus (5), Mercury (6), Mars (7), Jupiter (8), Saturn (9), Fixed Stars (10), then Outer Fire and Aither

its mathematical geometry, the other concerned with reckoning the positions of heavenly bodies for horoscopic purposes and based on arithmetic or linear methods. The second direction lacked, or was not interested in, geometrical models.[17]

Ptolemaios drew together all the main astronomic trends. His planetary theory dealt with the determination of longitude and latitude, but also with the stationary points, the first and last visibilities. His lunar theory dealt with parallax, distance and size of sun and moon, computation of eclipses, solar apogee, results of the precession of the equinoxes, fixed-star coordinates and their connection with lunar positions. Taking the earth as centre, he used a judicious superimposition of eccentric circles and epicycles to explain the cosmos. Many details were discovered or worked out, for example the change in position among the stars of the pole of the heavenly spheres' rotation, and the inequality in lunar motion known as evection. In his *Optics* Ptolemaios recognised astronomical refraction (the apparent elevation of sky-bodies near the horizon). He also described the deviation (refraction) of rays of light passing into a glass of water, a first faint anticipation of experimental physics. The result was that, until the time of Kepler and Newton, all astronomy consisted of modifications of Hellenistic science, especially of the contribution or codification by Ptolemaios.

The notion of a correspondence of high and low, of heaven and earth, was already well established in the Pythagoreans and in Plato. We have the Orphic myth of Time and the World-Egg cut into two halves, heaven and earth, but held together by the attractive power of Eros-Phanes. These images went back to cosmologies of the Tiamat-type and to early exchanges between Greece and the East; in the historical period, apart from the Pythagoreans, men like Pherekydes, Eudoxos, and Berosos provided links between the two regions.[18]

The Orphic-Pythagorean Egg was Eastern in origin. In Phoenician cosmology there was a primal Egg. A fire-flash created the First Body as a Sky-Egg or Sky-Mountain, from which twins emerged. One was the Upper Sky, Hypsouranios, the other seems identical with the fiery energy producing the egg-mountain. This latter was equated with Hephaistos and called the Opener; he was the fire-in-the-egg, while his brother was the outer shell or upper covering of the Egg. There are close analogies in all this with Iranian myth, where Ahriman split the world apart by dragging the lower half downward, away from the stars. In these cosmogonies Wind had affinities with the *Pneuma* of the Stoics, while Fire was the warm substance and energy of all genesis. Aristophanes was well aware of the Orphic cosmology; for he set it out in the *Birds* (415 B.C.): "In the abysmal Womb of Erebos, before all things Night brought forth a clear Egg, whence in due time sprang Eros the desired, with wings of shining gold upon his back." The Peripatetic Eudemos (in the fourth century B.C.) declared that an Egg is the embryo of the World and that the two halves of its broken shell become Earth and Heaven. While the Christian Rufinus in the fourth century A.D. summarised the myth:

According to Orpheus, in the beginning was Chaos eternal, immense, uncreated, from which all is born; neither darkness nor light, nor damp nor dry, nor hot nor cold, but all things mingled, eternally one and limitless. The time came when after infinite ages, in the manner of a gigantic egg, he caused to emanate from himself a double form, androgynous, made by the conjunction of opposites.

The same cosmogonic correspondences as are found in the Orphic

Egg appear half-humorously in Aristophanes' fable in Plato's *Symposium* of original double-sexed beings, rounded like the spherical universe, whom Zeus cut in halves "as one cuts an egg with a hair". An astral touch is added by making the male sex issue from the sun, the female from the earth, the androgynous or homosexual from the moon. Sexual coupling is an effort to regain the original (spherical) unity. Plato gives the serious version in the *Timaios* when he declares that "the gods contain the two divine revolutions in a spherical body in imitation of the rounded form of the universe", and that this body, "called head by us at present, is the most divine part of the human organism, that which has command over all the others".[19]

The Stoics thus held that the souls of men were spherical.[20] The concept is developed by a large variety of thinkers. Thus an hermetic text tells us:

Since the world is a sphere, that is a head, and since above the head there is nothing material, as, no less, below the feet there is nothing intelligible, but all is material, and since the intellect is the head, which is moved with a circular movement, *i.e.* a movement proper to the head . . . so every living being, like the universe itself, is composed of the material and the intelligible.[21]

An Orphic poem works the analogy out further. Head is equated with heaven, eyes are sun and moon, intellect is *aither*, shoulders and back are air, stomach is earth, legs are sea, feet are the roots of the earth, Tartaros, the world's extremities.[22] Macrobius states:

The soul, in creating and organising bodies—and in this connection it is nothing else than nature, which, according to the philosophers, is issued from God and intelligence—the soul used the purest part of the substance drawn from the source whence it emanated, so animated the sacred and divine bodies, *i.e.* heaven and the stars, which were the first to emerge from its bosom. So a portion of the divine essence was infused into this body, round or spherical in shape. So Paulus, speaking of the stars, says that they are animated by divine spirits. And coming down towards the inferior earthly bodies, the soul judged them too frail and perishable to be able to contain a ray of the divinity; and if the human body seemed to deserve that sole favour, it is because its perpendicular position appeared to distance it from the earth and approach it to heaven, towards which we can easily lift our eyes. Also because the head of man has a spherical form, which is, as we have said, the only proper one for receiving intelligence.[23]

Synesios of Ptolemais (Kyrenaika), in the later fourth century, used these ideas in playful fashion in his *Praise of Baldness*. Though the vulgar admire hair, as they do anything external, the spherical is the blessed form. As the moon waxes to the full, so does baldness till it exhibits the head "shining back with full-orbed circle to the light of heaven". The best of men, priests and philosophers, are all painted as bald men.

Macrobius further tells us that the tall hat or *kalathos* on Sarapis symbolises "the height of the sun and the power of his capacity, which is such that all earthly elements return to him, drawn there by the emitted heat"; and he cites an oracle said to have been given to Nitokreon of Cypros when he wanted to know the nature of Sarapis (then a new god):

> The nature of my divinity I'll now declare;
> My Head's the heaven's adornment, my Belly the sea.
> My Feet are earth, my two Ears are the air,
> My eyes, flashing afar, are the sun's light shining free.[24]

"Adornment" here is *kosmos*, carrying on the play on the word we shall soon discuss.

This kind of imagery occurs in the magic papyri, and is carried on into medieval times in such works as *Causae et Curae* of St Hildegarde.[25] Egyptian imagery appears in the following hermetic passage from Stobaios, in which the earth is depicted as a divine figure stretched out flat.

The Earth rests in the centre of All, laid on its back like a man looking up at the sky, and it is divided into as many parts as a man has members. It turns its glance towards the heaven as towards its father, so that, following the heaven's changes, it changes itself in what is proper. It has its Head situated to the South of the universe, the Right Shoulder to the East, the Left Shoulder to the West, the Feet under the Bear, the Right under the Tail, the Left under the Bear's Head, Thighs in the regions that come after the Bear, the Middle Parts in the Middle Regions.

Proof of this is that men who live in the South and dwell on the Head of the Earth have their tops well formed and beautiful hair. The Easterners are disposed to attack and are followers of the Archer—these characteristics belong to the right hand. The Westerners are secure against danger as they usually fight left-handed and all the effects that the others get by acting on the right they go by acting on the left. Those who live under the Bear have [splendid] feet and well-made legs as well. Those who come after that and a little further still, the geographic region now

called Italy and Greece, all these folk have beautiful thighs and fine
bottoms, and so, on account of the extreme beauty of these parts the men
there copulate with males.

As all these members, compared with the others, are lazy, they make
the people inhabiting them also lazy. But then in the middle of the
earth is situated the most sacred land of our ancestors [Egypt], as the
middle of the human body is the sanctuary of the heart alone; and so,
my child [Horos] the people of that land, as well provided with other
qualities as the rest of mankind, are in an exceptional manner more
intelligent than those others and endowed with wisdom because they
have been raised to the place of the heart.[26]

This is an unusual passage, though its components, apart from the
Egyptian image of the outstretched earth-deity, all derive from
astrological speculations. The astrologers worked out *klimata* of
the earth, each under its own star-controls and owning its own
character; but here the *klimata* are devised in terms of the earth
as a single human body. The characteristics allotted to each *klima*
seem to have no relation to facts but to be dogmatic derivations
from the part of the body in question—except in the case of the
Greeks where the (apparently) satirical remarks about bottoms
has some basis in reality. The rare term *toxianoi* seems to mean
"subjects of the constellation Archer and thus good archers
themselves"—perhaps a reference to the Parthians: in which case
we have some indication of the text's date. *Eukoryphoi* may mean
that the Southerners have large tall craniums or big upstanding
heads-of-hair: that they are Sudanese Negroes. *Oulotrichai*
would then mean "crinkly-haired". The division of the earth
into seven bodily parts appears also in the Hippokratic *On the
Week*.[27]

A text that seems of a related kind has been recovered from the
Essene library that was put into the caves of the Dead Sea. It is
written in code, mainly made up by reversing the normal order
of the letters, and substituting Greek or other alphabets for some
of the square-letter Hebrew script found elsewhere in the scrolls.
There are only fragments; the text has been put together from
scores of small pieces scattered on the cave-floor. But the work
clearly dealt with the physical and spiritual characteristics produced by birth under the various zodiacal sections. Thus, a man
born under the Bull would have long thin thighs and toes. Everyone's spiritual system was made up of so many parts of light, so
many of darkness; the total of parts was nine—apparently a

reference to the nine months in the womb. A person who had eight parts from the House or Pit of Darkness, and only one from the House of Light, had thick fingers, hairy thighs and short stubby toes. His zodiacal sign is lost, but perhaps it was the Lion. Someone with the opposite share of parts was curly-bearded, of medium height, with "eyes like black and glowing coals", well-ordered teeth and fine tapering fingers. The scheme of nine parts of light and darkness suggests the moon as the formative power.

An hermetic conceit was to call man the *kosmos* (adornment) of the *kosmos* (universe). "The demiurge has sent onto earth, as ornament of this divine body [the cosmos], man the living mortal ornament of the living immortal."[28] The early usages of the word *kosmos*, we may note, are all based on the idea of orderliness, with a suggestion of the customary. Something done against *kosmos* is shameful; when men sit in the correct order of rank, the result is *kosmos*. Homer and Hesiod also used the term in reference to women's decorations. In Crete the chief magistrate was called *kosmos* as the regulator of order and custom. The first use of *kosmos* as world-order or universe was made by Pythagoras or Parmenides; and though we have no means of deciding definitely which thinker had the priority, the ideas of the universe as a system of good order, with inner relations of hierarchy or proportion, and with an overtone of an effect of beauty and ornamentation (above all in the stars), seems especially appropriate for Pythagoras. Xenophon uses the phrase, "the *kosmos* as it is called by the Sophists", which suggests that the term still had in his time a certain strangeness.

The *Asclepius* says that if man is in accord with God, "he brings about that in a way he himself and the world are an ornament of one another—and further, as a result of this divine structure of man, there is accorded to him a world, or, as the Greeks say more correctly, an order [cosmos]".[29] Finally we may take an hermetic poem (often cited as Orphic) in which we are told that man has the planets in him:

> Seven stars turn circling on Olympos' threshold.
> With them Time accomplishes his endless revolution.
> The Moon that shines in the night, lugubrious Saturn,
> the dear Sun, the Paphian who prepares the bridal bed,
> impetuous Ares, swiftwinged Hermes and Zeus
> first author of all birth, whose issue is Nature.
> These same stars have shared out the race of men

and in us are Moon, Zeus, Ares, Paphian, Kronos,
Sun, and Hermes. And such is our lot; to draw
from the *Aither* flowing tears, laughter, anger,
generation, word, sleep, desire. The tears
are Kronos, the generation Zeus, the word
Hermes, the fury Ares, sleep the Moon, desire
the Cytherean, laughter the Sun; through him,
the Lord of Justice, the spirits of men rejoice
and all the infinite world.[30]

These ideas and positions are not abstract, not something worked
out by a dry logic. They beget trembling and exalted convictions
of unity with the whole universe, which is felt as a living thing
in ceaseless process of self-fulfilment. "Grasping in your mind
that nothing is impossible for you, consider yourself immortal and
capable of understanding everything. . . . Ascend beyond all

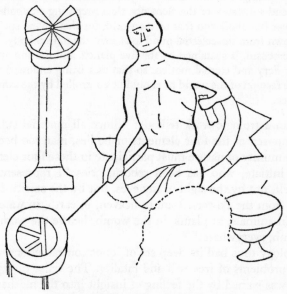

Fig. 29. Astronomer on Brading mosaic

height, descend below all depth. Gather into yourself the sensa-
tions of creation, of fire and of water, of dryness and of humidity,
imagining that you are at one and the same moment everywhere,
on earth, in the sea, in the heaven, that you have not yet been born,
that you are beyond death.'[31]

The astrologers thus expanded the doctrine that all things were composed of the four elements into one of dynamic correspondences between all parts of the universe. They were seeking to move beyond a general concept of a unitary material process into one which brought in the question of structure, of precise relationships between the parts; but they sought mathematical definition only of one section of phenomena, that of star-movements. Firmicus Maternus states:

In the first place you must know that God, that artificer of man, has produced under the direction of Nature the form of man and his whole stature and substance after the pattern and fashion of the world. He has compounded man's frame, as that of the world, out of the four elements, fire and water, air and earth, so that out of the mixture of these he might equip a living being after the divine fashion. He compounded man by divine handiwork, so that within the small compass of his body he might bestow under the requirements of Nature the whole energy and substance of the elements, thus preparing an abode, frail if you please but similar to that of the world, for that divine spirit which came down from the celestial mind to sustain the mortal body. So man, as a microcosm, is sustained by the five planets and the sun and moon by their fiery and eternal motion, so that as a being endowed with life after the fashion of the world he should be controlled by the same divine substance.

Again an astrologic work tells us: "Since all material substances are composed of the four elements or bodies, man too because of the community of nature must participate in these four elements." The initiate, who has been reborn, cries "I represent things to myself, not by the sight of my eyes, but by the spiritual energy I draw from the Powers. I am in heaven, in earth, in water. I am in air, in animals, in plants, in the womb, before the womb, after the womb, everywhere."[32] Astrology thus had its deep set of inner contradictions, centred on the problems of free will and fatality. The sense of rapturous release was gained by the feeling of insight into the mechanism of destiny, even of doom, as we noted with Seneca. The contradiction crystallised into the conflict of two schools: those with a rigidly mechanistic viewpoint, who held that everything was determined, and those who held that some things were determined, but not everything. The latter school held that it was possible by inquiry into the stars to learn how to make activities or procedures prosper, by choosing the auspicious moment. Free choice was nothing but the learned choice of the right time at which to start. So the astrology based on this outlook was called katarchic, from *katarchē*, beginning.

But both schools of astrology were hampered by the fusion of scientific methods with various irrational assumptions. Not merely the belief that the stars were alive, were gods; rather the conviction that the moral and psychological nature of each star was known, its peculiar qualities and powers, with which in turn it affected men and all life on earth. The astrologer was able to point, correctly enough, to the close link of the Sun with all earthly genesis and growth.

. . . the Sun, which nourishes the seeds of all plants, is the first also to gather from them the first fruits as soon as he rises; for this gathering of his uses his rays, if one may employ the term, like immense hands. What indeed are hands for him but those rays that gather in the first place the suavest emanations of plants?[33]

The hand-image is Egyptian. Under Akhenaten we find the sun's rays depicted as ending in hands.[34]

See then how in the earth, in the most central parts, there spurt many sources of water and fire, and you can see together in the same place the three natures of fire, water, and earth, all dependent on a single root. This has brought about the belief that there exists for all matter a single storeroom, which both provides for the supply of matter and also receives in return the sustenance coming from on high.

It is thus indeed that the Demiurge, I mean the Sun, binds together heaven and earth, sending substance down, raising matter up, drawing everything near to himself, right up, sending out from himself and giving everything to all things, and spreading liberally over all his light. For he it is whose good energies penetrate not only into heaven and air, but also on the earth into the deepest gulf, into the abyss . . .

The Sun is established in the middle, wearing the cosmos like a crown, and like a good chariot-driver he has assured the equilibrium of the world-chariot and has attached it to himself to make sure that it will not be carried into a disordered course. . . .

With the part of his light that tends towards the height—that is, with the rays the one of his two faces looking up skywards sends out—he nourishes the immortal parts of the world, while, with his light that is imprisoned in the world and bathes with its lustre the entire concavity of water, earth, air, he vivifies and sets in movement, through birth and transformations, the living beings that subsist in these parts of the world.

In short, the intelligible world depends on God, the sensible world on the intelligible, and the Sun, across the intelligible and the sensible worlds, receives from God, for his provision, the influx of the Good; that is, of creative action [*demiourgia*]. Besides, all round the sun gravitate the eight spheres, dependent on the Sun, that of the fixed-stars, the six spheres of the planets, and the single sphere that surrounds the earth. On these spheres depend the *daimones,* and on the *daimones,* men . . .[35]

There are eight spheres also in the *Epinomis,* but there made up of Sun, Moon, fixed-stars and five planets. Here the total forms an ennead. The six spheres are those of the five planets and the moon; the single sphere is that of the atmosphere.

But, while thus glorifying the Sun with a considerable degree of truth, the astrologer also assumed that the planet Mars was warlike, the planet Venus was feminine and concerned with love, and so on. The ancient associations of a god with a planet and the character which that god had developed were accepted as scientific axioms from which to deduce the sort of influences that the planet exerted. The stars were seen as beings with will, sex, strong emotions. Their living natures are reflected in the terms used about them. They rise and set, see, hear, rejoice, grieve, are gay or sad, obey commands, and so on, with many epithets to express their attitudes to men. Some astrologic writers went so far as to find the origin of all emotions in the planets, so that what men felt was only a reflection of the impulses and feelings in the sky. We saw the hermetic verses which said "The tears are Kronos . . ." We are further told that "the powers and passions", *dynameis* and *pathē*, are common to us and the planets. The soul took on the various qualities of the planets on its downward flight, and it would give them back as it returns upwards.[36] The signs of the summer semicircle command the signs of the winter semicircle, and the latter obey. In the complicated system set out by Valens some signs obey others, some look at each other, and so on. A papyrus sets out three kinds of relations between them: seeing, hearing, perceiving.[37] Plato, developing on Babylonian bases, had much to do with this way of regarding the stars. In the *Symposion* human bodies are presented as offshoots of the planets and the *Timaios* seem to make them the products, then the dependents, of the astral gods.

In the *Phaidros* we meet an allegorical picture. Across the heavens circulate the souls, winged charioteers each with a pair of horses. They attach themselves at will to the escort of one of the twelve (or rather eleven) gods making their round. (There are eleven since Plato follows a Pythagorean myth that makes Hestia remain "alone in the house of the gods"; the hearth was traditionally a centre.³⁸) Rising up to the groups that follow the chosen gods, the souls reach the top of the starry vault beyond which lie the supreme celestial spectacles. Then with the fall of the charioteer, who loses his wings, comes the imprisonment in the body until Eros gives the souls strength enough to make a new ascent. The picture is by no means clear; but ancient commentators all agreed in seeing Zeus as the sphere of the fixed stars, Hestia as the earth, and the ten other gods as planetary and other spheres. Hestia despite her suggestion of fire cannot be taken as the Pythagorean central-fire.

The number of the revolving gods (eleven) makes one think of one form of the early Babylonian Zodiac, which was made up of eleven signs, since the Scorpion and his Pincers were counted as one sign; the twelve-division was applied first to the equator. Later the Balance took place of the Pincers in Greek accounts. Plato combines his eleven sky-gods with twelve month-gods. Certainly he is not narrowly following any Babylonian scheme; his gods are bodiless and are not attached to the sphere of the fixed stars. However, in the *Laws* the system is getting more rigid and he is not satisfied with a suggestive picture of the revolutions of the great gods of Greece, Zeus, Hera, Ares, and so on. The gods of the *Phaidros* have links with the signs of the ecliptic; in the *Laws* they appear as gods of the months while the *daimones* who follow them become gods of the days.³⁹ Indeed even in the *Phaidros* they are, with all their immateriality, attached to the zodiacal constellations by a sort of patronage they exercise over them. In speaking of rank, domain, power, and escorts, Plato is using an astrologic terminology, which reminds us of the twelve Taxiarchs of the Book of Henoch—a work full of Babylonian elements. Here we must not exclude Orphic sources, which may be linked with Zervanite theology; the account of the chariots suggests the Chariots of the Elements according to the Mages (described by Dion of Prousa). And there may well have been Pythagorean versions of the same sort of thing.⁴⁰ Plato makes a sort of transference of horoscopic powers to Love, invoking astral influences on pre-existent souls to explain the particular forms that desire takes among men: love, friendliness, ambition, homicidal fury. "Ares' servants breathe murder and are ready to immolate themselves with those with whom they are smitten." (He is thinking of the homosexual battle-devotion of men like those in the Theban Sacred Band.) "Those who've followed Zeus seek his mark in the one they love; they find out if he is philosophic and fitted to lead; those who have made part of Hera's escort seek to meet a royal character." And so on.[41]

The attribution of god-natures to the planets was slow in its full development. Apart from Venus (called Dawn or Dusk Star), the Greeks before Alexander used terms like Star of Zeus, not Zeus; Star of Hermes, not Hermes. The *Epinomis* states that the planets have only surnames. Astronomers devised expressive terms, mostly related to the brightness of the planet, such as Phainon, Phaethon, Pyroeis, Phosphoros, Stilbon. The last word, Flasher or Twinkler, was used for Mercury by Eudoxos and Aristotle.[42] But these names had little effect on astrologic predictions; they did not last long and were never translated into Latin. The stars became directly identified with the gods to whom they belonged.[43] By the end of the last century B.C. they were called by the names of the Olympians: Kronos or Saturn, Zeus or Jupiter, and so on. The earliest known horoscopes with such names seem to be dated A.D. 4 and 14. The first one has the Sun in the Balance, the Moon in the Fish, Kronos in the Bull, Zeus in the Crab, Ares in the Virgin; the Bull was setting and Aquarius at the nadir. The text ends with a warning of dangers; the subject is to take care for a certain time on account of Ares.[44]

The astrologers did not attempt to link the planets with the various myths told of the deities; they simply drew on mythology for the character of each deity, the complex of associations roused by the name. This discarding of myth, with a concentration on the essential characteristics of each deity, was helped by the allegorical interpretation of myth favoured by Zenon and the Stoics in general.[45] The astrological Zeus merged the supremacy of the Olympian, Father of Gods and Men, with the astrological aspects of a God of the Atmosphere. Venus-Aphrodite remained the goddess of love and pleasure; Mercury-Hermes was the astute and tricky schemer or enterpriser, who was also eloquent and a stimulator of the arts. Saturn had a livid look and moved slowly: he was seen as a prudent, grave, and melancholy old man, indifferent to human fates and even a little malevolent. Through his age he was given a sort of primacy; but also through ancient associations with the moment of sowing, he was thought to possess a generating virtue—though paternity did not at all suit his years. Mars the flamboyant, *pyroeis*, with his red fire colour, his movement by leaps, was seen as a bloody and capricious tyrant, enemy of man, liable to throw all nature into perturbation.[46]

In general two planets were favourable, Jupiter and Venus, two unfavourable, with Mercury neutral or equivocal. Their temperaments were analysed in terms of the four qualities mingled in them to varying degrees, produced by the four elements of Aristotelean theory. Warmth and dryness combined to beget fire; warmth and humidity, air; cold and humidity, water; cold and dryness, earth. The proportions were said to be conditioned by a planet's distance from sun and earth. The sun was set in the middle; above him, in order, Mars, Jupiter, Saturn; below him, Venus, Mercury, Moon. Those above were less humid than those below; they grew colder the further they were from the sun. Humidity was thought to produce femaleness, so the upper trio were male, the lower female (except Mercury who was hermaphroditic).[47]

The scheme's smooth working-out foundered on the character of Saturn, who, through his association with seed, had to be humid. In the Zodiac he had as houses Capricorn and Aquarius, cold wet signs; he was patron of gardeners and water-carriers. Traversing his houses, he begot rains in the atmosphere and in the body movements of cold humours, intestinal fluxes and so on. The Moon in leaving him created rheumatism and dropsies. Many more examples of inconsistencies, which increased as the systems grew more complex, might be cited. A further strain was built up by the need to keep on fusing astronomic fact with the fantasies about the god-natures of the planets and the zodiacal signs. The signs had to be endowed with definite characters linked with the imaginary and arbitrary patterns which had been imposed on their constituent stars. At the head of the troop of signs was the Ram. Thinkers who held to the Egyptian origin of Zodiac saw in it the Ram of Ammon (Amun). Ptolemaios, with no liking for it as the first sign, invoked the generative virtue of the spring as evidence that the Ram was symbolic of the opening year: an identification that did not suit the sex of the sign, for humidity was female.[48] The Greeks saw the Ram as one with the Fleece of Gold, the ram fought over by Atreus and Thyestes, or the ram that led the thirsty procession of Bacchos to the Oasis of Ammon (Siwa). Nonnos extravagantly makes the Ram the world-centre:

When I reach the Ram, the navel-star of Olympos,
in my exaltation I let the Spring increase
and crossing the herald of the Westwind,
the turning-point that balances day and night
I guide the dewy course of the Season bringing the swallow.[49]

The Ram's subjects were woolworkers and men making fortunes out of textiles; but as the Golden-Fleeced Ram was once submerged (when he lost Helle in the Hellespont) and lost his fleece, and as mortal sheep also are shorn, so traders meet sudden reversals and are kept going only by hope of a change for the better. The Ram was thus also a sign of ascension. The traits of its subjects were timidity mixed with stupidity, sharp outbursts of anger (the buttings with the ram-horns), shaky and shrill voices. The Ram was not a brilliant constellation, as it had been shorn of its gold.[50] Incidentally the Ram provides evidence for the claim that horoscopes were introduced late to the Greeks or Egyptians. The common use of the Ram 8° as vernal point in astrological texts—compare the vernal point of System B in Babylonian lunar theory—suggests that the Greek calculations were made about the time of Hipparchos. Eudoxos used the Ram 15° as his vernal point, as did several astronomers or almanac-makers of the Ptolemaic period in Egypt; the earlier norm however was soon lost and does not appear anywhere in astrological literature— another argument for the lack of schools and continuity in the fourth century and the third as well.[51]

Hipparchos is often cited by astrologers for the moon's elongation. The method in question shows the use of an epoch (Augustus —1) which makes it much later than Hipparchos; yet it may well go back to him, just as other linear methods go back to Babylonian originals. Hipparchos in the second century may well have played a key-part in the maturing of Greek astrology about that time.[52] Plinius says of him:

Hipparchos, who can never be praised enough, no one having done more to prove that man is related to the stars and that our souls are part of heaven, detected a new star that came into existence in his lifetime.[53]

Thus astronomers and astrologers alike were inspired by the conviction that they were demonstrating the manifest existence of a divine world. Ptolemaios put the emotion succinctly in a quatrain:

> I'm mortal, I know, and though I'm born for a day,
> following the serried stars on their circling way,
> I ascend to Zeus. No longer on earth my feet
> are treading, and ambrosia I eat.[54]

So much rhetoric was poured out, serious or feebly imitative, on

Fig. 30. Dionysiac officient with spotted skin; and the Sons of
Horos-Osiris in the sky near the Father (Orion-Osiris)

the claims of star-study to put all other human activities in the
shade, that we find Arellius Fuscus, who had been Ovid's
professor of oratory, a sceptic in the Karneadic tradition, ironically
parodying the vast pretensions and scope of astrology:

He to whom the gods themselves reveal the future, who imposes their
will even on kings and peoples, cannot be fashioned by the same womb
that bore us ignorant men. His is a superhuman status. Confidant of
the gods, he is himself divine. . . . He may set his sire among the stars
and claim descent from heaven. . . . No narrow span of years can be his;
his soul must be exempt from fate who proclaims the future's secrets to
the world. If these auguries are true, why then do we not devote all our
days to the pursuit of this lore? Why from infancy do we not fix our
eyes on nature and on the gods, seeing that the stars unveil themselves
for us and that we can hold converse with the gods? Why exhaust
ourselves in efforts to gain eloquence or devote ourselves to the profession
of arms? Rather let us lift up our minds by means of this science which
reveals the future, and before the appointed hour of death let us taste
the pleasures of the blest. . . .

He ends with a direct attack, using some stock arguments:

Too many seers have foretold long life, and while they thought of no
danger the day of doom overwhelmed them. To some they have
announced the nearness of death, yet these have survived to worn-out
days. To others they have promised happy years, yet every kind of
misfortune fell swiftly on their heads. Our life's destiny is unknown.
These predictions are but arbitrary fictions of the seers, no treasures
from the mine of true knowledge.[55]

But to return to the laudations. With the correspondence-theory of up-and-down flow of forces and of similar patterns in heaven and earth, the upright human frame became a sort of world-pole, a small version of the *ziqqarat* like the *gnomon,* connecting earth and sky. Man alone was upright because of this role of his, made so that he might look at the stars. And he looked at them because he was their kin; he saw and realised them on the principle of like-to-like, which was deep in ancient thinking. Poseidonios said: "Light is apprehended by the light-like power of vision; sound by air-like hearing; and similarly the nature of the universe must be apprehended by the reason that is akin to it."[56]

The Orphic verse, "It is by brightness we see; with the eyes we see nothing," would have been accepted by the greatest physicists, philosophers, and mystics such as Plotinos and Plato. "That which sees must be akin to and made like that which is seen to be adapted for vision. Never would the eye have seen the sun unless it were constituted sun-like, nor could the soul ever have seen the Good unless it had first become good" (Plotinos). The same view meets us in Proklos and in a devotee of astrology like Manilius, who asks, in the famous lines, "Who could know heaven save by the gift of heaven, or find God unless himself were part of the Divine?" (Angus.)[57]

7

Hellenistic Astrology: Egypt

There is not much evidence for astrologers connected with the Hellenistic courts. We have seen how the Babylonians tried at times to impress the early Seleukid kings. Soudines was at the Attalid capital of Pergamon, but we do not hear of the rulers consulting him. Berosos dedicated his main work to Antiochos I Soter. Kleopatra, according to Ploutarch, used an astrologer as a spy over M. Antonius; he was presumably a court-adviser. "There was with him a seer from Egypt, one of those who cast nativities; and he as a favour to Kleopatra or in sincere counsel, used frank terms in speaking with Antonius."[1] When Ptolemy III went on his Syrian campaign (247–246 B.C.) his cousin-wife Berenike vowed her hair to the gods in return for his safety. Annoyed at finding her shorn, he called in his priests and they swore that the tresses had vanished from the shrine of Aphrodite at Zephyrion while the astronomer Konon declared that he had noted a new constellation in the sky: which was named the Hair of Berenike. Here was a kind of katasterism. The stars in question lay between the Virgin, the Lion, the Big Dipper and Arcturus. Kallimachos wrote a poem in celebration, which Catullus later translated.

> Kypris sent me a new star among the old,
> washt in the waters, rising close to the immortals.[2]

Another Ptolemaic katasterism appears with Queen Arsinoe, who died on the 9th of July, 270 B.C. Kallimachus again wrote a poem, of which we have some fragments from a papyrus. The prefatory statement reads: "*Deification of Arsinoe*. The poet says she was snatched up by the Dioscures, and that an altar and a holy enclosure were established in her honour by the Emporion"— close to the harbour at Alexandreia:

Fig. 31. Mithraic symbols of the Persian (sickle and scythe: Mithras is shown as reaper and there is a link with Kronos-Saturn); symbols of Sun-Courier (whip, radiate halo, torch): mosaics at Ostia

... O bride already up under the starry Wain
snatcht away you were speeding past the Moon
... loud laments ... one voice ... Queen Arsinoe's gone ...
having suffered what was [our Star] quenched?[3]

The younger sister Philotera, already dead and honoured as a goddess, asks Charis (Grace) to fly to the top of Mt. Athos to find out the cause of the huge smoke column billowing across the Aegean—from the pyre.

The Hellenistic kings claimed cosmic as well as earthly rule. Demetrios Poliorketes wrapped himself in a cloak decorated with stars and zodiacal signs; he took possession of the astral world as evidence of his right to rule the world below.[4] Kleopatra at the great festival of Antonius' Donations at Alexandreia "assumed a robe sacred to Isis and was addressed as the New Isis"; this robe was also cosmic, as we see from a funeral relief.[5]

The world-cloak reappears in Mithraism. The Capuan fresco shows the god's mantle bluish purple on its underside and studded with planets; several other representations have the same symbolism and often the mantle is puffed up to bring out its role as the dome of heaven.[6] The Capuan picture is especially interesting in view of its colours. The caps of the Torchbearers (Morning and Evening Sun) are red like the top-side of the mantle, expressing vitality and the burning sky or *aither*. Kautes has a red mantle like his star-fronted cap, the rest of his clothes are orange and brown; he stands for the barren part of the year (stressed again by the grey-bearded bust below him) while Kautopates has green and grey on his clothes, with a female bust below and the Moon-bust above; he stands for the verdant time of the year. (When the sun

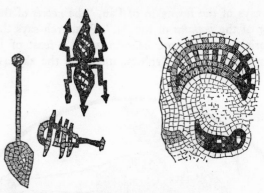

Fig. 32. Symbols of the Lion (fire-shovel, rattle or sistrum, Isiac, thunderbolt); symbols of the Bride (damaged: torch, diadem, lamp)

is in the Bull, indicating the spring, Kautes is shown with the bull's head in his hand; when Kautopates is seen with the Scorpion, the sun has passed into the Scorpion and autumn has begun.[7]) An Orphic poem sets out at length the cosmic robe:

> Here is the sacred costume in which to clothe
> the splendidly shining body of the Sun.
> First take a *peplos* resembling silver beams
> and hued with reds of fire, and cast it round:
> a spotted fawnskin shot with glancing colours
> spread broad on his right shoulder imitating
> the glorious Stars and all the holy Pole.
> Then over the fawnskin put a gleaming belt
> of gold, passed round his chest, a mighty symbol
> as when the Sun has just come up and shines
> dazzling at the far end of the world
> and slaps the waves of Ocean with his rays.
> That moment his enormous radiance,
> merged with the dew, makes light before him roll
> in whirls and eddies; and then, a marvellous sight,
> the vast circumference of the sea appears
> a belt that's simply claspt around his breast.[8]

The cosmic robe is a large theme; here we can only note a few details. Diodoros says: "Around Osiris is hung a garment of spotted skin, representing the *poikilia* of the sky"—*poikolos* means variegated, glinting with points of light, spotted, and in the epic of Nonnos it has a special force as expressing the play of light, the deep moment of metamorphosis in his alchemic universe.

Eusebios says of the fawnskin of Pan, "the *nebris* of the stars in the sky or of the *poikilia* of the All". Ploutarch says that priests at the burial of Apis wore *nebrides* as at a feast of Dionysos; Porphyrios, speaking of Orphics, mentions the sky as a *peplos*

Fig. 33. Mainad, possessed, with fawnskin, snake, and thyrsos
(cylix with white ground, Munich)

(mantle), "like the garment of the celestial gods". We may further note imperial coins that show the empress Sabina or Faustina going up to heaven on an eagle or peacock against a starry mantle.

The Mithraic colour-symbolism goes back into the Persian past and helps to clarify the whole question of Mesopotamian cosmic imagery, including the *ziqqarat*. An Avestan account states that the sky looks like a palace built of heavenly substance with a body of ruby, a garment inlaid with stars. We find the relevance to city-construction and world-mount if we turn to Herodotos' description of the royal city of Ekbatana, which the Median king had built in the eighth century B.C. on a low-topped hill with seven walled concentric circles, each higher than the one before. Palace and treasury stood at the top; the lower levels were correlated with levels of the court hierarchy, but the mere commoners were quite excluded and lived outside the walls. The wall-colours, going up, were white, black, scarlet, blue, orange, silver, and gold. The last two were certainly moon and sun; the rest were probably something like fiery morning, noon, earthfires of evening, earth (or murky air of the void and night, a Stoic concept), and waters-of-ocean (called the Wide Kasa in the *Avesta*). The same array of colours were used on the robe of warriorhood and sovranty as set out in the *Greater Bundashin* and the *Denkart*. This robe of purple, red or wine-colour was adorned with gold, silver and precious stones of various colours. Similar too in myth was the House Anagran (the Endless), the top of which reached to the Garodman (located in the realm of the sun and thus corresponding to the highest circle of the city). Here the robe was the sky-palace of the self-moving substance, both mansion and garment of the sky-gods. The many-hued clothes of Mithras and his Torchbearers seem meant to represent the ruling powers of the sky and of warriorhood.[9] The robe of Zurvan, however, the Long Selfcreated, whose body was the firmament, was said to be dark blue, which was the colour of the farmer; for the function of Zurvan was to rule the destinies of the world according to *aša*, just as the farmer had to till the soil to produce crops. Blue was the colour of genesis and fixed-law, just as the farmer was "bound to the law of the house" or to the lord's estate. (Necessity is thus correlated with the lord's power to order and control his dependents' lives.) The Deus Aeternus who divides the two halves of the Zodiac on the Barberini fresco stands on a blue globe; and the underside of Mithras' robe with its revolving planets on the Capua fresco is deep blue as against the fire-colour of the topside. We may add that the seven circular walls of Ekbatana correspond to the seven circles round the royal standards of the great gods of Syria, the upper two being sun and moon, or moon and sun.[10]

The colour-symbolism we are considering had a wide extension. Thus, in a Pompeian wall-painting we see Zeus seated in majesty, holding a long staff with a small sphere at either end and aureoled with an azure nimbus; he has been described as Zeus of the Blue Sky. A piece of Hellenistic tapestry from Arsinoe shows a god (a sort of Osiris-Dionysos-Sarapis) wearing a rich blue cloak that falls behind him; he too holds a staff or thyrsos with spheres at either end, and (like the Zeus) lifts his right hand to his head.

Fig. 34. Zeus of the Blue Sky (Pompeii); Zeus and Good Fortune (Pompeii)

In Egypt the blue lotus had an ancient solar significance. We see it in our tapestry in a place often taken by a pectoral, as also on the collar of Tutankhamen's mummy; blue-lotus flowers are found put into the bands of mummies. The sun-of-the-blue-sky had a revivifying effect.

Porphyrios, cited by Eusebios, shows these ideas in a clear form, though mingled with Egyptian imagery:

Having called the power of fire Hephaistos, they have made his statue in human form and have put on him a dark blue sky-cap [*pilos*] as a symbol of the circuit of the sky where exist the principle form and most unmixed of fire. But the fire of the sky that is carried down to earth is more diffused and in need of support and basis, that of matter. So he is lame because he is in need of matter for a support . . .

The Demiurge, whom the Egyptians call Kneph, is human shaped, but has a dark blue complexion, is master of girdle [*zonē*] and sceptre, and about his head lies a royal wing, because reason [*logos*] is rather elusive, hidden and not visible because he is a life-creator, and a king, and is moved intelligibly. So the nature of the wing rests on his head. But he [Porphyrios] says that this god ejects an egg from his mouth, from which a god is engendered, whom they call Phtha [Ptah] but the Greeks Hephaistos, and they interpret the egg to be the cosmos. . . .

Here the dark blue stands for the hidden *logos*, the girdle for the origin of life, the sceptre for kingship or controlling power, and the wing for intelligible motion. Porphyrios also says:

They fashion a representation of the cosmos by an anthropomorphic form with its feet together and clothed with a variegated garment reaching from above to the feet, and on his head he has a gold sphere, all because of no changing motion, because of the variegated nature of the stars, and because the cosmos is spherical.[11]

Reading these passages, with their direct Eastern relations, we feel again how close to the same sources was Plato, though he improvises freely and develops his own use of the imagery. What Porphyrios states in a single concentrated symbol, "a royal wing", expressing intelligible motion, appears in the *Phaidros* as the feathers keeping the soul in the intelligible world. "When it is perfect and fully feathered it roams in upper air and regulates the entire universe; but the soul that has lost its feathers is carried down till it finds some solid resting place"—the supporting matter of Porphyrios. The Phoenician Kronos-El seems a god of the world-order of time and motion; he and his correlatives lie behind the Platonic cosmos of the *Phaidros* and the *Timaios* as also behind the Aion of Mithraic religion.[12] The Egyptians had the cosmic Egg as well, but made no such important developments with it as the Mesopotamians and their neighbours.[13]

One Eastern prince who certainly did take astrology seriously was Antiochos I Epiphanes of Kommagene. High in the Taurus range a relief shows a conjunction of planets in the Lion; for long it was taken to depict the king's conception-horoscope, 17 July 97 B.C., but the date has now been shown to be 6 or 7 July, 62, his coronation-date after Pompeius had put him back on his throne.[14] The relief stands on the summit of Nimrud Dagh, about 7000 feet above sea-level. Here the king built his tomb, as near the stars as possible, with many colossal statues and long inscriptions dealing with the cult of himself, his ancestors, and his patron gods. He makes no self-abasing homage to the gods but meets them on equal terms with handshake, *dexiōsis*, in a pact of faith.[15] He makes a strong point of synthesising Greek and Iranian deities: Zeus-Oromazdes, Herakles-Artagnes. Mithra is called Apollo and at root is not much different from Helios-Hermes, while Ares is linked with Herakles-Artagnes. The tendency to triads or tetrads was perhaps stimulated by a Semitic tradition such as that found at Heliopolis (Baalbek). Details like the bundle of

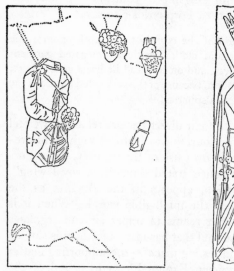 

Fig. 35. Scenes from Nimrud-Dagh: the King and Mithras

wands in Mithra's hand show borrowing from Mazdean ritual.[16] The inscribed law states that the priest in each sanctuary will put on his Persian garb for cult-rites twice a month, on the day of the king's birthday and of the festivals of his ancestors. Besides their obligations they are given certain privileges.[17] The motives are stated: a great purity is required of all celebrants and all subjects, together with a strict seclusion of the impure, those stricken with *miasma*. The stress here seems Mazdean. The king's celestial advantages and virtues, such as his *eusebeia* (piety), are seen as benefits for his people, who should be grateful for them. (We may compare the use of epithets like Pius or Felix by Roman emperors from Commodus to the Severi.[18]) The aspect of

Eternity is so emphasised that the first investigators thought they were dealing with a cult of Aion. What we see is a royal variant of Mithraism as it was developing into a mystery-cult, soon to invade the Roman world as it discarded its national basis. The mages who served Antiochos were however not identical with those bringing about the new direction of Mithraism; Antiochos was trying to organise and canalise for his own benefit certain cult-tendencies which were appearing over a wide area. Apart from the Mithraic aspects, his Graeco-Iranian pairs were ready for merging with such cults as those of Heliopolis.

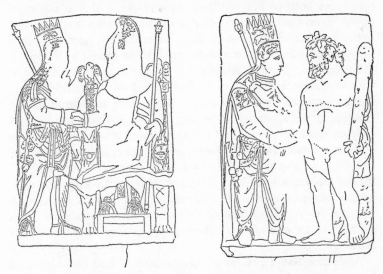

Fig. 36. More scenes: the King with Zeus, and with Herakles

On the western terrace, beside statues of the deities (who include the Goddess of Kommagene), is a huge relief of the Lion covered with stars and showing the Moon and three planets: Jupiter near the head, Mercury in the middle, Mars near the tail. The nineteen stars on or about the body agree well with the positions of the nineteen stars assigned to the constellation in the Katasterisms of pseudo-Eratosthenes.[19] The three planets are those of the three gods represented in statues and glorified in the inscriptions: Zeus, Apollo, Herakles; and the best evidence that the relief is not just a statement of the king's protectors plus a symbol of royalty (the Lion) is the crescent on the chest. Basiliskos—*regulus* in Latin—is the main star of the Lion; it was thought to make royal vocations and corresponded to an exaltation of the solar power in the passage through the Zodiac. The Lion too played an important part in the grades and symbol of the Mithraic cult as they developed under the Empire, and was connected with Kronos-Aion, the lion-headed god of Time. (A Lion often appears on funerary monuments in Asia Minor as a guardian; in a Cilician inscription we find him as the guardian of the estate of one Sandaios—incorporating the divine name Sanda—who seems to be still alive. Here the Lion is called "Mightiest of Beasts and *Mystes* or Initiate of the Gods". There are perhaps side-references both to the Mithraic mystery-grade and to the royal power incarnated in the beast. The Cilician Sandes was identified with Herakles.) There can be little doubt that the horoscope thus depicted on the rock was associated with the arrival of Pompeius in Syria after defeating Mithridates. No doubt the Roman victory, with its multiple repercussions, had stirred up the astrologic and magian groups. Here were events threatening or promising big changes in the allocation of power; and the diviners would want to learn what the stars could tell them about it all. Possibly some of them, realising that the future lay with Rome, put about prophecies of a world-ruler and saviour being born at this time, and these prophecies were later linked with Octavian-Augustus after he had beaten Antonius. The forecast said to be made by Nigulus Figulus (in 63) about Octavian's birth would then represent an attempt to fix one of these floating predictions on to a famous astrologic figure.[20]

Antiochos was a zealous commemorator of both his birth and his coronation: his text states:

I have sanctified the Birthday of my Flesh, 16 Aydnaios, and the Day of my Coronation, 10 Loos, to the Manifestations of the Great Gods who were for me the Guides of a Fortunate Reign and for the Whole Realm the source of Common Benefits. . . . And for the Rest of Time, each single month I proclaimed that the aforesaid Days—for my Birth the 16th and for my Coronation the 10th—be forever honoured by sacrifices.[21]

An inscription found in Selik near Samosata also mentions the monthly celebration of the Coronation.[22] We know of two more coronation-horoscopes: that of Leontios in 483 and that of Khosroes I (in Arabic) for 18 August 531. We shall later look at the Leontios horoscope.

Meanwhile it is expressive of the ways in which the Babylonian and Syrian ideas steadily moved westwards, that the handclasping equality between ruler and gods at last appears in the Roman world some hundred and fifty years later. On the Arch of Trajan at Beneventum we see the emperor being greeted on the Capitol by the supreme Triad and other deities. Juppiter hands over his thunderbolt, to express the fact that the emperor is now the highgod in an earthly form. A stage further appears when we find the two consorts of Capitoline Jove, Juno and Minerva, leaving him to guard the black stone Elegebal, a solar symbol (perhaps a meteorite) brought from Syria by Elegabalos the emperor. On a coin the same stone is guarded by the Eagle as it lies enthroned on a chariot guided by a star.

Fig. 37. The Lion of Nimrud-Dagh

We can now turn to Egypt and ask what contribution, if any, that land made to the general tradition. Though the evidence suggests that only in the last century B.C. did horoscopes come into much use outside Mesopotamia, there may well have been an earlier diffusion. Herodotos tells us of the Egyptians:

[they were] the first to assign to each month and day a particular deity, and to foretell a man's character by the date of his birth; a discovery which the Greek poets have turned to account. The Egyptians too have made more use of omens and prognostics than any other nation; they keep written records of the observed results of any unusual phenomena, so that they come to expect a similar consequence to follow a similar event in the future.[23]

The Greek poets of whom he speaks seem to be Hesiod and composers of occult works like those attributed to Orpheus and Mousaios. To foretell a man's future by his birthdate does not necessarily imply horoscopes; Herodotos seems merely to refer to calendars of lucky and unlucky days.[24] Such lists included predictions as to what would happen to someone born, say, on a certain unlucky day: death by crocodile, snakebite, and so on. Yet more rudimentary forms of birth-prediction are found in Hittite texts of the thirteenth century B.C., where a child's fate depends on the month of birth.[25]

It was inevitable, as Hellenistic astrology grew, that large claims would be made for Egypt. Fragments of early astrologic works have come down with Egyptian names attached, assigned to a distant past. Plinius avoids taking sides by saying that some persons take Atlas as the art's inventor, some look to the Mesopotamians, others to the Egyptians. But many scholars, after astrology had taken root in Egypt, challenged Babylonian priority.[26] In the later period, while some students were satisfied with claims to immediate revelations, others wanted a vast antiquity for the art. Berosos was said to have spoken of records covering 432,000 or even 468,000 years; Cicero reported 470,000 years; Diodoros, 473,000. Epigenes said the Babylonians had tablets of 730,000 years of star-observations as against the mere 490,000 suggested by Krito-demos. Simplikios went furthest with more than 1,440,000 years, though Kallisthenes, executed by Alexander the Great, was said to have mentioned only 31,000 or even 1,900 as the figures given him by Babylonian scholars. Hipparchos was said to have made the sum 170,000, while Iamblichos credited the Chaldeans with having gained in this period complete knowledge of the Seven Kosmokratores.[27] In reply, the Egyptians claimed figures ranging from 48,863 years to 400,000 or 630,000.[28] In the last century they were putting out strong propaganda on their own belief. Diodoros, about 59 B.C., begins by saying, correctly, that their geometry and arithmetic had been built up to deal with boundary lines on account of the endless disputes after the yearly flooding.

And arithmetic is useful in business affairs connected with making a living, and also in applying the principles of geometry, not to mention that it is of no small aid to students of *astrologia* as well. For the positions and arrangements of the stars, as well as their motion, have always been the subject of careful observation among the Egyptians, if anywhere in the world. They have kept to this day records about each of these stars over an incredible number of years, this theme of study having been zealously kept up among them from ancient times. They have also observed with the utmost keenness the motions, orbits, and stoppings of each planet, as well as the influence of each of them on the generations, *geneseis*, of all living things—the good or the evil effects, namely, of which they are the cause.

And while they often succeed in predicting to men the events that will befall them in the course of their lives, not infrequently they foretell destruction of the crops, or, on the other hand, abundant yields, and pestilences that are to attack men or beasts, and as a result of their long observations they have prior knowledge of earthquakes and floods, of the risings of comets, and of all things which the ordinary man regards as quite beyond finding out. And, according to them, the Chaldaioi of Babylon, who were colonists from Egypt, enjoy the fame they have for their *astrologia* because they learned that science from the priests of Egypt.

In fact Egyptian mathematics were very rudimentary in comparison with that of the Babylonians. They had a set of signs for powers of ten (1; 10; 100; 1,000; 10,000; 100,000). Numbers were written with the highest figures to start with, then those next in

Fig. 38. The Bull's Foreleg: tomb of Senmut

order, down to the units. There was no sign for nought, but some scribes left a blank to represent it. Addition and subtraction were easy. To multiply, the following method was used. Say the problem was 15 × 13. The scribe began by writing down: 1–15, 2–30, 4–60, 8–120. He stopped there as 13 was less then twice 8. From the left-hand column he took the numbers that made up 13: 1, 4, 8. He added together the numbers in the corresponding right-hand column (15, 60, 120), getting a total of 195. Numbers were divided by an inverse process. The only fraction they conceived was that with one as numerator, expressed by a sign like a long thin oval over the denominator. A complex fraction they reduced to the sum of two or three separate fractions with different denominators; thus two-fifths was not written as one-fifth plus one-fifth but as one-third plus one-fifteenth. There was however a sign for a third, and others, rarely used, for three-quarters, four-fifths, five-sixths. The Babylonians had devised algebra, but the Egyptians never made such a step of abstraction; their geometry, like their arithmetic, was severely practical. (One text deals with the division of various numbers of loaves among ten men so that each man gets the same share both in quantity and in number of pieces.) They, like the Babylonians, knew how to determine the area and volume of simple geometrical figures (triangles, rectangles, trapezoids, etc.); and they could work out the frustrum of a pyramid with a square base—a problem for which the Babylonians had an incorrect formula. Their formula for the area of a circle was a good approximation. But they always had a practical aim, e.g. the storage of grain in barns of different shapes, the amount of soil needed for a ramp. In general both they and the Babylonians used an essentially arithmetical method; the problem was stated in numbers and the procedure simply set out what to do with the numbers. There was scarcely any reference to the way that the rules arose, or any trace of a logically construc-ted system with analytical proofs.[29] However, at the end of some calculations in the Rhind Papyrus the author wrote, "It is equal", "It is just that"; a sort of Q.E.D. He thus shows a certain awareness of the power of reasoning, which went beyond a purely empirical approach.[30]

The Egyptians had in fact collected data about the stars, but their interest was connected with the fixation of the calendar, not with an obsession about omens. They wanted to determine the night-hours as furnishing the framework of the liturgy. Thus, we have a papyrus with a commentary on the doctrine of the Dekans, which served to indicate the hour of the night, and ano-ther dealing with positions of the moon, so as to establish a cyclic calendar of 25 years.[31] In the latter, the twelve first columns stand for the twelve months of the civil year; each column has 25 lines for the consecutive years of the cycle; and generally two consecutive entries are twice $29\frac{1}{2}$ days apart—though occasionally

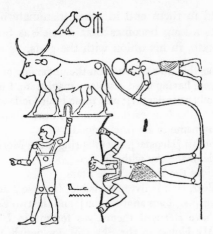

Fig. 39. The Bull's Foreleg: tomb of Seti

30 days are added: in which case we get a year of 13 months, the Great Year.[32]

As for omens, the priests were not concerned to draw up systematic accounts, though we know some birth-signs. The cries uttered by the newborn child were interpreted: a cry sounding like a negation was taken to mean an early death, and if the child turned his eyes towards the sun, that also was a death-sign. There were naturally many forms of omen-reading and oracular inquiry; dream (incubation), ordeal, lekanomancy (by cup), necromancy.[33] In later periods the practices took on more and more a judicial aspect. But the element of acute anxiety that we found among the Babylonians is not present. The world-outlook has the same basis of correspondences, but the much greater stability of the political system, the much smaller part played by trade, begot a more secure sense of the enduring order in the cosmos: an order that had its reflection in the temple-rites and was in turn sustained by those rites. Hence the comparative lack of interest in divination among the clergy. What was the sense of searching, at much trouble, in nature for signs of a future that would only turn out a repetition of the past? The whole culture aimed at perpetuating the repetitive cycle or cycles. So the Egyptians had recourse to an oracle only to learn the answer to some immediate problem which had already come up, such as the choice of a new ruler or the discovery of some guilty person.[34]

All this does not mean that the stars lacked importance. A god

F

was manifested in them and in other inanimate objects. In the Pyramid Texts a king becomes Star as well as Sun in his sky-ascent after death, in his union with the gods.

Lo, I stand up as this Star which is on the underside of the Sky. I give judgment as a god, having tried cases as a magistrate. I have summoned them [his heavenly attendants?]; and these Four Gods who stand at the Staffs of the Sky [the four cardinal points], bring them to me so that they may tell my name to Re [the sungod].

My sister is Sothis [Dogstar], my offspring is the Morning Star. I am on the underside of the sky with Re.

The King guides the Imperishable Stars.

The Sky is clear, Sothis lives [is visible] because I am a living one, the Son of Sothis [*i.e.*, I am another star], and the two Enneads [groups of nine gods] have cleansed themselves for me in Ursa Major, the Imperishable. My House in the Sky will not perish, my Throne on Earth will not be destroyed, for men hide, the gods fly away. So this has caused me to fly up into the Sky into the company of my brethren the Gods. Nut the Great has uncovered her arms for me, the Two Souls who are at the head of the Souls of On who attend on Re have bowed themselves, even they who spend the night making this mourning for the God.[35]

Nut, the heavenly vault, has thrown back her cloak and stretched out her arms in welcome. The Two Souls are probably Isis and Nephthys; the mourned god, Osiris the King, ends by flying up to the sky as a bird. Nut is thought to conceive the dead king in her womb and bring him forth as a Star.[36] The king's role was

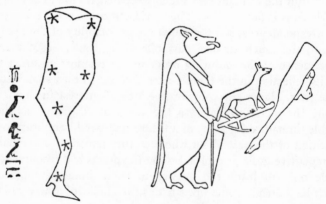

Fig. 40. The Bull's Foreleg: Herakleopolite period, Assiut; Roman period, Dendera

finally taken over by commoners, and from the New Kingdom onwards Nut was depicted on the inside of their coffin lids as well as on the king's.[37] Association with the constellation Orion gave Osiris in Heliopolian theology a strong astral basis, and in the form Osiris-Orion he became the father of Horos-Sopd (Sothis).[38] In the later period, according to Ploutarch, the soul of Isis was called Sothis, that of Horos, Orion, that of Typhon, the Bear. Elsewhere however Ploutarch took Typhon as the world of the parching Sun, Osiris as that of the moisture-yielding Moon; the dismembering of Osiris into fourteen parts represented the period when the Moon was on the wane, and the conflict expressed the destructive action of the Sun against the Moon. Typhon was beaten and restrained, but freed again to fight Horos (the earthly world). Other theorists said that Moon-Osiris was eclipsed because Sun-Seth was opposite and the Moon fell into the earth's shadow as Osiris into his coffin. Again the Moon hid and eclipsed the Sun on the 30th of the month, but did not wholly destroy it, just as Isis did not destroy Typhon-Seth. (Here Isis, not Osiris, takes over the Moon.) A further opinion was that Typhon was not Sun, but the earth's shadow into which the Moon fell during eclipse.[39]

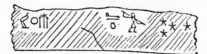

Fig. 41. Herakleopolite-period sky-design

In the *Book of the Dead* the dead man is aided in his ascent by the stars:

The god Shu has made me to stand up, the God of Light has made me to be vigorous by the two sides of the Ladder, and the Stars that never set [the circumpolar] put me on my way and bring me away from slaughter.

He is identified with the stars in the deification of his members: "The fingers of Osiris Ani: triumphant are the fingers of Orion."

You rise up like Sah [Orion]. You arrive like the star Bau, and the goddess Nut [stretches out] her hands to you. Sah, the son of Re, and Nut, who gave birth to the gods, the two mighty gods of heaven, speak to one another saying: Take the scribe and draughtsman Nebseni into your arms . . . You are raised up and hear the songs of commemoration through the doors of your house.

You shall come forth into heaven, you shall sail over the sky, you shall hold loving intercourse with the stargods.[40]

The texts are here taking over the king's star-role in the Pyramids: "My bones are iron and my limbs are the Imperishable stars. I am a star that illumines the sky . . ."

The Unsetting Stars are, as I have said, the circumpolar, the Unresting are the southern. Varying numbers are given for the Unsetting; twelve of them towed the sunboat through the Underworld at night and did constant homage to the god of heaven, they were the ministers and followers of Osiris.[41] Most important was Septet, Sothis, with its heliacal rising connected with the Nile-flood. In a Pyramid text it is called the Year itself. "It is Sothis your beloved daughter who prepares yearly sustenance for you in

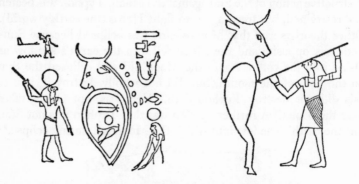

Fig. 42. The Bull's Foreleg: Ramasseum; Roman period

this her name of Year and who guides me to you." She was the Ba of Isis. As a dominant star identified with Hathor, she was shown as a cow with a star between the horns, lying in a boat. She was also the first of the Dekans.[42]

Not many constellations are known by name or position. Most important was Sah, Orion, "long of leg and lengthy of stride", who presided over Upper Egypt. He is Father of the Gods as well as the Ba of Osiris (as also was the Moon); a Great Star on his shoulder marked him out.[43] A female counterpart Sah-t seems included among the Souls of Heliopolis. Sah was associated with Septet and in late times confused with Canopus. He was represented as a god with sceptre in right hand and star in outstretched left; he looks back as he runs. Texts show him as the Heavenly Ferryman and he was probably the prototype of the ferryman depicted with backturned head in the *Book of the Dead*. He was Her-f-Ha-f, who is also called Doorkeeper of Osiris.[44]

Hathor assumed at times the form of Sothis; she appeared near the Sun in the second half of July. When Re entered his boat, she, as daughter-wife, went with him and took her place on his forehead as a crown. Her eyes are described as sun and moon. The Seven Hathors were Fates or Birth-Fairies who in tales possess the power of predicting the destinies of those they visit. At Dendera they were shown as lovely young women in close-fitting tunics, with vulture-head dresses, with cowhorns and solar disks on their heads; as goddesses of love and pleasure they hold tambourines. In Ptolemaic times attempts were made to identify them with the Pleiads, a constellation that seems unknown to the early Egyptians. The stars were said to be in the sign of the Bull; in a vignette of the *Book of the Dead* we meet the Bull with the Seven Hathors—in a chapter concerned with providing the dead man with meat and milk, cakes and ale.[45]

The Great Bear was a very important constellation; but it was seen as Bull rather than Bear. The seven stars were grouped in the pattern of the Bull's Foreleg—though after a while the shape become a sort of egg on which a bull's head was set, then again in the Ptolemaic and Roman periods it became the Foreleg, but now with a bull's head on it. Its name was *mshtyw*. We see it clearly on a coffin-lid of the Herakleopolitan period, called "*Mshtyw* in the Northern Sky". In the XVIII Dynasty we hear of "[the Foreleg] in the Northern Sky"; and in a mystical Graeco-Roman text, of "a golden calf's shoulder which is the Great Bear".[46] The Foreleg was imagined when the constellation was standing up in the eastern sky; when the stars were high up above the pole they lay in an extended position and were felt to compose the pattern of an Adze. In the Pyramid Texts *mshtyw* once has a determinate with both star and adze. In these texts an adze-shaped

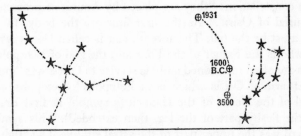

Fig. 43. Constellations: Mshtyw and the falcon-headed figure; and the positions of the Pole: dotted line between shows the path
(after Wainwright)

instrument for opening the mouths of the dead was also called *mshtyw*, and was thought of as made of iron. The earthly adze was then the mere reflection of the heavenly star-adze which immortalised the dead by opening their mouths. Perhaps through its iron composition *mshtyw* was closely connected with Set—as Ploutarch knew when he declared that Arktos (the Bear) was "the soul of Typhon" or Set, and that iron was "the bone of Typhon". (The Bedouin of the western desert still call the Great Bear *en Rigl*, the Leg.) In the drawings *mshtyw* is confronted by a falcon-headed man with extended arms who stretches a cord. Gradually (at least, by Ramessid times) the cord was changed into a spear, and the man and the bull were seen in conflict. By the Roman period this change was complete. This man was called the Uplifter of Wings or Claws—the wings or claws being represented by the arms he uplifts. He seems certainly to be made up of the stars now composing the constellation Cygnus. As *mshtyw* was Set, his opposer could only be Horos; thus the myth of their conflicts was transposed into the skies. By the New Kingdom the Uplifter had also given a name to one of the mouth-opening instruments, which is otherwise called *dwn-'* (*dwn* meaning to stretch). The name *Dwn-'nw* was given to a Horos with wings outspread.

The body of the Bull would apparently have been taken as the fleshy part of the leg; and the stars forming this must have been the four of which Ramses VI spoke as "the Four Northern Stars of pure *mshtyw*". These stars were in fact the Four Children of Horos, for in the XVIII dynasty we read the names of those children: "These are they who are behind the Foreleg in the Northern Sky." A little later on in the same text the Four Children are again named as a section of the seven stars making up the whole constellation: "they are placed by Anubis as protectors for the burial of Osiris." As the first four are the body, the other three must be the tail. The seventh star is called Horos *mhnty-n-irty*, who is the Father of the Four and the god of Letopolis. His thighs are often mentioned and his service to Osiris was "guarding this left arm of Osiris which is in Letopolis". Letopolis was the capital of the Nome of the Haunch (a symbol at first drawn as only the fleshy part of the leg, then extended). This symbol or standard was the upper part of the astral *mshtyw*. The High priest of Letopolis, to complete the interconnections, was the most important Opener of the Mouth in Egypt.

We thus find the Bull, or its Foreleg, connected with both Set and Horos. Since we find Horos at Letopolis as the guardian of the Arm of Osiris, we may conjecture that he was at first the guardian of the Bull in the sky; then as the myths of his battles with Set increased and gained in importance, he was imagined as fighting the Bull as Set.

The constellation represented in the sixteenth dekan had as its chief star the abode of the god Shesmu; his hieroglyph was a

Fig. 44. Deadman (Ani) addresses Her-f-ha-f, the ferryman with backturned head; the block of slaughter of the god Sheshmu

winepress and he was said to come bearing water and wine, but later he was known as the headsman or executioner of Osiris. A lion-headed man, he hacked the bodies of the damned. His female counterpart, Shesemter or Sebshesen, had the head of a lioness. There are many more figures hard to locate in the sky, a god wearing a solar disk and gripping a bull's tail, six stargods shown between Sothis and Sah, or Zwntw who goes round the sky is said to cross it nine times a night. The Street of Stars in the Pyramid Texts is no doubt the Milky Way.[47]

But there seems little attempt at any precise observations despite the keen general interest in the stars as divine bodies to which the king, and then others, were thought to be able to ascend if the correct rituals and spells were used. Attention was mainly turned, apart from Sothis, on to Sun and Moon; and the problem of assuring the Sun a successful passage through various danger-points, especially in the Underworld (the site of his night-journey), was given much ritual expression.

Interest in the planets was late, with the exception of Venus.

However, with the Egyptians, as with others, she attracted attention as star of the morning and the evening, not as planet. The Pyramid Texts speak of the "Morning Star, Horos of the Netherworld, divine Falcon". She is the Lone Star: "Open up your place in the sky among the stars of the sky, for you are the Lone Star, the companion of Hu." We saw above the dead king calling the Morning Star his offspring. In the late period the Star was shown as a two-headed woman, each head with a different crown; by this time it had been discovered that the morning and evening stars were the same star.[48]

8

More on Egypt

But if the Egyptians were not much concerned with careful observations of the stars, they certainly took much interest in time-divisions; and it was in this matter that they made a contribution to Hellenistic astrology. They had divided the sky into 36 sections or *bakiu*, called *dekanoi* by the Greeks. Each dekan had its spirit or god and corresponded to ten days of the Wandering Year of 360 days. This dekan-belt was superseded by the Zodiac. It contained 12 signs, to each of which was attached 3 stars; and each god had his boat. The Dekans were the Living Bas of Gods. (*Ba* is a term hard to translate; "soul" is too loose and vague. The Ba emanated from the body and it ultimately became divinised; it originally was a manifestation of the power of a dead king or a god; it developed into a sort of otherself of the dead man, a personification of his vital forces; and in Ptolemaic and Roman texts we find, "May his Ba live before Osiris."[1])

The Egyptians also contributed to the Hellenistic fund of ideas the division of the day into 24 hours (as opposed to the Babylonian division into 12). At first the hours were of unequal length, depending on the seasons; and we meet schemes for varying daylights: a Ramesside papyrus on lucky and unlucky days sets out a system for the lengths of days and nights, month by month, with linear variations of 6 hours minimum and 18 hours maximum.[2] But in the Hellenistic period, under the influence of Chaldean-Greek mathematics the 12 day-hours and 12 night-hours were replaced by equinoctial hours of constant length—even then only in theoretical work. As at times astronomers used the sexagesimal system, at least for fractions, the equal hours were divided into 60s, so that we still speak of 24 hours, 60 minutes, 60 seconds. The dekans have left no trace in our system, though they underlay the 12-hour division of the night, and so of the whole 24-hour system. In Hellenistic times the dekans were brought into a fixed relation to the Babylonian Zodiac; and in the end they merely became thirds of the zodiacal system, each standing for 10° of the ecliptic. However, with the extension of astrology they regained their importance as Masters of Time, Chronokratores, especially in connection with the magic lores of plants and medicines. In this relation they invaded India and returned in even odder forms to Islam and the medieval West.[3]

Fig. 45. Egyptian Zodiac (Budge): Ram, Bull, Twins (Shu and Tefnut)

But to get inside the Egyptian outlook we must consider their Year, which consisted of 12 months of 30 days each, with 5 intercalary days. The origin did not lie in observations of the sun and was not connected with Sothis. It seems that the Egyptians, aware of the Flooding of the Nile as a great cyclic event on which their world depended, made records of the dates when the Nile rose. Those dates were indeed variable, but would yield a yearly average of 365 days. After a while, however, weaknesses were found in this system and a new factor was introduced as a check: the rising of Sothis. The notion that a calendar was created on a Sothic basis as far back as 4231 B.C. must be dropped. The ancient calendar was agricultural, based on three seasons.[4]

How then are we to explain the 30-day month, found also in Mesopotamia? Its schematism does not tally with the actual behaviour of the moon, which was much more complicated. We must admit that at all periods of Egyptian history there were real lunar months. These were carefully worked out and noted, for they had deep religious significances; and they had their reflection in myth in the tales of the loss and return of the moon's eye and its magical virtues.[5] In a twelfth-century list of offerings at Benihasan we meet Short and Long Years, years with respectively either 12 or 13 moon-festivals (new moons). The same system appears in a demotic papyrus where a simple cycle of 25 years is set out, by means of which we can tell if a year has 12 or 13 new moons and on what dates in the civil calendar they will come.

Schematic moon-systems, such as that of a 30-day month, result from the tension between a calendar of real lunar months and the need felt by the government and by private business for some clear way of fixing dates ahead. Only a well-developed theoretical astronomy can predict with accuracy the length of

Fig. 46. Scarab (Crab); Lion

the real moon-month for any distance; and a schematic system obviates the need to keep or work out exact records of the actual lengths of a moon-month. We see the same situation in Babylonia where contracts that involved future deliveries were dated by the schematic calendar, and past rents or costs were computed in terms of a 360-day year and 30-day months. In astronomical texts as well the same schematism was used in dealing with solstice, equinox, lengths of day and night, shadow-length, rising and setting of fixed stars, and so on. All this shows that the schema was simply a way for dealing with dates in a rough practical way and was not meant to usurp the role of a more exact system. When necessary the relation to the true lunar calendar could be found; but in general men did not feel the need to draw the two systems together or make them influence one another.

In Egypt the relation of the schematic calendar and the new-moons of religious festivals were much the same. We see it in the twelfth century B.C., in the dekanal lists of coffins from Assyut or the star-calendars round the body of Nut in Seti's cenotaph or Ramses IV's tomb; and we might add that the same sort of situation reappears in the days of early Greek astronomy.[6] However, the development on this basis was different in Babylon and Egypt. In Egypt there was a central power imposing the same civil calendar over the whole land, while in Mesopotamia each community was free to devise its own calendar. Hence in Egypt the lunar calendar was pushed into the background, while in Mesopotamia in due time the schematic calendar was the one that was set aside.

The 365-day year in its origin then had no connection with the schematic month-system. It was based on the working-out of the average number of days between Floods, and then was linked with the rising of Sothis. It must have been devised at a time when the flooding coincided fairly well with the season called Inundation: that is, in the centuries round 4200 B.C. or those round 2800, the time of Djoser. The second date is by far the more likely.[7]

Fig. 47. Virgin (Tarpi); Scales; Scorpion

We may here then look closer at Sothis. As the stars come up over the eastern horizon each night, they show up at the same spot. But, during the twilight period, less and less stars will be recognisable as they come up, and at last, near sunrise, they all disappear. A star, seen briefly to rise and then be lost to sight, was glimpsed in its Heliacal Rising. The rising of a particular star that ends the night goes on for several days. Then things change. The sun shares in the daily rotation of the sky east to west and has a slow motion of its own (relative to the stars) in an opposite direction. Its eastward motion is completed once in a year; it delays the sun a little each day so that after a while the rising of the star in question becomes clearer and the star stays longer visible. A new star has to be found to take its place for the Heliacal Rising. Then, after a year, the sun returns to the region of the first star.

In this way the Egyptians used stars or star-clusters (dekans) to measure the time of night. A different star could have been selected each day; but the Egyptians felt that it was more in the key of order to have one star acting as the pointer for a decade, ten days. A year of 360 days needed 36 dekans, which corresponded to an entire sky-circuit; 18 could be seen rising in one night. But variations in the length of night and twilight had their effect; and at the summer-date of Sothis' rise, only 12 dekans could be seen to rise during the darkness. Hence the twelve-division of the night as found in the diagonal calendars of 1800–1200 B.C.[8] Behind this system lay the decimal order of the civil calendar. An inscription of Seti I (about 1300) shows that a similar system was applied to daylight. We see a sundial that indicated ten hours between sunrise and sunset, with two more added for the twilight of morning and evening.[9] The dekans, we may note, first appear on coffin lids of the Middle Kingdom, which depict the sky with the dekanal constellations inscribed: 36 columns with 12 lines each for the 12 hours of the night. The name of a particular dekan moves from column to column, each time one line higher, with the result of a diagonal pattern. The growing contradiction between civil calendar and natural year led to the breakdown of the system of dekans as hour-indicators; an attempt to substitute the culmination of stars for their rising failed. But the dekans held their own as representations of the year's decades in astronomical designs. Thus they survived till the Hellenistic age when they were linked with the Zodiac and began to play a strong part in astrological doctrine.[10]

Originally they had not been limited to 36. They were born out of the Egyptian conviction that every portion of time, great or small, should have its protecting genius or be the property of some deity. So all sorts of daimons were posted along the sun's route——not, in ancient Egypt, the circle of the ecliptic but rather a large band going from one tropic to another, with the equator forming a median line: on this band the stars were thought to rise or set at the same horizon points. The time-lords who dwelt along the band had to be placated or controlled by spells and rites

Fig. 48. Archer; Capricorn

to ensure the sun's safe passage. Which stars or clusters were considered to make up this set of time-lords on the sun's path it is hard to make out; but they included Orion and Sothis, perhaps Prokyon and the Hydra as well.[11] When they had to be related to the planets with their domiciles in the zodiacal signs, they were called the *prosōpa*, the faces or masks of the planets in their sector, their ten degrees of a sign.[12]

The full hermetic development of the dekans appears in a passage from Stobaios:

"Picture to yourself now that under the Circle of this Body [the enveloping Whole] are ranged the 36 dekans, in the middle between the Universal Circle and that of the Zodiac, separating those two circles: on the one hand in some sort raising up the Circle of the Whole, on the other hand circumscribing the Zodiac, moving in a circle with the planets—and conceive that they have the same force as the movement of the Whole, alternatively with the Seven. They restrain the Body that envelops the world (for it would move with extreme speed if left to itself) while they hasten the course of the seven other circles, since these move with a slower motion than the Universal Circle.

"Necessarily then the dekans move with the same motion as the Circle of the Whole. Imagine then the Spheres of the Seven and the Universal Circle [have been put under the dekans' power] or better still that these dekans hold themselves round the world like guardians of all that passes there, maintaining everything together and watching over the good order of the whole universe."

"I have pictured it all, Father, just as you've said."

"Consider again, Tat, that they were exempt from undergoing what the other stars undergo. In effect they are not held up in their course so that they halt. They do not meet any obstacle so that they go backwards. Even more, they are not even covered by the sun's light. All things that the other stars undergo. Rather, they are free, above everything, and as guardians and attentive overseers, they embrace the whole universe in the space of one day and one night."

"Have they then, Father, an influence over us?"

"The greatest influence, my Child. They exert their influence on bodies from on high. How then could they not act on us as well, on each in particular and on all men together. Thus, my Child, among all the catastrophes of universal scope due to forces emanating from them, we may cite as examples—mark well my words—the changes of kings, the uprisings of cities, famines, pestilences, flux and reflux of the sea, earthquakes. Nothing of all that, my Child, occurs without the influence of the dekans. And besides—pay attention to this—as the dekans have command over the planets and as we are under the domination of the

Seven, don't you see that a certain influence from the dekans reaches
down as far as us—whether it's a question of the Sons of the Dekans or
of the Planets as Intermediaries."

"What can indeed be the bodily form, Father, of these beings
[the Sons]?"

"They are those whom commonfolk call Daimons. For daimons do
not make up a particular class of beings. They have no specific body
made of a special matter and they are not moved by a soul, as we are, but
they have simply the force of these 36 gods. Besides, note again, Tat,
another effect of the action of the dekans. They further ejaculate on to
earth the seeds that we call *tanai,* some salutary, others destructive.
More, during their course in the sky they engender stars as ministers
whom they use also as servants and soldiers. These, mingled by them
with the aither, circulate there, suspended, and fill out the whole
expanse so that there may be in the heights no space void of stars. They
contribute to the ornamenting of the Whole and they have an energy of
their own, though subordinated to that of the 36. They are those who
cause from region to region the destruction of living beings in general
and who make swarm the creatures spoiling the fruits of the earth."[13]

Fig. 49. Aquarius (with Nile-springs); Fishes

The speaker goes on to discuss the Great Bear (made up of seven
stars in the midst of the Zodiac) and the Lesser Bear, who are
under these creatures; then minor choirs of stars, perishable
stars below the moon, and comets.

We may note a contradiction, found elsewhere as well. The
dekans each govern ten degrees of the Zodiac, but are assimilated
to the *monomoiriai* who each govern one. This confusion arises
through the connection of the dekans with the planets, which,
in terms of the theory of the *monomoiriai,* each control a single
degree, one after another.[14] The flux-reflux of the waters cannot be
the tides; it is rather some dangerous movement of the seas.[15] The
Egyptian tradition always calls the dekans gods; under the

Christians they became malign demons. The reason for the names of soldiers and overseers, *hyperleitourgoi*, is brought out by Firmicus Maternus:

Some [Egyptians], wanting to develop this point in more detail, have applied to each dekan three deities [*numina*] to which they give the name of Soldiers-on-Service [*munifices*] or *Leitourgoi,* in the sense that in each sign are found nine Soldiers-on-Service and that each group of three such Soldiers commands a dekan. In their turn these nine soldiers, established (they say) in each sign, they divide into an infinity of divine powers, to which, they say, are due all the sudden calamities, griefs, illnesses, cold fits, fevers: in short, all the events that come about unexpected and unforeseen. To them they attribute the birth of monsters.[16]

The sky-demons are felt to harry men on earth just as do the soldiers and imposers of (unpaid) public services or liturgies. Under the Empire the army became more and more the agents of the oppressive government in all matters. In Egypt they collected many taxes (in trades, in gold, on manufactures and supplies, and at least some of the yearly grain tribute). In the post-Severan period taxpayers looked on the army as the chief emptier of their purses; Ulpian, dealing with *tributum*, merely says "it is paid, *tributum*, to the soldiers"; and a writer in Valentinian's reign speaks of the soldiers who at Edessa "usually levied the taxes". The soldiers indeed in their rapacity grew so used to bureaucratic jargon that when they imposed an illegal tax for their own benefit they called it *cenatica superstatuta,* Superstatutory Dinner-Money. And they oppressed and harassed the common folk in many other ways.[17]

To return to the dekans: Sothis and Orion, we saw, were among them; Sothis indeed was the ideal example. The star rose after being visible for some 70 days through closeness to the sun; and so the priests assumed that the same interval applied to the other dekans. The commentary in Seti I's cenotaph told how one dekan after another died and was purified in the embalming-house of the Underworld, to be reborn after 70 days. The pattern was felt to be a necessary one, however much it lacked astronomic precision. So, for the decade following Sothis, a star was selected which rose ten days after Sothis had risen. Again here there was no exactitude; the priests were satisfied if the star was bright and fitted the pattern fairly well.

With the New Kingdom more elaborate documents survive

with information: for instance the ceiling of the incomplete tomb of the vizier Senmut with its representations of the deities of the hours and pictures of constellations of the northern hemisphere. Hippopotamus and crocodile appear among the star-systems. But faint lines of blue under the drawing show that the artist altered his design to gain a better effect, and it is clear that he was not concerned with any attempt to keep to the actual star-positions.[18] In the centre of the bullheaded cluster—our Great Bear, and the circumpolar stars—across the sky are drawn the twelve monthly festivals, each in a circle with its norm of 24 hours; below come the stars of the northern sky. Opposite, in the southern skies, Orion turns his face away from smiling Sothis; above them comes the dekan-list with Queen Hatshepsut's name among the heavenly beings.[19] Again, inside the wooden coffin of Her-Nedj-Tef-f, prophet of Amun and other gods at Thebes, we see the figures of the gods of the constellations, and several scenes from the *Book of the Gates*.[20] A demotic papyrus of about 1300 B.C. gives a translation and commentary on a much older hieratic text, the hieroglyphic version of which we find in Seti's cenotaph. It included an account of the travels of the dekans over the body of Nut the sky-goddess. The text began with a picture of her showing all the constellations, with the dates of their risings and settings. Deep in the Egyptian sky-image is then the picture of a huge woman's body sprawled all over the sky with the positions of the stars expressed in terms of her anatomy.[21]

In the tombs of Ramses VI, VII, and IX, we meet a new kind of sky-text, which sets out the observations made to determine the night-hours through the year. For the 1st and 16th of each month a seated man is drawn; above (or rather behind) him is a coordinate net with stars. The inscription names a star for the beginning of each night and for each of its 12 night-hours, and states when it will be visible: "over the left ear", "over the right ear", "over the left shoulder", and so on. Here we find another version of the sky as a single human figure. The horizontal lines in the network stand for the hours; the vertical ones give the positions. The stars are entered as named in the text (apart from errors made by a craftsman copying systems he did not understand). Here is a much more subtle way of time-measuring than the coffins of the Middle Kingdom show—though the texts were copied again and again past the period which they correctly covered.[22]

The Egyptians then for religious reasons were much interested in time-intervals; and they may have in time developed a finer astronomic knowledge in spheres that interested them than we have allowed for. Thus it has been claimed that the 24 tables dealing with transitions have been inadequately analysed, through a belief that they were based on a constant duration of dusk. Such an analysis leads to contradictions in terms of the modern theory which requires the declination of the sun to remain constant. But if we take account of the inclination of the ecliptic, of the eccentricity of the solar orbit, of the variation in dusk-duration, we get results that confirm the phenomena of the variation of the 13 stars by night in the 24 tables of the half-months. We seem to touch here on a very precise descriptive astronomy with the three seasons of four months each.[23]

Still, even if some aspects have not got their full credit, Egyptian astronomy was clearly far behind Babylonian and never even remotely approached its mathematical level. The Zodiac came in in the third century B.C., about 250; and several representations were made in temples. The most ancient (now destroyed) was engraved on the ceiling of a hall north of Esna, under Ptolemy III (before −221). Others are at Esna, the great temple of Khnum (under Titus and Commodus): and in the pronaos at Dendera, in the eastern chapel of Osiris and in the western. Another is preserved at Cairo, and yet another has been found at Athens.[24] Direct Mesopotamian influence is clear: for example in the fact that there are two signs (Balance and Scorpion) where the Greek tradition knew only the Scorpion. The Egyptians however added their own touches, calling the Balance the Horizon and using a composite symbol with the Balance surmounting a traditional sign for the Horizon in which the sun rises up. The reason for the changes here lay in the fact that at the time of the Zodiac's introduction the Balance rose up heliacally at the start of the Egyptian year.[25]

In general the Zodiac in Egypt appears as a mixture of Greek imagery with the Babylonian originals.[26] We learn the names from four Coptic ostraka, a Coptic papyrus, and a wooden tablet. First comes the Sheep (Ram); then in order *pa ka*, the Bull; *na htre* (two men clasping hands), the Twins; *pa kenhd*, a sort of Scarab, not a Crab; *pa-me*, Lion (shown by a Lion or a Knife); *tarpi*, Virgin; *ta ahi*, Horizon; *tadl*, Scorpion; *pa ent ath*, "he who draws a bow"; *ten pa her ankh*, Capricorn; *pa mu*, Waterman (a figure connected with the Nile-sources); *na tebte*, the Fishes.[27] Greek papyri of the second and third centuries A.D. usually have the name of Sun, Moon and Planets written out in full; demotic planetary tables have symbols for the planets and zodiacal signs, apparently based on the Egyptian names, unrelated to the medieval symbols.[28]

The Egyptians thus contributed very little indeed to astrology in its mathematical forms. What later writers grandly called the Egyptian System was in fact a Greek planetary one. The Eternal Tables in which the Egyptians were said to have set out their ancient planetary lore were compiled from Babylonian almanacs.[29] The Egyptian New-Moon tablets used crude arithmetic devices. The one genuine Egyptian element was the stress on time-divisions with the doctrine of the dekans.[30] At Dendera there are two zodiacal designs, one round, one rectangular; and all around the first one we see the 36 dekans represented. They turn up in astrological literature with Greek names that seem based on the old Egyptian ones, and now they are linked with the various ten degrees of the Zodiac. So we find a combination of the Egyptian way of determining time by the rising dekans and of the Babylonian method (come in through the Greeks) of using the parts of the Zodiac that rise up, plus their *paranatellonta*. The Hellenistic dekans in turn were connected with the 36 stars of the Babylonian astrolabe, the 36 stars of [mul]APIN, and the 36 Chaldean stars mentioned by Diodoros. The emperor Julian also tells us that in the Mithraic mysteries the Zodiac was divided into 36 "powers of gods"—a system connected with the old Babylonian division of the sky into the Roads of Enlil, Anu, and Ea.[31]

There are a few more points about the Egyptians we may note here. The concept of correspondences and of the microcosm was as strong in Egypt as in Mesopotamia, but was applied in different ways. It appeared especially in the concept of the temple as expressing the pattern of creation, the emergence of the primal hill out of the waters; and in this relation Steps or Ladders had the same significance as the stepped *ziqqarat*. In Papyrus Salt 825 we see that the House of Life is conceived as a microcosm. The papyrus describes its construction. Its walls are the four cardinal points; the ground is called Geb, the earthgod, to ensure its identification with the whole earth in a divine form; the ceiling is called Nut to ensure its identification with the heaven. Here, above all at Abydos, was kept a statue in a ram's skin (associating Osiris and the Sun); hostile forces were destroyed by magical spells; apotropaic spells were recited by priests enacting the role of Shu, Tefnut, Geb, and Nut—the four ancient deities, issued from the demiurge, who were wind, fire, earth, heaven, the four elements composing life. These rites maintained the cosmic order and its continuity. In the Houses of Life were kept the Books of theology, astronomy, magic, rituals, which in the late period were called the Bas or the Power of Rē.[32]

There are some further aspects of the year-reckoning and the rising of Sothis that concern us. As a result of the failure to insert an extra day every fourth year the civil calendar had fallen out of step with the solar year; the discrepancy amounted to 10 days in 40 years, 30 days in 120. Finally midsummer turned up in January and midwinter in August; then slowly the calendar moved round into harmony with the fixed phenomena. The Egyptians knew well enough that things went wrong, but could not see how to deal with the situation. Several times we find them recording the date in the calendar of some important historical event, the heliacal rising of Sothis (19 July in the Julian calendar). They assumed that the star gave the signal to the Nile to rise and thus was the cause of the flood. We know that the rising coincided with the first day of the civil calendar in A.D. 139, and on this basis can calculate backwards, as the Sothic year was about $365 \times 4 = 1460$ years. Not that this figure is precise. The length of the Sothic Year changed gradually as a result of the precession of the equinoxes; and by using a constant *arcus visionis* we get lengths varying from 1450 to 1453 to 1456 and 1458 as we move back to a year covering -4226 to -2768 B.C. However, when Sun and Sothis are apart in azimuth, the star will be visible near the horizon at a smaller solar depression than when they are close together; so the arc of vision may have been less in the past than now. We can guess at the year of a cycle-beginning only to within a period of four years, as heliacal rising occur at the same date for four successive years; the effect does not matter much for the first two cycles, but then grows more important. So we get lengths, going back, of 1449, 1452, 1454, 1456 years, bringing us to a year covering -4426 to -2770.[33]

The problem of the exact length of the solar year, and the intercalations required in the calendar, was insoluble until mathematical and observational astronomy had made big advances. In the Greek language even the term *isēhēmeria* (equal day-length:

equinox) was late; it appears in the Hippokratic collection (not earlier than the late fifth century), in Aristotle and in the pseudo-Aristotelian *Axiochos*. The first scientific attempt in Greece to grapple with the problem appeared with Meton and Euktemon with their 19-year cycle, which gave figures for the mean moon-month accurate to within two minutes, but was an hour too long for the solar year. About a century later Kallippos set out a 76-year cycle of 27,759 days (4 Metonic cycles minus one day) and 940 lunar months (with 28 intercalary): this gave a year of $365\frac{1}{4}$ days like the Julian calendar—some 11 minutes too long. Then, 200 years later, Hipparchos made the solar year $\frac{1}{300}$ of a day less than $365\frac{1}{2}$ days (365 days 5 hours 55 minutes 12 seconds): about $6\frac{1}{2}$ minutes too long. Ptolemaios used the Kallippic cycle plus the Egyptian system for dating purposes.[34]

A demotic treatise shows one way in which the Egyptians sought to grapple with calendaric disorders. We saw how the Middle Kingdom devised a system of Great and Small Years (years with 13 new-moon festivals, or with only 12). The demotic text sets out a periodic scheme based on the fact that 25 civil years (9125 days) nearly equalled 309 synodic mean moon-months. It grouped these months into 16 normal years of 12 moon-months and 9 great years of 13. Two consecutive moon-months were generally here given 59 days; but every fifth year the last two months were made 60 days long. The whole 25-year cycle then equalled 9125 days. By this system the dates of moon festivals could be worked out so that nothing would go wrong for several centuries—though the full moon might deviate by two days either way, or even more.

Sothis remained important in astrology as well as in the calendar. We see there an Egyptian characteristic, but Sothis was of much interest also to the Babylonians.[35] In tablet 1 of [mul]APIN the date of its rising was given as 15 Month IV, a key-date in the schematic calendar; in tablet 2 it appeared in rules for determining intercalation. And interest in the Dogstar (Sirius) went on through the Seleukid and Arsakid eras. In some kinds of non-mathematical astronomic tablets of these eras we find only two sets of dates for phenomena (which are to be spaced apart a year, tropical or sidereal). One set consists of the four dates of equinoxes and solstices; the other is a triplet of dates for the heliacal (or rather acronycal) rising and setting of the Dogstar.[36] A fragmentary Seleukid tablet from Uruk gives predicted dates for a series of summer solstices, setting out year, month, and day-number with a two-place sexagesimal fraction. The summer-solstice dates that follow (with fractions ignored) are those predicted by the almanacs and diaries of the period. The dates there given for autumnal and vernal equinoxes and winter solstice depend on the summer-solstice dates.

For Dogstar-phenomena we have nothing corresponding to the Uruk tablet. The scheme however may have gone back to −322, but not to −418; its date was perhaps around −384. The 19-year cycle, however, was dated round 380 B.C.; and we may conclude that a scheme for the prediction of the typical Dogstar phenomena, parallel to the summer-solstice scheme, was first used in the century after the Seleukid era began; and then went on at least till the third century of that era. The almanacs have only predicted dates; and all the dates for the Dogstar and the summer-solstice were derived from the two schemes outlined above. The Diaries however include both predicted and observed phenomena, but as far as we can make out not one Babylonian text of Seleukid times has a Dogstar-date based on observation. Probably some years before 380 the 19-year cycle was devised on the basis of a set of observed dates for the Dogstar's heliacal rising; the seven intercalary months were spread out over the 19 years so that these dates would always fall in the fourth month. Within less than a century of 380, the prediction-schemes for the summer-solstice and the Dogstar were worked out, using synodic months and *tithis*—with a rounded-off value for the difference, in *tithis*, between the twelve mean synodic months and a mean year. We may deduce that it was the date of the Dogstar-rising which determined the pattern of intercalations in the 19-year cycle.[37]

Syrian priests used the Sothic Year (or the Cosmic Year as they called it) in divinatory speculations. The same sort of practices are found in Asia Minor.[38] And Cicero tells us:

Posidonius thinks that there are in nature certain signs and symbols of future events. We are told that the inhabitants of Cea, Heraclides of Pontus reports, are accustomed to observe carefully the circumstances attending the rise of the Dogstar, so as to know the character of the ensuing season and how far it will prove healthy or pestilential. If the star rose with an obscure and dim appearance, it proved that the atmosphere was gross and foggy, and its respiration would be heavy and unwholesome. But if it appeared bright and lucid, that was a sign the air was light and pure, and therefore healthy.[39]

And Manilius states that after Orion:

> The Dogstar follows, straining in his rapid course.
> No star comes more impetuously over earth.
> Those who watch his rising as he first returns,
> stationed upon the topmost heights of Taurus,
> foretell what earth will produce, the times of seasons,
> what sickness comes, how far will concord reign.
> War he begets, brings peace back, as he varies
> his movements; by his aspect looking down
> he governs. As warrant of his power: his colour,
> vivacity, glittering, almost the Sun's equal,
> only more distant, emitting azure rays
> with weakened heat. Before him the other stars
> grow pale . . .[40]

The Taurus region was populated by *magousaioi* who mingled Babylonian astrology with old Mazdean traditions; from Cilicia the Mithraic cult reached the Romans. Ploutarch, in his account of Zoroaster and Mithras, described the dualistic system, then went on to say that Oromazes (Ahura-Mazda)

after increasing himself threefold, severed from the Sun as much space as the Sun is distant and adorned the heaven with stars; and one star he appointed before all others as Guardian and Overseer, namely Seirios. And having created 24 other gods, he shut them up in an Egg; but those produced by Arimanios [the evil principle], the same in number, pierced the Egg that had been laid, and so bad things were mixed up with good. But a time appointed by Fate was coming in which Arimanios, after bringing on famine and pestilence, must be destroyed by the same and utterly vanish; when on the Earth, becoming plain and level, there shall be one life and government of men, all happy, and speaking one language. Theopompos says that according to the Mages one of the gods will conquer, the other be conquered, alternately for 3000 years; for another 3000 years they'll fight, war, and undo each other's works. But in the end Hades shall fall and men be happy, needing no food and building no shelter . . .[41]

Teukros the Babylonian called the Dogstar the Royal Star of the 36 Dekans. The *Avesta* shows that Ploutarch was substantially correct. "We sacrifice to Tishtrya, magnificent and glorious Star, which Ahura Mazda has established Master and Overseer of all the stars."[42] This hymn, of which the old part goes back to the Achaimenid era, gives us the essential idea of Tishtrya, who is the author of rain and the enemy of the barren daimon of dryness;

when Earth is thirsty, he goes down into the Ocean and takes its waters up into the air, transforms them into clouds and carries them afar over the lands to fall as water. Once when Ahura was angered at the corruptions on earth, he made Tishtrya rain for 30 days and 30 nights, till the waters rose to the height of men; but generally Tishtrya is propitious. On account of his relation to fertility, he was approximated in Syria to Adonis.[43]

A demotic text of the Roman period, probably found in the Fayum, sets out predictions based on Sothis. It sets out the following system: (1) If Sothis rises when the Moon is in the Archer; (2) when Saturn is in the Archer; (3) when Jupiter is in the Archer; (4) when Mars is in the Twins; (5) when Venus is in the (Twins); (6) when Mercury is in the Twins; (7) when the (Sun) is in the Archer. . . . In Greek astrology Sothis was given a longitude in the Twins, which at the star's rising would be the horoscopic or rising system, with the Archer as the setting Sign. Assuming that a heliacal rising is being dealt with, Sothis would be in the Crab; the inner planets Venus and Mercury would probably be noted in the Twins and the Bull—in our text they are both in the Twins. (The sign for Venus is lost, but can be safely restored.) With the seventh section we are clearly starting a new system and the Sun must be the missing body. This new section marks the ending of conjunctions and the beginning of oppositions to Sothis. In horoscopes the normal order of the planet-gods is Sun, Moon, Saturn, Jupiter, Mars, Venus, Mercury. A heliacal rising of Sothis would involve a conjunction with the Sun, and so the text does not bother to start with that detail; but in the new section the Sun is in opposition and thus needs to be named.

The predictions themselves run:

The Influence of Sothis: (1) Grain in the field . . . in the country of the Syrian . . . death will occur . . . will abound in weakness by night and day . . . will go . . . and it will be tilled. (2) The King will fight . . . of his and he will . . . prince in Egypt. Pharaoh . . . will go to . . . the Flood will come to Egypt . . . will occur in the country of the Parthian. (3) The King of Egypt will rule over his country. An enemy will be [his and] he will escape from them again. Many men will rebel against the King. A Flood which is proper is that which comes to Egypt. Seed [and] grain will be high in price [in] money, which is . . . The burial of a god will occupy Egypt . . . [will come] up to Egypt and they will go away again. (4) Some men will rebel [against the King of] Egypt in the country of the Syrian. The King will proceed to them with his army. He will fight. The sky abundant with rain will not be able to [occur] in the country of the Syrian . . . distress for 5 months. (5) The King will do a good thing for Egypt . . . come at the end of the year . . . judgment of Sachmet will occur after . . . months. (6) The whole earth will . . . Grain will be high in price . . . (7) The King of Egypt will do . . . in . . .[44]

The prophecies deal with Egypt, Syria, and probably Parthia. Another papyrus was also part of an astral handbook; but unlike the Sothic text it dealt with predictions about individuals, which in the preserved portion were based on the presence of Venus and Mercury, in turn, in each of the horoscopic houses at the time of the person's birth. For the first text we may compare a passage in Hephaistion of Thebes, which deals with the heliacal rising of Sothis "on the 25th of the month Epeiph"; especially relevant is the section predicting events in Egypt and Syria on the basis of various zodiacal signs being present at the Star's heliacal rising.[45]

The first text seems to have originated about the mid-second century B.C. The predictions deal with people rebelling in Syria against the King of Egypt, who is going to attack them. The circumstances are vague and could refer to any of the conflicts between the Ptolemies and the Seleukids from the third century on; but if the term "rebel" (bks) is taken literally, the most suitable time is when the two dynasties were interrelated and Philometor campaigned in Syria against Alexandros Bala his son-in-law in 145 B.C. Philometor was killed in battle and the most bloody period in Ptolemaic history began. If the Parthians are in fact introduced, a date about mid-second century is made yet more likely; for they were not of much interest to the Greek kingships till their threat to Mesopotamia grew stronger and led in 140 to the taking of Seleukeia. The text then seems to belong to the period to which we may attribute the rise in Egypt of an astrology revealed in the corpus under the names of Nechepso and Petosiris—a period also in which there was a rising nationalist mood among the native population.[46]

Hephaistion makes clear the Egyptian basis of the scheme that uses the Sothis-rising as a calendar-key.[47] He deals with prognostications of all sorts, meteorological, nosological, political, which derive from the positions of planets after the Sothis rising. In combining the positions and aspects of those planets, the influence of their colour, the apogee and perigee of their orbit, and their reciprocal relations, plus the varying strength of the star's own colour and the winds or thunders at the moment of its rising, "the Egyptian sages of old times" had opened up a new area for the exercise of astrologic ingenuity. Hephaistion has behind him an hermetic work by the astrologer Palchos; and the Sothic method carried on into Arab days when we find it used in a treatise under the name of Hermes which deals with the star's risings and its effects on the events each year in the world, "as it has been revealed and taught to him".[48] This treatise was carrying on an old tradition. In the Anon of A.D. 379 we read, "Our Egyptian ancestors have mentioned these things and written of them; the first was Hermes and he has treated in his *Apotelesmata Kosmika* of the heliacal rising of the Dog." Antiochos of Athens also used this hermetic statement.[49]

9

Egyptian Astrology

Magic papyri often say that the rites must not be tried on certain days; for then hostile forces would make them useless, gods stronger than those called on were in the ascendant. The notion of lucky and unlucky days went far back, and was the one area in which, apart from medicine with its mixture of practical lore and magic, any kind of systematisation was applied to omens. The concern of the priests with calendars for festival purposes lay behind such division of days into good and bad. We find papyri with copies of the calendar in which each day is divided into three parts, and every part is marked as lucky and unlucky. Other papyri tell us why certain days are lucky or unucky or only partly so. Here is the system for the first month of the year, Thoth:

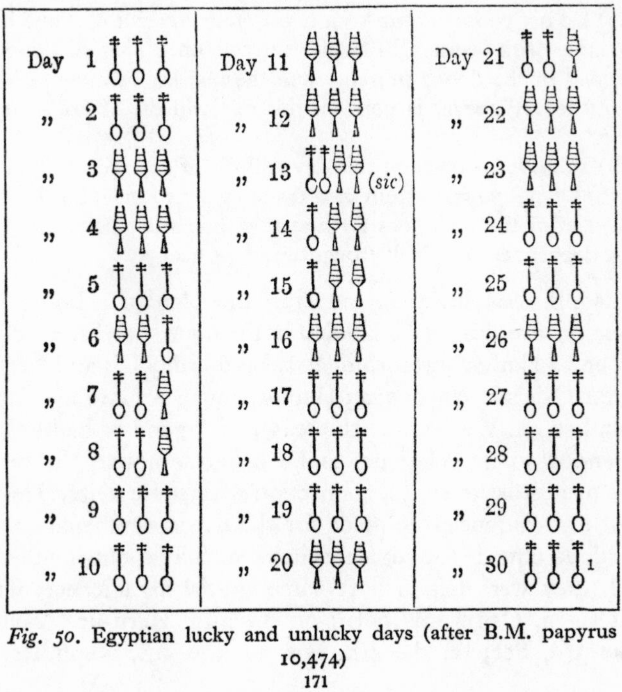

Day 1	Day 11	Day 21
„ 2	„ 12	„ 22
„ 3	„ 13 (sic)	„ 23
„ 4	„ 14	„ 24
„ 5	„ 15	„ 25
„ 6	„ 16	„ 26
„ 7	„ 17	„ 27
„ 8	„ 18	„ 28
„ 9	„ 19	„ 29
„ 10	„ 20	„ 30

Fig. 50. Egyptian lucky and unlucky days (after B.M. papyrus 10,474)

The signs for days 1 and 2 are lucky, that for day 3 is unlucky. Take Day 19. It is here wholly lucky and in papyrus Sallier IV we are told: "It is a day of festival in heaven and on earth in the presence of Re; it is the day when flame was hurled on those who followed the boat containing the shrine of the gods; and on this day the gods gave praises, being content," and so on.[1] Both papyri make the 26th wholly unlucky. "This was the day of the fight between Horos and Set." They first fought in the form of men, then in bear-form they fought for three days and three nights; Isis aided Set when he was being beaten and Horos then cut off her head; Thoth transformed the head into that of a cow and put it on her body. In another version of the myth Horos and Set fight as hippopotami in the river.[2]

Not all the calendars thus agree. In the above list 20 Thoth is unlucky but in Sallier IV it is lucky, though the reader is told not to work on it, not to slay oxen, not to take a stranger in. On this day the gods in the following of Re slew the rebels. On 4 Phaophi (the next month) Sallier IV says:

Do not go forth from your house from any side of it; whoever is born on this day will die of the disease *aat*.

(5th) Do not go forth from your house from any side of it and hold no intercourse with women. This is the day on which all things were performed in the divine presence and the majesty of the god Menthu was satisfied. Whoever is born on this day will die of excessive love-making.

(9th) Whoever is born on this day will die of old age.

(15th) Do not go forth from your dwelling at eventide, for the serpent Uatch, son of the god, goes forth at this time and misfortune follows him; whoever sees him will straightway lose his eye.

26 Phaophi was lucky for making the plan of a house; on 5 Hathor no fire was to be kindled in the house; to listen to songs of joy on 16 Hathor was forbidden as on this day Isis and Nephthys wept for Osiris at Abydos; 23 Hathor, a man would die of drowning, and so on. We see that the reasons for good or bad luck on a day tended to be religious, to be connected with the festival-myths or at least to seek a connection with some deity. The same sort of associations were made for the five epagomenal days. As days added outside the regular scheme of things, outside the lunar round, they were felt to have some special significance. On the 1st of them, Osiris was born; on the 2nd, Heru-ur (Aroueris); on the 3rd, Set; on the 4th, Isis; on the 5th, Nephthys. The

1st, 3rd, and 5th were unlucky and no work should be undertaken on them. The rubric dealing with the five days says that whoever knows them will never suffer from thirst, be smitten with disease, or be taken possession of by the goddess Sekmet. The Eye of Sekmet seems to take the form of noxious vapours at sunrise; she stands for the scorching fierceness of the sun's rays and so is called the Eye of Rē. The rubric also directs that figures of the five gods be drawn with unguent and *anti* scent on a piece of fine linen, evidently for use as an amulet.[3]

A papyrus dealing with gymnasion-debts dated about October, 180 B.C., oddly gives us a glimpse of devices used by the Egyptians. There are eight fragments; on the recto we find eight columns with marginal notes in a second hand. But at the start of the ninth column another hand sets out a method for dealing with moon-months and gives a table of equivalents; the verso was later used for an account drawn up by the days of the month. The names suggest a provenance of Philadelphia.[4] Interest on debts in money is at 2% a month; but there are also debts concerned with common or club funds and quantities of oil. So the document seems to deal with the affairs of a *synodos* or association, though some debts point to a gymnasion. A funeral feast is mentioned. The astronomic section is concerned with determining the character of the moon-month by using a 25-year cycle: which certainly has an Egyptian basis at least as far back as the fourth century B.C.[5]

Column ten deals with the relation of Egyptian months and the Zodiac. No exact correlation of zodiacal signs and a 30-day month is possible; the sun covers less than 360° in 360 days, slowing near the apogee in the Twins and hastening at the perigee in the Archer. Still, attempts at correlation went on in the lunar-solar calendars; in that of Dionysios, dated under Philadephos (282–246), the months are even named after the signs. The unstable Egyptian calendar made such correlations especially ineffective.

When did Thoth the month coincide with the Scorpion as in our text? The longitude of the sun for Thoth 1 (from the years −200 to −169) gives values that do not fit the text; but the problem fades if we bring in the Eudoxan norm for the division of the Zodiac. For the years round 180 B.C. we then get the Balance 27 or 26 for the sun's longitude at Thoth 1.[6]

A papyrus shows that a starting-point for the 25-year cycle was

Thoth 1 of Tiberius 6 (19 August A.D. 19); eight cycles earlier we come to Thoth 1 as −181, 8 October. (The minus sign comes from the astronomic custom of inserting a zero between B.C. and A.D.) Our papyrus states that the cycle's first year was "the same as the first year as reckoned by . . . Philomētor". That ruler's first year can be taken as going back to 1 Thoth −180. (He seems to have become king in summer −179; the reckoning of his first year would be from the actual date to Thoth 1 of −179, but retrospectively the year could be regarded as going back to Thoth of −180). So we may take the first year of the cycle as here given from 181–180 B.C.

The lunar phenomena indicated in our papyrus seem to be the dates of the first evening visibility of the new crescent.[7] Together with the New Moon, the deities Hermes, Demeter, and Hephaistos are named; which suggests a calendar of festivals. Perhaps therein lies the reason for combining so strangely a scheme of lunar months with the business-accounts of a gymnasion. Hermes and Demeter fit a gymnasion-context; but Hephaistos is odd. (He was identified with Ptah, whose centre was at Memphis and whose high-priest was called the Lord of the Mastercraftsmen.)[8]

We have already seen in the Sothic text an Egyptian form of astrology apparently going back to the second century B.C. What seems a yet older form of predictions occurs in a papyrus of the late second century or early third century A.D. There are two texts, both copied by the same scribe but in their contents clearly not derived from the same original work.[9] Text A deals with five countries, B only with Egypt. A opens with a general introduction to eclipses of Sun and Moon; then goes on to deal with the Sun and the concordance of Babylonian and Egyptian years, assigning the months in groups of four to three countries and dividing the sky into three regions, which are assigned to three countries again; it treats the eclipses of the sun by individual months and gives predictions for each month. In the section on the Moon we find a division of the sky into four; the concordance assigns the months in groups of three to four countries; eclipses of the moon are dealt with by individual months, with predictions for each month. The effects of an eclipse, it appears, could be concentrated on one land or spread out over two or more.[10]

Babylonian texts in general were concerned only with their own land Akkad and the three lands around it: Amurru to west,

Elam to east, Subartu Gutiu to north. Only in late Greek texts does the astrologic eye glance over the whole world, from Iberia to China.[11] In our text the only lands that can be made out are those neighbouring the Egyptian empire: the land of the Syrians (or Assyrians), here probably Amor or north-eastern mountainous Phoenicia, the land of the Hebrews, and Crete (*Grty*). The prophecies are of the following type: "The inundation will occur abundantly in the entire land," "Great hunger will occur in the whole land," "The land will be extremely happy," "That army of the land will fall to battle-swords."

What is decisive for the Babylonian origin of our text is the fact that in two tables of concordances a start is made from Nisan, the first month of the Babylonian year. An Egyptian, looking at things from the perspective of his own calendar, would have started with Tebeth, the tenth Babylonian month. Further the writing of the Babylonian names follows Aramaic rather closely. But there is no sign whatever of a zodiacal outlook. The most likely date then for the writing of the original text would be the late sixth or early fifth century B.C., when Mesopotamian influences were coming in through the Persians. (Furthermore, we must not forget that the Persians deported Egyptian priests to Asia—and then sometimes sent them back. The best-known case is that of Udjahorresne of Sais.) However, the Egyptian scribes did not attempt a slavish copy, as we see from their assignment of the months to lands that interested them. The sky-division for solar eclipses seems to correspond to the Three Roads of Anu, Enlil, and Ea in Babylonia, which are determined by the movement of the sun north and south in this way.[12] In that scheme Enlil, the northern sky where the sun is in summer, represents the southernmost land Akkad, and the southern sky (Ea, winter) represents the northern and western lands of Amurru and Subartu. Not that this set of correspondences, due apparently to looking on the sky as a mirror over the earth, is the only one in Babylonian texts.[13] The four places of the sky for the moon in the Egyptian text is a puzzle; in Babylonia we find no sign of a sky-division into Four Roads, though there is one into Four Fields. We do not know their extent or operation, but hear about the Fields of Akkad, of Elam, of Gutiu, of Amurru, which Jupiter approaches.

If we turn to text B, that on moon-omens, we find fuller predictions:

Great poverty will occur in the whole land. Death will occur to the King and Egypt will obey his foe. Barley and emmet will be abundant and every harvest likewise in the whole land, so that they [quarrel] and they eat . . . Snakes will occur in the houses.

The foreign countries . . . will attack Egypt, making quarrels and trouble . . . plentiful fish and fowl.

If you see the moon at a time when it is coloured, there being one disk inside it, you are to say about it: Death will occur in the whole land, but its life will be exceedingly good with barley and emmet.

If you see the disk [coloured], there being three stars inside it, you are to say about it; Great trouble will occur in Egypt.

If you see the moon [coloured] downward in it red, you are to say about it: Egypt will mourn exceedingly. A great wind will attack the sky, trouble being in . . . Pharaoh will be at peace with his enemies. Barley and emmet will be abundant and Egypt will be strong.

If you see the moon wholly black, there being one red disk inside it, you are to say about it: the army of Egypt will revolt against the chief of Egypt, they will rule him like a woman with her children.[14]

There are no certain Babylonian signs, here, but there is a strong suggestion of Babylonian influence. No earlier Egyptian text deals with moon-omens. Herodotos stressed the Egyptian interest in divinations, but he was writing after 460 B.C. and the Persian conquest. And we know that the Babylonians were very observant of lunar changes or effects: the moon's appearance on the first and last days of the month, its colour and brightness, the shape of its horns, the earth-shine ("the moon carries an *agu*, a tiara or royal cap"), a nebulous corona or ring (halo). Such a ring was often taken as a fence enclosing a sheep-meadow with the moon-shepherd in the centre; or it was seen as a river. At times it was taken to represent a siege, with planet or stars inside the ring indicating who was besieged; if the ring was broken, escape was possible.

When a halo surrounds the Moon and Jupiter stands within it, the King will be besieged. The halo was interrupted; it does not point to evil . . . From Nabu-shuma-ishkun.

When a halo surrounds the Moon and Sudun stands within it, the King will die and his land be diminished; the King of Elam will die. Sudun is Mars. Mars is the star of Amurru; it is evil for Amurru and Elam. Saturn is the star of Akkad, it is lucky for the King my Lord. From Irasshi-ilu the King's servant.[15]

There is good reason then to date B far back like A, though the two texts can hardly come from the same ancient work. They testify however to the strong impact that Babylonian astrology was beginning to make round 500 B.C. Again when we look at later demotic documents, especially the horoscopes, Babylonian influence is pervasive. The one early text that seems to stand on its own, denying this generalisation, is dubious: a reference to a partial solar eclipse of 610 B.C., which the writer explicitly states that he did not himself see. But even if this text is rightly interpreted, it includes no reference to any good or bad event connected with the eclipse.[16] There is a late Coptic record of A.D. 601, to an eclipse. Looking back, we can find prophetic references to disasters, as in a text of about 800 B.C., but with nothing said about any eclipse.[17]

Demotic documents provide us with collections of predictions, Zodiacs, planetary tables, horoscopes. The fact that such an early kind of document as that we have just examined was still being copied late in the Roman period, is proof that mathematical astrology had a limited diffusion and that people were ready to listen to any kind of predictions set out confidently. The Sothic text we looked at shows the intrusion of the full zodiacal systems.

The earliest astrologic text is an ostrakon:

List of the 5 Living Stars: Horos the Bull [Saturn], it is the Star of Re. Horos the Red [Mars], it is the Star of the Fierce Lion. Sbg [Mercury], it is the Star of Thoth. The Morning Star [Venus], it is Horos, son of Isis. Horos of the Secret [Jupiter], it is the star of Amun.

These are the names of the 5 Living Stars together with all gods constituting their names. The list of the Stars which are spread [over] the 12 months: VI the Ram. VII the Bull. VIII the Twins. IX the Crab. X the Lion. XI the Virgin. XII the Horizon [Balance]. I the Scorpion. II [the Archer]. III the Goatfaced [Capricorn]. IV the . . . of the Water [Aquarius]. V the fishes. Total 12 Stars, 1 [2] months, [one star] to the month.[18]

The order here separates the evil planets from the beneficient ones by putting Mercury (dubious) in between. In the list of the months, the first one coincides with the Scorpion. We see here then certainly an Egyptian calendar; in the Roman period the Sun never stood in that sign during the first months of the Alexandrian calendar, but it did so in 250 B.C. After that date there was a lessening coincidence of Sun and Scorpion, so that we may assume our document to have been drawn up well before 250. Further, the document follows a Babylonian order for the planets.

G

The suggested date of the document is supported by a consideration of the Egyptian sign for the Balance, which is that of the Horizon. Under the system shown above, the Balance became the sign of the last month of the year; but the Egyptians were apparently aware of one of the Babylonian names for the sign, the Claws or Pincers (of the Scorpion), and they did not want to use this term for the sign that was rising heliacally as the star of their year. They thought it would be more fitting to use the term Horizon (expressing the star's rise) for the sign that was, so to speak, the Horoskopos of that year. (The Greeks took over the Claws as the *Chēlai*; they substituted the term *Zygos*, the Beam (of the Balance) rather late. It appears once in Hipparchos and more often in Geminos. The Romans however preferred the term *Libra*, Balance. The Babylonians had known both names; Old-Babylonian texts already have the Balance, though in ^{mul}APIN the equivalent Sting of the Scorpion also is found.) The hieratic-demotic sign of the horizon thus stood for what was in Greek the Claws; and we find the fourth-century writer Hephaistion stating that it was pronounced as *chēlai*: "All the older ones called the sign following the Virgin the Balance and they used the following symbol" (the horizon); Ptolemaios however called it the *Chēlai* and used a modified version of the horizon-hieroglyph.

There is a jump to the next example, dated from −16 B.C. to A.D. 11. After that we have four tablets, surviving out of a total of nine, dated A.D. 71–132. These have been worked out according to arithmetic methods found in Babylonian documents of the last two centuries B.C.—methods less precise than the trigonometric ones used by the Greeks. Right on to the last one of these tablets, about mid-second century, the precession of the equinoxes is ignored. This tablet is also the only one to use the Julian calendar. The methods employed in such works (apart from the last one) must go well back into the second century B.C. The demotic documents thus reveal an extremely conservative tradition; they were closed against influences from Alexandreia, where the latest scientific discoveries of any kind must have reverberated.[19]

Despite the interest in Egypt shown by Pythagoreans, Herodotos, Plato, Hekataios and others, few Greeks seem ever to have learned Egyptian. The early Greek mercenaries were mostly absorbed into ordinary Egyptian life; Greeks of the lowest social class married Egyptian women. A few well-educated Greeks did learn the native tongue in varying degrees out of hope of acquiring the secrets supposed to lie hidden in Egyptian culture, especially in matters of religion and medicine. But in general the attraction felt for Egyptian mysteries created a sense of strangeness, even of something dark, sinister, frightening. There was no genuine cross-fertilisation. The Egyptian elements taken over remained unassimilated; and the two languages hardly penetrated one another. Despite moments of rapprochement, the Egyptian response to intrusive foreigners was to close in upon itself. In one papyrus Greek is kept for matters of daily life, Egyptian for religious matters. In the Nile Festivals at Oxyrhynchos we see juxtaposition, not fusion; Greek performers (mimes, homerists, trumpeters, dancers, pankratiasts, charioteers) and Egyptians (walking in the processional of the gods, carrying the sacred boat, hierodules), but nothing that we can distinguish as Graeco-Egyptian in any vital way.[20]

Of demotic horoscopes, we have five ostraka and a coffin-lid. The ostraka can be dated to the 43rd year of Augustus, 4th of Tiberius (twice), and 21st of Tiberius; the fifth is fragmentary. The coffin-lid of A.D. 93, with the subject dying at $31\frac{1}{2}$ years: early 125 at latest. The ostraka show that the method consisted of: (a) giving the date (regnal year, month, day, hour) and position of sun, moon, planets; (2) giving the four *kentra* (rising and setting signs, the lake of the sky and the Duat or Underworld), the three *swsp* (the Greek *apoklimata*, the signs inclined in the direction of the daily rotation and so preceding the three upper *kentra* by 30°), and the two *twr* (the left- and right-hand ones define a parallel line to the left and right *swsp*); and (3) setting out the houses in their relation to the Zodiac in its position of the given moment. All the four main texts deal with men in the first half century A.D. and may well have been composed by the same astrologer at Medinet Habu.[21]

The coffin-lid, found at Luxor, shows on the inside a large figure of Nut surrounded by images of the twelve zodiacal signs. The names of the planet among the signs are indicated in cursive script, later additions made by the priest Heter, who bought the sarcophagus, to show where the constellations stood on his day of birth. Egyptian terms like Horos the Bull, the Lake of the Sky, the Duat, are used; the House of Provision of Life is in Latin *lucrum*.

In a rough way the dates coincide with those of the planetary tables and with those of the oldest Greek horoscopes found in papyrus in Middle Egypt and the Fayum. (The literary tradition has preserved Greek horoscopes going back to −71 B.C.) Is this coincidence in dates significant? Perhaps, with the Roman era, there was a slightly stronger fellow-feeling between Greeks and Egyptians—at least in some areas—since both were now subject peoples. Rebellious texts like the Potter's Oracle were translated into Greek. But the Romans made every effort to make the Greeks a privileged class in comparison with the Egyptians; fraternising could not have gone on with any effect except at the lowest social levels. However in Alexandreia a certain amount of cultural exchange must have kept on at the higher levels, especially in and around the Mouseion. In the third and second centuries B.C. a fusion of Greek, Babylonian, and Egyptian elements in astrology did occur, issuing in the tradition of Nechepso and Petosiris; and some aspects of this may have spread out into wider Egyptian circles through the temple-priesthoods. Thus something of an Egyptian astrologic tradition did grow up, but quite without the ancient roots that it soon claimed.

The material in demotic, as we have seen, is scattered and slight; the theoretical and practical working-out of the so-called Egyptian School was done almost wholly in Greek.

10

Hermetic Correspondences

We have now come to the point where many strands converge. The planets are Mesopotamian; the dekans are Egyptian; the development of mathematical geometry is Greek. The mythology that becomes attached to the Zodiac is also mainly Greek, though there may well be Babylonian elements, recently or anciently diffused westward, in the tales told of the star-patterns. As with early alchemy, all sorts of legendary or famous names are attributed to treatises, ideas, systems: deities like Isis, Hermes-Thoth, Asklepios-Imhotep; priests or mages of Egypt and the Near East, Petosiris, Zoroaster, Ostanes; heroes of the Old Testament, Enoch, Abraham, Solomon. Greek mythology was raided for astrologers. Augustine was sure that Atlas "that great astrologer" was a contemporary of Moses; Servius declared Prometheus had shown astrology to the Assyrians; Euripides already attributed to Hippo, Cheiron's daughter, the art "of predicting by the rising of stars"; Cheiron predicted rain and storm for Peleus' wedding, and taught astrology to Herakles; Eumolopos, Musaios, Linos were astrologers; Teiresias discovered the sex of planets; Bellerophon, Daidalos and Ikaros (as sky-ascenders) were astrologers; so was Pasiphae, smitten with desire for the Bull; Pan, identified with Capricorn, was also an astrologer. Astrologic interpretations of myth were made. The Delphic Pythia was the Virgin; Didymean Apollo, the Twins; Ammon's oracle, the Ram; Aphrodite mating with Ares (in the tale of the *Odyssey*) was a planet in conjunction. Atreus and Thyestes, because their crimes halted the sun in heaven, were astrologers, and so on. A veil of oracular stylisations blurs out the individual writer. Sextus Empiricus later distinguished two kinds of horoscopy: the elementary and the more complex. The first was based simply on the relations between zodiacal signs and planets in the Horoscopic Point: hence the term horoscope for the whole nativity, *horoskopia* merely meaning "hour-observation". The second took into account also the signs and planets in the cardinal and other important points, not to mention finer details such as depressions. All planets, he stressed, had a specially strong influence if located in their own houses, e.g. the Sun in the Lion or the Moon in the Crab.[1]

At no time did the papyri use more than three symbols: a ligatured ō and r for hōros or hōroskopos; a crescent for the moon; and a circle with a slanted cone for the Sun. The modern symbol for the Sun, a circle with a point for centre, seems to occur first in printed books of the Renaissance; Copernicus used it rarely in the MS of his De Revolutionibus. Diagrams are very rare. Only one papyrus gives a crude circular design; and graffiti (three at Doura and one at Abydos) have drawings of the zodiacal system and its divisions. Diagrams grow more common in Byzantine codices.[2]

Apart from the time-divisions, the Egyptians did much to stress the aspect of revelation and mystery-lore. True, the hermetic works have come down in Greek and were apparently the work of Greeks, yet something in the whole Egyptian situation has contributed strongly to their character and doctrine—even if it were only through Greeks imagining themselves into what they felt to be the Egyptian atmosphere. Still, though it is mostly impossible to distinguish what is the precise Egyptian share in these documents, the important role of Thoth (Hermes), not to mention Isis and Horos, cannot have evolved without some sort of connection between the Greek dreamers and questers in Alexandreia and the Egyptian priesthood in various parts of the country. Tales such as that of Thessalos and his revelation at Thebes must reflect genuine contacts between Greek intellectuals and the old centres of Egyptian culture. Thoth-Hermes became a key-figure in at least certain aspects of astrology as he did in all occult matters of knowledge. An Astrologoumena was attributed to him; the fragments suggest, not so much a coherent system, as a mixture of attitudes and methods derived from many different schools and techniques. Our texts are late, but they point to a collection dated in the Ptolemaic era, priestly in origin, Memphite and not Alexandrian: what the Greeks called Hermaikai Diataxeis, Arrangements or Doctrines of Hermes.[3] Clement of Alexandreia tells us of the 42 Books of Hermes; others gave wilder estimates. Seleukos (according to Iamblichos) said 20,000; Manethon 36,525—a figure corresponding to 25 Sothic periods (each of 1461 years) or re-establishment, *apokatastasis*, of the world. Indeed the *apokatastasis* was treated in a chapter of the *Genika* attributed to Hermes.[4]

Among the hermetic works we find also citations from the *Salmeschiniaka* (on medical and genethliac astrology), the *Iatromathematika* concerned with healing relations, the *Sacred Book of Hermes to Asklepios*, which explained the names and actions

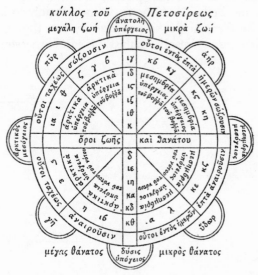

Fig. 51. Circle of Petosiris (after Bouché-Leclerq)

of the 36 dekans, and a *Liber Hermetis*, a detailed catalogue of the dekans which seems to go back beyond Hipparchos (about 150 B.C.) and to be used by Teukros a century later. But many other texts on the dekans circulated under the name of Hermes Trismegistos. Pamphilos in the first century A.D. used a book on the magical relations of simples with the 36 dekans. The botanical section of star-medicine indeed was very popular as we see from works like the *Book of Hermes to Asklepios* on the Plants of the Seven Stars (planets) and a treatise dealing with the zodiacal plants. The archetype probably treated only of dekanic plants, and one tradition asserted that botanical astrology was begun by Nechepso.[5]

Hermes was also considered to have written about the action of the 360° degrees of the ecliptic in 12 Books which Maternus called *Myriogenesis*; and to have composed a *Sphaera Barbarica*, a sky-system with non-Greek names for the stars. He was further credited with some *Monomoiriai*. Other works were put out under the name of Asklepios or Imhotep; and the Isaic cult attracted astrologic elements, e.g., in the aretology of Andros, Isis is said to have taught men the course of the stars. In hermetic texts she appears as the revealer of mysteries to Horos.

We come closer to actual persons in the works attributed to Nechepso and Petosiris. Alchemy seems certainly to have arisen in a definite form in the second century B.C. through Bolos of Mendes; it is easy to imagine in the same sort of way some Graeco-

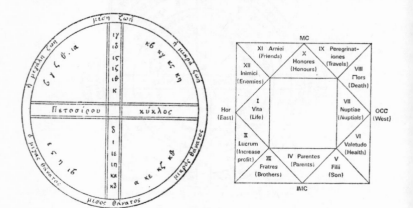

Fig. 52. Circle of Petosiris, and the squared circle of the Twelve Places in relation to the four Cardinal Points

Egyptian scholar making about 150 B.C. a synthesis of Greek, Babylonian, and Egyptian ideas on astrology, taking over the prestige of priestly lore (Petosiris) and of the Royal Science (Nechepso)—compare the *regales animi* of Manilius, who says of astrology:

> First then it deigned to move the minds of kings
> who touched the tracks of things nearest to heaven
> and tamed savage nations in the eastern lands.
> It's there the world's reborn and light comes up
> over darkened cities. Next priests, tending with rites
> the temples, age on age, and chosen to offer
> the people's homage to gods, and win their favour,
> felt in pure minds the deity's mighty presence . . .[6]

No doubt the process was more complex than is suggested by the advent of a single synthesising scholar; but there may well have been such a man, or a pair of men, who brought about some decisive turn, just as Bolos seems to have done in alchemy. And since all other names are lacking, we may as well call the synthesisers by the traditional names of Nechepso and Petosiris, and ignore such shadowy figures as Astrampsychos, Boumegas, Zodarion, or Kourites.[7]

The names Nechepso and Petosiris are often combined. Petosiris was at times made a contemporary of Plato; and it is not impossible that he was the priest Petosiris, whose tomb, dateable at latest as 341 B.C., enjoyed for many years a great popularity.[8] This priest was looked on as something of a miracle worker and many people flocked to his tomb, leaving many graffiti. It lay near Hermopolis, where he had held the office of *lesōnis*, chief administrator, of the temple of Khmunu (Hermes) in the last days of Persian rule. He was certainly well aware of Greek culture; in the tomb-decorations the artist has done his best to depict a Greek motive (the gathering of the family) in the style of a Greek relief; many of the figures on the wall are in Greek dress—though we also see Egyptian commonfolk, not in the single loincloth of Pharaonic days, but in a loose tunic girt up and falling to the knees.[9] There are Hymns to the Sun on the walls. Petosiris calls himself Prophet of Amun Rē and Thoth's representative. Later, Hippolytos made the astrologer a son of Thoth; and Petosiris in the *Astrologoumena* under his name was shown as gaining his revelation from Thoth-Hermes. The pilgrims certainly looked on the priest Petosiris as a wise man. One man cut on his chest "Hail!" (or should one translate *chaire* here less pompously as "Hullo" or "Goodday"?); another scribbled his own name, "Phibis Apollonos"; while a third, surprised at the behaviour of somebody there, wrote down, "Look at that chap!" A group of slaves used their holiday to pay a visit. One Greek was stimulated to verse:

I invoke Petosiris whose venerated body under the earth here lies.
Today he is among the Gods, he is now united with the Wise.

But another irreverently counted up the words, taking them as numerals, and declared: "Total of these verses: in silver 8,373 drachmai." Yet another disagreed: "2,720 dr." But these levities do not affect the impression of a wide interest and reverence for the priest, who as well as a wise man was also an apostle. "You who live, I'll see that you are instructed in the wishes of God; I'll guide you to the way of life."[10]

It is unlikely that the priest in the fourth century was an astrologer, except in a minor way; he may have acquired something of Greek and Persian ideas, but he could not have known of the Zodiac. What seems most likely is that his name survived as that of a disciple of Thoth with insight into the mysteries, and was used in the second century to father a body of astrologic doctrines. The pseudo-Manethon in a verse-compilation of the second century A.D. asserted that Petosiris borrowed from Sacred Books hidden in sanctuaries, which the Allwise Hermes had composed and engraved—aided by Asklepios and upheld by the Providence of the Stars; no one but Petosiris had attempted to gain such wisdom.[11] Hephaistion yet later declared that "illustrious Nechepso" drew on the *Salmeschoiniaka*, which would then (if the statement were correct) precede Nechepso and Petosiris.[12]

Petosoris seems to have considered the moon more important than the sun for individual fates; and Nechepso may have differed. But it is to the latter that Valens assigns a doctrine according to which the moon may be in "contact" with a planet in several ways. Thus the moon might be in a sign next to the planet so that she will soon come in conjunction with the planet as her longitude increases; or she might reach the diameter of the planet or the side of the quartile aspect. Attributed to Petosiris was a *sphaera* dealing with names and numbers, which was perhaps the first chapter of the *Anthologies* put out under his name.[13] Maternus tells us that he gives the version of the *Thema Mundi* (the horoscope of the Universe) "according to Petosiris and Nechepso, who have followed Asklepios and Anubis, to whom the all-powerful divinity of Hermes has revealed the secrets of this science".[14] A fragment on the planets with the title *Seven Gods* begins, "After inquiry in many books that follow the tradition coming to us from the ancient sages, I wish to read the works of the Chaldeans and Petosiris, but above all of King Necheus [Nechepso], on which they all together rounded their doctrine, borrowing it from our Lord Hermes and from Asklepios, who is Imouthes, son of Hephaistos [Ptah]."[15] The Anon of 379, citing his forerunners, mentions first the Babylonians and Chaldeans on whom Berosos had written, then "Our Ancestors the Egyptians", among whom was Hermes "who in *Cosmic Influences* has composed a work on the Rising of Sirius". After him came Nechao and Keraphoros (unknown), Petosiris and Nechepso, and so on till Ptolemaios, especially his little work *Phases*.[16]

Back in the first century A.D., Thessalos, in the account of his revelation, says that Asklepios remarked of King Nechepso that "he was endowed with a natural wisdom and understood the affinities of stones and plants with stars", but "did not know the moments or places where the plants had to be gathered".[17]

Among the attributed texts we find *Petosiris' Greetings to King Nechepso* (in Latin), which deals with the prognostics of sick persons confined to bed, fugitive slaves, gladiators or *monomachi*— all after a system of astrologic dream-prophecy; *Astronomic Instrument of Petosiris dedicated to King Nechepso, King of the Assyrians*, which is the first of the two Circles of Petosiris; and a fragment of a letter on a recipe for astrologic dream-prophecy, which deals with the relations between a name's letters and the zodiacal signs. This latter work mentions other letters to Nechepso on planets, their signs, their activities, their relations to zodiacal signs.[18]

The Spheres or Circles attributed to Petosiris remind us of the *Sphere of Demokritos*. They were rather childish devices used to formalise and simplify the question of prognostics; anyone could be shown how to employ them. The system attributed to Demokritos consisted of a rectangular table with the 30 days of the months ranged in three colours and mixed up in an occult order.

Sphere of Demokritos, Prognostic of Life and Death. Know under which Moon the sick man took to bed and the name of his nativity. Add the calculation of the Moon and see how many times there is 30 days in it. Take the remainder and seek in the Sphere. If the number falls in the upper part, he will live. If in the lower part, he will die.[19]

What is done is to add the numerical value of the name given at birth (in Latin, the *praenomen*) to that of the day of the month in question, and divide by four.

In place of the divisor 30, which corresponds to a fictive Moon, the *Circle of Petosiris* adopts 29 (the middle between the various ways of estimating the length of the moon's revolution). Otherwise the procedure is the same. Followers of Petosiris insisted that the method applied to all sorts of problems, not merely to sickness.[20] Always one added the name to the day, divided by 29, and then saw to which prognostic the remainder in the Circle corresponded. If two competitors were involved, the operation was done for each of the two names. Thus, the procedure applied to Achilles made him fall in the *zoē megalē* (great life), applied to Hektor it made him fall in the *mikros thanatos* (little death).[21]

Fig. 53. Heptagram of the Weekday Gods

In one *Circle of Petosiris*, we find a division into the four quadrants by diameters in the form of bands. The upper hemicycle (of the diagram) is attributed to Life, the lower to Death. The numbers 1 to 29 are set out in the quadrants and in a column on the vertical diameter. Two rectangular tables, one above and one below the Circle, enclose the computations of the days of the moon. The second Circle is divided into eight sectors making up a sort of compass-card, orientated, with the Rising, *hypergeios*, on top and the Setting, *hypogeios*, below. On the middle line, *mesogeios*, the north is to the left, the south to the right. The horizontal diameter is described as Hours of Life and Death; and the sectors below this line are called *hypergeia* of the South Wind, those above it, *hypergeia* of the North Wind. Numbers 1 to 30 are set out on the edge of the sectors and on the vertical diameter. On the Circle's outer edge are inscribed the prognostics: in the north-east quadrant (Great Life), "These

Numbers speedily save"; in the south-east (Little Life), "These save within seven days"; in the north-west (Great Death), "These speedily destroy"; in the north-east, "These destroy within seven days". Both Circles are dedicated by "Petosiris the *mathematikos* to King Nechepso".

Another way of manipulating the Petosirian Circle was to operate merely with the client's name and the moon's number (taking, not the day itself, which is not divisible by 29 or 30, but the numeric value of its name).

If the moon's number is found under earth and the man's name above, the man will be in danger, but will escape. If, on the contrary, the number of the man is under earth and that of the moon above, misfortunes will arrive in the guise of prosperity. But if both numbers, that of the man and that of the moon, are above the horizon, without doubt what they promise is a prosperous future. In the same way, if both are found under the horizon, only misfortunes will come.[22]

Another example has a table with only the 30 days of the month set out in two equal series of 15 numbers (in an odd order): the series of Life above earth, that of Death under earth. Here we make up the sum to be divided out of the day of the week, the day of the month, the client's name, and the number 10: perhaps the holy Decade, one of the keys with which the Pythagoreans penetrated the universe's secrets. In the *Book of Henoch* the history of the world is made up of Ten Weeks.[23]

Again we find a table of dekans formed of three bands of 12 numbers each. The upper band is bound up with Life and Good Things, the lower with Death and Adversities, the middle with mixed prognostics, long trials that end in deliverance. The sum to be divided by 36 is made up of the day when the client fell sick and went to bed, up to the day indicated. "If you find the answer in the first line, say that the sick man will live; if in the second line, the illness will be prolonged but without fear of death; if finally the number is found in the third line, it's death for the sick man."[24]

We have already seen how the founding astrologers were considered to have experienced revelations. Here are some more examples of the belief. The pseudo-Manethon, speaking of the way he had been favoured by a special providence of heavenly stars, goes on later to tell more openly of a divine revelation such as came to Petosiris-Nechepso.[25] We learn also that in an ecstasy King Nechepso felt himself ascend in the air and heard a voice, *boē*, out of the sky, while there appeared to him a form wrapped in a dark *peplos* that spread obscurity. The text is corrupt, but it seems that the ascension went on "all night". In the account that Thessalos gives of his own visionary experience, Asklepios remarks, "King Nechepso, intelligent man as he was and possessed of every magical power, did not receive from a divine voice any of the secrets you wish to learn."[26] Indeed the idea that the pioneers in star-lore were inspired became a commonplace. Vitruvius writes:

... Others followed up their discoveries and with the aid of astronomical tables discovered the indications of the constellations, of their setting, and of the seasons, and handed the explanations down to later ages. Their knowledge is to be revered by mankind, because they so applied themselves that they seem by a divine mind to declare beforehand the indications of the seasons.[27]

We may compare Henoch's ascent. He is "rapt up" and "no man has known where he was lifted or where he is or what has happened to him". He says, "As for me, I have seen in my sleep what I now tell you." He mounts into air (clouds, mist, star-courses, lightnings) up to a door which he enters; then he comes to a second house, where the door, of fire, is open; inside is a throne and on it the Great Glory. He hears a voice, "Come hither, Henoch, and hearken to my word."[28] In *Revelation* we are told, "After this I looked, and, behold, a door was opened in heaven; and the first voice which I heard was as it were a trumpet talking with me: which said, Come up hither and I will show you things which must be hereafter. And immediately I was in the spirit, and, behold, a throne was set in heaven and one sat on the throne." The hermetic *Poimandres* opens: "One day when I had set to meditate on beings and my thought had gone to soar in the heights while my bodily senses were bound down as happens to those overwhelmed by a heavy sleep . . . I thought I saw a being of immense size, totally beyond all definition, who called me by my name and said to me . . ." Later on the narrator sees a light, then a darkness which produces "a sort of sound, an indescribable groaning", and out of it comes an inarticulate cry "like the voice of fire".[29]

In a *Recipe for Immortality* the subject ascends through various heavenly zones; when he reaches the last he hears a burst of thunder and roarings in the air, then he sees the doors (of heaven) and the world of gods inside the great open doors; finally Helios appears and gives him his revelation. All the while he is in an ecstasy, yet able to retain and remember an oracle with thousands of verses.[30] The Christians had similar experiences. "I knew a man in Christ above fourteen years ago," said Paul, "whether in the body, I cannot tell, or whether out of the body, I cannot tell: God knows, such a one caught up to the third heaven. And I knew such a man, whether in the body or out of the body, I cannot tell: God knows—how he was caught up to paradise and heard unspeakable words which it is not lawful for a man to utter." He is telling of "visions and revelations in the Lord". Loukian on the other hand parodies the rapt ascents. In his *Ikaromenippos* the hero flies up 3,000 stades to the Moon, pauses, crosses 500 parasangs to the Sun, then on eagle-wing rises to the citadel of Zeus on the sky-summit. (Here is the Pythagorean threefold division set out by Philolaos: Ouranos below the Moon, Kosmos up to the Sun and planets, including the Moon, Olympos or the Third Heaven.)[31]

The authors seem to be thinking at once of an actual and a psychological event. Note Paul's "in or out of the body". There is often an emphasis on a part of the visionary remaining on earth while another part ascends to heaven.[32] Philon of Alexandreia echoes the mocking tone of Aristophanes in his attack on the Chaldeans, the astrologic priests of his time, "You have your seat on earth: then why frisk above the clouds? Why say you are able to touch things of the *aither* when you are quite rooted to the ground?"[33]

There was, however, a deep feeling that the ecstatic contemplation of the stars somehow lifted one up aloft; and behind these attitudes lay the shamanist experiences of levitation and ascension. In other passages Philon devoutly admires what he has ridiculed. He praises "all those among the Greeks or the Barbarians" who give themselves up to the study of wisdom and lead blameless lives, fleeing from the matters that absorb other people—law, politics, business, intrigues.

They excellently contemplate nature and all natural beings. They penetrate the secrets of earth, sea, air, heaven, as well as their physical laws. They accompany in thought the Moon and Sun in their circuitings, the choirs of other planets and fixed stars, attached below to the ground by their bodies, but giving wings to their souls, so that, walking on the *aither,* they contemplate the powers they find there. For they have become authentic Citizens of the Cosmos, they who have made it their City and who regard as its members all friends of wisdom.[34]

Stoic Cosmopolitanism means much more than feeling the whole earth as one's native land; it means primarily the sense of being part of the universe. The hermetic works insist that men can rise to the heavens.

No heavenly god will pass the frontiers of heaven and come down to earth; man on the contrary rises even to heaven. And he measures and knows what is in the heaven above, and what is below, and he learns all the rest with precision. Supreme marvel; he has not even the need to leave the earth to establish himself on high, so far his power extends . . .

Nothing can obstruct, neither the Sun's fire nor the Aither nor the heaven's revolution nor the bodies of other stars; but, cutting across all space, the soul will ascend in its flight up to the furthest heavenly body.[35]

These attitudes could take the form of a simple claim of having talked with the gods. "It has seemed to me," says Vettius Valens, "that divine beings have conversed with me, and I felt then that my intelligence was wholly clear and pure for research." Moments of particularly intense insight or concentration were interpreted as a sky-ascent into the dimensions of the gods.[36]

These experiences, an essential aspect of the new scientific inquiries, had a dual character. By clarifying the sense of correspondences and active relationships, by increasing the unified grasp of diverse phenomena, they gave men a deepened comprehension of reality and greatly enriched life. But these gains were made at the cost of a continually extended sense of alienation from the earth and of contempt for earthly activities. We are reminded how the concentration on the star-world was bound up with the breakdown of the democratic *polis* where, whatever the weaknesses, limitations, and contradictions, men could feel drawn together in shared and significant actions. The intellectual and religious worship of the stars may seem naïve in many respects, and the range of scientific interests and methods may seem restricted, in comparison with the attitudes and systems of post-Galilean science. But we must realise that the alienation from the earth into the mathematics of the stars was in fact the necessary precondition of the mechanistic universes of Galileo and Newton, in which the living concrete world of qualities, the world of the fullness of earthly experience, was thrown overboard in the name of quantitative measurements; the superior reality of star-movements became the superior world of pure quantities and mechanical motion. Science has still to outgrow the categories on which Plato crucified it.

We touch however one of the vital aspects in astrology, which links it with alchemy, in its use of basic formula expressing dialectical change: a nature is delighted by another nature, a nature conquers another nature, a nature dominates another nature. This formula certainly goes back to the early days of alchemy in Egypt and seems the work of Bolos of Mendes. It is then perhaps significant that Maternus links it with Nechepso-Petosiris. "A nature is conquered by another, a god by another." Nechepso is said to apply the principle to dekanic medicine. "Out of contrary natures and contrary powers he devised remedies for all diseases by methods of divine reason."[37] We see then that the astrologer, at least in his deepest moments, was not thinking simply of two or more gods or powers pulling in different directions and thus modifying the result in a mechanist way; he also was thinking of a dialectical conflict in which the struggling forces merged in order to bring a new unity. He was not able to develop a method which linked mechanism and dialectics, but it was important that he was haunted by the ghost of fuller comprehensions. The magical elements at times introduced into the purely mathematical calculations do not merely represent a surrender to irrationality; they represent also the effort to grasp the unknown forces or aspects of a dynamic situation in a way which the system of calculations failed to do.

A work that seems to have mixed magic and astrology was the collection variously cited as the *Salmeschoiniaka*, the *Salmeschoiaka*, or the *Salmesachanaka*. This manual, which Iamblichos calls "the shortest section of the Hermaic Doctrines" (*diataxeis*), was Hellenistic in origin, and has been claimed as Egyptian and as Babylonian.[38] A longish fragment, which seems related to it and which may come from another work of the same type, has been found in a papyrus of the late second century A.D.[39] It is an account of a calendar. The year is divided into weeks of five days, each week corresponding to the sixth part of a zodiacal sign; the same formula is used for each week. A brief astronomical statement is made of the relation between the month-section under consideration and one of the signs, probably the one making its heliacal rising during the period. Then comes the name of the presiding deity, male or female, and its explanation, introduced by the phrase: "Of which the Interpretation is". Then comes a detailed description of the *typos* of the deity, who is represented by a statue partly human, partly animal. Next we are given an

elaborate account of the omens, signs, portents, and favourable
or unfavourable influences characteristic of the period presided
over by the deity—introduced by the phrase "he signifies". In
conclusion the particular form of sickness derived from the
period is described. In one case there is added a passage about a
female deity's son, which carried on on the same lines and ends
with directions for medical prescriptions.

We also have a fragment on vellum, some centuries later, which
gives us a list of deities with an account of the signs, events, and
sicknesses associated with them; but here the plan of arrangement
differs. The deities are connected with various stars and constellations, each numbered so as to form a series.[40]

In the papyrus a distinction seems drawn between (1) the
superior gods who preside over each ten days, but more especially
over the first five, and of whom the first mentioned in each month
seems that month's god and (2) the lesser divinities called *krataioi*
or *hegoumenoi* (mighty ones or leaders, governors) who preside
over the 6th-to-10th, 16th-to-20th, 26th-to-30th sections of the
month. The gods or *theoi* can then be identified with the dekans,
whose strange names have a certain likeness to those mentioned
in the papyrus, particularly in one case, where *Tet . . . ysa.ē.e* may
be *Tet[ima]ysa.ē.e* who occurs in Hermes Trismegistos' *On the
Months, to Asclepius.*[41] In the latter work the account of the Fish
is also close to that on the Fish in the papyrus, while its *Soapphi*,
second in the list, is not unlike the name of the first dekan in the
papyrus [S]*aphthyn*. The only other reference to the lesser
category of deities in the papyrus is in a *Letter* from Porphyrios to
Anebon the Egyptian. Chairemon, mentioned there, wrote in
Nero's time; and the two terms "mighty" and "leaders or governors" are run together:

As for Chairemon and the rest, they don't believe in anything else prior to
the visible worlds, for they account as a ruling power the Gods of the
Egyptians and no others except the so-called Planets and those stars
accompanying the Zodiac and as many as rise near them. Also the
divisions into the *Dekanoi* and the Horoscopes and the so-called Mighty
Governors, the names of which are contained in the Almanacs, and their
power to heal diseases, and their risings and settings, and their indications
of future events.

For he saw that those who assert the Sun to be Creator twist the story
of Osiris and Isis, and all the priestly legends, into allusions to the stars,
their appearances and disappearances, and the solar distances at rising,

or else to the hemisphere of Night or of Day, or to their River; and generally that they interpreted all things of physical phenomena and nothing of incorporeal and living beings. And most of them made even their free will depend upon the motion of the stars, binding all things down by indissoluble bonds, I know not how, to a Necessity they call Fate, and making all things depend closely on these Gods, whom, as the sole deliverance from the bonds of Fate, they worship with temples and statues and the like.[42]

The lack of any references to the Romans and their institutions, plus several mentions of Kings, *Basileis*, strongly supports a Hellenistic date for the papyrus. Here are passages:

The presiding deity of that season is Neby, of which the Interpretation is that he is Lord of Wars and of Reason [*logos*]. He is represented by an upright statue with the face of a Vulture, wearing a Diadem on his head, and with the face of a Serpent behind, having two Wings and the feet of a Lion and holding four Swords—both faces being of Gold.

He signifies that the Governor [calls up] evils; there will be war, disgust, and battle, and he will take counsel with the people as a friend, and during his rule there will be war, and many cities of Egypt will perish on account of the rebel, for the signs of the time are of war and disgust and battle, and there will be destruction of many.

In that time many will live by staying hidden, and some will live by song and dance, and some by chanting in the temples, and some by singing at banquets with sweet voices—and they end well.

This deity causes, by *logos*, the conqueror to be conquered and the conquered to conquer, and many live by getting gratuities and register-ing and collecting from men what they have drunk up, and some live by . . . as servants. He causes men to be lame because one foot [withers up]. The sickness in this season is in the intestines and bowels, and there will be many deaths.

The persons registering, etc., seem to be tax-collectors forcing men to disgorge what they have already spent. The reference to the rebel reminds us of the Sothis-text and suggests a date round 150 B.C. The diadem, *basileon*, recalls Saopphi, the 35th dekan in the text of Hermes Trismegistos, who has a man's shape, naked, with wrappings (*peribelaion*) hanging from his shoulders down his back, a small pitcher in his right hand, his left fore-finger to his mouth, and a *basileon* on his head. The concise paradoxical phrases about conqueror and conquered are important: they suggest the triadic formula of dialectical change and the hope of social reversals which often lurks behind prophesies at the popular level—the first becoming the last, the meek inheriting the kingdom of heaven, and so on.

The Lord of Flame. His image is an upright statue with the face of . . ., and a young Pig behind, with snout on its face, holding four swords in his hands and a Knife. His tongue and face are Fire. He signifies that this season causes many to make a living by the mouth. And many shall be advocates and others magicians, and many singers of gods and kings, and many interpreters of languages, and many . . . migrating from place to place, and men earning much without labour or worrying how it was earned . . . are eaten up. Many however also consume the substance of others. He makes many bugger-boys and many copulate with aunts and stepmothers, so as to debauch them. . . .

    She is represented by an image in real lapis lazuli of a Woman seated on a Throne, with one eye like that of . . . and one like that of Typhon, her face being of Gold and her hands adorned by . . . [or folded], with a diadem on her head. She signifies that this time makes hidden writings [unsettle] many men, who are uninstructed in the soul. For this reason also it produces men ignorant of writing, and again those who know writing very different in character from this kind and from the hieratic writings . . . and there will be many sacred secretaries, and the life of many will be . . . This god causes. . . .

What kind of writing is meant? Demotic? Or is the text a translation from Egyptian, so that in the original it was Greek that was the intrusive tongue? With regard to the eyes, the missing word seems something like Typhōs or Typheus; but then it is hard to see where the contrast lies. We should expect some name like Horos. The idea of the two differing eyes however is Egyptian. We hear often of the Two Eyes of Horos, one injured by Set (Typhon); in late times the motive was taken as referring to the monthly waning of the moon—the injury produced an eclipse. There was also an interpretation of the Two Eyes as Sun and Moon: and in hermetic doctrine we find the right corresponding with the Sun, the left with the Moon.[43] The Hidden Writings seem to be hermetic, in view of the contrast between the instructed and the uninstructed (idiōtikoi)—the initiated and the uninitiated.

In this season men fall upon women and many children are born and there will be one male child who will be of service to him, but the rest will die, even the male children. This season causes men to copulate with their own slavewomen and beget children who will rule the lives of their fathers and of the free women. The God causes women to be childless and other children to be begotten, and these to rule our lives. The sickness in this season is in the shoulders [perhaps eyes] and . . .

The Son of the Goddess, whose name is . . . *tōrtensē.eutōououōphi*, which means Terrible Speaker. He is represented as a statue with the face of a Lion, the hair of a God. He holds a sceptre in his left hand, in his right . . ., with a crocodile's tail . . .

This is a favourable time for high priests. It produces many sacred scribes of gods and kings, and gives long life to each. It causes a king to confer many favours even on his former adversaries and upon . . . and cities as well to confer favours. It makes men behave well and strive for the good, above all with regard to the God. It causes the king . . . from the other kings who afford him great support [or supplies] as has been said in connection with another season . . .

. . . in the great city of Hermes. This deity causes long old age—until a man is bowed down by old age. He produces hunchbacks or makes men bent over by illness. He causes dwarfs to be born and beetle-shaped monstrosities and persons with no eyes and like a beast and dumb and deaf and toothless. He causes men to suffer being buggered and again manifest *kinaidoi* [pathics] . . .

The stress on priests, scribes, and worship suggests a temple-environment.

In general this text has a strong Egyptian coloration, aided by the system of time-divisions. It suggests some priestly scribe, or a group of such scribes, struggling to absorb the new doctrines, soon after the idea of the Zodiac had come in, and at the same time to give them a thoroughly Egyptian slant. The monster gods are in the key of many later magical images, especially that of Bes as a sort of All-god Wizard. Take for example an amulet such as this:

Naked genius with head of Bes, flanked by seven heads of animals among whom are bull, lion, and ibis, and surmounted by *atef* crown with several horns; four wings; falcon-tail and crocodile-tail; four arms—two arms stretched out along the wings hold lances and serpents, while the third on the left seizes a lion, the fourth on the right holds sceptre and whip. The erect penis ends in a lionhead; there are lionmasks on the knees, the feet are given the form of jackal-heads with pointed ears and prolonged as coiled snakes. Bes stands on an ouroboros [cosmic all-enclosing serpent] which contains various animals: scorpion, crocodile, tortoise.[44]

Incidentally we may note that Bes plays his musician's role in welcoming Hathor back from Nubia in rites dramatising the lunar cycle.[45]

II

More on Correspondences

The hermetic character of the *Salmeschoiniaka* seems to have been influential and the papyrus we have just examined may be ranked among the works connected with it. We have seen also hermetic positions in the *Horasis* of Kritodemos and the way in which Hermes-Thoth keeps turning up as the ultimate source for writers like Petosiris and Nechepso.[1] Julian of Laodikeia (fifth century) attributes to Hermes a doctrine of zodiacal signs and dekans taken up by others.[2] "Hermes Trismegistos and those who have used him have instructed us on the zodiacal signs, on the nature and energy of each of them; besides, if one wants to find out about the figure of the dekans, one will commit no error in learning from this author." The Anon of 379 knew a book by Hermes in which the dekans were related to illnesses.

When Saturn and Mars are in aspect by the right with the Moon and the Sun occurring in these places . . . those then born are inevitably diseased in the eyes, if neither Jupiter nor Venus are in aspect on the right with the stars responsible, or the places and the dekans, such as we have set down in our table [lost] according to the contents of the *Book of Hermes* in which he has dealt at length with iatromathematics.[3]

Hermes was considered an authority on astrologic botany. "Pamphilos mentions a plant named, according to him, *aetos*, of which he asserts that no Greek has spoken, but which appears in one of the Books attributed to Hermes the Egyptian where the 36 Sacred Plants of the Horoscopes are dealt with."[4] Paul of Alexandreia enumerates, after the hermetic book *Panaretos* or *The All-Excellent*, the Seven Lots corresponding to the Seven Planets; and in his commentary on Paul, Heliodoros (about 500) says:

It's necessary to know that Hermes Trismegistos has treated of these Lots in the book *Panaretos* where he reveals also the Influences of these

Lots, thanks to which one can, without further aids, foresee the future for all matters without the aid of any further research. This divine man has then taught that there are Seven Lots according to the number of the Seven Planets . . .[5]

We are also told of an opuscule on the *Dodekatemoria* and of a *Brontologion* (Thunderbook) which explained the meaning of thunder in each month of the year.[6] In this work the months are Roman in the headings, Egyptian in the text; and all the presages deal with the East, especially Egypt. The western Mediterranean is called the Land of the West. The original seems old, as it was the source for presages set out by the Roman Fonteius, from whom in turn John Lydos took passages.[7] Hermetic too is a poem on Earthquakes which some MSS attribute to Orpheus.[8] The date is uncertain, but is at least pre-Byzantine. Presages are classed according to the position of the Sun in the zodiacal signs, starting with the Ram (April). The poem thus opens:

> Hear then my discourse, Child. Whenever the Shaker
> with dark hair makes earth trembles, it prophesies
> good or bad fortune for men. When the Equinox
> of Spring is come and Helios crosses the Ram,
> if the god who clasps the earth brings violent quakings
> at night, the City will witness large revolts.
> If the quake arrives by day, it means there'll be
> grievings and maledictions, and a scourge
> will fall on foreign peoples and for us
> hardships and afflictions will multiply.[9]

The Shaker is Poseidon; and the City is not Rome, but Alexandreia. The first form of the work was possibly Ptolemaic. We possess also a paraphrase in prose, which has a stronger popular note, stimulated apparently by outbreaks of civil war at such times of disorder as followed the deaths of Nero and Commodus. Thus it covers the same period as the verses cited above.

April. The Sun in the Ram; if the earth trembles by day, those who approach kings will lay snares for one another, the towns nearby [to the quake] will be shaken with great troubles and know acts of violence and murders; an illustrious man will perish and his followers will be in danger. There will be great rains; the fruits of the earth and the trees will prosper. If the earth trembles at night, there'll be brawls among the people [or splits in the people and their groupings, *hoi dēmoi*], and there'll be revolt against the reigning tyrant; for the soldiers of the tyrant will leave him, will oppose him, and will rebel against their own king. There'll be troubles and revolutions among the people. The tyrants of the West will perish. There'll be great rains, seeds will multiply. In Egypt there'll be a famine and lack of Nile water.[10]

Again the atmosphere is strongly Eastern, Egyptian.

A small work is *The Secret Method of Hermes Trismegistos for every Katarchē*, which occurs in four MSS and is perhaps fairly old; there are no vulgarisms in the Greek. It says that we must begin by determining the position of the Centres, the Periods, the Planets.[11] Also in four MSS occurs *On the Denomination and Power of the Twelve Places*.[12]

Here we had better pause to consider the doctrine of Places. The key-moment for the casting of nativities was the moment of birth and what was then happening in the eastern sky—what point of the Zodiac was then coming up. This point was the *Horoskopos*, the ascendant point or degree. The astrologer looked for a fixed-star or planet which was "born" into the sky at the same instant as the child was born on to earth. Planets were too rare to supply enough horoscopes; so the Zodiac was what the watcher looked to for the hour, *hōra*. As the systems grew more elaborate, he sought for the degree of the zodiacal circle, or even for subdivisions. The geometric combinations imagined for the stars were applied equally to the pivot or point (centre, *kentron*, *gōnia, cardo, angulus*) called *Horoskopos* and to the three others determined by that starting-point. The *kentra* of the birth-circle were thus: *Horoskopos* or East (H), the culmination above, *mesanourēma* or *medium caelum* (MC), the Setting, *dysis* or West (W), the lower culmination, *hypogeion* or *imum caelum* (IMC). These were determined by the meeting of the zodiacal plan with that of the horizon and that of the meridian.

The early astrologers believed it was enough to consider the Zodiac as a circle to be divided into four equal quadrants; they thought they could then fix the positions of the Horoscope and the West (points of intersection with the horizon) or the two Culminations (points of intersection with the meridian). But some observers discovered that the Zodiac was turning on an axis oblique to its plane and therefore was never divided into four equal quadrants by horizon and meridian; they also saw that some signs went up faster than others and that these same ones came down slower. All this was important, for the calculations as to a subject's length of life were based on the value of the arcs of the zodiacal circle expressed as time. The Egyptian School clung to the idea of equal arcs of the Zodiac of 30° and resisted the more precise working-out of the *anaphorai*, the ascent of a sign measured in degrees of the equator.[13] They did not understand or accept the notion of the obliquity of the Zodiac, so that even in the late period we find Paul of Alexandreia drawing up a manual for his son Kronammon in order to reject the persistent errors and to assert "the *anaphorai* according to Ptolemaios".[14] Macrobius, setting out the Egyptian System, had no idea of what the problems were, nor had Servius, the commentator of Virgil.[15]

The *kentra* were thought to own a specific energy and speed, which they communicated to the signs and planets with which they coincided or which they pointed out. The West drew its significance from the fact that it was opposite to the birth-moment and was thus taken for death. Ptolemaios would have liked to drop IMC, but the Egyptians clung to it, making it stand for the North, with MC as the south. The stars were commonly taken to set in the west, go under the earth, and rejoin the Rising-point by the north.[16]

After the four *kentra* came the four *epanaphorai*, "those that ascend after"; they moved towards the future and their action was rather favourable. The other four compartments were the decliners, *apoklimata* or *epikataphorai* in relation to the *kentra*; they lacked energy in the sense that evil is the negation of good; they produced the bad effects.

The system of Places, *topoi* or *loci*, seems the work of the Egyptians, who wanted to break away from the tiring exposition of the Zodiac with its apparatus of houses, exaltations, limits, dekans, and other such matters, and to base their analysis solely on the influence of the planets considered in three sets of angular positions (*kentra, anaphorai, apoklimata*) in relation to the horizon.[17] Perhaps they meant to leave to zodiacal interpretation the question of forces acting on the body and to deal through their system with the moral aspects, the vicissitudes of conscious life, the succession of acts at different ages. The system itself can be imagined as arising independently of the zodiacal signs, though it may indeed have been stimulated into existence by the lines of thought evident in zodiacal horoscopy. What happened was something like a superimposition of the two systems, that of Places being used as one of the elaborations or complications of the zodiacal system.[18]

In the diagram of the Twelve Places the Horoscope is I,

representing Life, the whole basis of the prognostication; IMC is IV and stands for Parents, Patrimony; the West, VII, stands for Marriage; MC, X, is Life, Breath, Actions, Homeland, Home, Arts, Honours, all the occupations of mature age and civic ambitions. Next come four places called Seconds, favourable, being in trigon relation, V, IX, III and XI—Sons, Journeys, Brothers, Friends; and finally four that are unfavourable or ineffective, II, VI, VIII, XII—Profit (*lucrum*), Health, Death, Enemies. These are "slothful and dejected", without any definite relation of position or direct connection with the Horoscope at Place I.[19]

Place II, following I, is not in aspect with it; it keeps its name "Door of the Underworld" (Hades), but a note of hope is introduced by the motive of *lucrum*, growth of possessions. We are to think further about the subject after, perhaps, puberty; it is in trigon with XII, Honours. Place III, though *apoklima*, is favourable, and represents brothers, friends, perhaps also voyages; here is put the Moon under the name of the Goddess, starting off the series of planets. In IV or IMC are the parents and all they involve. Here should have gone Mercury, who represents education or wealth (but *lucrum* not patrimony); however he is left out, though Manilius put him in his Horoscope. Place V, for Sons, is set next to that of parents; here appears Venus, as goddess of generation, in the form of Good Fortune. Place VI, unfavourable, is the seat of Mars (as Bad Fortune), the source of diseases and infirmities. In VII or West we meet Marriage—and must not ask why it comes after the Sons. It is the turning-point, the middle of the career. Place VIII, unfavourable and opposite to another unfavourable place, gives us death. (Here in the eight-place system is Typhon.) In IX is the Sun, opposite to the Goddess, linked with Journeys; in X come Life, Breath, Civic Actions; in XI comes Jupiter as Agathos Daimon, pendant of Venus-Fortuna, gathering Friends who do services and repay benefits. Finally in XII lurks the Kakos Daimon, pendant of the female Bad Fortune; he is Saturn and all unpleasant things, troubles through enemies and slaves as well as chronic illness suggested by the image of old age.

Not that such a definitive system appeared all at once. Many attempts were made to round it off and eliminate incoherences.[20] We may note how the four great stages of life have been made to correspond to the four *kentra* (birth, maturity, old age, death), going from left to right like the daily movement. Mature age is at the top of the sphere, death below. Each *kentron* in turn forms the middle of a group of three Places which are counted in the time-order of their rising, *apoklima* first, *kentron* after, *epanaphora* third. Thus the groups are ranged from left to right, and the units of each group from right to left. The cycle starts at the Place (*apoklima*, preceding horoscope) where lie the pangs of gestation and birth. The Horoscope itself stands for the achieved act of birth and the first infantile years; in the next Place infancy ends. We pass on to the second group, at the top of which stands the middle-of-the-middle, with the new start on the right and the ending of middle-age on the left. The West represents the final phase, decadence starts on its right and ends on its left. The lower culmination represents death, with the time before it on one side, the time after it on the other. The time-after was taken by the scholiast to relate to the reputation left behind on earth— though we can imagine a Pythagorean astrologer seeing it as the stage before a reincarnation started the cycle off again. But astro- logy never, as we know it, concerned itself with any afterlife; it was wholly focussed on life here and now.[21]

Now back to the works of Hermes. The corpus under his name seems certainly, at least in its roots, to go back to the Ptolemaic era and to found zodiacal astrology in Egypt—though his role as founder is merged with that of Petosiris and Nechepso, whom he inspires. His work is cited by Thrasyllos under Tiberius and Antiochos of Athens, earlier still, as well as by Maternus, Paulos, and Rhetorios—and perhaps even by Sarapion, pupil of Hipparchos.[22] The picture we get of the religious world in the Ptolemaic period would suit well for the seeding-ground of Hermetism: a strongly organised hierarchy of priests, various kinds of devotees installed in temples as *enthousiastikoi*, diviners and dream-prophets, god- possessed men, *ekstatikoi*, who utter oracles, mystics seeking and finding secret books, half-naked ascetics in rags, lost inside their long hair and ready to break out into a confession of sins, magicians and exorcists. Men dedicated themselves to the gods with all their property and ended their days in the sanctuary's glooms, unable to cross the threshold. Hierodoules or temple- slaves are sometimes slaves who have been willed to a temple, sometimes they are men whom the god has possessed. Maternus groups together "beggars, naked men, madmen, temple-slaves", and speaks of men being made "to serve in the temples or compelled to prophesy".[23] (Strabon says of Kamana in Cappadocia that it was noteworthy for "the crowd of god-possessed and of hierodoules". Among the Albanoi of the Caucasus, the moonpriest was the most important person after the king and among the hierodoules were many who were inspired and who made prophesies; each year one of the sacred slaves, becoming possessed and wandering alone in the woods, was seized and later immolated.) The Egyptian temples were not only asylums for fugitives from the police; they also harboured the sick and the penniless. An astrologic text puts together, "poverty-stricken and raggedy folk or those held in sanctuaries"; Maternus, "beggars, poor folk, covered in rags and sunk with a disaster of wretched want", whom he then links with temple-servants and prophets.[24]

That a compendium of hermetic doctrine existed is shown by a Latin version, *Liber Hermetis*, taken directly from the Greek, not via the Arabs. In its existent form, however, it is hardly earlier than the fifth century A.D., as shown by the authors cited: e.g., the doctrine of the seven cardinal rules found in Rhetorios.[25] And by the fact that earlier writers like Sarapion and Antiochos of Athens seem to be ignorant of it. In any event it is a collection of extracts and could have been put together over a long period of time into its present form. It plunges straight into the theory of the dekans, without any account of zodiacal signs; and its text has much disorder, mixing general ideas and particular applications. Chapters of theory deal with the Brilliant Stars, the Twelve Places, the Fixed Stars, Conjunction of Planets, Position of Planets in Signs, and Planetary Limits. But these are preceded or followed by bits dealing with practice: the year, month, and day of death, useful or useless days, marriage, parents, bodily affections resulting from the moon's position in the signs, brothers, duration of life, persons dying a violent death (*biathanatoi*), the death of brothers. This last-named section abruptly ends the MSS.[26]

Many matters are summarily treated, when we would expect much greater length; others, such as *katarchai*, are hardly mentioned; and there are many references back to subjects not to be found in the text. When we compare late writers on various themes —Valens on the Seven Lots and Mutations of the Moon, Maternus on the quadrants, Maternus and Rhetorios on the Twelve Places— we see that at least in parts the work does go back to a Hellenistic original of an hermetic kind; and we feel the earlier Egyptian element most strongly in the sections that are most characteristic of the treatise, the chapters on dekans, brilliant stars, fixed stars (with indication of the degrees of the Zodiac in which they have their rising). The dekans have a special role in the *Liber*, which sets out how they exercise control over the human body. Far back in Egyptian medicine each organ was considered dependent on some god, with whom it was identified. The identification could take the form of seeing the organ as one with the organ of a god or as itself the god:

Your head is Horos of the Underworld, your face is Mekhenty-Irty, your ears and your eyes are the Twin Children of Atum, your nose is the Jackal, your teeth are Sopd, your hands are Hapi and Duamutef . . . (Pyramid Text)

The summit of your head is Re, the nape of your neck is Osiris . . . your ears are two king-snakes, your arm is Horos, your navel is the Morning Star, each limb is a god and each god protects your name . . . (spell)

These litanies often end with the sentence: "There is no part of the body without its god." Such correlations carried right on over the centuries: Paracelsus wrote, "The Sun governs the head, Jupiter governs the liver. . . ."[27]

The dekans also control both the whole of Egypt and its nome-divisions. Thus, the third dekan of the Virgin dominates the *klima* of Meroe and Elephantine.[28] The dekans further influence all the lands round Egypt or those with which it has contact; but remoter areas as well have crept in, doubtless during the Roman era, such as Britannia, Dacia, Sarmatia. The section on the brilliant stars seems old; the Anon of 379, in treating this subject, refers to the Author, who is Hermes Trismegistos.[29] Our text seems based on Hipparchos; and the calculations of star-positions seem even earlier in basis, going back to the earlier third century B.C., perhaps to men like Timochares and Aristyllos.[30] A Ptolemaic and Egyptian origin is further suggested by the chapter on the *monomoiriai* (divisions of a single degree), the stars presiding over each of the thirty degrees of each sign; Egyptian here again is the notion of the masters-of-time, the *chronokratores*. An hermetic work on the *monomoiriai* was known to Rhetorios, Maternus, Gregory of Nyssa. The *Asclepius* refers to it:

Since then the two elements making up forms are bodily and bodiless, it is impossible that two individual forms are born wholly like one another at different points of space and time; on the contrary these forms change as often as there are moments in the time of the circle's revolution inside of which resides the great god we've named the Omniform.[31]

We have already seen in the *Sphere of Demokritos* and the *Circles of Petosiris* a rather childish attempt being made to produce simple calculating-systems for dealing with illness. These systems were very popular. One which was attributed to Thrasyllus ran as follows:

LIFE	1	4	7	10	13	16	19	22	25	28	31	34	—happy end
MEDIUM	2	5	8	11	14	17	20	23	26	29	32	35	—long end
DEATH	3	6	9	12	15	18	21	24	27	30	33	36	—bad end

Put down the day when the patient went ill to bed, or when the child was born, or the runaway escaped, or someone went away; in short of anything about which you want certainty. Count then from 18 May to that particular day. Divide that number as often as possible by 36. Take into your hand the final remainder and address yourself to the Table. If you find the number in the first line, then announce that the patient will live, . . ., the traveller have a good journey, the runaway [slave] be caught, the newborn live long, and so on. If the number is found in the second line, then the patient will be long ill but in no danger of death, the runaway will be caught at last, the traveller will meet bad weather, and so on. If the number occurs in the third line, death carries off the patient, the runaway will never be recaptured, and so on.[32]

A more detailed Table, called *The table of Aristoboulos* sets out a series of 36 questions which are linked with the names of dekans and numbers (in the last column) on an unknown system. We may assume that the questions represent the sort of things that most worried people in these times[33]:

If someone will enjoy a just-begun love-affair	1	1 Bendonc	1
If lovers truly love or pretend to love	2	2 Mensour	5
If someone should get married this year	3	3 Carexon	9
If someone in marriage will gain what he seeks	4	4 Gizan	2
Which one, husband or wife, will survive the other	5	5 Tourtour	6
Who of a married couple loves more faithfully	6	6 Ballat	10
If a pregnant woman will bear a boy or girl	7	7 Farsan	3
If a divorced wife is pregnant or not	8	8 Vaspan	7
If a girl is virgin or not	9	9 Paquia	11
If he is jealous or not	10	10 Panem	4

If a young man will be prudent or foolish	11 11	Catarno	8
If a young man will be rich or poor	12 12	Hellors	12
If someone will profit in a business transaction	13 13	Jarea	13
If someone will carry out his plan	14 14	Efraa	18
If a dream bodes good or ill	15 15	Hayas	23
If stolen property will be recovered or not	16 16	Angaf	26
If a change of domicile will help	17 17	Betaphen	14
If it's good to continue the voyage	18 18	Baroche	19
If someone will return from abroad or not	19 19	Zercuris	24
If a messenger will fulfil his mission	20 20	Baham	29
If someone will make a good end or not	21 21	Pieret	15
If someone will live long or not	22 22	Haziza	20
In what field someone will do best	23 23	Nacy	25
If a tie is faithfully kept or not	24 24	Alleinac	30
If someone will have faithful friends	25 25	Ortusa	16
If someone has made anyone pregnant	26 26	Daha	21
If he has big gains from his property Which of the boxers will win	27 27	Satan	26
If a patient will recover or not	28 28	Eracto (Ero)	31
If a prisoner will be freed or not	29 29	Salac	17
If someone will be able to pay debts or not	30 30	Seros	22
If someone will get back his debts	31 31	Tonghel	27
If someone will win his lawsuit in court	32 32	Anafa	32
If a priest will be moved or not	33 33	Simos	33
If a priest *stolis perficiet* or not	34 34	Achaf	35
If a planned journey will profit or not	35 35	Larvata	34
If rumours someone heard are true or not	36 36	Ajaras	36

The system of assigning a part of the body to a god or to a dekan was worked out in detail: *melothesis* is the technical term.[34] But however many irrationalities were involved, we must at least realise that the astrologers were not making a mechanistic connection between a dekan or a star and a limb of the body. Especially in the notion of a vital influence of sun and moon on our bodies, they were carrying on the Stoic doctrine of universal sympathy, of a continuum of tensional fields dynamically interacting and affecting all bodies on which they impacted—the bodies themselves being composed of energies, of *pneuma*, which made them akin to the rest of the universe including the stars. The system also inherited the Pythagorean sense of endlessly entwining harmonies reducible to proportions and patterns and so to numbers which were seen as the constituent parts of bodies and as defining their relationships. To think merely of stars exerting some unexplained magical influence is to fail to get inside the astrologic systems and to vulgarise or trivialise them out of all resemblance to the complex doctrine which agitated at least the creators and the main handers-on of the tradition. Above all these men were thinking of bodies not as isolated mechanistic systems, but as bundles of energies, held together by what the Stoics called the *hegemonikon* and continually reshaped by a formative principle shared by the whole cosmos. The schemes of correspondences must be interpreted in terms of this world-outlook, however many arbitrary elements they contained.

According to the *Liber Hermetis* the third dekan of the Twins produced muscular pains; the first of the Crab, heart-troubles; the first of the Lion controlled the stomach; the second caused stoppages and boils; the first of the Virgin reigned over the stomach; the second over the liver, the third over the spleen; the first of the Balance, the kidneys; the second brought about stoppage of the urethra and retention of urine, and so on. The system had been worked out by taking a plan of the zodiacal band and setting on it another of the body. Head went over the Ram, feet on to the Fish, neck on the Bull, shoulders and arms on the Twins, chest on the Crab, flanks on the Lion, lower stomach and bladder on the Virgin, buttocks on the Balance, genitals on the Scorpion, thighs on the Archer, knees on Capricorn, legs on Aquarius.[35] The dekanic system was more detailed but based on the same sort of superimpositions, though in some matters the dekans seemed to control or affect general aspects of the body, *e.g.* muscles, fractures, abscesses. This latter kind of application may represent a carry-over from earlier Egyptian ideas before the precise astral patterns were applied. Planetary systems of *sympatheia* with parts of the body were not tied down to a geometrical lay-out such as the Zodiac and therefore could be applied more freely.[36]

The principles were thus stated in hermetic works:

Man, my dear Ammon, is called by the informed a World since he is wholly correspondent with the World's Nature. Indeed at the moment of conception there spurts from the seven planets a whole complex of rays that bear on each part of the man. And the same thing happens at the birth-hour, according to the position of the twelve signs. Thus the Ram is called the Head, and the head's sense-organs are shared out among the seven planets. The right eye goes to the Sun, the left to the Moon, the ears to Saturn, the brain to Jupiter, the tongue and uvula to Mercury, smelling and taste to Venus, all the blood-vessels to Mars.

If then at the moment of conception or birth one of the stars finds itself in a bad condition, there is produced an infirmity in the member corresponding with that star. For instance, a man has four main parts: head, thorax, hands, feet. One of these has become infirm at the conception-moment or at birth somewhere by its heavenly patron having been itself in a bad way; an eye, the two eyes, an ear, the two ears, or again the teeth have undergone some damage or speech has been blurred; the ray of a malevolent planet has come to strike one of those parts, spoil, and corrupt it.[37]

Hermes goes on to claim priority in the science he sets out. "And I have wanted it to be called the Servant of Nature; it is necessary for this science to conspire with nature, and thus one comes to the aid of nature herself." He could not put more clearly the basis in Stoic attitudes, which are shared by the alchemists. The quester seeks to enter into the formative principle of nature, learn how it works, then use it to overcome distortions or cankerings in the flow of energy. Later he says, "We must find out the day and hour when the sick man went to bed, and take a total view of the world-pattern at that hour. For nothing happens in a man that is not connected with cosmic sympathy."[38]

The inquiry thus leads on to therapeutic issues. Is the damage or distortion to be overcome by fighting it, by confronting it with its opposite, or is it to be cured by sympathetic methods, by drawing it more effectively into harmony with the flow of things? Both methods had a place in ancient Egyptian medicine. There was a deep-rooted belief that disease was spread through the vessels and eliminated in the excreta—by defaecation, urination, vomiting, sweat, wind, tumours, or nasal mucus. As a result, an important section of medical thinkers had held that *whdw* (a substance circulating in the body) resulted from the putrefaction of alimentary residues; it could circulate or cause a local illness.[39] (There may well have been in these ideas a rough form of what became with the Greeks the theory of Humours.) On the other hand there was a general idea of the need to restore a lost balance rather than to drive out toxins, and here the principle of *sympatheia* or like-by-like was used: a woman who suffered from the vulva when walking was told:

You say: What is the smell that she emits? If she says to you: I emit the smell of burnt meat—you say: It is the *nemsu* of the vagina. You do thus for it. You fumigate her with burnt meat, the smell of which she emits.[40]

The doctrine of expulsion seems upheld by Nechepso. At least

H

he drew on the triadic formula according to Maternus. "The famous Nechepso, that perfectly just king of Egypt and excellent astrologer, has related to the dekans all the infirmities, all the maladies, showing which dekan is the cause of which malady; and since a nature is conquered by another nature, and a god often triumphs over another god, from this opposition of natures and heavenly powers he has drawn the remedy of all evils, instructed as he was by divine reason." We may perhaps infer that he considered the set-back to be the result of an intrusive malevolence which had to be corrected by strengthening the force of the favourable planet or dekan.[41] Hermes however concentrated on the aspects of *sympatheia*. He too held that the damaging star was not the direct cause of the trouble, but had itself been attacked by the ray-force of a malign planet, so that it had no choice but to remit the weakening effect. The problem then was to find the creatures, planets, or stones sympathetically linked with the planet in question; by using these the medical astrologer could strengthen the favourable planet's influence and expel the malign influences. There was therefore no great difference between Hermes' doctrine and that of Nechepso; one stressed the building-up of the salutary forces, the other their effect in expelling the malign ones. Proklos in *On the Hieratic Art* sets out powerfully the doctrine of inter-related energies and vital correspondences. Here are a few of his words:

Just as the dialecticians of Love rise up from sensible beauties till they meet the unique principle itself of all Beauty and all Intelligibility, so the initiators into the holy mysteries start from the sympathy that unites all visible things to one another and to the invisible powers, and, understanding that everything is in everything, they have founded this hieratic science—not without wonder at finding in the first links of the chain the lowest of all and in these last the first one as well: in heaven, earthly things in their cause and under a heavenly mode, and here below, heavenly things under a mode proper to the earth.

Hence indeed it is that heliotrope moves in harmony with the sun, selenotrope with the moon, each one joining in the movement, in the measure of its forces, of the world's luminaries. For all beings pray according to the rank they occupy, they chant the chiefs who preside over their whole series, each praising in its own way, spiritual, rational, physical, or sensible. So heliotrope moves as much as it is feasible for it to move; and if we could hear how it strikes the air while turning on its stalk, we would note down this noise as the offering of an hymn to the King, as much as a plant can sing.

We can then see here below, in an earthly mode, suns and moons. In the heavens we can see, in a heavenly mode, all the plants, stones, beasts, living a spiritual life.[42]

We must recall that the stoic *pneuma* or *pneumatikos* did not refer to spirit as something cut off from body, but took it to be an aspect of the unitary stream to which body also belonged. Proklos goes on to mention more flowers and stones as well which owned affinities with sun or moon. "Everything then is filled with gods, the earth is filled with heavenly gods, the heaven with supracelestial gods. Each series proceeds, growing in number, up to its limits." Some plants or trees show the form of light-rays, like palms, or have an igneous essence like laurel (serving to light a fire), and so on. Other plants bring about a theophany, a cure, a purification. "By means of sympathy they attract certain divine powers and repel others by means of antipathy." Men can attract daimons and then rise "to operate on the gods, instructed by the gods themselves". Thus we end with a claim to theurgic powers.

Plinius knew of many works on the magic of plants, by Pythagoras, by Demokritos, by mages like Zoroaster and Ostanes; there was a work by pseudo-Aristotle (perhaps by Nikolas of Damas); others were attributed to Alexander the Great, Hermes, Henoch, Solomon, the doctor Thessalos, Harpokration, Alexius (or Flaccus Africanus, disciple of Belenos or Apollonios of Tyana). The *Sacred Book of Hermes* addressed to Asklepios sets out the dekanic plants in a set of medical recipes.[43] The practitioner is to find the stone and plant in sympathy with the dekan in question, engrave the dekan's image on the stone, place a piece of the plant under the stone, put the result in a ring, and wear the ring while abstaining from food antipathetic to the dekan. Often a name is taken to provide the clue of sympathy. Thus the first dekan of the Lion, which has a lion's head surrounded by sunrays, had for plant *leontopedon*, lion's-foot; the second, which had a crescent on its head, had moonstone for its stone. The Ram is defined as "the Head of the World; the Bull, the Neck", and so on. The dekans were originally accompanied with designs now lost, but we are told the name of each, its description, its effects, and the associated recipe. Thus:

Ram. Ist Dekan: its name is *Chenlachori* and it has the form here shown. Its face is that of a small child, its hands are raised on high, it holds a sceptre which it lifts above its head. It is swaddled from feet to knees. It dominated head-affections. Grave it on a porous stone of Babylon; set the plant *isophryn* below. Fix in a ring of iron and wear. Beware of eating boar's head. Thus you will gain the benevolence of each dekan by engraving it on its stone with its name.[44]

There are also two accounts of zodiacal plants, one short, one longer. The first, attributed to Hermes Trismegistos, gives, for example, *helelisphakon*, sage, as the plant of the Ram. All plants, it says, are to be gathered and have their juices extracted when the Sun is in the Ram. The longer version adds, "It is manifest that the Sun is the King of all the Stars. Well, the Sun has its exaltation in the Ram and in the sign it receives an incredible power. That is the moment when plants have the most virtue, not only because of the Sun but also because the Ram is the cause sharing in the influence that the gods [stars] exercise on the earth." It states that the juice must not be cooked. The short version tells us, "But it is also necessary for the Sun to be in the sign of the plant to be gathered and the Moon in the Sun's trigon or its horoscope. Let this be on the day and hour of the *oikosdespotes* of the sign"—the planet domiciled in the sign, the house-lord. "Do this to succeed, as the teacher [Hermes Trismegistos] says, according to the physical and cosmic influence."[45]

The longer version comes from the text of Thessalos (Harpokration) straight after the prologue. Again it is called the work of Hermes. The plant-series is the same as in the short version, except for Aquarius; and it adds more details:

Ram: first Sign. On Sage. Gather to start from 22 Phamenoth, i.e. Dystros [second Macedonian month, corresponding to March]: in Roman style, from fifteen days before the Kalends of April [18 March]. First plant: Sage. It has great virtues against flux of blood and for consumptives, for those liable to fall into syncope, for hypochondriacs, and for affections of the womb.[46]

Then come prescriptions for each of the maladies, with some further advice as to the use of the root against nephritis and sciatica, and with recipes for cataplasm. In another text attributed to Solomon the plants are very different; e.g., for the Ram we get *myriphyllon* (thousand-leaved), not sage. The recipes are very precise, with indications of measures and methods of use, in the Thessalos-text; but here all is much vaguer, concerned with magic rather than therapeuty; amulets and charms are important; and the language is later.

There are also three sets of texts on planetary plants, with differences in the attributions (Hermes or Solomon) and in the lists of plants. The magical element increases. The plant of the Soul is the Prolific, *polygonon*.

This plant gained its name from a certain likeness with the Sun. In effect the Sun is the author and sower of all beings, while this plant makes one apt to engender. Some call it chameleon since it has received as its Lot parts of the sun and the earth [*chamaileon : leon,* house of the sun, and *chamai,* on the ground]. Drunk as a potion, its juice stimulates the act of generation and the pleasures of love. Worn as an amulet with a prayer to God, who has given to both sun and plant such a virtue. It drives out all ophthalmia; he who wears it will never be stricken, for the sun has received as his share domination over eyes. [It dominates also the heart.] That is why the sun is retrograde at the start of the illness, the plant restores frenetics and lethargics, since these maladies come from the heart. As amulet, it cures as marvellously those with weak sight, and in plaster-form those beginning to be stricken with . . .[47]

One text bids the gatherer to pray as he plucks—to pray for the plant to give him aid. Then after uprooting the plant, he is to throw down in compensation a bit of wheat or barley. The peony makes a love-philtre: a small root got on the day and hour of Venus. The seed, enclosed in a piece of genuine silk, is to be carried by a woman near her genitals; it will make her "preserve the seed", but it can also be used to prevent conception.[48]

These passages will give some idea of the fullness with which astrology was linked with the magical lore of plant and stone in a new kind of medicine. There is every indication that the Egyptians played a large part in this development; their medical science had anciently been superior to that of Mesopotamia and had contributed much to early Greek medicine. It was natural that they should seek to link their curative systems with astrologic prognostics. Ptolemaios states that this was so:

. . . those who have most advanced this faculty of the art, the Egyptians, have in every way united medicine with astronomical prediction. For they would never have devised certain means of averting or warding off or remedying the universal and particular conditions that come or are present by reason of the ambient, if they had had any idea that the future cannot be moved and changed.

But, as it is, they place the faculty of resisting by orderly natural means in second rank to the decrees of Fate, and have yoked to the possibility of prognostication its useful and beneficial faculty through what they call their Iatromathematical Systems so that by means of Astronomy they may succeed in learning the qualities of the underlying temperatures, the events that will occur in the future because of the ambient, and their special causes, on the ground that without this knowledge any measure of aid ought for the most part to fail, because the same ones are not fitted for all bodies or diseases. And on the other hand, by means of medicine, though their knowledge of what is properly sympathetic or antipathetic in each case, they proceed, as far as possible, to take precautionary steps against oncoming illness and to prescribe infallible treatment for disease already existing.

We may then sum up what we know of astrology in Egypt by saying that the main impetus came from the Babylonians and was developed by Greek mathematical astronomers, but that the Egyptians made certain contributions, especially in the matter of time-divisions and on the iatromathematical side. Clearly there was a welter of influences in the third century B.C.; and since Alexandreia was the great cultural centre of the Hellenistic age, much of the development must have gone on there. Geminos in the last century B.C. hands over to the Chaldeans the theory of aspects in what concerns planets and the Zodiac; but that theory was a fundamental dogma of Graeco-Egyptian astrology and we have no evidence that the Babylonians knew of it till the spread of hermetic texts.[49] We cannot indeed trust any of the generalisations that now come up, without some objective evidence to test it. Thus, Cicero refers to Chaldean Science (perhaps on the basis of Poseidonios), but he deals with ideas (*monomoiriai*, aspects) that are not properly Chaldean but derive from the hermetic tradition.[50]

12

The Romans

If it is true that the Latin *considerare* embodies the word *sidus*, star, the notion of contemplation as star-gazing was common among the Romans by the mid-third century.[1] The Prologue of Plautus' *Rudens* is spoken by a Star, Arcturus (Bear's Tail), who acts as a spy for the gods:

> With him who sways all peoples, seas, and lands,
> I'm a fellow citizen in the realms of gods.
> I'm a bright and glittering Star, as you can see,
> a Constellation rising in its season
> here and in heaven. Arcturus is my name.
> By night I shine in heaven among the gods,
> I pass among mortals by day. Other such stars
> also descend from heaven to earth. For Jove,
> Ruler of Gods and Men, scatters us round
> in all directions among the peoples to watch
> their actions, manners, piety, faith, and all . . .
> The seawaves I aroused. Most violent
> constellation of all am I. I'm turbulent
> rising, and setting, I'm more turbulent still.

Arcturus rose in October: Plinius says on the 12th, Columella on the 5th. Probably Plautus drew on some folk-belief. Astrology was certainly getting known. Ennius (239–169 B.C.) is the first Latin writer known to speak of astrologers:

> They note the astrologic signs of heaven
> whenever the Goats or Scorpions of great Jove
> or other monstrous names of brutish forms
> rise in the Zodiac. But not one regards
> the sensible facts of earth on which we tread
> while gazing on the starry prodigies.[2]

Cato, who died in 149 B.C., warned the farm-overseer not to

consult Chaldeans; and if astrologers were circulating in the Italian countryside by this time, we can guess how much earlier they must have been at work in Syria, Asia Minor, Greece, Egypt. Itinerant prophets and quacks of all kinds were turning up at the fairs. Ennius again fills in the picture:

> Of little service are the Marsian prophet,
> the village-diviner, the astrologer
> of the crowded Circus, or the priest of Isis,
> or the charlatan interpreter of dreams.
> All these are lying conjurers with no skill
> to read the future: a pack of hypocrites
> urged on by hunger. Ignorant of themselves,
> they'd teach others, to whom they promise great fortunes,
> begging a penny in pay, paid in advance.[3]

The Marsians and the *haruspices* were traditional, but the astrologers, Isiacs, and dream-readers were aliens. In 139 B.C. astrologers were expelled from Rome.[4] Accius, a poet with a long life (born 170 B.C.), wrote of the Zodiac:

> Drive through the sky, through the glittering
> constellations that the universe holds painted
> with its twice six continuous signs.

When Marcellus took Syracuse, he had enough scientific interest to select as his share of the loot only the model of the spheres in Archimedes' house, Archimedes having been killed in the capture of the city. This model, with an even better one later exhibited, was brought to Rome; and G. Sulpicius Gallus used it to demonstrate to Marcellus' grandson the causes of eclipses.[5] The increasing influence of the Stoics at Rome must have helped the interest in astrology there. Most leading Stoics defended the discipline, though the attitudes varied. Chrysippos of Soloi had introduced a slightly sceptical note, but Poseidonios preached a return to sheer fatalism.[6] The problem of eclipses had been coming up as a serious matter. L. Aemilius Paulus defeated Perseus of Macedon at Pynda. On the battle-eve, 21 June 168, a lunar eclipse set his soldiers clashing bronze utensils and brandishing torches; the Macedonians too were scared, thinking their king's death portended. Paulus knew the theory of eclipses; but after the moon reappeared, he sacrificed eleven heifers to her. Gallus, says Cicero, tried to tell the legionaries next morning what an eclipse really was. In Cicero's dialogue, Tubero, Paulus' grandson, asks,

"Do you mean that he dared to talk like that to men almost totally illiterate and ignorant?" Scipio replies that "he performed a very noble action in thus freeing his countrymen from the terrors of an idle superstition".[7]

Among the spreaders of astrology were men brought in as captives and slaves from the East. Plinius says that Antiochos, who introduced astrology to Italy, was such a slave.[8] Astrologers seem to have played a part in stirring unrest. The 139 expulsion may have been connected with the attacks by the Senate (the aristocratic landlords) on the reform bill of the previous year. The fact that devotees of Zeus Sabazios were also expelled does not disprove this point; Eastern cults might well have been also considered politically unsettling with their grip on the slaves and commoners.[9] Athenio who for a while led the slave armies in the second slave-rebellion in Sicily was, says Diodoros, "an expert astrologer", who "insisted that the gods through the stars had revealed to him that he'd become king of Sicily". He was killed in 101–100 B.C. The leader Eunus was also a diviner. At this phase, astrology, like Stoicism itself, was raising up hopes of a world of brotherly equality. There were astral elements in the Utopia of Iamboulos, *The City of the Sun,* which played its part in the attempt to set up an egalitarian City of the Sun at Pergamon, which the Romans promptly wrecked.[10]

We must not forget the existence of a strong tradition of entrails-divination in Etruria, which had long affected the Romans and which was often closely linked with senatorial reaction. Tubero, affected by the Stoics (especially Panaitios), seems to have compiled the first relatively sophisticated weather-calendar, which related the phenomena to planets, fixed-stars and constellations.[11] Poseidonios had helped to stimulate such interests. Centred on Rhodes, he travelled much and was an envoy to Rome at a time of violent upheaval. Marius and Cinna took Rome, and the consul Octavius was killed; on his dead body was found the astrologic diagram that had lured him to his death.[12] The great men grew more and more taken up with horoscopes. Sulla brought one back from the East. It included his deathdate, which Ploutarch says he accepted, so that as it neared he concluded his *Memoirs.* But the tale that he died on the specified day is one of the bits of propaganda-gossip that we shall keep meeting. Later, astrologers provided all the great men with horoscopes.[13] "How many of these Chaldean prophecies," says Cicero, "do I recall being repeated to

Pompeius, Crassus, and Caesar himself, according to which each one of those heroes was to die only in ripe old age, in domestic felicity, in perfect renown."

About this time we meet full-blown Roman astrologers. The most important was P. Nigidius Figulus, who took over the complete Hellenistic system. Like Poseidonios, he was interested in astrologic climatology; and he wrote on the *Timaios* a work *About the Universe*, and a *Physikos Logikos*. A story alleged that he got his name Figulus (Potter) after having argued, on his return from Greece, that the earth span round as fast as a potter's wheel. An extreme conservative, he was a friend of Cicero, despite the latter's scepticism. (Cicero, Lucretius, and Caesar were among the few who refused to go with the astrologic trend.) A dubious tale was told about Nigidius having prophesied Octavius' future at his birth; but its inventors failed to get their dates right. Suetonius reports:

The Senate was engaged in a debate on Catilina's Conspiracy, and Octavius [the father] came late to the House on account of his wife being in childbed. It's a well-known fact that P. Nigidius, on hearing of his late arrival and the hour of the wife's delivery, declared that the world had got its master.

However, the dates of the birth and the Senate-meeting in September 63 do not tally.

It was true however that Nigidius took a prominent part in the Senate at the time of the Conspiracy, being in charge of the Minutes when the charges were made against Catilina. A strong member of the senatorial faction, he was praetor in 58, but never became consul. Cicero on his way to Cilicia as governor met him at Ephesos on some ambassadorial job; in the Civil War he was Pompeian and Caesar exiled him. He appealed to Cicero, his last known letter being dated August or September 46. Caesar would certainly have let him return, but he died soon after.[14] Cicero paid him a tribute:

Much has been written against the *physici* in our Academics and much has often been discussed with P. Nigidius. For that man was at the same time graced with all the other arts that suit a free man as well as being an eager and diligent investigator of those matters which seem by nature cryptic. In all I hold that after those lofty Pythagoreans, whose sect somehow became extinct after flourishing for several centuries in Italy and Sicily, he arose to revive it.[15]

Nigidius was thus an astrologic and mystical neo-Pythagorean, interested in magic in all its forms. The Eusebian Chronicle calls him *Pythagoricus et Magus*. Cicero in his oration against Vatinius accuses that radical of spirit-raising and boy-murder; a scholiast links the charge with Nigidius. "Very many men sought him out. His group was criticised by detractors as an objectionable faction, though they themselves wanted to be looked on as Pythagoreans." A pseudo-Ciceronian text attacked Sallust for having twice tried to join "the Fraternity of Nigidian Sacrilege". No doubt Nigidius used boy-mediums; we find them often mentioned in spells. Simon Magus was accused of murdering one; and the Christians, after being accused of the ritual murder of children, later accused the Jews of the same crime. The writer Apuleius, himself accused of magical practices which included the use of boys, told a story: "Fabius, who had lost 500 denars, came to Nigidius, to consult him. Then certain boys, inspired by him through charms, pointed out the place where the purse had been buried, together with some of the money, and how the rest had been distributed, and how even M. Cato the philosopher had one of the pieces in his possession. M. Cato then admitted he had received that very coin at the hands of one of his attendants for the contributions to Apollo." (Upper-class Romans felt it unseemly to carry money in the streets; they had footmen, *pedissequi*, to bear their purses.[16])

Aulus Gellius deals with Nigidius' linguistic analyses, and comments on his "obscurity and subtlety", which "have caused his works to be neglected as of no practical value". Other Nigidian writings included *On the Gods,* which set out the Magian doctrine of world-eras and of world-end by fire, no doubt using Stoic sources such as Poseidonios, and which may well lie behind much of Virgil's Fourth Eclogue; *On Divination,* which had at least two books on private augurium; *About Entrail-Divination*; a treatise or a pair of them on *Thunder Omens*; *On Countries,* probably setting out astrologic geography; *On Animals*; and two works on the Heavenly Sphere, one on Barbarian terminology, one on Greek. Nigidius was certainly much influenced by Etruscan tradition for, as we learn from John Lydos, he knew of Tages.[17] Despite his opposition to popular leaders like Julius Caesar, he willy-nilly helped the spread of the idea of astral immortality as the reward of the saviour-hero. In *De Signis* he set out the thesis that the appearance of constellations was linked with the disappearance of heroes.[18] For him as for Poseidonios or Cicero in his Pythagorean mood the

soul at death rejoined the concentric circles where the divine
Aither moved, at first that of the Moon (Hekate, Persephone),
then that of the Sun, who drew up the *pneumata* of the chosen,
on up to the Milky Way and then to the supreme circle enclosing
all the others. In *Scipio's Dream*, Cicero tells how that hero looked
down from the Milky Way:

From there, as I took a view of the Universe, everything appeared
beautiful and admirable. Those stars never visible from our globe are to
be seen, all things seem of such magnitude as we could not have
imagined. The least of all the stars was that furthest removed from
heaven and placed next to the earth: I mean our Moon, which shines
with a borrowed light. Now the globes of the stars far surpass the
magnitude of our earth, which at that distance looked so extremely
small that I couldn't but be sensibly affected at seeing our whole Empire
no larger than if we touched the earth, as it were, at a single point.[19]

Lucan introduces Nigidius as an astrologer at the outbreak of the
Civil War. After the flight of Pompeius and the Senate, there are a
number of portents which scare the citizens. It is resolved to follow
the ancient custom of calling in Etruscan prophets. The oldest of
these was Arruns,

> who dwelt in Luca's deserted walls, well-skilled
> to read the thunderbolt's course, the entrail-marks
> yet warm, the warning of each wandering wing.

He orders the destruction of all monstrous births, a procession
round the City, a lustration of the walls. He buries "the thunderbolt's scattered fires", sanctifies the spot where the bolt fell, and
sacrifices a bull, which inauspiciously struggles. From the cut
comes, not blood, but a slimy liquid. Arruns is alarmed at the
colour and malign marks of the patchy entrails with their blood-
spots; the liver is flabby "with boding streaks in its hostile heart".
The lungs and heart too are threatening. A second lobe is growing
on the liver-lobe: Caesar growing great at the expense of the State.
Then comes the turn of Figulus, "he whose study was to know the
gods and the secrets of the sky, he who was not matched even by
Egyptian Memphis in observations of the sky and calculations
keeping pace with the stars". He makes a dark speech, with
premonitions of all sorts of disaster. He sees "the madness of war"
in the disordered constellations, the flight of which represents
Caesar's "illegality". But he couches his speech mostly in terms of
"ifs". If baleful Saturn were now kindling his black fires in the

zenith, then Aquarius would drown the earth with a flood. If the Sun's rays were passing over the Lion, fire would destroy the world. "These heavenly bodies are not active now." But what dread purpose has Mars in kindling the menacing Scorpion? Benign Jupiter is hidden in the West, healthful Venus is dim, Mercury's swift motion is halted, Mars alone holds the heaven while sword-girt Orion "shines all too bright". A woman then prophesies in an exalted state.[20]

Even Kepler was beaten by this passage; and it has been shown (by Housman) that the planets were not at all in the parts of the sky mentioned, except Mercury.[21] But most likely Lucan is not ignorantly fabricating his account; he is much more likely to be citing an actual speech or text of Nigidius, a *katarchē* of the opening Civil War, which aims at denouncing Caesar for demoralising both heaven and earth. The scheme can be reconstructed, with the Scorpion in the ascendant (or first place), the Archer in the second, Capricorn in the third, and so on. The key lies in the continued visibility of Orion; for the image of the Scorpion rising to chase off the setting giant who had tried to molest Artemis was familiar in the stories of katasterisms. (An attempt has been made to identify constellations and the earthly actors: Scorpion as Caesar, Orian as Pompeius—not to forget Jupiter as Crassus, Venus as Julia, and Mercury as Cicero. But it is hardly convincing.[22]) Mars was in the risen part of the Scorpion, the only visible planet; so Mercury and Venus would be in the Archer, the second place or *templum*, with Jupiter in the Ram, the sixth. The trigon of Ram, Lion, Archer had a further significance: it was identified (as in Ptolemaios' *Tetrabiblos*) with the first of the four quarters of the *oikoumene*, that towards Keltic Galatia. Caesar, we must recall, was coming in from the Gauls.[23]

Disaster, however, seems held up, at least for a while, by the inactivity of the other planets. Saturn is seen apparently as the planet of the Sun (as in the *Epinomis*). But it was also the Sun of the Night; and the suggestion has been made that the reference is to the Etruscan doctrine of 16 sky-regions. We must not however forget the Egyptian schemes of the night-sun. Nigidius puts Saturn in the night-house of Aquarius at IMC, with the Lion, the Sun's house, opposite at MC. But could Aquarius and IMC in the middle of the infernal half-circle of the *dodekatropos* (the zodiacal twelve divisions) be imagined as *summo caelo* (on the topmost part of the sky), while the Lion and MC might surely be so described in the

centre of the upper half ? Yes.[24] Sextus Empiricus, dealing with the
kentra or cardinal points, says of IMC that it was also MC.
Clearly then the unseen pole is in the upper half, and people
living thereabouts are in the upper hemisphere and on the right,
while we are in the lower hemisphere and on the left. The Pythagoreans, however, said the opposite to all that; while they set us
above and in the region on the right, they put the others below
and in that on the left. These difficult questions of orientation have

Fig. 54. Mosaic of Seasons, Palermo, with Bellerophon on Pegasos,
etc.

been much discussed since Proklos. In passing we may note
Plato's doctrine (probably from the Pythagoreans) that, when souls
are judged, the righteous are sent to the right and up through the
heavens, the unrighteous to the left and down.[25]

Nigidius was by no means alone. Kastor of Rhodes, historian of
the late Republic, tried to interpret Roman customs by his sort of
Pythagoreanism. Thus he explained the ivory lunules or crescents
which decorated the senators' shoes as expressing the fact that
noble souls after death inhabited the Moon and trod on its soil.[26]
Aulus Caecina was the son of a man of Volterra whom Cicero
defended in court. He published a libel on Caesar and was
exiled; he then composed his *Querelae* in an effort to gain a pardon
and sent it to Cicero for revision. After the Pompeian defeat in
Africa, he surrendered to Caesar, who spared him. He was an
expert on the Etruscan discipline and Plinius in Book II used his
work. Seneca also cited him:

Caecina distinguishes three kinds of lightnings: those of counsel, of assertion, and what is called *status* (state or condition, circumstance). The first comes before the event but after the project. Thus, a man forms a resolution, a thunderclap confirms him in it and dissuades him. The second follows the event and indicates if it will be propitious or unfortunate. The third occurs to a man at peace, who does not do or even think anything about the matter: it brings threats, promises, or counsels.

There are also bolts that pierce, that overthrow, and that burn. The first is a subtle flame; the second is globular, enclosing dense and stormy *spiritus*; the third contains earthy matter. Bolts also discolour (change the colour-effect to some extent) or colour (totally change the colour: to blue, black, or pale white, *pallida*). "So far the Etruscans and philosophers agree." But, while the latter credit natural causes, the former maintain that Jupiter throws the bolt with his hand.[27]

There was also G. Fonteius Capito, another Roman astrologer, who in the Civil Wars finally threw in his lot with M. Antonius and Kleopatra. The passage from his works cited by John Lydos reads very much like the predictions we have already seen in Egyptian texts:

The Moon in Capricorn. If it thunders in daytime, a Tyrant will arise in lands from the Narrow Sea to the Nile, but will fail in his enterprise. There will be scarcity, especially in provisions. The Nile will subside, children will be at odds with their parents. . . .[28]

He was probably writing in the years just before the Battle of Actium.

The most outstanding scholar of these late Republican days was Varro. What survives of his work by the chances of time does not allow a proper estimate of his achievement. Servius remarks, "Nigidius is, apart from Varro, unique; while Varro excels in theology, Nigidius is an eminent universalist." By his time, Varro's *Human and Divine Antiquities* had made his other works fade out, together with such books as Nigidius' *On the Gods*. He seems at first sceptical. "Are not astrologers those men who scribble away with pictures of the heavens?" Then he was won over and wanted to be buried with Pythagorean ritual.[29] But he was never a horoscopic expert like Nigidius. When he wanted the nativities of Romulus and of Rome, he asked L. Tarrutius Firmanus to do the computation.

I grant indeed that L. Tarrutius of Firma, my own personal friend and a man especially well acquainted with Chaldean astrology, traced back the nativity of our own city, Roma, to those equinoctial days of the Feast of Pales in which Romulus is said to have begun its foundation, and asserted that the Moon was at that period in the Balance, and on this discovery he did not hesitate to pronounce the destinies of Rome.[30]

Ploutarch also records the astrologic tradition of Rome's foundation. Tarrutius decided that Romulus was conceived in the first year of the second Olympiad (772–771 B.C.) in the month Choiak of the Egyptian calendar, on the 23rd day, at the third hour, during a solar eclipse; and was born 21 Thoth at sunrise. Rome was founded 9 Pharmouthi, between the second and third hour. Ploutarch remained a bit dubious. "These and like speculations will perhaps attract readers by their novelty and extravagance rather than offend them by their fabulous character." The use of Egyptian months, like the idiom of Caecina's predictions, suggests that the influence of Egyptian astrology was dominant at Rome. Tarrutius' *cognomen* Firmanus seems to make him a native of Firmum in Picenum; but the name Tarrutius itself is Etruscan.[31]

Only 39 titles of works by Varro are given by Jerome, whose catalogue is however incomplete and also puts ten *libri singulares* under one head. It has been calculated that the full list would be 74 works in 620 books. Many were destroyed when Varro's library was plundered during the proscriptions of 42 B.C.—though Varro himself was saved by Fufius Calenus and lived till nearly ninety (27 B.C.). In his *Antiquities* six of the forty-one Books were devoted to units of time; three of these were on Days, Months, Years, and were much used by later writers, Dionysios of Halikarnassos, Suetonius, Gellius, Festus, Censorinus, Macrobius.[32] In his *Hebdomades* he celebrated the number Seven. "M. Varro in Book I of his *Hebdomades* or in his *On Portraits* speaks of the many and varied virtues of the number Seven, *Hebdomas* in Greek." *On Portraits* consisted of 700 accounts of famous men, arranged in seven categories of Greeks and Romans—with a 15th Book as Introduction.

"For that number (7)," he says, "forms the Greater and the Lesser Bear in the heavens; also the *Vergiliai* (from *ver*, spring, since their rising, 22 April to 10 May, marked the beginning of spring), which the Greeks call the Pleiades; and it is likewise the number of those stars [planets] which some call *erraticae*, but P. Nigidius *errones*." Varro also says there are 7 circles in the heavens, perpendicular to the axis. The two smallest of these, which touch the ends of the axis, he says are called *poloi* or poles; but that because of their small diameter they cannot be represented on what is termed an armillary sphere.[33]

We see then that the two small spheres on the end of the long staff (pole) held by Zeus and Osiris-Sarapis, which we discussed, represented these two small poles. Gellius goes on, summarising Varro:

And the Zodiac itself is not uninfluenced by 7; for the summer solstice occurs in the 7th Sign from the winter solstice, and the winter solstice in the 7th after the summer, and one equinox in the 7th Sign after the other. Then too those winter days during which the kingfishers [*alcyones*] nest on the water he says are 7 in number. Besides this he writes that the course of the Moon is completed in 4 times 7 completed days; "for on the 28th day," he says, "the Moon returns to the same point from which it started", citing Aristeides of Samos as his authority [error for Aristarchos]. He adds that one should not only note that the

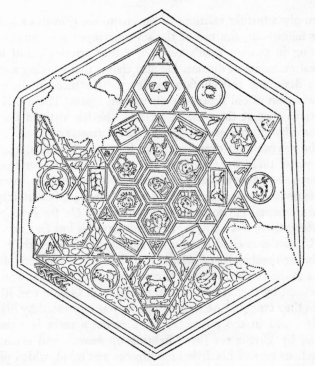

Fig. 55. Mosaic of Weekdays and Zodiac, Bir Chana, N. Africa

moon finishes its journey in $4 \times 7 = 28$ days, but also that 7, if starting with 1 and going on till it reaches itself, includes the sums of all the numbers through which it has passed and then adds itself making the number 28, the number of days of the revolution of the moon $[1+2+3+4+5+6+7=28]$. He says that the number's influence extends to, and also affects, the birth of human beings.

"For," says he, "when the lifegiving seed is given into the woman's womb, in the first 7 days it is compacted and coagulated and made fit to take shape. Then in the fourth *hebdomad* the rudimentary male organ, the head, and the spine which is in the back, are formed. But in the seventh as a rule, that is by the 49th day," says he, "the entire embryo is formed in the womb." He adds that the power has been noted in the number that before the 7th month neither male nor female child can be born in health and naturally, and that the regular time to be in the womb is 273 days after conception: i.e. not until the start of the 40th *hebdomad*.

Of the periods dangerous to the lives and fortunes of all men, which the Chaldeans call Climacterics, all the gravest are combinations of the number 7; and in addition the limit of growth of the human body is 7 feet.

Varro gives further relations of Seven: to the growth of teeth, or their falling-out, the use of the seven-stringed lyre curatively in "setting in motion men's veins or rather arteries", and in the critical moments of disease. He also claims that starving men last out 7 days, and collects famous Sevens: the races in the circus, the wisemen of old times, the champions against Thebes. He also mentions that at the time of writing "he has entered the 12th *hebdomad* of his age and completed 70 *hebdomads* of books". In all this he was probably drawing at least in part on Nigidius. Augustus was one of those worried when he reached his climacteric year.

Varro also wrote a weather calendar, *ephemeris navalis*, in 77 B.C.; it was revised or superseded by another after 46. It certainly had astral elements. He composed a Pythagorean *On the Principles of Numbers*; there was a chapter *de astrologia* in his lost *De Disciplinis*; and Cassiodorus cited him on the egg-shape of the earth.[34]

Through embassies or private visits leading Stoics were often at Rome in the last century B.C. Cicero was one of the men who were influenced by them there or at the schools in Greece and Rhodes where they taught.[35] At an early age he was impressed by his star-studies; and in the poem *On his Consulship* there is a passage spoken by Urania on Jove "lighting up heaven and earth with marvellous rays of his divine intelligence and mind, which pierces all the inmost sense of man and vivifies their souls held fast within the boundless caverns of eternal air". She stresses the orderly nature of the orbits; any disorder aloft foretells disorder below:

> For when as a wise Consul you ruled the State,
> you noted, and approached with the due victims,
> propitiating the rapid stars, the strange
> concurrence of the fiery constellations.
> Then when you purified the Alban Mount
> and celebrated the great Latin Feast,
> bringing pure milk, apt offering for the gods,
> you saw fierce comets bright and quivering
> with light unheard-of. In the sky you saw
> ferocious wars and dread night-massacre.[36]

Thus the stars justified Cicero in suppressing Catilina. The moon, he writes, was muffled and hidden; the sun set at midday; a thunderbolt came from a cloudless sky; fiery forms and visions wandered about, scarcely shrouded by the dark. And he drags in the "sad predictions in the dark pages of Etruscan Books". At all costs he wants to glorify himself and stress the horrors from which he saved the senatorial landlords. Again in his speech *On the Answers of the Haruspices* he is ready to accept the Etruscan system of omens when he can use it against the radical Clodius. But in critical works like *On Fate* and *On Divination* he sets out at length his strong opposition to astrologic doctrine. He is respectful when dealing with a man like Poseidonios, but steadily rejects all fatalistic views. He uses most of the anti-astrologic arguments which had now grown up: that twins have different destinies, not all persons born under the same stars have the same fates, astrologers would need an infallible sense of sight in observing the heavens. If the stars are so influential, why don't they control winds and seas? Besides, "parental seed" (heredity) is important; and a man by his own efforts or medical insight can cure defects he was born with. Environment and local traditions differentiate men born under the same constellations; the assertions about vast periods of observation proving the truth of astrology are a fraud. What of all the men that die together on the same battle-day?

Lucretius too was an Epicurean sceptic who set out the creed of the eternality of matter and the cosmos; of free will against fatalism. He dealt with eclipses and set out an incorrect Chaldean theory of the moon's surface plus a correct Greek one; in his exposition of lightnings, meteors, and earthquakes there was not the least concession to omen-mongering or to astrology.[37]

He sees astrology as part of the vast complex of guilt, cruelty, and oppression which has gathered together as religion or found there its sanction: an effort to lessen anxiety which in fact it nourishes and increases.

> When we gazed up at the great world's heavenly *templa*
> and aither fixed fast above the glittering stars,
> and turn our thoughts to the courses of sun and moon,
> then into our breasts oppressed with other evils
> this fear as well starts lifting its woken head,
> the fear that we'll find the gods' power to be boundless
> and able to wheel the stars in their varied motion;
> for lack of power to solve the question troubles
> the mind with doubts: did the world have a time of birth
> and will it end? how far the walls of the world
> can endure the strain of an unresting motion? . . .

Looking further afield, we do not know much of the leading astrologers of the epoch. Timaios is thought to have been of the last century. His works included a treatise, *Mathematika*, and another, *Peri Physeos*. Plinius is the first writer known to cite him, and knew also a theorist with opposed views.[38] Teukros of Babylon was perhaps some decades later. He laid stress on the dekans and their *paranatellonta,* and has been taken as of Egypt; but he also tried to vindicate Babylonian astrology. He transmitted many names from the *Sphaera Barbarica* and seems to have been interested in the magic powers of precious stones; he later influenced the Arabs.[39] Cicero mentions Metrodoros of Skepsis, together with Charmadas of Athens as possessed of an "almost divine memory". Each of these men "used to say that he wrote down what he wanted to remember in certain places conceived in his imagination by means of images (or symbols) just as if he were inscribing letters on wax". Quintilian also mentions the pair, though he takes Metrodoros as something of a braggart and charlatan; he adds that his memory-system was based on the Zodiac. Metrodoros was one of the Greek men of letters whom Mithridates of Pontos drew to his court, where he seems to have played an important cultural role, gaining the nickname of Roman-hater—though Ploutarch hints that he was finally put out of the way. Strabon says that he wrote in rhetoric in a way which "dazzled many"; apparently it was of the florid Asianic type. In his mnemonics he must have used the zodiacal signs as "places" with which to associate the matters he wanted to recall; he no doubt used the dekans too. Dionysios of

Miletos, under Hadrian, was accused of training pupils in mnemonics by "Chaldean arts", and in the Renaissance the Metrodoran system was revived and much expanded by men like Bruno.[40]

An historian such as Diodoros the Sicilian shows how wide the interest in astrology had grown; he varies between full acceptance and the Stoic views as modified by Panaitios.[41]

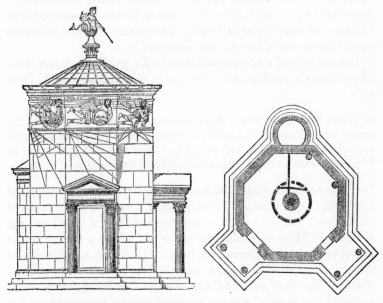

Fig. 56. Horological Monument of Andronikos Cyrrhestes at Athens; groundplan (Vitruv. i, 6, 4; Varro RR iii 7, 17)

The revolutionary epoch, from Sulla to the Battle of Actium, was marked with an endless number of prodigies, prophetic dreams and omens. Comets and stars were used to point out the saviour of the new dispensation. Virgil's Fourth Eclogue set out the Roman hope of a world-end leading into a Golden Age without any convulsions; the Sibylline verses set out the opposing version of the oppressed eastern masses, at points manipulated by Kleopatra and her agents. The *haruspex* Spurinna who warned Caesar of his murder may have been an astrologer; he was perhaps the *summus haruspex* who advised Caesar not to cross to Africa before the winter solstice.[42] Cicero knew him. He jestingly refers to him in a letter of complaint to the rich Epicurean, L. Papirius Paetus, in February 43, about his failure to go out to dinner. "Spurinna,

indeed, when I pointed the thing out to him and described your
previous life, showed that the whole State was in peril unless you
reverted to your old habits, when Favonius [the west wind of
spring] begins blowing. For the moment, he added, such conduct
might be tolerated since possibly you can't endure the cold."[43]
Astrology entered into the symbols chosen by either side in the civil
wars. In using the Bull as legionary emblem, Caesar seems to have
been thinking of the Bull as the house of Venus, the ancestress of
his *gens*, whom he claimed as his protectress. Augustus in turn
used Capricorn; Tiberius, the Scorpion.[44]

Comets played a special part among the prodigies. Seven days
after Caesar's murder, says Ploutarch, a comet appeared. Dion
tells us:

A certain Star appeared in the north towards evening. Some called it a
comet and claimed it foretold the usual events, while the majority,
instead of believing this, ascribed it to Caesar and took it to mean he
had become immortal and been received into the number of stars.[45]

Instead of a king's death, the Star announced his katasterism. Like
Ploutarch, Pope Gregory I still believed that righteous men lived
on as stars; but held that he had support for the idea from the
Gospels.[46] "The only place in the world where a Comet is the
object of worship is a temple at Rome." It appeared apparently at
the games given by Octavian after Caesar's death in honour of
Venus. "The common folk," says Plinius, "believed that this Star
signified the Soul of Caesar received among the spirits of the
immortal gods. But privately," he adds of Octavian, "he rejoiced
and interpreted the comet as born for his own sake and as containing his own birth within it." Baebius Macer said a *haruspex*
Vulcatius (an Etruscan name) went before an Assembly and said
that the comet indicated the end of an age or *saeclum*; but he
collapsed and died on the spot.[47]

Christ's birth was less than fifty years ahead. The link of a new
star with a saviour went far back in the East, into the Zoroastrian
past. Consider Balaam, who in *Numbers* is described as living in the
city of Pethor in Mesopotamia and who was called on by the King
of Moab to curse the Israelites. Instead he blessed them. "I shall
see him but not now. I shall behold him but not nigh. There shall
come a Star out of Jacob and a Sceptre shall rise out of Israel."
Zoroaster as Babylonian mage had predicted the advent of a saviour,
the Saosyant, bringing justice and happiness to earth. So the

Saosyant and the Star-out-of-Jacob tended to come together.[48]
One tradition told how Balaam's prophecies were collected by the
Kings of Assyria and handed on, reign after reign, and reaching the
Kings of Iran, till the time of Augustus. When the Star of Jesus
appeared, the Persians, scared, recognised in it the prophecy of
Balaam and sent offerings by the Mages whom the Star led to
Bethlehem. Later the Mages were turned into the Eastern Kings
themselves. From Origen on, Christian writers took the Mages of
Matthew for Balaam's inheritors and disciples; and we find
Balaam's Star in ancient catacomb-paintings. Thus, at Rome,
near SS Marcellinus and Peter, is represented an eight-rayed
Star at which Balaam points.[49]

Caesar found the Roman calendar in disorder through failures to
carry out intercalations. Down to 153 B.C. the year had had two
starts, the natural year on 1 January, the civil year on 1 March
(earlier, 15 March). That is why our twelfth month, December, is
still called the tenth, *decem*; November, *novem*; September,
septem. The Romans like other peoples had begun with a lunar
month, but in their effort to link it with the solar year they devised
a clumsy system of a four-year period of years consisting success-
ively of 355, 377, 356, 378 days: an average of $366\frac{1}{4}$ days, or one
day too much. The extra month was put into February on alternate
years, but a special announcement of it by the College of Pontiffs
was needed. And the College was at times careless or demoralised
or controlled by pressure-groups who might like a long year, for
instance a company of tax-collectors.

Caesar set about stopping this irresponsible system. In 46 B.C.
he had to make the year run for 445 days. On 1 January 45 the new
calendar came into action, making the normal year 365 days with
an extra day inserted between 23 and 24 February every fourth year.

Caesar laid the problem before the best philosophers and mathematicians, and out of the methods of correction already at hand he compounded one of his own more accurate than any. (Ploutarch.)

There were three main schools, the Chaldean, the Egyptian, and the
Greek; and to these a fourth was added in our country by Caesar during
his dictatorship; for with the aid of the learned astrologer Sosigenes he
brought the separate year back into conformity with the sun's course.
(Plinius.)

Dion does not mention any helpers, but says, "He got this

improvement from his stay in Alexandreia." Caesar did not use the Egyptian system of 30 days in each of 12 months, with 5 extra days at the end; he wanted to break as little as possible with the accepted patterns of festivals. As *pontifex maximus* he was responsible for the calendar; and things had got so bad that the spring Floralia was liable to turn up in summer.[50] Cicero had to

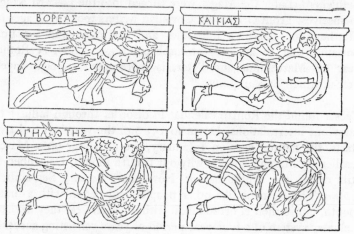

Fig. 57. Four of the Monument's eight reliefs of Winds

admit that the laxity of the pontiffs had brought the mess about; but he resented the hated Caesar making the reform.[51] Working with one scribe, M. Flavius, Caesar was credited with devising the final form of the new calendar. Sosigenes, however, may well have been the consulted expert.[52] We know little of him, but he doubtless provided Caesar also with material for his work *On the Stars*, a new Latin *parapegma* or almanac, an up-to-date version of the old farmer's book of weather-signs.[53]

After the Julian calendar, *menologia* or farm-calendars of a simple sort were cut in stone or laid out in mosaic: rather for display than use. Two have come down from Rome, one almost certainly of the first century A.D. There are twelve columns, one for each month. At the head of each is set the month's zodiacal sign, then come the features most interesting for a farmer:

May
31 Days
Nones on 7th
Daylight: 14½ hours

September
30 Days
Nones on 5th
Daylight: 12 hours

Darkness: 9½ hours
Sun in the Bull
Protector: Apollo
Weed Corn
Shear Sheep
Wash Wool
Break in Young Bullocks
Cut Vetch
Bless the Cornfields
Sacrifice to Mercury, Flora

Darkness: 12 hours
Equinox: 24th
Sun in Virgin
Protector: Vulcan
Pitchpaint Winejars
Pick Apples
Loosen earth round Treeroots
Feast in Honour of Minerva[54]

A day of 24 hours, each containing 60 minutes, is used.

There was a complete system of lucky and unlucky days. *Dies fasti*, marked F on calendars, were open for public business; *dies comitiales*, marked C, for election-assemblies unless the day coincided with one of the *nundinae*, the eight-day holidays at the end of the seven-day weeks, with a regular festival or with one of the moveable *feriae conceptivae*. When there was no public meeting, legal transactions took place on a C Day. There were probably some 193 or 195 C days before Caesar, 191 after. In the Republican calendar F days numbered not more than 29, though we must add a number of *nundinae* to them; and there were 14 split days on part of which no legal business was legitimate. The 10 days added by Caesar were all made F days, which now numbered 52; and Augustus made alterations to increase the *fasti*. It worked out that under Caesar 243 days a year could be used for legal and other public business. *Nefasti* were 106 or 107 of the Republican year, 108 of the Julian, not available for public business of any kind; of these 45 were festivals and the rest had religious significances of some sort.[55]

At some time in the Hellenistic era the seven days of the week got their planetary attributions and names, becoming the days of Saturn, the Sun, the Moon, Mars, Mercury, Jupiter and Venus. Romans must often have first encountered the seven-day week through the Jews with their Sabbath, day of Saturn; but with the quick spread of astrology the idea of such a week must have grown familiar. Thus, quite apart from the old official list of *dies nefasti*, certain days were liable to take on an aspect of planetary malevolence, especially Saturday, Saturn's day; and we find that day considered unlucky for starting a journey. Of Tiberius we are told:

The grammarian Diogenes, who used to hold public disquisitions at Rhodes every Sabbath day, once refused him admittance on his coming to hear him out of course, and sent him a servant with a message, postponing his admission till the next seventh day. Diogenes afterwards came to Rome and waited at his door to be allowed to pay his respects; but Tiberius sent him word to come again at the end of seven years.[51]

Pompeii shows that the seven-day week was well known before A.D. 79. The way that common folk reckoned is shown by graffiti such as this: "In the consulship of Nero Caesar Augustus and Cossus Lentulus, 8 days before the Ides of March, on Sunday, on the 16th of the Moon, Marketday at Cumae, 5 days before the Marketday at Pompeii." Josephos' statement, echoed in the early third century by Cassius Dion, claims the whole world, Greek and barbarian, knew and used the seven-day week; and Juvenal suggests that by the early second century schools were following a seven-day timetable.[57] From the third century the Christians had accepted the custom despite the pagan and astrologic nature of the day-names; but Mithraism and sun-worship in general had displaced Saturn's day and made Sun-Day the first of the week. The Romans had always jeered at the Jewish use of the Sabbath as a rest-day, but Constantine ordered the observance of Sun-Day as one of religious worship at the official recognition of Christianity in two edicts of A.D. 321. Theodosius stopped the use of that day for law and business; games too were barred, except for imperial birthdays falling on it—though in 409 even those games were disallowed. The earliest evidence for the Christian observance of Sunday as the *dies dominica,* the Lord's Day, comes from Tertullian in 202; in 386 Valentinian and Theodosius spoke of "The Day of the Sun, which our ancestors rightly called the Lord's Day." But it is likely that the Christians, wanting a day of rest and feastings *(agapai)* which was not that of the Jews, had felt that Christ was their Sun and so had long claimed the *Dies Solis.*[58]

To return to Caesar: we are not sure if his new calendar and his almanac were put out together, or if the almanac followed.[59] An amusing passage on the Pleiades, cited by Plinius, can hardly be Caesar's work; it is rather in the vein of Petronius:

(For 10 November) Even clothes-dealers go by the constellation and it is very easy to identify in the sky. So dealers, out for profits and careful to watch their chances, make forecasts as to the winter from its setting. Thus by a cloudy setting it foretells a wet winter and they at once raise the price for cloaks, whereas by a fine-weather setting it foretells a hard winter and they screw up the price of all other clothes . . .

Between the rise of the West wind and the spring equinox, 16

February for Caesar marks three days of changeable weather, as also does 22 February by the appearance of the Swallow and next day by the rising of Arcturus in the evening, and the same on 3 March. Caesar noticed that this bad weather took place at the Crab's rising, but most authorities put it at the setting of the Vintager. On 8 March at the rising of the Fish's northern part, and next day at Orion's rising . . . Caesar also noted 15 March, day that was to be fatal for him, as marked by the Scorpion's setting, but stated that on 18 March the Kite became visible in Italy and on 21 March the Horse sets in the morning.[60]

Plinius elaborated the idea of harmful astral influences over certain crops. He sees two kinds of damage done by the heavens: one directly by storms, by "exceptionally violent weather, originating from noxious constellations", and the other "occurring when the sky is quiet". Arcturus, Orion, the Kids are noxious. He seems here to be drawing mainly on Caesar. However, *De Astris* does not appear to be based on fatalist astrology. It does assume a strong and occasionally decisive influence by stars and constellations on plant-life through the weather; but nature is often described as merciful. Human affairs, e.g. in seasonal disease, are also seen as affected by the weather.[61]

A decree of the Greek Cities of Asia in 9 B.C. on the introduction of the Julian Calendar shows how far the deification of its author had then gone:

What could be more pleasant or more fraught with blessing than the Birthday of the most Divine Caesar, which we might rightly regard as like the First Beginning of All Things? . . . He gave a different aspect to the whole world that would otherwise have readily fallen a prey to ruin . . . It is difficult to give thanks commensurate with such acts of blessing by him . . . whom Providence filled with such virtue to do good to mankind . . . The Birthday of the God was the Beginning for the World of the Good Tidings [*evangelia*] which he brought.[62]

We saw how, from the fifth century BC., ordinary people also aspired to reach the stars. Here are some more examples of epitaphs from the Augustan period onwards, which show how the emotion persisted:

Mother, don't weep. What use is now your moan?
Marvel, admire. A star among gods I've grown. (Amorgos)

The body is hidden under this dusty heap.
But the soul, escaped from the body, the wide heavens keep. (Athens)

He has returned his soul to the *Aer,* his body to Earth. (Rome)

The coffin may hold my glorious [*aglaos*] body, the soul has
    gone hence to the *aither*. (Thasos)
Stand by the tomb and behold young Chorō.
Diognētos' unwedded daughter,
Hades has set her in the Seventh Circle. (Miletos)
Approaching the altar to pay her vows, she went to the stars,
    respected of all.
Without sickness, she obeyed the demigods' call. (Megalopolis)[63]

This last was of a priestess of Isis. In a late inscription from Smyrna
the dead man tells how his "winged soul ascended the sky and has
been pleasantly welcomed by the gods, drinking cheerfully in their
company. Hermes is his patron."[64] These were all Greek, but the
same ideas and images invaded the Latin area:

Eight years you reached. Now, privileged, the aither you see
and shine in the stars that shine eternally.[65]

A Cologne epitaph declares that with death "the body remains on
earth, the spirit follows the heaven, the spirit moves all things,
the spirit is as a god". A poet in Rome, perhaps of the Augustan or
else of the Flavian era, tells in a long set of elegiacs how in the midst
of tears he is confronted at dawn by his dead friend Nepos who
bids him not to weep. He has not gone down to gloomy Hades
with Charon, judge Minos, and the rest of the underworld
apparatus.

Holy Venus bade me not know the seats of the silent dead,
to the lucid temples of the heavens she bore me on high.

The poet then hails the dead man as a member of one or other of
the heavenly choirs (Liber, Phoebus, Attis, or the sky-charioteer
Cyllarus); but ends with the statement that "whatever god or
hero he'll be called, Nepos is beyond the reach of dissolution".
Another inscription declares, "The Sun snatched me up."[66]

13

The Early Principate

We may now glance at the different uses of the terms *astronomia* and *astrologia* in ancient works. Olympiodoros later stated, "Formerly the theory of the heavens, *astronomia* and *astrologia* formed a single science: the first teaching the essence of the stars [*ousia*], the second their movement, the third their influences." The Ionian thinkers in fact used two general terms, *astrologia* and *meteorologia*; all those studying the stars were *astrologoi*, concerned with the *logos* or rational system to be found there. The study had certain practical bents. *Nautikai astrologiai*, for sailors, were composed: one was attributed to Thales, another to Phokos of Samos. Kleostratos was said to have written an *Astrologia*; Pherekydes was called *astrologos*. Proklos remarks: "*Astrologia* deals with the cosmic movements, the size and form of the heavenly bodies, their luminosity, the distances separating them from the earth, and all such things."[1]

The first time we hear of *Astronomiē* is in a book attributed to Demokritos. Thrasyllos in his list put it under *Mathematika,* with works on arithmetic and geometry; it must, then, have included computations of star-movements. The nature of stars would have been dealt with under *Cosmographiē*, in the works on *Physika*. *Astronomos* means the man who regulates the stars, as *oikonomos* means he who regulates a household; it belongs to a group of terms designating magistrates or controllers. The *astronomos* seeks to grasp the laws of the cosmos in a mathematical form, while the *astrologos* deals with the nature and origin of the world.[2]

Plato uses only *astronomia,* even in the *Timaios* where we might expect *astrologia*. The Hippokratic treatise *On Airs* says that "astronomy plays in medicine a role that is not at all small, that is indeed among the most important". The Pythagorean Archytas remarks, "From Quantity are drawn the four sciences. Continuous Quantity without movement gives Geometry; with movement, Astronomy: discontinuous, without movement, Arithmetic; with movement, Music." The *Epinomis* compares the childish astronomy of the ancients, concerned only with the rising and setting of stars, with the advanced science of its day, so complex in its combinations that the mind needs a special initiation.[3]

Aristotle, however, uses only *astrologia*. He wants a science that is both physical and mathematical; for nature is double, he says—made of form and matter. Theophrastos wavers. He speaks of the *astrologia* of Demokritos, but otherwise uses *astronomia*. Many writers such as Xenophon now used either term indifferently. Aristophanes prefers *astronomia*; for the populace looked on the astronomer as a man who lived in the moon. The term was

Fig. 58. Charioteer Eros in quadriga, with acclamation "Eros, Everything through You!"—Mosaic of Dougga, N. Africa

ambiguous: a man who regulated the stars, a man who studied the regular movements of the stars, a man who lived in the stars (as *pezonomos* meant a creature living on earth, a quadruped, and *agronomos,* a man who lived in the field or who administered the countryside). *Astronomein* was equated with *aerobatein*: walk on air. The satiric outlook appears in the tale told by Plato about Thales *astronomōn* and looking aloft, so that he falls down a well. Plato took the view that, apart from the mathematical *astronomoi,* there were fantasists, *meteoroskopoi, meteoroleschai.*[4]

Another trend is to admire. Sosipatros writes, "He possessed all the *logoi* concerning nature; first of all he taught us *astrologein.*" *Astronomiai* were attributed to Orpheus and Hesiod. With the growth of mathematical astronomy we meet the term *mathematikoi* for astronomers, used by Hipparchos about 150 B.C., and three hundred years later Ptolemaios called his book *Mathematikē Syntaxis*. But *mathematikoi* also came to be used for astrologers, like the term Chaldeans.[5] After astrology proper became firmly established, a distinction was gradually drawn: *astronomia* for the mathematical and observational aspects, astrology for the application to predictions. The word *astrologoi* was used for the Mages who taught Demokritos and Oinopides, for the Egyptian initiates. Strabon used *astrologoi* for astrologers; but *astronomia* was their science—Nikolas of Damas confused the two terms, Cassius Dion linked *astronomia* and *mantikē* (prophecy), and so on. Still, despite many such confused usages, the distinction grew. Theon of Smyrna, Proklos, Pappos, and Ptolemaios used *astronomia* for the mathematical disciplines. And the latter in *Tetrabiblos* distinguished two sciences: one dealing with successive configurations of the movements of sun, moon, and stars in their mutual relations and with the earth, and a second by which we examine, through the physics of these configurations, the particular characters and the vicissitudes brought about, which they controlled. So *astrologia* came definitely to refer to astronomy in its mantic and horoscopic forms.[6]

Epitaphs helped us to see the influx of astrologic ideas at the popular level. More important still is the way in which they invaded the Circus. Ennius at his early days gave us a glimpse of astrologers there selling tips as to winning horses; and if they were so busy at Rome we can imagine how much more active they must have been in eastern cities. We have many later references to the way in which everything connected with the Circus was given an astro-logic interpretation; and the ideas in question must have had their roots far back in Hellenistic days, building in turn on simpler cosmic images which underlay the structure of the original rounded or oval racing-ground. (*Circus* is from *Kirkos*, a species of hawk or falcon, which must have had a circling flight; *Kirke* or *Circe* is the feminine form, the daughter of the Sun with magical powers.) Writers who give us clues to the astrologic Circus are Cassiodorus, Corippus, Isidoros, Malalas, Kedrenos; and Malalas for example seems to have drawn on the *Histories* of Charax, which he cited in his *Chronography*. Another source was Suetonius, an enthusiast about both Circus and astrology.[7]

First, we meet a general imagery of sky and stars. The concept of the charioteer as the solar driver reached its climax in the Byzantine

period, with the full growth of the circus-factions, but the idea itself
went far back. We may note that in the Mithraic system the
Heliodromos or Courier of the Sun was the deputy on earth of
Helios-Sol, under whose care he was set. In the Santa Prisca
fresco we see the Courier approaching the seated Father with his
right hand raised in salute. He wears a red garment with yellow

Fig. 59. Triumphal procession (shown like the sun-quadriga),
opus sectile, Albani palace (fourth century)

belt, and has on his shoulders the sky-mantle, on his head a blue
nimbus with gold rays. He clasps a blue globe in his left hand.
The Father of the fraternity wears a red robe.[8] The four parties of
the Circus were linked with the Seasons and the Year, and each
had its Colour. They were also linked with the Elements.[9]

In the colour-symbolism the Red represented Summer, Fire,
Mars; the Green, Spring, Earth and Flowers, Venus; Blue,
Autumn, Air of Heaven and Water of Sea, Saturn or Neptune;
White, Winter, Air and Zephyrs, Jupiter.[10] According to Minucius
Felix, Blue is sky and sea (autumn), red is Mars (mainly strength
or summer), white is zephyr (winter), green is Terra Mater
(spring).[11] (We find the identification of the elements and colours
in tribal society. Thus the Na-khi, of the Tibeto-Burman family in
south-west China, had a tale of an ancient hunter who decided to
visit the land of the dead; he was told at the entry he would not be
able to return. His children, searching, found his arrow without
the five coloured strings, which represented the elements making
up the body.)[12]

The Hippodrome was the universe in miniature, its microcosmic image. The arena was the earth, the euripus the sea, the central obelisk the pinnacle of heaven, consecrated to the sun whose course it shared. The Circus was again the circular year, its twelve doors or *carceres* the twelve months or signs. Its limits were marked by the ends of East and West, the rising and the setting; it had three turning-points at each end as each zodiacal sign had its three dekans. Each course consisted of seven turns, expressive of the seven days and the seven stars. The 24 courses of each festival corresponded to the 24 hours of day-night. In turn the imagery of the Circus was imported into the sky. The emperor Julian spoke of the Sun "rounding Capricorn as if it were a goal post" in the races.[13]

The full working-out of these ideas took a long time, but clearly astrologic ideas had a central effect at each phase. The system, in the last resort, rested on tribal notions of orientation and so on, which we noted in chapter 1; and it is surprising how deeply rooted such notions were, surviving among the people and reasserting themselves in new situations. At Antioch the factions stood for the four city-quarters; Constantine Porphyrios noted the hair-colours in the names of Pecheneg tribes, corresponding to the sky-region towards which the tribe in question was oriented; and still in the nineteenth century B.C. some Wallachian towns had quarters marked by colours.[14]

Astrology entered the prayers and curses of the faction-backers. On the spell-tablets found at Rome, Carthage, Hadrumetum, are set down the names of drivers and horses, sometimes of one or two of the parties, but never three or four—showing the way in which pairs of them were allied. On one *lamella* of the third century from Apheka in Syria the dedicator begs the *daimones* to break the aid that his rival Hyperechios might get from "the 36 dekans, the 5 planets, and the 2 luminaries".[15] Three late texts show the planetary connections fully worked out:

(1) Saturn, Mercury, and Venus have affinities with the Blue Party; the Sun, Mars, and the Moon with the Green; Jupiter is shared by both. Among these stars, that which is set on a centre, that which comes near it, that which is in its house, its exaltation or its own limits, or finds itself diametrically opposed to or in trigon with Jupiter at the Hour of the Contest, is the one giving victory to the Party with which it corresponds. The star of the ascendant and that from which the Moon is distancing herself, designate the questioner about the Contest; the star

of the setting and that which the Moon is approaching, the adversary. The preceding conjunction of Moon and Sun is linked with the Blues, the Full Moon with the Greens.

(2) You must know that the Moon aids the Greens, the Sun the Reds, Saturn and Venus the Blues. So, when the Sun meets Venus, if at that moment the Blues are launching out on the course, they'll win. When it meets Mars, it's the Greens who win, for Mars is their ally; and when Jupiter is found at a *kentron*, then infallibly the Blues will win, above all if the Moon is at this moment deprived of light and if she inclines towards the region which descends lower than the [*mesēbria?*].

(3) The ancients, having examined also the question of the Hippodrome, spread out the colours also among certain stars. Thus it was they gave Blue to Mercury, Red to Mars, Green to the Moon, Victory to Jupiter and Defeat to Saturn. That is, according to them the star which regards Jupiter wins, that which regards Saturn loses. As for the Sun, some have argued that it aided the Red because of its igneous substance; but most have been of opinion that it dispenses good equally—they consider it a mixed and shared star.

According to others, the Moon near her start and finish, that is from its dichotomy [its division into two sectors] or from the 21st day, and also during its conjunction with the Sun till the 7th day, helps on her side the Blues—then from that moment, the Greens. But while maintaining this view, they add that the weakness she seems to experience when receiving insufficient light, prevents her from helping. As a result it's her very weakness that favours the affairs of the Blues.

And since the stars have their full power when in their own houses, exaltations or trigons, or when they are *horiokratores* [lords of their own limits, of certain degrees in the zodiacal sign], or when they move quickly or when they regard Jupiter or the Sun under good aspects, the astrologer naturally looks on these positions as preferable to others, and predicts victories from them. If on the contrary they have a retrograde movement or they are regarded by harmful planets or burned by the Sun, or they find themselves in places opposed to them or in the strange confines of harmful planets, or if they regard Saturn under bad aspects (I mean, of trigons), and again if they set or go down, all that enables us to predict defeat.

Still, this procedure often produces erroneous prophecies. That's why the famous Theodoros of Alexandreia, so expert in the science and above all a specialist in hippodrome-questions, discovered yet another method, quite infallible. Not ignoring the other matters, but adding new points, he made his subtler observation. He decided that stars above the earth have more power than those below; he attributed victory then to them.

An example: when Venus is found above earth at the hour of the course, and Mars at the same time below, he gave the victory to the

Whites. If the two stars were above earth, but one in the supra-terrestrial *kentron,* he gave the victory to the star on the *kentron.* He kept his observations to himself till a certain moment, then he used to say to the faction he chose, "Let the event take place at seven hours, or at eight, or at six . . ., the other side will win." So many people, indeed almost all, through not knowing his reasons, took him for a magician. Such a thing happened at the race of the Indiction Ten, year 6450: normally the race took place at the seventh hour, at the start of the eighth, or during the whole eighth. But this time it was prolonged until the ninth. The Moon moved from the seventh place towards the sixth, the place of disaster. At once the Greens were ruined. For at the same moment Venus, arriving at the upper culmination, aroused all the energy of the Whites . . .[16]

It is an instance of how many gaps there are in our records that we know nothing else of this Theodoros with his racing-tips.

The wild glorification of charioteers in the Byzantine period led to their identification with the Sun. An hermetic doctrine ran:

The Sun is established in the middle of the world, wearing the world like a crown; and as a good driver he has assured the balance of the world-chariot and attached it to himself out of fear that it might be carried away on a disordered course. The reins are life, soul, *pneuma,* immortality, and generation. He has loosened the reins a little so that the world can run its course, not apart from him, but, if we must speak the truth, with him. And thus it is that all things are continually created.[17]

Dion Chrysostom in his 36th Discourse has an elaborate myth which he attributes to the Mages. The chariot of Helios, he says, is recent when compared with that of Zeus:

They assert that the Universe is constantly being driven and propelled along a single path as by a Charioteer endowed with the highest skill and power, and that this movement goes on unceasingly in unceasing cycles of Time. And the coursing of Helios and Selene, they say, is the move-ment of parts of the whole and thus is more clearly perceived by men. And they add that the movement and revolution of the Universe as a whole is not perceptible to most men, but that they on the contrary are ignorant of the magnitude of the Contest [*agon*: the word used for the races].

The Horse of Zeus is on the outermost tract and is incomparably superior in beauty, size, speed; winged and brilliant with the colour of purest flame. "In it Helios and Selene are to be seen as conspicuous signs or marks—like, I fancy, the marks borne here on earth by horses, some crescent-shaped, some of other patterns. And they say those 'marks' seem to us in close array, like great sparks of fire darting about amid brilliant light, yet each has its independent motion." The planets are directly associated with the Horse of Zeus, "the most shining and most spangled of stars". Next is the Horse of Hera, obedient and gentle, black by nature, but bright where Helios lights her. Third is the Horse of Poseidon (of which the earthly counterpart is Pegasos). Fourth is the wingless

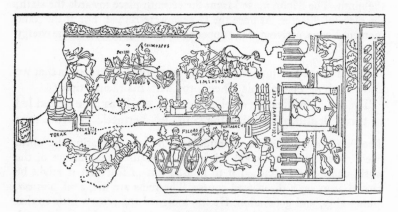

Fig. 60. Chariot-races (mosaic of Girone): along the middle is a statue of Cybele on a galloping lion: cf. mosaic of Barcelona at Madrid

unmoving Horse of Hestia (the hearth or cosmic centre). For long the Horses are in harmony; then at last a blast from the Horse of Zeus sets the whole universe on fire, or agitated sweat from that of Poseidon creates a flood. Dion is right in giving an Iranian origin to this myth, though he has decorated it with Greek trimmings. The *Avesta* tells of the team of Mithras, god of light, crossing the firmament; and the Mithraic mysteries, we saw, carried on the symbolism.[18]

The gladiators in the Circus, with their dangerous lives, naturally looked to the stars for aid or blamed them for defeats. Thus a *retiarius* or net-man at Verona, who, married, died at the age of 23 in his 8th engagement, made his complaint: "Observe, every man, his own planet. That's my advice. Have no trust in Nemesis. She deceived me." Deceived is a common term for killed: "Deceived by Fate, not by Man."[19] Under the empire Nemesis had a considerable cult in the circus-area. She spread from the East westward, especially into the Danubian provinces; the evidence is to be found in the amphitheatres of the West and East. She was an example of a comparatively unassimilated Greek deity, who had no intermediary stage of a public cult at Rome before getting into the western provinces.[20] If we take Cisalpine Gaul we find her cult centred on Istra and Aquileia, with a few inscriptions as far west as Brescia and Verona.[21] The social status of her devotees is not always clear; but at least four seem slaves; a fuller at Pola honoured her, also a Greek-named *sevir* (probably a freedman) at Aquileia, and a soldier. Half of the dedications are ex-votos; two are in compliance with visions. We meet wheel and tiller in her representations, showing her link with Fortuna; an Aquileian gem shows her directly as Fortuna. She is twice seen girt like Diana, with a griffin. On an Aquileian altar she is identified with Diana the Huntress in a relief of dogs dragging down hare and hind. Her role in races, gladiatorial fights, and staged hunts provided the basis of her assimilation to both Diana and Fortuna.[22] Among the Lingones in Gaul she appears as a goddess of the race-course. Dedications to her have been found in the theatres of Samnite Venafrum and Illyrian Carnuntum and Aquincum; the two latter sites had temples annexed. The Attic Theatre of Dionysos had an altar to her; she had statues in the stadium at Olympia; and her cult existed in the theatres at Patrai and Antioch. In Cisalpine Gaul two altars to her were found in the ruined theatre at Pola; at Aquileia was a College of *Kynagetai Nemesiakoi*, Hunters of Nemesis, who frequented a theatre of the Ephesian Artemis.[23] We see how the anxieties of this world turned people to Fate-cults, whether of Fortuna (Tyche), Nemesis or the Planets.

There was an expulsion of astrologers in 150 B.C. Various restrictive measures were taken against prophets of all kinds by Octavian in his struggle with Antonius and Kleopatra. In 33 Agrippa as aedile issued an ordinance against astrologers and sorcerers. Later, in 12, Octavian, now Augustus, burned prophetic and divining books; but we do not hear of further steps against astrologers till A.D. 16 under Tiberius. There seem to have been two *senatus consulta*, the second resulting from the inadequate provisions of the first. The cause was the plot of Libo, which we shall consider later.[24]

But however much the emperors might reprobate other persons having recourse to astrologers to pry into their death-date, they

246 ORIGINS OF ASTROLOGY

themselves could not resist the hope of seeing into the future. Augustus does not seem to have had any court-astrologer, but we are told that when in his youth at Apollonia he went with his friend Agrippa to visit an astrologer Theogenes in his roof-gallery. Agrippa first had his fortune told and was promised "almost incredible things". For some time Augustus refused to declare his nativity

out of a mixture of shame and fear, lest his fortunes should be foretold as inferior to those of Agrippa. He was persuaded, however, with much importunity, to give the date. Theogenes started up from his seat and paid him adoration. Not long after, Augustus was so confident in the greatness of his destiny that he published his horoscope and struck a silver coin bearing the sign of Capricorn, under the influence of which he had been born.[25]

He did not publish his horoscope until he was near death but adherents may have started stories about his great future. Many tales collected round his birth. We have noted that in which Nigidius was involved. We have accounts of his mother's prophetic dreams; and, according to Julius Marathus,

a few months before his birth there happened at Rome a prodigy by which it was signified that Nature was in travail of a King for the Roman People. The Senate in alarm came to the resolution that no child born that year should be brought up. But those among them whose wives were pregnant, to secure to themselves a chance of that dignity, took care that the decree was not registered in the Treasury.

We see by comparing this story with that of Herod killing the firstborn that it falls into a folk-pattern of themes in which a threatened tyrant tries in vain to kill off a champion or saviour.

Octavian-Augustus was in fact born on 23 (really 22) September 63 under the Balance; but officially he put himself under Capricorn, signifying fortune and domination, a sign in which Mars found his exaltation; the earliest coins with the sign are dated 28–26 B.C.[26] One theory is that, being born before sunrise, he was under the moon, not the sun; and on 22–3 September 63 the Moon was in the sign of Capricorn.[27] But the texts cited in support of this interpretation do not make the Moon dominate the zodiacal sign of birth; generally for her position in the horoscope she combined her influence with that of two zodiacal signs; only in a single case does she affect the one in which she is found.[28] However, the prominence of the Moon in genethliac astronomy might excuse an overstress on her part. In the one Babylonian horoscope dealing with conception we find the position of the Moon with regard to what is called a Normal Star, the date of the nearest equinox, and an obscure statement about the Moon and a second sign (Fish); there is no mention of planetary positions. Generally in Greek nativities the main effort is to determine what are the masters of the Horoscope and of the Moon: what stars hold them in their houses at the birth-hour. Why is the Moon so important here? Because she allowed the astrologer to determine the star that was master of the geniture. Maternus gives various methods of calculation, but adopts that of taking such a star, the house of which was occupied by the Moon at the rise of the sign she inhabited at the birth-moment. A text dealing with circus-factions begins by distinguishing the two main parties, considers two competitors in each faction, and provides the means of recognising them in the astrologic sky by the position that the ascendant or the setting of the Moon occupies. We also noted the stress on the Moon by Nechepso. But to return to Augustus, there is another theory that his Capricorn refers to the moment of conception. Oddly, there is the same sort of difficulty with Tiberius, who, born on 16 November under Scorpion, seems to have used the Balance for official purposes. That however appears to have been before the death of Augustus; after he became emperor he gave the Scorpion as badge to the praetorian cohort.[29]

Virgil in his scheme for Augustus' astral ascent makes him go up between the Virgin and the Scorpion, and take the place of the Balance.

> New constellation, yourself to the dragging months
> you add, where yawns a gulf between Erigonē
> and the Claws that pursue her; already the ardent Scorpion
> compresses his arms and leaves you of heaven more
> than a just part.[30]

Virgil is using the old zodiacal system in which, as Hyginus said later, "the front part of the Scorpion" is "called the Claws". He uses the fact of the gap between the Virgin and the Scorpion, corresponding to the date of Augustus' birth, to take him up and identify him with the Balance, which could be said to give equipoise to the universe, knowledge of right, discrimination, infallible justice, the power coming to the rescue "of all that's in uncertainty and needs a guide", in Manilius' words. Under the Balance a blessed person is to appear one day, "judge of life and death", who will "impose his yoke on the lands" and "make towns and kingdoms tremble".[31] Virgil in the Ninth Eclogue represented Julius Caesar's comet as taking the place of the old constellations or zodiacal signs to announce and bring about agricultural prosperity. So naturally in the *Georgics* he thinks of the same benefits when turning to the signs themselves which rule over the rustic calendar. The Balance means autumn, the temperate month providing fruits, and is in union with, and in opposition to, the Ram which gives spring-flowers. It dispenses wine, the gift of the Italian Bacchus, Liber, but it promises too the future, the crops of Ceres. Manilius manages to link the foundation of Rome and the birth of Augustus under the Balance, probably to help in supporting the cult of Augustus and Roma.[32]

Virgil connects the ascent of Augustus with that of other heroes such as Herakles, Bacchus, Romulus, Castor and Pollux; Horace merely names him in such company. For full measure Virgil makes him son of Phoebus Apollo as well as a descendent of Venus. Augustus preferred Apollo as his god-guise, but on occasion could be called Mercury. Virgil in short fused three concepts: astral immortality for great men, a country's benefactors; the status of the ruler as intermediary between man and deity, as a sort of god on earth; the descent of a divine spirit, which was destined to return to heaven. But he left a certain vagueness as to the question: Will he truly become a constellation, as for instance Caesar became for Ovid?[33]

Manilius carried on these ideas in the next generation. Virtuous heroes after death go up to the Milky Way; and yet higher than that Way are the men-gods, Augustus, Caesar, Romulus-Quirinus, up in the zodiacal circle, where the Stoic God, the World-Soul, Jupiter (with the cosmic epithet Thunderer and no mythological name), is the universal consciousness. In the Zodiac they dominate all human life. As in Virgil, Augustus goes aloft, not to forget the world, but still to aid and control. The connection of Milky Way and Zodiac fixes attention on the two points where the two circles seem to cross. One is where, at an equal distance from Capricorn and the Balance (Augustus' two signs), the Galaxy cuts the equinoctial circle and is partly in the Scorpion (of which the Balance had been in the old Zodiac no more than a section). Besides, the Balance is symmetrical with the Ram, but, with its clear symbolism, is more than that sign the expression of equinoctial equilibrium. Manilius then seems to be recalling Virgil and coming round to the same point in a rather complex way.[34]

But there is a profound difference in the world-outlook of the two poets. Virgil strives to use astrologic formulations to define an arc of human development, with a persistent hope of renewal on a new level; Manilius reveals the collapse of the hope. All is ruled by Fate. There survives a remnant of the positive Stoic outlook, which strives to transform the deadening sense of Fate into an acceptance of the rule of law, an *amor fati*.

> Fate rules the world, all is based upon fixed law . . .
> What use to gaze at the world with our frail reason
> when everyone's mind is at variance with itself
> and fear grasps hope and from heaven's dome destroys it.
> Something indeed by nature swells in the vast of space
> and eludes our mortal vision, our mortal sense.
> Nor can it help us. All's governed by the Fates,
> while Fate stays hidden, whatever method's tried.

And at the end we see that the fate governing the cosmos is one with the absolutist power governing the Roman State; the heavens have the same hierarchy as the earth.

> As the people are distributed in large cities,
> The Senate keeps highest rank, the middle order
> the next, the swarm of *equites,* and below
> this group, as you might see, the inert mass
> and the host already nameless. Thus there exists
> a sort of State in the Universe as well,
> a State of great dignity, created by Nature
> who has founded the Heavenly City.

He goes on to attack democracy, which is counter to the cosmic order; hence his scorn for the *turba*, the mob, like Horace with his *profanum vulgus*. As we read such passages we begin to realise the appeal of astrology to men who felt themselves trapped in a mechanism of power quite outside their control, a monstrous historical process in which individual will (apart from that of the ruler) seemed to count for little or nothing.

In the work of Virgil and Manilius, Nigidius, Varro and Cicero we see how strongly and subtly astrology had got to the heart of the cultural situation. Suetonius says that Virgil paid special attention to medicine and mathematics (which could include astrology); and we may note, apart from the complex role played by astrologic concepts in his poems, the way in which Aeneas flatters Helenus for his star-lore.[35] Earlier, Catullus had translated Kallimachos' poem on the Lock of Berenike. Horace was well-versed in astrologic terms. In one of his Odes he tells how he and Maecenas are linked in fate, with the same time-ruler in their horoscopes. Maecenas has been helped by Jupiter overcoming Saturn, but his own helper he makes Faunus. He has a sort of belief in *katarchai*; divine power can modify fate. Maecenas did not, it seems, accept the view that identities of horoscope meant that he and Horace would die together, for he recommended his friend to Augustus on his deathbed. Horace, however, did die less than two months later, on 27 November 8 B.C.[36]

Propertius, dead by 16 B.C., was more of a fatalist. He upholds astrology and jeers at all other methods of divination. An elegy written near his end is astrologic. An astrologer speaks:

> I'll give you certain proofs, or I'm no seer,
> unskilled to show stars spun in a bronze sphere.
> I'm Horos; my father was Oropos, Babylonian,
> son of Archytas. Our family comes from Konon . . .
> The gods attest I've not disgraced my race
> and in my writings nothing's preferred to truth.[37]

Others turn the gods to profit and use Jupiter as they cheat for gold; the truth lies in the Zodiac. Finally the astrologer warns the poet: "Dread the ominous back of the eight-legged Crab"—that is, avoid an avaricious woman like Cynthia born under the Crab.

Ovid had Arellius Fuscus for professor of oratory, but he knew astrology. In his *Ibis* he writes:

> You are born of ill-omen. So the gods willed. No star
> was favouring or propitious at your birth.
> Venus did not shine that hour, nor Jupiter.
> Neither Sun nor Moon were in an auspicious place,
> and the Son that lovely Maia bore great Jove
> lent you no rays with kindly influence.
> You're crusht by the star of Mars presaging still
> only things ruthless, never things of peace,
> and by the star of the Old Man with the scythe.
> To darken all things, your days of birth began
> with filthy weather, a glooming bed of clouds.[38]

His *Metamorphoses* have a Pythagorean background; we could use them to fill out the picture of Virgil and Manilius from his

more independent angle. And as we shall see, he may himself have
dabbled in predictions.

A court poet wrote verses of Consolation to Livia when
Augustus' stepson Drusus died in 9 B.C.; he declared that the
skies mourned with her, Lucifer left his course and did not rise on
the day after the death. Venus (Julian ancestress) also mourned.
An educated person was expected to have a good smattering of
astrology. It has been estimated that apart from directly astral
works there are 132 references to the planet Venus, 170 to the Big
and Little Dipper, in poems between Plautus and Claudian. In
this relation we may cite the poem *Aetna* (of uncertain date, but of
the early Empire, before A.D. 63) with its call for the study "of the
colossal work of Artist Nature":

> . . . to know the Sun's track-bounds; how much lesser the moon's
>   orbit
> (flying through twelve rounds in her shorter course,
> while he has a year's path): to know which stars are constant
> in order, which stray from their gyre in irregular ways;
> to know the Zodiac changes, their immemorial laws
> [six sped by night, as many returning with dawn]:
> to know lowering Phatne warning from heaven of rain,
> why the Moon-goddess reddens, her brother reveals pallid fires,
> why the year's seasons vary, why Spring its first youth
> dies into Summer, why Summer itself grows old,
> why Winter on Autumn creeps, coming back in the cycle:
> to know Helike's axle, discern the ill-omened Comet,
> on which side gleams Dawnstar, and Duskstar, and Bearward,
> which Star is of steadfast Saturn or warrior Mars,
> under which groups the sailor must furl or outspread
> his sails: to know the sea-paths, the heavenly courses,
> where Orion hurries, where ominous Dogstar broods:
> in short, to refuse to allow all the various marvels
> of the mighty universe remain unordered,
> buried in a heap of things, but arrange them clearly,
> each marked in its proper place. All is indeed
> the divine and grateful pleasure of the mind.

Phatne is the Manger constellation, which Aratos links with storm;
Helice is the Great Bear. This poem is not without intellectual
force, and, with the better side of Manilius' work, brings out the
positive side of the interest in astrology under the Principate. Its
author also, however, cannot help projecting on to the universe the
social system in which he is imbedded. He says of Fire: "In itself it

lacks motive force. Where Spirit is commander, it obeys. Spirit is *Princeps*. Fire serves in the army of this great General."[39]

The way in which astrology had penetrated into court-culture is shown, not only by the work of Virgil and Manilius, but by the fact that a prince, Germanicus, made a version of the poem by Aratos. The name Hyginus is attached to a work generally called *Poetica Astronomica,* which is based on some Greek work making use of Eratosthenes, a commentary on Aratos, and a star-map. We have only excerpts, but the compilation seems certainly of the second century A.D. and cannot be the work of the learned Spaniard, G. Iulius Hyginus, who became librarian on the Palatine and who tried to follow in Varro's steps as a universalist, writing on agriculture, bees, history, geography, and antiquarian matters. His *On the Gods' Characteristics* included the stars among the deities to be worshipped and declared that birds were the right victims for them, presumably as winged aerial creatures and perhaps because they brought messages or signs from the gods.[40]

P. Vitruvius Pollio, another Augustan, wrote on architecture and built the basilica at Fanum. It is significant that while taking architecture as his theme he felt it necessary to cover also astronomy, meteorology, and time-measurements. He used *astrologia* to cover all star-matters, drew on many Greek sources, and accepted the Mesopotamian origins of Astrology.[41] Agrippa built the Pantheon, which he dedicated in 15 B.C.; this building must from the outset have had cosmic conceptions as its basis, though the present roof and most of the walls date from the reconstruction by Hadrian, to whom are due the seven niches for the seven planetary deities, the central opening, and the vault-decorations. Of Hadrian's edifice Cassius Dion wrote, "My own opinion of the name is that because of its vaulted roof it resembles the heavens."[42] At the apex a window (9 metres across) opened into the sky, an *oculus* or eye looking up straight into the blue of heaven or the starry night, and making the building change its lights and shadows, its moods, every hour of the day. "Just as the use of the two circles of equal diameter for plan and elevation seems like the revival of the old Pythagorean worship of numbers, so does this almost literal pantheism reveal Hadrian's attitude towards religion—a half intellectual, half aesthetic yearning for the vastness and the everlasting, everchanging life of the heavens" (Hanfmann). There may well however have been astrologic elements already in Agrippa's conception; for we know he put in his temple the statues of Divus Julius with starred head, Mars Ultor and Venus Genetrix: the last two being planets as well as gods. The trio thus in a sense represented the astral forces predicting, protecting or expressing Augustus. But there was nothing horologic in these associations.

Among the astrologers who came into conflict with the government about the time of Actium was Anaxilaos of Larissa, exiled in 29–28 and perhaps expelled from Rome in 33. Jerome calls him Pythagorean and Mage, and he seems also to have been an alchemist. Larissa was in Thessaly, an area famed for witchcraft, as we learn from the opening of *The Golden Ass*. But the considered and lasting basis on which actions against astrologers were taken was the edict of A.D. 11 brought in when Drusus was quaestor. The development of an imperial system under a single ruler, whatever the pretences and the forms used, meant that treason laws must change and be tightened up. The crime of Literary Treason seems introduced about A.D. 8; offending works were burned. In serious cases the author was exiled, though the only known Augustan case was that of Cassius Severus. He wrote satirical verses and attracted attention by accusing a friend of Augustus, Nonius Asprenas, of poisoning; Augustus in his last days exiled him to Crete for his poems. He went on writing and under Tiberius was removed to the desert island of Seriphos. Caligula permitted his proscribed works to be read again.[43] Under Tiberius came death for literary traitors. The first case seems that of G. Luterius Priscus. He had been well paid by Tiberius for a poem on Germanicus' death; when the emperor's own son Drusus fell ill, he anticipated his death by writing an elegy, which he recited in a private house before some ladies. The Senate seems to have taken this act as semi-magical, liable to bring about the event it foresaw; they condemned Priscus to instant execution. Tiberius, annoyed, caused a decree to be passed that ten days should elapse between a senatorial decree and its carry-out.[44] But in A.D. 23 Aelius Saturninus, under a charge of literary treason, was killed with the emperor's consent.

Dion gives a summary of the edict of A.D. 11. "It was forbidden for diviners [*manteis*] to prophesy to anyone alone or to prophesy death even when others were present." Astrologers were no doubt the main *manteis* aimed at; Dion's text states that Augustus in an edict revealed his own horoscope and thus his (astrologic) death-date. Rumours of his death in A.D. 11 had been strengthened by the advent of a comet and other portents linked with the loss of three legions in Germany; by publishing the horoscope he hoped to show that his death was not near. In A.D. 14, says Dion, his death was in fact foretold by a sun-eclipse, fire and embers falling from the sky, and a comet of ill omen.[45]

The danger of death-prophecies was that they stirred up slaves, wives, husbands, heirs and enemies who, on finding the stars too slow in action, were stimulated to make the predictions come true; in the case of an emperor they might raise the hopes of heirs or pretenders to the throne. The prohibitions against astrologers remained in force until the fourth century, but were hard to apply. Tiberius reminded the *haruspices* that they too must abide by the law; he further clarified the question as to whose *salus* or safety was being queried. To inquire about the emperor and his house was still severely punished four hundred years later.[46] Slaves who inquired about their masters were harshly treated; but what the law was mainly concerned about was the political motive. Most evidence at trials was given by the secret police. Yet, while it was true that astrology could have an unsettling effect on many ambitious people, the dread that rulers felt at any probing into their stars had a strong element of plain superstition: as if the act itself somehow created instability, unrest, sapping their power at its secret source.

Ancient police systems were never very effective. Rome at this time had a fire-fighting and police corps of about 7,000 freedmen. Hellenistic cities like Alexandreia and Pergamon had long had their police, and the Latin West now developed municipal systems, which took over what had long been a senatorial matter. But offences such as those created by the A.D. 11 edict were too complex for *municipia* to handle. A considerable body of secret police grew up, *curiosi* or *speculatores,* at first soldiers or officers in mufti. After Caesar's death their number and importance had already increased and with the empire they became a settled institution of much importance, rarely written about but providing an element of fear and insecurity in social life, from which no one was exempt. Epiktetos in his fearless way is one of the few writers who admits this fact.

When someone appears to us to chat frankly on his own affairs, we are in some way induced to expose our secrets to him ... Thus it is that the thoughtless are caught by the secret agents in Rome. A secret police-agent sits by you and begins to speak ill of the emperor. Then, as if you'd been given a pledge of his fidelity by his starting off the abuse, you say likewise what you think. And so you are led away in chains to execution.[47]

The historians mention only the big trials; but there must have been hosts of lesser folk trapped, as Epiktetos describes, by some rash outburst of indignation. Most astrologers would be obscure men. Unless they were entangled in an upper-class scandal, we should not hear of them.

In art as well as literature there was astrologic propaganda for the imperial idea. Thus, the Great Cameo of Paris seems to show the star-assumption of Germanicus, who is going up to rejoin the Divus Augustus. His Triumph in Germany is transformed into an astral exaltation. His birthday in fact became an important festival, *Natalis Germanici*; we find it still set down for 24 May in the *Feriale Duranum*, the army-calendar used at Doura on the Euphrates in the mid-third century.[48] Ovid had attached himself to the prince, and it is possible that the fault which earned him exile on the Black Sea was an act of divination connected with Germanicus. Augustus interpreted the act as a consultation on the *salus* of the prince or his near relations. Germanicus was certainly much interested in astrology, as his translation of Aratos shows; and in the East in A.D. 18 he may well have come to know many mages and astrologers.[49]

A sidelight on Ovid's links with both the prince and with magic is perhaps shown by the Suilli. P. Suillius Rufus, quaestor of Germanicus in 15 (perhaps again in 18), married Vestilia who under Tiberius asked for the right to prostitute herself. Plinius has some odd remarks on the abnormal lengths of her gestations.[50] She bore Suillius a son of the same name; and Suillius, after separating from her, married Ovid's stepdaughter, the girl borne by his third wife in a previous marriage. About 15, Ovid in Tomi wrote an elegy to Suillius begging him to intercede with Germanicus on his behalf. It follows that Suillius was on close terms with the prince; and he appears to have been of the neo-Pythagorean school founded by Nigidius. In 24 he was banished by Tiberius for what seems a money scandal, but was recalled by Caligula. (He may have been related to the empress, Caesonia, as we hear of a Suillius Caesonius). Under Claudius he became a wretched informer. Later, another Suillius, apparently a son of Ovid's stepdaughter, turns up as a flatterer of Nero, with a *cognomen* Nerullinus showing how he had been taken to the imperial bosom. Nero sacrificed the informer father to the Senate, but saved the son.[51] In the second century Athenagoras speaks of pagans in Asia Minor concerned with healing-oracles in the Troad and a magical statue of a hero Neroullinos. The name here may have been that taken by some prophet-agitator in the East cashing in on Nero's Eastern popularity; but it may also well be that of our Nerullinus or of one of his descendants—we know of at least one proconsul of the family in Asia: M. Suillius Nerullinus appears on coins of Smyrna under Vespasian. These are all only suggestive points, but they have a certain accumulative force.[52]

To return to Germanicus: at his death an Arch was raised on Mt. Amanos in Syria as well as a cenotaph at Antioch where he was burned, and a tribunal at Daphne where he breathed his last. Such monuments helped to keep his memory alive in a semi-orientalised army. Certain eastern kinglets cut their hair when he died, and shaved their wives' heads; the Persian king abstained from hunting or receiving the great nobles at his table.[53] On the Great Cameo we see Aquarius (as Ganymede) holding the globe in front of Divus Augustus, while Germanicus rides a winged horse whom we may call a Pegasos. In Aratos the name of the constellation is merely Horse, but the Latin scholiast says, "Some indeed think him Pegasus, who flew up to the stars after Beller-ophon's death." Here is an Eastern connection; for Pegasos appeared on coins of the great Mithridates and was taken over by the kings of Cappadocia with the name of Ariarthes. On imperial coins up until the time of Hadrian the sign seems to refer to a pact with the Parthian king. Could the constellation Horse-Pegasos have played a part in Germanicus' horoscope?[54]

The globe has been seen as an offering to the Rider as *kosmo-krator*, universe-lord: a detail with political significance but also perhaps meant as a compliment to the prince's astrologic knowledge. And the offerer? His oriental clothes—*anaxyrides* and bonnet—have attracted the epithet of Chaldean. But it would be odd to show a mere human flying in the sky amid such divine figures, and the clothes seem Phrygian rather than Chaldean. Chaldean suggests heavy garments and a high headgear. Later Alexandrian coins, under the Antonines, show Aquarius in much the same garb; he wears a semi-oriental dress through being merged with Ganymede, rapt to the sky to pour liquor for Zeus.

Here however a globe supplants the water-urn, and perhaps stands for *chronokratia* or time-control. We find Aquarius holding a globe on Augustan coins; and the Horse can be taken as one of his *paranatellonta*, one of the constellations whose heliacal rising seems to accompany that of the zodiacal sign. A scholiast on Germanicus' poem says, "When Aquarius rises, there set the horse-part of the Centaur, the head of Hydra, but Pegasus rises." The areas under Aquarius' influence were Syria, Germany, Sarmatia, in the Latin list of Hermes; only Syria in that of Paul of Alexandreia. Germanicus had strong links with both Germany and Syria.[55]

Germanicus was born on 24 May, while Aquarius reigns from 15 January to 15 February. But, as we saw in connection with Augustus and Tiberius, the sign allotted to an emperor at this period seems to have been worked out using some complex system. In the year's calendar Aquarius follows Capricorn, who reigns over the Vienna Cameo between the head of Augustus and that of Roma, but is missing on the Paris Cameo where the Scorpion appears on a shield of the lower register. In the latter design the astrologic conception may be taken to centre on Germanicus, its main theme. His father Drusus hardly makes a probable competitor for the scheme; the court-poem already mentioned seems to make the Morning Star (Venus) his planetary connection. The theme of the Dawn leads on to Nero.[56] We may note however that the Aquarius-figure has been taken for Alexander the Great; and though this is more than unlikely, it is relevant that in the *Alexander Romance* he is given a birth-theme halfway between Aquarius and the Fish—the theme of a *kosmokrator*. Here we seem to meet an Egyptian idea, as shown by the role that Nektanebos plays in the story.[57]

$I4$

Tiberius and Gaius

With Tiberius the court-astrologer fully emerges. The man was
Thrasyllus and Tiberius met him when in retirement on Rhodes.
Suetonius tells a story of those early days in a chapter devoted to
the omens predicting the future greatness of Tiberius: altars
lighting themselves, an eagle perching on his house at Rhodes, a
tunic seeming to be on fire:

He then also had a remarkable proof of the skill of Thrasyllus the
astrologer, whom, for his proficiency in philosophical researches, he had
taken into his household. For, on sight of the ship bringing intelligence
(Tiberius' recall to Rome), he said that good news was coming. Yet
everything had gone wrong before and quite contrary to his predictions.
Tiberius had meant at that very moment to throw him into the sea as a
charlatan and as a man to whom he had too readily entrusted his secrets.[1]

This is obviously a folk-tale. Recall the story of Thales regarding the
stars and falling into a cistern. Alexander in the *Romance* kills his
astrologer-father Nektanebos:

And when it was night, he took the child out of the city and looked up
into the sky and showed Alexander the stars. And Alexander seized him
and took and threw him down into a pit. And he suffered severe blows
on the neck in falling, and he said, "Alexander my child, why did you
want to do that?"
    And he replied, "Blame yourself, astrologer."
    And he asked, "Why?"
    "For," he replied, "while not knowing the earth, you seek to study
the affairs of the heavens."
    And he said, "I am dying, Alexander, for I suffered grievous harm in
falling. But nothing and no man can conquer fate."[2]

Tacitus in his account of Thrasyllus brings out the full force of
the folk-tale, which is muffled by Suetonius:

Whenever he chose to consult an astrologer, he retired with him to the top of the house, attended by a single freedman chosen for the purpose, illiterate but of great strength. This man led the prophet, whose talents were to be tried, along the cliff-ridge on which the mansion stood; and as he returned, if his master suspected fraud or a vain pretence of knowledge, he threw the impostor headlong into the sea. Tiberius was thus left at ease with no witness to tell tales. Thrasyllus was put to the same test. Led along the cliff, he answered a number of questions. Not only did he promise imperial splendour to Tiberius but opened up a vista of the future in a way that filled his imagination with astonishment. Tiberius asked if he had cast his own nativity: could he foresee what was to happen in the course of the year? on that very day?

Thrasyllus consulted the position of the heavens and the aspect of the planets. Stricken with fear, he paused, hesitated, sank into meditation, was shaken with fear and amazement. Breaking silence at last, he said, "I see the crisis of my fate. This very moment may be my last."

Tiberius clasped him with congratulations on his knowledge and on his escape from danger. After that he considered Thrasyllus' predictions as the oracles of truth and the astrologer was ranked among his confidential friends.

Tacitus then digresses on fatalistic astrology, on the possibility of an immutable law of fate being consistent with the events of moral law. "So law does not depend on the course of wandering planets but is fixed in the first principles of things, supported and sustained by a chain of natural causes. Man all the same is left at liberty to choose his sphere of action; but once the choice is made, the consequences follow in a regular course, fixed, certain, inevitable." Also, "Indeed the colour of our existence is settled in the first moment of our life." He considers that the fallacy of astrology does not lie in the art itself but in the vanity of its pretenders. Now and then in his own times there is proof of the astrologer's powers. "In fact the reign of Nero was foretold by the son of this very Thrasyllus."

Rhodes was a leading academic centre at this time. Cicero and Caesar had been there in Poseidonios' time. Thrasyllus was a grammarian by profession, though interested in astrology and numerology. Tiberius had arrived there in 6 B.C., rather in disgrace. Many Roman travellers ignored him; and he was grateful for those who then paid him attention. He recalled, for instance, how an official, Quirinus, had called on him.[3] On returning to Rome he took Thrasyllus with him and they remained friendly for the rest of his life. Suetonius tells us an anecdote of the astrologer during Augustus' life; here he appears as complaisant grammarian rather than diviner.

Augustus called an island near Capri as Apragopolis [No-Business-Town] from the lazy life led by several of his party there. A favourite of his, Masgabas [apparently of African origin], he used to call Ktisis [Founder] as if he had been the planter of the island. And noting from his room a large number of people gathered with torches at the tomb of this Masgabas, who had died the year before, he spoke very distinctly this extempore verse [in Greek]: "Blazing with light I see the Founder's Tomb."

Then, turning to Thrasyllus, a companion of Tiberius, who reclined on the other side of the table, he asked him, who knew nothing of the matter, what poet he thought the author of the line. When Thrasyllus hesitated, he added another, "Honoured with torches you behold Masgabas." And put the same question. Thrasyllus answered that whoever the poet was he wrote excellent verses. Augustus set up a great laugh and fell into an extraordinary vein of jesting about it.[4]

When in A.D. 14 Tiberius became emperor, Thrasyllus was in a powerful position. His daughter married the *eques*, L. Ennius, about A.D. 15; for her daughter Ennia Thrasylla was herself married some fifteen years later. Ennius was brought before the Senate in 22 on a *maiestas* charge, accused of melting down a statue of Tiberius and using the material for household purposes.[5] Tiberius stopped the case. Ateius Capito uttered a servile warning that such clemency would encourage malcontents. The charge against Ennius may have been the work of a group jealous of Thrasyllus' court-role.

In the summer of 16 came the case of Scribonius Libo, a spend-thrift whom Tiberius had let become praetor. Tacitus, as an anti-Tiberian, depicts him as a giddy-headed fellow, half-innocent, entangled in ambiguous tactics; Seneca accepts the charge of treason. Tacitus says he was charged with planning a coup; Suetonius speaks of a plot; Dion says, "He apparently planned a coup." What he seems to have done was to seek "the promises of the Chaldeans, the rites of the sorcerers, as well as dream-interpreters", at the suggestion of an agent, Firmus Catus.[6] One question he asked of the diviners was: "Would he ever be rich enough to pave with money the Appian Way from Rome to Brundusium?" The chief of the four accusers, Vibius Serenus, began by arguing that the Augustan Edict was violated. Tiberius wanted proof of *perduellio* if he were to apply the Lex Julia in all its rigour. The accusers alleged that

Libo had made "frightful and secret" entries behind the names of the Caesars and certain senators. Libo denied that the notebook with the entries was his. But among the first informers against him was a necromancer named Junius, who testified that he'd been asked to use magic on Libo's behalf. Libo did not wait for the verdict, but killed himself. He was then convicted after death and his property divided up, though Tiberius vetoed a senatorial damnation. The date of the plot, 13 September, was to be put in the *Fasti* as a day of deliverance to be remembered for evermore. But it is hard to take Libo at all seriously.[7]

Two men, astrologers or sorcerers or both, seem connected with the Libo case. The Senate rapidly passed two decrees against astrologers and other diviners after the trial, and L. Pituanius and P. Marcius were arrested. "The first was hurled headlong from the Tarpeian Rock," says Tacitus, and the "latter, on the consuls' order, was executed, at the sound of the trumpet, outside the Esqueline Gate, according to the form prescribed by ancient usage." Suetonius tells us that the custom was to strip the criminal naked and then lash him to death, with his head fastened in a forked stake. We see the sort of thing that happened to astrologers of humbler status who attracted the attention of the authorities.[8]

The position of Thrasyllus was not affected. Dion says that Tiberius "was forever in his company and daily made use of his divinatory art, *manteia*, growing himself so skilled in it that when he was once bidden in a dream to give money to a certain man, he realised a daimon had been cheatingly called up before him, and put the man to death".[9] The theme of the friendship between emperor and astrologer became a classroom topic. Julian, accepting the tales of Tiberian cruelty, comments, "Thrasyllus by becoming intimate with the harsh and naturally pitiless tyrant Tiberius would have incurred indelible disgrace for all time had he not cleared himself in the writings he left behind and thus shown his true character." The account by modern scholars of his marriage with Aka, princess of Kommagene, is due to a misread inscription and and incorrect idea of his relation to the later astrologer Balbillus.[10]

He wrote on astrology. Valens used his work, and Porphyrios refers to a controversy waged by Apollinarios and Ptolemaios against their predecessors Thrasyllus and Petosiris. Hephaistion knew his work; and we have an epitome of one of his treatises, the *Pinax*, dedicated to Hierokles, perhaps another astrologer. In it he cited Petosiris, Nechepso and Hermes. But in his neo-Pythagorean aspects he wrote a work on Numerology, which continued to be much used; we saw one of its tables earlier. Perhaps he and not Thrasyllus of Mendes wrote a book on the Properties of Stones, since, as we noted, such matters interested astrologers. We have a reference to a work of his on the Seven Stones; Porphyrios, in the third century still thought of him as an authority on Pythagoreanism. He was certainly a considerable scholar. With Derkyllides he published the edition of Plato that became the standard arrangement of the dialogues in tetralogical form, which has come down to us. He also edited a complete Collection of the Works of Demokritos.[11]

To return to the trials. We know of five under Tiberius and in the first eight years of Claudius. The accused were tried before the Senate as a sort of supreme court, with the emperor (if in Rome) presiding. The A.D. 11 edict was expanded to make its violations treason involving the *salus* of the emperor, and then of any members of his family. At first a certain sense of shame made men feel it was necessary to throw in more traditional charges such as that of conspiracy to overthrow the State, adultery, or fraud; and then the edict came in for a final blow. Originally *maiestas* was an attribute of the gods, but the State had claimed the same sanctity during the period of war-expansion against Carthage, and that of empire-building. Under the Republic and the larger part of Augustus' reign, only action against the State provided a basis for a *maiestas*-prosecution.[12] But the last century B.C. with its violent party-strife had seen a fusion of actions for *Minutae Maiestatis* (Impaired Majesty) and those for *Perduellio* (High Treason) into a single *Maiestas*-indictment. Prosecution was then before a public assembly, the Comitia. But the Comitia were abolished in A.D. 14 and nobles were henceforth tried before the Senate. For high treason the penalty was death. The emperor might grant a noble the choice of suicide instead of execution; at times the wife joined her husband. The accused might of his own accord kill himself before conviction in the hope of saving his property for the heirs; but there was no guarantee that he would succeed. A formal *damnatio memoriae* automatically ensured confiscation of the entire estate. In the early Principate, however, most *maiestas*-cases seem of the second degree, not for *perduellio*.[13]

There were no public prosecutors. As in private lawsuits, private persons prosecuted; but there was inevitably much imperial intervention and control. The accused might be forced to sell his slaves so that they would lose the position of being legally unable to testify against their master and as State-slaves, would be liable to the rack. (Tacitus says that Tiberius first used this trick, but it certainly went back to Augustus.) The emperor at need might quash a case or give orders for the accused to be found guilty. There was no lack of informers, men seeking for political advancement or financial gain. Charge was piled on charge to make conviction as sure as possible; and even if a man were acquitted, his reputation was blasted. An informer who lost his case could be charged with *calumnia*, and sentenced to exile of one kind or another if found guilty, but probably few men wanted to reopen an unpleasant case.[14]

Late in the summer of 20, Aemilia Lepida, a highborn matron, was accused of astrologic consultations, with charges of adultery and fraud, *falsum*, thrown in, plus an accusation of trying to poison a former husband. She was of suspiciously high status. Sulla and Pompeius were among her ancestors; her grandfather was Lepidus the Triumvir; Augustus at one time had betrothed her to his grandson though he dissolved the betrothal before the young man died. In A.D. 4 she married an elderly general, P. Sulpicius Quirinus. Suetonius says that Tiberius had her charged to gratify Quirinus who was very rich and childless and who, after divorcing her twenty years before, accused her of an old design to poison him. Tacitus says that she had also married (and perhaps was now divorced from) Mamercus Aemilius Scaurus, to whom she bore a daughter. She must now have been in her late thirties. The statement that Tiberius was after her huge fortune is ridiculous; after the trial he let it go to the second husband. Also, he quashed the indictment of conspiracy "through astrologers against the House of Caesar". He did not even have her slaves racked.[15]

Was she really ambitious? Germanicus had died in 19 and the question of the succession was in the air. Lepida could hope to rise only through some man. She is hardly likely to have been thinking of her brother Manius Lepidus, though he was allowed to defend her before the Senate, with Tiberius presiding. Her second husband Scaurus does not seem to have been driven by ambition, though we shall see him wrecked by a *maiestas* charge fourteen years later. She might have hoped to remarry, perhaps into the imperial family. Convicted of adultery and perhaps *falsum*, she was exiled. Her case seems the first based solely on the A.D. 11 edict.[16]

If we turn to the general political field, we find Drusus sent to quell three revolting legions soon after Tiberius' accession; a moon-eclipse terrified the soldiers, who beat bronze instruments and blew trumpets. "Religious panic spread through the army," says Tacitus, "the appearance of the heavens foretold eternal labour to the legions." Drusus took advantage of the men's demoralised condition to draw them back to allegiance. In A.D. 19 Germanicus died, his death probably hastened by fear of magical practices. That year saw unrest through a Sibylline prophecy; Tiberius expelled all Jews who would not renounce their cult; some four thousand went to Sardinian quarries. And there was an Isiac scandal which is said to have led to the destruction of Isis' Temple; a man had bribed the high priest to convince a woman that the god Anubis desired her, took the god's part himself, and then was imprudent enough to boast of his ruse.[17]

In 26 or 27, Claudia Pulchra, widow of the Varus who lost the legions in Germany, was charged with *impudicia,* adultery, and *maiestas*: she had tried to poison the emperor and use magic, *devotiones.* Demetrius Afer, who accused her, gained the hatred of Agrippina's youngest son Gaius, who, as emperor thirteen years later, had him tried for *maiestas.* The Claudia case is said to have started off the feud between the Claudians and Julians: Tiberius and his grandson on one side, and Agrippina (Claudia's close friend) and her children on the other. Claudia and her latest lover were found guilty of adultery; the treason aspects of the charge do not seem to have been taken seriously.

Next comes Scaurus. He had been a member of the Sejanus-faction at court. Livilla secretly poisoned her husband Drusus, son of Tiberius, in order to marry Sejanus but Tiberius forbade the marriage. The passion of the guilty pair lessened and Livilla took other lovers, Scaurus among them. In 34 two men accused him of partaking of rites of the Mages and of adultery with Livilla (now dead about three years). He and his wife committed suicide. The Mages may well have been astrologers.[18]

Drusus had disliked both his father's favourites, Thrasyllus and the praetorian prefect Sejanus: which fact brought the two men together. Thrasyllus, however, seems too wary to have become involved closely in any of Sejanus' schemes. In 29 the latter rigged the trial of Agrippina and her son Nero for treason, and they were deported to the islands. About 29–30 Ennia, the granddaughter of Thrasyllus, married a young Roman *eques*, Naevius

Sutorius Macro, who played a key-part in bringing Sejanus down. He is said to have started the latter's decline by citing lines from his play *Atreus*, which advised subjects to bear with patience the folly of princes. Finally he was the man who left from Capri with Tiberius' secret instructions that destroyed Sejanus, and was himself appointed to the vacant post of praetorian prefect. He handled the critical situation at Rome with skill and for the last five and a half years of Tiberius' life he wielded the power which had belonged to Sejanus. Ennia was one of the most influential court-ladies, but Macro did not aspire to more power than he had gained.[19]

Thrasyllus seems to have been backing the claims of Gaius, the youngest son of Agrippina (who had starved herself to death in exile). In any event Ennia decided to seduce the prince. An episode, reported by Suetonius, shows Thrasyllus in an ambiguous relation to Gaius:

"When I was a boy, I heard my grandfather say that the reason assigned by some courtiers" for Gaius as emperor making a bridge of some 3½ miles long from Baiae to the Mole of Puteoli "was that when Tiberius was in some anxiety about the nomination of a successor, and rather inclined to pitch on his grandson, Thrasyllus the astrologer once assured him: Gaius would no more be emperor than he'd ride on horseback across the gulf of Baiae." On the face of it, this is a belittling remark; but we do not know the full circumstances. Thrasyllus may have meant to soothe Tiberius and lessen his distrust of Gaius. Tiberius in fact had meant to exclude him from the succession, but changed his mind.

Clearly the building of the bridge of boats, across which Gaius crossed and recrossed for two days, had some deep symbolic value for him. The first day, riding a richly-caparisoned horse, he wore a crown of oak leaves and a cloak of cloth-of-gold; he carried a battle-axe, a Spanish buckler, and a sword. The second day, he drove a two-horsed chariot, attended by a young Parthian hostage named Dareios. He seems to be making a solar and world-conqueror masquerade. Suetonius says that most people thought he was imitating Xerxes with his bridge across the Hellespont, or that he wanted to strike terror into Germany and Britain, which he meant to invade. The boy Dareios suggests that he may also have been thinking of himself as Alexander the Great on the Granikos.[20] We can perhaps connect the episode also with his behaviour in the northern wars. He "presented the companions and sharers of his victory with crowns of a new form, with a new name, having Sun, Moon and Stars depicted on them, and which he called *Exploratoriae*". On the Atlantic coast he drew up his engines of war (as if meaning to attack the Ocean) and bade his men fill their helmets and clothes with shells as "the spoils of Ocean due to the Capitol and the Palatium".[21] Perhaps the image of world-conqueror and ocean-tamer was for him merged with that of Aquarius. From Manilius to Maternus, that was taken as a very favourable sign— though all depended on the degree of the dekans observed in the horoscope, the opposition of planets in relation to the sign, and so on. Generally those born under it could easily become masters of hydraulic matters. For Manilius it gave the power of "discovering waters underground", of "sprinkling the stars with drawn-up waters" (waterspout or bore), or of "deceiving the sea by creating in luxury new shores". The last point would suit Nero, a great builder of ports and canals, rather than Gaius; but the latter was an Egyptianiser and Aquarius was important in Egypt with its Nilotic cults.[22]

Suetonius, telling of various omens that picked out Galba, says that Augustus pinched his cheek as a child, saying, "And you too, child, will taste our imperial dignity," while Tiberius, when told that Galba would become emperor, but at an advanced age, remarked, "Let him live then, since it doesn't concern me." Who was involved in his horoscope, we do not know.[23] Tacitus declares that the last years of Tiberius saw many *maiestas*-trials, a continual slaughter. Suetonius makes Thrasyllus play an honourable role in these matters: "Had not death prevented him, and Thrasyllus, designedly as some say, prevailed with him to defer some of his cruelties in hopes of longer life, it is thought that he would have destroyed many more, and not have spared even the rest of his grandchildren; for he was jealous of Gaius and hated Tiberius as having been conceived in adultery."[24]

Ennia often visited Capri; and on one of her visits she began her affair with Gaius, the last surviving male of the house of Germanicus. The sources, guessing as usual, contradict one another, stating that the liaison was all her own work or that she was acting at her husband's suggestion. Thrasyllus was said to have correctly forecast his own death at the moment when his house's fortunes were at their zenith. He died a year before his master; and his death seems to have been a blow to the ailing Tiberius, who died on 6 March 37.[25] Ennia played a vital part in gaining the throne for

Gaius, using her influence with her husband to have him proclaimed sole emperor. (Tiberius had divided his estate between
Gaius and Tib. Gemellus.) Philon says that Macro was thought
"to have contributed more than anyone else" to Gaius' accession;
he had praised him "vociferously" when Tiberius spoke of him
as the Julian enemy of the Claudian line.[26] All the while Ennia
urged Macro to support Gaius "for an unmentionable reason",
and behaved more affectionately than ever to Macro to hide her
infidelity. Suetonius also recognises Macro's important role, and
Tacitus adds that Tiberius "taunted Macro in no obscure terms
with forsaking the setting and looking to the rising sun".[27] Dion
makes Macro bid his wife seduce the prince "and bind him by an
engagement to marriage. And the lad, as long as it helped him to
the throne, shrank from no conditions. For though of an excitable
temper, he had thoroughly learned the masks of hypocrisy under
his grandfather's loving care."

However that may be, Macro broke down all opposition and soon
afterwards Gemellus died. But he had succeeded all too well, and
Gaius was now afraid of him. Macro imagined he still had to deal
with a docile lad; but Gaius complained bitterly of him as a
disciplinarian, of being made to feel belittled by his presence. He
played Macro off against a friend, Flavius Avillius, prefect of
Egypt (who had tried to win Macro to support Gemellus), and
suddenly condemned Macro, Ennia, and their children. Philon
says that Macro had to kill himself. Believing that Ennia had won
Gaius by a love-magic, he commented, "There seems no love-
potion that works forever."[28] That year Gaius married Lollia
Paulina.

In his reign there was much conflict between the Alexandrian
Greeks and Jews. An Apollonios was arrested in Alexandreia
for prophesying "in his native land the actual fate of Gaius". He
was sent to Rome "and brought before the emperor on the very
day", says Dion, when the latter was destined to die. His punishment was postponed till a little later, and his life was saved.
Apollonios may have been a Roman citizen who appealed, or the
prefect maybe thought his case of enough importance to go to Rome
—in the hope, perhaps, that he'd implicate high persons. According
to Dion, Gaius tried him on 24 January 41, but was in a hurry to
attend the Palatine Games. Claudius pardoned Apollonios.
Suetonius also tells us that "Sulla the astrologer, consulted by
Gaius on his nativity, assured him that death would speedily and

unavoidably overtake him"—not a very plausible tale; nor is it likely that Sulla was an error for Thrasyllus (the son) or for Balbillus, of whom we shall soon hear more.[29]

Summing up this period, then, we may say that together with the systematic persecution of astrologers who in any way touched on imperial politics, there came the elevation of an astrologer to a position of unofficial but considerable power. Thrasyllus was probably of Alexandreia, or had at least studied there, and his skill as a grammarian, shown by his important editions of Plato and Demokritos, plus his Egyptian type of astrology, strongly suggests that. Despite his role as a close friend and adviser of Tiberius, he seems to have had no political ambitions or policy: his interests were those of a scholar. But with his grand-daughter things were very different. She unscrupulously used the family-position to make a bid for power, and wrecked herself and her husband in the process. What happened to the son of Thrasyllus we do not know; but he seems to have survived Ennia's disaster.

We may cite here the few horoscopes in Greek up to A.D. 40. First comes one from 21 January —71 (B.C.), extant in two versions. It is an excerpt from Balbillus on the "method concerning the length of life from starter to destroyer", and deals with technical details. The second, probably dated 27 December —42, treats a life of 70 years, and is from the same source. The third is of 14 August —9; only a few lines of it survive. The fourth is of 2 October —3, and ends: "There are dangers. Take care for 40 days because of Mars." These two were on papyri from Egypt, as is the fifth, which, dated under Tiberius, includes a rough circular diagram and is addressed to "dear Tryphon". The sixth is of 26 May A.D. 32 and has an Homeric verse on the other side. The seventh, from Valens, seems of 15 December A.D. 37. We get no personal details from these; but an eighth, preserved by Hephaistion from Antigonos, is of much interest as it apparent deals with the father of the emperor Hadrian; we shall deal with it when we come to Hadrian's reign.[30]

15

Claudius and Nero

Claudius was much interested in antiquarian subjects. In 41 an embassy came from Alexandreia to inform him of honours voted on his accession and to gain support against the Jews. A papyrus gives a list of the leaders:

Tiberius Claudius Caesar Augustus Germanicus Imperator, Pontifex Maximus, Holder of the Tribunician Power, Consul Designate, to the City of Alexandreia, Greetings. Tiberius Claudius Barbillus . . . Chairemon son of Leonidas . . . Tiberius Claudius Archibios . . . your ambassadors discoursed at length about the City . . . Of the two Golden Statues, the one . . . as my most honoured Barbillus suggested and entreated . . . shall be erected in Rome . . .[1]

Claudius warned them to stop rioting against the Jews, but added that he would in turn warn the Jews not to ask for more than their old privileges. He ended, "I bear witness to my friend Barbillus of the solicitude which he has always shown for you in my presence and of the extreme zeal with which he has now advocated your cause. . . . Farewell." The date was 10 November 41. Barbillus was a Greek misspelling of Balbillus. The man in question was the second astrologer to win high imperial favour.

How he and Claudius had become acquainted, we do not know. But he, like Thrasyllus, was a scholar, and it must have been literary interests that drew the two men together. Balbillus wrote a history in 41 Books, starting from the end of the Civil War; an *Etruscan History*; a *Carthaginian History* in 8 Books; and a treatise *On the Latin Alphabet*. But Balbillus, unlike Thrasyllus, was also a man of civic position, as we see from his ambassadorial work. Many modern writers have taken him for the son of Thrasyllus whom Tacitus briefly mentions; but we have no evidence whatever linking him with the Thrasyllus family. That he would have shared the *praenomen* and name Tiberius Claudius with Thrasyllus' son proves nothing; thousands of Roman citizens of provincial origin at this time were similarly styled as expression of their naturalisation—or if they had been slaves, of their enfranchisement.[2] It seems also that modern historians have confused two Balbilli: the friend of Claudius and a son whom Nero sent to Egypt in 55 as prefect, and who there held various posts concerned with the Mouseion, with cults, and so on. We know the latter's career mainly through an inscription at Ephesos where he founded Games, and we shall have more to say of him later.[3]

Dion tells us of A.D. 45 that, "since there was to be an eclipse of the sun on his birthday, Claudius feared there must result some disturbance, inasmuch as other portents had already occurred. So he issued a proclamation in which he not only stated that an eclipse would occur, and for how long, but also the reasons why this was bound to happen."[4] This slightly pedantic form of proclamation was in character. We see that the government must have had astronomers or astrologers to advise it, or the eclipse would have taken them by surprise. Whether Balbillus worked with Claudius on the statement we do not know.

Soon another highborn woman was in trouble. Lollia Paulina, a woman of immense wealth and fabulous jewellery, had been taken by Gaius from her husband, married, then divorced with orders to stay chaste. In 48 Claudius was a widower (Messalina having died), and court-groups were intriguing to have their favourite the next empress. Lollia was put forward, but failed against Agrippina (II). But the latter still resented her and arranged a faked trial with charges of consulting astrologers, sorcerers, and the oracle of Klarian Apollo.[5] Claudius demanded that the Senate convict her of "pernicious designs against the State". Probably she had attempted to foresee the future during her struggle to get hold of him, and had asked how long Agrippina would live. So far such an inquiry about an empress was not *maiestas*, but Agrippina was the first woman to get the formal title of Augusta. She had her way, Lollia was exiled; but Agrippina, unsatisfied, sent a soldier after her. Lollia committed suicide. Agrippina had a look at the teeth in the cut-off head to make sure of the identity. Then, after Nero had killed Agrippina, his mother, he had Lollia's ashes brought back to Rome and put in a worthy tomb. Now the Augustan edict was no longer needed; all divinatory inquiries about the *salus* of an emperor and his family were *maiestas* in themselves.[6]

Three other important prosecutions came under Claudius.

Furius Camillus Scribonianus was the son of a legate of Dalmatia who had been executed for rebellion. He seems to have made astrological inquiries about Claudius' death; and the fact that he was a lineal descendant of Pompeius told against him. Exiled, he soon died. Naturally it was whispered that he had been poisoned. What happened to his mother, who was included in the charge, we do not know. Soon after the trial, in 52, all astrologers were expelled from Italy.[7]

Next year T. Statilius Taurus was acused of *maiestas*, mainly for divination. Possibly Agrippina pushed Claudius into these two trials; she was perhaps genuinely suspicious, believing that her previous husband Germanicus had indeed been killed by magic. Still, it seems she had her eye on Taurus' fine park. He had been consul and governor of Africa; and one of Agrippina's followers, Tarquitius Priscus, served under him as a spy and tried to bring him down with a charge of *repetundae* after he returned to Rome, but failed. (When years later Tarquitius has to meet the same charge, he was enthusiastically found guilty by the Senate.) Tarquitius then charged Taurus with magical practices. Not long before, a subterranean sanctuary, dedicated to some cult (perhaps Mithraic or Pythagorean) had been found on what seems part of Taurus' estate in Rome; the assumption was that he carried on forbidden rites there. The whole case was highly dubious, and Taurus committed suicide before the verdict. Statilia Messalina, perhaps his daughter, married Nero in 66 after the latter had killed off her husband.[8]

Another feud of Agrippina's led to a trial. The victim this time was Domitia Lepida, who in 54 was accused of attacking Agrippina with black magic and of spreading unrest in Calabria through her many slaves there. Tacitus calls her shameless; Messalina (Claudius' wife) was her daughter. She had three husbands, the second of whom was fatally indicted with Messalina's support—perhaps because he rejected her advances. Domitia then formally broke with her daughter. The girl was said to have committed incest with her brother (father of Nero by Agrippina), and she was finally killed in Domitia's house where she had taken refuge. The long struggle of Agrippina and Domitia ended in the latter's trial. Domitia may have had hopes of her grandson Britannicus succeeding to the throne, while Agrippina was determined to see Nero enthroned.[9] These trials however tell us more of the discord and intrigues in and around the imperial family than they do of astrology; but the important part played by astrology in the charges shows how much it had come to the fore and how much it was both trusted and feared. Claudius lacked the interest in Mages and the like that Germanicus, Gaius and Nero had. It is probably significant that a neo-Pythagorean (Nigidian?) sect, who had begun an underground basilica, abandoned it in the latter part of his reign.[10] Seneca in his squib, *The Pumpkinification of Claudius,* makes Mercury address one of the Fates: "Do let the astrologers tell the truth for once. Since he became emperor they've never let a year pass, never a month, without laying him out for burial. Yet it's no wonder if they're wrong and no one knows the hour. Nobody ever believed he was really quite born."

Soon after the trials we have discussed, Claudius died and Agrippina's ambitions were realised in Nero. There were no more of our treason cases till 65, with the Pisonian Conspiracy. In the medley of ensuing prosecutions, two were connected with magic: those of Barea Soranus and his daughter, and that of P. Anteius Rufus and M. Ostorius Scapula. Soranus had opposed one of Nero's freedmen who was stripping Asia of paintings and statues. Tacitus mentions only political charges against him, but Dion says that he was involved in magic through his daughter Servilia who had lavished money on mages (astrologers?). Tacitus says she erred only through "the thoughtlessness of youth" and affection for her father; she was aged nineteen. She had made inquiries as to the *incolumnitas* (unsafety) of the imperial house and wanted to know if Nero would relent. Dion adds that she had her father "make a certain sacrifice when Nero was ill". Tacitus gives a moving picture of the girl before the Senate.

When the accuser asked her if she'd sold her bridal presents (her husband Annius Pollio had been recently exiled) or stript her neck of its ornaments to raise cash for performing magic rites, she at first flung herself on the ground and wept in silence. After a while, clasping the altar-steps and altar, she cried, "I've invoked no impious deities, no spells, or anything else in my unhappy prayers but only that you Caesar and you Senators might preserve unharmed the best of fathers. My jewels, my clothes, and the signs of my rank, I gave up as I'd have given up my life-blood if they'd demanded it. They must have seen this, these men previously unknown to me as to the name they bear or the arts they practise. No mention was made by me of the emperor except as one of the divinities. But my most unhappy father knows nothing, and if it's a crime, I alone am guilty."

Soranus asked to be tried separately and his daughter to be charged only with acts of misguided filial devotion. But his case was damaged by a crown-witness, P. Egnatius Celer, a client of his and a Stoic philosopher, an easterner from Berytos. As a Stoic he was likely to approve of astrology, and he seems to have been the person who induced Servilia, his pupil, to make the consultations. He had been named with Soranus and he sought to save himself at his patron's cost. With them was also a rich Bithynian, Cassius Asklepiodotos, who, refusing to admit the charges, was exiled with loss of property; and the Stoic Thrasea, who however was not accused of magic. Soranus, his daughter, and Thrasea were convicted and let choose their own form of death. The implication of the Bithynian suggests that Soranus was suspected of stirring up disloyalty in his former province, Asia.[11]

Shortly before this episode, two men were found guilty in a summary trial, apparently held in secret before the praetorian prefect and Nero. They were Anteius and Ostorius Scapula. The evidence against them was drawn from the files of the Egyptian astrologer Pammenes. They were accused of an attempted coup and of inquiries as to their future and the emperor's. Both were men of the highest class and Anteius was certainly a devotee of astrology. Pammenes, one of his advisers, had been exiled; and Anteius kept on sending him money and inquiries from afar. Scapula seems to have been another client who kept in touch—though Anteius may of his own accord have sent to Pammenes the horoscopic material about Scapula. The latter was a courageous man who had won a civic crown in Britain and who in 62 defended Antistius Sosianus in a case of literary treason. Sosianus had recited some verses (said to be libellous) on Nero while dining at Scapula's house. Guests, who had heard the verses, testified against Sosianus, but his host denied the charges. Sosianus was exiled with loss of property. Four years later, on the same island of exile as Pammenes, he stole some papers from the astrologer, including the horoscope of Anteius, and sent them to Nero, who permitted him to return to Rome. (Two years after Nero's death the authorities remembered that he had not been formally pardoned and sent him back to the island.)

If Anteius was the father of the Anteia who married the Stoic Helvisius Priscus, then he must have belonged to the Stoic opposition around Thrasea. After his trial he was given his choice of death. The poison he took was slow in working, so he cut his veins. Scapula was on his estate in Liguria, where a centurion sur-

K

rounded the house with soldiery; he severed his veins and stabbed himself.[12]

We have three horoscopes of persons born in the reign of Claudius. One birthdate is 3 January 46 and the text is on a papyrus from Egypt. It calls the Sun "the ruler of the world", and the Moon, "the mother of all", and merely gives the astral details. A second papyrus is very fragmentary. A third horoscope, given by Valens, has the date 25 October 50 as an example of a distinguished nativity.

L. Annaeus Seneca, rhetorician and philosopher, had been exiled to Corsica by Claudius, apparently because he was friendly with Julia, sister of Gaius, whom Messalina disliked. As we saw, each of the three powerful freedmen at the court backed a candidate for Claudius' fourth marriage; Agrippina II, Julia's sister, won and Seneca was recalled. She invited him to act as tutor for her son Nero, then twelve years old. A co-tutor was Chairemon, who may be the Alexandrian figuring in the same document as Balbillus. A Stoic, and a member of the Egyptian priesthood, he had studied hieroglyphics and written a book on them; he also presided at one time over the Mouseion and wrote on comets, suggesting that they could herald good as well as bad things. As a Stoic he interpreted Egyptian religion as an allegory of nature-worship; and Origen studied his works. Martial wrote an epigram addressed to him, mocking his asceticism, but not questioning its genuineness.

> Stoic Chaeremon, because you praise death loudly
> do you want me to admire, look up to your mind? . . .
> What a great man you are, who can do without
> dregs of red vinegar, black bread, and straw? . . .
> In straightened means it's easy despising life:
> he acts the strong man who's wretched and can endure.[13]

Seneca as a Stoic was also interested in all natural phenomena, including comets and stars. In *On Providence* he says that Fate leads and does not drag men along, "yet cause is linked with cause". In *Consolation to Marcia for her dead son* he defines birth as an entry into cosmic communion:

You are going to be born into the city common to gods and mortals, which embraces all things, which follows constant and eternal laws, which sees the heavenly bodies perform their tireless revolutions. There you'll see stars beyond number, and that marvellous star which alone fills all space, the Sun . . .

And so on in rapturous style. On the least movements of the heavens "depend the destinies of peoples; the greatest and the smallest events are shaped by their malign or favouring influence". And he ends the Letter with a vision of world-end, mountains crashing down; new ones rising up; the earth opening to swallow towns; floods and universal fire. Then the universe will arise anew. "Happy is your son, Marcis. He is already initiated into these mysteries."[14]

Again and again he returns to the problems of Fate and Freewill, and of the nature of omens. He tries to resolve the contradictions:

When this matter is discussed, I shall say to what extent, without eliminating Fate, something is left to the Freewill of man. For the moment I have explained in what way, even if the sequence of Fate is fixed, sacrifices and the interpretation of omens avert perils; for they do not fight fate, but themselves happen according to fate. What then, you say, can an haruspex do for me, since it's fated I make a sacrifice even without his advising me to do it? But the advice is useful, since he is a minister of Fate. Thus while good health is due to Fate, it is also due to the Physician since the blessing of Fate comes to us through his hands.[15]

He wavers between demanding a purely physical cause for phenomena and finding omens and signs in them. Can people be so conceited as to imagine that "the gods send out previous intimations of the death of great men? Do you think anything on earth is so great that the Universe should perceive its loss?" Yet he can remark, "Lightning portends the future too. Nor do the signs it gives refer to only one or two events. Often a complete series of Fate's succeeding decrees is intimated." He repeats that astrology is true, but insists on its complexity and on the over-simplifications of practising astrologers:

The Chaldeans confined their observations to the five planets. But do you suppose that the influence of so many thousands of other bright stars is nothing? The essential error of the men pretending to skill in casting horoscopes lies in limiting our destinies to the influence of a few of the stars, while all that float above us in the heavens claim some share in us. Perhaps the lower stars exert their force on us more directly, and the same may be true of the stars which, by reason of their more frequent movements, turn their looks upon man in a different way from that in which they are turned on other living creatures.[16]

Astrologic ideas intrude in his plays. In *Hercules Furens* the hero sees the skies darken and the Lion shake its tail; then he wonders if he is at the point where the Sun rises or under the heart of the icy Bear; he suspects the stars will leave their courses and roam at will—an image that grows increasingly common to express disorder in the universe: a projection on to the stars of the oppressive disintegration that men feel worsening in earthly life. Seneca's Hercules insists on his necessary katasterism. "I seek the skies that I myself have borne." He sees the Zodiac as the representation of his own Twelve Labours. His wife cries out, when she hears his voice declaring that he has reached the stars, "I know, I know, Chaos is conquered!" He has become the Saviour.

Seneca dealt with Comets in his *Natural Questions* (VII).[17] They continued to be a matter of much interest, usually taken as portents of evil, but now and then heralding a new king, a new dispensation. One was said to have been seen at the great Mithridates' birth and to presage his accession; a copper coin of his shows an eight-rayed star, one ray elongated into a tail. Caesar's comet was said to have been blood-red in colour, and some northern stars over which it had appeared were named Caesar's Throne.[18] Dion says a comet warned Cicero of his death; other comets heralded the Battles of Philippi and Actium as well as the Varus' disaster and the death of Agrippa.[19] (Manilius ascribed the plague at Athens during the Peloponnesian War to a comet, and Silius Italicus the Roman defeat at Cannae to another.)[20] The comets of A.D. 9 and 11 were taken to threaten Augustus; in 14, when he did die, there was a third one, blood-red. Seneca refers to it. "Let's not believe the comet seen under Claudius is the same as that which appeared under Augustus, nor that which showed itself under Nero . . . has resembled the one rising after Caesar's murder." A comet of 54 was taken to predict the emperor's death, but that of 60 was a harbinger of good tidings.

Calpurnius Siculus in his First Eclogue describes the ushering in of Nero's reign by a comet which marks it out as a new Age of Gold; and he contrasts this comet with that of Julius Caesar.

> Do you mark for the twentieth time the night shining
> in cloudless skies, a comet in tranquil light
> radiant? Fully it burns, no bloodshed portending.
> Is there trace of blood-hued flame, in a comet's way,
> sprinkling the poles? Does it flash with gory fire?
> Not such as this, when Caesar was rapt away,
> told of destined wars for luckless citizens. . . .

This is one of the poems announcing that the promises made in Virgil's Fourth Eclogue had been realised under Nero. Another Eclogue on the same subject, whose author we do not know, declares:

> Such was the divine power
> which begot the world and inwove with seven borders
> the Artificer's Zones and blends them all with Love.

While a third, probably by the same poet as the last, cites directly from Virgil:

> Saturn's days have returned with the Virgin Astraea . . .
> Chaste Lucina be gracious. Your own Apollo reigns.

Virgil merely mentioned the Virgin, but he certainly meant the constellation also called Erigone or Astraea, identified with Justice. Apollo, ruler of the tenth age or *saeculum*, has now definitely become the emperor—but Nero rather than Augustus.

To return to Comets, Plinius seeks to explore the subject:

People think it matters in what direction a comet darts . . . what shape it resembles . . . If it forms an equilateral triangle . . . In relation to certain positions of the fixed stars it portends a man of genius and a revival of learning; in the head of the northern or southern Serpent it brings poisonings . . . Aristotle also records that several may be seen at the same time and that this signifies severe winds or heat . . . Some people think that even comets are everlasting and travel in a special circuit of their own, but are not visible when the sun leaves them. There are others that hold they spring into existence out of chance moisture and fiery force and eventually are again dissolved.[21]

The comet of A.D. 11 may have been Halley's Comet and some scholars have taken it as the Star of the Gospels. Origen took that star to be a comet, but no comet is known in the years in question.[22]

In 64 came the Great Fire of Rome, possibly started by the Christians who were anxiously waiting for the world to end by fire and who did at times start fires in order to prompt God. Lightning and a comet were said to accompany the event. Poppaea Sabina had an affair with M. Salvius Otho, then married him. In his house she met his astrologers, among whom was one named Ptolemaios and who may have been the same as the Seleukos that we meet.[23] But she was after Nero, who got rid of Otho by sending him to govern Lusitania. Ptolemaios seems to have attached himself to Poppaea; but there were many astrologers around and not all in her entourage. Nero killed her when she was pregnant, with a kick; Ptolemaios went off to Otho and promised him the throne by the stars.[24]

A tenth-century MS has a tale of Nero expelling the astrologers, who retorted by publishing the day on which he would die; and he duly died then. The whole account is highly dubious. Tacitus says that the proclamation of his accession was planned by Agrippina with the astrologers; things were held up until "the auspicious moment established by the astrologers arrived". And Suetonius depicts him as much addicted to astrology. When Vindex revolted in Gaul:

Nero had formerly been told by astrologers that it would be his fortune to be at last deserted by all the world; and this occasioned his famous saying: An artist can live in any country. He meant to make excuses for his practice of music by saying that it was not only his amusement as a prince, but that it would serve to support him when reduced to a private status. Yet some of the astrologers promised him in his forlorn state the rule of the East, and some in express terms the Kingdom of Jerusalem. But most of them flattered him with assurances of restoration to his former fortune.[25]

He died in 68 and the exact date is proved by an astrologic document. On the basis of Jerome's statement that his reign lasted 13 years, 7 months and 28 days, his death-day has been taken as 9 June. But Dion warns us that emperors of the period did not succeed formally on the death of their predecessor, for instance Galba. Josephos gives the reign as 13 years and 8 days, amended to 13 years, 8 months and 8 days, or 13 years and 8 months. Dion gives the length as that last figure, making the interval between Nero's death and Vespasian's accession as 1 year, 22 days. Both these computations make the death-date 11 June. Vettius Valens the astrologer gives Nero's birth as 15th December 37 at sunrise: compare Suetonius, "the 18th of the Kalends of January [15 December] just as the sun rose so that its beams touched him before they could well reach the earth". Valens mentions the return of Jupiter to the same latitude (18 of the Virgin), which gives us 11 June for the death. So astrology verifies the date of Dion and Josephos. (Valens seems to have taken his figures from a work by Kritodemos.)[26]

We have yet to consider the role of Balbillus at Nero's court. The Ephesian inscription gives us the main details of his career. He began as Praefectus Fabrum or Chief Engineer in 44; he was also Tribunus Militum of XX Legio and distinguished himself in the conquest of Britain. Claudius then gave him a civil-service ministry—*ad legationes et res* (*ponsa Graeca* (*?*)); he was promoted to the procuratorship of the Shrines of Divus Augustus (and other shrines) and of all the Sacred Groves in Alexandreia and Egypt as well as the Mouseion and its Library. Then under Nero he became Prefect of Egypt.[27] At Ephesos he had a strong position as a benefactor; perhaps he had been a procurator there. Plinius mentions that he arrived in Egypt in record time, six days after leaving the straits of Messina.[28]

Fig. 61. Sol kneeling to Mithras, Nersae, Italy; Mithras and Sol at the sacred meal, Sol with bunch of grapes, Heddernheim

Tacitus names him among the friends of Agrippina and implies that he was given Egypt at her request. She had her astrologers, but we have no reason for including Balbillus among those whom Tacitus mentions: "Of her own dreadful end Agrippina had warning many years before, when, consulting the Chaldeans about the future lot of her son, she was told that he would reign at Rome and kill his mother. 'Let him,' she said, 'let him kill me, but let him reign.'"[29] These men may however have included the young Thrasyllus. In one episode only are we definitely told that Nero consulted Balbillus. "A blazing star, vulgarly supposed to portend destruction to kings and princes, appeared above the horizon several nights in succession. He felt great anxiety at this phenomenon. Balbillus, astrologer, told him that princes were accustomed to expiate such omens by the sacrifice of illustrious persons and to avert the danger foreboded to themselves by bringing it down on the heads of their chief men. So he resolved on the destruction of

the principal nobility in Rome." If true, this anecdote shows
Balbillus as cynically shrewd; but it seems more likely to be the
sort of tale circulating among the Senators who disliked any of
Nero's favourites and who would have looked on Balbillus as a
Greekling upstart. In any event it testifies to the closeness of his
relations with Nero.[30]

The period in question was that of the 60s, after Balbillus had
returned from Egypt. What Nero's zodiacal sign was, we do not
know; but clearly he claimed a solar role—as shown by the tale of
his dawn-birth. He called himself Helios Basileus, the Sun King,
and his Golden House was designed as a cosmic setting for his
solar splendour. He set up a colossos of himself as the Sun Apollo.
Greeks hailed him as the New Sun. But the episode that brings out
most clearly his image of himself was that of the visit and coronation
of Tiridates of Armenia. The ceremony occurred in a setting of
brilliant gold, under a *velarium* embroidered with stars, on the top
of which Nero was represented as the solar charioteer. The day was
to be called the Golden Day. The Arsakid Tiridates, a Mazdean,
saluted in Nero his temporal ruler the god Mithras, his Fate and
Fortune, his Moira and Tyche. We are reminded of the Mithraic
reliefs in which Mithras invests Helios or the two gods partake of a
banquet together.[31]

We have no evidence that Balbillus was connected with this
event, but it is likely that he played a part in the inspiration of its
cosmic setting. At Ephesos he was a leading citizen, founding
Games that lasted for a long time; a marble base dated 200–12 at
Philadelphia in honour of an athlete, Aurelios Polykrates, sets out
the various Games in which he was victor, including the Balbillea
at Ephesos. Balbillus seems to have spent much time between
Ephesos and Pergamon. At the latter place, under Domitian, a
Claudia Capitolina was honoured as his daughter and given
the Greek title of Queen, *Basilissa*. The inscription shows that
she was the wife of a Roman, Junius Rufus, so that the title did
not derive in any way from her marriage. The most likely thing
is that Balbillus, her father, had married near the end of Nero's
reign an eastern princess, a close connection of Antiochos IV of
Kommagene. However, it is possible that Claudia had been
earlier married to a Kommagene prince, C. Julius Antiochos.
Certainly the two families intermarried in some way, as we know
from an inscription left by Julia Balbilla under Hadrian on the
Colossos of Memnon in Egypt. One of her poems there ends with

the proud statement: "Pious indeed were my parents and my ancestors, Balbillus the Wise and the King Antiochos, Balbillus father of my mother of royal blood, and the King Antiochos father of my father. It's from their race that I draw my noble blood, and these verses are by me, Balbilla the pious." She seems the sister of Philopappos the heir of the dynasty, who left a well-known monument to the Athenians. Her father was then the son of Antiochos IV whom Vespasian deposed—he was probably the elder Antiochos Epiphanes, not the younger Kallinikos. The princess Aka whom some scholars have made the wife of Balbillus is however a figment, a misreading of the inscription. We must remember also that Balbillus may have had another daughter besides Claudia Capitolina. But however we interpret the evidence, it is certain that the Balbilli and the Kommagene dynasty had become closely related, and thus it is highly probable that Balbillus had an important finger in Nero's Eastern policy. We saw how the Kommagene dynasty was early a fervent apostle of merged Mithraism and astrology, and we may surmise that Balbillus thus introduced into the Roman court a kind of royal astrology which was different in its implications and coloration from the con-

Fig. 62. Coin of Antigonos IV of Kommagene; scorpion with foliage around

ventional Greek-Egyptian system used by Thrasyllus. Coins of Antiochos IV have a scorpion surrounded by laurel-foliage on the reverse, so that the Scorpion seems his sign.[32]

The role of Balbillus in Asia Minor is stressed by the fact that he may be the person denounced in *Revelation*, whose excessive idolatry contributed to unloose the author's rage. "And he has power to give life to the Image of the Beast, so that the Image of the Beast should speak." The identification is based on the numerical analysis of the symbols, and it seems to fit the historical phase underlying the work. The author had gone from Ephesos to

Pergamon, the two places where Balbillus was responsible for the exaltation of the imperial cult in a theurgic way. (We may recall Nerullinos and the cults in the Troad, also connected with Nero.) Renan in his *Antichrist* writes: "These characteristics point to a false prophet, an enchanter, in particular to Simon the Magician, an imitator of Christ, who in legend became the flatterer, the parasite and wizard of Nero, or to Balbillus of Ephesos, or to the Antichrist of whom Paul speaks with some obscurity in the second epistle to the Thessalians." Balbillus' close relations to Nero give him a special claim to be the animator of the Image of the Beast.[33]

We have a manuscript with the tantalising heading, "What I found useful in the work of Balbillus", followed by the comment, "This chapter was omitted as useless." There is however a synopsis.

First he deals with the spans of life, starting his survey with the life-determining Planets. He considers as life-determining stars, Kronos, Ares, Sun, and Moon. He takes as the life-determining Lord the one in Mesuranema, or when none is present there, he takes the life-determining star from the Horoscopic Point or Dysis, or Hypogaeum [Anti-M.].

If, however, several planets are in the same sector, then one is held to be the only one of the life-determining star which is closest to the Mesuranema, and deathstar that one of the life-determining stars reckoned among them as the closest according to [Fate] to the point called Tyche . . .[34]

It goes on thus and ends, "Balbillus was born . . ." The compiler meant to add a biography, but either could not find the material or changed his mind. This manuscript enables us to identify another synopsis, with fragments, given by Palchos: *Astrologoumena,* dedicated to Hermogenes. Other passages in manuscripts have been tentatively assigned to Balbillus, one of them about the time of his death. An epigram by Seneca on three very intimate friends may refer to him and Hermogenes. "You think them brothers, such *pietas* they enjoy, but you may deny it: such a single love is in three."[35]

Before we pass on, we may glance at the fortunes of the Kommagene dynasty. Antiochos IV was for a while on the best of terms with Gaius, who seems to have restored him. Dion speaks of him and Herod Agrippa as instructing the emperor in the art of tyranny. But somehow he annoyed Gaius and lost his kingdom

again. Claudius restored him. After Nero's death he supported
Vespasian and was spoken of as the richest of the tributary kings.
He sent his eldest son (who was apparently the one married to
Balbillus' daughter) at the head of his troops. This prince,
G. Julius Antiochos Epiphanes, looks a bit uncouth on coins, but
was a capable soldier. (He had first fought on Otho's side and been
wounded.) In May or June 70 he was heading a native contingent
to aid Titus before Jerusalem and led the assault on the walls.
There were rumours that the king and the prince were plotting
with the Parthians—though the governor of Syria, Caesennius
Paetus, may have spread the tales for his own ends. Vespasian
decided to annex Kommagene and Paetus marched on Samosata.
The king did not resist, but his two sons did. A long battle ended
in stalemate. The king fled to Tarsos and surrendered; his sons
went to Parthia. Vespasian let the king settle in Sparta with a large
revenue; and soon the sons also were allowed to enter the empire.
The family was reunited in Rome. These later events must have
provided an anxious time for Balbillus, but he does not seem to
have been involved in them. Certainly he did not fall into disfavour.
Dion tells us of Vespasian in his dealings with astrologers, "He
was in the habit of showing favour to Barbillos, a man of the
profession, even permitting the Ephesians to celebrate some Sacred
Games, a privilege he granted to no other city."[36]

We have already seen how Lucan cited Nigidius at length with an
astrologic prophecy at the outbreak of the Civil War. He opens his
epic with an over-pitched passage in which Nero makes his advent
as the final vindication of history and the cosmos, and is offered the
choice of taking over from Jove, mounting the fiery chariot in
place of the Sun, or settling in the clearest regions of the sky. Lucan
seems to have his tongue in his cheek as he begs him not to lean on
any part of boundless space: otherwise "the axle of the sphere will
be weighed down. So keep the equipoise of heaven by staying right
at the system's centre." He goes on to an account of world-end
with the stars falling into the sea, the moon moving in opposition
to the sun, and "the whole distracted fabric of the shattered
firmament subverting its own laws". Later he makes Caesar say,
"In the thick of battles I have always studied the heavenly zones of
the stars and the sky." An Egyptian priest, expounding his
country's lores, discourses on the Planets.[37]

Persius (about 34 to 62) pays a tribute to a Stoic friend in

astrologic terms, thinking of an ode of Horace and of pictures of
Fate holding a balance or marking a horoscope on a globe:

> Don't doubt there's a fixed law brings our lives
> into accord, one star that guides them. Whether
> in the equal Balance, tenacious of truth, Fate
> hangs our days or the birth-hour sacred to true friends
> shares our united faith between the Twins
> and we break Saturn's shock with our common Jove,
> some star, I'm sure, fuses my life and yours.[38]

The Greek epigrammatist Loukillios knew Nero and apparently
dedicated a book to him; the money that Nero gave him enabled
him to start a second book, of which we have some verses forming
a part of the preface. He mocks at Chairemon, probably Nero's
tutor, making him an air-treader in an Aristophanic vein of
mockery at star-gazers:

> Chairemon, caught by a gentle breeze, went drifting
> lighter than a straw along the airy track.
> He'd have been swept away but his feet were tangled
> in spiderwebs. He lay there on his back.
> Five days and nights he hung there overhead
> and on the sixth climbed down along a thread.
>
> Chairemon fell down flat. A poplar leaf
> windborne struck him. Like Tityrus he's downed,
> or like a caterpillar heaving in grief
> his skeleton frame, he's stretched out on the ground.

An ascetic, Chairemon was doubtless rather gaunt; so the poet
uses his light build for these fantasies. Astrologers are generally
mocked at:

> Aulus the astrologer made out his own nativity,
> said his deathday was come; just four hours left.
> The fifth hour came. He lived, a fool and daft.
> Ashamed of Petosiris, he hanged himself.
> High up he's dying, but dying ignorant.

Again the "high up" is a jeer at the pretence of getting high in the
stars.

> Boxer Onesimos came to Olympos the prophet
> to learn if for old age he yet might hope.
> "Yes, if your profession—you just drop it.
> Box on, and Saturn is your horoscope."

All the astrologers told my father with one breath
my brother would live to a ripe old age. Alone
Hermokleides truly foretold his premature death . . .
while over the corpse in the house we made our moan.

This last quatrain has a note of personal anger, which explains the poet's attitudes.[39]

We have already mentioned Thessalos of Tralles with his revelation from Asklepios and the treatise in which he set out the astral affinities of 19 plants, their links with the zodiacal signs and the seven planets. Both Latin and Greek versions survive; the Greek one is ascribed to a physician, Harpokration. Thessalos may well have been the famous practitioner who made a headstrong attack on prevailing medical theories. He excerpted Nechepso, and a Greek scribe refers to him as an astrologer.[40]

Columella in *On Agriculture* (about 62) provides us with the most comprehensive weather-chart that has come down. He has many omens and mentions a book against astrologers, apparently those of the fatalist type. He denies the "impudent assertion of the Chaldeans that changes in the air coincide with fixed dates". Better use motherwit and experience than persuade yourself "that the influence of a star makes itself felt sometimes before, sometimes after, and sometimes on the actual day fixed for its rising or setting".[41]

The elder Plinius in his *Natural History* cites many astrologers, Horos and Zoroaster, Petosiris and Nechepso, as well as historical figures. He himself has a touch of the solar cult, but is something of an agnostic. "I consider it a mark of human weakness to seek to discover the shape and form of God. He consists wholly of himself." He derides polytheism and thinks that men have made things even more dark by inventing an intermediate deity, Fortune. "Another set of people banish Fortune as well and attribute an event to its star and to the laws of birth, they hold that for all men who are ever to be, God's decree has been enacted once for all, while leisure has been granted to him for the rest of time. This belief begins to take root, and the learned and the unlearned alike go on marching towards it at the double." He argues that experience shows that the gods take an interest in human affairs and that Man wasn't born next of kin to God for the purpose of approximating to the Beasts. But not even to God are all things possible; he cannot commit suicide or make twice ten other than twenty. God indeed is for Plinius in his strict Stoicism "the power of Nature". He rejects fatalist astrology but accepts in a general way the influence of the stars, since all things are interconnected.[42]

Philon of Alexandreia could not take things so easily; he was agitated by questions of Providence and Fate. He wanted to devalue astrology and set out many of the stock arguments against fatalist systems. If man acts only by fate, it is unjust to punish criminals and an accused man in the courts has a full answer, pointing to his horoscope. Similarly virtue is not praise-worthy if it comes merely by fate. But he too does not deny astral influences, though he sees them as secondary causes. Thus he does not mind the theory that the Big Dipper affects sexual intercourse. Like the Christians later, he uses Biblical texts to define the stars as signs: to shed light and indicate the future. Men can conjecture what is to happen, from star movements, eclipses, configurations, weather, and so on. Steady observation can enable students to find in heaven the events of earth in similitude, but not in a fated form. The astrological part of astronomy is assigned to a place above the "encyclical disciplines", that is, on the highest level. Despite his emphasis on a God beyond the universe, he is always responsive to the notion of organic correspondences.[43]

Petronius gives us a good glimpse of how astrology had penetrated into the lower or less-learned social levels. Trimalchio at his dinner-party provides a surprise-dish:

There was a round plate with the Twelve Signs of the Zodiac set in order, and on each the artist had laid some food fit and proper to the symbol. Over the Ram's head ram's-head pease, a piece of beef on the Bull, kidneys on the Twins, over the Crab a crown, an African fig over the Lion, a barren sow's-paunch over the Virgin, over the Balance a pair of scales with a muffin on one side and a cake on the other, over the Scorpion a small seafish, over the Archer *oclopeta,* over Capricorn a lobster, over Aquarius a goose, over the Fish two mullets. In the middle lay a honeycomb on a sod of turf with the grass green on it. An Egyptian boy took bread round in a silver chafing-dish.

Most of the associations are obvious enough. *Oclopeta* is the most obscure object, connected with the Archer. It has been translated as "bull's eye", derived from *oculus* and *peto* and based on the idea of the crow as the seeker of, or striker at, eyes. Another reading is *oclopecta, oculus-pektos*: with fixed or staring eyes (an unknown fish). It has also been taken to mean peewit or lapwing, or to be connected with cranes, whom we find described as arrow-swift and straight in their flight. It might mean "eye-guider" as *heredipeta* means "heritage-getter", or it might be a sort of word-play for *oscopeta*: Eros as bowman is a kiss-seeker.[44]

What we are given in this passage seems not so much a joke at Trimalchio's philistinism as a sample of popular notions about the Signs, but a little later on he does discourse at length on the Signs, again giving a popular version of the sort of thing set out learnedly in works like Ptolemaios' *Tetrabiblos*.

"No one can bring me anything new, as the last dish proved. The firmament where the twelve gods live turns into as many figures and one time it becomes a ram. So anyone born under that sign gets plenty of flocks and wool, a hard head and a brazen forehead and sharp horns. Under this sign are born big herds of pedants and young rams." We applauded the wit of his astrology and he went on. "Then the whole sky changes into a young bull. So now are born men who are free with their heels, and oxherds and people who've got to find their own food. Under the Twins tandems are born, and oxen and looselivers and those who daub the wall on both sides [sit on the fence]. I was born under the Crab. So I've got lots of legs to stand on and many possessions by land and sea, for either of them suits a crab. And that was why just now I put nothing on top of the Crab. I didn't want to weight down the house of my birth.

"Under the Lion big eaters and masterful men are born. Under the Virgin, women and runaway slaves and chain-gangs. Under the Balance, butchers and perfumers and in general people who put things to rights. Under the Scorpion, poisoners and murderers. Under the Archer, cross-eyed men who take the bacon while looking at the vegetables. Under Capricorn the poor folk whose troubles make horns sprout on them. Under Aquarius innkeepers and chaps with water on the brain. Under the Fish chefs and rhetoricians.

"So the world turns like a mill and always brings something bad to pass making men be born or die. You saw the green turf in the middle of the dish and a honeycomb on the turf. I don't do anything without a reason. Mother Earth lies in the world's midst rounded like an egg and all blessings are there inside her as in a honeycomb."[45]

As the guests go into the house, they see on wall-paintings, "Trimalchio with long hair holding a Mercury-staff. Minerva had him by the hand and was leading him into Rome . . . At the point where the wall-space gave out, Mercury had taken him by the chin and was whirling him up to his high official throne. Fortuna stood by with her flowing horn of plenty and the Three Fates spinning their golden thread." A doorpost was "painted with the Moon in her courses and the likenesses [*imagines*] of the seven stars. Lucky and unlucky days were marked too with distinctive knobs."[46]

The table with the Zodiac on it was a cosmic symbol; the table in itself also had the same meaning. In Ploutarch's *Symposion* one of the diners says, "As for me, I find that the Table is a representation of the Earth. For besides feeding us it is round in shape, it is fixed, and very suitably it has been given by some the name of Hestia." The Table of food-communion is thus equated with the Hearth-goddess; and among the Romans we find it consecrated to Vesta. The idea goes far back. Anaximenes had remarked, "The Earth is like a Table in form." (We may recall the part played by Hestia, the central hearth, in the cosmogony of Plato and the Pythagoreans.) In Aithiopia, Pomponius Mela tells us, "There is a place always filled with ready dishes, which is called Table of Helios, for everyone can come there as he wishes to take a meal. The people say that the dishes, served all around, are ceaselessly renewed by the will of the gods." We see there a folk-paradise, a Land of Cockayne, which is lavishly described in a fragment of the comic poet Krates. In the *Life of Apollonios of Tyana* the Indian sages offer a meal to the Greek. "And the earth strewed beneath them grass softer than any mattress. And dried fruits and bread and vegetables and the dessert of the season all came in, served in order and set before them more agreeably than if cooks and waiters had provided it. Now two of the tripods flowed with wine, but the other two supplied, the one a jet of warm water, the other of cold." Thus the image of the cosmic Table merged with the dream of happy plenty in a utopia of brotherhood; and the particular table in any household carried some of this benediction of hope. It owned such potency that it was held, said Plinius, "medicaments lose their virtue if, before being administered, they are put down by chance on a table".[47]

The transformation of the table or room into the cosmic image appears in such an act as that of Trimalchio, or in the constructions of Nero's Golden House:

. . . in other parts it was wholly overlaid with gold and adorned with jewels and mother-of-pearl. The dining-rooms were vaulted, and compartments of the ceiling, ivory-inlaid, were made to revolve and scatter flowers, while they contained pipes that shed unguents upon the guests. The chief banqueting-room was circular and revolved perpetually night and day, in imitation of the motion of the celestial bodies.[48]

Trimalchio again has his imitation. There is a crash in the ceiling and the whole room trembles. "The entire ceiling parted asunder and an enormous hoop, apparently knocked out of a giant cask, was let down. All round it were hung golden crowns and alabaster boxes of perfumes"—gifts for the guests Further, to drive home the cosmic point, when the big Zodiac dish is lifted up by four dancers, "we saw in the well of it fat fowls and sows' bellies, and in the middle a hare prankt up with wings to look like Pegasus. Four Marsyas-figures at the dish-corners also caught the eye; they let a spiced sauce run from their wine-skins over the fishes, which swam about in a sort of tide-race." The Marsyas-figures seem Dionysiac quarters of the world, comparable to the four winds, sky-supports, or compass-points, providing the Ocean for the Earth (the flesh-food) and the Heavens (Pegasus). Later, Justinian, Kedrenos tells us, had a Sacred Table made in which the metals, stones, woods, represented everything that sea and earth, the whole world, produces.

16

The Rest of the First Century

We heard above about Ptolemaios (also named Seleukos?) who visited Otho in Lusitania; he and others kept up Otho's courage and stimulated him to make his bid against Galba in 69. Galba on the other hand refused to accept as ominous a thunderstorm which burst out as he went to tell his soldiers that a third claimant, Vitellius, had risen up, in Germany. Tacitus contrasts the behaviour of Otho: "The Chaldeans and soothsayers about him would not let him drop his hopes or quit his design, chiefly Ptolemaios, insisting on a prediction he had made that Nero would not kill Otho but himself die first and be succeeded by Otho."[1] He also records a crowd of omens that afflicted Otho, complicated by a bad flood of the Tiber, which caused much damage in Rome and made his route out of the city impassable (over the Campus Martius and the Via Flaminia).[2] When he was killed, his astrologers dispersed; we do not know what happened to Ptolemaios. Perhaps he was again exiled.

Vitellius was another devotee of divination. Suetonius says that "his parents were so terrified at the astrologers' predictions on calculating his nativity that his father during his lifetime did his very best to prevent him being despatched as governor to any of the provinces. When he was sent to the legions and when he was proclaimed emperor his mother at once mourned him as utterly ruined." We are told that "he had great regard for omens and did nothing however trivial without consulting them". We see how dependent large numbers of the noble families had become on astrology. Dion however makes him scoff at the predictions, but if the tale is true it rather shows prudence on his part than disbelief. "Vitellius held himself of so little account that he mocked at the astrologers and used their predictions as evidence against them, saying, 'Obviously they know nothing when they assert that even I shall become emperor.' Nero, hearing of it, also laughed and felt such contempt for the fellow that he did him no harm." He seems to have been a passive homosexual.[3]

He entered Rome on a bad day, *dies ater*, the anniversary of the defeat of the Allia; and in every way seems to have come up against the astrologers, who had been on Otho's side and predicted Vitellius' discomfiture.

There was no person more severe than he against jugglers and astrologers; and as soon as any of them were informed against, he put them to death without the formality of a trial. He was enraged against them because, soon after the proclamation by which he commanded all astrologers to quit Rome and Italy before the Kalends [1st] of October, a bill was at once posted about the City with this text: Take Notice: The Chaldeans also decree that Vitellius Germanicus shall be no more by the day of the said Kalends. He was even suspected of being accessary to his mother's death by not allowing her to have food while unwell, a German witch whom he held to be oracular having told him: He would reign long in security if he survived his mother. (Suetonius.)[4]

The astrologers' notice was in the form of a public edict. In fact Vitellius lived almost three months after 1 October.

Vespasian, when revolting in the East, welcomed the astrologers as allies against Vitellius. Tacitus comments: "These are the sort of men whom the powerful cannot trust and who deceive the aspiring." He also suggests that Vespasian had been supported by the diviners from the start; for in describing the effect of his speech announcing the revolt, he says that the listeners "pressed round him, exhorting him to undertake the enterprise; they recalled to him the responses of oracles and the predictions of men skilled in astrology. Nor was Vespasian unaffected by that credulity. Even when he had gained supreme authority, he retained the *mathematicus* Seleukos, to assist his councils with his insight into future events." Tacitus then records a number of omens favouring Vespasian in earlier years including one connected with entrails-inspection.[5]

Meanwhile there were the usual crop of prodigies, a comet, two eclipses of the moon on the 4th and 7th day, two suns at once: "One in the west weak and pale, one in the east brilliant and powerful." And a rumour that the world's master or saviour would come out of Judaea, as Vespasian had.[6] The moon-eclipses terrified Vitellius' army: not so much the darkness as "the fact that it appeared both blood-hued and black, and gave out other frightening colours". Yet even so the men pulled themselves together. Then, despite the aid that omens and astrologers had been to him, even before he reached Italy Vespasian renewed the Vitellian edict of expulsion—for Rome and probably for all Italy. Also, soon after his arrival, he exiled the philosophers (except Musonius Rufus); he wanted to get rid of any dissident Stoics. His regulations seem to have been well-enforced. It is some years later that we hear of a few Cynics "managing somehow to slip into the city"— as appeared when some of them rose up in the theatre to denounce Berenike, the Jewish mistress of Titus.[7]

Suetonius says an old oak sacred to Mars near Rome on the Flavian estate put out a new branch with each child of Vespasia's: the first soon withered, the second was strong, but the third "grew like a tree". *Haruspices* told Vespasian's father what the omen meant, and he informed his mother that "her grandson would be emperor of Rome". Vespasian himself remained sceptical of such things, even if he was ready to use astrologers. When his friends warned him that Mettius Pomposianus had an imperial nativity, he made the man consul. He jested till the end. "When among other prodigies the Mausoleum of the Caesars suddenly flew open and a blazing star appeared in the heavens, he merely remarked that the first omen concerned Julia Calvina, who was of the Julian family" (and not himself who was a Flavian, with his own family-tomb); while the second omen concerned the Parthian King "who wore long hair". And when his distemper first seized him, "I suppose," he said, "I'll soon be a god." An earlier comet had proved harmless and had been made the theme of a poem by Titus, who was thus following in the steps of Germanicus as a princely poet of the stars and who was perhaps helped on the technical side by Balbillus.[8]

Of Titus, Suetonius says that "he was born on the Third of the Kalends of January [30 December] in the year remarkable for the death of Gaius near the Septizonium, in a mean house and a very small dark room, which still exists and is shown to the curious". The building called the Seven-zoned was probably circular with seven niches for statues. We shall later examine this type of building when we come to Septimus Severus; but it is interesting to have this early testimony to such a structure in Rome. Titus, like his father, refused to take action on the basis of astrologic consultation. He seems to have taken a fatalistic attitude to the stars:

Two men of patrician rank, convinced of aspiring to the empire, he merely advised to desist, saying that the sovereign power was disposed of by Fate. He promised them that if there was anything else they wanted of him he would grant it . . . More, he not only invited them to dine with him, but also next day at a gladiatorial show he purposely placed them near and handed them the weapons of the fighters for inspection. It is likewise said that he had their nativities cast, then was assured that a great calamity was impending on both of them, but from another hand, not from his.

His death was preluded by his bursting into tears at the public games; after which he went off for the Sabine uplands, "rather saddened because a victim had made its escape while he was sacrificing, and loud thunder had been heard from a serene sky". Seized with a fever, he drew back the curtains of his litter and "looked up to heaven, complained heavily that his life was taken from him though he had done nothing to deserve it; for there was no action of his that he had reason to repent of, but one". His belief in Fate and the way he looked complainingly up to heaven suggests that he had been threatened with an early death by his horoscope and died through loss of nerve, as Germanicus also may have done.[9]

His brother Domitian took horoscopes with the utmost seriousness. "He had not failed to take careful note of the days and hours when the foremost men had been born, and as a result was destroying in advance not a few who did not feel the least hope of gaining power." Whether or not Titus was haunted by his horoscope, Domitian certainly was. "He had long entertained a suspicion of the year and day when he was to die, and even of the very hour and manner of his death: all which he had learned from the Chaldeans when he was a very young man. His father once at supper laughed when he refused to eat some mushrooms, saying that if he knew his fate he'd rather fear the sword. So, being in ceaseless apprehension and anxiety, he was keenly alive to the slightest suspicions. . . ." Mettius Pomposianus, whose imperial horoscope Vespasian had laughed at, became an object of fear to Domitian, who was upset further at learning that "he used to carry about a map of the world on vellum, with the speeches of kings and generals extracted out of T. Livius, and that he had given his slaves the names of Mago and Annibal."[10]

He seems to have taken two actions against diviners, who certainly included astrologers, though only Jerome and the *Souda* are specific on this point. One astrologer arrested was Ascletarius (Asclepion, Asklation, perhaps Ascleparion), who seems Egyptian by his name. On 17 September he was brought before Domitian, who had, we are told, received several astrologic warnings of near doom. Ascletarius seems to have admitted the charge against him. The fullest account of what happened is found in an astrologic manuscript, which states that the man came before the emperor "and told him definitely that he'd be killed next day, before the 5th hour had come. The other asked jestingly if he had something to predict about himself. The man then said he would very soon be eaten by dogs. The other, wanting to prove him a liar, ordered him

Fig. 63. Coin of Domitian, with Minerva; coin of Vespasian with goats

to be chained to a stake and burned. But when they lit the fire, a very violent rainstorm burst and put the fire out. And when the guard had hurried off because of the rain's fury, dogs came and tore him to pieces. When Domitian heard of it, he began to fear the man had told the truth about him as well. And so it turned out." Suetonius adds, "The emperor learned of the matter with the other news of the day from the actor Latinus who chanced to see it all when passing the place." He says that the body was being burned when the pyre was blown down; Dion, that the man was at the stake with hands tied.[11]

The story sounds very much like a folktale of the kind used to glorify astrologers. That such tales clustered round Domitian is proved by the fact that a variant of the tale-type is also attached to him. A man known as astrologer, *haruspex* or mage, Larginus Proculeus, had been arrested in one of the two provinces of Germany for prophesying the emperor's end. He seems to have admitted the charge, but claimed the right of appeal as a Roman citizen; anyhow the governor sent him to Rome and he was brought before Domitian on 18 September. Asked the meaning of a thunderbolt that had fallen, he said that it portended a change of ruler. Domitian sentenced him to death. An astrologic manuscript version makes him tell Domitian the day of his death (that very day); Domitian replied that he'd keep him in chains as he wanted to witness his execution. The man riposted, "You will not kill me nor am I fated to die by you." Shortly after that Domitian was killed; and the next emperor Nerva gave Larginus 400,000 sesterces.[12] What Domitian's horoscope was, we do not know.[13]

Dion says that Domitia, Domitian's wife, learned of her husband's plans for a massacre and told the senators involved, who went to Nerva, a mild persecuted man. "He had been in peril of his life through the denunciations of astrologers who declared that he'd become ruler. This last circumstance made it easier for him to be persuaded to assume the imperial power." Whether his own astrologers or others gave him away is not clear. Domitian would have killed Nerva "if one of the astrologers friendly with the latter had not stated that he'd die in a few days. So Domitian, trusting this would happen, did not want to be guilty of an unnecessary murder since Nerva was to die soon in any case." We see the illogicality of all such proceedings: if a man was executed for having a royal horoscope, the horoscope lied and there had in fact been no reason for the execution.[14]

Philostratos in his *Life of Apollonios* tells how his hero on arriving in Rome is arrested and brought before Domitian, who suspects him of complicity with Nerva (then exiled in Tarentum) and has his hair and beard cut off. Apollonios magically strikes the fetters off his legs and gives a discourse on magic. Interrogated in court, he astounds Domitian by disappearing. He is transported to Dikaiarchia (Naples) and mistaken for his own ghost.[15] Here is another fable of the Tyrant baffled by the Wiseman.

Nerva adopted Trajan as his heir and astrologers assured him that his choice was a good one. Trajan himself, a good man of action, seems to have had no interest in astrology. The younger Plinius in his *Panegyric,* however, praises him: "You raised your father [Nerva] to the skies" after his death on 27 October 97: "not from fear of the citizens, not in affront of the deities, not in your own honour, but because you believe him a god."[16]

We do not know when Balbillus died; but around this time his children, Julia Balbilla and G. Julius Antiochos Epiphanes Philopappos, were flourishing. The latter was an intellectual, not a soldier. Athens was his favourite place, where he was *archon* probably in the mid-eighties, perhaps again in the nineties—unless there was another Philopappos. He gained the office through his wealth and lineage, and was let keep the title king. Ploutarch knew him and dedicated to him a discourse: *How to distinguish Flatterer from Friend*. Perhaps he felt that a man surrounded by so many flatterers needed instruction on such a point. When we consider the sumptuous tomb that he left, we feel indeed that he may have needed a nudge from the philosopher. Of poems, the *Hypomnemata* or *Dissertations, Memorials,* of Q. Pompeius Capito seems dedicated to him. He was made a member of the aristocratic

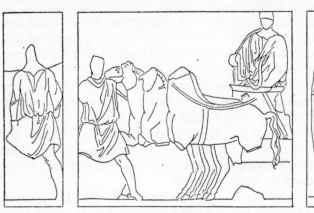

Fig. 64. Monument of Philopappos at Athens

cult-group, the Arval Brothers, and was chosen for the imperial guards and for consul in 109. Trajan was no intellectual, but his wife Plotina was; and Philopappos clearly remained in the court-favour. He wanted to be buried in Athens, where his fine mausoleum was built. Pausanias seems referring to him when he says of the Mouseion there: "this is a hill right opposite the Akropolis inside the old city boundaries, where legend says Mousaios used to sing and, dying of old age, was buried; afterwards a monument also was erected here to a Syrian." Philopappos would certainly have enjoyed the association with such a site.[17]

Quintilian, a Spaniard, professor of oratory, came to Rome with Galba. He considered that mathematics demonstrated the order of the heavens, with nothing fortuitious: "a concept that may at times be of value to an orator". He also brought out how pervasive the use of astrology and other omen-systems had now become, so anyone practising the law had to know how to deal with such matters in evidence.

If . . . anyone should want to bring in evidence of the sort known as supernatural, based on oracles, prophesies, omens, I would remind him there are two ways of treating these. There is the General Method, about which there is endless dispute between the adherents of Stoicism and of Epicureanism, as to whether the world is governed by Providence. The other method is the Special, which is concerned with the particular departments of the art of divination . . . The credibility of oracles may be established or destroyed in one way, and that of soothsayers, augurs, diviners, astrologers [*mathematici*] in another, since the two classes differ wholly in nature.

Equally instructive in another way is the pseudo-declamation of his, which is supposed to have been delivered before the Senate. It deals with the rights to suicide and burial. A son has had his horoscope taken before his birth; it predicts (correctly) his sex and fine military career, but adds that he will kill his father. So the son claims the right to kill himself. All the prophecies have so far come out as true, except that the murder still remains to be done. "Not that the astrologer alone has predicted the deed of these hands specifically as to period and time, but I myself am convinced that I shall commit parricide." He goes on to show how the astro-logic prediction has created his state of mind, the conflict of father and son, an impossible contradiction. The dilemma is that if the Senate agrees with him, it contradicts the decree of Fate. "Nor should you decide in favour of my life because I seem to be engaged in a struggle with the astrologer to defeat Necessity, to conquer Fate." His father opposes him and wants to take his chance

Fig. 65. Monument of Philopappos: he is shown as consul in chair and as Athenian citizen; also a statue of Antiochos IV

The son pleads that, if he continues to live it is an intolerable burden on his father, who completely believes in astrology. He argues that the courage of the astrologer in telling the dark as well as the bright side of his life gives good reason for accepting his picture in its totality. The father nobly did not expose his child: all the more reason not to repay kindness with murder.

My father knows how great is the lack of guilt in the predicted crime and he thus tries to persuade you not to trust in the astrologer's art. So he contends there is no Fate and all happens by Chance, haphazardly. Or that even if all were governed by Providence, it still could not be found out by human science . . . I however assume the man spoke the truth because certain stars, so to say fixed and linked, shine jointly for all eternity once they are joined to each other, while others in unchanging orbits pursue their measured courses dispersed all over the sky. Do you really believe that all these have been casually and accidentally distributed? . . . Hence what is born is assigned its role . . . and accepts the future as it does life itself.

He goes on to argue that astrology is the "most certain science" and to trace the steps by which from terror of the stars, then admiration, knowledge has been born through observation.[18]

The declamation is worked out as a piece of complex casuistry, yet it does bring out with genuine force and subtlety the conflicts in mind and spirit created by the existence of astrology and its contradictions as they sink integrally into the lives of people. Deep in their hearts was a desperate need to learn and act out the fated parts, and yet at the same time somehow to use knowledge to transcend the whole situation.

The poet Martial also came from Spain. Domitian made him a tribune, and patrons gave him a small house at Rome and another in the Sabine hills. He accepted the idea of katasterisms and played about with it, as with the ideas of Fortune and Fate. An epigram on a dilettante, who does all things prettily, remarks:

> he composes pretty mimes and epigrams pretty witty,
> a literary man and astrologer, pretty well.

And on a prodigal spender he writes:

> An astrologer said you'd have a speedy end,
> Munna. He didn't lie, it seems to me.
> You fear so much you'll leave one coin to spend,
> you waste your inheritance disastrously.
> Less than a year, two millions gone, we see.
> Isn't that coming to a speedy end?[19]

He makes a show of astronomical lore to describe Domitian's return from the north. When the latter has a spendid lion in the arena:

> . . . did your brother or your father, afar,
> send this fierce Lion down from Hercules' star.

Vespasian and Titus, now in the sky, send down the Nemean Lion, killed by Hercules out of the constellation: here we have an example of the way in which the zodiacal signs were identified with the Twelve Labours. Again, in telling how snow fell thickly on Domitian's face and breasts, Martial says that the latter, after the fatigues of his Dacian and German campaigns, is so used to "Bootes' North Star and rain-drenched hair", that "he pays no notice to the Greater Bear, who frolics in heaven with dry showers in his play. These snows are sent by Caesar's child, I say." That is, by Domitian's infant, who died and was deified.[20]

The poet is echoing an idea of Domitian himself. Undated *aurei* and *denarii* of Domitia show a naked baby boy (Divus Caesar as the baby Jupiter) seated on a globe which is marked with cross zones. The boy stretches out his hands; above and around are seven stars. These stars have been taken to represent Ursus as a symbol of royalty and eternity, with the globe as the Earth where Zeus and the baby spent their first years before being rapt to the stars. The globe could however simply stand for the cosmic role; and we find seven stars as an emblem of Aion (Time, Eternity). Also seven stars with a half moon appear on a denar of Septimus Severus to express *saeculi felicitas,* the Felicity of the Age, the return of a golden age of peace and plenty.[21]

Legio I Flavia, a favourite legion, was called by Domitian "Minerva Pia Fidelis" after his patroness, with the Ram as his emblem: since the Sun in the Ram was sacred to Minerva—17 March to 16 April. On the legionary standards on the Column of Trajan we see the Ram; and on the reverse of a coin of Victorinus is Minerva holding a crown and followed by a Ram, with the inscription LEG PRIMA MINERVINA PF.[22] We may note that both the legionary *signum* and that of the maniple in the army normally had signs drawn from the Zodiac, though at times the signs had other relations (to the founder, to the legion's own birthday, to the god whose *cognomen* the legion bore, or some famous incident in the legion's history). Legions with the Bull were Caesarian in origin, since the Bull is the zodiacal sign for the month 17 April–18 May sacred to Venus the ancestress and patroness of the Julian *gens*. Those with the Capricorn were Augustan. II Augusta had both Capricorn and Pegasus, and the second sign seems added by Vespasian. He was first hailed emperor in Alexandreia in July 69, and no doubt he knew of the oracle saying that the new master would come forth from Judaea; he may well have taken Pegasus for himself as the Horse of the East. It is noteworthy that II Augusta had been his first command and that he gave Pegasus also to II Adiutrix, which seems the first legion created under his rule.[23]

Statius in his *Silvae* produces for Domitian an hyperbole that can stand by Lucan's picture of Nero at the start of his *Pharsalia*: describing a statue of the emperor he says, "Your sole neck will give a place for all heaven's stars." As he uses the word *locus* for place, he is perhaps giving it a technical meaning: it would indeed be the end of astrology if all the stars found their locus in a single spot, buzzing madly round the imperial neck. He also outdoes Martial in pleading that though Domitian may be tempted by "some shining quarter of the sky", let him "remain content with the governing of men, be lord of Earth and Ocean, and give the Sky constellations". That is, stay alone on earth and keep on begetting children who die and populate the sky.[24]

Valerius Flaccus in his epic on the *Argonauts* takes the stars as the causers of weather-conditions. Thus it is the Dogstar that harms the earth:

> When the god's immense anger and Sirius,
> ravager of Calabrian fields, has swooped on pen
> and cornland, a scared band of countryfolk
> gather in an ancient grove and there a priest
> speaks out reverent vows for their distress.

The rainy weather comes. "By the law of heaven", *polus,* "Jove has drawn down the Pleiads, that stormy constellation, as he carried on the eternal revolutions. At once rain poured. . . ." That is the time of fear. For then Justice, *Astraea,* "urges her plea, imploring Jove's wrath against the peoples, and leaving earth she importunes Saturn's star with her complaint". The departure of Justice for the stars, seen by Virgil as an ancient event which only a totally new start can reverse, is here defined as happening yearly.[25]

Juvenal, with his unrelenting satirical eye, inevitably tells us of astrology at work demoralising upperclass Roman Society:

The Chaldeans are still more trusted. Each word uttered
by the astrologer they take as from Ammon's fountain:
For now, with the Delphic oracle dumb, man's doomed
to face a darkened future. Chief of these
was one, often in exile, through whose friendship
and venal ticket of prophecy there died
the great citizen that Otho feared. For now
no astrologer's credited who's not been jailed
in some far camp, chains clanking on either arm.
No one trusts his powers if he's not been condemned
and almost done-for, contriving to get deported
to a Cyclad or to escape from little Seriphos.

Seriphos was an exile-island of the smaller Cyclades. From Juvenal's
picture we can see that very many more astrologers suffered than
the few who managed to get into the full light of history. The
"chief of these" was Ptolemaeus. Elsewhere he asks what use he is
at Rome. He cannot tell lies, and

> I don't know the star-movements. I cannot, will not,
> promise a man his father's death. I've never
> examined the entrails of a frog.

Again he writes:

> The astrologers know your horoscope, you say,
> but it's boring to wait for the slow-running spindle;
> you'll die before your thread is snapt. Already
> you're in your son's way, you delay his prayers.

Not only heirs are concerned about their father's nativity. Wives
are also waiting for husbands to die. Tanquil makes consultations
about her husband and her jaundiced mother; she wants to know
when she'll bury her sister or her uncles:

> and will her lover outlive her? what greater boon
> could the gods bestow? Yet Tanaquil herself
> doesn't understand the darkening threats of Saturn
> or under what constellations Venus smiles,
> which months will be times of loss, and which of again.
> But beware of meeting one whom you see clutching
> a worn calendar like a ball of clammy amber,
> one who doesn't inquire, but is herself inquired of;
> who, when her husband's travelling abroad or homing,
> won't go if Thrasyllus' *Numbers* call her back.
> If she wants a drive to the first milestone, the book

> tells her the hour; if her rubbed eye itches, she checks
> her horoscope before she asks for a salve,
> and if she's ill abed, the hour for food
> is that prescribed for her by Petosiris.

There's also the woman with tales of calamities. "She's the first to notice the comet threatening the Kings of Armenia and Parthia."[26]

Tacitus we have already seen with his concern on questions of Fate. Suetonius was much interested in astrology and wrote on the Roman Year. Epiktetos was exiled with other Stoics in 93, but returned under Hadrian. He opposed the divining art to the diviner within, conscience and morality. He holds to the Stoic idea of Fate, and, secure in his deep inner life with its ceaseless attempt to find security and peace in a complete acceptance of the total frame of things, he rejects all forms of divination.

What then is it that so often leads us to divination? Cowardice, the dread of events. Hence we flatter the diviners. "Pray, sir, shall I inherit my father's estate?" "Let's see, let me sacrifice upon the occasion." "No, sir, just as Fortune pleases." Then if he says, "You shall inherit it," we give him thanks as if we'd actually got the inheritance from him. The result is that they play upon us.[27]

And he says, "The Chaldeans and astrologers, after foretelling the deaths of many, were themselves surprised by death." At the same time he is full of Stoic sense of *sympatheia*: "The things of earth are in sympathy with the things of heaven." Philon had used almost the same words, "Earthly things depend on heavenly things by a kind of natural sympathy." And this side of Epiktetos is close to the views of the astrologers. Man, says Maternus, "is an animal made in imitation of the World, and is governed by the substance of divinity".[28]

If we turn to the extant horoscopes of the later first century A.D. we find them multiplying after 61. In the following rapid summary the sources are literary (that is, they come from astrologic manuscripts) unless the item is described as from a papyrus. A text in which the birth is dated 1 May 61 states of its subject that "in the first period he owned high political prestige and affairs and positions of trust", but later "he was brought down in life and became a vagabond". The next, probably of 7 October 61, mentions that "it is necessary to examine the hostile places and stars not only with respect to the other planets but also for the Horoscope and

Sun and Moon; for these also when they come into diameter during their travel indicate crisis and death". The third, probably of 22 January 62, deals with a person who "fell into a great many troubles and losses and offences against governor and king". He was a eunuch priest assigned to the Goddess, presumably Cybele or the Great Mother. "The ruler of the Lot [of Fortune] happened to be in Scorpion, the [9th] locus of the God and the rulers of the [diurnal] Sect, Saturn and Mercury, were found in the 11th locus Agathos Daimon, but in opposition." Hence the troubles. The birth was in the daytime and so was allotted to one of the day-planets (Sun, Jupiter, Mercury as Morning Star, Saturn) and not one of night-planets (Moon, Venus, Mercury as Evening Star, Mars). The zodiacal signs were also divided into those of the day and of the night.[29]

A person born at 8 a.m. on 31 October 65 "was destined to very great property even in childhood". Another born on 6 January 72 had a nativity which "at the beginning was mixed and mediocre but later was raised and had a share of chaplets". The man became an archpriest. Of another born on 19 April 74, in the *klima* of Alexandreia, we hear only that he lived 70 years and 1 month. A man born on 26 November 64 in the night has left two versions of his horoscope.

He lived the first [years] humbly and in poverty and [experienced] captivity and servitude, and was caught up in many perils. But since the [planets] of the same Sect happened to be in operative positions, he came into friendships and associations, and received positions of royal trust. Indeed he became highly esteemed because the [nativity's] exaltation was found in the Lion and [its] ruler, the Sun was in Mid-heaven with regard to the Lot [of Fortune] and he was found worthy of leadership and a position of power.

[2nd version] In the 69th year he was considered worthy of governor-ship and became feared and most highly regarded and blessed by many, but was envied and became entangled in mob-uproar and riots and did not complete his term of office, but was overtaken by painful illness and death.

The man may be Valerius Eudaimon who was eparch of Egypt in 142, but was no longer in office by 144.[30]

A man born in July 75 lived 69 years. "I took physical [life] from the Lion," the Lot of Fortune, says the astrologer, "giving first to the Lion itself 19 years, then to the Virgin 20, then to the Balance 8, then to the Scorpion 15: it makes 62 years." As for the man:

In these years he had many crises, both falls from a height and broken limbs. And the remaining 8 years from the Archer, Saturn being located there by Sect [?]. In these years he had to expect shipwrecks and bodily disorders. We get the cause of the injury from the sign where the ruler of the Lot of Fortune was found passing through: that is, the Lot was found in the Lion, and the ruler of the Lion, the Sun, was found in the Crab; and the Crab indicates breast and throat. We say then that the injury was from the Crab . . . He died diseased in the throat and afflicted with coughing. . . .

Up to 27 years he was an intermittent vagrant. His adequate property was squandered by guardians . . . [Then] he lived this whole period in success and was entrusted with public and royal affairs, and as a result became rich, but destined to reversals and ups-and-downs in the course of time . . . and he came to the end of his career and lost much through misplaced trust, and he undertook pledges for relatives and slaves, through whose negligence and need he fell into debt and was found abject, because the whole foundation [of the nativity] bore in this direction.[31]

The next test, of a man who lived 76 years, is hard to date with precision. Then comes a man born on 1 April 78:

This person was commanding and despotic, for the rulers of the Triangle [of the Sun] were found to be at a *kentron* [H] and in the Horoskopos, and it also fell the Lot [of Fortune] and the Daimon and the Basis and the Exaltation [of the nativity]. But Mars the ruler of these being unfavourably situated and not in aspect to the place had opposite effects, both in exile and violent death; for it was the ruler of the conjunction [of Sun and Moon]—

which occurred in the Ram. For 28 May 80 we have a text from Manethon, detailing his own horoscope:

But I'll proceed by a new turn in verse
and recall the stars of my own nativity
and in what sign did oft-sought Eilithyia
deliver me from the womb, so that for all time
they may teach and prove what Fate has granted me
to teach, the wisdom and beautiful poetry
of the stars. The sun was in the Twins. There too
was lovely Kypris, and also belovèd Phaeton
and golden Hermes; and in Aquarius then
were the Moon and Phainon. In the many-footed Crab
was Mars, and the Centaur was turning about Midheaven,
trailing his weapon. Thus Fate determined my birth.

He uses some poetic or old terms. Kypris is Aphrodite, Venus; Phaeton (Phaethon), Zeus, Jupiter; Phainon, Kronos, Saturn. The time was about two hours after sunset.[32]

An elaborate papyrus text gives a computation for 31 March 81 by Titus Pitenius. It opens with an unfounded claim for the Egyptians:

The Egyptians of old, who had faithfully studied the heavenly bodies and discovered the motions of the Seven Gods, compiled and set out everything in Everlasting Tables and generously left us their knowledge of these matters. From them I have accurately calculated and set out for each [of the Seven Gods] according to Degree and Minute, Aspect and Phase, and, simply, not to waste time by listing each item, whatever is relevant to its inquiry. Thus the path of astrologic speculation is made straight, unambiguous—that is, consistent. Goodbye, dearest Hermon.

Then comes the nativity composed in high-sounding terms. The Sun is the Mightiest and Ruler of All; the Moon is Divine and lightbringing; Saturn's Star is called Phainon; Mars is Pyroeis. The exposition is elaborate. Pregnancy is computed as 276 days, with a mean value of 273 assumed. (The Egyptians assumed a length of 275.) Thus runs the paragraph on the Moon:

Waxing in crescent she had advanced in the Bull 13° and a thousandth part of a degree; in the sign of Venus; in its own Exaltation; in the terms of Mercury; in a female and solid sign; like Gold; mounting the back of the Bull; in the second dekan called Aroth; its *dodekatemorion* again was shining on about the same place in the Scorpion.

Pitenius uses the measure "a finger" apparently for 0.5°, a norm in both Babylonian and Greek astronomy. "Like Gold" is unusual for the Moon, which is connected with silver, but astrologic texts call her *chrysampyx*, "with gold fillet or frontlet", and Bacchylides uses that epithet for the heavens, Ourania. Pitenius also oddly links crystal and Venus. In al-Biruni's *Astrology* crystal is linked with the Moon and gold with Venus, while the Moon represents crystal in Hindu doctrine.[33]

We have two versions of a horoscope of 9 July 82. "The nativity was brilliant and distinguished. He was entrusted with royal office and considered worthy of the high priesthood." The text ends, "The [11th locus of] accomplishment was irregular and unstable, sometimes too full, sometimes lacking; for Saturn and Venus were in aspect to it." The second version adds, "The total

L

is 70; so long he lived." We have again two versions for a birth sometime in 83. The man's life "at first was troubled and lowly; but the Moon being found in a *kentron*, he came into military and advantageous circumstances". He then reached "the greatest fortune and governorship". After a gap we read, "property and plunder and theft and violence; they were wickedly plundered after his death". The second version adds, "This person had mange on the head and leprosy and lichens on the body; for the ruler of the Daimon was in the Fish."[34]

A man born of 5 February 85 again "came from a humble and ordinary fortune to one of governorship and wealth". Another of 24 November of the same year had a worse time. "The sun being found in the places [house] of Jupiter, which indicate things concerning the groin and the thighs, caused infirmity in the [parts] and gout; for it is the ruler of sinews. And as Saturn was found in the Lower Midheaven, he had Visions of Gods and of the Spirits of the Dead."[35] A luckier man was born sometime in August about 86: "such a person was commanding and master over life and death, because the stars were found in their own domains." He was perhaps a *strategos* or nome-governor in Egypt. Another, born on 27 December 86, "was beheaded", while the next, of 9 January 87, "was disabled on account of the Pleiades and of maleficent Saturn, and he had unmentionable vices as a result of both signs. Further, Jupiter, ruler of the Daimon in the Fish, was found in Capricorn: from these it was clear that he had gout. Enough to have ascertained from the Lot [of Fortune] and its ruler both the infirmity and the disease." A man of 9 July of the same year had a bad horoscope. His lot of Fortune was in the Twins. "In this [sign] Saturn, Mercury, Mars, were accompanied by one another, destructive and in aspect to the Moon. Further, the ruler of the Full Moon was turning away, and Jupiter, being in the [8th] locus of death and in opposition, could not aid. The man was beheaded."[36]

Also bad was the nativity of a man of 29 July 89. Saturn was in the same locus as, and in dominant aspect to, Mercury, ruler of the Lot of Fortune, and to the Moon, with Mars opposite the locus of Death. "He hanged himself." For a man of 4 April 91, the locus of Death was in the Crab, with Saturn, ruler of the Full Moon, turning away, and so on. "He was killed by wild beasts." Another of 17 November 92 was "disabled in the penis as Saturn in particular was in dominant aspect to the conjunction, and the luminaries [Sun and Moon], and the ruler Mars was unfavourably placed".[37]

Now we have another papyrus, with birthdate as 13 April 95, in the latitude of Alexandreia. The papyrus seems to have been bought in Thebes, perhaps found with wooden tablets that held demotic planetary tables for at least A.D. 71–132. It begins with an almost-lost introduction, then sets out the position and character-isation of Sun, Moon, and five Planets. At times demotic signs are used in spelling the names of dekans. The end of the horoscope proper gives the four cardinal points and the four lots. After a mutilated passage we get what seems a discussion on the single periods of life, first in Greek, then in Old Coptic with some Greek insertions. The man's fortune begins well (for 6 years, 9 months (?) 25 days) with (well-being and) lots of pleasure. If he is a slave, he'll be freed; if poor, he'll become rich; if rich, he'll become richer and the number of his slaves will increase. His crops will do well; his children of any union will have a fine inborn nature like their parents, and he will have excellent associations extending every-where. But he will suffer from cold, fevers, and other illnesses. Saturn being in trine to Venus shows that he will be cold towards women. He'll be tried in court for "unspeakable charges", will suffer wretchedly, and live a miserable life abroad.

The Coptic text expands the details of his fate, using the "if" formula. Thus:

If Jupiter were a hostile star at his nativity, perhaps he'll pass by his wife or be at enmity with her, or his children will misbehave in turn, or he'll part from them in mercantile affairs. If there were an evil star . . . a wife won't make a term for [for ever], a child won't come to him for ever . . . and a wife will burn into the hair . . . A woman of . . . [will] . . . him, and his heart will . . . through her . . . A woman will cause him to take shame, or he'll be hunted [?] from year 42 on. A woman will be to him. He'll take one until year 94. He'll see a wife's death or be parted from her and they'll examine him . . . He will take counsel of a woman and [she] will take counsel from him . . . His heart will become good for a wife and sent him to a child from year 42 . . . God said: one woman and . . . become good for one woman. His heart will love . . . six. His life will come to . . . through him. His heart will become good . . . pity . . . in his heart . . . and he will drink his . . . and he'll take a wife and she'll leave . . . pity . . . someone . . . to him . . . his dream . . . A scorpion was not dumb.

Except that a woman or women will play a large part in his life, it is not easy to see what is going to happen. The text is unusual among early horoscopes in its detailed exposition as well as its addition of a long statement on doctrine. It reads more like one of the treatises of the fifth century. But in fact we know little of astrologic theory before the second century, when we have Valens and Ptolemaios. There are many difficulties. We cannot make out the principle used in the numbering and the names of the Lots, which do not agree with the Lot of Fortune or the Lot of the Daimon. Dekans 1, 2, 3 are cited with regard to the *dodekatemoria*, and the names in general harmonise with the Egyptian names; but 36 Horoscopes are also listed, with names clearly related to those of the Egyptian dekans. We might consider the dekans to be those of the *dodekatemoria* and the horoscopes to be those of the longitudes; but the order of the dekans as known from the Egyptian sources of Hephaistion hardly support this idea.[38]

Back now to literary sources. A man born 14 May 95 "had many ups-and-downs in the first period of his life and though his parents' property was good he lived in debt. Then later he got an inheritance and improved his means by shrewd enterprise. He grew ambitious, lordly, munificent, popular, and a friend of kings and governors; and he provided temples and public works, winning perpetual remembrance." A man born 4 days later "rose from mediocrity" and became governor and *strategos*. One born on 23 February 95 "was beheaded", and another of 6 November the same year had a different fate. "The rulers of the [Moon's] Triangle and of the Lot, found in Lower Midheaven, made him miserly, unambitious, and niggardly."[39]

These nativities, then, give us an interesting series of side-lights on individual lives in the period. Inevitably most of the persons concerned belong to the propertied classes; but we see how hazardous life could be even for those with a good start, while now and then we see a man rising up in social status.

17

Hadrian to the Severi

Aelius Hadrianus, an uncle of a cousin of Trajan, was an amateur astrologer who was said to have forecast that his grandnephew, P. Aelius Hadrianus, born 24 January 76, would mount the throne.[1] We possess a horoscope of Hadrian. After the technical details it states: "Such a person was adopted by a certain emperor, akin to him, and having lived with him two years, he became emperor about his 42nd year, and was wise and educated, so that he was honoured by shrines and temples; and he was married to one wife from maidenhood and was childless; and he had one sister [Domitia Paulina]. And he was at discord and conflict with his own relatives. When he had reached about his 63rd year he died, a victim to dropsy and asthma." He died on 10 July 138, about 62½ years old.

He became emperor [*autokrator*] because the two luminaries [Sun and Moon] were in the horoscopic sector and especially because the Moon was of the same Sect and in conjunction to the degree with the horoscopic sector and with Jupiter, which was also due to make its morning phase after 7 days. And the Moon's attending stars themselves were found in favourable positions, Venus in her own exaltation, Mars in his own Triangle, both in their own domains and in *apanaphora* with regard to the Moon. And besides the cosmos-ruling Sun was the Moon's attendant in the subsequent degrees and had as attending stars Saturn in his own house and Mercury, both at their morning rising. It is also significant that the Moon was about to come in conjunction with a certain bright fixed star that is at the 20th degree. For it is necessary to look at the conjunction of the Moon not only with the planets but also the fixed stars.'

One manuscript has an insertion:

That he was honoured and received the *proskynesis* [adoration, prostration] from all men was due to the fact that Jupiter was in epicentric attendance on the Sun. For a planet that thus attends Sun and Moon has the effect that a man is highly esteemed by his equals or betters, and has attendants and receives the *proskynesis*. And the beneficial qualities he got from the cited position of Jupiter. That he was beneficial to many, and, as I said, got the *proskynesis*, was due to the fact that epicentric sun and moon were equally attended by the five planets. For especially if Sun and Moon or both are in active [? cardinal] points—that is, the Horoscopal Point or the Mesuranema—and are attended in this way by all stars [planets], they make those born under such constellations into kings ruling over many nations. (Antigonos of Nikaia.)

This is a royal horoscope though the term is not used; it is however implied by several words.[2]

There is also a horoscope that is very likely that of Hadrian's father, P. Aelius Afer. The *klima* is that of southern Spain and the birthdate is 5 April 40. The text states that the person "who has the stars in this way will be very distinguished, of very distinguished ancestors, a person of authority and a punisher of many, and very wealthy", but "not unjust and not accused". He was "indifferent to female intercourse and sordid towards males, especially because Mars had his position with Venus and Mercury in the Ram, which is a vicious sign, and Venus was looked on by Saturn in quartile, and all these stars were in male signs". Also the man had "a happy and very wealthy theme", and "provided many dedications and gifts for his fatherland".[3]

We have a third horoscope connected with Hadrian. This seems to be of Pedanius Fuscus, who, together with his parents, was executed, apparently in 136. The text comes from Antigonos:

All of his family suffered in the same reversals because the Sun was in the Horoskopos, attended by Mercury and Jupiter. He [Antigonos] says about it: He was ill advised because Mercury and Saturn were found in a male sign and destroyed someone of those of the family because of this configuration. And he himself was cut down because the Moon was in the Scorpion, a misfortune-causing sign, and projecting her rays against Mars, who was in Epanaphora with respect to Midheaven. The damage would come to a person because Mars was in a human-shaped sign [Aquarius]. He was erotic and fond of gladiators because Mars was in epanaphora with respect to Midheaven and Mercury was in the house of Mars. He died about his 25th year, in a bad way, because this [the number 25] and the rising time of Aquarius were the same.[4]

Cassius Dion gives his age at death as 18, but he may well be wrong. From our text the execution took place in 137–8. Pedanius was grandson of Servianus' daughter, who was Hadrian's niece.

Hadrian himself had long been interested in astrology. When about 20, serving in Lower Moesia, he consulted astrologers, who reassured him. He himself mastered the technique and was said to have foretold his own death-hour. His liking for divination made him also use the Virgilian Lots (turning up passages blindly from the poet); and he was the only Roman emperor who visited the site that had been Babylon. He matched Nero's colossos (on which Vespasian had substituted a star-encircled head of Helios for the head of Nero) with one of the Moon Goddess; and he restored the Pantheon, making it an astrologic symbol of the cosmos.[5] The death of his favourite Antinoos in the Nile had some astrologic overtones. Dion suggests that the death was sacrificial, since Hadrian "was always very curious and employed divinations and incantations of all kinds". The death then may have been a vicarious sacrifice, "it being necessary for a life to be freely surrendered for the accomplishment of the ends that Hadrian had in view". We are reminded both of the charges of boy-sacrifices against Nigidius and others, and of the alleged advice of Balbillus to Nero to kill others in order to prolong his own life. Such an act however hardly fits in with what we know of Hadrian. In any event the death led to a star-apotheosis. "Hadrian declared he had seen a star which he took to be that of Antinoos and gladly lent an ear to the fictitious tales woven by his associates that the star had

Fig. 66. Ephesian relief in honour of Marcus Aurelius and his triumph over the Parthians; he enters a solar chariot, ushered by Victory, with Earth and Child under the horse

really come into being from Antinoos' spirit and had then appeared for the first time." It is still called by the name of Antinoos.

We saw how Julia Balbilla, descendant of the astrologer, was with him when he visited Egypt. Here is one of the Greek poems she left on the so-called statue of Memnon, which was supposed to utter a cry as the sun rose:

By Julia Balbilla when the Augustus Hadrian heard Memnon

    I'd heard how Egyptian Memnon, warmed by the rays
    of sunlight, sent his voice from Theban stone.
    When all-king Hadrian he saw before the sun
    had risen, as he might he gave him hail.
    When Titan springing in *aither* with white hair
    held in shadow the second section of the hours,
    it seemed an instrument of bronze was struck;
    a sharp cry came. A third sound broke in welcome.
    Then the emperor Hadrian lavished salutations
    on Memnon and for posterity he inscribed
    lines on the stone to tell what he had heard.
    All clearly saw he was cherished by the gods.

She seems to say that the oracular statue accepted him as a sun before the sun rose.[6]

He used astrology in seeking a successor. His choice of Aelius Verus is explained as having been made out of desire to possess him sodomitically, although he knew that Verus' horoscope was unsatisfactory. "For Marius Maximus represents him as so expert in astrology as even to assert that he knew all about his own future." A scholar tried to console him. "What if a mistake was made in taking his horoscope?" Hadrian replied, "It's easy for you to say that when you're looking for an heir to your property, not to the empire." The advent of the method of adoption for choosing a successor gave a special value to the use of horoscopes. We may note the play on the name of Aelius Helios or Sun, and the fact that Hadrian raised colossi of Aelius in several places—colossi being specifically monuments of the Sun.[7]

There is not much sign of astrologic activity under Antoninus Pius and Marcus Aurelius. Under the first the Alexandrian mint issued many coins with astral and zodiacal symbols; and the so-called Rain Miracle of Marcus' Dacian campaigns was linked with an Egyptian mage, Arnuphis, who has been identified with Julian, son of Julian the Chaldean.[8] Marcus in his *Commentaries* has much of a Stoic nature to say on Fate, Order, Justice. He accepted

dreams as revelations of Providence, and astrology as well. After
his wife Faustina "had given birth to Commodus and Antoninus,
the latter for whom the astrologers had forecast an horoscope as
favourable as that of Commodus, lived to be only four years old".
Apparently they did not forecast Commodus' disastrous life and
murder. Marcus merely comments, "How many astrologers, after
foretelling in great display the deaths of others", themselves died.[9]
He has a deep sense of *sympatheia*. The cosmos is "a web spun of
one texture", and "all things have been interwoven and holy is the
bond. Nothing can really be said to be alien to anything else. Things
have been marshalled and combine to make an ordered universe.
There is one universe consisting of all, and one god through all,
and one substance and one law, and one reason common to all
intelligible beings, and one truth." This sense of a unitary process,
Stoic at basis, was an essential aspect of both astrology and
alchemy.[10]

Fig. 67. Companion piece: Selene, pursued by Hesperos, entering
chariot, with Ocean under

Commodus was a devotee of Isis and Mithras rather than of the
stars. The trend now was towards a solar cult as a form of monotheism, reflecting the role of the single earth-ruler. But astrology had
gone too deep not to leave many marks and to determine much of
the direction of the new trends. The age was too wearied, too
broken down, too submissive despite its capacity for savagery, to
be as interested in an intellectual discipline like astrology as in

mystery cults and saviours. Commodus saw himself as a sort of Hercules. In the cult of Hercules there was now merged both a saviour-worship (with star-apotheosis) and an astrologic concept of Time as the repetition of the zodiacal signs and the twelve labours. Sol Invictus thus merged with Saviour Herakles to provide the ideal protector of the empire and image of the emperor. The Gallic secession of the third century under Postumus used Herculean symbols; and at the same time solar Apollinism, semi-messianic, was drawing strength from cult-centres like Emesa, Palmyra, Baalbek, in which there were many astrologic elements. The trends in question were converging to the point where under Constantine they could lead into Christianity, modifying and strengthening it as they were absorbed or demolished.[11]

After his twelve labours Hercules went to heaven via the Zodiac, through a door taken to be the Crab. A typical monument expressing the new stress on Hercules is that at Igel, on the line of the Roman road from Trèves to Rheims. On the rear wall is shown the apotheosis of Hercules, who mounts in his chariot up to the zodiacal circle. Minerva is not at his side, as in earlier representations, but emerges from the clouds to greet him with outstretched hand—just as the Christian God holds out his hand to heaven-ascending emperors on later medals of consecration. In the spandrels are the heads of the four Windgods. The link with the Sun appears in the Genius above Hercules bridling two griffins (sacred to Apollo and the solar gods); on the pediment is Sol Sanctissimus on a quadriga. There is also a representation of Ganymede rapt to heaven by the Eagle (astrologically standing for Aquarius).[12]

We may compare an ivory leaf showing the deification of (probably) Constantius Chlorus, the father of Constantine the Great, where we meet the eagles, the chariot ascent, and part of the Zodiac circling round the sky. Here emperor and sun are entangled. We see the emperor or his image in a chariot; above the pyre a youthful figure in a chariot is the sun, with his arching drape over his head for the sky; and above again is the emperor carried aloft by Sleep and Death, to be welcomed by five deities out of the clouds.[13] Aspects of all this symbolism appear in the funerary monuments of lesser people. Thus a sarcophagus of the late second century in the Palazzo Barberini shows a couple inside a medallion (in the form of a *corona triumphalis*) decked out with the twelve zodiacal signs. The medallion is held by the four Seasons, two on each side; below love-gods pile up grape-clusters to represent the blessed hereafter. In humbler form is a little *stēlē* at Carnuntum. Inside the *corona* is an eagle with outspread wings, the Winds are in the spandrels; Sol crowns the pediment within which are two dolphins (expressing the journey over the waters to the Blessed

Fig. 68. Igel Monument; northern face with Zodiac and Apotheosis

Isles)[14]. The message the Emperor Julian received from the oracle reflected the spirit of such monuments: "Then when you have put off the grievous burden of mortal limbs, the fiery car will bear you through the midst of the eddying whirlwinds to Olympos; and you will come to that ancestral home of heavenly light from which you wandered to enter the body of man." We may compare the chariot and horses of fire which parted disciple and master asunder, and Elijah ascending "by a whirlwind into heaven".[15]

As we have noted, some of the monstrous animals which Herakles had fought on earth were linked with zodiacal signs; and we are told by Festus-Paul that "Hercules is called Astrologer because on the day he threw himself into the flames there was to be an eclipse of the sun". The idea was no doubt taken from some tragedy or poem, and links the hero and the sun.[16] We may compare the darkness said to fall when Jesus was crucified.

If we look back, we see that, apart from some use of the Heraklean apotheosis to glorify Augustus, it was the orientalising emperors of the first century, Gaius, Nero, and Domitian, who took up the idea of being Hercules Redivivus. Trajan was the ruler who brought Hercules strongly into the current of imperial ideas. He, a practical man, preferred a hero who had struggled for the good of mankind before reaching heaven. Also, he was a Spaniard, and the cult of Hercules of Gades was important in his native land. And he had in his entourage a keen propagandist of the Heraklean Idea, Dion Chrysostom, who represents the trend in Stoicism to accommodate itself with autocracy by servilely identifying *autokrator* and Sun—while, of course, blandly moralising the situation. Dion used the parable of Herakles at the Crossroads (between Virtue and Vice), changing it into a choice between *Basileia* and *Tyrannis,* True Kingship and Despotism. Herakles chooses True Kingship and Zeus "hands over to him the government of the whole human race".[17]

Thus Herakles became the symbol, protector, and guarantee of the imperial unity.[18] Antonine coins and various votive inscriptions bring out this role. On an issue of L. Verus he appears for the first time as Pacifer. Commodus thus had a considerable tradition behind him when he took up Hercules with special fervour. The way in which he appropriated him appears in the appellation Commodianus which now replaces the traditional epithets on coins; and the emperor has himself represented with the attributes of club and lionskin; finally he is called on coins Hercules Romanus and he gave himself out as Founder of Roma Commodiana.[19] He even directly imitated Hercules as lion-hunter in the arena. (The Greeks had had at the Olympic Games some complete winners who were styled as "of the Line of Herakles".) One aspect of his Herculean masquing is however hard to comprehend. It was as Amazonius that the Lord of the Amphitheatre had his eternal victory acclaimed by the senators.[20] His *Life* takes effect for cause and links the choice of epithet with the portrait he had had made of

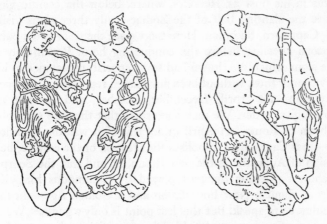

Fig. 69. Amazon and Greek fighting; Herakles (cheekpieces of Roman helmet from Palestrinum)

his mistress Marcia as an Amazon. But clearly he had the picture painted because of his Amazonian enthusiasm, just as it was that enthusiasm which made him appear in the arena "in Amazonian dress".[21]

It has been suggested that the epithet refers to the hunter Hippolytos (who died after resisting his stepmother Phaidra).[22] True, Ovid calls him *Vir Amazonius*; and his legend appears on second-century sarcophagi (where for the first time on Roman funerary reliefs the goddess Virtus is shown in a hunting scene). But the chaste Hippolytos seems wholly out of harmony with a character like Commodus. The adjective was late in use and comes to the fore only when Commodus gave all the months one or other of his names—in the following order: Amazonius (January), Invictus, Felix, Pius, Lucius, Aelius, Aurelius, Commodus, Augustus, Herculeus, Romanus, Exsuperatorius, inaugurating a golden age, *Saeculum Aureum Commodianum*. The Heraklean

coloration is clear. Herakles did on one of his lesser exploits fight
the Amazons (as did also Alexander the Great and Achilles).
Gaius had earlier clothed his Caesonia as an Amazon; Nero carried
round with him the statue of the Amazon of Strongylion (doubtless
a replica) and at the last moment he had his concubines' heads
cropped, and dressed the women with double-axes and *peltae*
(the crescent-shield characteristic of the Amazons).[23] Finally we
have the proof of Heraklean and zodiacal associations for Commodus in his bust as Herakles, where, below the cosmic globe,
we see the slanting belt of the Zodiac—only three signs visible,
Bull, Capricorn, Scorpion. Here too we see the *pelta* and a pair of
Amazons kneeling before the conquering hero. Presumably the
three signs which are shown had some special importance to him.
They cannot thus, without even any planet, represent a horoscope.
They stand for April, December, October, and are not in a
chronological order. We may conjecture that the Bull symbolises
the birth of Rome—21 April under this sign was the traditional
date—that Capricorn symbolises the creation of the empire, being
the sign of Augustus as the new Romulus; and that the Scorpion
somehow represents the part played by Commodus himself in
bringing about a New Foundation and a Golden Age—the third
Romulus, so to speak. But this last point is only a guess.[24] We can
indicate no October event in his life warranting such an emphasis
on the sign. True, he became Caesar on 12 October, but that was
hardly an event able to stand up against the importance of April
and November as foundation-moments. We may note however
that in his month-system October was Herculeus; and it seems
clear that for reasons unknown to us Commodus connected with
October his assumption of the Herculean role and his creation of
a new era.[25]

The Amazons we may note had a strong lunar coloration with
their single breasts and crescent-shields; but what Herakles had to
take from their Queen was her Girdle. It is perhaps not too far-
fetched to see in Commodus-Hercules, defeating the Amazons
and taking the Girdle, the Conqueror of the Zodiacal Circle—that
is, of the whole universe. *Zōnē*, girdle, was used for a zone of the
terrestrial sphere, or for one of the planetary spheres. And in the
plural *zonai* it was used for an order of divine beings presiding
over, or engirdled with, cosmic zones. *Zonaios kosmos* was the
universe over which they presided[26]: The month Amazonius
came after Exsuperatorius (Conqueror) and Commodus dressed

as an Amazon (owner of the zone) in his arena-victory. We may
note that in the passage cited earlier from Accius the Zodiac was
seen as a Girdle painted or embroidered with the Zodiac; a copy of
the statue called Apollo-and-the-Goose in the Vatican has a sash
draped across the body or over the shoulder with the Zodiac
embroidered on it. The same imagery has got into the account of
the sacred breastplate and its golden chains in *Exodus* (by some

Fig. 70. Amazons fighting with pelta-shields: painted sarcophagus
of Corneto (at Florence)

revision) and into the picture of the angels in *Revelation*: "And the
seven angels came out of the temple, having the seven plagues,
clothed in pure and white linen, and having their breasts girdled
with golden girdles." If the popular vision was thus so filled with
imagery of divine or holy beings with their heavenly girdles, why
should not Commodus have been englamoured by it in one of his
moments of excitement?

The man who was to found the next dynasty was Septimius Severus
of Lepcis in Africa. An ambitious man, coming up from below, he
was keenly interested in all forms of divination, especially
astrology.[27] Thus, probably when he was legate in Africa in 175
and there was a rebellion in the East against Marcus Aurelius, "he
had recourse to an astrologer in a certain African city. The
astrologer, after casting his horoscope, saw high destinies in store
for him, but said, 'Tell me your own nativity and not that of
another man.' Severus swore an oath that it was really his and the
astrologer revealed to him all the things that did later come to pass."
(This repeats the story of Augustus and Theogenes.) In 178 as
praetor Severus had promising dreams. As legate of Legio IV, in

189–90(?), he visited the popular oracle of Bel in Syria. (Macrinus as future emperor also visited this shrine, was given good news, and after his accession made a pilgrimage there.)[28] Later, Severus, considering marriage, inquired into the horoscopes of possible women. Learning of one in Syria whose horoscope stated that she'd marry a king, he sought her out and through the mediation of friends he won her as wife. She was Julia Domna, whose father was high-priest of the Sungod Elegabal, whom Greeks called Heliogabalos, to link him with Helios. Julia was an intellectual who gathered round her a group which included astrologers.[29]

Severus no doubt had the horoscope of his first child Bassianus (Caracalla) cast, as we are told he did with his second, Geta (27 May 189). "On learning the horoscope, a study in which like most Africans he was proficient, he is said to have remarked [to Flavianus Juvenalis, praetorian prefect in 193], 'It seems strange to me, my dear Iuvenalis, that our Geta is destined to be a deified emperor, as in his horoscope I see nothing imperial.' "[30]

While in Sicily, he was indicted for consulting seers and astrologers [*Chaldaei*] about the imperial dignity, but because Commodus was now detested, he was acquitted by the prefects of the guard to whom he had been handed over for trial, while his accuser was crucified.[31]

He became consul. Prosecuted for adultery, he won his case. In 192 came a comet and Commodus was killed.[32] But Pertinax became emperor, only to be murdered after three months and replaced by a rich profligate, Didius Julianus. Severus felt that his hour had come.

And what added not a little to his encouragement was the remembrance of several dreams, oracles, and other predictions, which seemed to foretell his future grandeur. For all these kinds of prophecies are credited when the course of events seems to verify their predictions. Most of them have been since published in his *Autobiography* and represented in sculpture and painting on his public images.[33]

Before he gained power, Didius Julianus was holding Rome and there were three challengers. While the senators pondered, the stars spoke out. Three of them suddenly became visible round the Sun as Julianus was offering sacrifices of Entrance in front of the Senate House. Cassius Dion, an eye witness, tells of the event. "The stars were so very distinct that the soldiers kept all the while looking up at them and pointing them out to one another, while declaring that some dreadful fate would befall the emperor. As for us [the senators], however much we hoped and prayed that it might so prove, yet the fear of the moment would not allow us to gaze up at the stars except by furtive glances. So much for the incident, which I give from my own knowledge."[34] Julianus, who was said to have used human sacrifices in his anxiety to probe the future, fell, and Severus emerged as the victor. Dion further tells us that his own *History* developed out of his interest in Severus' dreams and portents.

I had written and published a little book about the Dreams and Portents which gave Severus reason to hope for imperial power; and he, after reading the copy I sent him, wrote me a long and complimentary acknowledgment. This letter I received after nightfall and soon after I fell asleep. In my dreams the Divine Power commanded me to write history. Thus I came to write the narrative with which I am at this moment occupied."

He began on an account of the troubles leading up to Severus' accession, then decided on a larger work dealing with the whole history of Rome, from the foundation up to the point "that will seem best to Tyche". "That goddess," he adds, "gave me strength to carry on with my *History* when I grew timid and inclined to shrink from it. When I grow weary and would drop the task, she wins me back with dreams."[35]

Dreams could thus help a man in this world; they could also damn him. Popilius Pedo Apronianus was accused because his nurse had once dreamed that he'd be emperor; he was therefore suspected of using magic to gain the throne. Dion once more gives us a striking instance of the strange dreads under which people lived in such a world.

Now when the evidence about him, taken under torture, was read to us, there came up the statement that one of the persons conducting the examination [of nurse and household-slaves] had asked who told the dream and who heard it, and the man being examined said among other things, "I saw a certain bald-headed senator peeping in." On hearing this, we found ourselves in a terrible position . . . and although no one was very cheerful except those with unusually long hair, yet we all looked round at those not so fortunate . . . I actually felt with my hand to see whether I had any hair on my head. And a good many others had the same experience. And we were very careful to direct our gaze on those who were more or less bald, as if we'd thus divert our own danger upon them.[36]

Finally a former aedile was named. Dion suggests that he was innocent and only pointed out after the witness had been given "an imperceptible nod from someone". The man was at once executed. Apronianus was condemned in his absence as governor of Asia, then killed.

Severus as emperor executed many men. "He even went so far as to bring charges against several of his friends on the grounds of plotting to kill him. He put many others to death on the charge of asking Chaldeans or prophets [*vates*] how long he was destined to live." He was especially suspicious of "anyone who seemed qualified for imperial power, for his sons were still very young and he believed or had heard that this fact was being noted by those who sought predictions as to their prospects to the throne."[37]

Not wanting to lose any of the sanctions that had been used by the Antonines, he venerated Hercules, giving him the title of *deus patrius*.[38] An astrologic monument which he constructed in 203 was the Septizonium, built on the Appian Way where it would strike the eyes of travellers coming up to the Porta Capena of Rome; he wanted to impress, it was said, his fellow-Africans on their way to the City.[39] It was not a mausoleum. Most of the Severans were put in Hadrian's tomb—though Spartianus does state that Geta was buried in the ancestral tomb which Severus had beautified as a Septizonium. The building was pulled down in the sixteenth century by Pope Sixtus V, who wanted to use its stones; pictures made before this act of vandalism show three terraces or floors supported by columns.[40] We have seen that Suetonius knew a septizonium which existed under Vespasian. About fifty years before Severus we meet the term *heptazonos* in a Greek astrologic text; and later Valens used it for a series of the seven planets with the Sun as the middle one—in this sequence they were the deities of timekeeping. A suggestion has therefore been made that the Severan building had a clock denoting each of the seven week-days. Not that that is very likely.

The *Forma Urbis* shows two exedrae preceded by a large podium which a perpendicular return of the wall closes on the left. The colonnade follows the track of the wall; and we can restore a third exedra on the right. Clearly such a building did not suit any normal kind of planetarium. The structure was in fact a monumental façade dominating the Via Triumphalis, the palace of Domitian which was being reconstructed. It was in a part of the palace, constituting a false entry to it. If there had been a door into the main building, it would have led straight into the Baths. Further we are told that a statue of Septimus Severus stood in the middle: that is, in a central niche, at the point where a door, if it had existed, would have been been. The imperial statue thus stood at the same sort of place as did the Augustus in the Aulia Regia of Domitian, when he welcomed visitors on his throne, sheltered by the apse that framed, opposite to the entry, the two passages leading to the great peristyle. It follows that the Severan statue in the middle niche represented the emperor as the Sun, with three planets on either side. Severus we know had himself shown as Sarapis, who now was looked upon as a solar deity.[41]

A misunderstanding of a passage in Ammianus has attributed a Septizonium in the form of a Nymphaeum to Marcus Aurelius; and efforts have been made to reconstruct the Severan building with fountains on either side of the imperial statue, with waters pouring into a big basin in front of the edifice. Other efforts have produced a *ziqqarat* structure of seven storeys or a system of seven concentric enclosures.[42] All these were fanciful. The nyphaeum-reconstruction put the images of the planets on the third floor and considered that they consisted of three mosaic panels. The building would then be a monumental form of the plaque calendars found in contemporary Gaul.

If we turn to Africa we can get a more correct notion of what was involved. There we find Septizonia at Carthage, Avitta Bibba (Henchir Bedd), and Lambaesis.[43] The second site is known through a dedication to an aedile; the third by an inscription saying that the legate of Numidia had restored it. A text of 262 speaks of a Nymphaeum, which was either identical with the septizonium or one of its annexes: here was a big apse with two connected columns at the back and a column standing out on the side of the opening, with entablatures on all of them. The apse was flanked by two wings, each preceded by four columns supporting an entablature. Niches stood in the apse and the wings, made for statues. Another structure has been found at Cincari (Henchir Tounga) in northern Tunisia. This is thermal, not unlike the lay-out of the Baths of the South at Timgad. The building was several times reconstructed; and the first change consisted in the construction of a Septi-zonium. Here have been found the heads of some planetary statues: those of Saturn, Mars, and Sol—three of the first four of the series, Jupiter being lost. A cippus shows a young female head and bare breasts; on the sides jutted out in strong reliefs what seem to be the heads of dog and ram. Here perhaps we have Luna or Venus, but more likely an altar consecrated to the deity. The Mars with its deep frown, the creases below the cheeks, the thick lips hanging under a heavy moustache, is very reminiscent of portraits of Caracalla, who liked to think of himself as the wargod. The Saturn shows the classicising tendency found in the years 220–40. It does not belong to the Numidian type of the Old Man, nor to the baroque variant (as at Dougga), but is Jovian and lifts its eyes to the heavens.[44]

From these monuments it is clear that the Septizonium belonged to the same family as the *frons scaenae* used in theatres and also as a decoration for all sorts of building, private houses, baths, mausolea. The fundamental element is the exedra (a hall with seats, often used for discussions or lectures) framed by two rectangular wings, which we find in isolation at Lambesis and which, in a triple form, produced the Roman Septizonium. The Cincari structure represents a type popular in the fourth century.[45]

Severus, we may note, made use of his gentilic name Septimius, with its root of *septem,* seven. "We feel from the time of the siege of Byzantium, a hazardous episode in which so many ominous signs appeared for and against him. Was there not a seven-secret hidden in the very walls and gates of the future Constantinople?"[46] The seven towers of the enclosing walls gave out exactly the same echo from the first to the last: an acoustic perfection that conformed to the theory of the music of the seven spheres.

He made a direct use of his horoscope, perhaps recalling the tradition of Augustus' disclosure. "The stars under which he had been born he had had painted on the ceilings of the palace-rooms where he was used to hold court. There they were visible to all— with the exception of that part of the sky [the Horoscopic Point] which, as the astrologers put it, observed the hour when he first saw the light. For this portion he did not have depicted in both rooms." If the Horoscopic Point were shown, any astrologer could compute his death-hour; his birthday, 11 April 146, would enable men to use tables and establish the relative positions of the five planets and the Moon within the Zodiac on that day. What he kept hidden was the hour of birth.[47]

Severus went on his last campaign to Britain. Dion says that he knew he would not return. "He knew this mainly from the stars under which he had been born," but he knew it "also by what he had heard from the seers".[48]

His son Caracalla carried on his concern for divination, but in a more paranoiac way. Herodian says he was "of a very inquisitive nature and loved to pry, not only into the affairs of mankind, but even into the mysteries of the gods and daimons. Suspecting everyone about him to be a traitor, he was so often making the most thorough researches into oracles and sending for Mages as well as *Astrologoi* and Soothsayers that not one professor of wizardry, *goēteia,* escaped his notice." At last he suspected even the diviners and wrote to Maternianus, who managed all his affairs in Rome and whom he looked on as his most faithful friend, to seek out the best Mages that could be found. So he made use of the necromancer's art to learn the time and manner of his death, and whether anyone was plotting to seize power. Dion makes things more precise; with his high rank he was more in the know of imperial politics than Herodian. He tells us that a prophet in Africa had declared that the prefect Macrinus and his son Diadumenianus were fated to hold the imperial power; and the matter was so much talked about that he was taken to Rome, where he spoke out to Flavius Maternianus, "who at this time commanded the soldiers in the City and who at once wrote" to Caracalla in the East. Herodian remarks that "whether the demons really gave the information or it was through some private vendetta against Macrinus", Maternianus wrote to tell that Macrinus was plotting treason. While the letter was on the way, says Dion, an Egyptian, Sarapion, told Caracalla to his face (only a few days before his death) that he had not long to live and would be succeeded by Macrinus. "So he was first thrown to the lions, but he merely held out his hand, it is reported, and the animal refused to touch him. He was then killed; and he might have escaped even that fate, or so he declared, by invoking certain spirits if he had only another day of life." Meanwhile the letter arrived, but was diverted to Caracalla's mother Julia at Antioch. "She had been instructed to sort out everything that came along, and thus prevent a mass of unimportant letters being sent to him while he was in enemy country." At the same time a warning letter from Ulpius Julianus, then in charge of the census, went by other couriers direct to Macrinus. Herodianus has a different version; he says that the letter from Maternianus did go to Caracalla "just as he was off to the races and had already mounted his chariot". The couriers handed him the packet of letters in which was the one about Macrinus; but, eager to get to the Games, the emperor handed the package to Macrinus to open and inspect: "to send him word if there was anything of extra-ordinary importance; otherwise to carry out his duty as prefect in the usual way." And so Macrinus, reading the letters, found the one that contained his death-sentence. He quickly collected his adherents and arranged to kill Caracalla on a desert excursion.[49]

Dion insists that the day of the murder, 8 April 217, was that of the prediction; and he adds that Septimius Severus appeared to his son in a dream, "wearing a sword and saying: 'As you killed your brother, so I'll kill you.'" The excursion was to have been to the shrine of the Moon near Carrhae—perhaps to appease the goddess after news had come of a great fire in Alexandreia, with strange stars seen in the sky. Accounts disagree as to whether the attack was made as Caracalla went from Edessa to Carrhae or on the way back. Macrinus on becoming emperor promptly had Maternianus killed.

In the Severan period the East had been asserting itself in the whole cultural sphere. The Mages grow more important. Carac-alla gave a cult to the Mage Apollonios of Tyana in Asia Minor. Egyptian magicians too were prominent; Dionysios of Alex-andreia accused them of surrounding the damned soul of Valerian.[50] With the Severans also there came to a climax the concept of Royal Astrology, which we saw full-blown in the early horoscope of Antiochos of Kommagene and which had been invading the Roman world since Augustus, given a strong stimu-lation by Balbillus under Nero when all with a drop of Augustan blood, of *sangius caelestis*, were in danger, their inherit-ance seen as something both physical and astral. Valens makes no distinction between royal and imperial power; and we meet a Syro-Iranian version of the predestination of all power, which in Egypt defined the *kosmokrator*.[51]

Caracalla carried on something of the Commodian claim to be a Hercules.[52] He had an Eastern orientation in his thoughts. At first he welcomed the Parthians in festival fashion, then turned on them. He penetrated deeply in their land, and returned to Syria with the claim of conquering all the East; he is said to have wanted to marry a daughter of the last Arsakid. (Shortly the Parthians were to be replaced by the Persian Sassanid dynasty.) In all his athletic exploits he manifested a devotion to Herakles and Alexander the Great. Alexander's combat with a lion had been the prologue to the hunt-combats of imperial Virtus; the lion-killings by which from Commodus to Caracalla we are expected to measure the Heraklean virtue of the emperor become more and more linked with the igneous Lion of Mithras or of Kronos. That is, the actual lion becomes lost in the astral lion, proving the emperor to be a new Alexander. We may recall how Martial had anticipated this outlook by suggesting that Domitian's Lion had been sent from the stars.[53] Eznik of Kolb, an Armenian of the mid-fifth century, says that according to the Chaldeans, "When it's the Lion that has just been in the astral residence, it's a King who is to be born; if it happens several times, many kings are to be born." The Lion thus came to be taken as the sign of the *genitura* of Alexander the Great.[54]

The death of Caracalla shook the army, who felt it as a world-end. Without an Antoninus the state would break up. The soldiers had only a vague idea as to how many Antonines there had been, but they identified the family with imperial power. Macrinus tried to overcome this emotion by deifying the man he'd murdered, and by giving the Antonine name to his young son. But the latter's prospects were dim, as believers in divination pointed out. He and his father ruled only one year—"as Fate has decreed", observed Herodian.[55]

Macrinus was from Mauretania and must have known the cult of Tanit, Moon-goddesss, guardian of Carthage. As Caelestis she was popular in North Africa and Spain, and was worshipped as Astro-arche, Queen of Stars.[56] Her prophecies went all over the empire. One of her priestesses, inspired by her under Antoninus Pius, uttered the name Antoninus eight times. The repetition was interpreted as meaning that the emperor would rule eight more years; but he lived on. So devotees suggested that eight Antonini were to rule, then the empire would perish. (That such an oracle had to be re-interpreted to fit in with the facts of history shows what prolonged importance was attached to it.) The Tanit priestesses were propagandists for the Roman regime; for when Pertinax, under Commodus, was proconsul of Africa, "he suppressed many rebellions by aid of prophetic verses issued from the temple of Caelestis".

The Sun-cult now came to the rescue. A Phoenician woman, Maesa of Emesa, sister of Julia Domna, had been at Court; Macrinus ordered her home. She had two daughters, Julia Soaemis and Mammaea; each girl had borne a son who became a Sun-priest. "This deity the natives [of Emesa] worship with singular devotion, calling him in the Phoenician tongue Elegabal."[57] Maesa used bribes, promises, and declarations that both boys had been fathered by Caracalla; she brought Macrinus down. Her grandson Elegabal, aged fourteen, became emperor and ruled some four years. The three women tried to control him, but his fanatical passion for the Sun made him persevere with something of a religious revolution, with Elegabal as the one great god.[58] As astrology had come to see the stars arranged in a sort of class-system, so Elegabal tried to reallocate the gods in various levels of dependency on his Sun, El, "calling some his chamberlains, others his slaves, others his attendants for different purposes". Also "he kept about him every kind of mage and made them all perform daily sacrifices". The old charge of human sacrifice came up: children were killed so that their entrails might be inspected. Astrologers were much in demand. When Elegabal planned war against the Marcomanni, he was told that Marcus Aurelius "through the aid of astrologers and mages had made the Marcomanni forever the liegemen and friends of the Roman People, and that it had been done by means of magic chants, *carmina,* and a dedication".[59]

He tried to draw Tanit in as the sungod's wife, bringing her from Carthage (her cult-image?) and demanding huge sums for her dowry.[60] Finally the praetorian guards killed him and his mother, and his god was banished. We may note that Julia Domna had begun the introduction of Syrian deities into the imperial cult; she was worshipped as Caelestis Dea by the troops of the Rhineland; and at Carvoran in north Britain a zealous officer, M. Caecilius Donatianus, had set up a slab in verse, which stated that he had learned the truth, aided by Caelestis.

> On a Lion the Virgin rides in her Heavenly Place
> town-founder bringer-of-corn inventor-of-laws
> we know the gods because of her gifts and her grace
> therefore she's Mother Divine, Ceres, Virtue, and Peace,
> the Syrian Goddess: life and law in her slaves she weighs.
> Syria sent the Constellation seen in the Skies
> to Libya for worship. Thence have we learned her praise.

A statue must have stood on the slab showing Julia Domna with a wreath of corn, riding her lion, and holding scales. A centurion at Corstopitum set up an altar to Juppiter Eternal Dolichenus, Celestial Brigantia, and Salus. He was thus identifying the tribal goddess of the Brigantes with Tanit as Dea Caelestis and with Juno Regina the usual wife of Dolichenus. Tanit appears as a lion-rider on coins of Severus. Much more might be said of the spread of the name Caelestis and its applications; but even these few will give some idea of the way that Tanit was taken into the Severan system and linked with Julia Domna's Syrian cults and with astrology in general.[61]

Before Elegabal died, his grandmother and mother got him to adopt his first cousin, Mammaea's son, to whom he gave the name of Alexander—at the god's orders, he said. Mammaea declared that she had borne the boy to Caracalla. Alexander was now proclaimed emperor; and we may note that, despite the high esteem of astrology when it served the imperial interests, it was now that the two jurists, Domitius Ulpianus and Julius Paulus, summarised the anti-astrology code.[62] Alexander was a highly talented man, played a number of musical instruments, studied geometry, painted, sang, composed a poem *On the Lives of Good Emperors*. He encouraged the higher education. "He was also well versed in haruspical techniques and so skilled a bird-observer that he surpassed both the Spanish Vascones and the augurs of the Pannonians." Further, "he was an expert in astrology and so great a supporter of it that on his orders *mathematici* set themselves up publicly in Rome and announced that they'd teach their art".[63]

The *Augustan History* says that "on the day of his birth", 1 October 208, "a star of the first magnitude was visible for the entire day at Arcena Caesarea; further, in the neighbourhood of his father's house, the sun was encircled with a gleaming ring"—the house was also in that Syrian city. "And the soothsayers, commending his birthday to the gods, declared that he would someday hold the imperial power." The date was thought to be the deathday of Alexander the Great, which however was in June. We are further told that the "*haruspices* prophesied that he would indeed be emperor, but not for long, and that he would early succeed to the imperial power."[64] His expedition against the Parthians in 231 or 232 failed; then came news of grave perils on the northern frontier. "When Thrasyllus the astrologer, with whom he was on most friendly terms, told him it was his fate to fall by a barbarian's sword, he first expressed joy, thinking he was to die in battle in a way worthy of an emperor. . . . But the result deceived his hope. He did indeed fall by a barbarian's sword—by the hand of of a barbarian guardsman [of his own army], but not in battle, not in the course of a war."[65]

He had in fact been called at first Alexianos. But he was born

near a temple of Alexander the Great, and clearly the name
Alexander did much to form his career. We do not know the day of
Alexander the Great's birth, but 1 October corresponds to the
date of his decisive battle of Arbela.[66] The birth fell in the month
Hekatombaion, which is conventionally made to correspond to the
July of the Julian calendar; but we do not know of anyone carrying
it on into October. Still, there does seem a link of that month
with Alexander. Macedonian coins of the first half of the third
century, and some inscriptions, attest a celebration in October of
games in the form of an *agon* or contest, under the auspices of a
koinon meeting at Beroia.[67] And we hear of Severus Alexander
presiding at an Agon Herculeus in honour of Alexander the Great;
the national dynasty of the Argeads in Macedonia were Heraklid.
Was the Agon too held on 1 October?[68]

Two other points linking Alexander the Great with this period
are worth mentioning. We are told that the descendants of
Macrinus all kept images of that hero on their persons, the men in
rings and their silver plate, the women on their toilet ornaments
(in embroidery), their hair-ornaments, and so on. To wear such an
image was felt to ensure the success of any enterprise.[69] There is
also an horoscope scratched roughly on the wall of an important
house in Doura on the Euphrates, in six more or less complete
versions, one of them with a crude diagram:

Year 530 month Aydnaios 9 according to the Moon 5, Saturday, about
3rd hour of the day, was born Alexander Macedonios son of
Apollonikos . . . Horoscope: Aquarius.

After Apollonikos comes *en ichthydiōi*, which has been interpreted
as "in the Fishes", *Ichthyes*; but, apart from the odd diminitude,
Ichthydion, this does not make sense. It seems that the word
modifies the proper name, adding a locality, profession, or
nickname. It thus seems impossible to link the text with the
horoscope in the Alexander Romance and use it to amend a
corrupt passage there.[70]

Finally a few words on Alexander's birth-star. Apparently the
death of Commodus was heralded or followed by the advent of a
comet; for Pertinax, who briefly held power after him, issued
coins with an imperial allegory in which Providentia (of the gods)
is associated with a Star; and this has been plausibly taken as an
effort on his part to turn the comet to his own advantage.[71]
Severus Alexander certainly made good use of his birth-star, as

we see from a mosaic of the Months found at Thysdrus (El-Djem), which are shown in the order March to February. Some of the images show festivals occurring during the month; and in such a case the use of an accusative plural, *Octobres,* suggests that the Kalends or the Ides are indicated. So, for October we are shown two males, facing one another, who stare up at a star above their heads. There can be no doubt that this is the Star of the Kalends of October, Alexander's birthday.[72]

After the death of Severus Alexander there was a period of anarchy; then from 260 came the emperors Gallienus, Aurelian, and Diocletian. The conflict of the pagan State and Christianity was maturing; and socially and economically there was a dire crisis. The arc of history which had reached with fair stability from Augustus to the Severi, despite periods of temporary difficulty, had now reached an end; and a new Star, with new basis, was required. We shall therefore stop here our detailed examination, though a few points about the period between Severus Alexander and Constantine the Great may be made.

First the cult of Hercules. Under the Severi the *vota* made by soldiers for the emperor's safety multiply; under Gordian II the words Virtus Augusti appear with the hero's image. The Gaulish emperor Postumus (in the late 250s) had an extreme devotion to Hercules and mingled traditional images and titles with local elements; we find Hercules Magusanus and Hercules Duesoniensis on his coins. Gallienus was stirred to take up the theme. All this while the cult of Hercules was both being aided by that of the Sun and yet competing with it for primacy. Ploutarch had noted that according to Egyptian mythology Herakles had his seat in the Sun and went through the universe with it; the voyage of the hero in the golden cup across the waters had long been given a solar interpretation; Porphyrios declared, "As the Sun drives evils away from the earth, he has been called Herakles, for he cleaves the air in his course from rising to setting; besides he has been imagined as accomplishing twelve labours, symbolising thus the sky-divisions of the Zodiac." Hero and Sun both claimed the epithet *Invictus.* But the Sun had stronger forces; and the henotheistic trend triumphed under Aurelian with the solar cult. Hercules was no longer *Conservator,* the force that preserved and held things together, nor the *Comes Dominorum Nostrorum,* the Companion of Our Lords, but simply *Consors,* Partner; and a coin-issue from Sardis shows him leaning on his club, with his foot

on a captive, while he receives the glove from Sol. Later Diocletian
had himself called *Jovius*, while his colleague Maximian was
Herculius, a lesser though eminent figure. And this relationship
prefigures what was to be accepted under Constantine of God the
Father and God the Son, as was plain to Christians like Arnobius

Fig. 71. Arch of Galerius, Salonika: sacrifice by Diocletian and
Galerius in honour of Jupiter and Hercules, surrounded by
deities (Jupiter, *Oikoumene*, Peace, etc.); on right, Nike image
above a round buckler; below, easterners with gifts from Persian
king

and Lactantius. (Cornutus had already made Hercules into the
Logos, and Epiketos had said, "Herakles had no more intimate
friend than God; so he has passed for the Son of God, and that is
what he was.") This theology appears in the panegyrics where we
find Jupiter as *rector caeli*, governor of the heavens, and Hercules
as *pacator terrarum*, the bringer-of-peace on earth.[73] We cannot

here follow this aspect out, but a quotation from the emperor Julian will bring out the cogency of the point:

For what is there impracticable for Herakles? what is there that would not have yielded to his body so divine and pure, since all that we call elements [*stoicheia*] obey the demiurgic and perfective power of this pure and unmixed spirit, whom the great Zeus has begotten to be the Saviour of the Universe.[74]

Julian is polemising against Christianity, but he could not write in this vein unless there was a genuine and widely-held tradition behind him. A hermetic sect in Gaul, we may note, tried to combine the worship of Christ and Helios: the Heliognosti and Deinvictiaci.[75] And the Christians themselves had taken over the Sun's Birthday, 25 December, for the Birthday of Christ.

18

Horoscopes and Astrologers

We shall now run through the extant horoscopes of the second and third centuries A.D. for various points of interest, including the side-lights thrown on individual lives and social attitudes. Where not otherwise indicated, they are from literary astrologic sources. For 28 January 101 we have this text:

Sun and Venus in Aquarius, Moon in the Twins, Saturn in the Scorpion, Mars in the Crab, Mercury and Horoskopos in Capricorn, the Lot of Fortune in the Virgin, the locus of Death in the Ram. The Lords of these places were in opposition to one another in watery signs, and further Mars happened to be in the Dysis. This person was burned to death in a bath.

For 5 March of the same year, "Since the co-rulers of the Triangle were unfavourably located and the rule of Daimon was turning away, this person was exiled and committed suicide." Next we have two horoscopes dated 20 April 102, both of the subjects dying at the age of 67 years. The sum was reached by adding up two rising times for Babylon and then adding 15 for the cycle of Mars: 24 + 28 + 15. Valens was pleased at the coincidence of the deaths and considered it a significant confirmation of the theory. For a subject of 4 December of the same year we read: "In the 45th year birth of twins non-effective [? stillborn]. In the same year also high priesthood. In the 51st year a distinguished public office. In the 52nd year death of a child." For a man born 14 December that year, about midnight: he began as deputy-governor but fell into disfavour with his superior and was condemned to the Quarry. In the 36th year "by the aid of greater persons he was freed from confinement as disabled". The beneficent stars were then strong. "In the 39th year his affairs were in a bad way through the former enmity and he was condemned to an Oasis." In the 40th year he "lived precariously and fell ill. But his wife, who had accompanied him, affectionately comforted him and shared her property with him." This must have taken place in Egypt.[1]

For a subject born 10 January 103 we find among the positions the Lot of Fortune in the Lion and Mars "in a fiery and solar sign" opposed to the Horoskopos, with Mars and Saturn in a dominant aspect in the locus of death. "This person was burned alive." A man born on 23 April 104 "was short-armed". For another of 17 July, Sun and Jupiter were found "in the death-bringing month Archer; and besides Sun and Jupiter, Mars yielded in the 54th year from the [8th] locus of Death to Saturn in the Archer. The yielding was grievous." For the first day of 105: "The nativity, though well supplied and prospering at first, was later to be reversed and hard-up, with forecast of burning and plunder." A second version says of the 48th year, "He witnessed a very grave sorrow, the death of a beloved child, and in the same year also the death of the mother." The geographical latitude was of Babylon–Syria. For 16 January 106: "In opposition to the Daimon, who forecasts the intellectual and the spiritual, was Saturn, and he was in dominant aspect to the [preceding] full moon and to the phase at that time and the ruler of the Lot of Fortune. So this person had in the fated places injury and tender feet and above all he was lunatic." For 8 May 107: "In the 51st year he went abroad, and going to the king's court he won a case for the high-priesthood of a friend." In the same year "came the death of a child, for Mars in the [8th] *locus* of death transmitted to Saturn in the [10th] locus concerned with children".[2]

For 28 March: "This person was possessed of a god like a madman because Jupiter the ruler of the Lot [was] in the Balance, the [9th] locus concerning god and Saturn, the ruler of the Daimon, in the Horoskopos, and Venus in Lower Midheaven." For 6 November: "In the 52nd year he had a great dispute and lawsuit with his sister about property and inheritance, and at the royal [court] he won. . . . Thus all stars were operative but Mars. So he was ill at this time and had a close escape at sea and had big expenditures, but the beneficent stars were destined to be in dominant aspect to Saturn and prevailed." We have the horoscope of this man's sister for 15 December 110, *klima* of Babylon. She is called "the defeated woman". In the 53rd year "she had the prospect and expectation of victory through the aid of influential persons, so she was persuaded to go to court". But next year "she was abandoned by her helpers, as the beneficent stars did not combine their times". For 2 June 109, "this person was born a slave; but he entered a *gens* [became a Roman citizen], attained political office, and enjoyed honours". At last Mars, Saturn and Mercury were unfavourably located, "so they reduced his livelihood and made it embarrassed". He died in the 45th year. For March 110: A man who died in his 51st year. For 27 September: "In the 47th year he was a friend's heir and was separated from his wife because of jealousy and abuse."[3]

For 24 April 111: "In the 42nd year he was a woman's heir." In the 45th "he held a distinguished office for public affairs; for Venus at Midheaven gave over to Mars, which indicated trouble, and to Jupiter, which indicated esteem. And the star was from Horoskopos to the Sun, so he won royal recognition at that time. The same year he freed concubines because Jupiter in the [6th] locus of slaves took over from Venus. In the 46th year he had troubles and reverses in matters of property and through females; for the transfer [of power] was from Venus to Saturn in the [7th] locus of marriage, and from the Sun to Mars and Jupiter. From these quarrels then he stopped." For 30 September: "In appearance he was guarded all round, but he had to look for reverses and loss through a woman."[4]

For 27 July 112: "In the 24th year he profited from the dead [through wills] and from friends. In the 26th, marriage and woman's aid. In the 29th, by the death of someone else's slave and allegation of poison he had legal affairs and disputes. For Saturn made *paradosis* to Sun, Moon, and Venus in the [12th] locus dealing with slaves. But he got help from the friendship of greater persons, male and female." At last in the 45th year "he was freed by the influence of greater persons on grounds of illness." For 17 August 112: "This person was hunchbacked"—or suffered from some disease with humps. For 1 April 113 we have the horoscope of Pedanius Fuscus. For 1 July 113: "In the 20th year the parents were both killed by a guardsmen in an assembly of robbers." The man was involved in the tumult but "escaped the danger". A second version repeats that he was in grave danger and would have met a violent death but for Jupiter's presence. The *klima* was of Alexandreia. For 13 May 114: a man who lived 28 years 9 months. For 26 July: "the crisis was double". For 24 September: the man was exiled in the 30th year. Valens comments: "He had, then, crises in the earlier times; but for comparison with the preceding nativity (for it's a brother) we watched the 39th year. One must marvel then at the natural law [*physis*] that it brought the periods to the same result even though they were born in different *klimata*." The horoscope to which Valens refers was for 8 December 120: the subject was the younger brother: in the 27th year "he was in danger because of Capricorn, and in the 30th and 40th years bodily illness of eyes and feet"; in the 33rd year he was exiled through a woman's treachery.[5]

For 10 November 114: in the 42nd year, "quarrels and confusions and notoriety through a woman". In the 44th, "violent death of a slave and crisis of his father and accusation of ignoble descent and rape. But he received help and gifts from friends. He got into trouble with the law about the writings (?) and went through punishment and fraud and false accusation, and was harassed by treachery and fell physically ill." For 15 February 115: The man lived 32 years 5 months. "The place of the conception did not have the start; for the full moon of the conception"—the full moon occurring about 6 June 114—"and the ascending node happened to be at the same degrees. So he had a dangerous birth and a violent end." For 26 December 115: the man was killed by wild beasts. For 21 January 116: he was effeminate and "had unmentionable vices, for Capricorn is lascivious and its ruler [Saturn] was in the Bull, the sign [indicating the kind of] weakness, and the Scorpion indicates the kind of lewdery". For 30 June 117: in the 38th year, after serving in a distinguished army post he was entangled in an accusation and lost his standing. From the 38th "he had to look out for enmities and oppositions". In the 39th, "he was accused and bound and lacked the power to set things right". Then, "at this time he was abroad and a woman betrayed him by writings [? in a lawsuit]. He grew poor and was troubled about slaves, one of them by alienation, some by loss and penalty, and he himself was physically ill."[6]

The writer, P. Aelius Aristeides, born in Mysia, kept a sort of neurotic diary of his long illness, *Sacred Logoi*. Among his many dreams he records one in which he saw Plato. He engaged an astrologer to explain it in terms of his horoscope; the details given could apply to 8 October 117 or 16 October 129, but 117 is the more likely year and fits in better with what we know of his biography. The dream occurred at Smyrna.[7]

For 30 July 117: a man who was castrated. For 26 November: we have four versions. The first mentions an injury of genitals and baldness of head. "But Jupiter the ruler of the Daimon was found

M

Fig. 72. Liturgical calendar at Athens (preserved in church of
Panhagia Gorgopito: or Hagia Eleutherios), cross added by
Christians. The months are indicated by zodiacal signs, festivals,
etc. (date variously given third century B.C. to third A.D.): Twins
(Thargelion), athlete with crown; bull-sacrifice; Crab (Skiro-
phorion); Panathenaic procession; Lion and Seirios (Hekatom-
beion)

in the [9th] locus of the god and affected his recovery through the
god. And he became a seer." The second version mentions that in
the 19th year his father died violently and he had eye-trouble;
he went abroad and was in danger at sea. Next year recovered,
following an oracle of the god (? Asklepios) "by treatment and
ointment". The third says the 36th year was critical. The fourth is
much like the first and for the sea-danger it cites the Ship Argo in
the Archer. This man was one of five survivors of a shipwreck in
A.D. 155. We have also a horoscope for 24 April 133 which gives
more details:

These six men on a voyage with many others encountered a violent
storm and the rudder was lost. They were in danger of death by
drowning as the ship took in water. But by the draught of the blowing
wind and the helmsman's management of the sails they escaped.
They met with other dangers at the same time from a roving pirate.[8]

For 8 February 120 we have four versions, the first dealing with the
method for predicting the earlier death of father or mother on the
basis of the relation between Sun, Moon, and Venus. For 12 May:
in the 36th year, "disputes and legal matters on account of his wife
and his friends' hostility". For 28 September 120: in the 40th
year, exile. "The forecast was effective by a female and prospect of
profit." For 8 December: again exile, this time in the 33rd year,
through female treachery; danger in the 27th year; illness of eyes
and feet in the 40th. For 27 October 121: "This man at 35 years
happened to be a soldier, and he began among prisoners and in
prison. In the prison he was loved by a woman through whom he
got out of a troublesome accusation; he made his way out and

Fig. 73. The same: Child with olive bough (Pyanepsion); vintager; *kanophoros*; Scorpion; dancer

escaped the danger. At the same time he caught and bound a runaway slave."[9]

For 22 January 122: in the 39th year, he was in danger "of being imprisoned for sedition and violence". Star-relations "caused hardships and disturbances"—Mars, Moon, Saturn. However, Jupiter came to the rescue in relations that portended travel: "which was voluntary but risky, and help and co-operation of friends". For 30 January: a crisis in the 33rd year. For 12 June: "Suppose we investigate the 42nd year." Then "flight from battle and fall from his horse as the enemy came up, and many killed, and he himself wounded, he was mixed up with the rest of the fallen and thought to be dead, escaped the danger and stayed in the enemy country till the 44th year, leading a campaign". The war must have occurred at the end of 163 or early 164; it might well have been the campaign of Avidius Cassius against the Parthians, which ended in 166.[10]

For 4 December 122: in the 36th year, "the malevolent stars hemmed in Venus". His wife's death was suspected to be the result of a plot, he "was to go to trial, accused at the royal [court], but fled". In the 37th year, fortune was kinder. Valens says, "Many other facts were significant for past and future, but I've thought it necessary to set out only those which I myself knew more exactly and which I chanced upon." The second version puts the wife's death in the 32nd year; in the 36th the man was tried for plotting her death but escaped. For 3 January 123: "He was a dancer and in his 25th year" (about A.D. 148) "was put in confinement on the course of a public riot, but was defended before the governor and freed through the aid of friends and the crowd's entreaty, and became more esteemed." Valens adds, "The nativity was precarious as to the loss of reputation and condemna-

Fig. 74. The same: Labourer; Sower; Centaur Archer

tion and danger of life." Venus aided the man. But in the 32nd year, "he was deprived of honour and reputation and livelihood, and lived unhonoured". He was to blame for his own fall, having become a braggart and pretender. This charge is odd, for Valens gives the astral causes of his downfall.[11]

For 29 July 124: In the 37th year, "through his wife, from whom he had hoped for great profit, he had to meet an inheritance-suit and was beaten at the royal [court]. Still, the time wasn't wholly harmful to him, though disappointing to his hope." He had won the same suit in the 35th year, but was worsted on the appeal: years 159 and 161. We have the wife's horoscope, for 23 June 134, which repeats the tale of the lawsuit. For 23 November 127: a male died in the 12th year through an encounter with Mars; otherwise "he'd have lived the years of Venus, 84". For 16 January 129: "In the 35th year he escaped from slavery and carried out many thefts, and though undetected for a short while was caught the same year": this text from Valens seeks to explain the events in the subject's life as reflecting the passing of rulership according to various cycles, e.g. "Venus in the Ram, 10 years and 9 months." For 4 November 134: in the 20th year, "a petition for honour to the king's [court] was made, but failed". That year the man became ill and "fell from an animal and was dragged so almost to lose his eyesight. And fault and deception and penalty had to do with a female." In the 23rd year, Jupiter "provided by means of gifts a powerful colleague. Thus nothing can make a man to be possessed of the friendship of kings and great men if the periods [of his life] work against it," Valens comments.[12]

For 20 January 135: the man died in his 34th year. For 27 October: the man was the son of the priest in the horoscope of 8 May 107 given above. Valens says he reached his 22nd year in accord with the father's horoscope and died, as stated, when his

Fig. 75. The same: Cockfight, Capricorn; Phrixos on Ram

father was in his 51st year. We have three horoscopes in papyri, dated 137–9; but they give no biographies. One, the subject of which is Ophellinos, mentions Eros and Necessity; and another, dealing with Anoubion son of Psensnois, has a passage that begins: "*The Seven Gods.* After examination of many books as it has been handed down to us from ancient wise men, that is, the Chaldeans, and Petosiris and especially King Necheus [*sic*], just as they themselves took counsel from Our Lord Hermes and Asklepios, that is, Imouthes, son of Hephaistos." The month-names are Egyptian like the name of the subject. For 25 March 142: the subject in his 18th year "went abroad with a distinguished woman because of friendship and esteem and for further intimacy and erotic passion". The woman died that year, "and he himself failed in his hope, so he went back home with little profit". Next year he got aid and gain, "but had disagreements and mental troubles and enmities with relatives", and looked forward "to greater hopes and profits, but then was disappointed because she died". In the 21st year "he had friendship with a prominent and royal person from whom he expected the right to wear the wreath and an archpriesthood. And this would certainly have happened if Mars had not been in dominant aspect and operative." As a result the "climacteric was illness and bloodshed and frustration of hope, treachery of slaves, attacks, injuries, wants. Then later he did well, and with an upward trend for the following period." Valens adds, "There will be troubles, great expenses, or else independence resulting from previous affairs or from some other income and help from friends." It would be interesting to know what was the business of this young man who seems to have mixed love-affairs and other ambitions.[13]

For the rest of the second century there are about eighteen odd horoscopes, none of much interest. First three papyri: one mentions the Egyptian month "Pharmouthi according to the ancients", another has as its subject a woman, Philoe. Then come four literary texts, of 152, 153, 158, and 159. Of the second subject, the father died in his fourth year; the third was a child, born on 14 August 158 and dying in May 161—it was "afflicted with eruptions and eczema, e.g. in the 15th, 17th, and 23rd month, and in the rest, but above all in the 27th; and supposedly [?] he fell into an animal snare [?] and was struck in parts of his body". From the 28th month "he lived precariously", in the 32nd "he was dangerously ill and in convulsions", in the 33rd he died. Then comes a papyrus of 29 July 161 with regnal dating "according to the Greeks", and Egyptian months; the name Harpokration appears. Next a literary horoscope (9 February 162) of a boy who lived 11 years. A baby born on 3 February 173 died a fortnight later. A Doura graffito of a horoscope in a private house is dated July 176. A literary horoscope of 10 August 188 remarks that "such a person [will be] fortunate, a leader, despotic, possessed of royal fortune, and established in great property". Then comes a papyrus with the date 25 January 190.[14]

We may now glance at some of the astrologers whom we know from the texts. First, four of them who appear to be all of the second century A.D.

Antigonos of Nikaia seems to have flourished about 150; we can fix his date by the fact that he refers to the death of Hadrian while his works are cited by Porphyrios in his *Introduction to the Tetrabiblos* in the late third century. The latter writer mentions him with an Egyptian Phanes, straight after dealing with Ptolemaios in a chapter on the geometrical patterns (triangles, squares, hexagons) of constellations.[15] There seems no reason to identify him with a physician of the same name, probably of Hadrianic date, who invented a useful antidote.[16]

Vettius Valens of Antioch, probably flourishing about 144–70, is of first importance for horoscopes, since he cites some hundred and thirty examples in his *Anthologiae,* ranging in date from A.D. 39 to 188. He was drawing on material gathered by himself or his predecessors to illustrate various aspects of theory or practice; each item can be shown to be astronomically correct for a date in the first or second century. Valens keeps on claiming that he uses his own experience. A large amount of his material covers the years 140–70: which may be taken as the period when he was at work collecting and analysing. He added some borrowings from earlier sources and inserted a few additions reaching up to 184. Most of the persons he deals with were born between 100 and 140.[17] Several times concerned with the rising times of zodiacal signs (for determining length of life or critical years) he has to consider geographical latitude and gives the *klima* in which a subject was born. He himself works with the sequence based on Alexandreia, *klima* 1. Only for this *klima* does he use the rising-times which he has instructed us to compute; he violates his rules for *klima* 2 (Babylon) in dealing with Palestine and Syria, though still using a consistent scheme: the classical rising-time for Babylon. After that he merely selects rising-times that enable him to get the results he wants for his explanations. All this suggests that the theory of the seven *klimata* was not yet widely known or worked out in a precise and systematic form. Also, not much stress is yet put on the careful determination of the culminating-point (M); and the lunar nodes (which later, especially in Hindu astrology, gained the same significance as the planets) play a slight role. So we feel that despite the large amount of astrological theory set out, development is not yet at its highest point, despite Ptolemaios. Both he and Valens use simple arithmetical schemes (e.g. for handling rising-times) which in astronomy proper had been left behind.[18]

Valens' *Anthologiae* was copied more often than almost any other ancient astrological work, wholly or in part. His bent was practical and he conveys a good effect of the life of the professional astrologer, struggling with rivals and detractors, and not finding things at all easy.[19] He wrote also treatises and a *Teacher's Manual* now lost, and added to his income by running a school for astrologers, dedicating his *Anthologiae* to one of the students, Marcus. Such a school was not an innovation; he tells of his own experiences with Egyptian teachers.[20] Unoriginal of mind, he wanted to vindicate and explain the earlier writers. His hope for fame does not seem to have come true during his lifetime, but he later was much used, and his texts show many emendations and additions, which complicate the question of his date. *Anthologiae* is divided into nine books. Climacterics are a common theme, with the usual apparatus for determining the date and mode of death. Valens deals with both fatalistic and katarchic astrology; but like other practising astrologers he was not much concerned with philosophic problems. We saw how he commented that a man was responsible for his own downfall, though he had set out the star-mechanism which brought it about. Neither he nor Ptolemaios refer to one another; they may well have been contemporaries.[21]

Ptolemaios in many ways brought ancient astronomy to its climax. His earth was a sphere in the centre of the cosmos. If it were at one side, the stars would there seem bigger. The heaven or cosmos is a sphere turning on a fixed axle, as is shown by the circumpolar stars and the fact that other stars rise and set at the same horizon-points. If the earth were nearer one pole, the horizon would bisect not the equator, but one of its parallel circles; if it were outside the axis, the ecliptic would be divided unequally on the horizon. The earth was a mere speck in comparison with the heavens; for the stars seem of the same size, and at the same distance from one another, wherever we are on the earth's surface. The earth had no motion of translation: to translate in mechanics is to cause a body to move so that all its parts follow the same direction. For there must be, he thought, some point to which the motions of other bodies could be referred, and heavy bodies sink to the cosmic centre (the earth). Also if there was such a motion, it would be proportionate to the great mass of the earth, and all the animals and objects on earth would be left behind, thrown violently into the air. He also held that these points disproved the argument of some thinkers that the earth, while unmoving in space, turned on its own axis—though he admitted that such a thesis would simplify a lot of problems.[22]

Thus he discussed the development of the notion of the circle and of the sphere on the construction of the cosmos:

It's reasonable to assume that the first idea on these matters came to the ancients from observation in the following way. They saw sun, moon, and others stars moving east to west in circles always parallel to one another; they saw the bodies begin to rise from below, as if from the earth itself, gradually up to their highest point, then with a corresponding decline tracing a downward course till they at last disappeared, apparently sinking into earth. Then they saw these stars, after staying invisible for a while, make a fresh start, and in rising and falling repeat the same periods of time, with the same places of rising and setting in regularity and virtual similarity.

But they were led to the view of a spherical heaven mainly by the observed circular motion described about one and the same centre by those stars which are always above the horizon. This point was necessarily the pole of the heavenly sphere, since the stars nearer this pole revolve in smaller circles, while those further off make larger circles, proportionately to their distance—till the distance reaches that of the stars not always visible. And of these latter they noted that those stars nearer the always-visible ones remained invisible for a shorter time, while those further off stayed invisible for a correspondingly longer time.[23]

So the images of the circle and the sphere settled down in men's minds as providing the primary basis for a model of the cosmos. As more inequalities or deviations from uniform circular motion were noted, astronomers used their mathematical ingenuity to introduce further complexities without giving up the circle. Yet Menaichmos had described conic sections (375–325 B.C.) by examining the cross-sections of a cone, and had shown how they could be circles, ellipses, parabolas, or hyperbolas. Later Apollonios continued this study by working out the equations for these curves as fully as Eukleides had dealt with the equations and properties of the circle. Several times thinkers suggested that the earth rotated, even that it revolved in an orbit round the sun, with the heavens stationary. But the image of the sphere was so firmly established that such suggestions seemed wilful and irrational.

The astronomical observations in Ptolemaios' *Mathematikē Syntaxis,* now called by its Arabic name the *Almagest,* belong to the years A.D. 127–51; and as he seems to have lived 78 years, his span covered, say, 190 to 268 or 200 to 278. The astrologic treatise *Tetrabiblos* is certainly his. Also *Phases of the Fixed Stars,* a collection of prognostics, and a set of star-tables. But *Karpoi* or *Centiloquium* (astral aphorisms) is generally rejected. He dedicated his two main works and others to Syros, who seems an Alexandrian physician.[24]

Very few considerations are needed to make anyone realise that a certain power [*dynamis*] emanating from the eternal aitherial substance is dispersed through, and permeates, the whole region about the earth, which throughout is subject to change. For, of the primary sublunary elements, fire and air are encompassed and changed by the motions in the *aither,* and in turn encompass and change all other things, earth and water and the plants and animals in them.

The Sun, together with the ambient [*periechon*], is always in some way affecting all things on earth, not only by changes that accompany the year's seasons to bring about the generation of animals, the productiveness of plants, the flowing of waters, and the changes of bodies, but also by its daily revolutions supplying heat, moisture, dryness and cold in regular order and in correspondence with its positions relative to the zenith. The Moon, too, as the heavenly body nearest to the earth, bestows her influence most abundantly on earthly things; for most of them, animate or inanimate, are sympathetic to her and change in company with her. The rivers increase and diminish their streams with her light, the seas turn their tides with her rising and setting, and plants and animals in whole or in some part wax and wane with her.[25]

Even if some of the facts were incorrect, in these general principles the astrologists were nearer to twentieth-century physics than most of the soberer scientists in between. We now see the earth bombarded by physical influences from outer space, cosmic rays, light-rays, perhaps even gravitational waves, and we are beginning to get a faint glimpse of the magnetic and radio network that pervades the universe. In the same way the alchemists had a vision of continuous tensional forces operating in fields and of the ceaseless transformation of matter. Where both astrologers and alchemists went wrong was in the narrow oversimplified systems within which they thought that influences, waves, rays, and transformations were at work. Thus Ptolemaios goes on:

Further, the passages of the fixed stars and the planets through the sky often signify hot, windy, and snowy conditions of the air, and earthly things are accordingly affected. Then too their aspects to one another, by the meeting and mingling of their dispensations [*diadoseis*], bring about many complicated changes. For though the sun's power prevails in the general ordering of quality, the other heavenly bodies aid or oppose it in particular details, the moon more obviously and continuously, as for example when it is new, at quarter, or full, and the stars at great intervals and more obscurely, as in their appearances, occultations, and approaches. If these matters be so regarded, everyone would judge that it follows, not only that already-compounded things must be affected in some way by the motion of these heavenly bodies, but likewise the germination and fruition of the seed must be moulded and conformed to the quality proper to the heavens at the time.

The more that astrology gets down to details the more it is liable to tie up its generalisations in applications based on a narrow dogmatic system with a large set of irrational presuppositions derived from religion. But, given those applications, men like Ptolemaios did their best to work out a rigorous system embodying as much of astronomy proper as was possible. How far astrologers had gone in efforts to meet critics who objected to the way in which a complex set of facts or causes were crammed and crushed into a limited and rigid pattern, is shown by many passages in Ptolemaios:

Differences of seed exert a very great influence on the special traits of the genus, since if the ambient and the horizon are the same, each seed prevails to express in general its own form [*diatyposis morphomatos*]: for example, man, horse, and so forth; and the places of birth bring about no small variation in what is produced.

If the seed is generically the same, human for example, and the condition of the ambient the same, those who are born differ much, both in body and soul, with the difference of countries.

In addition, all the aforesaid conditions being equal, rearing and customs contribute to influence the particular way in which a life is lived. Unless each one of these things is examined together with the causes derived from the ambient, though this latter be conceded to exercise the greatest influence . . . they can cause much difficulty for those who believe in such cases everything can be understood (even things not wholly within its jurisdiction) from motion of the heavenly bodies alone.

Since such is the case, it would not be fitting to dismiss all prognostication of this sort because it can sometimes be mistaken; for we do not discredit the art of the pilot on account of its many errors. But, as when the claims are great, so also when they are divine, we should welcome what is possible and consider it enough. Nor, further, should we gropingly and in human fashion demand everything of the art; but should rather join in the appreciation of its beauty, even in instances where it could not provide the full answer. And as we do not find fault with physicians, when they examine a patient, for speaking both of the sickness itself and of the patient's idiosyncrasy, so too in this case we should not object to astrologers using as basis for calculation nationality, country, and rearing, or any other already existing accidental qualities.[26]

Ptolemaios particularly likes the analogy with medicine. He shows how astrology, in the hands of thoughtful practitioners like himself, was begetting a many-faceted approach to the question of causation, especially of human development. He rejects the simple fatalism of some of the early Stoics, and takes the position of men like Chrysippos and Diogenes of Babylon. Some things are directly under fate, others under chance. Some things occur "through more general circumstances and not as the result of an individual's natural propensities"—e.g. great fires, plagues, cataclysms. "But other events accord with the individual's natural temperament through minor and fortuitous antipathies of the ambient," the environment.[27] He keeps on making this kind of distinction, anxious not to create a closed system of a mechanistic kind; he wants to leave the way open for an analysis of the complexity and the interaction of factors of all kinds, arguing only that some factors will be more important in any given situation than others. He had been much affected by the consideration of medicine. The doctor had to work with the laws of the body, which left to themselves would produce certain inexorable results; but knowledge could modify and even change the way that the laws operated. He specially praised the way in which the Egyptians, "who have most advanced the faculty of the art, have wholly united medicine and astronomical observation".[28]

Antiochos of Athens seems of the late second century; a fragment of his in verse survives and there is much of him in Rhetorios. Whether he, Dorotheos or someone else was the author of a much-copied set of astrologic verses we do not know.[29] Perhaps his most important work was *Thesauroi*. But we know little of him and cannot place him with any certainty.[30] The Anon of 397 puts him between Valens and Antigonos; Maternus, between Ptolemaios and Dorotheos. Rhetorios, in an epitome of Book II of an *Introduction* by Antiochos, says that he approved the methods of Ptolemaios and Dorotheos—and so was later than they.[31] Hephaistion calls him an Athenian, but a catalogue of his was meant for Egypt.[32]

We see from him that astrologers used verse. Other such versifiers were Astrampsychos, Anoubion, Manethon, Dorotheos. The first-named is called an ancient mage, living before Alexander the Great; but if there ever was an early writer of this name, the works assigned to him in the tradition are much later. We have 101 verses under his name, in a strictly alphabetical order, which seem to date before Manethon's poem.[33] Hephaistion cites twelve lines by Anoubion, but we also have many fragments of his in prose. The name is Egyptian; but in these later days the fame of the Egyptians might invite anyone to assume an Egyptian name.[34]

Dorotheos tried to put into good verse-form an earlier work either in prose or verse, and was much used by Maternus, also by Hephaistion. For the Arabs he was a leading authority; Marsala sets him in a sequence where only Ptolemaios, Hermes, and Plato precede him. His main work was referred to as *Pentateuch*.[35] Omar-ben-Farchan mentions its topics: Births, Eras and Periods, the Lords of the Horoscope, the Computation of Birthyears, Undertakings. The first author citing him is Antiochos of Athens.[36]

Manethon's poem is called *Influences*. We know nothing of him, though the same name was borne by an historian and a physician. He is linked with Nechepso and Kleopatra; and an horoscope in his poem, cited earlier, puts his birth at A.D. 80. But he seems later than Dorotheos and shows a fear of dealing with royal horoscopes as liable to stir up trouble. This attitude does not seem characteristic of the Principate, but appears strongly in Maternus.[37]

Julius Firmicus Maternus is of the first half of the fourth century. He tries to accept both free will and the rule of the stars. The stars are part of God's creation, his signs in heaven; the astrologer, dealing with such things, must be upright, unselfish, pious, a model to men. He cites Hermes, Nechepso, Petosiris, not to mention Abram (Abraham); but he also knows Hipparchos and Ptolemaios. His *Mathesis,* which survives, refers to two previous works of his. He became a Christian under Constantine and wrote *On the Error of Profane Religion,* addressed to that emperor and his son Constans. (Which of his two extant works comes first, has been debated. But it makes little difference, Maternus had a conformist mind. A professional astrologer, he wanted to prove to the authorities that he was a loyal citizen and to accept whatever religion they adopted. *On the Error* has no reference to astrology, but both works servilely put the emperor on the level of the sky-bodies and the supreme God.)[38] In *Mathesis* he is anxious to placate the authorities. He deals with arguments against astrologers. He admits that some practitioners are inexpert and some even cheat; the science is difficult; but the human spirit which conceived religion and the various disciplines of knowledge can unravel astrology too. Horoscopes are not so hard as is the mapping of the courses of planets; yet the *mathematici* have managed that. All about us we see Fate at work; otherwise how explain the failure of the good, the success of the wicked? In dealing with the casting of horoscopes he makes many references to contemporary religion and its practices, to temples, priests, and divinations. Magic and divination are often connected with holy exorcists who "stay in the temples in an unkempt state and always thus walk abroad", frightening demons and evil spirits out of their human abodes. Maternus mentions religious games and contests, and men who grow rich on religion; and he recognises magic as a valid science, even if it is one that has its secret practices frowned upon.[39]

He is particularly keen to remove the shadow from astrologers. He warns the practitioner:

You will indeed always give your replies in public; and this must be mentioned in advance to those inquiring about information, that you will speak out in a loud voice your answers about whatever they may ask, so that perhaps some question may not be put to you, the asking or answering of which is forbidden.[40]

Constantine had issued two decrees attacking the private consultation of *haruspices*; in the second he derided even a public inquiry as mere superstition.[41] Maternus repeats, "Never take place in night-sacrifices, whether public or private. And never discuss matters with anyone in secret. Do it publicly as I have said before. In front of everyone's eyes ply the practice of this divine art." He stresses:

Be careful never to give an answer to anyone inquiring about the life of a Roman Emperor. For it is neither necessary nor permitted for us to learn anything about the State of the Realm through nefarious curiosity. But anyone who when asked says anything about the Fate of the Emperor is both criminal and worthy of every punishment . . .

And no astrologer has ever been able to find out anything true as to the Fate of an Emperor. For the Emperor is alone not subject to the Courses of the Stars, and he is the only one whose Fate the Stars have no power to determine . . .[42]

This is an odd change from the high claims of royal astrology. Perhaps the ruler-worship established by Diocletian had meant that the emperor as a god was raised above fate. But more likely the astrologers were now badly scared.

Since he is Lord of the Whole World, his Fate is directed by the Supreme God. And since terrestrial space of the Whole World is under the Emperor's Power, he has also himself been placed among those gods to whom the Supreme Deity has entrusted the Creation and the Preservation of All Things.

This statement is not quite consistent with Maternus' earlier prayer to the Seven Planets to protect Constantine and his sons.[43] The identification of the emperor more or less with the Christian God brings out the social aspects of the heavenly hierarchy from a new angle:

This matter disturbs the *haruspices* too. Whatever divinity is invoked by them, its power is weaker; it has therefore never been able to unfold the substance of superior power which indeed is contained within the emperor. For all freemen, all ranks, all rich men, all nobles, all dignitaries and all power serve him. He has gained the might of a deity and of immortal freedom, and is ranked in the forefront of the gods.[44]

All the same he feels that the astrologer, however loyal, should do his best to keep out of all scandals and law-suits. Once he gets into court, there is no knowing where the charges are going to end. The kind of trouble that an astrologer or his clients were liable to meet at this time is exemplified by what happened to the rhetorician Libanios who was pushed out of the place he had hoped to gain at Byzantion, and who set up on his own. He did so well that the public professors were jealous and had him charged with consulting an astrologer and using sorcery. The crowd was roused; a praetor who tried to protect him was promptly ousted and another installed; and Libanios had to leave the city to escape death (A.D. 346). An important case about twenty-five years later (in 371-2) shows how seriously charges about astrology were still taken under a Christian emperor. A hireling poisoner and an astrologer began the whole thing when under interrogation they earned pardon for their own crimes by revealing that attempts had been made to find the next emperor "through detestable presages". Three men were named, and one of these betrayed many others while a second betrayed three more. One of these three named Theodoros the Notary. So it went on till the jails were full. Ammianus, who knew the episode well, gives the names of fifteen accused. The examinations were carried out with the utmost brutality; one man dropped dead with terror in the witness stand; and Ammianus, years later, looked back on the events "as among shadowy things", and recalled the racks, the scourges, the yells of the tortured reverberating in the prefect's palace. Two of the arrested men had made a tripod of laurel wood, consecrated it with incantations, and set it in a room purified with incense. A metal plate on the tripod was inscribed round the rim with letters of the alphabet. "A man clothed in linen, shod with linen shoes, garlanded and bearing twigs from a tree of good omen, propitiated the divine in prescribed verses," then set swinging over the letters a ring hung on a linen thread. "Who will succeed Valens?" was asked. The ring stopped at *Th, E, O, D*—and there the inquirers also stopped, sure that Theodoros was meant. The executions were ruthless, panicky, inflicted on anyone at all suspected: chancellor of the treasury, vice-prefect, proconsul, Palatine trooper, ex-governor, and the theurgist Maximus (teacher of the emperor Julian). Of two philosophers, one was sentenced to the stake. "Laughing at the sudden breakdown of human fates, he died motionless in the flames, like Peregrinos Proteus the famous philosopher" (who achieved apotheosis by throwing himself into the flames at Olympia). Next, books in vast quantities were taken from houses and burned under the eyes of the judges as prohibited. Throughout the eastern provinces men burned their whole libraries in fear. "In those days," says Ammianus, "we all crept about as in Cimmerian darkness." John Chrysostom, a young man, chanced on a book of magic and expected to share the fate of the executed. So it is no wonder that Maternus writes:

So I don't want you with a truculent and stern reply to scare anyone who may have asked something about the Emperor. No, persuade him with learned speech that no one is able to ascertain anything about the Emperor's life, so that, his mind's error corrected, he may be impressed by your arguments to leave off the white heat of his boldness. Nor do I want you to denounce anyone who may have inquired about something else in evil manner, lest, when he's subjected to a death sentence through the illicit desires of his mind, you appear the cause of his death. That is improper to a man in a priestlike position.[45]

Some fifty years later all astrologers were banned. However, that did not halt the practice or stop works of astrology being written. Hephaistion was writing about 400. What seems his one contemporary horoscope is dated 22 February 380; and this date fits in with three longitudes of stars cited from him; he himself quotes other texts that he ascribes to Antigonos.[46] Palchos comes somewhere in the later fifth century. A horoscope dated 479 shows him to have been in Smyrna when a ship from Alexandreia was expected. Three of his horoscopes deal with sea-travel, and one discusses the prediction of a letter's contents. These themes seem to fit in with two chapters in a work of his which he took from a much earlier treatise with Zoroaster's name attached. We may assume that he was using some recent examples to furbish up old doctrines.[47] His name is Egyptian; but a passage which has been taken to prove that he came from Egypt is a quotation from the Anon of 379.[48]

Rhetorios is probably to be set about 500; this date accords with two of the seven horoscopes preserved under his name. Efforts have been made to prove him of Egyptian origin; but his use of rising-times which suit Alexandreia may only mean that he took the passages from Antiochos. He contrasts the rising-times of Ptolemaios, "accurate to minutes", with the cruder schemes of "the Egyptians and of Valens".[49] Eutochios may have written an Introduction to the Almagest which is extant; and a reference makes him the author of a horoscope dated 497, but the horoscope in question is also given to Paul of Alexandreia and appears in *Astronomical Observations* of Julianos of Laodikeia—an example of the difficulties in pinning down these astrologers and in trusting the references.[50]

There was an astrologer called Stephanos. He has been assumed to be the Neoplatonist Stephanos of Alexandreia (under Heraklios), who was probably also an alchemist. But the horoscope attributed to him shows an awareness of events up to 775; and the argument that some parts had been interpolated cannot be sustained. He is thus more likely to have been Stephanos the Philosopher, of whom an astronomical treatise is partly extant, *On the Mathematical Art*. Its author came from Persia to Byzantium. As he states that the art was transmitted from the Romans to the Saracens, he cannot have been writing before 800. Bagdad was not founded till 762, and Masha'allah, with whom Islamic astrology became heir of the Graeco-Roman tradition, lived till about 810.

After discoursing on the philosophy of astrology, Stephanos reports the visit of his friend Epiphanios, an Arab merchant, who has told him of a prophet Mōamed. This prophet promises his followers "victory in war, rulership over their enemies, and the pleasures of paradise". Stephanos knows that Mōamed was of the Quraysh tribe and had appeared in the desert of Yathrib in April 609 (Islamic tradition says 610), though he calls his father Ismael instead of 'Abd Allah. He feels the need to cast a *katarchē* on the merchant's visit. "O misery, alas the change of things." He sets out the horoscope and goes on: "The horoscopic premise then indicates a nation of Saturnian type and a State akin to Venus, rising quickly and mastering many nations; for the rising Balance brings servitude to all men." It is interesting thus to find that the Balance, associated with Augustus as the lord of a new dispensation, now ushers in Islam. However, its appearance here seems the result of a pun rather than an astrologic proof: for the Greek word means literally a Yoke.[51]

Stephanos goes on to give a full-length "prediction" of what the new State will achieve:

It prevails over all Egypt and Libya—Egypt as belonging to Mercury and Libya to Mars—and also Palestine and Syria as belonging to the Moon and Mercury. It drives the Roman nation from all Syria and the other countries, and subdues, slaughters, and imprisons Cilicia; and it will entirely devastate Cappadocia because of Mars. But it will not overwhelm the kingdom of the Romans itself, because of the Sun and because of Mars being near Midheaven . . .

The account, dealing with loci and starters, concludes with account of events reaching up to the Abbasid period (A.D. 775), the date when it was written. The author then does try to make some genuine predictions of what is to come after that, but goes quite wrong.[52]

19

Writers, Magicians and Horoscopes

Though a completely sceptical position was rare, many philosphers and other writers sought to take a middle position in the second century. Thus, Ploutarch kept to a generally Stoic attitude, believing in the rule of law or fate, but distinguishing possible from inevitable consequences, and allowing for the providential intervention of gods. This position was set out in *On Fate,* probably not by him, but in line with his views. As a believer in divination, he could criticise only blind fatalism, asserting that intelligence gave men free will, unlike beasts. He seems to avoid a full confrontation of the problem of astrology, though he praises it as useful, even for women. The ignorant women of Thessaly were persuaded by Aglaonike, well-versed as she was in *astrologia* and able to draw down the moon from the skies: a power given effect by her predicting a lunar eclipse. He twice uses this tale. His repugnance however appears in his comment on children delighting more in rainbows, haloes, and comets than in the sun and moon, like people who prefer riddles to a plain statement— though in Lampridios' Catalogue he is given a (lost) essay on Comets. The myth in *The Face in the Moon* tells of how the body goes down to dust, the soul up to the Moon, and the mind up to the Sun. In this work there is a strong hermetic note.[1]

Maximos of Tyre, a rhetorician late in the century, holds to a somewhat similar position in *If Divination Exists, What is Left for Us?* He sees a divine power pervading the cosmos, and wants to keep faith in oracles, but leaves men a limited area of freedom, citing physicians, pilots, army-commanders. Divination, piercing the veil that cuts us from the divine, lets us decide what can and what cannot be avoided, so that we pray as well as accept our lot. However, in *Should One Pray?* he ridicules prayers, for the gods since Homer's day have been themselves subject to Fate.[2] He is in some sort a Platonist, writing *God according to Plato*; but he uses

Aristotelian categories, and his argument that evil was necessary for the production of good looks to the Stoics and the neo-Platonists. He is thus an example of the wide eclecticism in thinkers, who are largely concerned with making the best of a bad job rather than with consistency of thought.[3]

Favorinus of Arles in Gaul, born about 85, was at his height under Hadrian. The *Augustan History* calls him the most esteemed of scholars at the court; he at times argued with Hadrian, but observed that it would be folly not to give in to the master of thirty legions. A universalist in scholarship, he was a foe to fatalist astrology which he attacked with missionary zeal, mustering forcibly all the sceptical arguments. He jeered at those who consulted the stars on the issue of law-cases, and he cites in example suits about partition-walls and the water-supply.[4] Diogenianos, probably an Epicurean, but also rather eclectic, added his voice to the attacks on fatalism and was later cited by the Christians. He repeats Favorinus' cry: "Why take the joy out of joy by long anticipation, or aggravate sorrow by prolonged worry?" (Ptolemaios tried to answer these points.[5]) Diogenes, another Epicurean, who died about 200, is known because of the long inscription he had engraved in his native Oinoanda on the walls of a portico. He attacked divination and fate as making a mock of all moral reproaches or legal punishments. He wrote, he says, for all men to read since they are all equal "citizens of the world".[6]

Alexandros of Aphrodisias, the last important Peripatetic, though wandering eclectically from Aristotle's empiricism, was given the Peripatetic school at Athens by Septimius Severus. He was another who accepted a limited area of life dominated by the stars and fate, but denied sheer fatalism. He admitted that changes in our world were reflected in the stars, but only on the physical level; he dodged the issue of fate by stressing the dualism of body and soul.[7] Often he stated ideas without making clear how far he agreed with them; but he seems to hold that the power of the heavenly bodies created both simple and complex organisms in form as well as in essence. According to the star-positions, heat and dryness, or their opposites, were engendered in earthly bodies by astral influences. The planets circling the Zodiac bestowed on those particles closest to them qualities like heat or dryness (that is, elements of fire), and the stars created the other three elements, air, earth and water. Besides creating the four elements (of which all matter was composed) the stars also brought about the compounds (mixtures of the elements). From the physical angle the stars brought about the creation, destruction, and transformation of matter.[8] While many Peripatetics of the day were drawn into equating soul or even intelligence with the *aither*, Alexandros managed to save the three aspects of Aristotle's kinetics by declaring that both *aither* and stars shared in responsibility for the motions of heavenly bodies and that (with them) soul was their nature.

Fig. 76. Atlantes as world-supporters used architecturally (Agrigentum); Atlas in Mithraic cosmogony, Neuenheim

The Cynics, like the Epicureans, were alone consistent in attack. Of them we may take Demonax and Oinomaos of Gadara, both under the Antonines. The latter, strong on free will, wrote *Unmasking of Wizards,* which pleased the Christians. He mocked at political divination, but was careful to use only very ancient examples.[9] Demonax was milder, rather close of Loukian.[10] The latter indeed can be called an amiable Cynic. Born about 120 at Samosat, he grew up as a rhetorician. Hating all forms of quackery, he attacked various popular prophets and saw the Christians as simple-minded adherents of a crucified sophist. A work falsely attributed to him, *Astrology,* is not at all scathing and put errors down to human fallibility. It declares that the science was devised by the Aithiopians, though Greeks developed it independently through Orpheus; it stresses the ancient importance of divination, but declares for modern scepticism. The stars are not concerned with us, but revolve by their own necessity. To know what can't be altered is useless. The value of astrology is moral and emotional; it enables men to delight in a coming good, or prepare themselves for a setback. In *Zeus Catechised* Loukian sets out all the anti-fatalist arguments. A Cynic harasses Zeus till he admits that the gods are controlled by fate, but claims they have a role as prophets. In the 30th *Dialogue of the Dead* a robber puts up the fatalist thesis in his own defence before Minos and baffles the hereafter-judge. In *True Story* and *Ikaromenippox* Loukian guys the tales of sky ascent in an ironic form of embryonic science-fiction.

Galen reluctantly admits iatromathematics. He has a keen sense of Stoic *sympatheia* but tries to apply it only to ascertainable facts. With his interest in cosmogony he wrote at least two commentaries on the *Timaios*; one survives in an Arabic version.[11] Among the aspects of a disease to be inquired into before diagnosis he lists the constellation prevailing at the time the patient fell ill. But this, *katastasis*, is mentioned without comment; he seems to have included it only out of professional convention.[12] He had little respect for astral botany and "the sacred herbs of the dekans and the daimons". He attacked Thessalos and Pamphilos. "Perhaps Pamphilos like very many others had idle time on his hands to spin useless yarns."[13] But with his strong Stoic sense of organic relations, he often could not resist ideas of correspondences when they had little or no direct evidence. He disliked atomists as Necessitarians, "who hold in contempt omens, dreams, portents, and any kind of *astrologia*". He accepted the influence of stars, e.g. the Dogstar, on the course of illness and the preparation of drugs. Aischrion devised a medicine against rabies "after the rise of the Dogstar when the Sun had moved into the Lion and the Moon reached her 18th day", and Galen didn't object. As for his own famous theriac, he noted that "many of the most highly placed Romans take this medicine on the first day of the moon; some choose the fourth day. . . . They take it about the third hour." He even had attached to his name a work on numerological medicine, the influence of numbers and critical days.[14] There exists under his name (also under that of Hippokrates) a work of astrologic prognostications connected with the time the patient went to bed; but this seems certainly not his. "Astrology is the foreseeing part of the [physicians'] art; and if not all, at least most of them have accepted this concept of astrology." Twelve chapters are given to the influence of the moon in each of the zodiacal signs, starting with the Ram.[15]

Plotinos as a Neoplatonist was opposed to fatalism. But he saw the heavenly bodies as divine and considered the Gnostics to be blaspheming when they denied this divinity and asserted that the elect were superior to the stars in spiritual dignity—a viewpoint also held by the Christians. He held that there was no evil in the bodies of the star-gods, which were wholly dominated by soul. (Much of the Plotinian views here were carried on by the Christians in their contrast of "natural" and "spiritual" or post-resurrection bodies, as Augustine admitted.)[16] Macrobius as a Neoplatonist of

Fig. 77. Triple Hekate (Bucharest)

the fourth century, a passionate advocate for solar monotheism, made an effort to uphold Pythagorean ideas (as well as those in Ptolemaios' *On Harmony*) and to bring in astrologic notions of influences by a back-door. He argued that one can still think Saturn and Mars baleful "despite the fact there is only one nature in things divine". He invoked the Pythagorean-Platonic ratios of the sesquitertian, sesquialter, super-octave, double, triple and quadruple. The sun and moon are the guardians of our lives; in our associations and activities we rely as much on them as on the other five planets combined; but Venus and Jupiter are favourably aspected, while Saturn and Mars are not. He then cites Plotinos as saying that while planets do not exert a direct influence on the individual, his fate is yet revealed to him by the way the seven planets aspect each other, just as birds in flight or at rest reveal the future by their direction or their cries.

Macrobius sets out a Plotinian explanation of rotation. The soul, whose essence is motion, has created out of itself the heavenly sphere, which it keeps rotating; for a sphere embracing the universe can only have a rotatory motion. It seems to be pursuing the soul, but cannot catch it up. If it did, it would cease to move, it would cease to be. As the soul, "leading the chase, is forever pouring itself out into the universe, the body [of the latter] is forever commingling with it". A sort of ceaseless copulation and orgasm of the embraced soul and cosmos, the driving energies and the material structures. The heavenly sphere was filled with constellated and single stars. Many thinkers held that the stars were fixed in the sphere—Macrobius and others considered that they moved, but owing to the sphere's vastness they took ages to complete their revolutions. There were eleven great circles girdling the sphere: the Milky Way, the Zodiac, and nine others (in fact mere mathematical lines). Macrobius made the Milky Way cross the Zodiac at the Crab and Capricorn, not at the Twins and the Archer: an error he took from Porphyrios, who was trying to make the Gates of Souls correspond with Homer's Ithacan Cave. The Zodiac was bisected by the ecliptic, so-called because the eclipse occurs only when sun and moon are both on this line at the same time. The extra nine circles included the Arctic and the Antarctic, two Tropics, the Equator, two colures, and the Meridian and the Horizon. Under each heavenly parallel was an earthly one, so that each earth-zone directly corresponded with a heavenly one, and climate on earth was regulated by the climate of the heavenly zones.[17]

We see then that almost all thinkers had to come to terms in some way with astrology. They had in varying degrees to orientate their systems towards the fundamental concepts of astrology and explain their relation to those concepts. Here we have been able only to point out certain key-aspects of this connection; but from Plato onwards it provided the main current of ideas on the nature of the universe. Only the Epicureans made a consistent effort to build a world-picture from which astrology was excluded; but the deep urgency which they felt in working out that world-picture was largely derived from their passionate desire to deny the claims of all the divinatory arts and undermine the system on which they depended.

When a thorough-going sceptic turned up, like Sextus Empiricus, who wanted to deny the possibility of any form of knowledge and to demolish the whole structure of ancient culture as based on fallacies, he had to pay much attention to astrology. Sextus set himself against the Science of Birth-Horoscopes [*Genealogia*] by means of which the Chaldeans, decking themselves with highsounding names like Mathematicians or Astrologers, have inflicted a not-inconsiderable injury on human life; against a discipline with which they are creating within us a mighty superstition, while preventing us in any way from acting according to common sense.

Yet he oddly excludes astronomy and astrometeorology from his universal attack on knowledge.

Nor will the power and possibility of prediction be discussed, which is possessed by Eudoxos, Hipparchos, and men of their type, i.e. the discipline called astronomy. For there is observation of phenomena in certain fields (such as agriculture and the art of navigation) in it, from which one may predict droughts, rains, plagues, and earthquakes, and other changes of the surrounding air.[18]

Sextus stressed the contradiction between fatalist and katarchic astrology, and mentioned a third class, which assumed that some things happen according to fate, others do not. If fatalism were true, all knowledge would be useless; if free will determined a category of events, they remained unpredictable. Then he argues that all astrology was based on the Horoscopic Point, so if that were shown to be uncertain, the whole structure broke down. In fact, a truly accurate observation of the birth moment and the specific zodiacal sign then rising was impossible. The moment of conception? That, in any event, could not be established. Even with a gong on a mountain top, the time taken by the sound waves to reach the calculator would spoil things. (He ignores tables and the possibility of estimating the gong's distance, the air's temperature, and so on.) Further, the border-lines between the signs were not clearly defined; atmospheric motions could pervert observations; some signs even overlapped one another; nor did the observation-place (hill, roof, etc.) remain constant. Also there was the phenomenon of refraction, especially strong near the horizon; and the time of the rise of signs varied with the locality. Then he goes on to the old arguments about men born at the same time or dying at the same time, with different horoscopes. All drowned men weren't born under Aquarius. The crude identification of the signs with animals and men was a ridiculous pretension. Unlike medicine, astrology had a hopelessly inadequate set of observations. In any event, as the world ended periodically by fire, there was not time enough to amass sufficient material about the stars.[19]

As an example however of how certain aspects of astrologic thinking had sunk deep into the culture, we may take a passage from the Carthaginian poet Nemesianus of the late third century. Thus, in dealing with the nurture of dogs he advises a "lessening of their regular fattening food":

> When burning Phoebus attains the hot heights of heaven
> entering his slow paths and the sign of the lingering Crab.

Discussing rabies, he asks:

> if it emanates from taint in a heavenly body
> when Phoebus shoots languid rays from a saddened sky
> raising a pallid face on a world dismayed;
> or, striking the burning back of fire-maned Lion
> he drives his feverish heats in our friendly dogs;
> if Earth breathes out contagion from her bosom . . .

We have already noticed how astrology slid off into magic and magic into astrology. The two arts could not but strongly affect one another; and a large body of astrologic doctrine moved over into the world of spells and incantations. The hopeful side of astrology had a natural link with the theurgic aspects of magic.[20] Astral deities loom up importantly in spells. For instance, the Sun in his boat, the Sun who, a man, is born, grows old, ages and dies. Macrobius, speaking of the identity, in his view, of Liber Pater and the Sun, says of Liber that his images

are shown, some in the form of a child or youth, others in that of a bearded man, and even as an old man, such as those of the Greeks who scall him Bassareus or Briseus, and those of the Neapolitans in Campania who honour him under the name of Hebon. These varieties of ages are connected with the Sun. He is considered as a Child at the winter solstice, a period when the Egyptians took him in this form out of his shrine. Then, because of the shortness of the day, the Sun seems in his infancy. Towards the spring equinox, the days grow longer and like a youth he gains in forces and is represented as a young man. Then at the summer solstice he enters into the fullness of his growth, expressed by a beard. Then also the day has come to its fullest growth. After that lessening days make him resemble an aging man; which is the fourth figure under which the god is shown.[21]

Or he is imaged as a child in a lotus, seated: Horos Harpokrates, an image which Augustine got from Porphyrios, and so on. Here is a magical application:

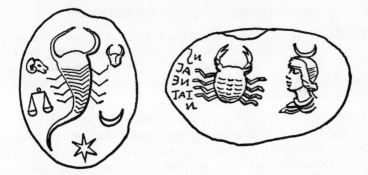

Fig. 78. Magical astrological gems: Scorpion surrounded by Ram and Bull (heads;) Balance; Sun; Moon. Brown and yellow jasper. Woman with crescent on head (Moon) and Crab (the Moon's domicile: *Tetrab.* 17). Sanguine Jasper

Take a pure boy and recite the formula of the spirits which is prescribed for this end. Take him out in front of the sun and place him upright on a new brick at the moment when the sun rises. When the whole solar ball comes up, put on him a new linen shirt and bid him close his eyes. Then get behind him and recite in a low voice over his head, striking his head with the solar finger of your right hand after rubbing his eyes with a previously made unguent.

"Nasira, Oapkis, Shfe-shfe, Bibiou, Bibiou is your true name [twice]. Lotus, open for me the heaven in all its width and depth. Bring me the pure light. Send me the god between the hands . . ."[22]

So the incantation to force the Sun to speak goes on, including a formula to be repeated seven times. There is also a spell for questioning the Moon directly or through a boy. If you perform the spell alone, you do it at full-moon on your house-top, after rubbing your eyes with green and with black ointment.[23]

Then there were the ancient beast-images. The wizard like the astrologer needed to take account of hourly changes. To each of the twelve hours of the day was connected a beast and a magical name. The hours and their animals corresponded to the bestiary of the *Dodekahoros* found in hermetic texts and in Teukros. Some are grotesque. The Sun has the form of a crocodile or the tail of a snake; he rides two dekans represented in turn by crocodile and serpent. He is the master of the stars; he has created the five planets considered as the gathering-points of the five animals; his rays are assimilated to angels, archangels, or daimons of the sky. The dekans too are represented in much the same way, each with its own name.[24] The Sun reigns over the Seasons and the Winds.

The Sun in his name of Attis is given as attribute a wand and a reed-pipe. The pipe shows a sequence of unequal breaths [*spiritus*]. For the Winds, in whom nothing is equal, draw their proper substance from the Sun. The wand or rod expresses the power of the Sun, which regulates all things. (Macrobius.)[25]

Sympatheia links the Sun to planets, stones, and animals.

The Moon is traditional in night-spells, invoked as Selene, Mene, Hekate, Persephone, Artemis, Isis, Astarte, Ereschigal (Sumero-Babylonian deity of the underworld and sorcery), Moira, Dike, Erinys; she is many-named, many-shaped, at times hermaphroditic as Hekate. Prayers celebrating her powers remind us of the aretologies of Isis or the litany of praise near the end of the *Golden Ass*. She is assimilated to Hermes-Thoth as being quadrangular (four-phased); but other terms recall the older idea of three phases, and she is represented with three heads or faces as triple Hekate. "The Trivian Titaness is Diana," says Varro, "called Trivia from the fact that her image is set up quite generally in Greek towns where three roads meet, or else because she is said to be the Moon, which moves up in the sky by *tres viae*, three ways, upwards, sideways and onwards". Her revolution gained her twenty appearances in which we find the old bestiary of Egypt asserting itself.

The Zodiac played a large role; we find magical names corresponding to the signs and symbols of the constellations.[26] Various aspects of astrologic doctrine infiltrate without any obvious system, probably often through systems of correspondences in the wizard's mind. Here is a spell against gout:

You write these names on a band of silver or tin, you fix it on the stag-skin and bind it on the man's foot. The stagskin should have two fillers. *Thembarathem Nournembrenoutipe aoïkhthousemmarathemmou naïoou.* Heal N to whom N has given birth of all the maladies of his feet and in the soles of his feet.

Do it when the Moon is in the constellation of the Lion.[27]

The following charm, supposed to be practised by the god Imhotep, gains the magician the favourable stars he needs. He takes a four-legged bench of olivewood on which no one has sat; puts it in a room, in the middle, near his head; covers it with an apron from top to bottom and puts four bricks on top of one another underneath; before it he sets a stone with olive charcoal

Fig. 79. Astrologic gem: BARKABA, 7 stars, 2 arrows, IAO; ADONE
between star (? sun) and crescent, and ABRASAS—grey agate.
Mithraic gems: Mithras with Dog, Scorpion, Torchbearers and
astral sign, snakes in cosmic image; Lion with Bee in mouth and
7 stars with magical (Greek) letters

burning in it. He makes pilules of the fat of a wild goose brayed
with myrrh, throws one in the stove, keeps the others, and recites a
Greek formula. Then he lies down, quite silent, and sees a god
looking like a priest, clothed in the finest of stuffs. The formula
runs:

I call you that reside in the invisible darkness, who are among the great
gods, who are strong and reign over the solar rays, who send the
luminous goddess Nebutosualeth and the great god Barzan to night,
your angel Zeburthaunen, acting in truth truthfully and infallibly,
with no contradiction of my interest. I conjure you by him seated in a
cloak of fire on the good spirit's head of silver, the all-powerful spirit
with four faces, who is supreme, who is dark, the chief of the soul's Fox.
Don't refuse to hear my call and send me quickly tonight this connection
with the god. (Thrice.)

When the god has appeared and told the magician what he wants to
know, the latter puts on the plaque for indicating the hour, he sets
stars on it, writes his design on a new sheet of papyrus, and puts it
on the plaque. The plaque will then reveal "the stars favourable for
your design".[28]

With the magician, predictions by number and iatromathematics
are often mixed, and they take the place of astrology proper.
Speculations about the zodiacal *melothesis* are also mixed with old

beliefs about the parts of the body linked with a particular demon.[29] As with astrology and alchemy all sorts of famous or mythical names are used; but now and then what seem the names of actual persons come in, Pankrates (known to Hadrian for his naming a red lotos after Antinoos), Ptolemaios, Klaudianos, Manethon. Hermes here as elsewhere is a character with whom the magician seeks to identify himself. Thus he addressed the Sun:

I am Thoth, inventor and initiator of magical methods and magical writing. Come here to me, you who are underground, rise up for me, the greatest daimon, Nun of the underworld, and you, gods of Nun of the underworld, for I am Heron, enjoying great glory, the Eye of the Ibis, the Eye of the Falcon, the Eye of the Phoenix wandering across the airs, enveloped in mud . . . . and skin . . . . I don't learn what is in the souls of all the Egyptians, Hellenes, Syrians, and Aithiopians, and of any other tribe or nation whatever, if I don't learn the past and the future, if I don't learn anything concerning their art and their occupation, their works and their way of living, then I shall shed the blood of the black Dog-headed into my vase, without hurting myself, I'll put the pot on a new pedestal, I'll burn below it the bones of the Drowned One [Osiris] . . .[30]

The amalgamation of Greek cosmological ideas with the other aspects of astrology helped to weaken the indigenous beliefs in Egypt, but those beliefs carried on in a zoomorphic demonology. Among the multiplicity of strange and sacred animals that populate the world of magic, certainly some come direct from the Zodiac: the Scorpion, the Crab, Capricorn. The Scorpion protects against the evil eye, and in this case there may seem at first glance no particular association with the constellation.[31] There was however an easy link of prophylactic magic with the zodiacal image of a man superimposed on the band, each sign presiding over the organs it touched. Also, there were the various links of planets and signs with plants and stones, which we have discussed. In the zodiacal system the Scorpion corresponded to the genitals, and so the stones on which its image was engraved might well have been thought to protect that part. To protect the genitals was to protect against the evil eye, which was thought to strike especially at the penis. In Mithraic cult-imagery the Scorpion aims at the testicles of the cosmic Bull. In astrology the Scorpion constellation was the house of the planet Mars, who protected it; Macrobius tells us that Mars was in the Scorpion at the birth of the world; in Mesopotamia it was an attribute of Ishtar-Ishara, one of whose functions was to rule war and death. *Skorpaioi,* born under it, loved war, gladiatorial combats, brawls. The scorpion however also had its beneficent qualities; as it could kill, it could also fertilise. Scorpion-men and scorpions played an ancient part in Meso-potamian myth and ritual-imagery; the scorpion, associated with astral signs, had the task of guarding the sun's path; it was a sort of Atlas or sky-supporter. It was thus a very potent creature and was both dreaded and appealed to for protection.

The *Sacred Book of Hermes to Asclepios* connects the Scorpion and cornaline; but we find many scorpions cut on yellow jasper— not that this fact need bother us. Ancient lapidaries often disagree on the particular sequence of star, stone, plant; we find contradic-tions even in various versions of the same text, as also between magic papyri and the intaglios that correspond to some of their recipes. If then we are right in linking the Scorpion with the genitals, the Crab would go with the flanks, lungs, and spleen; Capricorn with the knees as an anti-rheumatic.

Intaglios with a zodiacal sign do not attempt to follow the more complex rules of astrology; they merely bear the sign under which the wearer was born. The belief in the efficacy of such a sign was strong in Byzantine times, but certainly goes far back, as is shown by the passage from Petronius we discussed.[32] Still, if the signs were used mainly in this way, we'd expect a much larger assortment of them than we do find. Most of the signs on the gems, e.g. the Scorpion, can best be understood in astrologic medical terms. Further, the signs are accompanied by formulas which reappear in spells and show that they had in themselves a magical force.

On a blood-red jasper we see a woman's head with a crescent on it, turned to a Crab with ten feet; to the crab's right five lines, *Ns/as/ne/iat/nn.* Here we certainly have an astrologic representa-tion, for the Crab was the traditional house of the Moon. A yellow and brown jasper stone has a ten-footed Scorpion surrounded by the Ram and the Bull (shown by their heads alone), the Balance, the Sun, the Moon; on the reverse is a palm and a sign suggesting a chrism. The legend says, "Keep away from injustice [or the unjust man] and fear will not come near you."[33]

A strange stone purports to set out a horoscope. Above a serpent bounds a goat-figure, apparently with a large cock-headed genius on its back. In place of the latter's legs are five scallops which make us think the torso is meant to be covered with a cuirass closely modelled to the body (as on the statues of emperors).

Its head bears a crest radiating with five rays; the left hand holds a spiral-shell, the right hand a heart. On the right we see traces of a second goat-figure (lost by the breaking of the stone). The legend runs: *Con(iunx) Div(i) Aug(usti) Livi(a) Drusi(lla)*. In the field are the signs of the Virgin, Mars, Venus, Jupiter, Capricorn, also the number XXIII—all back-to-front as for a seal. The signs indicate a date determined by the position of Venus in the Virgin, of Mars in Capricorn 23.

But the signs are not in any known ancient form; they are of Renaissance-date. The heart likewise is not ancient in shape. The shell suggests shells in late medieval miniatures. No cock-headed god with snake-legs is known in association with a pair of (strange) goats; and both the birth and the marriage of Livia fell in the early year, but Venus in the Virgin means July–August—and for neither of Livia's dates is Mars near Capricorn. The date intended can hardly be that of her death or apotheosis.[34]

And yet the work cannot be a simple fabrication. An hermetic passage dealing with creation (in the *Kosmopoiia* of the Leyden papyrus) states that the god brings about the seven primordial deities by seven successive bursts of laughter. "When he means to burst out laughing for the third time, through his anger appeared Nous (or Intelligence) holding a heart in his hand. He was called Hermes, he was called *Sēsēsilam*." Also a text at Esna tells how Thoth was born from the acerbity or bitterness of the creator— Thoth and "acerbity" being assonances in Egyptian. Such verbal play or punning was felt to hint at mysterious links or correspond-ences, and was common in Egyptian. The Leyden passage is thus proved to have a genuine Egyptian basis, and the "forged" intaglio is shown to have genuine elements that could not have been devised by any Renaissance artist or scholar. In both papyrus and intaglio the god is characterised by the heart he holds in his hand. Thoth-Hermes and Heart were closely associated. Thus Hora-pollon tells us: "When they want to write Heart they paint an Ibis. For that creature is put into relation with Hermes, the Lord of every heart and every reasoning. And also since the Ibis has itself a likeness to the Heart, on the theme of which the Egyptians give many accounts." The value *ib* (heart) was used for the hieroglyph of the ibis. The equation scarab-ibis has not been otherwise proved; but the scarab in mummies was a heart-substitute and scarabs called "hearts" are countless.

The best conclusion is then that the intaglio is a genuine one with later additions or that it embodies elements from a genuine one that has since become lost.

The Christians carried on a great deal of the magical outlook and procedure in their exorcisms. We find these invoking the angels in their choirs or as individuals with control of some particular set of demons, the Throne of God with its 24 Elders, its eternal fire and its Sea of Glass, Christ's Seven Thrones, the Breasts and Milk of Mary, the Seven Days of Creation, the Seven Heavens, the Heaven of Heavens, the Earth, the Sun, the Moon and the Course of the Moon, the Stars and their Names, the Secret Names, and the symbolic Names of Christ. A link is afforded by the Jewish exorcists mentioned in *Acts*, who use the Name of Jesus, and the *Hebraikos Logos* of a magical text.

We may round this chapter off with the remaining horoscopes, from 207 to 488. First come some 34 examples from papyri or graffiti, mostly with bare astral informations. We have already noticed the Doura graffiti of 219, probably cast when the child was five months old. All the versions are scratched roughly in wall-plaster, one with a portion of a diagram (circular, with horizon and meridian as diameters). "I have made the sphere in Daisios I, according to the Moon 30. May the writer be blessed. Monday." He uses *sphaira* for the circular drawing, a usage that probably stems from the meaning of "circular orbit" in astronomic literature. His comment must mean that the first day of the Macedonian month Daisios in the civil calendar corresponded with the 30th of the preceding lunar month (Artemision). This coexistence of a schematic civil calendar and a strict lunar one reminds us of the calendar of the Hellenistic era.[35]

We find papyri starting with "good Fortune" and ending with "good Luck". Thus, "With Good Fortune: according to the date you gave me, dearest [lady], you were born in the Blessed Reign of Diocletian, according to the Greek calendar, the month Athyr, the 14th–6th hour of the night." Another ("with Good Fortune, nativity of Hermesion") makes part of a group of eight, all possibly copied down by Hermesion himself, plus two accounts and a large multiplication table. One page had previously been used for a housewife's complaint against her husband, but there seems no connection with Hermesion. A graffito at Abydos, in the temple of Sethos I, again has a diagram, a circle divided into twelve segments. Below is written, "Artemidoros Health By Bes

N

may I not be wiped out." Perhaps the man was alarmed at finding the horoskopos in a house of Saturn. Does the graffito mean that astrologic consultations were held in places like this ancient temple? Or that someone had slipped in to consider what he had learned elsewhere? The first supposition seems the more likely.[36]

Some eighteen examples come from the fifth century. A literary horoscope from the start of the century shows an elaborate effort to determine the duration of each planet's role as *chronokrator*; the length of these periods, ending with Saturn's rule, is the length of the life. For 2 July 419: a man killed at 36 years, *klima* of Spain. For 25 April 463: "this was the child of a king and died at 5 months, in Byzantion". The child cannot be that of Leon I and Verina, born 25 April 464 and dying at 2 years 2 months, but the similarity of day and month is odd.[37]

Next come two enquiries about journeys. First: "*Katarchē* of a Ship", 1 October 474: A man left Caesarea (probably in Palestine) 191st year of Diocletian, month October 1, fifth (hour) of day. There was "a storm and delay in the voyage", the oars were damaged and there were "quarrels and fights in the ship". But this aspect "did not harm the *katarchē* because of the ruler of the Horoskopos". As for the subject, "thrown on land, he was loved by a woman". He embarked in another ship at Abydos, in the Hellespont. Then: "Inquiry about a *Katarchē* concerning Fear of a Journey to Athens," 16 July 475. There was a suggestion of "danger and loss" because Mars and Saturn were in the Horoskopos. Also, because of "the presence of Venus and the Venus contacting towards Jupiter, they had fallen into trouble and, given 15 [days?], they were saved". The discussion, which cites Dorotheos, shows that the ship must have carried four-footed animals; and indeed it brought camels. "I said that when the Moon would be in the Archer or the Fish the ship would arrive; and when the Moon came into the Archer, they arrived. If one reads through the chapters of the ancients, one will find not a few excellent suggestions." If the camels were consigned to Athens, they were an odd cargo.[38]

For 29 June 479 (papyrus): the first line has a monogram of an unusual kind for Christos, but line two ends in "the Lord Anoup", who may be the god Anubis. It was common for Egyptians to call a god the Lord of a locality. For 19 August the same year: another *katarchē*, this time "about the lost linen of a [slave] girl". The computation showed that the thief was in the household and not from outside, and that he was an old man. Also, "he was an educated person and a rascal, and frustrated in intercourse". The loser, a female, was also "a humble person or slave", and the article, "old and wretched". One wonders why the inquiry was put.[39]

For 14 July 479: again a ship-inquiry, like the list from Palchos:

Another inquiry, in Smyrna, about fear for a ship; for it was expected long before to arrive from Alexandreia and had not arrived . . .

I said the ship had met with a great storn, but was saved . . . And because the Virgin was a winged sign, as also the Archer, I said they were bringing some feathered things. And because the Moon was in the house of Mars and terms of Mercury, I said they were probably bringing books and papyrus with them and some bronze objects because of the Scorpion. Noting that Asklepios [Ophiouchos] was rising with the Moon, I said they were bringing musical instruments with them.

They arrived on the eighth day:

and being asked, they spoke of the delay and said there was an upheavel at sea, and, as the sea parted, the rudder struck a rock and was broken, and they were much driven about by the storm. On reaching a harbour, they transferred the cargo to another ship, on which they came, bringing indeed ostrich feathers and plain papyrus, because Mercury was retrograde, and cooking implements, because of the Scorpion, and a shipload of medical supplies because of Asklepios and Hygeia.[40]

Fig. 80. Graffito at Abydos (in schematic form)

Hygeia (Health) was a name also used for Ophiouchos (Snake-holder).

For 21 March 482: we meet stillborn children—non-viables (those who die in less than a year). For 8 July 483, Palchos again deals with animals (on shipboard). "About a Small Lion, whether he will be tamed." The Horoskopos indicated a quadruped and the question of tameness. "All this showed it would be tamed and brought up with man." Also it would go abroad in a ship because the setting sign was watery. "And the fact that the Moon had left contact with Venus to make contact with Jupiter, linked the fortunes of sender and of receiver. For the sender was to become consul and the receiver was consul." The consuls for 483 were Anicius Acilius Aginatius Faustus in the West and Flavius Trokondos in the East. We may assume that Trokondos wanted the lion for Games; but if it were to be tamed it would not be of use for beast-combats.[41]

From Palchos also comes "*Katarchē* when Theodoros the Augustalian Prefect entered Alexandreia": 17 March 486. "He began well and caused prosperity, he was not a thief, and was truthful and in good repute with the City [Alexandreia]. But he was soon dismissed in disgrace and under punishment for thievery." In explanation: "You will find Saturn in *apoklima* and fallen under the disgrace of eclipses, which caused the overthrow with disgrace." A total eclipse did occur on 19 May 486 (two months after the *katarchē*), visible in Alexandreia and coming between two lunar eclipses (7 December 485, 23 April 487). The text also mentions that the subject was "obstinate and insolent". We do not know elsewhere of this Theodoros; but he may have been caught up in troubles in Alexandreia following the abortive revolt of Illos and Pamprepios, with which we shall later deal.[42]

For 5 September 487: "Saturday, 7 Thoth, first hour of daytime, distressing letters were brought to a certain person with everything contrary to his expectations." The *katarchē* of Palchos explains why. One MS adds, "an efficacious *katarchē* in which I failed and went astray, then afterwards, finding the reason, marvelled at its force". The horoscopes for 1 April 488 and 28 October 497 have no points of interest.[43]

20

Pagans and Christians

We have seen how astrology continually affected the religions of the empire. The triumph of solar monotheism as a prelude to the acceptance of Christianity was closely bound up with astrologic doctrine; the Sun which emerged had many ingredients, but Stoic and astrologic elements were of central importance. Indeed almost all the cults which stirred men and women in these years (when the old city-cults had weakened) assimilated astrology in some degree. Take the cult of Adonis. We saw earlier how Syrian priests used the Sothic or Cosmic Year. The date of the Adonis festival seems to have been mid-July, the 19th. When in 362, about that date, the emperor Julian entered Antioch, the women throughout the city were celebrating the Adonia and weeping with loud cries.[1] The crowd welcomed Julian, shouting that a Saviour Star was lighting up the East. Some scholars have seen a reference to the planet Venus identified with Astarte; but the revolutions of a planet cannot fix a yearly festival.[2] A fixed star is needed, and the one here must be Sothis. In Egypt 19 July corresponded to its heliacal rising and marked the start of the Sothic year. The geographical differences of Syria and Egypt meant that the rising would occur in Syria on a different day; but probably the religious links of the two regions had grown so close that the Egyptian date was taken over for the start of the religious year.[3] Theokritos, describing the Adonis festival at Alexandreia, makes the god return from the underworld with the twelfth month; hence the prayer, "Be propitious to us, dear Adonis, and favourable for a New Year." Ammianus states that at Antioch the festival was performed at the year's end.[4] Manilius writes on the Syrian rites that went on at the Dogstar-period and lasted, like it, seven days. Alburni, astrologer of the eleventh century, says that the Egyptians sowed all sorts of grains in bowls in the days before the rise of the Dogstar, and on 25 Tammuz (last of the Dogdays) tried by means of the plants to predict the crops for the coming year. So those days of the Dog-star were taken to determine the whole of the next year; they were *krismoi hēmerai*. The Syrians had a similar custom.[5]

Macrobius gives us the sort of learned exegesis that had grown up:

No one will now doubt that Adonis is the sun if he considers the religion of the Assyrians among whom used to flourish the cult of Venus Architis and Adonis; which has passed on to the Phoenicians. The physici have attributed the name of Venus to the upper part, which we inhabit, of the terrestrial hemisphere; and they have called Prosperpina the lower part of that hemisphere. That's why Venus, among the Assyrians and the Phoenicians, weeps when the sun, running through the twelve zodiacal signs in his yearly course, enters into the lower part of hemisphere. For, of the twelve signs, six are considered lower, six higher.[6]

He goes on to interpret the Sun's course in terms of the death and rebirth of Adonis.

The lid of a silver box found at Parabiago, of Antonine date, shows how astrologic (and Mithraic) elements entered the Attic cult. The scene is the wild cosmic journey of the Great Mother rather than a sky-ascent. She and Attis are seated in a chariot, which is decorated at the side with a Maenad, drawn by lions, and surrounded by three Kourētai who beat their shields with daggers in an ecstatic dance. Aloft is Sol in a chariot, preceded by Phosphoros and going up to heaven, while Luna descends in a *biga* drawn by two oxen and heralded by Hesperos. Below are the four Seasons (three shown as children) and the Earthmother with two naked children who point up at Cybele. Beyond the Seasons are two River-nymphs, and between Earth and the nymphs lies Ocean represented by Triton and Nereid. Before Cybele's chariot stands a naked young man upholding an oval ring on which the zodiacal signs are engraved; he is inside the ring and has a long staff in his free hand. He is the young god of Time; by him is a thick obelisk entwined with a large serpent (the Tree of Life). Cybele is here shown as the Mistress of All Living, of all growth and movement, of Time itself. She moves from light and life to darkness and death, from east to west, fertilising as she goes. She will return out of death in the eternal cycle.[7]

At Palmyra was the dominant triad of Bel, Iarhibol, Aglibol (known from A.D. 32 to the third century).[8] Bel presides, Iarhibol is solar, Aglibol is lunar. The last two gods were Palmyrean and had names of Canaanite origin; Bel was Akkadian, but with an image like those of his partners, indeed of a long series of beardless Syrian gods. He was doubtless once the chief god Bol, and was merged with Bel by a priesthood who had absorbed Babylonian doctrines. We know of Bolstar: Bol of Ashtar, the goddess's consort, or he whose image is set up in Ashtar's temple. Belastar is probably the same god.[9] However, the triad was so cohesive that we do not know of any representation of Bel by himself. The triadic form had a long background. We can trace it to the fourteenth century B.C. in a treaty of the Hatti and Mitanni; and a Cilician inscription, probably of the fifth century B.C., cites as guarantors: Baalshamin the Great, Shar, and Shamash. The triadic form was common in Hellenistic times and in Roman times we meet Greek-Oriental cult-images or symbols of the Sun, Moon, and a supreme deity, Jupiter of Baalbek, Zeus Hagios of Tripolis, Jupiter Dolichenus, or Artemis of Perge.[10] But here in Palmyra the Sun and Moon are not mere appendages to the high god; they have clear characters and Iarhibol gives oracles. Bel becomes Zeus in Greek inscriptions and is represented as master of the planets and the Zodiac; he has no connection with thunder. We find him in a relief with a secondary god, Keraunos (Thunder). Nor is he a solar god; any solar aspects are part of the general syncretic trend. Baalshamin also appears in Palmyra, but in a small temple on a side-site, showing that he is no city-god like Bel; he remains a stranger, connected with the Phoenicians, who set up his earliest monuments.

In Bel's temple the sculpture on the soffit of the lintel in the north *thalamos* shows a starry sky borne on the wings of a great eagle. Among the stars winds a serpent flanked by six globules. The left end is gone; but on the right we see Iarhibol as a radiated god, with sun-symbol at his side. Certainly on the left would have been Aglibol and moon. The eagle we may take as belonging to Zeus Belos; the serpent is the planetary system; the six spheres stand for the six planets with the serpent itself as sun; the undulation is the yearly movement of the sun—a form of symbolic design that we find in Egypt as well.[11] We may add that the celestial eagle, as attribute of the high god, gives immortality in the form of a serpent held in its beak or claws—though the serpent can be replaced by a palm or crown of leaves. The god of heaven, Baalshamin, in human form, when not shown with an eagle, wears a

cloak covered with snakeskins: that is, he possesses immortality.[12]
We may compare the sculpture on the lintel of the temple at
Rahlé on the slopes of Hermon: here the eagle has a crown in his
beak and a palm in his claws. At the left end is a star and above the
palm a long serpent, but no globe. On a Haurian relief the eagle
with outstretched wings is flanked by Hesperos and Phosphoros
with torches.[13]

The ceiling of Bel's niche in the north *thalamos* is also astrologic.
In the middle rises a dome divided into seven hexagonal medallions,
each with a bust. In the peripheral six we see a radiate Sun, armed
and helmed Mars, the Moon in her crescent, Venus veiled in
Syrian mode, Saturn with his *harpē*, Mercury with caduceus.
The centre must have held Jupiter. The Moon here is represented

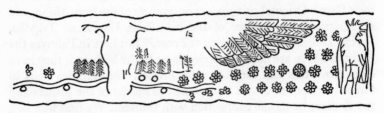

Fig. 81. Lintel of north *thalamos* of Temple of Bel, Palmyra

in Hellenistic style as Selene—in a temple where she was
worshipped as a male deity according to the Semitic tradition.
It is odd to find Jupiter at the centre; we expect the Sun. But
Jupiter was the star of Bel at Palmyra, as of Marduk at Babylon.[14]
Marduk, we are told, created the seven planets and fixed the point
of exaltation of his own Nabiru-Jupiter. The Sabians consecrated
the fifth day of the week to the planet Jupiter under the name of
Bal.[15]

Around the dome is a Zodiac representing the fixed stars. The
Scorpion has huge claws that embrace the sign of the Balance
(shown as a man holding scales). As we have noted, the Balance
seems introduced into the Zodiac only in the last century B.C. in
place of the Pincers of Scorpion. The first known references to it is
in Varro's *On the Latin Language*: "*Signa* are so called because
they sign or indicate something, as the Balance marks the equinox."
The dome-decoration here probably goes back to the era of Tiberius. Four eagles uphold the firmament. No particular horoscope is
illustrated; the Sun and Venus accompany opposed signs, the

Fig. 82. Ceiling of same room, with zodiac and seven planets

Bull and the Scorpion: which could be astrologically meaningful only if the earth passed between Venus and the Sun.[16]

We may compare the account in *Apollonios of Tyana* of a room in the palace at Babylon:

where the roof had been carried up in the form of a dome, to resemble in a way the heavens. It was roofed with lapis lazuli, a stone that is very blue and like heaven to the eye; and there were images of the gods they worship, fixed aloft and looking like golden figures shining out of the aither. Here it is the King gives judgement, and golden wrynecks are hung from the ceiling, four in number, to remind him of Adrasteia [a title of Nemesis] the goddess of Justice and to engage him not to exalt himself above humanity. These figures the Mages themselves say they arranged; for they have access to the palace and they call them the Tongues of the Gods.[17]

The situation at Palmyra was not unlike that at Baalbek. The highgod there was Jupiter Optimus Maximus Helipolianus; a dedication to him at Beyrouth precedes IOMH with *Regi Deo* (or *deo(r)um*); another at Baalbek follows it with *Regulo* (second century A.D.). Rex and Regulus are Latin translations of the Semitic Melek, king, common in Oriental cults; but they also probably have an astral sense as they are followed by the names of the consorts Venus and Mercury. In the astrologic interpretation of the Heliopolitan triad these three deities represent the three planets whose conjunction, says Valens of Antioch, "produces princes capable of royal acts". Regulus cannot mean the derogatory "little king", it must rather refer to the star Basiliskos with its role of king-making.[18] The closure of the Kommagene centres of the royal cult by A.D. 72 must have sent their priests afield to places like Baalbek-Heliopolis, taking with them their ardent ideas of royal astrology.[19]

If we turn more south to the trading state of the Nabataians, we find again a permeation by astral symbols.[20] Outstanding is the relief of Tyche (Fortune Tutelary Power) found in a ruined temple at Khirbet Tannur and dated perhaps in the first quarter of the second century A.D. With her mural crown and her veil representing the heavenly vault, she rises from the nearly circular panel surrounded by a raised zodiacal band. Above her right shoulder is a crescent; above her left an astral symbol apparently made up of two staffs bound together, one tipped with a crescent, the other seemingly with a torch—the pair thus standing for light and darkness. Tyche and Zodiac are upheld by winged Victory or Nikē. The Nabataian Tyche was inseparable from the dominant deity Atargatis with her strong moon-element. Here she appears both as protectress of the nation and as mistress of the cosmos, of its star-movements, winds, seasons, and of the fortunes of men. The zodiacal signs are oddly presented. Instead of running continuously round, one half goes clockwise, one half anti-clockwise. We see six from the Ram going anti-clock, six from the Balance going the other way. The reason for this division may lie in the existence of two New Years to be celebrated, one in the spring, one in the autumn. On the right are the signs of spring and summer, of warmth and light; on the left, those of autumn and winter, of cold and dark.[21] The zodiacal Tyche at Khibet seems connected with the high importance of the sanctuary itself; probably the seven main characters of the Nabataian pantheon, identified with the seven planets, were thought to visit the temple on special occasions when the signs were in their most beneficent positions; and worshippers would bring offerings in some sort of communion with the deities at such a favourable moment.

Three of the signs are given an unusual form. The Ram is shown as an Athena-Minerva figure; the Archer appears as a young man with rather jovial looks (in bust form) and a spear or arrow jutting above his right arm; Capricorn (also a bust) seems feminine and may indeed be meant to represent one of the Nereids of the constellation. However, the figure may be in fact a Pan. We may note that a number of anti-clockwise Zodiacs exist; and we meet a central panel showing a horned and goatlegged Pan.[22]

There are several angles from which we can approach this important monument. First we may take the Nikē or victory. We are reminded of monuments in which Atlas, the mythological sky-bearer, upholds a globe or sphere. One important example at Rome, probably of the second century A.D., shows an enthroned Zeus-Jupiter inside a Zodiac which rests on the back and upraised arms of an Atlas.[23] A Hellenistic relief from Askalon shows an Atlas supporting a sphere on which stands a winged Tyche. A medallion of terracotta from Vienne in France provides what is a sort of halfway-house. Here a large crown of laurel surrounds a woman's bust, her head bearing a mural crown; she is described as Tutela, the Latin form of Tyche. A bearded head on high represents one of the Winds, under it is a Victory holding the laurel-crown, with a palm branch in the free hand. On the left of the terracotta (now lost) there would have been another Wind and another Victory. Below is a bearded figure with rounded veil blown up over him, representing the terrestrial universe and its sky. He is not actually supporting the crown-medallion—that is being done by the Victories—but he could easily become a crouching Atlas.[24]

From another angle we can see the Nabataian Tyche as belonging to a long series of works that carry on into the medieval world, in which a winged creature, dressed in a long drape that falls to the feet, upholds above his or her head a medallion with a portrait or symbol, while standing on a disk or sphere. We need not follow up this line, but we may note that our Nikē probably stood on a globe of some sort as do other examples at Khirbet Tannur. Ancient Eastern representations of winged genii bearing the solar disk have a certain similarity; but the disk there has no portrait or symbol and is winged in Egyptian style, while there is no globe underfoot. Globes also form a common base for an Eagle, and are often associated with Zeus-Hadad or Jupiter in his capacity as the Baalshamin or master of the heavens.[25] The normal significance of such globes is cosmic; but some discoid bases, it has been suggested, may symbolise sacred mountain tops, where such deities as Zeus-Hadad loved to live. A Syrian bronze sculpture shows an eagle perched on a discoid base on which is incised in Greek: *Helios*. Here then the reference is solar.[26] An ancestry for the caryatid has been claimed in the Egyptian picturings of the god Shu upholding the curved-over sky-goddess Nut, with the Dendera Zodiac showing the first adaptation and with the theme taken over by the Greeks in the images of Atlas or Herakles bearing the heavenly sphere. In Christian art the upholders become the four archangels. Winged caryatids often appear as Victories or funerary genii. No doubt the origins are more complex than this scheme suggests; but it has a certain truth. The caryatid Victory does express a triumph over death, a successful movement from earth to a heavenly home. In Coptic funerary art, birds lift their wings above their heads to uphold crosses inscribed in crowns. In the nekropolis of el-Bagawat four birds, standing on spheres, lift up on their wings a circular motive filling the centre of the vault.

We may now turn to the zodiacal aspects. Scenes enclosed by a zodiacal belt are not uncommon. The oldest seems the scene of *anodos* or rising-up, the yearly resurrection of life, depicted on a disk of Brundisium, dated at latest in the last century B.C. The commonest subject in such works is Mithras, born of the Rock or killing the Bull. But at times a single deity is enthroned in the circle: Zeus, Helios, Astarte, Sarapis, or even a private person. We have already noted one with Zeus; and there was also the Zodiac of the Parabiago patera, where the young man makes the same gesture as does the Nikē of Tannur. We must also recall the Zodiac and four eagles at Palmyra in Bel's temple.

A stranger analogy can be found in an Argive relief. In a niche is the bust of a young woman, her head surrounded by seven eight-rayed stars and surmounted by a crescent from which emerges the highest star. The crescent is placed so as to look like horns coming out of the skull. Round the niche is shown the zodiacal signs in anti-clockwise movement, while on the monument's lower face is a gnostic inscription. (The inscription may have

Fig. 83. Nike supporting Zodiac with Tyche of Khirbet-Tannur

been added later; but even if that is so, the engraver felt the work to be suitable for such an addition.) The handle of a sort of patera from Egypt perhaps throws some light on the gnostic or hermetic links of both the Argive and the Tannur reliefs. It is made up of a naked female figure with crossed legs; she holds above her head a crown with a cross inside, and, what is unusual, is attached to the vessel by her feet. (The patera, being round, would be a sort of sphere on which to stand.) Against her legs are two upended

Fig. 84. Terracotta medallion, Vienne, France

dolphins—and the great goddess of the Nabataians with whom our Tyche is in some sort identified was a dolphin-goddess. We cannot imagine ordinary Copt Christians using a naked woman to support a Cross, but Gnostics often had a different idea of the body. Markos, disciple of Valentinos, was told in a revelation, "I want to show you Aletheia [Truth] herself. I have made her come down from dwellings on high so that you may see her naked and observe her beauty, and even so that you may hear her speak and may admire her spirit." The following description shows

Aletheia a cosmic figure, the primordial element, source of every *logos,* each part of her body corresponding to a letter of the alphabet. The first words she pronounces are "Jesus Christ". And in the Coptic *Pistis Sophia* we meet a Virgin of the Light. In the cosmology here various entities and mysteries emanate from God and are distributed in three spheres. The lowest sphere, that of the cosmos, encloses our earth. Next is the sphere of *kerasmos* or mixture, where the lower region, called the sphere of Fate, *hiermarmenē,* is inhabited by the twelve Aions (the twelve zodiacal signs); above the twelve, but still in the sphere of mixture is a thirteenth Aion, then an intermediary place where lives the Virgin of Light, whose task is to make proof of souls and decide which can pass on upwards to the higher realm, the Treasure of Light. Above that is the third sphere, that of Light, where dwells the supreme deity. We can perhaps in some ways assimilate the Tyche of Tannur to the Virgin of Light. The Tyche appears as a heavenly deity, mistress of light and darkness, connected with the Moon though not identical. The Moon, we have seen earlier, was often under the empire taken as the threshold of the dwelling-place of souls, some of which stayed there for ever while others went on upwards.

If there is then a link between the Tyche and such Gnostic conceptions as Truth and the Virgin of Light, we might interpret the antithetical lay-out of the Zodiac in a different way. It has been broken in half; its power has been shattered, the power of Fate. Those who truly believe can trample Fate and the stars underfoot. This interpretation is perhaps too far-fetched for a public monu-

Fig. 85. Argive relief

ment such as our Tyche, which can still, however, help us to understand how such images of heavenly power, tutelary and watchful, could shade off into hermetic images of judgment and salvation. In the same way the Victory upholding the Tyche of a city or a people could turn into that of a private individual confident of defeating the stars and their Fate, and of ascending through the Moon to the upper fields of light.

These correlations seem less strange if we realise how astral or cosmic imagery had more and more invaded the area of imperial ideology and of thought in general. The notion of cycles of breakdown and renewal had remained partly tethered to schemes of the heavenly Great Year, but had to some extent broken off to stimulate hopes of somehow getting through the worsening crisis of Roman society into an enduring condition of harmony and happiness. The empire, we saw, had been ushered in by Caesar's Star and by the imagery of world-redemption, of a Golden Age, uttered in Virgil's Fourth Eclogue and in the Sibylline poems of the Eastern masses (which Cleopatra sought to claim); the mass-disillusion at the imperial settlement was expressed by the Star of Bethlehem, by the turn to a Saviour not of the State. As things worsened, the rulers continually attempted to claim the achievement of a Golden Age in defiance of all the facts and to elevate themselves to a divine and cosmic status. Let us look again at the Globe. In the later empire the abode of the Caesars was approximated to a Heavenly Place; and the *Castrum* or Camp, as a centre of their rule, became synonymous with *praetorium* and *palatium*: an emblem of the Justice, Wisdom, Beneficence emanating from the emperor. On coins of Diocletian and Constantine the cupola over the *Castrum* is often changed into a globe. The *sphaira* is associated with the domical cover or celestial canopy. A fresco at Herculaneum shows one under a celestial *skēnē* or tent flanked by griffins. On the silver *lanx* found at Corbridge (dated late fourth or early fifth century) Apollo stands in his world-*ciborium*, which is a tent, with the Sun and Moon over it, the *sphaira* on a pedestal in front of the shrine and the griffin at his feet. The continual assertion of a divine role by the State, with a complex involvement of imagery and symbol, in turn stimulated the use of similar or related systems by groups opposed to that State or expressing their disillusion by a total rejection of the political world and by an escape into hermetic or other fantasies. To set private symbolism beside the *lanx* of Apollo, we may take a mosaic panel from Brading, Isle of Wight, where a cock-headed man (perhaps the Gnostic Abraxis) stands before a ladder or steps, with a pair of griffins (facing in different directions). The scene is probably of some initiation, with a bird-masked neophyte about to make a spirit-ascent; heaven appears as a temple at ladder-top and the griffins are guardians of the dead. In the same villa is a mosaic of an Astronomer with a sun-dial on a pillar, and a globe on a three-legged stool; the man points at the globe with a rod.

We may now turn to two cults that invaded the Empire from the East: First, Mithraism. This cult developed astrologic elements at its core. Some 16 of its monuments show the complete Zodiac: three at Doura (two of them frescoes), two at Rome, one at Sidon, one at Salona, and others in German areas and other parts of the West (one in London). The Zodiac also appears on other Mithraic monuments from Italy, Britain, Gaul.[27] There are some peculiarities. The equinoctial signs shown with the symbolic trees (wintry-barren or in full leaf) and torchbearers are a bullhead (*boukranion*) for the Bull and a scorpion for the Scorpion, instead of the usual Ram and Balance; also a combination of Lion and Bowl may be used for Lion and Aquarius to mark the solstices instead of the Crab and Capricorn. The sign for the vernal equinox, the Ram, starts off the series, or the Ram and the Balance, when the circle is shown in two separate halves; but the more ancient signs for Bull and Scorpion are still used when they appear separately.

At times the opposite halves have as much significance as the

Fig. 86. Mithras and Zodiac, London

complete cycle. Thus in the Mithraeum at Ostia the first six signs go along the face of the left bench, starting from the end where the bull-sacrifice is represented, while the other six go along the right bench starting at the entrance end. The northern signs on the left express the sun's course from spring to autumn, while those on the right express the course of the winter sun. Again, at Doura in the larger relief and on the frescoes of the middle and late periods of the Mithraeum the Zodiacs are cut into two by a representation of the Deus Aeternus or Skygod—the first at the autumn equinox, the second at the spring. On a statue of the Deus Aeternus the two halves run from the head down. We see then that the Nabataian Tyche with her divided Zodiac has good company; the first meaning we gave to the division seems upheld by the Mithraic examples, even if they do not make the two halves run in opposite directions.[28]

In the Mithraic Zodiac two differing orders are used: the eastern which runs anti-clockwise and the western that runs clockwise. These variations seem linked with questions of orientation. The Mithraeum itself was a cosmic image, as we see from the way the signs were placed along the side-benches at Ostia or round the arch of the cult-niches at Doura or on the Barberini fresco. The cosmic image is made even clearer when stars were shown in the ceiling, as at Ostia and Doura. Several mithraea, cut from solid rock, were circular or elliptical. At Sidon the cave was made deep underground with twelve sides to the innermost room, each side decorated with its zodiacal sign. Euboulos, cited by Porphyrios, says that "the cave conveys an image of the cosmos, of which Mithras was the demiurge, and things at measured intervals within the cave convey symbols of the cosmic elements and *klimata*".[29] The *klimata* here seem to refer to the winds, seasons, and planets in their control of earthly life. Porphyrios himself says, "They have made the caves symbols with reference to their being natural, night-like, or dark and rocky, but certainly not only with regard for their shape, as some have assumed, since not every cave is spherical." It is clear then that Mithraics did discuss the sphericity of their caves, and in the picture of the bull-sacrifice were especially concerned with this shape.

We find caves oriented approximately east; from southeast to southwest; from northeast to northwest. The first set are of fairly early date (second century) and are under strong Greek influence from the East; the second set show Latin or North-European influence; the third are Iranian or Semitic. The few turned to the

West are Graeco-Iranian and tend to stress the grades of initiation
in their pictorial symbolism. The relation to the Zodiac, with
connected ideas of sky-ascent, played a strong part in orientations:

The theologians have established the Crab and Capricorn as the Two
Gates, but Plato spoke of Two Mouths, that of these the Crab is the
one through which souls descend but Capricorn through which they
ascend. The Crab is northerly and descending, but Capricorn is southerly
and ascending. The North is for souls coming down into birth and

Fig. 87. Mithraic relief, Heddernheim. Cloak billowing as heavenly
dome

correctly the cave-gates to the North are descents for men, but the South is not for gods but rather for those going up to gods. For this reason Homer said the way was not for gods but for immortals, which term generally has to do with souls or self-existing beings or immortals in essence . . .

So, not to Sunrise or Sunset has Homer set the Gates, nor to the Equinoxes, i.e. to the Ram and Yoke [*Zygon-Libra*], but to the South and North, and to the most southern Gates at the South and the most northern Gates at the North, because the Grotto was consecrated to souls and to water-nymphs, and these places are most suited for souls "in birth and from birth". For Mithras therefore they arranged the appropriate seat that is at the Equinoxes, for which reason he carries the Dagger of the Ram of the Zodiac and is conveyed on the Bull of Aphrodite, as the bull also is a demiurge and [Mithras] a lord [*despotēs*] of generation.

He has been placed at the Equinoctial Circle, with the northern signs on his right and the southern on his left, the hemisphere being arranged for him at the South which belongs there on account of its heat, but at the North the one belonging there through the wind's coldness. For souls going into birth and withdrawing from it they properly arranged Winds, because of souls being called a *pneuma,* as some have thought, and because of their having the same kind of essence. Now the north wind is appropriate for souls going into birth, and so also those on the point of death the northern breeze "revives by blowing on him who has unfortunately breathed out his hot breath". But the southern breeze disintegrates. For the colder one integrates and prevails in the coldness of chthonic birth, but the warmer one disintegrates and sends upwards to the heat of the divine.[30]

The Mithraeum here is oriented due east, with the northern signs (those through which the sun passes while in the northern hemisphere) on the right: these run from the Ram in the east to the Virgin in the west, the most northerly being the Crab at the summer solstice. The northern signs are thus hot and lie on the south side of the Mithraeum, the side of Apogenesis, the period from birth to youth, until the soul withdraws from the body and makes its ascent. The southern signs are the cold ones, from the Balance in the west to the Fishes in the east: here is the side of Birth or Genesis, where souls go down into bodies. The Death of the Bull, in at least one group of representations, marks the change from the time of Kautopates to that of Kautes. These latter are the two genii closely associated with Mithras. Kautes presides over the descent of souls into genesis, while Kautopates over the life after genesis. Kautes holds his torch up to express the kindling of life, *thymos,* while Kautopates lowers his to express the hiding of life in the body. At death the soul-heat ascends to the *thermon* of divinity.[31]

In the later classifications the seven grades (Corvus or Raven Nymphus, Miles or Soldier, Leo, Perses, Heliodromos, Pater) were linked with the seven planets in the order: Mercury, Venus, Mars, Jupiter, Luna, Sol, Saturn. Also with the seven parts of the Bullman. We can express these grades thus: (1) Raven or Mercury, perceptivity as the motion and cause of mental concepts and imagery; (2) Nymphus or Venus, attracting love which inclines towards physical birth; (3) Soldier or Mars, the motion of nature as a fiery force or substance; (4) Perses or Luna, the power of visible and physical growth; (5) Lion or Jupiter, the *physis* or

Fig. 88. Mithraic relief (Coll. de Clercq)

natura of the lordship and vitality of bodily existence; (6) Sun-driver or Sol, the power and embodiment of perceptivity; (7) Father or Saturn, the power of reason and intelligence—or more simply: motion of the perceptive mind, motion of physical desire, fiery motion of nature, physical force, physical growth, perceptivity and imagination, rationality and intelligence.

We thus meet a scheme of human growth conceived in both spiritual and physical terms, and a system of perfectibility: the whole pattern also projected as a system of otherworld-ascent. The initiate could either go down through the Lion to a perfected body and thence upwards through the Father to spiritual unity with Logos and Nous, or he could become developed by stages to the final perfection. The materialist element strong in original Stoic and Iranian thought makes thinkers like Iamblichos and Julian try to get the best out of both worlds by combining Aristotle's material and moving *aither* with the immaterial and intelligent mind and form of Plato. Thus an unresolved conflict appears, an uncertain balance which could tip towards an organic pantheism or an other-world transcendence. We may note the powers of growth attributed to the Moon and the dialectical principle set out by Porphyrios: "The harmony of the drawn bow shoots by means of opposites."[32]

The Bull-sacrifice was the great primal act, the separation creating union, the death creating renewal of life; Mithras killing the Bull was the saviour bringing new life to the world. The Bull was linked with the Moon. A crescent was carved on the Bull's body, as we see on the Esqueline relief (which shows the influence of Egyptian sculpture). A smaller crescent is set above the back of the Bull in the Zodiac of the larger Doura relief, while the other five of the first six signs merely show a star as companion. Capua and the Barberini bull-sacrifice, strongly Iranian in inspiration, show the bull silver-white, the moon-colour that makes the bull manifest. The *Bundahišn* says that the Only-Created-Bull in the Middle of the Earth was "white and bright like the Moon". On the Barberini fresco the killing occurs under the Deus Aeternus who stands on the blue sky-globe of genesis and fate, and is flanked by the zodiacal signs. The Bull of the Doura reliefs was originally white, but later made orange-red (physically vital). Euboulos says the Persians call Hekatē "horse, bull, lioness, dog".[33] Indeed the association of Bull and Moon was especially Iranian. The Phoenician Astarte Megistē "put a bull's head on her own head as a characteristic sign of royalty", writes Eusebios. The Syro-Cappadocian cylinder-seals show a naked goddess between a solar and a lunar god, seated on a bull. She was the Phoenician Europa whom Bull-Zeus carried on his back to Crete, where Pasiphaē (Shining One) mated with a white bull. Astrologically the planet Venus had its exaltation in the Bull.[34]

Mithraism took in deeply the idea that the soul in its descent assumed the qualities of each planet, and in turn shed them in going up. But the same system had a wide hermetic expansion.[35] The zodiacal circle in a sense represented the cosmic egg. At Trier the god is shown as born into it; he holds at the same time the globe and thrusts up against the edge of the circle with his right hand; he is the emerging god of fire who cracks the cosmic Egg.[36] And for a last point we may note that on the Sidon relief the signs of the circle are so arranged that the Scorpion is in the position for attacking the Bull's testicles; thus the scorpion often shown in

Fig. 89. Mithraic Aion, Modena

the reliefs is given an astral significance.[37] A passage from the
emperor Julian is important in showing that very old Babylonian
ideas were still alive in the fourth century A.D. and that they were
propagated by Mithraism.

The sun's disk, moving in a starless region, is far above the fixed stars.
Thus it is not the middle of the other six planets but is of the three
kosmoi, according to the Mystical Hypotheses, it is not at all correct to
call them hypotheses and not *dogmata,* and the spherical schemes hypotheses. For the *dogmata* are said to be revealed by God, of great
Daimons, whereas the hypotheses are only assumed as probably by
their harmony with the phenomena . . .
  Besides those already mentioned there are a large number of heavenly
Gods, known to those who contemplate the heaven well and not like
beasts. For Helios, intersecting fourfold the three [worlds], because the
zodiacal circle communicates with each of them, divides it into twelve
powers of Gods and each of these again into three, so that thirty six
[powers of Gods] results. Hence, I presume, the threefold gift of the
Charites [Graces] comes to us from heaven, from the circles; for the
God, by fourfold dividing them, sends us the Grace of the Seasons.

We must go back to ᵐᵘˡAPIN to grasp what he means. The three
kosmoi are the Ways of Enlil, Anu and Ea. The Sun's path (the
zodiacal circle) divides each of the Ways into four segments
corresponding to the four seasons; and each segment is divided

into three zodiacal signs or "powers of God". Each segment is again divided into three, so that thirty-six dekans result. He calls the doctrine Mystical Hypotheses or rather *Dogmata* because it has been taught to him in the Mithraic Mysteries, of which he was a devoted initiate; and he contrasts it with the spherical systems of the Greek astronomers, which have been merely devised by the minds of men.

The cult of Dolichenos, a high god, was spread through the empire by soldiers from Asia Minor and Syria. His cult began its movements when in 72 Vespasian annexed Kommagene to the province of Syria and auxiliaries were recruited from the Kommagene area

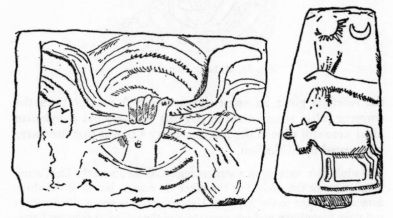

Fig. 90. Relief of Kefr-Kelbine: hand and bolt inside triple nimbus. *Stēlē* of Tell Sfir: above the Hadad or Teshub bull, hand and lightning with sun and moon above

where the god's home of Dolichē was situated.[38] We find him called *Deus Aeternus* or *IOM Aeternus*; like Mithras he has a pair of companying genii, who for him represent the two hemispheres; and as we would expect from his origins he had a strong nexus of astrologic systems and images. Take for example a monument to him at Lambaesis by a soldier of *Legio III Augusta*, probably before A.D. 238. The base held a statue of the god (not standing on a Bull as he so often did). On it is a thunderbolt with undulant lines, to which two palm-boughs are joined. A line runs vertically through, with a star at the bottom end, a circle just below the jointure with the boughs, and a smaller circle above the point where the lines meet. Across the top are three stars linked by a curve, representing the heavenly vault—the three stars may stand for the three stages of the Sun, at dawn, noon, and setting: symbols of his eternal death and rebirth. (But they also might well signify the divine triad, the god flanked by Sun and Moon as often shown on the tops of Dolichenos monuments; or else the morning, noon, and night that express the triadic nature of Saturn on a Palmyrene altar.) The front side of the slab has at each end a ram's head; and a Ram was the emblem of the African Saturn, who may be paired off with the Syro-Phoenician Baalshamin. In any event we see a clear astral element at work, used to stress the cosmic powers of the god.[39]

In a triangular bronze plaque, at Kömlöd, dedicated by a centurion of *Cohors I Alpinorum Equitata*, we see a Victory crowning the god on his bull, with a palm in her left hand. Near the god's head and above his thunderbolt is a star with eight rays, an astral or planetary symbol of his divinity. In the register above are

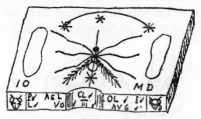

Fig. 91. Dolichenos base at Lambaesis

Sol and Luna, as busts, with stars behind the god, a crescent behind the goddess. These two busts express the god's eternity.[40] Another such plaque at Mauer-an-der-Url, a hand with thunderbolt is shown on the back in a circular medallion; this motive is of Eastern origin. Below it here are two eagles, and above is a peacock—Juno as the starry sky: a symbol probably taken from the cult of Hera at Samos. On the top of the plaque is an eight-rayed star; on front at the top is an Eagle, Sol with a nine-rayed star, and Luna with crescent—the Divine triad. This sort of imagery, which multiplies under the Empire, illustrates the way in which astral thinking invaded so many cults with a popular appeal. As with Mithraism, questions of Time and Eternity are implicated.[41]

An interesting set of cosmic monuments at which we can only glance is that of the Jupiter Columns of north-east Gaul. The column is surmounted by a god rider trampling a snake-footed monster or upheld by him. Below at the base are represented four lesser gods; and above them are shown the seven days of the week, the seven planets. The exact interpretation is uncertain; but we can say in general that here we see the cosmic struggle depicted: the god of light and good triumphs over the forces of darkness and evil—though in fact he is at least in part identified with the Empire triumphing over its adversaries as the symbol of civilisation against barbarism. (Humble soldiers over the Empire liked to be shown on their tombstone riding down or killing a prostrate barbarian.) The cosmic struggle, which also produces its dynamic balance or equipoise, goes on over the foursquare or stable base and the revolving planetary cycles.

If we turn to the Christians, we see that strong in their original impulse had been the same sort of resolve to reject the rule of Fate and the Stars which we noted among the Gnostics. The rule of the stars was identified with the power-role of the State, and was utterly rejected; and emotionally in this rejection was included the

Fig. 92. Jupiter and anguiped giant on column-top: Neschers, Puys-de-Dôme

whole world of fate or necessity that was implied by the existence of slavery, the whole dead burden of the alienating world.

Paul declared, "I am persuaded that neither the ascension of the stars nor their declination will be able to separate us from the love of God," in a denial of astral Fate. And in admitting that once "we were enclosed to the elements of the world", he was saying that before the advent they had been in the same control of star-fates as were still the profane. As for the relation of the conviction of an oppressive fate-mechanism to a world based on slavery, we may take the phrase of Epikouros: "the servile artifices of the astrologers". I take him to mean, not merely that the astrologer was himself the slave of the stars he served, and that he enslaved others by means of his art, but that the whole system was itself somehow a reflection of a world in which both the slave and his master were alike dominated by forces of alienation, even if the master had a false-consciousness of freedom.

The Gnostics held that the advent of Jesus destroyed the power of the sky-forces; in the preamble of *Pistis Sophia* Jesus, returned to Earth, explains the triumph to his disciples. Henceforth fatalism is ended; the stars can no longer influence and control the lives of men. Indeed, in the face of all the evidence, Christ was taken to have imposed on the stars a course different from their usual one. The power of the Archons up aloft, the Rulers, was over. In Gnostic cosmology the Seven Archons (Planets) moved below the spheres of the stars. Believers were sure they could see in profile the Virgin of Light who in *Revelation* is crowned with the constellations and has the Moon under her feet as she is threatened by the dragon with seven heads. Lightning-flashes represented the light of which the Archons, after being seduced, were being violently dispossessed. And the phases of the Moon were spiritually significant; at its waxing it was being filled with the light it had gathered in, while at its waning it was sending that light back to the higher world.[42]

The idea of Christ's demoralisation of the zodiacal signs long persisted. The Spanish poet Prudentius writes: "We have seen then, they say, the Child borne through the stars and burning above the ancient course of the signs." The astrologer trembles at what he sees. The Snake yields, the Lion flees, the Crab contracts its claws, the tamed bull lows.

> Repulsed, the Water-boy falls, and there the Arrows;
> astray the Twins are parted in flight, the unchaste Virgin
> betrays her silent lovers in the world's brothel;
> other fires hang in the terrible clouds in fear
> at the Morning Star. The Sun sticks with wan wheel
> and feels that now at last his end will be . . .[43]

But there was no consistent position. The Christians were against astrology in so far as it put natural law in the place of God, but often they were ready to accept the stars as the Signs of God and therefore in some sense signalling his thoughts and decisions. Abraham was at times taken as an astrologer who was able to recognise God in the rational system of the stars at a time when all other men were in error; he thus understood that all things were regulated by Providence.[44] We find the Twelve Apostles taken as the Twelve Months of Christ, and Simon Magus as an astrologer.[45] But any official attitudes could not but be hostile, even if now and then they wavered. Origen attacked magic but was mild towards astrology. He even went so far as to say that Christ "did not die on behalf of men only, but on behalf of all other rational beings . . . It would be absurd to declare that it was only for human sins he tasted death, and not also on behalf of every other creature beyond man who has been involved in sins, such as the stars." In this view the stars had quite changed their function after Christ's advent and ceased to be the ministers of compulsive Fate.[46]

Early Christians indeed could not easily disentangle themselves from the elements of astrology pervading their environment, especially those elements that had become imbedded in popular culture. *Revelation* is full of astrologic ingredients as shown by the frequency of astral images and the stress on numerology, with 7 and 12 especially prominent. The same elements pervade oracular and hermetic literature in all sorts of orthodox or bizarre forms. Sabaoth reigned over the Pole with his throne in the constellation of the Chariot; close to him was the Serpent; the Dragon was neighbour to the Great Bear "at the great commencement of the heavens"; Ialdabaoth was identified with Saturn and the Archons were the other planets, the sun and moon replaced in the seven planets by the Dragon's Head and Tail supposed to produce eclipses. Indeed a Gnostic, or for that matter any early Christian, would be able to look up at the night-sky with an awed and fascinated recognition of the various glittering powers manœuvring against him with their uncanny movements and coherent patterns of menace.[47] We have seen how Christ's natal star and its relation to the Mages was a matter of much interest. The romance of Cyprian, in the form of a biographical *Confession*, gives us a good idea of the sort of experiences that men went through in the early Christian era, even if in it there are packed almost all the possible variants of magical devotion. While he was young, his parents wanted him instructed in all that there is on earth, in air or in the sea, not only in what concerns the generation and corruption of herbs, trees and bodies, but also all the virtues with which the Lord of this Age has filled them. Still quite young, he was dedicated to Apollo and "initiated into the dramaturgy of the Serpent". At seven he was an initiate of Mithras, at ten, of Demeter and Kore as well as of Athena's Serpent on the Akropolis. At fifteen he spent forty days on Olympos, where under the direction of seven hierophants he took part in all sorts of strange rites. Then he participated in the mysteries of Hera at Argos, where "he was initiated into the designs of the unity that air and *aither, aither* and air, earth and water, water and air created among themselves". He then went to Elis and on to Sparta where he was initiated in the mysteries of Artemis Tauropolos "to learn the mixture and division of matter and the sublimity of the ambiguous and wild doctrines". Then in Phrygia he studied prophecy and hepatoscopy, and among the Barbarians (whoever they were) he acquired all the kinds of divination, "and there was nothing on earth, in the sea or in the air that I didn't know, no phantasm, no object of *gnosis,* no artifice of any sort, and I was even able to change writings by my spells and all marvels of that nature." But still he knew nothing. So he went to Egypt at the age of twenty to gain the key to the mysteries. In an underground temple at Memphis he learned how to recognise the communications of daimons with earthly things, the places they hated, the stars, magical bonds and objects that pleased them, the means of hunting them off, the ways they inhabited darkness, the resistance they set up in certain domains, and the ways in which they succeed in souls and bodies communicating with them, and the effects they gain by these instruments, effects of a superior knowledge, of memory, of terror, of illusion, of motion without a word being said, of sorceries by which they disturb the crowd. He discovered the likeness of earthquakes and rain, the art of producing motions of the earth and cyclones; he grasped the relation of demons and oaths, of spirits of the air and men. He even penetrated into a sanctuary where the demons beget the illusory forms that deceive us, the 360 passions which are so many figures assumed by the demons to lead us into evil, figures loaded with ornaments, but without substances. (The number 360 has a clear reference to the demons of time-divisions.) At thirty years, after ten years in

Egypt, he went to Chaldea and learned all the secrets of astrology, all the mysteries of the *aither* which some people relate to fire, but which others more shrewdly relate to light. He learned to distinguish stars as one does plants, their choral evolutions, their conflicts, the house of each one, and the chain that links them on earth with some food, drink, bodily combination, the division of the aither into 360 sections, each under a demon whom one can conciliate by efficacious words in sacrifices and libations. He came to know the Intermediaries (spirits connecting heaven and earth) and was astounded at the force of the oaths that bound them. After that, he had finished his schooling. He went to live at Antioch, where after various adventures, he ended by becoming a Christian.[48]

Tertullian was scathing about attempts to accommodate Christianity to astrology. "Astrology indeed treats of Christ. It is the science of the Stars of Christ, not of Saturn or Mars." It was legitimate till Christ was born; then it became inadmissible and went wrong. Presumably men were released from the rule of astral fate and so star-systems no longer applied. "For since the Gospel you will never find sophist or Chaldean or enchanter or diviner or magician who has not been manifestly punished." Hardly a factual statement. It was a good thing, Tertullian added, that the *mathematici* were forbidden entry to Rome or Italy as they made calculations about the emperor's life.[49]

Celsus in his polemic with the Christians attacked magic and had no doubt as to its harmful power, and he considered that the Christians were good at exorcising evil spirits through their proficiency in magic, and that Christ performed miracles by magic. He had the greatest respect for the stars. They were "the most manifest heralds of things from on high"; they were "the true heavenly messengers [angels], announcers of so many natural phenomena"; he was surprised at the Christian indifference towards the Sun.[50] The Christian poet Commodian gave up one of his *Instructiones* to the Septizonium and the Stars, which he saw as demons.[51] Origen, arguing against Celsus, maintained that angels acted as agents between men and God; he attributed to them the powers that the astrologers gave to the favourable aspects of the stars or the lords-of-time. "It is by these administrators, these unseen guardians, set over the fruits of the earth, the water that flows, and the breezes that blow, that the soil makes the so-called natural products sprout, water jets from springs and spreads out

into rivers, air keeps its purity and vivifies those who breathe it."
We see how strongly the idea of social categories intrudes into the
unseen world. Origen believes in the magic hidden in words, names,
formulae, and in its possibilities for good. If the Mages made
their way to Bethlehem, it was that they had been troubled and
held up in their magical operations; they sought the cause,
observed the star, and let it guide them. However, magic is a
dangerous activity, to be used only in the cases allowed by the
Scriptures.[52]

Hippolytos draws on the arsenal of objections prepared by
Sextus Empiricus against astrology; Gregory of Nysa in 328 in
On Fate attacked astrology as pagan. St John of the Golden Mouth
was worried about the tale of the Mages in *Matthew*; the ignorance
underlying it was shown by Jesus being called the King of the
Jews; the star was not a real one. "Some invisible Virtue assumed
a star's form." And St John was not the only Christian whom the
tale upset. Basil condemned astrology and horoscopes but admitted
the influence of the moon in her variations on the organisation of
all living things. Not that all these condemnations seem to have
had a great effect. Eusebios reproaches his fellow-Christians
with their too simple and naïve reading of the Gospels, and with
their complaisance for the chimeras of astrology.[53] From
Augustine's polemic it is clear that large numbers of people in
Africa applied to astrologers for almost every enterprise they
undertook, even the most trivial ones: not only when to sow,
plant trees or vines, but when to mate their cows or mares, or to
learn how to deal with stock or dogs. In arguing against astrology,
he uses many old arguments, such as that about twins, and he tells an
anecdote. The father of his friend Firminus, together with a crony,
had made a collection of horoscopes, even those of their animals,
and compared them with one another. "Thus the proofs or tests
[*experimenta*] of this so-called art." Then Firminus' wife and a
woman slave of the friend became pregnant at the same time.
What a problem was set by this event, a slave and a free child
born at the same time! One may doubt the exact synchronisation of
the two conceptions and births, but the tale provided Augustine
with ammunition against astrology. Incidentally he demolished
the idea of synchronisations in astrology by another of his tales.
Citing Nigidius Figulus on twins, he says that that astrologer
turned a potter's wheel as fast as he could, throwing some ink at
what seemed a single point on it. When the wheel stopped, there

were several stains far apart. "Even so is the swift course of heaven that though one child be born after another in as short a time as I made these two marks, yet in the heaven a great space will have passed." Augustine then says the whole astrologic case is "far more brittle than the pots made by that wheel"; if the question of twins is so hopeless, how can astrology predict the fates linking anyone precisely with the stars? He himself had been a devotee in his youth, doubtless affected by his father; but was later weaned by two friends, Vindicianus and Nebridius.[54] In Spain the Council of Toledo in 400 and that of Braga in 560–5 condemned *astrologia vel mathesis*; and it is interesting to find the heretic Priscillianists accused of believing that each part of the body was under a zodiacal sign.[55] The grandfather of the poet Ausonius, Caecilius Argicius Arborius, had to leave Aquitaine for political reasons; he went to Aquae Tarbellae (Daix) and used his astrologic skill to set up as a professional. His grandson recorded these facts:

> In time a small sum gathered with lots of pains
> relieved, but not with wealth, his wearied age.
> You hid your acts, but knew the heaven's measures,
> the stars that hold the secret of man's fate.
> You saw the outline of my life, set down
> on a sealed tablet, which you never mentioned.
> But then my mother's forward care revealed
> what my shy grandfather had sought to hide.

He died at ninety, grieved at a son dying when thirty years old: "Yet you would say some consolation cheered you, though far remote, since high distinction awaited my destiny." Ausonius imagines the dead astrologer looking down in gratification at a grandson who has become quaestor, prefect, consul.[56]

But we cannot here continue the long story of what happened to astrology in a Christian world. We may end with this section by turning back to Lactantius who shows both the rejection of astrology and the acceptance of astral myths. He attacks the Stoics and their glorification of the stars as deities. "Inasmuch as they have fixed and rational movements by which the changes and vicissitudes of successive times are constantly governed, these objects possess no voluntary motions." Demons had babbled to men—"Astrology, Augury, Divination: these things are indeed fallacious, but the authors of evil so regulate them that people believe them to be true." (Evil spirits either rig events to fit the

prediction or *vice versa*.) They carry out miracles in the temples—
false miracles because they are not the work of the Christian God.
They creep into men and cause diseases which they expel if duly
placated. They send dreams, terrible dreams, so that they may be
invoked; or dreams that may come true. But they do it only to be
venerated the more. Thus Lactantius has no disbelief in divination; he merely sees it as bad since demons give the answers. He
ends with the destruction of the world and the millenium, carrying
on from the Iranian myths, the Stoic attempts to reformulate
those myths in terms of astronomic science, the fantastic developments in Sibylline verses and in Gnostic, Jewish, and early
Christian apocalypse. There will be many astral signs, "miraculous
signs from heaven". Comets "will be seen. The sun will be
darkened with endless gloom, the moon will be dyed with blood
nor will it renew its lost light, all the stars will fall nor will the
Seasons observe their proper course, for winter and summer will
be confounded. Year and month and day will be shortened." Later,
"fire will come down from heaven, the sun be stayed in its course".
When Christ comes, "then shall the heavens be opened in the dead
of night and Christ descend with great power; before him will go a
fiery brilliance". When the millenary kingdom of the saints is
established, "the light of the stars will be magnified, the sun's
brightness be increased, the moon's light no longer suffer
diminution or eclipse". When the prince of evil is unchained, the
Last Judgment arrives "amid showers of fire, brimstone, and
hail for the wicked".[57]

o

21

Two Poets

Though we are not carrying on in any detail after about A.D. 300 there are three matters of the fifth century that need to be brought in to round off our picture: the *Dionysiaka* of Nonnos, and the horoscopes of two men, Proklos and Pamprepios.

Nonnos in his huge epic on the Labours of Dionysos is in one sense producing a picture of the hero who like Herakles achieves heaven and the star-world. He ends with Dionysos setting the Crown of Ariadne in the skies and "then the vinegod went up to the paternal *aithēr*". But there are many aspects, meanings, and levels to his poem. I have shown elsewhere that he is above all the poet of alchemic transformations deep at work in life at all levels; he conveys his sense of transformation in his style, diction, imagery, psychology, and general theme. But he also seeks to find an astrological frame for the events, in order to stress the cosmic significance and to relate his theme to the time-structure of a life-period in the Stoic sense—at the same time to link it with the actual social and political crisis of his world when the ancient systems were giving way to strong feudalising pressures. But he is less expert at astrological techniques than he is at evoking imagery of the transformative process; and after a bold start he fails to build the astral meaning consistently into the movement of the poem.[1]

For instance he once puts Venus into quadratile aspects with the Sun (i.e. 90° away), though her maximum distance from him is 46°.[2] At the outset he is at much pains to bring out the theme of cosmic change and upheaval. He divides time into world-months making up a world-year, and after the cosmic month that brings the Flood and that of Typhon's attempt to grasp and upset the frame of things, Summer comes to the universe and the blessing of the new god (of autumnal fruitfulness) is due. That maturing triumph is worked out in the later books in the birth, growth, victory of Dionysos. But in following out his many stories about the god, he tends to lose sight of this basis. The astral ideas gather thickly in the first two books, then begin to fade out. Nonnos however might retort that he only wanted them to set out the cosmic dimensions and time-system of his conception, and that for the rest of his poem he was concerned with the working-out of the transformative imagery within the given perspective.

Fig. 93. Sun in Zodiac, mosaic, Munster near Bingen

At the start he makes an extended use of the imagery of reversal, of a topsyturvy world, to express cataclysm or deep change. The idiom here goes far back in prophetic and apocalyptic literature. We noted its roots in a certain paradoxical conciseness in Babylonian astrologic reports. "The conqueror will be conquered. . . ." The theme of reversal takes deep social roots in periods of violent and far-reaching change. "The first shall become the last, and *vice versa*." Such phrases express the fear of the ruling classes, the hope of the underdogs.

The first full-length use of the idiom that we know appears in *Admonitions of a Prophet* (or Sage) which emerged out of the political chaos in Egypt with the breakdown of the Old Kingdom, at the end of the Sixth Dynasty. "The highborn are full of lamentations and the poor are full of joy. . . . The son of the highborn man is no longer recognised. The child of his lady has become the son of his handmaid." All distinctions are lost. "Ladies are like slavegirls. . . . All female slaves have power over their mouths. When their mistresses speak, it is irksome to the servants. . . . He that had no shade now has shade. They that had shade are in the full blast of the storm. . . . Serfs become lords of serfs."[3] We may further compare songs of happiness, on the advent or accession of a Pharaoh: here of Ramses IV. "They that had fled have come again to their towns and they that were hidden have come forth. They that hungered are satisfied and happy, and they that thirsted have drunken. They that were naked are clad in fine linen, and they that were dirty have white garments. They that were in prison are set free, and he that was in bonds is full of joy."[4] The accession is a liberating god-advent, bringing the reversals of joy instead of those of disaster. In these texts the social change is not linked with a cosmic event; but in Egypt we do at an early date, in the Pyramid texts, find the idea of world-cataclysm linked with that of a passage-rite obstructed in its completion. The death of the king threatens such a disaster if a place is not made for him among the gods in the sky.[5] Thus, in a wider application, reversal and cataclysm appear when a period of great human change is held up, prevented from fulfilling itself.

To return to Nonnos. Europa is on her bull; the land-pasturing bulls swim over the sea.

> Does Zeus create navigable Earth?
> will the far waggon trace a watery rut through the salt deep?
> It's a bastard voyage I see on the waves. The Moon
> has got an unruly Bull, leaves the Sky to traipse
> on the High Seas. Or deepwater Thetis drives a coach
> on a floating racecourse . . .[6]

and so on. (Nonnos uses the term "bastard", *nothos,* when he implies that what is seen is not the reality, but a veil for the truth of what is happening.) The cosmic turmoil is at the same time limited and prettified by the charming conceits with their system of correspondences, and yet brought within the human sphere. The Moon here drives a Bull because her astrologic exaltation is in the Bull; we have already seen the deep link of Moon and Bull.

Then comes the outburst of Typhoios, the uprising or loosening of the deep elemental forces which have got out of control. The outburst is described as a War against the Stars. Typhoios steals the bolt of Zeus from a cave and attacks with his hand—"that battalion of hands".[7]

> One throttled Kynosouris near Olympos' ankletip;
> one grasped the Parrhasian Bear's mane as she rested
> on heaven's axle and dragged her off; another
> caught the Oxdriver and knocked him out . . .

One hand grasps Cynosura in Ursa Major; the Ankle of Olympos suggests the lower (southern) part of the sky near the equator. If so, Nonnos seems to confuse the star with Canis Minor which is some 70° from the Pole. The Bear is Kallisto, once daughter of the king of Arkadia, where Mt. Parrhasion lies. The Oxdriver is Bootes, called Arktophylax or Bearward, immediately behind Kallisto. Nonnos goes on to say that Venus, rising on the horizon before the Sun, is "under the circular turning-point" of the sky; she drives round the edges of it. *Nyssa* (Latin, *meta*) was the post round which the chariots turned in a race. We noted earlier in dealing with the Circus the use of driving imagery for the stars or the Sun; and the notion of war among the stars appears in the Sibylline poems to express world-end and renewal.[8] By interfering with the Bull, Typhoios prevents the Sun from passing through the constellation. So the season, Spring, cannot be completed.

Here are some more of the moves in the sky. By grasping at once Auriger (Charioteer) and Capricorn (here called Hail-storm as the sign of the winter solstice), Typhoios reaches clean across the sky from east to west. Next he tackles the Ram, which is Mid-Navel of the heavens, being the sign from which the astronomic year takes its start. The Sun is called its Fiery Neighbour, since he is in the Ram in Spring. Typhoios next "shadows the clear radiance of the cloudless sky by darting out his entangled army of snakes". One runs right through the rim of the polar circuit and skips on the spine of the heavenly Serpent (Draco near the pole); another twines round Andromeda; a third dangles coiled over the Bull's horns and harasses the Hyades opposite, "ranged like a crescent moon". This sort of thing goes on all over the sky. The crest of Mt. Atlas is dragged along with the Evening Star to the Morning Star: extreme west meets extreme east. Since Atlas supports the stars, the Titan's head is torn away and brought with them; Nonnos ignores the fact that morning and evening stars are one and the same.[9] There is total confusion in the heavens.

> The undaunted Seasons armed the starry battalions
> and the line of heavenly constellations came shining
> in a disciplined circle to the fray. A varied host
> maddened the upper air with clamour and flame . . .
> The unshaken congregation of fixed stars
> with unanimous acclamation left their places
> and caught up with their travelling fellows. The axis
> passing through heaven's hollow, fixed upright,
> groaned at the sound . . .

Typhoios attacks the seas and all their creatures are agitated. "The waters piled up and touched Olympos with seas precipitous. . . ." The tumultuous imagery goes on, mingling elegant conceit with elemental vastitude. In Book II Typhoios struggles with Zeus, but Olympos triumphs. The ideas of topsyturviness and dissolution are elaborately exploited.

> The foundations of the steadfast universe
> under Typhon's hands are already shaking;
> the four blended elements are melted.[10]

There are some effective pictures, such as that of the astral watch kept round Olympos before the attack. In Book VI comes the account of the Flood, again with many astrologic trimmings, and a wealth of topsyturvy imagery. "Sea lions now leaped with dripping limbs in the land lion's cave, among unfamiliar rocks, and in the depths of a mountain torrent a stray boar met with a dolphin of the sea."[11]

Fig. 94. Mosaic of Sentinum (at Munich)

Finally Astraios appears as a god of prophecy, the Sky itself turned into an astrologer. We meet him making a diagram which consists of a circle (Zodiac) with a square and an equilateral triangle inscribed in it. He is studying the position of certain stars which are in trine with each other (120° apart and thus on the points of a triangle) or in quadratile aspect (90° apart and on the four points of a square). These are two of the most important aspects, or relative positions, of the stars. Demeter enters and consults him. He sends for his orrery or planetoscope, a model (presumably in metal), with movable parts of the solar system.

On adjusting it, he finds that the Moon is right opposite the Sun
with the Earth in a straight line between: that is, she is totally
eclipsed at the zenith, the sun being at the nadir. Further, Mars
is in conjunction with Venus (both are in the same sign) in the
7th House (West) which governs marriage, Jupiter with the Sun
in the nadir, the House of Parents. The zodiacal signs at these
positions are respectively the Archer and the Virgin. Saturn has
for companion the Dragon. The eclipsed Moon indicates grave
trouble for Demeter; the conjunction in the House of Marriage,
adultery—while Drakon hints at the snakeform which is taken by
Zeus for accomplishing his desires. But Jupiter is shedding his
good influence on the House of Parents, and he is also in quadratile
aspect with Mars, thus indicating honour and glory. Also good is
the fact that Venus is in the same aspect with the Moon (here
standing for Demeter). So the horoscope is generally favourable,
though it bodes irregularities and troubles before the glorious
end is reached.

Later in the book Nonnos sets out the horoscope of the Flood:

> The Sun in his four-horse chariot drove shining
> over the back of the Lion, his own House.
> The threefold Moon rolled in her onrunning car
> over the eightfoot Crab. Kypris moving
> in equinoctial course under the dewy region
> left the Ram's horns behind and held her House
> of Spring in the heavenly Bull that knows no winter.
> The Sun's neighbour Ares possessed the Scorpion,
> that herald of the Plough, encircled by
> the blazing Bull. He ogled Aphrodite
> opposite, with sidelong looks. And Zeus of nightfall
> the twelvemonth traveller who completes the period,
> was treading the starry Fishes, on his right
> the roundfaced Moon in trine. Kronos passed through
> the showery back of Aigokeros drenched
> in frosty light. Round the bright Maiden was Hermes
> poised on his wings; for he as dispenser of Justice
> had Justice for his house.[12]

I have used here the Greek names: Aigokeros is Capricorn. Nonnos,
even in dealing with cataclysm, cannot but be hopeful. While his
stars presage the Flood, with a hint of Fire to follow, they also
suggest a better world to come out of it all.

Dionysos in these years had become something of a solar deity, in the sense of a conqueror, a bringer of light. As early as Alexander the Great, Philodamos in his Delphic hymn compared him in his Lion Chariot with the rising sun; a fragmentary inscription from Sousa of a hymn (probably first century A.D.) identifies Dionysos, Apollo, Sun. Nonnos made the god's war against the Indians a battle of Light versus Darkness. "I liken the light-bringer Dionysos to the Sun again shining, the bold black Indians to the dense Darkness." We see him on textiles in his cosmic mission across the

Fig. 95. Dionysos with mural crown on textile (Hermitage, Leningrad) from Egypt, burial site of Roman period at Akmim (Panopolis), third–fourth century

sky. The stepped triangular projections on Iranian monumental structures seem symbols of heaven; and the towered galleries of Syrian and other Eastern cities seem to have a similar significance. The turreted crown which Dionysos is at times shown in late imagery is like the crenellated crowns of the Sassanid kings, probably also has a miniature *ziqqarat* aspect, making the god or the king a heaven-ascender, a sky-pillar.

Now the horoscope of the philosopher Proklos, which comes from from the *Life* by Marinos. "So that those who love the higher things may be able to conclude from the configuration of the stars under which he was born how the Lot [of Fortune] fell to him, not in the lowest place, but in the very best, we shall give their schemata as it occurred at birth": with the Sun in the Ram 16;26 degrees, the Moon in the Twins 17;29, and so on, we obtain the date 17 April A.D. 412. Proklos lived 73 years and 2 months, dying in 485. Marinos adds that before his death there were signs in the sky: "a solar eclipse of such magnitude that it became night in the day; deep darkness fell and the stars were visible. This happened in Capricorn towards the rising centre. The calendar-makers also recorded another eclipse to happen at the completion of the first year after his death." The solar eclipse happened on 14 January 484.[13]

Marinos was a pupil of Proklos and wrote the *Life* soon after the master's death. Proklos, keen on theurgy, observed all the old Egyptian holy days; his astral bent was shown by his statement that "prayer is a turning to God as the sunflower turns to the Sun and the moonstone to the Moon."[14]

The horoscope which we may certainly attach to Pamprepios is of a more important nature. It opens:

This man was a grammarian of Thebes, poor up to the age of 32. From 33, having married, he began to rise at Athens, and, afterwards, fleeing, he was connected in Byzantion with a great person. Presenting himself as a magician and initiator, he became quaestor, then consul, then patrician, and later at the age of 44 years 2 months, he was slaughtered in a fortress for the crime of treason. He was also a dissolute man.[15]

There follows his horoscope in some detail. Mercury was the master of the Lot of Fortune. He was born 29 September 440 at 4 p.m. We learn further that he was in his 36th year when he went to Byzantion; when he was 38 years 4 months "his fortune shone with a new brilliance". Then when 41, "he returned to his native land with a powerful escort and immense pride". After that came disaster.

There can be no doubt that the subject was Pamprepios, a grammarian of Panopolis close to Thebes. (The *Souda* also says he was of Thebes.) This was a town with a strong cultural and nationalist life of its own; Nonnos was one of its citizens. Pamprepios in youth showed literary talents and went to Alexandreia, where he wrote poetry and worked as *grammatistēs*. Then he moved to Athens and studied under Proklos, distinguishing himself for his poetic gifts and literary knowledge. He married a Greek, acquired somehow the rights of an Athenian citizen, and became *grammatikos,* professor, in the city-schools. Probably at this time he wrote *Etymological Explanations (Souda).* He seems to have been envied by other philosophers of the schools, who persuaded Theagenes, the last archon of Athens, against him. Anyhow, after an affront from Theagenes, he left for Byzantion. There he soon gained the favour of the Isaurian Illos, a leading official of Zenon's court, by a discourse on the soul or a reading of his poems; he was appointed professor with a salary partly paid by Illos, partly by the public treasury. His open paganism and the rumours that he practised magic gave a weapon to his enemies and enviers; further he was involved in the politics of Illos.

Illos had been hostile to Zenon, whom Basiliskos, brother of the dowager empress Verina, had expelled in 475. Illos and his brother led the army in pursuit of Zenon into Isauria. They defeated him and blockaded him on a hill; but during the siege they were won over to Zenon's side, united armies with him, and marched on Byzantion. At Nikē in Bithynia the army of Basiliskos opposed them; but its commander, the usurper's nephew, also came over to Zenon. Basiliskos was dethroned and executed in 477. Illos was sole consul in 478 and next year put down a strong revolt under Markianos (son of Anthemius, emperor of the West, and grandson of the Byzantine emperor Markianos). The rebel had married a daughter of Verina, who was the sister of Zenon's wife, and he rose against Zenon in Byzantion itself, defeated the royal troops, and besieged Zenon in the palace. Illos wavered, but was confirmed in his loyalty to Zenon through an Egyptian diviner (? Pamprepios) whom he patronised: that is, the diviner told him that Zenon would win. Illos won over the rebellious forces and captured Markianos. He was now in a very strong position.

Pamprepios, who seems of an arrogant character, was disliked by Zenon and Verina; and when Illos went off on some business to Isauria, they banished him on the charge of seeking to divine the future for Illos' benefit and Zenon's detriment. Illos however received him into his household and brought him back to Byzantion. (The date of this episode is not clear, but it was probably after Markianos' revolt.) Verina employed an Alan to kill Illos, who is said to have been wounded. Zenon banished her to the fortress Papourios. (Again the date is not clear.) Ariadne, the emperor's wife, strove to get her mother restored and in turn had a try at assassinating Illos. (Jornandes says that Illos had done his best to make Zenon jealous of her.) This time the killer managed to cut off Illos' ear.

Illos and Pamprepios now retired to Nikē and then went on further east, on the pretext of needing a change of air to cure the wound. Marsos, an Isaurian officer who had introduced Pamprepios to Illos, went with them, or joined them later. In 483–4 they raised the standard of revolt, defeated Zenon's army near Antioch, gained Papourios, and freed Verina. They induced her to crown one of their adherents, a patrician named Leontios, at Tarsos. But a fresh army of Zenon's defeated Illos near Seleukeia (probably the Isaurian town of that name) and drove him and his followers into the fort of Papourios. The brother of Illos, Trokondos—the name is variously spelt, even as Sekoundos—tried to slip out, but was caught and killed. Illos and Leontios were encouraged by Pamprepios to believe that the mission would succeed, and held out for some three years. Then Trokondos' death was discovered. Illos in rage put Pamprepios to death and flung his body over the rampart. Soon afterwards the fort was taken and Illos and Leontios were executed.

Pamprepios seems to have had a key-role in the revolt and to have worked out a plan of diplomatic actions aimed at detaching Egypt from the Empire and raising all its neighbours against Zenon. After winning over Verina, the rebels arranged for her to write a letter to the imperial officers at Antioch, in Egypt, and all over the East, which sought to draw them into the new camp. All this was certainly part of Pamprepios' strategy. In 484 he was named *Magister Officiorum* in the new government. As the astrologer of Illos he must have given advice at each decisive step and convinced Illos that the stars were on his side. He must also have named the favourable day for crowning Leontios. Palchos gives us a comment on *Leontios Crowned at Antioch*. "This person, taking a *katarchē* from two astrologers, was crowned and at once expelled from lordship and fortune." Pamprepios and his colleague, whoever he was, gave a favourable interpretation of the day; for Palchos tells us:

Those who gave the *katarchē* were much misled by the Sun and Jupiter and Mars being in the Horoskopos and Mercury in Epanaphora and the Moon in the [5th] locus, Agathe Tyche towards Saturn and Jupiter. But they did not turn first to [the fact that] Mercury the ruler of the day and hour had fallen into passivity, for it had the greatest elongation from the Sun and was in aspect only to Saturn. And this indicates violent death.[16]

He adds that he had observed "that the Moon, being ruler of the Sun and of the Horoskopos and of Jupiter and Mars and of the [preceding] conjunction, was in depression and in the [12th locus] Bad Daimon". The date is 18 July 484.

We may note how well the horoscope with which we began accords with the historical facts. It was near the end of 478 that Illos was able to promote Pamprepios; from that date he made him his chief counsellor and Pamprepios began his active part in high politics. Rhetorios says that he went through almost the whole *cursus honorum* of the imperial administration. As for his journey to Egypt, this is corroborated by allusions found in the fragments of the *Life of Isidoros* by Damaskios. These stress its political import and set it in the period when Illos had retired to Antioch (early 482). Pamprepios, then quaestor, went to Alexandreia to draw Egypt over to the projected rebellion and perhaps to intervene in the fratricidal quarrels of the Christians there. It seems however that he temporised when pressed by scholars of Alexandreia with plans for re-establishing the cults and traditions of the Hellenistic era. Also his pride irritated those with whom he parleyed. The philosopher Isidoros and the seer Heraiskos got the impression from the conversations that he meant already to betray the cause of Illos and hoped to regain imperial favour.[17]

His death? The end of the horoscope seems clumsily set down by the copyist or abbreviator. It says that he died in late November 484; but from the historical accounts the date has been made 488. Which is correct? First we must note that the precise dating of Illos' career is throughout difficult; and it seems highly unlikely that it took years for Trokondos' death to leak out. Theophanes says: "Illos and Leontios, besieged, waited for him four years, deceived by the *magister officiorum,* Pamprepios, the sorcerer. Having learned that Trokondos had perished, they had Pamprepios beheaded because of his deception and thrown over the ramparts."[18] This is given under 484; Theophanes then goes on with the years 485, 486, 487, and under 488 states that Illos and Leontios were taken. Only he says that Pamprepios was killed for deception; Damaskios, Malalas, Josuah the Stylite, and Rhetorios all say that the rebels executed him on suspicion of treason. We may dismiss then the idea that he was killed in 488, and put his death in late November 484, when Trokondos' mission was seen to have failed and the whole structure of Pamprepios' counsels, founded on astrology, was proved to be illusory.[19]

Damaskios saw him as a demonic incarnation, sent to earth by the spirit of evil to combat Philosophy and treacherously prevent the re-establishment of Hellenism. This judgment may be largely coloured by the failure of the revolt in which he played such a guiding part, and by his ignominious end. As to the attributions of motive to him, we cannot judge; but taking his story as a whole and considering his connection with Panopolis, a city with a strong element of pagan nationalism, we feel that he was probably moved throughout by a devotion to those very ideals which Damaskios denied him. The tendency to depict him as a double-dealer may well be derived from an arrogance of behaviour that alienated others with the same cause at heart, who felt shut out and belittled, and who became distrustful. Pamprepios may have wanted to play a lone hand and become the sole champion bringing about the success of Hellenism; his failure stimulated his detractors to see him in the worst light. Though we cannot prove a connection, the katarchic horoscope we noticed earlier, dealing with Theodoros the Prefect, suggests that upheavals in Egypt accompanied or followed the revolt of Illos, and the imperial acts of suppression may have increased bitterness.[20]

Luckily we have two poems that we can attribute to Pamprepios with a fair degree of certainty. One of them opens with a prologue in comic iambic trimeters: six lines that seem only a small part of the original. The theme is to "sing of the Hours and tell of their Actions". That is, to describe successive phases of a day and the activities of country-life going on at each phase. In the background we hear of the weather-changes, and a symbolic unity is gained by stressing the conflict of light and dark, storm and sunlight. The season is early winter, in November. The poem is thus an original sort of development on the astrological almanac. It belongs to a genre, the *ekphrasis synezeugmenē*, a description of paired themes or subjects, which Aphthonios defined as "paired-off in the sense of combining *pragmata* [matters or affairs] and *kairoi* [times]", but the weather-basis gives an astrometeorological aspect—though, apart from the reference to the Dogstar, there is nothing directly astral.

An introductory passage tells how in an early-morning storm a shepherd is driving his flocks to shelter from the rain; hail is expected. Sitting under a cliff, he pipes. The scene then shifts to the tree-nymphs, when the storm breaks and assails them, scattering their twigs and leaves, and swelling the streams. The storm starts clearing. The sun slowly comes out; the world rejoices. The snow melts and floods the waterways. A tree-nymph good-humouredly speaks to a spring-nymph. The happenings of the sunlit afternoon are then told. The countryfolk gather to honour Demeter with song, dance, sacrifice. They return to work, plough and sow in the fields, build hedges, scare the birds from seed. A farmer sings of the coming harvest; his song is repeated by a girl tending her flocks at evening, who dries her still drenched hair and clothes. The sun goes down, a thunderstorm gathers in the twilight. Then, in an epilogue the poet asks favour of the audience and says he's been called to Kyrene. The poem thus seems to have been composed and recited in Athens, when the poet was about to visit Libya. The style is very Nonnan or Panopolitan, though it generally lacks Nonnos' idiom of incessant transformations. It has often been abused. Thus, "Its theme and structure are well-planned and highly poetical, but the composition is weak and vicious. The writer is of the school of Nonnos, to whom he owes his excessive ornament and fullness of description, erotic colouring, monotonous rhythms, and inclination to grotesque allegory. Verses 144–8, in which the sentimental may seem to find a touch of true tenderness, are in fact a conventional copy of an outworn tradition, and a vulgar appeal to susceptible emotions. The poem is carefully, indeed laboriously, written by a person eager to impress an audience with his cleverness; in that limited ambition he cannot fairly be said to have failed." (Page.) But the whole of that criticism is merely misconceived; it applies the wrong criteria. The Nonnan rebirth of poetry, out of a disintegrated classicism, is based on a system of romantic symbolism developed in a subtly glancing and evanescent way, fanciful and digressive, yet owning its own complex structure of allusion and overtone.

The second poem strongly supports the Pamprepian authorship; it fits in well with Pamprepios' Athenian period and is in honour of Patrikios Theagenes (of Ichthyon); one text says "by the same". It is only a fragment; the papyrus is a portion of a published book, not an odd autograph.[21] The poem begins conventionally and hyperbolically with an account of Theagenes' distinguished ancestry, and probably, in the method of the genre, went on to deal with his *anatrophe* and his *praxeis,* ending with a *synkrisis*: rearing, deeds, and comparison. In style and method it is far inferior to the first poem. Indeed it is worth while looking at the latter in more detail:

The audience must greet my song.
When the words come together and throng,
they draw the poet's subtle mind
discreetly; courage too they blend,
to tell the doings of the Hours,
though anxieties distract his powers.

Today a revel rings round me, but not of pipes,
nor that which, singing, the lyre's seven strings arouse,
responding with sweet cries of song, nor that which the swan
uplifts on the slope of the prophetic mountain,
changing to freshest youth his weight of melodious age
when the breezes blow through his whistling feathertips—
no, a song which the blast of wind from the snows of Thrace
dancing along the wintry waves of the sea
chants to the surges at dawn.
                         And charmingly sings
how the snowbright lustre of the outblazing Sun
is quenched by the rain that bursts from the womb of the clouds
and the fire-power of the Dogstar
is damped out by snowstorms in their watery progress.
Even the stars go pale at the pouring, no longer
we see the Moon the dark-eyed Lady who treads
on the Sun's heels: she's frosted among the clouds.
No longer the dawn with redness embraces night's circle.

Lately the snow-winds out of the East had . . .
the downpour of rain from heaven as fertile as milk.
The revolving sky-axis had hidden the Pleiads away . . .
There a bridal shower of Lovegods in guise of rain
strewed wedding-gifts on the couch of Mother Earth
and clasped the rich furrow with hope of ploughing-luck.
A herdsman, near the mountain-stables, expecting
a storm of hail from the clouds, propitious prelude
of a goddess bringing rain to birth, goes driving
his heifers lately relaxed from pangs of travail
high up to a resting-lair dry among crags.
Round his back he bound the shag-circles of his ox-horn coat
and piping to his herds went under the cliff.
So thin was his breath the pipe could scarcely puff
the dwindling notes of its undercover song . . .

She untwined the twisted shoots that were her tresses
and shook off on every side her glistening locks.
At the jut of a snowlockt hillock another nymph
drew virgin water with arms clean-stript of twigs . . .

Snow rushed on the nymph, mingled
with volleys of thickening hailstones. She refused
to beat off the stony cloak, but joyously welcomed
the snowclad nurse who'd aid her wood to grow.
But she wasn't fated long to sustain the surge
of rain or wear the wet snowveil around her head.
Already a ring with reddening rim shone in the clouds,
A frail gleam opened, grazing what sky was unclouded,
and blazed a track out into the azure. At first
the light of the sun was like the ox-eyed moon's
soft glow, then soaring it burned in broad abundance
routing the shores and hills with arrows of light.
Hard it must fight to scatter the mist that rolled
and swirled on high, the rayless mother of frost.
There was laughter all over the land. Peace smiled again.
The sun spread a fiery brilliance on air and ocean
and warmed them. Upleaped the dolphin, halfseen by ships,
and splashed in the air as he rowed across the sea.
Nymphs girdled their breasts with brightness that fought the snow
with flourishing forces. The nature of hail was changed
to a showery stream. Snow, shaken to ground, was vanquished
by light. Declining to combat the sheen it flowed
in myriad dapple-tears across the calm.
Loud roared the sinews of springs, hard-pressed by snowfloods
of heaven's downpour. Their breasts were taut with the streams.
And from its bed the rivulet rose and turned
back to where nymphs coeval with the trees
were rooted in the thicket-depth of pines.

A Hamadryad peeped from the leaves and spoke
to a fountain-nymph, her neighbour with rosy arms:
"Good day, dear daughter of father Ocean, queen
of the plantation, how should I need your waters,
loaded with bounty of blackbosomed clouds?
Don't you see how huge a shower, poured on my bushes,
drips down inside my locks. That's why, my dear,
your flood's so deep. What rouses me to speak?
Words go to the heart, so better plans are framed.
The time is nearing when the Dogstar scorches,
and that's when your cool gifts will help us most.
Then, lady, spread your waters on thirsting gardens,
a present pleasant indeed." She spoke with smiles
and an overbrimming grace shone out of her
as to merry conflict she raced . . .

After the snowdance of lovegods from the sky
corngoddess Dēo is wedded to the farmer
who knows his work. And all men prayed, and each
had the sacrifice at heart, to raise an altar
to Dēo. The bull that loves the crags obeyed
the crook and went to the sacrifice. The troops
of kids pressed up against the herdsman kindling
the fragrant torch of Eleusinian pine.
The countryfolk gathered, they encircled the altar
and laid upon it an offering of dry sheaves,
an excellent omen of the coming harvest.
The old men sang, the young men danced in time
revering great Keleus for generosity
and hymned the kind goddess of the Rarian Plain.

Keleus in myth was king of Eleusis, who became the first priest of
Demeter in the Mysteries there and whose son Triptolemos
mythically played an important part in the spreading of agriculture.
After the sacrifice the country-folk get on with their labours. Their
skills are the work of "all-subduing Nature with persuasive Art".
The poem ends:

He cut off the wheatland with hedges and stayed with staff
to scare away the enemy swarm of cranes
that swallow the wheat . . .
                awoke so great a song . . .
singing a harvest-hymn . . .
So the old man sang. A girl sent back a tune,
tending a herd at his side and hiding her sex
under male clothes, male sandals on her feet,
all her body denied and tightly tied inside.

There are internal rhymes and assonances here: *boukoléousa . . .
eousa . . . phérousa . . . nymphē . . . engythi.*

A shepherd's belt wound round her. She squeezed from her head
the spiral ringlets; and all her manly back
was streaming. Sunbeams failed to dry her out
as there she dripped with water in the evening.
Evading the track in the chilled forest, she sought
a brightening hilltop. Fastening the snow-lasht vest,
she bared to the sun the top of her body down
down to the cleft between her shapely thighs.
Still she was not neglectful of her flock;
the straying mother-ewe . . .
lightly gripping the rondure of its gushing udder
drew out a milky flood as an offering to Pan.

P

Already Phaethon's horses under their hooves
trampled heaven's path and towards the drinking-pool
in the western sea were drawing the dew-moist rail
of their twilight-chariot. Again the cloudmists
were gathering, rising from the earth, and all
the deep-rooted stars were hidden, the moon unseen.
A great thunderstorm was fiercely hurrying on high
and a torch leapt from the clouds as either side
they burst and mixed with one another.
                                        A father,
lifting his baby-son upon his lap,
presses hands across his ears to close away
the crash of cloud that pounded on cloud above.

The heavens clanged. A little girl, as well,
in trailing clothes was woken, and called her nurse.
Earth yielded up the fruits of her teeming flanks
and committed her children to the sky and clouds.

It is a good thing to be able to end with the story of Pamprepios
and with his poem. The story brings out the strong political role of
astrology, and its final failure; the poem brings out the strong
cultural role of astrology and its manifold stimulations. In the
poem the impact of astrology has been fully absorbed; uppermost
is the positive aspect of a fuller sense of man's integration in a
living universe where the movements of sky and air have a subtle
and profound connection with what happens below. The wet girl
baring her body to the sun and throwing off the distorting garments
of toil, the children awakening to the sense of mighty forces at work
in nature—in one sense these are commonplaces. The picture of
the girl is drawn from statues of Aphrodite; that of the children
looks back to other poets. And yet the total effect is not
imitative.[22] Here, as in the *Dionysiaka,* poetry is being truly reborn
and facing in new directions.

We have seen "a snowdance of lovegods out of the sky".

22

Conclusions

If the alchemists were the first experimental scientists, seeking to repeat processes under laboratory conditions and to test out a coherent theory, the astronomers were the first devisers of exact science, consistently applying mathematics to phenomena and thus evolving clear notions of structure and movement. And, as we have seen, in the ancient world, astronomy could not be separated from astrology, since practically all observers of the sky shared a concept of the divine nature of the bodies moving aloft, whether or not they agreed about the possibility of giving precise form to the influences emanating from above and of relating them to life on earth. The main motive-force driving men to watch the stars was a hope of reducing their movements to regular patterns which could be understood and foreseen. Since this activity went on within cultural systems in which the notion of vital correspondences between heaven and earth was central, it at no time asserted itself as a disinterested and abstract search for knowledge. To know more of phenomena was to know more of man's place in nature and the ways in which the phenomena illuminated and affected human life. This in itself was a valid enough attitude; what we now see as fantasy was the extremely oversimplified way in which correspondences, connections and influences were seen and treated. The reaction came in the sixteenth century with the slow foundation of scientific attitudes which totally excluded men from the world of natural phenomena.

Astrology has had a lot of hard things said about it. "That desperate error on which the intellectual powers of countless generations were spent," said Cumont, one of its most sympathetic historians. "The scientific theory of waning heathenism," said Boll, though its roots went back far into the first millenium B.C. "The chief tendency of the time, the most impious and immoral of all religions," said Dobschütz. The denigrations could be indefinitely multiplied. And yet, as we have seen, it was not simply a misapplication and distortion of astronomy; it was linked with the main impulses and needs driving men to study the stars; astronomy could not have developed without it. It was embedded in a complex system of ideas about the organic relation of man and cosmos without which we should have had no human culture at all. Whatever its weaknesses and misdirections, to isolate it from the complex of ideas in which it played a vital part, and to consider only what was irrational in it, is to show total irresponsibility as an historian of culture.

Let us turn and make a similarly one-sided analysis of the post-Galilean science which supplanted alchemy and astrology with their deep sense of man himself as implicated in all the processes he examined. Scientists from Galileo on till the present have had almost no sense of the limitations of their outlook and the irrational assumptions on which it has been built up. Yet a non-scientist can fairly easily see what those assumptions were. The systems of purely quantitative analysis emerging from Galileo and Newton and others of their times distort reality in an extreme fashion. They have assumed that cause equals effect and that action and reaction are equal and opposite. But a child could see that if these laws were universally applicable, there would be no universe, or that if they suddenly asserted themselves in the existent universe there would be a total deadlock, as of an irresistible force meeting an immoveable object. There would be an ubiquitous symmetry; and as Curie noted, "It is the asymmetry that creates the phenomenon." That is, there would be no phenomena at all in a symmetrical universe; Time would there be wholly reversible and a mere ghost of Space. So post-Galilean science began by assuming a universe in which nothing happened. It could in fact deal effectively only with stable states in which its irrational assumption of absolute symmetry might be made to apply effectively within the terms of the questions asked. It invented a world of symmetry and reversibility, and imposed it on the real irreversible and asymmetrical world, defining stable states alone as real and ignoring everything else—all points of critical change, all aspects of qualitative development. The limits of usefulness in this attitude have now been essentially reached. Hence the general crisis in physics and related fields, which has set in since Einstein, quantum mechanics and the new problems raised by penetration into the particle-level. From any general aspect the post-Galilean scientists have been far more blinkered than were the astrologers—though this fact has been masked by the very much greater range of possible effective applications of their ideas and methods within the given categories.

In making these points of criticism, one is not denying the permanent value of much of the work done by the post-Galilean scientists. Their method was highly effective in dealing with stable states; and their insistence on quantitive methods created a situation that cannot be reversed. What I am arguing for is an outlook which includes all that was valid in their achievements, within a dialectical approach which sees reality as made up of a ceaseless struggle between symmetry and asymmetry, stability and instability. Such an approach can give the purely quantitive viewpoint its place in an enlarged system which is also capable of dealing with points of critical change and with the structure of development. All that lies outside our scope here, but it is relevant to note briefly the way in which many new directions of science move closer to the world of the alchemists and astrologers (considered in the totality of their ideas) than to that of the post-Newtonian mechanists. A generation or two ago biologists thought in terms of protoplasm, of a colloidal concept of vital organisation, a kind of primitive slime or glue. Such a viewpoint was becoming out of date by the 1930s; in its place we now have electron microscopy, which has shown that cells contain micro-organs, anatomical structure with firm and definite shapes.

Moreover, there is no dividing line between structures in the molecular and in the anatomical sense: macro-molecules have structures in a sense intelligible to the anatomist, and small atomical structures are molecular in a sense intelligible to the chemist. (Intelligible *now*, I should add: as Pirie has told us, the idea that molecules have literally, that is, spatially, a structure, was resisted by orthodox chemists, and the credentials of molecules with weights above 5,000 were long in doubt.) In short the orderliness of cells is a structural or crystalline orderliness—a "solid" orderliness, indeed, for "the so-called amorphous solids are either not really amorphous or not really solid". (Medawar.)[1]

These ideas of micro-organic structure would have been seen as nothing strange by Philolaos or Plato, or indeed by Demokritos; and the alchemists and astrologers would have seen them as vindications of their schemes of micro-macro-correspondences and of a unitary stream of matter.

If we turn from the very small to the very large world we find that now we admittedly live in a world of endlessly impacting rays, waves, fields, and all sorts of emanations. Thus, we know of the presence of strong magnetic fields round certain fast-rotating stars, and of stars with periodically variable magnetic fields. So the hydrodynamical laws on which the construction of stellar models has been based is out of date; and we need to formulate the laws of a new science of magneto-hydrodynamics.[2] Or we may take the direct-action theory of Hoyle and Narlikar. "We now know that particle couplings are propagated essentially along null geodesics— i.e. at no distance in the four-dimensional sense. Strictly, the phrase 'action-at-a-distance' should be changed to 'action-at-no-distance'." The distance between two locations here becomes distance in the four-dimensional space-time continuum.

With this extension "null geodesics" become virtually the paths of light rays or electro-magnetic radiation. It merely means that action at a distance propagates itself in the same way as light along a world-line in the space-time continuum, any two points of which are at zero interval—the null geodesic. It therefore results that action at a distance between particles, occurring as it does via lines of null interval, boils down to action at *no* "distance", i.e. at zero interval.

With the action-at-a-distance difficulty having been conjured away even though only formally by a sort of mathematical jugglery, Hoyle and Narlikar proceeded to incorporate fully into their theory of gravitation Mach's principle, for which there is now growing observational support, which Einstein never did. As a result, mass or inertia of matter, according to Hoyle and Narlikar, is not its inherent property but is deemed to stem completely from the long-range interaction of distant masses. Indeed, they have produced an equation that neatly ties up the mass of any body to the total mass in the observable universe—a universe that is moreover assumed to be a conglomeration of discrete particles that any particular observer can possibly include within his observational ken. (Jagjit Singh.)[3]

We are not concerned here with supporting this particular point of theory, but to use it as an example of the way that thought is moving, and the change in attitudes that appears. What finally will emerge as an effective synthesis of the new material and the new points of theory is impossible yet to formulate with any clarity except in a highly general way, but we can surely see that any such synthesis must be incomparably closer to the world-view of the astrologers than to any of the mechanistic theses from the seventeenth century on to the present day.

Now let us glance at some recent views on the sun and moon.

Almost 99% of the living parts of living organisms are made up of four elements, hydrogen, oxygen, nitrogen, carbon. These elements, through hydrogen, play their part in generating sunlight; they are coupled through that light (i.e. through photosynthesis) with the same elements mainly composing life on earth. On the long-term aspect: carbon and oxygen, originating in the depths of the red giants, are thrown out into space to become part of the circulating matter of the universe and finally to condense and form new generations of stars, planets, and living creatures like ourselves. We see that there is a functional parallel in the metabolisms of stars and organisms, which involves the central role of hydrogen. What sunlight (derived by "burning" hydrogen to helium) does in photosynthesis is to activate hydrogen—free it from molecules of low potential energy, so that it can be incorporated with molecles of high potential energy. Organisms can later free the energy for their uses by returning hydrogen to lower energy states. All this would seem perfectly natural and logical to an astrologer or alchemist, vindicating the correspondence theory by its linking the metabolisms of stars and human beings.[4]

The moon-cycles affect the weather (argues a geophysicist of Leningrad); it can be shown that the earth's temperature goes up and down as the moon travels up and down in the sky on its 9-year and 19-year cycles. The higher it is above the horizon, the colder the weather, whether in summer or winter. Temperature may thus depend more on the lunar cycles than on the 11-year solar sunspot cycle.[5] The ancient notion that the full moon is the best time for sowing rootcrops has been claimed as correct. The radicle of a seed emerges first, thrusting the root deep down towards the earth's centre as if pulled by gravity; the plumule or shoot sprouts afterwards, moving up towards the light. At full moon the earth lies between sun and moon and the gravitational field (or waves, if such exist, as is suspected) are exerting their maximum effect.[6]

These are only a few instances taken at randon to bring out the fact that nowadays the worlds of the astrologers does not seem such a mad one. What was fantastic in their concepts was the attribution of certain characteristics, drawn from mythology, to sun, moon, stars, and planets and the belief that a comparatively simple pattern of star-positions could be related to a time-moment such as birth, conception, the starting of some enterprise, in such a way as to reveal the totality of cosmic forces operating on any given point of space.

But the mere analysis of such a system does not explain why it exerted such a tremendous influence on the men of the ancient world—or, for that matter, of the medieval world as well. In the course of our narrative we have paused now and then to show how men tended to project on to the screen of the cosmos a social structure—what they would like to see existing on earth, if they were dissatisfied and hoping for a more brotherly and harmonious system, or what actually existed, if they were defenders of the *status quo*. It was of the utmost importance for men to feel that the cosmic structure reflected and thus vindicated what they felt to be the right structure for human society. The conviction that heaven and earth existed as the two halves of a whole, vitally inter-connected and revealing in even the smallest matters an endless series of correspondences, was deeply imbedded in all thinking and feeling; and provided the basis which gave astrology such a vast force, such a desperate appeal.

Again we are faced by the paradox that at the heart of the irrational elements in astrology there lay what was the most valuable aspect of ancient thought—the sense of being organically a part of a living universe. A key-problem for the modern world is to regain what was valid and creative in this sense without yielding to the irrational elements. The latter were in part bound up with the general level of social organisation and of technological development at that time. Men were aware of vast potentialities, especially at times of economic and political crisis; but they also felt bound down and surrounded on all sides by ungraspable forces of oppression and frustration. At the core of the dilemma was the existence of slavery, which affected everyone in the societies, free or servile—in the same way as Hegel and Marx have shown that the master-and-servant relationship involves aspects of alienation, of limitations of humanity, in every person in a class-society. The effects of slavery as a key-institution was thus infinitely wider and stronger than can be assessed by any simple analysis of its economic and social effects. They included the crushing sense of necessity or fate which increasingly pervaded the ancient world as its crisis grew more comprehensive and unslackening. The philosophical argument about freedom and fate, carried over into astrology where it found its most powerful and constant centre, was emotionally linked with the pressures of the slave-system—

however much it also included problems which are timeless in the sense that they must reassert themselves in any social system, since every individual has his limits of development and fulfilment, his inner conflicts, his private compact with death.

Thus we can understand why, with the breakdown of the city-state and its cults, the cult of the stars and building-up of astrologic systems of thought became ever more important. Because of a distaste for astrology as an outmoded superstition, thinkers and historians have been averse from admitting the enormous significance, the centrality, of the astrologic viewpoint in ancient life, from the days of Plato on till the triumph of the solar cult under Aurelian. I trust that this book has done a little to correct the balance.

Definitions

Agathos Daimon : Locus 11 after Horoskopos; as starting-point inferior only to Mid-heaven and Horoskopos.

Anomalistic : (1) year: the time that the earth takes from perihelion to perihelion; (2) month: the time that the moon takes from perigee to perigee.

Aphelion : the point furthest from the sun in the orbit of a planet or comet.

Apogee : the point furthest from the earth in the orbit of any planet; the greatest distance of the sun from the earth when the latter is in aphelion.

Aspect : a planet is in dominant aspect to another if it precedes the second planet by 90° (quartile) in the sense of the daily rotation. The *Tetrabiblos* (i 13) distinguishes four combinations or symmetric arrangements of points of the ecliptic (BL 185 ff): Opposition or Diameter; Trine; Quartile; Sextile—endpoints of a diameter; equilateral triangle; square; regular hexagon.

Azimuth : arc of the heavens extending from the zenith to the horizon, which it cuts at right angles.

Centres (Kentra) : the four points which the ecliptic has in common with the horizon and the meridian at a given moment. So the points are the rising and setting points, and the points of upper and lower culmination. The rising point is also called the Horoskopos; the upper culmination is Mid-heaven. The setting point is *dysis* in Greek; the symbol M is used for Mid-heaven, IMC for *imum caeli* or low culmination.

Colure : one of the two great circles rectangularly intercepting at poles and dividing the equinoctial and the ecliptic into four equal parts, one passing through the equinoctial, the other through the solstitial, points of the ecliptic.

Conjunction : apparent proximity of two heavenly bodies.

Dekan : a third of a zodiacal sign; a section of the ecliptic of 10° length.

Diameter : aspect in which two heavenly bodies are located in opposite end-points of a diameter of the ecliptic.

Dodekatemoria : if we assume a point A of a zodiacal sign as sigma degrees from the beginning of the sign: with A is then associated as Dodekatemorion another point B whose distance from A is 12 sigma.

Dysis : see Centres.

Eccentric : of heavenly bodies, moving in an eccentric orbit—i.e. not concentric to another circle.

Ecliptic : the sun's apparent orbit.

Ephemerides : astronomical calendar or table.

Epicycle : small circle having its centre on the circumference of a larger one.

Exaltation : In Valens (ii 18) the exaltation of a nativity is defined by means of the sun (in daytime) or of the moon (at night). One counts the distance from the sun to the point of the sun's exaltation (or from the moon to the point of the moon's), and the same distance is assumed to separate the Horoskopos from the exaltation of the nativity.

426

Horoskopos : see Centres.

Houses or Oikoi : each planet has two, symmetrically located, which are assigned to the moon or sun respectively—by arrangement of the planets according to their distance from the earth.

Katarchē, beginning : astrologic investigation of the influence of a momentary configuration of heavenly objects, *e.g.* at the start of some enterprise.

Klima : the notion of geographical latitude plays a lesser part than the characterising of a locality by its longest daylight or the ratio of longest to shortest daylight. The longest daylight is directly related to the rising times.

Loci : astrologers made two other 12–divisions of the ecliptic besides the Zodiac, counting either from Horoskopos or the Lot of Fortune. In each case the 12th locus is given a special significance for a certain sphere of life.

Mean : equally far from two extremes; the mean sun is a fictitious one moving in the celestial equator at the mean rate of the real sun.

Meridian : circle passing through the celestial poles and zenith of any place on earth's surface.

Monomoiria : system by which each degree of the ecliptic is associated with a planet: there was much variety in the system.

Opposition : position of moon or planet diametrically opposite to the sun; less accurately refers to moon or planet rising in east when sun sets in west.

Paradosis, Yielding : transmission of rulership from one planet to another according to the sequence of the periods of life.

Parallax : the angular amount of apparent displacement of an object, caused by an actual change of observation-point.

Parameter : quantity constant in case considered, but varying in different cases.

Perigee : the point in the orbit of a planet, especially the moon, at which it is nearest earth.

Perihelion : the point in a planet's orbit when it is nearest the sun.

Periods : seven are often used: (1) 19 solar years = 235 moon-months, so-called Metonic Cycle; (2) 25 Egyptian years = 409 moon-months; (3) 30 years, approximate synodic period: (4) 12 years, approximate synodic period; (5) 15 years, ditto; (6) 8 years ditto, 99 moon-months; (7) 20 Egyptian years = 63 synodic periods.

Phases : aspect of a moon or planet according to the amount of illumination: the term is often applied to the moon as new, in its first quarter, as full, in its last quarter. Ptolemy wrote on the *Phases of the Fixed Stars.* The idea probably arose from the observation of bright fixed stars; in Greek calendars the first or last appearances of stars at morning or evening are called the phases.

Precede : a planet precedes another if it is further ahead in the sense of daily rotation (or smaller longtitude).

Precession : of the equinoxes: earlier occurrence of the equinoxes in each successive sidereal year, due to retrograde motion of the equinoctial points along the ecliptic.

Rising Times : indicate how many degrees of the celestial equator cross the horizon of a given locality at the same time as the consecutive zodiacal signs.

Sects : planets as divided into diurnal or nocturnal.

Synod : conjunction of planets or stars; as adjective, related to such a conjunction.

Terms or Horia : sections of the signs associated with planets.

Notes

Apart from the usual abbreviations for periodicals, I have used several of my own for writers often cited as follows: B: Boll; BL: Bouché-Leclercq; C: Cumont; Cr: Cramer; D: Dicks; F: Festugière; G: W. Gundel; JL: Jack Lindsay; N: Neugebauer; Nou: Nougayrol; S: Sachs; W: van Waerden.

1. BABYLONIAN BASES

1. *De div.* i 52.
2. N (1) 98.
3. *BM Guide Bab. & Ass. Antiq.* 1922 205–7.
4. Lassoe 54.
5. B (3) 14; Cr (1) 5.
6. Oppenheim (1) 160; Waterman 895.
7. Oppenheim (1) 157; Waterman 657.
8. Oppenheim (1) 158; Waterman 652.
9. Oppenheim (1) 161; Waterman 407.
10. Oppenheim (1) 161; Waterman 687.
11. Oppenheim (1) 162; Waterman 355.
12. Oppenheim (1) 195; Eberling 304.
13. *Enuma Elish* iv 55–146; Walcot ch. ii (rel. to Greeks); Brandon 99 ff; transmission by Berosos, 111–13.
14. Landsberger. Overstress by e.g. W. Volgraff in *Mél. Bidez* 999 f as part of the general unbalance of the pan-Bab. school.
15. Jacobsen (1) 205 f; Falkenstein 64 f.
16. Jacobsen (1) 145; *Maqlu* tablet iii 151 f; vi 1–8.
17. JL (1) 210 f; also Eisler (3) 578 and (4) 12; Hopfner (2).
18. Nou (3) 34; other methods by oil, flour, smoke, abnormal births, dreams, human features or behaviours.
19. Nou (3) 35 f.
20. Nou (3) 43.
21. *Cun. Texts BM* xx 44, 59–61; Gadd (1) 26 f; *Cun. Texts* xx 34, 3; xxx 16 (K. 3841, 8); xxxi 20, 22; Boissier (1) 226, 22 etc.
22. CT xx 44, 49; Festus 289M cited by Blecher 191; Fossey (1). Cf. for dreams, Artemid. i ch. 57.
23. Nou (3) 43–5.
24. Contenau (2) 115.
25. *Ib.* (2) 114; Jastrow (4).
26. V. Scheil, *Rev. Ass.* xxvi 1929 9; also Contenau 119.
27. Contenau (2) 116 f (K. 159); Klauber no 105.
28. For medical texts, Contenau (2) 17 f; Boissier (3) and (1) 209 ff, with BM 2896, K 3988; for ravaging by Nergal, underworld god, who represents noon-sun, Fossey 23 no 70.

29. Nou (3) 41.

30. Nou (3) 7–9.

31. Nou (3) 8 f.

32. Laroche (2) with *Or. Lit.-Zeit* 1957 135; 1962 28 f, and Laroche (3); Goetze (1), (2), and (3). Further Nou (4); Goetze (5) for Taurus; Alalakh, Woolley, *A Forgotten Kingdom* 120 n1; Gadd (3) 2507; S. Smith, *The Statue of Idrimi* 16 ff; 74 ff. Ugarit more doubtful, Virolleaud (2) and (3) i 118; Dussaud CRAI 1937 279 ff and *Syria* xvii 378 ff etc.

33. Contenau (2) 108; Merx; King; Jastrow (1); Dhorme 129 f.

34. Sacrifice of kid on stèlè of Ur-Nammu founder of 3rd dynasty at Ur: L. Legrain, *Rev. Ass.* xxx 111–15; Meissner (3) 59.

35. Contenau (2) 111 f; Jastrow (2). Weapon: Jastrow (3). For full anatomical analysis, Hussey.

36. Contenau (2) 20.

37. *Archives roy. de Mari* ii 139, 9–13; Finet 89 f.

38. Finet 90.

39. Nou (3) 42.

40. Lassoe 53 f. For following account of Falerian model: Nou (4). Origins: Syria (Dhorme), Lydia (Virolleaud), Hdt. i 94; Phoenicia (Nou). Diotima: Picard in N (4) 518. Haro- is not an Assyr.-Bab. name, Nou 518 f. For Hittite variations: Laroche (2). For terms: N (4), further Piganiol.

41. Plin. ii 54, 143; Mart. Cap. *de nupt.* i 45 ff; Pallotino 163–6; Thulin; Weinstock; Grenier (1) 18 ff and 34 ff; A. Fabretti *CI Ital.* 69 for man both *fulg.* and *harusp.* Also Grenier (2), and Nou (4) for Etruscan left and right: with Pottier; Fotheringham (6); Cuillandre 325 ff.

42. G. Thomson 53–7; Frazer, *Totemism* 501–7; P. Radin, *The Winnebago Tribe* (ARB 37) 185, cf. Sioux and Central Algonquil. Ponkas: J. O. Dorsey, *Siouan Sociology* (ARB 15) 228; Zunis: Cushing ARB xiii 367–70. Aztecs: G. C. Vaillant, *The Aztecs of Mexico* 1950 175; for sociological basis of cosmic structure 172.

43. Kramer. Kritodemos: i 258. Intestines: Meisnner (2) ii 268. On some tablets the scribes schematise the signs on liver; lines notched or bent, returning on themselves, to teach the pupil, better than any description, what he'd see on the liver: Boissier (3) i 120 & 139–43; Jastrow (5) 123–5.

44. Smith; Thureau-Dangin (1).

45. Art represents entrails, e.g. relief, period Teklath-phalasar (8th c.) showing vulture bearing them off from battle-corpse: Contenau (2) 123.

46. Bauer 258; and 262 n18 for possible Hurrian link. We know that as well as Sumerian and Bab. texts (read as far afield as Megiddo, Palestine) there was a Hittite and a Hurrian version.

47. Seal: Barnett (2) 83. Tell H.: Oppenheim (4) pl. 36; Hogarth i pl. B13; Nimrud: Barnett (3) figs. 6 f; Layard *Mons of N.* ii pl. 65. This area has contacts with N. Syria & Phoenicia.

48. TC: Louvre AO 12475; Barnett (1) pl. 1a. Clay mask, ib. 1b & Contenau (2) fig. 51. *Oscilla*; Virg. *Georg.* ii 289. Dawkins, *Artemis Orthia* pls. xlvii–ix, lix–lxii. Y. Yadin, *Hazor in Galilee* (BM 1958 fig -8); V. y Escudero. *La Necropoli de Ibiza* 1917 pl. xxxix; Delattre, *Necrop. puniques de Carthage.* In general, Barnett 147 f.

49. Gadd (1) 28 f; Daiches 14 f, 28, 7 & 23 f; in general Gadd (2) 78; Oppenheim (5) 196. Jewish commentator on *Ezek.* xxi 21 speaks of diviners sharpening and polishing iron of arrow, and looking into it "as they look in the thumb of the hand, into the nail . . . and also they look in the liver, because it has brightness". The use of the nail not known in Bab.

50. Cumont (5) 11.

51. Du Mesnil 7–29 for refs.

52. More refs. could be cited, showing beliefs and images covering an area from Egypt to Caspian.

53. See JL (3) esp. chs. 22–3.

54. Nou (4) and Cadd (1) 57 n 4. For role of Adad (of northern mountains ?): Nou (4).

55. Gadd (1) 33 f; Nou (2) plus *Assyr. Dict.* (Chicago) iv 281 ff & 285 ff.

56. Jacobsen (2).

2. BABYLONIAN ASTRONOMY

1. N (1) 97 f. Nothing is known of Sumerian astronomy.

2. N (17) 41.

3. N (1) 100.

4. N (1) 101–3.

5. W (3) & (7); Kugler (1) ii 259–66 & 276.

6. N (1) 105 f: problem: when is a month 30 or 29 days long? The answer needs an estimate of both lunar and solar motion, 106–9; more problems 109 ff.

7. W (2) 21; Schott 302 thinks original of astrolabe was circular; but we do not know if it had the numbers indicating duration of daylight; an astrolabe in Berlin (B) lacks the numbers. W (2) for rel. of astrolabe B and Nippur text of 12–11th c. for date, Weidner (1) 172.

8. W (2) 9 & 18. They assumed weight to be proportional to the watch-duration; not quite true. N (16) the other series refer to halfwatches and quarter-watches (seasonal hours, one hour equalling a twelfth of day or night). In this text the equinoxes are in months xi and xii, longest day in iii, shortest in ix; ratio of longest day to shortest night is 2:1.

9. Craig 17.

10. W (3).

11. In general, debt to W here.

12. Second system: in the later system the ratio of longest day and shortest night is 3:2; but the old scheme is used in Sargonid compilations for computing day and night for different months, and the daily retardation of moon's rising or setting. Only the equinox now is on 15 Nisan. N (16) 38 & 41; Weidner AfO xii 144 Taf xii; W (3) 24 f.

13. Hd. ii 109; W (3) 25 f; D (2) 165 f.

14. Kugler (1) i 71; Ptol. *Syntaxis* v 14. For previous moontexts: Thompson (2) 124; 140; 271 & 273 f; Pannekoek (1) 42–7; Virroleaud (4) Sin xix 19; Weidner (6) 23.

15. Fotheringham (2); W (3) 26 f. For more elaborate methods as to moon in Persian era, W 29, and rules from a Uruk text, some based on Saros period, others on old rule that daily retardation of moon is one fifteenth of day and night. For Seleukid era, *ib.* 30; Kugler (1) ii 538. For Saros: N (1) 116 & 141.

16. W (3) 30.

17. Huxley 10; ACT i 76 f.

18. W (3) 30 f.

19. Huxley 7.

20. N (17) 41 & (1) 103.

21. Schiaparelli 22; N (1) 153.

22. Ephemerides and tables for eclipses of II form a coherent whole; not so with I. Similar distinctions can be made in theory of planets, where use of step-functions has advantages over use of linear zigzag; but the relative chronology of lunar and planetary theory is unknown: N (17) 43. For ephemerides: N (1) 115 ff.

23. S (6). Normal Stars never cited in mathematical astron. texts of the era.

24. Problem of norming the Zodiac; some may have first used as norming

fixed star *v Piscium* for Ram O°, dropped it for brighter *xi Tauri* to define Bull 30°, at last changed to fix Virgin in Zodiac. But all this in one century seems unlikely. Term Normal Star applied by Epping to some 30 stars in the ecliptical belt, with ref. to which observations of lunar and planetary positions were made; for list, Kugler (1) ii 550 f.

25. Sachs (6).

26. In A, col. B is derived without direct mention of velocity (col. A) since in system A only two velocity values are used; so no need repeat separately. N (1) 116.

27. N (1) 118 on differences of A & B here.

28. The *kalu* are said to be in charge of god-appeasal by rituals, e.g. the New Year festival (T.–Dangin *Rit. Accad.* i & 86), while *mashmash* interpreted omens, including those of heavens.

29. *BM Guide* (see ch. I n 3) 161 (42, 262). Colophons: N (17) ii 11.

30. Olmstead (1) states N. set himself to determine true date of new or full moon, which was linked with determination of lunar and solar eclipses.

31. Lassoe 117 & 121. For *bit mummu*: Heidel (3); Luckenbill 259 ff. Animation: Ebeling (2) 100–14; T.–Dangin (1) no 42; Allbright (1). Narbonid: refs. in Heidel and Ebeling MAOG vii 1–2 1933 79. Patrons: Tallqvist 429 & 287 ff and Meissner (2) ii 17 & 12 ff. Deilem, *Pantheon* no 862. Ea: Lambert. *Mummu* in creation-legend: Heidel (3) and (2); Walcot 34 & 114. There are perhaps two to four homonyms.

32. Olmstead 200 f; Kugler (1) i 45.

33. Olmstead 200; Kugler (1) *Erganz.* 128; Weidner (5). Regulus: D (2) 164 and W (9) 67 f.

34. Olmstead 202; Kugler (1) i 61 ff; Ptol. v 14; J. Strassmaier *Kambyses* 1890 no 400.

35. N (1) 169.

36. BM (see n 29 above) 162 (92, 688); 161 (33, 837).

37. *Ib.* 184 f. (K. 15; 716; 184; 78; 480; 88).

38. N (1) 7: same basis in two of earliest Indian astron. works.

39. N (1) 17 & 19.

40. Lewy 11.

41. N (1) 33 f.

42. N (1) 44 for related problems considered including some that went beyond an algebraic character; geometric rels. 46; level 48. For limitations of Greek algebra, J. Klein (1968). S (2) for crude methods with cube roots and approximations of reciprocals of irregular numbers; also (1).

3. THE FIRST HOROSCOPES

1. Sachs (1) and (2). Strab. xvi 739, he says Borsippa was "sacred to Apollo and Artemis", manufacturing linen.

2. Friedrich; similar Bab. text, Virolleaud; S (3) n 17a.

3. BL 49 f; Eisler (1) 165.

4. Arrian, *anab.* vii 17, 3; Bidez (3) 41 f. Temples: Furlani.

5. S (3) 52.

6. S (3) 54. Several words uncertain.

7. Sachs works out the day by lunar longitude. The text dated 17 March to 15 Dec. 258 deals with both conception and birth.

The tale that a Chaldean predicted to Euripides' father the fortune of his newborn child (Aul. Gell. xv 20, 2) must be a late fabrication: "When E. was born, his father was assured by a Chaldean that the boy, grown up, would be a victor in the Contest [*Agon*]; for that was his fate." So the father reared him as an athlete; E. participated in the Eleusinian and Thesean Games, and won crowns. Then he turned to intellectual pursuits and at 18 attempted a tragedy.

8. 2 (3) 60 f. Greek names at Urk: R. A. Bowman, *A. J. Sem. L. & L.* lvi 1939 237 f & 242.

9. S (3) 61–3.

10. For kind of astron. document from which excerpts made: S (3) 64. Another text seems to give dates of 3 births for which H.s cast (of 115, 117 & 154 B.C.).

11. S (3) 65–74.

12. BL 216 n 3 & 209–303; Housman, Manil, Bk. II 1937 pp. xxii–xxvi; N (20) 6. For order of planets S (3) 73; two methods of computing second set of longitudes in GR computations, 72 f.

13. W (3).

14. W (4) 218.

15. W (4) 221 anx (2) 9.

16. Campbell 45 f.

17. Schwabe 23–37; Campbell 45 f.

18. Du Mesnil 131–7; *Mél. Univ. St. Jos.* xliv 1968 39 fig. 5.

19. *Persica* iii 1967–8 18–28 figs. 6 f.

20. Du Mesnil 132.

21. Amiet, *La Glypte Mesopot.* pl. 50, no 698.

22. Du Mesnil 134 fig. 35; H. Haas *Bilderatlas zu Relig.* 2–4 *Aeg. Relig.* 1924 fig. 55; *Riv. d. St. Or.* 1967 349 fig. 3. New Kingdom representations of Ashtart, Du M. 133 f.

23. Faulkner PT 1180, cf 1285, 1348, 1564, 1749, 1995, 2103, 2128.

24. Kugler (1) Erg. 2, 207; Gössmann.

25. B (10) 41–3; Gundel (10) 51–4

26. S (3) 70.

27. Kugler (1) ii 550. For 36 Stars: W (2) 10–2 & 23–5.

28. The Signs: W (4) 220. No basis in Sext. Emp, *adv. M* xxiii. Magnitudes of solar eclipses computed from latitudes of new moon. Zod. scheme, W (4) 221.

29. W (4) 222. limiting points of signs; precession 223.

30. W (4) 223.

31. W (2) 25; Rehm (7) 33.

32. Diod. ii 30 f; W (2) 22 f. Bidez (3) 53 n, 2–3 & 55–6; *Axiochos* 37 a & R.E. vi 2419, 35 ff. Names of planets Ungnad (2) 251.

33. Q. Curt. Ruf. iii 3, 4.

34. Justin xii 13; App. ii 9, 58; E. Taverner 1 ff.

35. Diod. xvii 112, 2 ff; Arr. vii 16 ff; Justin xii 13; Diod. ii 31, 2; Bidez (3) 43: Relations to priests: Arr. iii 16, 5; vii 11:8; Kornemann.

36. G. Radet, *Alex. le Gr.* 1931 373; Wilcken *Alex. d. Gr.* 1931 131 & 215, etc. Penetration of Hellenism at Bab., Koldewesy, esp. fig. 248, theatre. Gardens etc., Q. Curt. v 1, 24 ff; Radet 113.

37. Appian *Syriak.* lviii; Streck RE *Seleukeia* 1150. Note Antiochos I, who restored temples. Also, Bidez (3) 45; Schnabel 7 ff; H. Diels *Elementum* 1899 10; *Klio* 1922 131 ff.

38. Diod. fr. 21, 1, 1; Plout. *Eumenes* xix 2.

39. Strab. xvi (739); Dion *ep.* lxviii 30, 1.

40. App xi 9, 58; Diod. ii 31, 2; BL 368 n 1.

41. Cic. *de div.* ii 47, 98; Plout. *Rom.* xii 3 on Firmanus.

42. CCAG ix 2 177–9. Coins: Syria, Cumont (5) 81. Alex.: Anson vi 1 ff nos. 126 ff; Saglio-Pott. *sv* Zodiacus 1048; Cr (1) 12.

43. Ps. Kall. i 12; for heptagram of the weekday gods, B (3) 67; Cr (1) 21.

44. Syriac version (in English), Budge; Ryssel; Weinreich; Kroll (4): B (2). Magical works closed in Alex. tomb by Sept. Sev: Dion lxxvi (lxxv) 13, 2.

45. Valens *Ant.* ix 11 (Kroll 35, 4).
46. Bidez (1) 68 ff.
47. *Ib.* 86 f.

4. THE GREEKS AND THE EAST

1. Astronomy: Fr. 178–9 (Rzach); Diod. iv 85; Athen. xi 491 d; sch. Pindar *Nem.* ii 16; on Arat. 254; *Kat.* fr. i & xxxii. It may have been appended to *Divination by Birds,* which we know from Proklos (on *Works and Days* 828) was rejected by Apollonios of R. as spurious.

Homer: his long-days and sun-turns: D (2) 32 f; starts 30 f; (?) eclipse *Od.* xx 356 f.

2. *W. & D.* 564 ff; 383 f. D (4) 37; stars 35 f.

3. Huxley 4 f; a later copy from Assurbanipal's library is marked as from Babylon itself.

4. Dicks (1) 35.

5. For rels. of Greeks and Assyria 750–690 B.C., see A. R. Burn, *Lyric Age of Greece* 1960 49–52. Greek pottery from Tarsos (Hanfmann, *Aegean and Near East* 1956 165–84) is to be compared with evidence from Al-Mina: Walcot 140 n 46.

6. Walcot 21–2; Kirk, ch. on P. n 47 & 61.

7. *Vors.* 71. B 2; Kern (2) 277 n 46; Diels (4) ii 91 ff & 656 ff; T. Gomperz *Penseurs gr.* i 93; Diog. L. i 20 (*Vors.* 71. A 1) Eis; er (2) 346 ff & 220 n 4; *cf.* fr. 506 Euripides *Melanippe*; G (12) 38 & 106, line 5; and winged tree of Shamash. Plato *Rep.* x 614d; Kohl RE xi 598. T. Dombart *Deut. Philol.* 1928 64 ff.

8. Du Mesnil 16–18 & 129 f.

9. Walcot 93–7. For following summary, D (4); *parapegma,* 84 f, with list of writers including Egyptians with *episemasiai,* 189 (Eudoxos), and n 97–8; D (4) 73 f for Hiketas & Ekphantos; 77, Diogenes of Apollonia.

10. Diels-Kranz (9th ed.) 3B 24.

11. Kleos. 6A1; Plin. ii 31 (Kleos. 6B2). Cycle: Kleos. 6B4; Censor. ND xviii 4. For problems of 8–9 year festival of much earlier systems, Thomson (1). In general, D (4) 87.

12. N (1) 97; Rehm.

13. Hdt. i 74, 2; Huxley (1) 5; D (1) 37 & (2); N (1) 142 and (18).

14. Heath (1) 13–16; Fotheringham (3) & MNRAS 1920 108; Boll RE *Finisternisse* 2353; Oppolzer 60 no 1489. For further examination of eastern links: Bidez (1) & (2); JL (1); Cr (1) 5–7; Duhem i 5–27 on Pythag.; B (3) 90 against Frank who holds Philolaos taught complete astrologic system. Riess (2) & Jessen (1) holds contacts only after Alexander. Against them, Orfele; Cumont (9); B (3) 85 f; a century earlier, Capelle & Gressman etc.

15. N (1) 119.

16. Ptol. *Synt.* (Heiberg) i 269, 18 f; cycle wrongly called Saros, N (1) 116 & 141.

17. Kugler (1) ii 58 f; N (17) i 68 f, 115, 160 f; D (2) 296.

18. Plin. ii 31; discussion Fotheringham & Webb; Rehm (7); D (4) 89, 157, 172. JL (3) wrongly accepts Pythagoras and obliquity of ecliptic, 37.

19. W (3) 21.

20. Kroll i 15; Plin. ii 58.

21. Bidez (2) ii 176.

22. Bilfinger (2) 488; W (1) and (3) 27.

23. *Mem.* iv 7; Arat. 553–61.

24. B (10); Gundel (10).

25. W (3) 28.

26. W (3) 28 f.

27. W (3) 29. Fixing time from stars a consistent interest of the Babs.; in ^{mul}APIN is a list of simultaneously rising and setting stars; another list is of stars rising as others culminate; another gives difference between culmination-times expressed in weights of water (from water-clocks): Kugler (1) 1–49, 141–81, 207–24 etc. (1st & 2nd *Ergänz*).

28. Hdt. ii 109; Aristoph. *Ekkl.* 652; Menandros fr. 364 K.; D (1) 29 f; Ptol. *Synt.* iii 1 (205, 21 H.) citing Meton & Euktemon.

29. W (1) 34; Weidner (3) 198; N (1) 158.

30. Olmstead 204; Vitruv. ix 1, 1 f.

31. Olmstead 337. Polos in Hdt. seems portable hemispherical sundial D (2) 308 & (4) 165, 252.

32. Diog. L. ii 1 (DK 12A1); Euseb. PE x 14, 11 (DK 12A4); *Souda, sv* (DK 12A2).

33. D (1) 33 n 35.

34. Kirk 102 f.

35. Vitruv. ix 8, 1; D (1) 29; Huxley (1) 5 oversimplifies.

36. II *Kings* xx 8–11; *Is.* xxxviii 8.

37. M. von Gumpach, *Die Zeitrechtung d. Bab. u. Ass.* 1862 25; Layard *Nin. and Bab.* ch. xxii, note A p. 498.

38. Heath (2) 45 for perpendicularity; derived from *gignoskein*, know.

39. Heath (2) 52 & 51; for cube, JL (1) 13 f.

40. Stapleton (1) 2.

41. *Ib.* 2 n 4.

42. All this section from Stapleton, who gives refs. and fuller account.

43. Olmstead 337. I have no space in this book to go into clock mechanisms and dials.

44. C (24) 7; Gundel RE *Planetes*.

45. *Tim.* 38 cd, cf. 39 cd. For debt to Pythag., Jahn.

46. *Meteor.* i 6, 343 a (20), and 343 b.

47. D (1) 30 and Simplik. *de caelo* 471, 1: DK 12A19 cf. Aetios (ii 5, 6: DK 12A18 cites Anaximandros with Metrodoros of Chios & Krates); Heath (1) 42 f is unconvincing.

48. JL (1) index Mages, Ostanes, Zoroaster etc.; B (2) etc.

49. Diog. L ix 46. *Diakosmos*: Arist. *Met.* 986 ab; Plout. *Per.* iv; Diod. xii 20; Sext. Emp. *adv. M.* ix 27; Porph. *de antro* vi. Also Diels *dox.* ii 15, 3, Demokritos dealt "first with the fixed stars, after that with the planets", cf. C (24) 7.

50. *Vors.* 55B14.

51. Olmstead 337.

52. *De div.* i 57.

53. JL (1) 125.

54. Vitruv. ix 5, 4; in Loeb ed. F. Granger interprets as I do; Dicks disagrees. See also D (1) 27 and (3) 148 f. Olmstead 336 swallows the lot. Lucret. v 621 ff; D (4) 139. For Anaxagoras: Zafiropalo's ed. of the *Frogs*. For sphere 320; eclipses 321; stars as burning stone or metal 316 f; Milky Way as underearth-sun's shadow 320.

55. For cycle, N (1) 7, 95, 102, 140, 142, n 3; date W (8) 170.

56. Olmstead 342 n; *Clouds* 423 & *Birds* 414; Ail, VH xiii 12.

57. Arat 753. For confusions in Attic calendar about this time, D (4) 89.

58. S (4) 113; N (1) 140. Papyrus: D (4) 88, ed. F. Blass 1887, based at least in part on genuine Eudoxan ideas.

59. *Tim.* 39 c; circles 36 cd; against the denial of his concept of sphericity, D (1) 39 n 66.

60. Diod. i 98; *de plac. phil* (ascribed Plout.) ii 12; Ail. VH x 7; Cens. xix.

His geometry: Prokl. *Comm. Eukleid.* & Sext. Emp. *Hypot.* iii 4 & *adv. M.* 367. On the Nile: Diod. i 41. For Philolaos' Great Year: D (4) 75.

61. Ach. Tat. *Isag. in Arat.* xxiv; D (4) 88 f. *Daktylos*: D (4) 9 f.

62. W (4) 227 f; D (4) 164 f & 251: he takes a rather sceptical attitude to Bab. origins. Webb 33 on Virgin and Spica; but the connection seems to me clear. We must realise that, with the lack of reliable sky-charts or spheres, there was sure to be much confusion in detail in such transmissions, esp. in the early and perhaps decisive phases. For Amaxa: Kugler (1) i 250 & (3) 55. Papyrus: Oxy. 1802.

63. Sollberger; JL (3) 358 etc.

64. Strab. ii 119 & xvii 806; Sen. QN vii 3; Aristot. *Met.* xii 8; Vitr. ix 9; Diog. L. viii 86 ff, citing also Sotion. See D (4) 151 ff; calendar 188 f.

65. Diog. L. as cited; *Dialogues*, (?) Egyptian beastfables. Quarrel: denied by Tannery (1) 296 n 4 & Heath (1) 192. Note Nich. is really Aristotle—*Nich. Ethics*: i 12, 1101 b 27; x 2 m 1172 b 9.

66. Diog. L. viii 90 f; AP vii 744.

67. *De Div* ii 42; Cr (1) 9.

68. N (1) 188; Aristot. *de caelo* ii 12 (29 a7) Strab. xvii 1, 29 (806), Bidez (1) ch iv; F (1) i 17 & 44; Koster 25 ff etc.

69. N (1) 153 f; Simplik. cited Dreyer 126; plants 127 f.

70. Boker; W (4) 225.

71. N (1) 183.

72. W (1) 32–4; N (7) 251; Mich. Pap. iii 149, *klima* of Syria. In the principle of half the ecliptic rising during the day, etc., we find also links with Aratos (already discussed).

73. N (1) 185.

74. N (25) on two tables discussed by Ugnad.

75. N (1) 146, also 158 & 80. Cun. texts: N (25). For Deiphantes giving numbers "merely an instrumental significance" (cf. Aristot. post. anal. 74 a 20–4 & Prokl. *Eukl. comm.* viii 5–8) and the link with 16th c. algebra: J. Klein 1968 135.

76. D (4) 168–71.

77. D (4) 175 & 228.

5. THE WORLD OF THE STARS

1. Am. J. Sem. Lang. & Lit. xxiv 333.

2. Idiotai is contrasted with the State: Thouk. i 124 & iii 10: SIG (Chios 4th c.) 1013, 6; opposed to phatries, *ib.* 987, 28 (4th c.). Split in Plato and Iranian links: Des Places 139 with refs.; Bidez (1) 19 & 91.

3. Eilers.

4. Gatha iv 10 f, Darm. 306; Bousset (2) 160 ff; Rougier is wrong.

5. C (5).

6. Wheelwright 45; Aetios-Pl out. i Dox. 276.

7. Wheelwright fr. 43 p. 58 and 63; Dox. 471.

8. Delatte *Etudes* 308: Carcopino (2) 267: Detienne 94. 105 f, 108 & 140 ff; Kastor in Pl out 282 a (FGH 250 F16); Kratylos, Detienne 106. Plout. *de gen.* Sok. 591 c, on stars as islands kept for gods, but moon for *epichthonioi* daimons: G. Méautis 63. For catechism: Aristot on philos.: A. Delatte 274 f; P. Capelle 6 ff; also Iambl. in Stob. i 49, 39 (W. i 378, 14); Herakleitos: fr. 87 (Wehrli) and RHR 1957 132 ff; F (1) iii 218.

9. CI Att. i 442; Rohde *Psyche* (2nd ed.) ii 258; *Peace* 831.

10. Sogliano *Not. Sciav.* ii 1905 377–80; Wiegand *Abh. Ak. Berl.* 1905 (Miletos) and Haussouiller (2).

11. Helen 1014–6; *Melanippe* fr. 487 N; *Peace* 832 f and Schol. on 835; C (28) 95 & 104 f. For Ion, Diehl RE ix 1864.

12. Katasterisms: C (28) 104 f, the whole third lecture; L. Friendländer iii 280, *Darstellung aus d. Sitt. Roms* (10th) 1922.

Shuttle Maidens: Ant. Lib. *met.* 25; Korinna fr. 28 (Edmonds). Australians: the Bora: Meston, *Science of Man* i 10, cf. i 79, R. H. Mathews, also in *American Anthropologist* n.s. iii 339; also F. E. Williams in JRAI 1923; G. Roheim, *Australian Totemism* 1925 53, 112, 441; J. W. Gregory, *The Dead Heart of Austr.* 1906 229; E. Palmer JAI 1883 xiii 293. Ascent: E. M. Curr, *The Austr. Race* 1886 i 303. Milky Way as road to heaven, Palmer *l.c.* General material and discussion, JL (7). The Budera man was connected with the class-mark.

13. (1) AP vii 670, cf. 64, 391 (2) EG 41 (3) IG ix 6, 241, 6 (4) IG xii 1, 143 (Rhodes); EG 184, 4 (Korkyra, 3rd c.); BCH li 1927 387 (Kyme) (5) Athens EG 90 (6) EG xii 7, 123, 5 f. Cf. Cicero's desire for an apotheosis of his daughter Tullia.

For Cock: C (31) 292; Diog. L. viii 31; Delatte *Vie de Pyth.* 1922 34; Plout. QC iv 5, 2 (670 d); Ail. VH iv 17; Iambl. *Vit. Pyth.* 84 (49 Deubner); Boehm, *de symb. pyth.* 1905 20 ff. Moon Ail. NA iv 29; sun, Iambl. *protr.* xxi. (Pythagoras opposed to Abaris who examined entrails of chickens: Delatte 192 ff.) Coins: C (31) 290. Mēn and months: Strab. xii 557 & 577; Prokl. *in Plat. Tim.* iv 251; Spartian. *Carac.* vii. Kratinos: Athen. ix 374 a; Babr. 124, 12. Mazdeans: C (31) 297. Plin. x 21, 46.

14. Tim. 40 cd. For rel of *Tim.* and *Laws* x: Bidez (1) ch x. 78 ff; Duhem (1) 1,274; Koster (2) 48 ff—polemic v. Reitzenstein, ch. viii; Cr (1) 7–9. Also Grube 176; Harward 19 f.

15. A. E. Taylor; Raeder; Des Places; F. Müller; Theiler; Frits; Pavlu (1–5); Dicks (4) ch. iv, with refs. Autolykos: Dicks (4) 255 & 322.

16. Bidez (1) 1 f.

17. Er: Bidez (1) 3, 43 ff & 91. The ref. to Sirens suggests Pythag. allegory, C (23) 529; Delatte *Etudes* 1915 261; Frank *Plato* 28 ff & 201–15, cf. *Rep.* vii 530 d. Cycles in *Politicus,* Bidez (1) ch. ix. *Philippika* of Theopompos and Iranian sources, Bidez (1) 77.

18. See n. 17 above, also later passage from *Life Ap. Tyana* i 25, 2 & 34.

19. *Epinomis* 978 b7 to 979 b3; 986 b8–d4; 977 e5; 978 a6–7; 977 e5; 973 b2 & 989 e1. In general F (1) ii 196 ff with refs.

20. *Ib.* 980 a8–9 and 984 d3.

21. *Ib.* 985 c1 ff; 984 b2 to 985 c1; 981 c5 ff. Contact with unseen by dreams, revelation, oracle, no ref. to astrology.

22. *Ib.* 987 d; to 988 b, cf. 987 a, also *Laws* vii 821 a.

23. *Ib* 986 b8–d4; Theiler 353. "World, Olympos, Heaven," 977 a6–b5, cf. these names in ps. Philolaos, *Vors.* 44 a 16; Theiler 351; F (1) ii 210.

24. *Ib.* 991 b5 to 992 c3; geometry and stereometry, 990 de.

25. F (3) ii 213 f. For following paragraph: *Apolog.* 26 d; *Krat.* 397 cd; mechanistic, *Laws* 967 a, *Epin.* 983 c. *Lysias,* fr. 73 Th. (53 Sch.): Athen. 551 e. Kinesias: *Birds* 1372–1409 (insulting Hekate shrine); schol. *Frogs* 366. Nilsson, *Gesch.* i 685 f (Plato *Gorg.* 501 e). Shamans: JL (5). Anaxagoras: Dodds 188 f; F. Detenne 30 ff; J. S. Morrison CR xxxv 1941 5 n 2; Taylor CQ xi 1917 81–7; Davison CQ iii 1953 42–5; Plout. *Perik.* vi; Dicks (4) 227 f underestimates the stress of the situation, Africa overestimates, as does Bury CAH v 383. Diviners: Nilsson, *Gr. Pop. Rel.* 133 ff; Dodds 190 & 202; Diod. xii 38 f; Plout. *Perik.* xxxii; Adcock CAH v 478. Nikias: Plout. *Nik.* xxxiii; Farrington (1) i 96 f. *Apol.* 26 d.

26. Jaeger *Aristoteles* 133 ff; Des Places (2); Bidez (1) 37; Bignone, *Aristot. perduto* ii 341 ff. Fr. 10 for Seizure of God in sleep or at approach of death, cf. *Tim.* 71 & *Epin.* 985 c; later dropped by Aristot., *de div. per sonnum.* Bk. iii

of *peri philos.* echoes Epin. 878 ce and cavern allegory. No early astral cults: Nilsson (4).

27. Cr 9; Jaeger 136 ff & 156 ff; B (3); Bidez (2) ii 257; Plin. xxx 2, 3; Diog. L. i pr. 8—on mages, whom Aristot. declares to be more ancient than Egyptians, as also Hermippos, Eudoxos in *Voyage round World,* and Theopompos. Aristot. on East: D (4) 146; *de Caelo* 292 a8.

28. *De Meteor.* i 6; Gundel (1).

29. Graubard 28 f. Symmetries: D (2) 204; Met. 1072a 9–17 with Ross' note. Kalippos: D (4) 190 f.

30. N (1) 187; Prokl. *in Tim.* (Diehl) iii 151; Duhem (2) 1, 275.

31. Diog. L. vii 87 f; F (1) ii 286 f. Daimon: *Tim.* 90 c5; Plout. *de virt. mor.* iii 441 c.

32. Fr. 675 R; Edmonds *Lyra Gr.* iii 400; composed a little after 342–341.

33. *De Mixt.* 142.

34. Angus 266; D. L. vii 138; Macr. *comm.* ii 12, 11; Philon, *de migr. Abr.* 39 (C.-W 220), *de plant.* 7 (C.-W. 28) *de prov.* i 40; *Quis rer. div. haer.* 31 (C.-W. 155).

35. Following quotation from Stobaios ii 7, 11: SVF i 216, perhaps from Zenon's *Politeia,* Van Straaten 186 f. Inherent necessity: Cic. *de fin.* iv 14; Chrysippos SVF iii 4 & iii 12; i 555; F (1) ii 282 where Kleanthes would put universal nature, Chr. human nature.

36. Jos. C. Ap. i 129; Vitr. ix 6; Schwarz sceptical, cf. Schnabel; Kugler (1) ii 2, 603–30; Bidez (3) 48–52.

Athens: Plin. vi 37, 123; Kos, Herondas iii 54; B (3) 96; Cr (1) 14; D (2) against overlarge claims by Schnabel. *History:* Schnabel 350 ff for frags.; E. Schwartz RE iii 314 Lehmann-Haupt. *Klio* xxii 1928 125 ff.

37. Bel: Schnabel 76; moon and earth-shadow: CCAG v 2, 132, 31; *Dox.* 358 ff & 582, 26. Possibly an earlier work on Chaldeans before Berosos, used e.g. by *Epinomis*; Eudemos fr. 117; Schnabel 108, 226 & 246; also RE v 672, 40 ff. In general *sv* Zoroaster index Bidez (2) ii 159, 15 ff etc. Dualism: cf. Zosimos, *Alch. Gr.* ii 229 ff; Reitzenstein, *Poim.* 102 ff.

38. Plin. ii 191; Bidez (5); Kroll (15) 50; Gundel in B (3) 200 ff. Berosos does not seem to unite the 2 luminaries and 5 planets: Vitr. ix 6, 2; Schnabel 350, 15.

39. NQ iii 29, 1–9 on to 30 end.

40. Farrington (1) i 94.

41. *Tim.* 42; F (1) ii 109 ff.

42. Isok., *Philipp.* 121, with Soph. *O.T.* 1029; Eur. *Iph. T.* 417; Isok. xi 6; *Trag. adesp.* 100; Farrington (1) i 94–6.

43. Athen. ix 22.

6. MAN AS THE UNIVERSE

1. Plin ix 56, 115; vii 59; xxxvii 2, 25; ii 34; vi 90 & viii 115. Kroll (5) suggests there is much more of him in Plin., cf. Schnabel 130 & 132; Oder i 861. Stones: H. Martin; Gundel (2) 583.

2. Posidonios, meteorology: Graubard 30 f.

3. Vitr. ix 6, 2; BM Rm. iv 224; Kugler ii 2, 558–62; Schaumberger; dates by Sachs.

4. Plin. vii 57, 193 (Berosos); B (6); Valens *anth.* (K) 301, 27, cf. 150, 22 & 142; Maternus *Math.* iv pr. (K); Bidez (3) 84 f; CCAG viii 3, 102.

5. *Horasis:* Val. *anth.* iii 12, 150 & ix pr. 329, 18; C (3). Synopsis: Cod. Par. Gr. 2425: CCAG viii 3, 102. *Pinax:* Heph. ii 10, see CCAG viii 2, 64. Ideas: B (6) (7) (8) 372 (9) 340 f.

6. Book of Mysteries of Dorotheos of Sidon: CCAG v 3, 115, 22, cf 117, 33; C (16) 159 with n 35 & 28 (208 ff); B (6) 1928 ff; C (4) 311 ff.

7. Boll RE xi 1929; Diod. ii 29, 6; Psellos, or rather Iambl. & Proklos *Cat. MS Alch. Gr.* vi 85 ff & 163, 26, cf. Plato *Phileb.* 29 b.

8. C (4) 311; Christ, *Gesch. gr. Lit.* 1924 vii 2, 2, 906; Kroll (2) pref.

9. Schnabel 18–210 for all frags. Plin. ii, vii.

10. B (6) 1928 ff; C (4) 311 ff; N (19) 185 f.

11. N (1) 183; Sen. QN vii 17, 1 & iv 1; CCAG i 80, 8 & 113 n 1; C (10); Gundel (1); B (10) 368; Kroll (6) 115; Bidez (3) 80 & 83.

12. Sen QN vii 3–4; BL 575; Rehm (2).

13. Bidez (1); Dicks (4) 167; Simplik. *in de caelo* 495, 28 f H.; Diod. ii 30, 3; Damask. in Phot. 242; Euseb. PE i 10, 16; BL 93 n 2 for further material; Nonnos xl 369 ff—patterned, *poikilos* (starry).

14. *Dox.* Diels 224 f; Sen. QN vii 4, 1.

15. Teukros: Gundel (6); RE xviii 3, 122, 158 ff; C (19); Porphyr. etc. call him Babylonian. For Seleukeia: Tarn, *Greeks in Bactria* 15. Not the fortress on Nile as taken by Eisler and Gundel. Importance, B (10). Translated into Pehlevi etc. N (1) 189.

16. N (1) 157.

17. N (1) 158.

18. Ziegler (3) 570 ff; C (16) 277 n 46 & 273 n 11; Bidez (1) 40 & 168 n 11.

19. *Symp.* 190 b. Link with Empedokles, Dümmler (1) 222.

20. C (23) 122 n 4; *Tim.* 44d; Selene double-sexed, Orphic Hymn ix 5; Lobeck *Aglaophamus* 932; correspondence in Pythag. theory: H. Berger 206 f. Also Campbell 173–5; Sanch. in Euseb. PE i 10; Gaster *Thespis* 183; Arist. *Birds* 693 ff; Plout. *mor.* 926 f.

21. CH x 11.

22. Orph. fr. no 168 (Kern 201).

23. Macrob. *Comm.* i 24.

24. Macrob. *Sat.* i 21.

25. Same imagery in magic papyri: PGM iii 243: xiii 776–2; xxi 3–7. In the *Kaphalia* of Mani (lxx, 1, 169–72), C (25) 26; West, *Sacred Bks. of East* 123 for Persian Bundahish; Blochet RHR xxxi 243 ff; *causal* etc. 10, 28, Kaiser.

26. F (3) iv 55–7 & 61–3.

27. *De hebd.* xi; Boll NJ xvi 1913 137–40 & (2) 211 ff. Egyptian basis: Roscher, *Abh. Sächs. Ges.* xviii 5 (1911) 12 & *Memnon* v 3–4 1912 fig. 1; Scott iii 501; F (3) iv 63–42 Archer: F (3) iv 62 n 34; BL 330 f; Cumont (17).

28. CH iv 2; v 5; ix 2; xii 21; *Asclep.* 1 = F (3).

29. K. Kerenyi (2) 51: Heloid. x 4. For *kosmos*: sit, *Od.* xiii 77, shame viii 179; Pythag. *plac.* ii 1, & D.L. viii 48, cf Philol 21; Parmenides, Theophr. cited DL *l.c.* Xen. *mem.* i 1, 11. Hermetic astrology: *Iatromath. Hermetis* xxvi 1 (Ideler 1, 387 ff; F (1) i 94 & 130.

30. Stob. Exc. xxix, cf. CCAG viii 1, 265, 8 & n 1; Scott *Hermetica* i 532. See also JL (1) 175 f and index Microcosm; F (1) i 126 f; Maternus *math.* iii pr. 2 & CCAG i (Cod. Flor.) 146.

31. CH xi.

32. CH. xiii 11.

33. CH xviii; F (1) i 91.

34. Akhenaten: F. Preisigke. *Schr. d. Pap. Inst. Heidelb.* i 1920 5–10.

35. CH xvi 4–17: F (1) i 91 f. For Sun: Plin, ii 5, 13; Cumont, *Théol. Sol.* 459 f & 456 f; *Epin.* 986 a. Sun fed by earth-exhalations: D (4) 230. Plato and Sun D (4) 99.

36. F (1) i 95; also Serv. *Aen.* vi 714 & xi 52; *Poimandres* & CCAG iii 100.

37. Ptol. *Tetrab.* i 14; BL 163 f; Valens i 8; P. Mich. 149; *Symp.* 190b.

38. *Phaidros* 246 e; *Vors.* 32A16, cf. B7. Also B (10) 186 & n 2; Gemin. (Manit.) 263; Kerenyi ARW xxii 274; Bayet (1) 146–9. And D (4) 115, 65 & 108; certainly not the 12 gods set up by younger Peisistratos in Athenian agora,

Thouk. vi 54. For Pythag. influence on Plato: D (4) 111 (8 whorls), 117 & 130 (math. harmony and number), 95 (relative speeds).

39. *Laws* viii 828 bc & 737 e (with C. Ritter's commentary 131) cf. 988 b & *Epinom*, 986 bc; *daimones* 828 b, cf. 828 c7 & 848 d2. D (4) 114; development from *Rep.* to *Tim.* 113 & 149.

40. *Phaidr.* 347 a3; *Archontes, Laws* 903 b7; 246 eg (*stratia* of gods and daimons) 247 a3; taxiarchs, Kerenyi 251; B (33) 82; Bousset (1) 326, 11 & 12, angels of apoc. xxi 12. Chariots: Kerenyi; Robin, *Notice* in *Phèdre* 1933 p. lcxxiii.

41. Bidez (1) 62 & 174; *Phaidr.* 152 c, 252 e & 253 b.

42. Stilbon: Eudox v 10 (Blass); Aristot. *de mundo* 392 a 26. *Stilbon Apollonos* at Kommagene: cf. Plin ii 39; Apul. *de mundo* ii; BL 100 f.

43. BL 88 ff; A. E. Taylor (2) 194 f on *Tim.* 38 d2; C (24); *Epin.* 986 e; F (1) i 95 n 3.

44. Oxy. 804 & 235.

45. C (24) 35; B (3) 48–50.

46. BL 97 ff. Saturn: B (3) 126 f.

47. B (3) 48–50 & 127–39; Gundel (7) ch. vi.

48. F (1) i 97; BL 95; mnemonic lists PLM iv 143–6; Firmic. ii 10 k calls it the royal sign, cf. *Anecd. Ludwich* 107, 6; Nonnos xxxviii 268.

49. Nonnos *l.c.* See also Piccaluga esp. 197–209 for much on Aries and water-cults, with astrologic interpretation of Golden Fleece, etc. I have no space here to analyse.

50. BL. 131 f; Manil. iv 123 ff & 502 ff; Ptol. *Tetr.* i 8; *Philosophum.* iv 3 (physignomists); Serv. *Aen.* xi 259. Shorn of gold: Eratosth. *Rel.* 124 Robert; anger and fire: Firmic. ii 10 K; *Anec. Ludwich* 105 & 109; BL 132.

51. N (1) 188.

52. B (14); C (17) 268; N (1) 187.

53. Graubard 16.

54. C (5) 81 & (2) 206; AP ix 177; B (34) 19 & 39.

55. Sen. *Suas.* iv; C (5) 82 & (1) 88, cf. Cic. *de div.* ii 47, 97 ff.

56. Sext. Emp. *adv. math.* vii 93.

57. Upright: Angus 260: Kern *Orph. Fr.* 337 f; Plot. *enn.* i 6, 9; Prok. *in remp.* ii 164, 12 (52, 10 Kroll); Manil. ii 115. JL (1) ch. i.

7. HELLENISTIC ASTROLOGY: EGYPT

1. Plout. *Ant.* xxxiii 2.

2. Justin xxvi 3 ff; Kall. poem & Catullus lxvi; Wilamowitz (1) i 197 ff.

3. Loeb. Kallim. *Aitia* no 228.

4. Douris in FHG ii 477: Athen. xii 50 (535 f, 536 a); cf. Plout. *Demetr.* xli 3; C (2) 27 n 2; Eisler (2) 39 ff.

5. Plout. *Ant.* liv; Jeanmaire *La Sibylle* 128; Bayet (1) 168; Eisler (2) fig. 19 & 260. Sabina: Strang (1) pl. ix.

6. Campbell 39 & 91.

7. Vermaseren (1) 74. Mithras = Noonsun.

8. Macrob. *Sat.* i 18 end. Porph. *de antro* xiv (N); Diod. i 11; Euseb. PE iii 11 (PL xxi 205); Plout. *de Is.* xxxv, cf. Hdt. ii 42. Kern *Orph.* fr. 37, 59; *nebrizo* Magnien *Mystères d'Eleusis* 196 & 199–203; Dardanos, Lykophron 75; Mayassis 593 f; JL (2) 380 f etc.

9. Campbell 97; *Yasht* xiii 2 f; Hdt. i 96–100; Plout. *mor.* 749 e; *Greater Bundashin* iii 5; *Denkart* (Madan) 203.

10. RHR cli 1957 12; Cook *Zeus* i 1915 frontispiece; Picard-Schmitter 30 f & 36 f; V. Loret *Flore pharaonique* 56.

11. Euseb. PE iii 11, 23; 45 & 47; Campbell 143 & 175.

12. *Phaidr.* 246 c; Campbell 143 n 67; JL (1) *sv* Kneph.

13. Budge, *Book of Dead,* Egg of Sun 120 and 458; cosmic 173 etc. Reymond *sv* index: Island of the Egg.

14. BL 439; N (19) no 61 pp. 1–6.

15. Gagé (1) 144–6.

16. C (16) ch. iv.

17. Dörrie.

18. Cf. *RG divi Saporis*; A. Maricq, *Syria* 1958.

19. Humann 328 f; Olivieri 15; BL 439 fig. 4 (one star at tail left out).

20. Gagé (1) 220 f. Inscr.: *Anatolian Stud.* xix 1969 141 f; for Sandes, Nonnos xxxiv 192; Roscher *Lex.* iv 322, 39.

21. N (19) 15.

22. Puchstein 369; Jalabert-Mouterde IGL SYR i 3, 51; N (19) 16. Also CCAG i 107 f; vi 66, 16 to 67, 7; N (1) 147 f; BL 514 ff. Trajan: Toynbee, *Art of Rs.* 1965 pl. 41; Strong (1) 85 & 93; Elegebal: Strong, *R. Sculpt.* 308 & pl. xciv; Studniczka. Coin: Cohen iv 240.

23. Hdt. ii 82.

24. Chabas (1) & (2) 127–235; Read 19–26 & 60–9; Bakir 429; Brusch on Hdt. ed. Stein 1881 99 n; P. Sallier in BM, New Kingdom.

25. N (1) 198; Meissner.

26. Plin. vii 57, 20; he has Atlans.

27. FHG ii 499 & 510; Cic. *de div.* i 19, 36; Diod. ii 31, 9; Plin. vii 57, 193 & 160; Censor. xvii 4; Simplik. *comm. de caelo* i 3 (Heiberg) 117, 27 f. And Simplik. ii 12 (H. 506, 13–15) citing Porphyr.; Prok. *in tim.* (Diehl i 100, 29 f).

28. D.L. i pr. 2; Mart. Cap. viii 812; Simplik. i 3 (H. 117, 25 f.)

29. Diod. i 81. D (2) 307 f. Loaves: Gillings.

30. F. Le Lionnais in Posener, *Dict. Eg. Civil.* 1962 160–3.

31. N (21): Pap. Carlsberg 1 & 9.

32. H. Schäfer.

33. J. Capart CE xix 38 1944 263; S. Davis *Man* lv 1955 132–5.

34. Morenz; Černy in Parker (4) 35–48.

35. Faulkner 347 f; 357 (see JNES xxv 159); 373; 458–60.

36. PT 374 a & 782 e; Griffiths (1) 27 n 41 & 41; Rusch 16 ff; Zabkar for dead king as Ba. Morning-star: Griffiths 43 & 41.

37. Černy, *Anc. Eb. Relig.* 1952 82.

38. Griffiths 41; Breasted 146; Zander *Death as an Enemy* 1960 8; Zabkar 36 etc., see 74 pyramidion of Amenehet III.

39. Griffiths (2) 108 f for refs.; de is. 359 c, 21 & 368 d, 44; Wainwright (2). Also N. M. Holley JHS lxix 1949 43.

40. Theban Rescension, Budge 1960, ch. xcviii & xlii: pp. 183 & 433; ch. clxxii 36–9. Budge, Pap. of Ani xv 40; PT 1454–8.

41. PT 1155 c; 749 e, cf. 491 b.

42. Year: 956b. Headband: 1048 b.

43. PT 959; 409; 882 b.

44. PT 1210 a; Budge (2) 240 f.

45. *Bk. of Dead* xxxix Budge (2) 232; also 644 f for names of the seven and Bull (Pap. Ani); and 242.

46. Wainwright (2) for refs.; also for changes in position of Great Bear. Note Dwn-'mw became god of Hipponon, XVIII nome of Upper Egypt: Kees AZ lviii 95; cf. god Anher or Onuris who had similar attitude; he lifts only one hand, but stretches a cord between them: Daressy *Statues de divinités* nos. 38025, 38028; cf. possibles, 38024 & 38023. GR text: Nock JEA xv 231. More on Set iron in Wainwright (1) and JL (3). What we call Cassiopeia seems in Egyptian skies to have been the man who stretches arms, no cord, between Uplifter and Bull.

47. Sheshmu: PT 403; 1019; 1250 and Budge (2) 245. See also PT 1098. Street: 334 (Faulkner p. 77 n). Also Griffiths (2) 126 f.

48. PT 1207 & 251; morning and evening stars as Ba of Horos of Edfu, Zabkar 14. PT 1720 on Gt. Green; 929. Also 821.

8. MORE ON EGYPT

1. Zabkar in general; 14 for dekans. Names: Budge (4) ii.
2. Černy (1).
3. N (1) 81 f.
4. N (3); Winlock.
5. Griffiths (2); JL (3). Demotic pap., N (21).
6. Autolykos *de ort.* etc., theorem 6 (Hultsch 118).
7. Winlock 462 thinks Djoser installed the 365-day year, which may be true, though his historical scheme is based on the incorrect idea of Sothic observations.
8. F (1) i 115 f; Gundel (4); BL 215 ff.
9. N (1) 86.
10. N (1) 87 f.
11. F (1) i 115; BL 215 ff.
12. Scott vi; Stob. i 21, 9 (i 189, 9 W.); F (1) 118–20 & (3) iii 35–43.
13. Ejaculate: Gundel (4) 235 n 2; F (3) iii p. liv; Scott iii 380. Cold: CH ix 3 (97, 9). Gt. Bear: Valens xiii 27. Demons: C (26).
14. Gundel (4) 226 & 240; F (3) iii 40 n 15. Gundel (10) 338 f; BL 229 n 1.
15. Plin. younger vi 16, 11; 20, 9.
16. Firm. Mat. *math.* ii 4, 4–6, cf. Iambl. *myst.* ix 2; Mart. Cap. ii 200.
17. R. MacMullen, *Soldier and Civilian* 1963 exp. 60 ff for refs.
18. N (1) 88 f.
19. Winlock in Budge (2) 247.
20. BM Guide, 1st 2nd 3rd Eg. Rooms 1924 133, date 500–350 B.C. coffin no 6678.
21. N (1) 58 & (6).
22. N (1) 89.
23. E. M. Bruins in Derchain (1) 157 f.
24. Schott in Gundel (4).
25. W (4) 226; Derchain (1) 153.
26. Schott (2) 176; W (4) 229 f.
27. Spiegelberg; Budge (2) 246–7 with refs.
28. N (1) 67.
29. W (1).
30. N (21) & (6).
31. W (2).
32. Derchain (2) 19 & 13–6 on establishment of order and Ma'at.
33. Ingham.
34. D (1) 33 f. For earlier *oktaeteris* cycle, G. Thomson (1); also on Euktemon D (1) 34 n 44.
35. S (4).
36. N (24).
37. S (4) 113 f.
38. CCAG iv 24; *Mél. Glotz* 1932 i 257 f on Adonis; *Syria* xvi 1935 46 ff.
39. Cic. *de div.* i 57, 130.
40. Manil. i 401–6; cf. Bidez (2) Zoroaster fr. 40.
41. Plout. *de Is.* xlvii.
42. Bidez (2) 124 f; *Yasht* viii 44 (Darm. ii 426) etc.
43. *Yasht* viii 32 ff, 45 ff; *Bundahish* vii 1 ff; ix 3, Cf. *Geponika* on effect of Dogstar on harvest. *Yasht* viii 36; Bidez (2) i 126 f.

44. Hughes (1); Pap. Cairo 31222; Cr (1) 16; N (1) 90 f & 95, also (21). Ptol. knew the system well, *Alm.* vi 3; he arranged his tables of syzygies on it; no connection with Metonic cycle.

45. Pap. Berlin 8345; Englebrecht 94 ff Riess (7); B (32). In the Nech.-Pet. tradition. Spiegelberg *Dem. Pap. Berl.* pl. 97.

46. At no point are the predictions for the same heavenly bodies in the same sign identical in the two texts; in one item alone are they at all alike: Hughes n 45.

47. Hughes on error BL 367 n 1; Gundel (11).

48. Heph. i 23 (E. 91–7); Derchain (1) 151 f.

49. CCAG v 1, 204, 17; F (1) i 104 f & 95 n 2; CCAG iv 154 cf. 124; C (13).

9. EGYPTIAN ASTROLOGY

1. Budge (3) 224–6; Chabas (1) 24.

2. Griffiths (2) 40, 97 & 107; Schott Urk. vi 89, 18 f; P. Sallier iv 2, 6 ff; P. Chester Beatty i 8, 9 ff; De Buck *Coffin Texts* ii 37 bc & ii 38 g; ii 4 ih. Weakened form in Ploutarch: Horos takes diadem from mother's head.

3. Chabas 104 & 78; Budge (2) 159–61.

4. N (15). The gods too could be Philadelphian. All names but Persian Arsakes and Egyptian Sarapammon (marginal) are Greek. Which helps the gymnasion hypothesis.

5. Cf. Ptol. Alm. vi 2, 3 (used for computing the mean syzygies); P. Carls. ix; Ryl. 27; P. Lund 35 a. Other elements in the last two papyri are known from Bab. texts of Seleukid period. Months named after signs: RE v 991 (no 43); Oxy 465.

6. Pap. Paris 1 (of same period) says that according to Eudoxos and Demokritos summer-solstice falls on 20 or 19 Hathor: incorrect for period of Eudoxos but right for about 185 B.C. Hibeh 27 gives fixed dates for equinoxes and summer-solstices that lead to c. 300.

7. P. Carlsb. ix.

8. *Kata selenen* in Doura horoscopes (Dura Rep. iv nos 220 & 236, 3rd c. A.D.); probably in our text a complete list of 25 years was given. It is of interest to find Egyptian forms of computation in a gymnasion-document of a wholly Greek provenance.

9. Parker (5).

10. Thus a solar eclipse in first 4 hours of day, and in southern sky, was thought to affect Egypt alone; but one in IIII part, in last 4 hours and in northern sky, would seem to affect Egypt, Crete, Amor, and the Hebrews.

11. C (17).

12. Schaumberger, *Ergänz.* 3 1935 321 ff. For troubles in 2nd c., R. W. Pestman CE xl 1965 157 ff, and omen xv 4–9. Priests; J. Schwartz BIFAO xlviii 70 f; Posener IFAO Bibl. Et. xi 22 ff.

13. Ungnad (2) par. 66 b.

14. Parker (5) 35 f for disks.

15. B (17) Abh, 7, 25–37; Weidner (1) (1a) (2). More on moon, van Wynghene; Pannekoek 43 & R. C. Thompson (2) 95 & 107.

16. Erichsen; N (1) 95; Derchain (1) 148.

17. E. B. Allen; Caminos 88..

18. Spiegelberg (3); N (22) 121 ff, with refs. Strasb. D 521. Coffin-lid: N (22) 115 f. Planetary order in Egypt is (a) acc. to synodic period (b) acc. to Houses: Hathor temple of Dendera (c) acc. to exaltation: Osiris-chapel of same temple: 122 n 21. For Scorpion: Ptol. Tetr. i 19.

19. Berl. 3279; and P. Dem. Berl. 8279; N (7) 209–50; Spiegelberg Dem. Pap. Berl. pl. 97 & Stobart tablets (Brugsch, *Nouv. Rech.* 1856); F. L. Griffith.

20. Rémondon, esp. 142 f; A. Swiderek *J. Jur. Pap.* vii–viii 259; C. Préaux

Mus. Helvet. x fasc. 3–4 (July 1953) 204 & 210–15; Peremans AC iv 1935 403–17; CH xvi.

Works on Egypt by Egyptians: Manethos & Chairemon. Greeks: Leon of Pella, Hekateios, Palaiphatos, Philistios of Naukratis, Asklepiades of Mendes, Seleukos of Alex., Ploutarch; the Peripatician Aristokles, Iamblichos, neoplatonist Asklepiades—Otto *Priester* ii 215 ff.

21. N (22).

10. HERMETIC CORRESPONDENCES

1. Sext. Emp. v 33 ff.
2. N (13) 163; Oxy. 235.
3. Clement *strom.* vi 4, 35–7; JL (1) 169.
4. Iambl. *de myst.* viii 1.
5. Gundel (1) 9–40; Turcan (1) 394 f.
6. Manil. i 40 ff; C (2). Gundel has reserves.
7. F (1) i 79 f; RE ii 1796.
8. Gundel (1) 31.
9. Lefevre (1) 33, 95 ff; Piper (2).
10. Suys 14; Picard-Schmitter 32 & 74. Groups visited funerary chapels, conducted by priests who read the hieroglyphs.
11. *Apotelesmata* of M. vi 738 etc.; Garnett; Kroll (7); Riess (3) with B (35). For date Boll 129–31.
12. CCAG viii 2, 87, 1 f.
13. BL 185 ff. Moon: Valens vii 5 (K. 290, 14–23); CCAG i 103, 1–30; vi 64, 26–65, 21; viii 1, 231–5 to 31; BL 245 ff.
14. F (1) i 103.
15. CCAG viii 4, 95.
16. Anon, 204, 13 & 18; 205, 17. For the actual king, Manetho (Loeb) fr. 68, 69 a, 69 b (26th dyn., 663–522); but no evidence he ever dabbled in astrology. For relevation: CCAG vii 178; v 2, 143; viii 4, 131 f & index 271. Kroll erred in thinking A.D. 200 too early; Gundel (4) 92 suggests "Petosiris" used some 6th c. Egyptian MS—unlikely. Mathematician Timaios (c. 1st cent. A.D.) held N. & Hermes among earliest astrols. (Antiochos, CCAG viii 3, 116, 9–11). cf. Kroll (8) & (6) 2; C (13); CCAG viii 3, 111 n 2. Texts, Riess (3) & (4); bits in Valens and Antiochos as also Thessalos: B (10) 372 f & 144 n, 146 n; (3) 23 f; Darmstadt; Kroll (9); C (14). Boll takes latest date for N. & P. as 146 B.C.; Eisler 193 f not convincing for date after 132.

Salm. much imitated. Harpokration: C (11) & (12); CCAG viii (3) 135 f; viii (4) 235 f; Reinach (1) 367; Pietschmann-Pagel i 335. Further: CCAG v (1) 118; v (3) 140; vii 87; BL 556 & 576–8; B (15); Reitzenstein (1) & (2); B (3) 97; : Thorndyke (2) 850 f.

17. F (1) i 58 & 138; JL (1) *sv* index.
18. CCAG vii 160.
19. A. Dieterich *Pap. mag. Mus. Lugd. Bat.* 813 f (*J. f. kl. Phil. Suppl.* xvi 1888); BL 538.
20. Riess, fr. 37–42.
21. *Ib.* fr. 40. For Circles etc., BL 538 n 2.
22. Riess p. 383; BL 339 f; Ms 2419 Bibl. Nat. fol. 32; BL 538 n 2. Also fol. 156; the figures 44–5, BL, incorporate some corrections.
23. BL 9 & 540.
24. BL 541; Cod. Flor. 128.
25. Fr. 1, Riess; F (1) i 104; in general B (3) 96–9.
26. Valens vi *pr.* 241, 6 (K), cf. Reitzenstein (2) 5. Thessalos: CCAG viii 3, 137, 14. Hermes and Zeus talk: CCAG v 1, 149, 27.

27. Vitr. ix 6, 3.
28. *Henoch*, xii 1; xiv 1 & 8; F (1) i 314 f.
29. *Rev.* iv 1; *Poim.* CH i 1–4.
30. Door: PGM iv 624; *Apoc. Joh.* iv 1; xi 4; xiii 4; *Henoch* xiv 15.
31. *II Cor.* xiii 1–4. Philolaos: fr. A16 (Diels: Aet. ii 7, 7. Not forgotten by Christians of 5th c.: Carcopino (2) 267 n 3; Migne PL liii 756.
32. B (33) 6; C (8) 279–86.
33. Philon *de somn.* i 10, 54.
34. Philon *de spec. leg.* ii 3, 44 f.
35. CH x 24 f, cf. xi 19.
36. F (1) i 317; JL (1) e.g. Zosimos, Kleopatra etc.
37. Mat. *math.* iv 16; F (1) i 232; JL (1) *sv* index Triadic Formula.
38. See n 16 above. Oxy. iii p. 127; B (1) 152 f (10) 378 ff (11) 152 & (12). Also Pieper (1) 1048 & (2) 187; Eisler 128 f; Kroll (6) 843–6; Gundel (4) 86 & n 1.
39. Oxy. 465 (pp. 126 ff); B (14) 44; Sudhoff (1); Gundel (4) 413 f & (5) 135–93, esp. 176 ff.
40. B (13). For link with technical phrases of astrologers, B (13) 498.
41. Pitra (1) v 2, 279.
42. Euseb. PE iii 4.
43. *De Is.* 372 d52, 373 de55. Griffiths (2) 109, 125, 207, & 28 ff, 41. See next ch. here n 37; also PT 1287; Mayassis 216.
44. Delatte (4) 126 ff; Budge (2) 132 f; JL (3) 24.
45. Junker in *Abh. Berlin* 1911.

11. MORE ON CORRESPONDENCES

1. F (1) i ch. iv; JL (1) esp. ch. viii. BL 576–8 for more on Atlas etc. Augustine CD xviii 40; Serv. Ecl. vi 42; Clem. *Strom.* i 15; FHG iv 505 & Schol. German. v 292 (Eyssenhardt 410): Herakles. Pan: Tzet. *Lykophr.* 482 f. Further, Ps-Louk. *Astrol.* 10; Hygin. *Fab.* 258; DL *pr.* 3. Arnob. ii 69 on Thoth and Atlas, cf. *Not. et Extr.* xviii 2, 236. Babylonian Venus teaches Hermes (Hyg. *Astron.* ii 42); Bel invents star-discipline, Mart. Cap. vi 701 etc.
2. CCAG v 1, 188, 23.
3. F (1) i 105; CCAG v 1, 209, 2.
4. Galen xi 798 (Kühn). See F (1) i 77 & 56; M. Wellmann, *Physika d. Bolos Dem.* 32 n 2. Otto. *Priester*, thinks Greek influence on Egyptian priests was minimal. Were there hermetic groups or fraternities? Yes: Reitzenstein (2) 248; Geffken *Der Ausgang d. GR Heidentums* 1920 80; no says F (1) i 82–5; no trace of rites. Two different positions: world penetrated by God, world wholly evil. F 85 for refs. to Egypt.
   Planets clothe soul in descent with vices, CH i & xiii; their gifts are mixed KK 28 f; infl. of demons of planets xvi 13–16; Zod. signs xiii 7, 11 f; KK 19 f; dekans Exc. vi, xxvii; *Asclep.* 19.
5. Paul, *Eisagoge* (Schato) K 2–4; BL 207 n 1; CCAG v 1, 75. Heliodoros: CCAG iv 81, 1 cf. v 3, 63. Cf. Anon on *Kleroi*: CCAG viii 3, 190, 20.
6. CCAG viii 3, 106, 16, cf. viii 4, 126; F (a) i 105 f. List *ib.* 106–8.
7. CCAG iv 41; vii 59; vii 226 ff; BL 363 f; F (1) i 109; Lyd. de ost. (W), cf. CCAG vii 226; BL 363 & n 3. See JL (4) for Capito Fonteius.
8. BL 365 f; CCAG v 1, 34; v 3, 71; Kern Orph. fr. pp. 283–7.
9. For address "child" *teknon* (here *tekos*), *pai, puer*: Dieterich 160 ff; Norden 290 ff; B (33) 139 & n 1; F (1) i 332 ff; Reitzenstein (1) 40 f.
10. CCAG vii 44 & 167–71; B (17) 12. Other MSS start with Sept. (iv 41; vii 59 65) or March (v 3, 5).
11. CCAG viii 1, 32 & 172–7; also vi 79 & v 3, 58 for two more works on *katarchai*. Also BL 257 ff.

12. Four MSS: CCAG vii 48, 78; viii 1, 63, 69, 74; viii 4, 261 & 127–74; F (1) i 111 f; C (2) 19 & (11) 63 ff. Places: BL 280–8; C (11).

13. Ptol. *Tetr.* 134; V. V. (Riess 334; BM pap. no xcviii 40 f; Firm. Mat. ii 11 (Kroll).

14. BL 262; Paul *praef.*

15. BL 263 n 3; Egyptians and kentra, 269 f.

16. BL 270 f; 273.

17. Anon 158 & 139; BL 273 n 2. Angular positions, 273 f.

18. System of 8 places and Manilius: BL 276—which excludes the two favourable aspects, trigon and hexagon.

19. BL 280 ff.

20. BL 286.

21. BL 287 f; circles 188 ff. Afterlife: C (2) 201 ff; F (1) i 122.

22. Kroll (14).

23. C (2) 147 ff & 151 ff; Firm. Mat. i 168, 13 & 225, 5; Strab. xii 535 & xi 503.

24. G (10) 82, 8; Rhet. 140, 14; Mat. i 225.

25. These can be interpolations. G (3) 343 & 348 f.

26. G (3) 311, 316 & 321.

27. Ghalioungui 38 f. PT 148; Erman (1) Zaub. ii; Paracelsus, *Liber de Podagra.*

28. L. H. 21, 29 & 21, 23.

29. CCAG v 1, 194–226; viii 4, 174–82; G (10) 12–17. Hipparchos: Rehm (6), 30. G (10) 131–4.

31. G 142.

32. Cr (1) 23; Cod. Par. Gr. 2419 cf. 2327; Tanner (2) 240–50; G (4) 405 Egyptians: Cod. Neap. Gr.: CCAG iv 56. Gundel and Tannery cannot think that T. would lower himself to such a thing, but see Weinstock, CCAG ix 1, 14.

Hermetic works of astrologic medicine and botany: F (1) i 123–31, B (3); Kroll (26); Sudhoff (2); Stemplinger ch. vi; Ptol. *Tetr.* i 3, 18; BL 517 n 1. Organon of H.T.: Berthelot *Alc. Gr.* i 23 8–17 & *Intro.* 87.

33. Cf (1) 24; Cod. Pal. Lat 1367; G (4) 406 f.

34. CCAG viii 3, 106, 4; Porph. *in Ptol.* 201; Paul Alex. *T* ii.

35. BL 318; Manil. ii 453–65; genitals BL 319 n 3; F (1) 129.

36. Ideler i 387–96; CCAG v 4, 217–19; C (27); Hopfner *Fontes* 396; F (1) i 130 f.

37. Valens index ii 373 & 380; Ptol. *Tetr.* 110, 4. Cf. Chaldean Oracles; JL (1) 175.

38. F (1) i 131; Ideler i 296, 27–30.

39. Ghalioungui 76–8; Serv *ecl.* x 65; BL 519 n 1 & 517 f.

40. Ghalioungui 35; Griffith (2) 5–8 no 2.

41. Mat. *math.* ii 4, 4–6 & iv 22, 1 ff; F (1) i 132.

42. Cat. MSS Alch Gr. vi 1928 148–51; Bidez (6); F (1) i 134–6. For *hoi hieratikoi,* cf Prokl. in *remp.* ii 154, 5 ff.

43. F (1) i 139 n 2 for refs.

44. CCAG vi 73; G (7) 283 ff.

45. F (1) i 143–6, cf. BL 193 ff.

46. CCAG viii 2, 159–62.

47. Ib. 146–70.

48. Delatte (3) 19 n 3 etc. F (1) i 160–86 for plants and stones of the 15 fixed stars. Anon, 171; Theophilos of Edessa, 172; Teukros and Rhetorios 172.

49. Ptol. *Tetr.* i 3, 15 f; BL 517–20. Geminos, *Isag.* ii; Turcan (1) 397.

50. Diod. ii 29 ff, a farrago with perhaps a mark of Poseidonios and Epigenes. Source of Plin. ii, an anon Chaldean (Kroll)? But the main theories here come from the Greek-Egyptian vulgate.

446   NOTES

12. THE ROMANS

1. Cr 45; note also the suggestion as to *desidero*.
2. Cic. de rep i 18, cf Plato *Thaiet*. 174 a.
3. *De re rust.* i 5, 4; Ennius in de div. Cicero i 58, 132. Accius: *Trag. R. Fr.* 678–80 (Ribb. 3); *R.O.L.* ii 572 f Warmington.
4. Expelled: Val. Max. xiii 3; Cr (2).
5. Polyb. viii 37; Liv. xxv 23 ff; Plout, *Marc.* xix; Cic. *de rep*, i 14, 21 f. Gallus: Cic. *Brut.* xix 77; de div. i 58, 132.
6. Amand 6–12; Sen. *Epist.* cvii 10; Epikt. ii 8, 4; Cr (1) 51 more refs.
7. Cr 49 f for refs. Soon after, in 129, a comet heralded the death, prob. by murder, of Scipio Aemilianus, de nat. deor. ii 5, 14.
8. Plin. xxxv 17, 199.
9. C (30).
10. Klebs in RE ii 1896 203, 9–41; Diod. fr. 36, 5, 1 (Dind. v 129).
11. Cuntz 49; see Kroll (11); Plin. xviii 66, 235 but cf. xviii 68, 271; Alex. of Aphrodisias, *in Arist. Meteor. comm.* 152, 10; Rehm (3). Diagram: Plout. *Marius* xlii 1–5.
12. Cr (1) 61–3.
13. Plout. *Sulla* xxxvii 1; Cic. *de div.* ii 47, 99. For variations in Stoic doctrine Cr (1) 50 ff.
14. Cic. *pro Sulla* xiv 42; Plout. *Cic.* xx 1 f; Cic. *ad fam.* iv 13, 2, 7. Octavian: Suet. *Aug.* xciv 5; Dion xlv 1, 3–5; CCAG viii 4, 99; Cr (1) 63; Kroll (11). Other refs., *ad att*, ii 2, 3; ad Q. i 2, 66; Cic. *Tim.* i 1–2 (eulogy); *ad att.* vii 24: Lucan i 639.
15. Cic. *Vat.* xiv, with schol; Apul. *apol.* xliii.
16. Dion xlv 1, 3; Cicero *l.c.*; Thorndyke 428 f.
17. A.G. iv 9; x 11; xiii 10 & 26; xix 14; Jerome *in chron. Euseb.* 01. clxxxiv; August. CD v 3. Works: Persian elements: J. Geffcken (1) esp. 327 & 337; Birt, esp. 386 f. Users of his work: Hertz; Klein; Roehig; Phloratos 15 citing Diels-K. *vors.* i 442, 19 f & 404, 1–3. Virgil: Geffcken 327 ff; J. Kroll. *Augurium*: A. G. vii 6, 10; *de extis, ib.* xvi 6, 12; thunder, Lyd. *de ost.* 99, 17 Plin, i, list in 7–11; Serv. *aen.* xi 715; spheres, B (10) 349 f (cf. Lucan i 639 f). Tages: Ferrero 295–7: Lyd. 27 f.
18. Schol. *ad Germanic. Arat.* 80, 8 ff; ed. of Nig. by Swoboda lxxxviii ff.
19. Cic. *de rep.* vi 16, 16; Alex. Polyh. in DL viii 31; Delatte (6) 226; Cic. *l.c.* 17, 17. Pythag. Sources: Diels *Vors* (3rd) i p. xlii; Wellmann (2) 215; Delatte *l.c.*; Carcopino (2) 269. For moon: Serv. *Aen.* v 735; C (28) 92 & 99 for woman whom Hades set in 7th Circle (*i.e.* moon), cf. Cic. *de rep.* vi 17, 17 for 9 circles, supreme god, 7 planets, earth—here 7th is Venus, Moon 8th, but inscr. of Didymoi (that above) is certainly Pythag., though see Vollgraff, *Mnemos.* 1922 256; Carcopino (2) 269. Nig. and *oikoi*: BL 185 n 2.
20. Aquarius as Deukalion: Hyginus, PA, *sv* index Piccaluga.
21. Housman: astron. app. to his *Lucan* 1924 1950 327.
22 Phloratos, who thinks Getty wrong in taking lines 663–5 as dealing with atmospheric not astronomic phenomena; see Cic. *de div.* i 57, 160.
23. Ptol. *Tetr.* ii 3, 59 f. Getty (2) thinks himself wrong in (1) putting Saturn at IMC and in Aquarius; for there he'd bring about disaster complementary to that of Sun in Lion.
24. Etruscan regions: Weinstock (3) 120; B (3) 155. Weinstock 119 on two articles of Cumont, but also des Places 138 f and C (5) 28. Weinstock agrees ultimate source of Mart. Cap. on regions is Nig. rather than Varro; BL (2) iv 24 ff shows the 12 regions there are compatible with 12 *sortes* of Manilius iii 43 ff rather than *templa*. See Housman ed. 1916 and addenda 1937 v–xi, with

Weinstock 103 & 108. R. Enking 84 f sees allusion to Etruscan sky in *domus* of winds, Georg. i 380 f. See for all this, Getty (2) 315.

25. Sext. Emp. *adv. math.* v 12; Ptol. *Tetr.* iii 10, 135; Manil. ii 892; Housman, 2nd Bk. Manil. 1912 & 1937, xxvii f. Orientation: Aristot. *de caelo* ii 2, 285 b, 22–7. Plato: Weinstock (3) 120 & n 117.

Note *Georgics* i 231–51 changes the original, *Hermes* of Eratosthenes with its antipodeans; Virgil has N. pole as high above us, and S. pole as under our feet; with frigid zones to right and left. Aratos mentioned one pole as unseen, other as facing it in N. and high above Ocean, but like Eratosth. said nothing of left and right. Getty (2) 315–17. As the Pythags. knew the 5 heavenly zones, it is possible that astrologers, describing IMC (thought of by some as Northern, as if it were MC) as *summum caelum* (as it seems here in Figulus-Lucan), and so were giving a Pythag. attitude. See Getty (2) 317 ff for math. symmetries which seem Pythag., cf. Duckworth on Virgil TAPA 1960; V. Capparelli *Sophia* xxvi 1958 197–210; J. F. Scott 23; Gruelle *Et. Class.* xvii 1949 139–225 etc.

26. Fig. and Etruscans: n 17 above, and H. Bardon 314 ff for Aulus Caecina, father and son. Kastor: C (28) 97.

27. Cic. *ad fam.* vi 9; Suet. JC lxxv; *Bell. Afr.* 89; Sen. QN ii. 39; Veronese schol. *Aen.* x 198 (Mai); Sen. QN ii 56, & 41 for further threefold division.

28. JL (4) ch. xv.

29. A. Gell. xix 14. 1 f; Serv. *Aen.* x 175; Varro *Sat. Men. Lex Maenia* 6, 1 (Riese 154), *Maripor* 12, 19 (R. 163). Burial: Plin. xxxv 12, 160, cf. Charisius *Gramm. Lat.* i 29, 28.

30. Cic. *de div.* ii 47, 98; Plout. *Rom.* xii 3 ff.

31. Plout. *Rom.* v: QR xxxv; Macr. *Sat.* i 10; Augustine CD vi 7.

32. *Ant.* Hahn 17ff.

33. A. Gell. iii 10; Plin. xxxv 11; August. CD vi 3 is based on Varro.

34. Cr (1) 66; Dahlmann; Schanz. On Numbers: Schmekel 76ff; Dahlmann 1261. Cr (1) 67; Eggshape: Cassiodoros PL lxx 1218 d–1219 a.

35. Cr (1) 69 for Cicero's contacts.

36. De div. i 11–3.

37. Cr. 73. Lucret. V. 1, 204 ff.

38. Kroll (15) 10 f; *Souda*; Valens *Anth.* ii 31; Antioch. CCAG viii 3, 116, 3; Palchos, CCAG i 97; CCAG viii 4, 253 d; Kroll (13).

39. BL 224 & 227. Arabs: B (10) 6–12; Ruska *Tab. Smarag.* 1926 129 & 136; F. v. Lipmann *Enstehung d. Achemie* 1919 356 & 515.

40. F. A. Yates *sv* index Metrodorus.

41. Diod. i 81, 6; ii 29, 2 to 30 2 f; also ii 30, 5—as well as 3 & 8.

42. *De div.* ii 24, 52. In general JL (4).

43. *Ad fam.* ix 24, 2.

44. Domaszewski (1) & (2); BL 554 n 2 points out that xxii Primigeneia, formed by Claudius' doubling of xxii Deioteriana, made bricks marked Capricorn and Lion: M. Cagnat, *Rev. Epigr.* 1897 no 148; but this does not disprove, see JL (4).

45. Dion xl 7, 1; Ovid *Met.* xv 843–51; Plin. vii 55, 189 sceptic. Also Gagé (1) 246 & 262 n 63.

46. Migne PL lxxvi 21 ff; Plout. *Mor.* xvii.

47. Plin. ii 23, 93 f; Nilsson (3); Serv. *Ecl.* ix 46 f; Star: Plin. ii 23, 94; Dion xlv 7, 1 f; Virg. *Ecl.* ix 56 ff; Horace *Ep.* xvii on witch; also *Carm.* i 12, 46 ff & 13 ff; Serv. *Aen.* 681, "Augustus did the persuading for the belief that the star was Caesar's."

48. *Numbers* xxiv 17; Gagé (1) 262 n 67. Origen, *in Num. homil.* xiii 7; Bidez (2) i 48 n 1.

49. Gagé (1) 246 and 262 n 66; Bidez (2) i 48 f.

50. Suet. JC xl 1 f.

51. Plout. JC lix 3; hence joke about Lyra, see JL (4); Cic. *de leg* ii 12, 29 admits laxity of pontiffs.

52. Macr. *Sat.* i 14, 2; Plin. ii 8 & xviii 25; Macr. *l.c.*; Censor. xx, both last two probably using Suet. *De anno romanorum.* Earlier effort by Ptol. Euergetes failed: Plin. ii 6, 39—239 B.C.

53. JC's book used by Columella, Plinius, Ptol., Maternus, Lydos: Cr (1) 76 n 329. For weather-signs, Aratos *Phain.* 733-1154; Theophrastos may have written *Peri Semeion.*

54. Balsdon 59 with refs.

55. *Ib.* 75 f, with more details.

56. Suet. *Tib.* xxxii 2; Balsdon 61 f & 39 n 22.

57. Balsdon 63 f: CIL iv 4182; Snyder 17 f; Jos. *C. Ap.* ii 282; Dion xxxvii 18, 1 f; Juv. vii 160 f.

58. Balsdon 64 with notes; B (7); Halkin; Snyder; CT ii 8, 18; Tert. *de orat* xxiii. What was Lord's day of *Rev.* i 10 we cannot prove. See A. Robertson, *Origins of Christianity* 1953 147, 188 & 196; *The Teaching of the Twelve Apostles* (xiv) has common meal on the Lord's Day of the Lord; that is, it was a festal day, not like the Sabbath of rest; Justin claims Sunday as first day of the world and day when Christ rose, *Apol.* i 67.

59. Plin. xviii 57, 212; Rehm (4); Mommsen thinks both together, *Röm. Gesch.* iii 550 n 1; Plin. made much use of it: viii 56, 201 ff & 57, 214. See further Cr (1) 75.

60. Plin. xviii 60, 225 f; xviii 65, 237. Taken straight: xviii 68, 268-71 etc.

61. Plin. xviii 69, 278 f; later in section draws on Varro, then back to Caesar with 74, 309. Effect of Little Dog on vines: 272; Cr (1) 76.

62. Ditt. OGI 458.

63. IG xii 123; G (8); Haussoulier (1) 6. EG 104 b 3 f, cf 148; 164; 225; 243; CIG 2467; SEG ix 193; Peek *Hermes* lxvi 1931 474 f; CIG 9319, 30, 3 f (Christian). Rome: EG 642. Thasos: EG 325, 5-8, cf. SEG i 449; Christian 570; iv 192; CIG 3847; IG xiv 1868; EG 652; 654. Miletos: Wiegand. *Abh. Ak. Berl.* 1908 6, 46; C (28)—105 see n 19 above. For Olympos as heaven: Lattimore 33 f; underworld 51; Isles of Blessed IG vii 2541 (Thebes).

64. EG 312; Lattimore 35 f.

65. G (8) & (7) 116; CIL vi 3, 2244.

66. CE 2152 b. CE 1109 16–18 (Rome), with Lattimore 39 f. Sun: CIL vi 29, 954; Simon 156; C (35) 102. For return to heavenly fatherland: Cic. *rep.* vi 11, 11; vi 16, 16 & 17, 17; *Tusc.* i 12, 28; Carcopino (2) 370.

13. THE EARLY PRINCIPATE

1. Laroche (1); Olympiodoros *in Arist. Meteor* 19 ff; Prokl. *comm. Eukl.* xli 19; more refs. Laroche 119.

2. Laroche 119 for full refs.

3. On Airs ii; Archytas, *Fr. Phil. Gr.* i 572; Epin. 990 a.

4. Laroche 120 f; DL v 43 & 49; *Clouds* 225; Plato *Thaiet.* 173 e; *Rep.* 488 c, 389.

5. Athen. 378 a & 491 cs; Diels 470, 5; Laroche 122.

6. DL ix 34; Theon 198 (Hiller 14); Diod. i 98; Strab. xvii 1, 29. Nikol. *Hist. Gr. Min.* 3; Dion lvii 22; Ptol. *Tetr.* i *pr.*

7. Wuilleumier 194 for refs.

8. Campbell 311; Vermaseren (1) 151 f.

9. Lyd. *de mens.* iv 30; Malal. *Chronog.* 175 (Nieb.): Isidor. *Etym.* PL xviii 36; Cassiod. *Var.* iii 51; Coripp. *In laud. Just.* i 317; Isidor. *ib.* 41; Kedren, i 258.

10. Wuilleumier 191 f for refs.

11. Minuc. Felix *de spec.* ix; Campbell 98.

12. J. F. Rock, *Bull. de l'Éc. d'Ext. Orient* xxxvii 1937 45.

13. Wuill. 193 f; Julian *Hymn to Helios* 156 a (*Orat.* iv).

14. Wuill. 206 and JL (6) 116 f.

15. Wuill. 208; Audollent *Def. Tab.* 1904 no 5; Wuill. 191.

16. CCAG v 3, 127 f; Cod. Ambros. 886, C.222 inf. f 42; Cod. Paris. Gr. 2423 f 17 v. Wuill. 184–9. *Horiokratores*: Ptol. *Tetr.* CCAG ii 198; Paul Alex. *Q* iv *S* iv (Sch).

17. CH: F (3) ii 234.

18. Dion Chr. xxxvi 42 ff; Gomperz *Gr. Denker* i 65 holds Greeks did not know Avesta. For the Stoic 4 concentric spheres: Zeller, *Philos. d. Gr.* iii 1, 172. Iran: Bidez (2) i 91 f & 248; ii 142 ff & 153 n 3. For *heniochein* (cosmic): Leisegang. Mart. Cap. ii 189 for rel. to elements. Note that the 4 horses seem yoked to the same car.

19. Balsdon (1) 296; A. Mau *Pompeii* (2nd) 1908 229; English 1902 226. East: L. Robert, *Les Glad. dans l'Or. gr.* 1940 21 f, 86, 182, 187, 169 & 306 f. Nemesis and Circus: A. v. Premerstein; H. Volkmann, AfR xxvi 1928 296–321 & xxxi 1934 73 f; ILS 5121 Verona (CIL v 1466); *deceptus* ILS 5111–2 2151–2. Griffin with wheel on Alex. coin: J. Vogt 83 pl. i no xi; Nemesis-Nike: BCH xlviii 1924 276 ff.

20. Toutain i 392. For possible link of statue of Nemesis-Pax and first Balbillus: Rostovtzeff. Isis-Nemesis at Delos.

21. Pascal 38–40 for refs. Fortune gem: A. A. Napolitano *Aquil. Nostra* xxi 1950 25–42. Cf. CIL iii 1125 "To the Goddess Nemesis or Fortuna." See Roscher *Lex.* iii 117 ff; Zingerle in AEM xx 1897 228; Amm. Marc. xiv 11, 26; Mommsen CIL iii 10430; BGU vi 1216 (110 B.C.) on shrine of 2 Nemeseis and Adrasteia at Smyrna; Paus. vii 5, 1, etc. Vienne: *R. arch-du centre* iii 1964 101–23.

22. Von Premerstein, see n 20 above; FHRC 213.

23. Brusin, *Homm. à L. Hermann* 1960 219–27; Von P. 406 & 404; Paus. vii 50, 9; Malal. *Chron.* xii 407 etc.

24. Suet. *Aug.* xxxi 1; Dion liv 27, 2 f & 15, 8; Tac. *Ann.* vi 18 (12) Sen. *Controv.* x pr. 5; Rogers; Allen.

25. Suet. *Aug.* xxv; Cr (1) 83.

26. Bayet 153; Suet. v 1 & xciv 18.

27. Bayet 153 n 3.

28. *Ib.* 153 f; Manil. ii 726. Moon: Firm. Mat. i 2, 2; iv 19, 31; Wuilleumier 205 f; S (3) 58 & 64; CCAG i 138.

29. Bayet 154 n 2; Horace *Carm.* iii 17, 17–20; BL 155.

30. Bayet; cf. Manil. ii 559; prologue of *Georgics* 32–5.

31. Manil. iv 205–16; iv 547 ff; Bayet 156 n 6.

32. *Ecl.* ix 46–9; Manil. iii 658 ff & 672; ii 424–32. Liber: ii 658 ff; iii 662 ff; iv 204; Ceres iii 664. Bayet 159 n 2; Erigone, Bayet 159. Also Manil. iv 772 ff; Bayet 160 n 5; JL (4) 8 n 4th Eclogue.

Further: Manil. iv 773 ff; Suet. *Aug.* lii; vii 4 (Aug. & Roma).

33. Hor. *Carm.* iii 3, 9–16; Suet. *Aug.* xciv; Bayer 126 n 6; *Georg.* i 31; Bayet 163 n 4. Aug. as Apollo: JL (4). Ovid *Met.* xv 834 ff, cf. Hor. *Carm.* i 2, 45; Ovid *Met.* xv 868–70; *Tristia* v 2, 51 ff (combining Virgil & Horace).

34. Bayet 165 ff; Manil. i 798 ff (Milky Way—in general Rohde *Psyche* 395 n 35; 517 n 53; 330; 517; Thiele (2) 148). Manil. i 689–91; Bayet 169 f; for Virgil's steps towards Stoic worldview, Bayet 170 f. In general on Manil. Cr (1) 97–8.

35. *Aen.* iii 360. Manil. iv 14 & 866 ff; ii 236 ff.

36. Hor. *Carm.* ii 17, 21 ff; B (19); BL 491 n 1 & 491 ff. Hor. *Ep.* ii 2, 187; *Carm.* i 11, 2. Astrologic view of i 28, 5 too farfetched; BL 551 n 4.

37. Prop. iv 1, 109 etc., esp. 77 ff; B (20).

Q

38. BL 552; *Ibis* 207–16.

39. PLM Baehrens i 104–21, esp. lines 405 ff. List: Harder; C (1) 89. Cf. the imagery in *Elegy on Maecenas* (lines 129 ff): PLM i 122–36. *Aetna* 231 ff & 216–18. "Motive force": *impetus*. He adds, "Some help," *auxilium,* "is needed for the propulsion of bodies." For limitations of ancient notions of motion, see JL (1) ch. i. For Strabon and his modified acceptance of astrology: Cr (1) 89 f. Egypt: xvii 787; 806; 816—also xvii 1, 29; Phoenicians: xvi 757; Mesopot. xvi 739. Astronomy & geography: iii 110–12; xiv 642; ii (132).

40. Macr. *Sat.* iii 8, 4; H. J. Rose, *Lat. Lit.* 445–7; Rose *Hyg. Fab.* 1934; M. A. Grant *Hyginus* 1960; Rehm (5) and (6); C (1) 84 f. Virgil said to have been a pupil of his.

41. Bk. ix & xi. Berosos on moon-phases (wrong) ix 2, also in Lucret. v 720 ff, cf. Stob. *Ecl.* i 26, 12.

42. Dion liii 27, 2 f. Hamann (2) 73; K. Lehmann for the Dome of Heaven.

43. Anaxilaos: Jerome *Chron.* 01. 188 (Abr. 1989); Helm 62; D. L. iii 2 & i 107; see Cr (1) 85 f for refs.; JL (1) 99, 123, 126 & 403.
Lit. treason: Sen. *Controv* x pr.; Rogers; Allen. Cassius Sev. etc.: Suet. *Aug.* lvi; Plin. xxxv 12, 146 & vii 10, 12; Quint. x 1, 23; Macr. *Sat.* ii 4; Jerome *Chron.* 2048 in Euseb.; Sen. *Controv.* iii (start). Tac. *Ann.* i 53 & iii 18 etc.

44. Rogers; Allen; Ciaceri.

45. Dion lvi 24, 3 & 25, 4; Cr (3) 50 f; Suet. *Tib.* lxiii 1.

46. Paul. *Sent.* v 21, 3 f; Ulpian *de Off.* vii; see Cr (1) for further details right on to 3rd century.

47. Epikt. iv 13, 1; Suet. *Aug.* xxvii 3.

48. Gagé (1) 45, 13 & 62; also 37, 25 f n 38, & 65; for Prima Porta 31 f.

49. Gagé (1) 35; Ovid and Claros, 36.

50. Tac. *Ann.* 85; Plin. viii 39.

51. Gagé (1) 68 n 67; Tac. *Ann.* xiii 43. S. may have assumed Ner. name at time Claudius adopted Nero, cf. Commodianus in an imp. procurator of 177, CIL vi 632. But recall also town Nerulum, Lucania. Caesonius: Tac. *Ann.* xi 36.

52. Gagé (1) 68 n 64; Clarian Apollo 38 f & 68 n 65–6; Eckhel ii 556, coin. Tac. *Ann.* xiii 43 & xii 50 for M. Suillius consul with L. Antistius under Claudius.

53. Gagé (1) 45 f nn 76–7.

54. Gagé (1) Pegasus: 69 n 84; schol. 70 n 85; Ariathes, 39. CAH pl. iv 156; Gagé (7); Schrader. The originals of such cameos may be triumphal pictures or reliefs: Strong 67 ff; Gagé (7) 28 ff.

55. Gagé (1) 50–2 and n 87, 89–93.

56. Gagé (1) 52 & n 96; 53 & n 97.

57. Gagé (1) note 98 *bis*. L. Curtius took the figure to be Alexander: *Röm. Mitt.* 1934 x 568, 634.

14. TIBERIUS AND GAIUS

1. Suet. *Tib* xiv: also for tale of egg and of "highest numbers" coming up at the oracular fount. Dion lv 11, 1 f; Tac. *Ann.* vi 20 f; Krappe for various versions.

2. *Romance of A. the Gt.*, transl. of Armenian version, A. M. Wolohojian 1969 34 f. For Tales; W. Heryz, *Gesammelte Abh.* 1905 203; Eisler (2) 259. See Krappe 364.

3. Suet. *Tib.* lix, xi & xxxii; Tac. *Ann* vi 21; Suet. xiv 4; Dion lv 11, 2 f; *Cod. paris. gr.* suppl. 607 a 44 v: CCAG viii 4. 99 f; Krappe; Cichorius (2); Cr (1) 94.

4. Suet. *Aug.* xcviii.

5. Roger (1) 70; Tac. *Ann.* ii 70; Gagé (1) 77.

6. Rogers (1) 15 & (5); *Ann.* ii 30.

7. *Fasti Amiterni* CIL i (2nd ed.) 244, cf. v 15 nos 91–4.

8. *Ann.* ii 32; Cr (1) 270 f & (2) 21 ff; Rogers (1) 12 ff. Astrologers?

9. Dion lvii 15, 7–9.

10. Themistios *Or.* v (5th c); viii; xi; xxxiv (Dind. 76; 129; 173; 451). Julian 265 cd.

11. Valens *Anth.* ix 11; CCAG v 4, 1940, 185–228, esp. 203, 4 & 212, 15. Heph., CCAG vi 110, 11 cf. viii 2, 39 n 1. Epitome: CCAG viii 2, 99–101. Juv. vi 576. Stones: G (2) esp. 582 f; Delatte; no astrologic lapidaries in Mély and Ruelle 1898. For literary work: Cr (1) 93 for refs.

12. Tac. *Ann* i 72. See also Cic. *de orat.* ii 25, 107; *Nat. deor.* iii 10, 74; *de incend.* ii 105; *ad fam.* iii 11, 2; *in Verr.* ii 1, 5, 12; *pro Clu.* xxxv 97; *in Pis.* xxi 50.

13. More details Cr (1) 253 f.

14. Strachan-Davidson ii 138; Rogers (1) 197 f.

15. Suet. *Tib.* xlix 1; Tac. *Ann.* iii 22 f; Rogers (1) 52; *Ann.* i 13; Cr (4).

16. Cr (1) 255 f.

17. Tac. *Ann.* i 28. Germanicus: C (16) 292 n 74. Sibyl: Dion lvii 18, 4 f. Jews, Jos. AJ xviii 3, 5; Suet. Tib. xxxvi; Dion. lvii 18, 5 a. Isis: Jos. AJ xviii 3, 4.

18. Cr (1) 257–9, poem (?) based on *Phoinissai* 393. Mages: Rogers (1) 152.

19. Gagé (1) 118 n 6.

20. Suet. *Calig.* xix; xlvi & xlv; Cr (1) 111.

21. Suet. *Calig.* xlvi; Dion lix 25; Gagé (1) 72 on *musculi*.

22. Aquarius: Manil. iv 59 ff; Gagé (2) 642. See further Gagé 57 f, n 106–9: Ganymede picture on Palatine; Alex. geniture; sacrifice of birds etc. 58 f: Suet. *Calig.* xxii.

23. Suet. *Galba* iv; more refs. Cr (1) 106. Tale of Phoenix: Cr. *l.c.*, who thinks Thr. gave Tib. promise of ten more years against omen taken as meaning a change of emperors.

24. Rogers (1) 144–55; Tac. *Ann.* vi 29; Suet. lxii 3 & lviii 27, 2. Also Suet. *Nero* v.

25. Krappe 361 untenable.

26. Did Thr. make ominous predictions about the two young men? CCAG viii 4, 109, 9 ff; Dion lviii 23, 2. Main source for tale of Macro etc. is Philon, *in Flacc* iii 11 f; Jos. AJ xviii 10; also Phil. *Leg. ad G.* vi 33–8; *in Flacc* iii 13; Suet. *Calig.* xii 2 & xxvi 1.

27. Further. Dion lix 10, 6; lvii 28, 4; Tac. *Ann.* vi 46; potion, *Leg ad G.* viii 61.

28. More refs. Cr (1) 109 f.

29. Dion lix 29, 4; Cr (3) 40–2. Notice credulity: Suet. Vit. xiv 4 and then Dion. lxiv (lxv) 1, 4. Mania for gold: Gagé (1) 59. See also Suet. *Nero* vi. Gaius and his claim to be under influence of Cassiopoeia who was said to have power of producing metal artisans; rel. to the name Cassius? Gagé (1) 59.

30. N (19) 77–8, 16–19 & 79.

15. CLAUDIUS AND NERO

1. Bell, *Jews and Christians in Egypt* 1924 1–37; M. P. Charlesworth *Docs. Illustr. Reigns of Cl. & Nero* 1939 nos 1–2; Loeb *Sel. Pap.* ii 78 ff; R. Laqueur *Klio* 1926 xx 86–106; M. Wengers *ib.* 168–78; T. Reinach *Rev. Et. Juives* 1924 lxxiv 114; H. Grégoire, *Le Flambeau* July 1924 278 ff; A. Cameron CQ 1926 xx 45; Cichorius (1); Cr (1) 113.

2. For identification of young Thrasyllus and Balbillus: Cichorius (2) 390–8; Cr (1) 99 ff; on name B., Gagé (1) 81 f; Jouguet.

3. Keil nos 41 f; but see later here.

4. Dion lx 26, 1.

5. Suet. *Calig.* xxv 2; Tac. *Ann.* xii 22.

6. Cr (3) and (1) 259–61.

7. Cr (1) 261 f; Tac. *Ann.* xii 12; *Hist.* ii 75.

8. Tac. *Ann.* ii 69–72 & 59; Cr (1) 262 f.

9. Cr (1) 263 f; Nero and Royal Astrology, Gagé (1) 108 f.

10. Carcopino (2); ? rel. to Statilius T., *ib.* ch. i. Also Sen. *Apokoloc.* iii.

11. Dion. lxii 26, 3; Rogers (5) 287 ff, but see Taverner 1–12; Juv. iii 161 with schol. to i 33 & vi 552.

12. Tac. *Ann.* cvi 14; Cr (1) 265–7. Horoscopes: N (19) 20 & 81.

13. Chairemon: *hierogrammateus*, teacher of Dionysios who succeeded him. As preceptor of Nero: *Souda sv* Alexandros Aigaios; attacked by Jos. *C. Ap.* xxxii-xxxiii; Tzet. *Chil.* v 6; *Souda sv* Origenes and Euseb. HE vi 19. Martial xi 56.

14. *On Prov.* v 6 f; *Letter to M.* xvi 1–3.

15. QN ii 37, 1–3, cf. ii 35 etc.

16. Grabaud 68 f; Clarke 9.

17. *H.F.* 945 ff; 1332 f; *On Oeta* 61 ff; *Thyestes* 82 f; *On Oeta* 1925. Simon 106–9. Saviour: Dion Chrysost. *Or.* i 84, cf. *Or.* xxxiii 47; CIS (Tyre) 122. Also cf similar terms for Christ, *Aets* v 31.

18. Justin. xxxviii 3, 1; Imhof-Blumer *Giess. Anz.* 31 March 1910. C.'s Throne: B (25) 122 n; G (1); Alföldi (1) 80.

19. Cic. *in Cat.* iii 18; *de Cons.* ii (*de div.* i 11, 18); Dion xxxvii 25, 3 & (comet) xlv 17, 4.

20. Manil. i 897 ff; Dion 1, 8, 2 & xlvii 40, 2; Manil. i 907 ff; Virg. *Georg.* i 488. Also Dion liv 29 (death of Agrippa). Plague: Manil. i 880 ff; Sil. It. viii 638; Dion lvi 24, 3 f & 25, 5; Cr (4) 1 ff Aug.

21. Sen. QN vii 17, 2; Suet, *Claud.* xlvi; Plin. ii 23, 92 f. Cf. Sen. QN vii 21, 3; 23, 1; 29, 3, also vii 6, 1; 17, 2; 21, 3; 23, 1; 29, 3. Calp. Sic. i 74 ff; Tac. *Ann.* xiv 22; Suet. *Nero* xxxvi; Sen. *Oct.* 235 Anon poet: Einsiedeln Elegies i 29–31 & ii 23, 38. For his identity and that of Calpurnius see refs. in Loeb *Min. Lat. Poets*; Rose *Lat. Lit.* 381–3.

22. Stentzel, *Das Weltall* vii 113; Orig. *C. Cels.* i 58; B (26). Also Sen. QN vii 3 on Konon of Lock; he cited Epigenes and Apollonios.

23. Suet. *Nero* xxxvi; Tac. *Hist.* i 22.

24. Tac. *l.c.*; Suet. *Otho* iv.

25. Suet. *Nero* xl. 2; Tac. *Ann.* xii 68, Cf. Alex. Romance; tale of Seleukos Nikanor etc.

26. Reece; Holzapfel; Suet. *Nero* vi 1; N (19) 78 f & 186, for dates 176. Also Kroll (2) 233 f; Jer. *Chron.* 36 (Schöne); Jos. BJ iv 499 & 491; Dion lxvi 17, 4; lxiii 3; Suet. *Galba* x 1 & *Vesp.* vi 3.

27. Rainer Pap. 27922; Ditt. *Or.* 666; JL (3) 324 f. Tac. *Ann.* xiv 9 & xiii 21 f; Cr (1) 127.

28. Plin xix 1, 3; Sen. iv 2, 13 as to tale of dolphins and crocodiles (or was this of his father?). Prediction of death of Agrippina: Tac. *Ann.* vi 22; xiv 9.

29. *Ann.* xiii 21f; xiv 9; Cr (1) 127.

30. Suet. *Nero* 36; Gagé (1) 109 f; Tac. *Ann.* xiii 22 & xvi 23; xvi 14.

31. Gagé (1) 111; Robert REG 1956 esp. no 345; *Domus Aurea*, Gagé 113.

32. Gagé (1) 161 f; Buckler.

33. Renan, transl. W. G. Hutchinson (pref. dated 1899) 209; St. Giet; Gagé (1) 179 n 79.

34. Cod. Angel. Rome 29, 125; cf. Ptol. *Tetr.* iii 10; BL 307 & 436. Epitomy etc.: CCAG viii 3, 103, Palchos; frags. 4, 235–8, 240–4; life-length: Ptol. *Tetr.* iii 10. Rome: BL 307 & 436; also CCAG viii 3, 103 n; 4, 233 f.

35. Cumont CCAG viii 4, 233; Baehrens PLM i 72 no 38.

36. Tac. *Hist.* ii 81; son, Kirchner: Jos. BJ v 11, 3 & vii 7, 1–3; Dion lxv (lxvi) 9, 2, cf. Exc. Val. 271.

37. *Phar.* i 70 ff; x 185 f; x 193 ff.

38. Pers. v 45 ff, thinking of Hor. *Carm.* ii 17; for Twins, Manil. ii 628; H. Nettleship. *Satires of P. F.* 1872 91; Jahn, *Arch. Beit.* 170.

39. Geffcken; PA ix 572; xi 106 f; xi 164; xi 161; xi 159.

40. CCAG viii 3, 134–51 & 4, 254 ff (Latin, only first part after T.); Plin. xxix i, 9: Galen *de Meth. Med.* i 2 (K. x 7); C (1) 123; astrologer, CCAG viii 3, 134; JL (1) *sv* index.

41. Col. xi 2; Rehm (3) 1309 ff; Kapelmacher RE x 1910 1054–68; book, xi 1, 31; also ix 14, 2.

42. HN ii 4, 12 f; 5, 18 f; 6, 28 f etc.

43. Wendland; Amand 81–95; Bréhier 167 takes Panaitios as main source; Amand takes Karneades; Wendland, Poseidonios; see also Zeller (2) iii 2 422 ff. Fate etc., Bréhier 165 f; *de Opif. Mundi* 58; *de Spec. Leg.* i; *de Monarch.* i; *de Sacerd.* 89–92; Amand 88–90. Place: Bréhier 167 f; Bousset in *Alex. u. Romo* 1913 101 f.

44. *Sat.* xxxv 4; *Latomus* 1967 (34) 1010–4; de Vreese 14–16; Colin; J. Préaux—for refs. and discussion.

45. *Sat.* xxxix.

46. *Sat.* xxix.

47. Deonna 46 ff; Plout. *Symp. Gr.* 4 (704 b). Vesta: DS *sv* Lares 942; Hercules Epitrapezos: Deonna 15 & 47–9, & JL (4) *sv* Index. Anaxag., Diels *Vors* (6th) i 94, 20; *A. of T.* iii 27 (c. table of Psyche in Apuleius); M. Meunier, *A. de Tyane* 1936 95. Plin. xxviii 2, 28. See JL (4) ch. 9.

48. *Sat.* lx; Suet. *Nero* xxxi 3; cf. Hor. *Sat.* ii 8, 54–6 (accident); Kedr. (Stucki) ii 15, 314.

16. THE REST OF THE FIRST CENTURY

1. Tac. *Hist.* i 22–3; Plout. *Galb.* xxxiii; Suet. *Otho* vi 1; Stein (2); Juv. vi 557–9. Suet. *Galb.* iv, vi, ix, x & xviii; Zon. xi 16.

2. Tac. *Hist.* i 86; Zon. *l.c.*; Suet. *Otho* viii.

3. Suet. *Vit.* iii 2p Dion. lxiii 4, 3 & lxii 11, 2.

4. Tac. *Germ.* viii; Suet. *Vit.* xiv; Tac. *Hist.* i 62 & 78; ii 62; Dion lxiv 1, 4; Suet. *Vit.* xiv 4; Zon. *l.c.*; Tac. *Hist.* ii 91. Vit. died 20 Dec.

5. Dion lxv 9, 2; Suet. *Otho* iv & vi; Tac. *Hist.* i 22; Plout. *Galb.* xxiii 4. Vesp. and astrols., Tac. *l.c.*; Suet *Vesp.* v 1–7; vii 1–3; Dion lxiv 9, 1; Tac. comments, i 22. See *ib.* ii 78 suggests he accepted Ptol. publicly after his accession.

6. Dion lxiv (lxv) 8, 1; Zon. xi 16; Suet. *Vesp.* iv 5; Tac. *Hist.* v 13 (Jud.).

7. Dion lxv 15, 5 & 12, 1; Suet. xxv.

8. Suet, *Vesp.* v; xiv, xxv, cf. Dion lxv 12, 1. Suet. xxiii 4, cf. Aurel. Vict. *epit.* ix; Dion lxvi 17, 2 f. Titus and comet: Plin. ii 22, 89; C (21) 33; BL 360 n 3.

9. Suet. *Tit.* i; ii; ix 2; x cf. Dion lxvi 26 1 f.

10. Dion *ep.* lxvii 15, 6; Suet. *Dom.* xiv 1 f & xii; fear, iii 2 & xiv 3 Dion *ib.* 9, 1–5 for tale of dark room and death jest. Expulsion: Jerome *Chron.* ad 89–90; Suet. xiv 4 & xvi; Dion *ib.* 16, 2–17; Cr (1) 273–5; CCAG viii 4, 101 2–12 & 100, 28 ff.

11. Cr (1) 245 f; 273 f Suet, *Dom.* xv 3; CCAG viii 4, 101 n; PIR (1933) 239 no 1198; Malal. (Bonn) 266, 14; Asclepius in *Chron. Pasch.* (Bonn) i 68, 13; CCAG viii 4, 101, also i 79, 19; v 1, 205, n 1; v 2, 49, 3; viii 4, 101 n; Kroll (13) cf. Plin. v 9, 55; xvi 22, 82; *Souda sv* no 4; Cited by Valens *Anth.* ix; Anon (CCAG v 1, 204, 22 ff); Palchos CCAG i 80, 15; Lydos *de Ost.* ii (Wachs. 61); CCAG i 81. End: Dion lxvi 16, 3; CCAG viii 4, 101, 2–21; Suet. *Dom.* xv.

12. Dion lxvi 16, 2 (used by Kedr., Xiph., Zon.); CCAG viii 4, 100, 28 ff; Suet. *Dom.* xvi 1; Cr (1) 274 f.

13. Gagé (1) 224.

14. Stein (4).

15. A. of T. vii; on liberal arts xiii 7; viii 7 sacrifice of boy; his predictions ascribed to commerce with demons, treatise of Eusebios xxiii ff.

16. *Paneg.* xi 1 f.

17. CIG ii (2nd ed.) no 351 (? A.D. 87–8); P. Graindor *Chronol. des Arch. ath. sous l'emp.* 1920 95–100 holds improbable he held office after 87. Plout. QC i 10, 1. and *quomodo adulator* i 48 e; QC 628 b. Arvales: Kroll (16); Cr (1) 153; Paus. i 25, 8.

18. *Inst.* i 10, 46 ff; G. Lehnert 4, *decl. maiores.*

19. Mart. viii 82; ii 7 (pretty).

20. *Ib.* viii 21 & 65; iv 3; K. Scott 70 ff.

21. Coins: Mattingly dates 81–4; BMC ii 311 nos 61 & 63, also p. lxxxix; Dieudonné says royalty; see Cook *Zeus* i 1914 51; Schlachter 73. Aion: Alföldi (2).

22. Scott 179 f; Ritterling; Parker *R. Legions* 1928 App. Ab; Victorinus, Cohen vi 74 no 58; Carausius, Webb in Matt. *R. Imp. Coinage* vi 2 (1933) 468 & 487.

23. Parker 106 & 263.

24. *Silv.* i 1, 98; *Theb.* i 31 f.

25. Val. Fl. i 682 ff ii 362 ff.

26. Juv. vi 554 ff; iii 41–4; vix 248; vi 406; vi 565 ff; vi 407.

27. II 7, 1 f; cf *Ench.* 32.

28. III 3, 1; Angus 263 f.

29. N (19) 81–4.

30. *Ib.* 85–7.

31. *Ib.* 87–9.

32. *Ib.* 91 f.

33. *Ib.* 89 f. Gold, CCAG i 173, 2 & ii 82, 7; Bacchyl. v 13.

34. *Ib.* 92 f.

35. *Ib.* 93 f.

36. *Ib.* 94 f.

37. *Ib.* 95–7.

38. *Ib.* 28–38; Nock in F ed. of CH ii 319.

39. *Ib.* 97–9.

17. HADRIAN TO THE SEVERI

1. SHA *Hadr.* ii 4; B. W. Henderson *Life & Princ. of Emp. H.* 1923 90 f.

2. Gagé (1) 229 f: N (19) 90 f.

3. CCAG viii 2, 84 f; N (19) 79 f. SHA *Hadr.* xxiii 3 & xxv 8; Dion lxix 17, 1; Cr (1) 176 f.

4. N (19) 108; Cumont CCAG viii 2, 85 n; Dion lxix 17, 1 f; SHA *Hadr.* xxiii 3; xxv 8.

5. SHA *Ael. V.* iii 8 f & iv 5.

6. JL (3) 324 f; Gagé (1) 217–19; Bernard *Inscrs. de Col. de Memn.* 1960 nos 28–31, cf. 32 f. Antinoos: SHA *Hadr.* ii 28 cf. 9 (*sortes*); xix 13 (Col.); Dion. lxix 11, 2 f; Cr (1) 171 f; *Souda sv Hadr.* & *Paidika*; Dion *l.c.* 4; Gregorovius *Der K. Hadr.* 712 f Cf. JL (2) 214 ff.

7. Gagé (1) 226–8. Athenaeum: SHA xvi 8 & 10; Mouseion xx 2; *Vit. Soph.* ii 37, with Julius Vestinus as president CIG no 5900.

8. List in Cr (1) 181 f; Arnuphis, Cr (1) 180; JL (3) 215 ff.

9. Comm. xii 14 & 1; x 20; iv 23; viii 5; vii 48 & 75; v 8, 1. Dreams: i 17, 8 cf. SHA *Marc. Aurel.* v 2. *Comm.* iv 48.

10. Angus 263; *Comm.* iv 40; vii 9; cf. v 21; vi 38.

11. Bayet (2); Simon (1); Gagé (1) 237.

12. Strong 222 f; Simon 154.

13. H. Graeven; Strong.

14. Matz-Duhn *Ant. Bildw. in Röm* 1881 ii 301 bo 3016; Strong.

15. Strong 228 f.

16. Festus-Paul (Lindsay) 89. Rel. to Hadr., Gagé (1) 243 f.

17. Simon (1) 131 f; Dion Chr. *or.* i 84; Derichs; Anderson. Alexander etc., Simon 130 f.

18. Derichs 58.

19. Simon 133; Gagé (1) 239–41.

20. Cass. Dion lxxii 20, 2; Gagé (4) 378; L. Robert (1) 111 n 2; Aymard (2) 549.

21. Lamprid. *Vit. Commod.* xi 8. An enigmatic medallion, Gnecchi *Riv. It. Num.* 1907 379.

22. Grabar 141 f.

23. Suet. *Gaius* xxv; Plin. xxxiv 82; Suet. *Nero* xliv.

24. Aymard (1) 361–4. For H. festivals: Aymard 364; Gagé (1) 291 n 24 & 239–42.

25. For Hercules sarcophagus, early part of C.'s reign, with 8 or 12 labours including the Amazon exploit: ILN 3 April 1963 Arch. no 2131.

26. *Zonai:* Damaskios *de Princip.* 96, cf. 130, and Prokl. *in Plat. Parmenid. comm.* 494 s; *zonaioi*, Damask. *ib.* 206. Apollo statue: Eisler (2) i 96; Seyrig *Syria* xviii 1937 24 f fog. 16; Glueck 212; *Exod.* xxviii 15–21; *Rev.* i 13; xv 6; xxi 19.

27. SHA i 6–10 Dion lxxvii 11, 1 f; SHA ii 8 f; iii 4 f; i 8 f; Dion lxxiii 1; Herodian ii 9, 3–5.

28. Dion lxxix (lxviii) 40, 4–6.

29. Philost. *Vit. Soph.* ii 30 (32); SHA *Geta* i 5.

30. SHA *Geta* ii 6 f.

31. SHA *Sev.* iv 3.

32. SHA *Comm.* xvi 1; Herod. i 14, 1.

33. Herod. ii 9, 2 ff; SHA v 1; Dion lxxv 3, 1 ff.

34. Dion lxxvii (lxvi) 11, 1; lxxiv 14, 4 f; Herod. i 14, 1.

35. Dion lxxiii (lxxii) 23, 1–5.

36. Dion lxxvii 8, 1 ff.

37. SHA *Sev.* xv 4 f.

38. Simon 133; Gagé (1) 271.

39. SHA Sev. xix 5 & 24; xxiv 3 f.

40. Dombart; SHA Sev. xix 3; opened 203 from inscr., Jerome A.D. 201 is wrong. SHA *Geta* vii; *Sev.* xix 24.

41. Dombart (2); E. Maass (4); Huelson (1) & (2); Petersen; Picard (1). Sculpture: L'Orage.

42. Picard (1) 79; Amm. Marc. xv 7, 3. Canina: *Edifizi di Roma Ant.* iv 1856 266 ff, and Lubke. Reigel *Das Haus der sieben Zonen* 1898; J. Durm *Baukunst* fig. 472; Dombart.

43. CIL viii 14372; 2657 (JRS xl 1950 60–2); 2658. A. Audollent *Carth. rom.* 316 ff; S. Gsell *Mons. ant. de l'Alg.* i 241–3. (For site near Basle, Picard 82.)

44. Picard 82 ff.

45. *Ib.* 90 ff for full discussion including origins.

46. Gagé (1) 236; Dion lxxiv 14, 5.

47. Dion lxxviii 11, 1; Cr (1) 211. For variants Septizodium & Septidonium, Picard 78 f & 89.

48. Dion lxxvii 11, 1; Dion knew him well personally. Gagé (1) 234.
49. Herod. iv 12, 3; Dion lxxix 4, 1–4. Herodian says that after a court at Carrhae he was setting out for Moon temple, some days' journey. For more on the age: Gagé (1) mages 211; Egypt 271 f; Balbill. descendant 324.
50. Gagé (1) 216 f; 268 & 269 n 3.
51. C (2) 25 ff; Gagé (1) 361–4.
52. SHA *Carac.* v.
53. Gagé (1) 254; 264 n 86. Egypt see n 49 above; Gage 271 f (Carac.) & Aymard (2) 45 f, 175, 178, 546 f.
54. Gagé (1) 348 n 57 f.
55. SHA *Diad.* i 2; *Macr.* iii 4–7 & *Diad.* ii 6–10; Dion lxxix 19, 1 ff; Herod. v 3, 1 (Fate).
56. C (16) 262 n 77 for rel. to stargods; Herod. v 6, 4; SHA *Macrin.* iii 1 f; Pert. iv 2; starqueen Herod. v 6, 6; ded. to Jup. Serapis and Fortuna Caelestis: CIL xiii 7610 (Marienhausen). Apulum; *Lat.* xxiii 1964 473–82.
57. Herod. v 3, 2 f & 3 f; Dion lxxix 30 2–4.
58. Herod. v 3, 4 & 5–7; SHA *Eleg.* iii 4 f; Dion lxxix (lxviii) 11, 1; Herod. v 5, 7; O. Butler *Studies in Life of Heliog.* 1908 75 ff.
59. Dion. lxxx 8, 1 & 11, 1; Herod. v 6, 9.
60. Dion *l.c.* 12, 1; Cr (1) 226 f with refs.
61. JL *Romans were Here* 320 f; Merlat *Rep. Dolich.* no 273. Corbridge has *iussu dei.* Dea Syria: CIL vii 759. The deds. are explained as evidence of official army-cult (Domaszewski *Die Relig.* 52) but the ded. here could hardly have stood on the parade ground. Dea Syria also at Catterick. Julia Domna as Mater Castrorum rep. on handle of trulla in Capheaton hoard. Also Marlborough cameo: JRS 1957 267. In general, Cook *Zeus* i 604 ff; iii 1897 ff. Venus Caelestis at Puteoli: Carcopino (3) 61 f, cf. CIL x 1596.
62. Dion. lxxx 17, 2 f; SHA *Sev. Alex.* xxvii 7–10; Cr (1) 229 f.
63. Dion lxxx 17, 2 f; SHA *Sev. Al.* xxvii 7–10 & 5 f; xliv 4 (higher educ.). He gave lecture-rooms to teachers, rhetoricians etc., astrologers, engineers (*mechanici*), and free rations to students.
64. SHA xiii 1 & 5 f.
65. Cr (1) 230; his two visits to Alex., Gagé (1) 271 f.
66. Gagé (1) 251 f & n 78.
67. Gagé 250 & 263 n 74, rel. to prophet Alex. 263 n 75; Glykon and serpent of Olympias.
68. Gagé (1) 254 & n 85.
69. SHA xxx *Tyr.* (end of Quietus); Gagé (1) 284.
70. N (19) 54 f; Gagé 248; H. Stern (2).
71. H. Stern (2).
72. Also *Mél. Piganiol* 597.
73. Simon 134–41; L. Homo; coin, Matt.-Syd. *Imp. RC, aur.* 38; Derichs 100. Rel. to Mithras, Simon 150 f; Matt. (1). *Paneg. Lat.* i, 11 (Galletier) i 1949, cf. 2, 14; Epikt. ii 16, 44. H. & Sun; Simon 154 f; Plout. *de Is.* xli; Porph. In Euseb PE iii 11, 25.
74. Jul. *C. Herakl.*
75. Cumont *Textes et Mons. Mithras* i 49 n 5.

18. HOROSCOPES AND ASTROLOGERS

1. N (19) 99–101.
2. *Ib.* 101–3.
3. *Ib.* 104–6.
4. *Ib.* 107–8.

5. *Ib.* 108–11 & 118.

6. *Ib.* 111–13.

7. *Ib.* 113 f.

8. *Ib.* 114 & 125.

9. *Ib.* 116–18.

10. *Ib.* 119 f.

11. *Ib.* 122 f.

12. *Ib.* 38 & 123–6.

13. *Ib.* 126–8 & 39–46.

14. *Ib.* 47–51 & 128–31.

15. Cumont CCAG viii n 1 & RE i 2422 no 24 (Riess), Suppl. 1, 90 (Cumont), Suppl. 5, 2 (Kroll). Porph. CCAG v 4, 223, 18. Palchos, CCAG i 80, 24; v 1, 205, 14; i 107, 4, 13; vi 64, 14, 23, Rhetor. ii 188, 23; viii 1, 242, 15 f; Lydos CCAG i 81, 8; Anon. *ib.* ii 44 f 111 & *de Ost.* ii (W. 6).

16. N (19) 186 f; M. Wellmann, *Die pneum. Schule* 13. Date: Riess (6) and Kroll (6) 2.

17. N (19) 176 f; Hombart: Tables, N (19) 179 f.

18. N (19) 184 f.

19. Cr (1) 190 n 376; Kroll (2) 301, 14 ff; 329, 15–17.

20. CCAG. v 2, 143; Valens, Kroll 172, 3 ff.

21. Cr (1) 184 f. Shadowy figures, *ib.* 138.

22. Dreyer 192.

23. Cohen Drabkin 122 f.

24. B (15) & (25).

25. *Tetrab.* i 2. Also B (16) 133 ff for parellels and basis in Poseidonios (whom the Germans tend to overdo). *Aporrhoia*: *Tetr.* i 24 & Robbins on P. Mich. 149 col. iii 33.

26. *Tetr.* i, 2, 8.

27. *Ib.* i 3, 11 f, cf. i 3, 11 & 13.

28. *Ib.* i 3, 15; BL 5517–20.

29. Palchos CCAG i 108–113; Kroll (18) esp. 126 thinks Dorotheos, cf. B (28) and CCAG vi 91.

30. *Thesauroi*: CCAG i 142. General: Roess (5); Kroll (6) 2; C (15). Frags. Cr (1) 287 n 330; CCAG vii 107–28; i 42 ff.

31. CCAG i 80, 24; v 1, 205, 14; *Math.* ii 29; CCAG viii 2, 104 ff.

32. B (19); Porph. *Isag.* xxxviii (194), CCAG v 4, 210, 6 ff. Porph. & Antioch: Kroll (6).

33. D.L. pr. 2; Riess (2) 1796 f; B (27). Verses: ed. J. R. Harris 128–60; Cr (1) 185 more refs.

34. CCAG viii 1, 147, 10–22; against attrib., J. Heeg, *ib.* v 3, 124 n 1 & Heeg (1).

35. CCAG vi 92 ff; Palchos *ib.* vi 67 ff; Rhet. *ib.* i 146 & vi 91. Probably 5 books, but Antiochos once cited Bk. XI: Kroll (18); Kuhnert. Arabs: Cr (1) 186.

36. CCAG viii 2, 89 & 2 ff; Kroll RE Suppl. 3 1918 414 says between 50 & 300.

37. Lequeur; Kind; Cod. Laur. 73, 1 (142 v); Wellmann *Hermes* 1900 367. Horoscope: Garnett; Cr (1) 186. Sources: Kroll (19). Anoubion: Kroll (7) & (20). Petosiris: Darmstedt (2).

38. Ziegler 53 f cf. 15, 38 f, 64, 67, 81 f. Thorndyke (1) & (3) i 525 & (4); Boll RE vi 2365. Correspondences: *Math.* iii pr. 2.

39. Graubard 78–80.

40. *Math.* ii 30, 3.

41. CT ix 16, 1 f (A.D. 319), see later CT ix 16, 7 (364); *Lex Visigoth.* vi 7, 3; Zos. iv 3, 2 f. Maternus: ii 30, 10.

42. *Math.* ii 30, 10 & 30, 2.

43. *Math.* i 10, 14.
44. *Math.* ii 30, 6.
45. Thorndyke (3) i 538; Liban. *de Fort. Sua* xxv–xxx; Eunap. 131. Mac-Mullen (1) 135 f; Ammian. xxix 1, 29–32; Zos. iv 13 f; Hopfner (3) ii 144; Ammian. xix 1, 41 & 2, 4.
46. N (19) 187 & 131 f; CCAG viii 2, 86, 21–3; Cr (1) 190.
47. N (19) 187; Bidez (2) ii 209–224 (Zor.).
48. Anon: CCAG v 1, 194 f & 204, 18 (mistaken by Cumont).
49. N (19) 187 f; Cumont CCAG v 1, 219–26; C (21) 43; B (10) 15. Egyptian: C (21) 44 f. Rhetor., CCAG i 152, 9–16. Julian of Laod. C (32).
50. N (19) 188 f; Mogenet (1) 1–33 on Eutokios.
51. N (19) 190; CCAG ii 182, 2. Usener took as the Neoplat., *Kl. Schr.* iii 1880 247–322; Cumont rejects, CCAG ii 181; BL 371; Theophanes *Chronog.* i 512 (Classen 1839).
52. C (1) 138.

19. WRITERS, MAGICIANS, AND HOROSCOPES

1. *Mor.* 145 bc & 416 f–417 a; eclipses, 164 e to 171 f; riddles 409 cd (*End of Oracles at Delphi* xxx); 838 c, sphaira astrologike, celestial globe (Schlachter). Barrow 95 ff, providence; 86 ff daimons—also Merlat 60, cf. Apuleius, ib. 71 f on stars as visible gods: fr. 23 Rose & *de Deo Soc.* xv.
2. Hobein ed. 1910 58–60; Zeller (2) iii 2, 219–25; Christ *Ges.* vii 2, 21; E. de Faye *Origène* 1927 ii 154–64.
3. Merlan 81.
4. SHA *Hadr.* xvi 8–20; xv 11–3; Christ *l.c.* 764–6; Schmid (1) & (2); Amand 96 ff on tale of Ath. highpriesthood; Philostr. VS i 8 (490); fatalism, A. Gell. xiv 1; Cr (1) 197 f. Suits, A. Gell. xiii 1, 4.
5. Ptol. i 3, 10; Arnim; Amand 120 n 4; Euseb. PE iv 3 & vi 8.
6. Ed. J. Willian 1907; Amand 118 n 1; Epicureans, Caster 84–90; AJA 1970 51–62.
7. Moraux; Gercke (2); Norrisson; Amand 135 ff; Zeller (3) iii 1, 817–30; Duhem (2) 302; Bruns ii 2, 165 & 225; Wilpert 269–71.
8. Cr (1) 119 f; *Mixture and Growth* xi (Bruns ii 2, 225); Merlan 117 ff.
9. Mette (2); Zeller iii 1, 796–8; Euseb. PE v 19–36 & vi 7, 1–42; Vallette 27–68.
10. Louk. *Demonax* v; arguments with Favor. xii; smoke xxxix. Louk. *Apolog.* viii; Amand 110 f.
11. Kraus & Waltzer, *C. Plat. med. aev.*; *Plato Arabus* i 1951; H. O. Schroeder *Corp. Med. Gr. Suppl.* 1 1951; G. Sarton (2).
12. Thorndyke (3) 178 f; Gal. *de Meth.* ix 5; 14; 17; x 1, 5; xi 1, 9; 14; xiii 3.
13. Kuhn xi 798; xiv 285 & 298; xii 357; ix 769–94; xix 529–73; xix 530 & 533; Cr (1) 189.
14. Kuhn xiv 285; ii 357; xiv 298; ix 769 ff; omens ii 29.
15. Kuhn xix 529 ff, esp. 530 & 533; Cr (1) 189 f.
16. *Enn.* ii 3, also ii 9, 8, 35 f; ii 1 (40) 4, 6–13. Merlan 120.
17. *Comm. in Sc. Som.* i 19, 27; Angus 265; *comm.* i 19, 19–26; i 19, 27; Plot. ii 3, 3, 7 etc.
18. Vollgraff; Haas (1) & (2); von Arnim (2); Hartenstein; Cr (1) 203–5. Sextus: v 1 f; 4; 7 f; 12 f etc. In chamber: v 71.
19. Sextus: 88 ff; cf. Aug. CD v 7 etc. Nemesianus: *Chase* 157 ff; 203 ff. Varro has *signum candens* LL vii 14.
20. Gundel H. G. & Turcan (4).
21. Macr. *Sat.* i 18, 10.
22. Lexa ii 138, demotic spell of London and Leyden.

23. *Ib.* 139.
24. Tables in H. G. Gundel 21–3.
25. Macr. *Sat.* i 21, 9. Goes on about Hilaria.
26. Varro LL vii 16. List in Gundel 53 f.
27. Astrologic doctrines in magic papyri, Gundel 65–70. Example: Lexa ii 150.
28. Lexa 137.
29. Basic astrol. representations, Gundel 70–4; mentions of authors and works 74–8; image of world 78–82.
30. Lexa i 163. For Alchemy: JL (1). Gundel has app. on representation of child on lotus between two falcons under great winged solar disk.
31. Eitrem (1): Deonna (2). Mars: BL 143 n 3; 184; 190; 191 n 2 f; 535; Saglio-Pottier *sv* Zod. 1062; RE *sv* Skoprios 602; Macr. *Sat.* i; Manil. ii 433. Ishtar: Deonna (2) 27 n 7 & Amiet 113–15. Scorpion guards sun from times of Gilgamesh epic. It lifts its pincers to sky to uphold stars; the bust of the scorpion-man reproduces the same attitude. See Toscanne for satyr-scorpions, demon-scorpions, scorpion-griffins 193, 197 f. In Greek astral myth he bites and kills Orion and Panopeus. For part in Mithraic cult: Deonna 31. For Shadrafa or Satrapes (found in Greece, Paus. vi 25, 5 f): *ib.* 30 f.
32. Cf. Hippolyt. *Ref.* iv 15–26; CCAG x 101; 171; 192; 211 & 228.
33. Delatte (4) 268–70. Also 270–4, moon; no 248 Aphrodite.
34. Delatte (4) 274–6; PGM xiii 175. Heart: Sauneron BSFE xxxii 1961 47 and Mel. Mariette 235.
See Delatte further: Kronos as harvester 196 ff; solar themes, ch. iv sun in boat, sun as cosmic charioteer or rider, and lion etc. Lion no 316 f.
Exorcists: L. Delatte 142–4; *Acts* xix 13 & PGM iv 3019; for names of power Delatte 139 n 2. Seven Heavens: Pradel 21, 20; PGM, P 10, 15; heaven of heavens PGM iv 3060; Sun, Pradel 64 & Damask. *Life Isid.* lvi "Rays of the sun and the God of the Hebrews." *Rev.* iv.
35. N (19) 52–6.
36. *Ib.* 56–73 & 131 f.
37. *Ib.* 73–4 & 132–42.
38. *Ib.* 142 f.
39. *Ib.* 74 & 144.
40. *Ib.* 145 f.
41. *Ib.* 164 f.
42. *Ib.* 148 f.
43. *Ib.* 149 f.

20. PAGANS AND CHRISTIANS

1. Ammian. xxii 9, 14; Bidez, *Vie de l'emp. Julien* 274 ff.
2. Frazer, *Adonis*; W. Baudisson *Adonis und Esmun* 124.
3. Atallah 20.
4. Theok. xv 143; Ammian xxii 9, 15; Manil. i 401–6; C (33) & Syria 1935. Atallah on feasts of Andalusian Saints Justus & Rufinus.
5. Theophr. HP ix 1, 6.
6. Macr. *Sat.* i 21 start.
7. Vermaseren (3) 27–30 & (2) 179 ff; cf. mosaic at Sentinum MMM ii 419 f; Englemann AZ xxxv 1877 9 ff.
8. Ward Perkins 198; Seyrig (2); Curtius.
9. Seyrig 239–41.
10. Seyrig *Syria* xiii 1932 55 n 7. Hatti: Weidner, *Polit. Dok. aus Kleinasien* 33 1.54; Cilicia, Lidzbarski *Ephem. f. semit. Epig.* 3, p. 64; cf. II *Kings* xxiii 5.

11. *Syria* xiii 1932 59; Seyrig (2) 256.

12. Du Mesnil 137; *Mel. Univ. St. Jos.* xxxviii 1962 14–59.

13. *Syria* vii 1926 331 pl. 65.

14. Seyrig (2) 258 fig. 5. Star of Bel: Jastrow (7) i 144 f; Jeremias 176; Gressmann (2) 120.

15. En-Nadim *Fihrist* 4. Planets: B (3) 3rd ed. 48.

16. Varro LL vii 14; B (10) 186; Cumont DS *sv* Zod. 1050 b; Wuilleumier (2); Gundel RE *sv* Libra 116 f. No horoscope: Seyrig (2) 259 f. For Dome in general: JL (2).

17. *Ap. of Tyana* i 25.

18. Gagé (1) 204 f & 211 suppl. note; Mouterde (1) & (2); Gagé 210 n 40.

19. Gagé ch. iv for rel. to "wands".

20. Glueck.

21. Site, Glueck 73 ff; account 412–5; two new years, n 710; full analysis of each side, 45 ff.

22. Roscher *Lex.* iii 1, 1468, fig. 26. *Pan*: All, the whole.

23. Glueck 433, pl. 49 a, n 748.

24. *Ib.* 434 n 749, pl. 49 b.

25. *Ib.* 451, n 807–11.

26. *Ib.* 451 n 813, see also n 812. Triadic form: 453–67; Helios 454; eagle and serpent 479 ff; morning & evening stars 464–8; Tyche as moon 397; Baalshamin 409.

Atlas: Bunnens 392 n 1; medallion 392 n 3 f; portraits 393–6; globe 391; genii 397; caryatid 396 with refs.; coptic exs. 399; Brundisi disc 401 n 3; list in Gundel n 2. Argive relief: 401 f; dolphins 403; Truth 403; *Pistis* 404.

Globe: E. Baldwin Smith 53–7; Brendel; Schlacter (1); Alföldi (3). For Hellenistic rulers, Smith 109 & 112; emblem of *kosmokrator*: C (2) 27 f & Hombert (2). Herculaneum: Lehmann, *Art Bull.* 1945 xxvii fig. 67; Corbridge: JRS 1941 xxxi 100; *Bonn. J.* 1928 cxxxiii 155; JHS 1915 xxxv 198; J.M.C. Toynbee, *Art in R. Brit.* 1962 172 (scene of recipients of cult at a temple, Delos). See Smith and JL (2) for more on *ciborium* etc. Brading: Toynbee 202. For another astronomer, perhaps Anaximandros, from Trier: K. Parlasca, *Die röm. Mosaiken in Deut.* 1959 pls. A, fig. 1; 28, fig. 2. For Genius of Year holding zodiacal circle on African mosaics: Foucher 138 f.

27. Campbell 44 f.

28. *Ib.* 47 for refs. For ex. of Aion cult zodiac-encircled globe and snake of Eternity: L. Deubner *R. Mitt.* 1912 xxvii.

29. *De Antro* vi. Also vii–ix.

30. *Ib.* xxii–xxiv; *Iliad* v 608—see JL *Clashing Rocks* 272 & 362. Campbell 54 f.

31. Campbell 66–9.

32. *De Antro* xxix; Campbell 66 ff.

33. Campbell 260, 383 & 385; *de Antro* iv 16; Bundahisn i 49.

34. Euseb. PE i, 10, 31; G. Contenau (3) 949; Plout. *de Is.* 359 b & 368 c; moon, 368 c & 372 d. Campbell 71 f.

35. Serv. *Aen.* vi 714 & xi 52; cf. *Poimandres*. Take in qualities: Stob. i 77 (Wach.); Scott *Hermet.* i 532; Angus 259.

36. Campbell 196; 272; 275.

37. *Ib.* 26. Julian *Hymn to Sun*. This was briefly cited earlier without analysis.

38. Merlat (2) 9–24; C (16) 104 f; Toutain ii 67; A. H. Kau *de Jovi Dol. Cultu* 1901 13–19. *Aeternus*: RA xi 1888 185–7; RE i 69; C (16) 268 n 107.

39. Merlat no 291. Triad = Saturn: Jastrow (6), cf Palmyrene triad, C (34). Caduceus: R. Cagnat, *Mus. de Lambèse* 55 ff. See JL (1) on Caduceus as spine and conducting post between heaven and earth.

40. Merlat no 65, see p. 25 n 4 and index for Bolt.

41. No 152. DS *sv* Juno 674. For Jup. Columns: Cook *Zeus* iii 57–93; P.

Lambrechts *Contribs. a l'étude des divs. celt.* 1942 64 ff; Strong JRS 1911; for planets, Duval in *Gallia* xi 1953; *ib.* 1956 par. 33; 47 (Bavai). Also F. Benoit, *Les Mythes de l'Outre-tombe* (Lat. iii 1950); C. Picard *Karthago* iv 1953.

42. Dieterich (2) i 1 ff; Bousset (3) 223 ff. *Pistis* xv–xvi; *Rev.* xii; Clem. Alex. *Excerpt. ex Theor.* lxviii–lxxviii. Epikouros 2, 93 & 113.

43. Prudent. *apotheosis* 615 ff.

44. Thorndyke (3) i 411.

45. Athenasios found in *Job* a proof of planetary houses: in Petr. v, 1, 25.

46. Origen *in Joh.* i 35 (Brooke i 48); in Euseb. PE vi 11.

47. Doresse 270; Thorndyke (1) 402.

48. See summary in F (1) i 38–40 and app. II.

49. See JL (1) 38, 162, 179; *de Idol.* ix.

50. *Word of Truth* i 6; v 6; viii 66.

51. *Instr.* i 7; see JL (4) on date etc.

52. *C. Cels.* viii 31; ii 51 & i 24; v 45; i 59 (mages); i 6 and i 38.

53. Euseb. Quaest. cxxiii, 1 (Souter 314, 13 cf. 81, 91) and cxv 50 (S. 334, 10).

54. *Conf.* vii 6 & iv 3; in gen. CD Bk. v. Cited: CD v 7, cf. *Epist. classis* ii, ep. lv (PL ii 210).

55. H. Leclerq *L'Espagne chrét.* 155; Babut, *Priscillien* 279–82 tries to rebut the charges.

56. De Mirmont 29 ff; C. Jullian *Ausone et Bordeaux* 9–11; *Parentalia* iv.

57. *Epit.* chs. xxvi, xxviii, lxxi–ii; see further JL (4).

21. TWO POETS

1. Rose in Loeb ed. i p. xvi; Stegemann 122 ff.

2. *Dionys.* vi 82.

3. Erman (2) 92 ff; Gardiner, *The Admonitions of an Egyptian Sage* 1909.

4. Erman 279; *Rec. de Trav.* ii 116.

5. Pyr. Text utterance 254.

6. *Dionys.* i 94. For idiom JL (2) last two chs.

7. *Ib.* ii 165 ff.

8. JL (4).

9. Rose i 42 f.

10. Astral watch, ii 170 ff.

11. *Dionys.* vi esp. 229 ff; 249 ff.

12 *Ib.* 58 ff; Stegemann 88–94. Lenzen 22 f; hymns, Matz 760; C (16) 191; Nonnos xxxviii 80–2. Architecture: Pope; Ackerman 833 f & 869 f; E. B. Smith.

13. N (19) 135 f; L. J. Rosan, *The Philosophy of Proclus* 1949.

14. *On the Hieratic Art.* see earlier ch. xi n 42 here.

15. Delatte (5); Asmus (1–3); N (19) 140 f; RE xviii 3, 409 ff.

16. Palchos CCAG i 107 f; vi 66, 16 to 67, 7; N (19) 147 f; BL 514 f. Cumont (CCAG i 107) says L. was crowned at Tarsos; for dates N (19) 148 n 24.

17. Asmus (3) 1038.

18. *Chronogr.* ed. Classen 201 204 (CSHB xxv).

19. Delatte 73–5.

20. Palchos CCAG i 100 f cf. vi 63 n 1.

21. Gerstinger; Loeb. *Sel. Pap.* iii no 140; Graindor; Barner; Schissel; Maass (4) & (5); Korte; Horna; JL (2) 362. Page is cited from Loeb ed. For genre, Buecheler RhM xxx 2878 57 & 73; Reichel *Quaest. Progymn.* 1909 89. For Theagenes: *Souda* and Photios; for eagle cf. Julian *ep.* xv.

22. Bared girl: cf. figures like Vatican *Gabinetto delle Maschere* 433; v. Amelung *Vat. Kat.* ii 696–8; Brendel *die Antike* vi 41–64.

22. CONCLUSIONS

1. *The Art of the Soluble*, P. B. Medawar 1967 105.
2. J. Singh *Modern Cosmology* 1970 49.
3. *Ib.* 205.
4. G. Wald in *Penguin Science Survey* 1968 33–8; cf. W. A. Fowler *Nuclear Astrophysics* 1967 and in *Procs. Am. Philos. Soc.* lii 1964 524–48; H. Reeves in *Stellar Evolution* ed. R. F. Stein and A. G. W. Cameron 1966 83–122; J. L. Greenstein *Am. Scient.* xlix 1961 449–73 and *Procs.* lii 1964 549–65.
5. *Times* 3 April 1970.
6. B. H. Smith *New Scientist* 42 1969 37.

Bibliography

Aaboe, A., *Centaurus* iv 1955 122–5. Ackerman, P., in A. U. Pope, *Survey of Persian Art* i 1938. Africa, T. W., *Science and the State in Gr. & Rome* 1968. Alfoldi, A., (1) *Bull. Soc. roy. Lettres de Lund* no 1 1953 (2) *Hermes* 1930 lxv 373 (3) *RMitt.* 1935 l 118–201. Allbright, JAOS liv 1934 118–23. Allegro, J. M., (1) JSS ix 1964 291–4 (2) *The Sacred Mushroom and the Cross* 1970. Allen, E. B., JAOS 1947 lxvii 267. Allen, W., TAPA xlii 1941 18. Amand, D., *Fatalisme et la Liberté dans l'ant. Gr.* 145. Amiet, P., *R. d'Ass.* 1956 1. Anderson, A. R., *Harv. St. Cl. Philol.* 1928 7–58. Anson, L., *Num. Gr.* 1916. Archibald, R. C., *Outlines of the Hist. of Maths* (6th ed: suppl. *Am. Math. Monthly* 56 no 1, 1949). Armstrong, A. H., as Merlan. Arnim, von H., (1) RE v 1905 778 (2) 2 Reihe ii 2 1923 2058. Asmus, R., (1) *Byz. Zeit.* 1913 xxii 320–47 (2) *ib.* xviii 1909 467 ff (3) *Das Leben d. Philos. Isidoros v. Damaskios* 1911. Atallah, W., *Adonis* 1966. Aymard, J., (1) REL 1936 361 (2) *Essai sur les Chasses rom.* 1951.

Bagrow, L., *Geografiska Annaler* 1943 318–87. Bakir, Abd el-Mohsen, ASAE 1948 xlviii. Balsdon, J. V. P. D., *Life and Leisure in Anc. Rome* 1969. Barber, C. R., xliii 237. Bardon, H., *La Litt. lat. inconnue* 1952. Barnett, R. D., (1) *Elements or.* 143–3 (2) *Cat. Nimrud Ivories* (3) *Iraq* ii 1935. Barrow, R. H., *Ploutarch and his Times* 1967. Barth, F. (with Goedeckmeyer), *Die Stoa* (5th ed.) 1941. Bauer, T., JNES 1957 xvi. Bayet, J., (1) REL 1939 141–71 (2) MER 1929 1 ff. Beckmann, F., *Zauberei u. Recht in Roms Fruehzeit* 1923 1928. Berger, H., *Gesch. d. wiss. Erkunde d. Gr.* (2nd ed.) 1903. Bidez, J., (1) *Eos ou Platon et l'Orient* 1945 (2) with Cumont, *Les Mages hellénisés* 1938 (3) *Mél. Capart* 1935 41–89 (4) *Bull. Lettres Ac. roy. Belge* xix 1933 195–218, 273–319 (5) *Mél. P. Fredericq* 1904 9 ff (6) *Mél. Cumont* 1936 85–100. Bilfinger, G. (1) *Die Zeitmesser d. ant. Völker* 1886 (2) *NJ Philol u. Pädog.* liv 1884. Birt, T., RhM 1914 lxix 342–92. Blecher, C., *De Extispicio Capita Tria.* Boer, E., *Ptol. op. omnia* 1940. Boissier, A., (1) *Docs. assyr. rel. aux présages* (2) *Procs. Soc. Bibl. Arch.* 1902 xxiv 229–33 (3) *Choix de textes rel. à la Divination ass.–bab.* 1905. Böker, R., *Die Enstehung d. Sternsphäre Arats* (*Ber. Sachs. Ak. Wiss.* xcix 1952). Boll, F., (1) Bibliog. by K. Meister *NJf Wiss.* i 1925 329 f (2) *Kleine Schr. z. Sternkunde des Alt.* 1950 (Bibliog. xxv ff) (3) with Bezold and Gundel, *Sternglaube* etc. (4th ed.) 1931 (4) *J. f. kl.Alt.* 1908 xxi 103–26 (5) *Mem. d. sc. Ist. de Bologna* 1920–3 v–vii 1 ff (6) RE xi 1922 1928 no 4 & 1930 (7) RE 1912 vii (*hebdoma*) 2547–78 (8) *Z. f. Assyriol.* 1911 xxv (9) *in.* 1913 viii (10) *Sphaira* 1903 (11) ZfAS 1901 xxxix (12) with Bezold, *Aufsaetze z. Kult. u. Spra. vornehmlich d.Orients*, E. Kuhn *gewidmet* 1916 226–35 (13) *Archiv* i 482 ff (14) in A. Laudien, *Gr. Pap. aus Oxy.* 1912 (15) *Stoicheia* i 1914 4 ff (16) *Studien ueber Cl. Ptol.* in *J. f. kl. Philol.* Suppl. 21 1894 (17) with Bezold, *Sitz.-Ber. Sk. Heidel.* vii 1911 (18) with Bezold and Kopff, *Zenit u. Aequator. am bab. Fixtsternhimmel, Sitz. d. Heidel. Ak. d.*

Wiss. (ph-kl.) 1913 no 11 (19) *Z. f. Gymnasielschulwesen* 1911 lxv (20) RM 1900 lv 219 f (21) RE xi 1921 843 f (22) *A. f. Relig.* 1910 xiii 475–8 (28) *NJ f.d.kl. Abh.* 1913 xxxi 89–146 (23) *Wochenschrift f. kl. Phil.* 1913 xxx 919 f (25) *Sitz. Bayer. Ak.* 1899 (26) *Z. f. neutest. Wiss.* 1917 xviii 40–8 (27) RE Suppl. i 1903 155 (28) RE Suppl. 3 1918 412 (29) as (17) no 1910; no 1 1911 (30) with Bezold, *Hémérologies et ménologies d'Assur* 1939 (31) *Das Kalendar des Antiochos* (32) RE 1912 xv 309 f (33) *Aus der Offenbarung Johannis (Stoicheia* i 1914) (34) *Vita Contemplativa* 1922 (35) CCAG vii 129–51 (36) *Archiv f. Relig.* 1916–19 xix 342–6 (Kronos-Helios). Bonnet, H., *Reallex. d. aeg. Relig.* 1952. Bouche-Leclerq, A. (1) *L'Astrologie grecque* 1899 (2) *Hist. de la Divination* 1882. Bousset, (1) with Gressmann, *Der Religion d. Judentums,* 2nd ed. (2) *Himmelsreise d. Seele* 1904 (3) *Hautprobleme.* Bowman, R. A., *Am. J. Semit, Lang.* 1939 lvi 237 ff. Brandon, S. G. F., *Creation Legends of the Anc. Near East* 1963. Breasted, *Development of Religion & Thought in Anc. Egypt* 1912. Brecht, C., RE xix 1 1937 615–39. Bréhier, E., *Les Idées philos. et relig. de Philon,* 2nd ed. 1925. Brendel, O., *RMitt.* 1936 li 1–95.

Caminos, R., *Osorkon Chronicle.* Campbell, L. A., *Mithraic Iconog. & Ideology* 1968. Capelle, P., *De luna, stellis, lacteo orbe animarum sedibus* 1917. Capelle, W., *Hermes* 1925 lx 373–95. Carcopino, J., (1) *Rencontres de l'Hist. et de la Lit. rom.* 1963 (2) *La Basilique pythag.* 1943 (3) *Aspects Mystiques* 1943. Caster, M., *Lucien et la Pensée relig. de son temps* 1938. Cerny, J., ASAE 1943 xliii 179 f. Chabas, F., (1) *Le Calendrier des Jours fastes et néfastes de L'Année Egypt.* 1870 (2) *Oeuvres diverses* iv. Cherniss, H. F., *The Riddle of the Early Academy* 1945. Christ, W., xx *HB kl. Alt.,* 6th ed. 1924. Ciaceri, E., (1) *St. Stor. per l'ant. cl.* iii 1910 1–30 (2) ii 1909 377–415. Cichorius, C., (1) RhM 1927 lxxvi 102 ff (2) *Röm. Stud.* 1922 390 ff. Clarke, J., *Seneca, Physical Science* 1910. Clere, J. J., (1) *Kêmi* 1949 x 3–27 (2) JNES 1950 ix 143–52. Cohen, M. R. (I. E. Drakkin), *Source Book in Gr. Science* 1948. Colin, J., *Riv. di fil. e di istr. class.* 1951 xxix 92–144. Colson, F. H., *The Week* 1926. Contenau, G. (1) *La Divination chez les Assyr.* 1940 (2) *La Médecine en Ass.* 1938 (3) *Manuel d'arch. or.* Cook, R. M., JHS 1946 lxvi 67–98. Craig, *Astron. & Astrol. Texts.* Cramer, F. H., (1) *Astrology in Rom. Law & Politics* 1954 (2) *Class. et Med.* 1951 xii (1–2) 14–7 (3) *Seminar* 1952 x 49 ff (4) *ib.* ix 1951 ix 24–31 (5) *J. Hist. of Ideas* 1945 vi 2, 157–96. Cullandre, *La droite et gauche dans les poèmes homeriques.* Cumont, F., (1) Bibliog. A. & L. Delatte. *Ann. philol. orient.* iv pp. vii–xxxi 1936 (2) *L'Egypte des Astrologues* 1937 (30 see Bidez (2) (4) *Lux Perpetua* 1949 (5) *Astrol. and Religion among Grs. & Rs.* 1912 (5a) *ib.* 1960 (6) RHR 1920 lxxxii 229–40 (6) *Ac. des Inscrs.* 1909 xii 447–79 (7) *Bull. Ac. Belge* 1909 256–86 (9) *NJ f. d. kl. Alt.* 1911 xxvii 1–10 (10) RE 1896 ii 111 no 114 (11) *R. de Philol.* 1918 xlii 85–108 (12) CRAI 1918 225 f (13) *Mél.* Bidez 1934 ii 135–56 (14) as (9) (15) RE Suppl. 1 1903 92 (16) *Les Religions Or.* 4th ed. (17) *Klio* 1909 ix 263–73 (18) *Mystères de Mithras* (MMM) 3rd ed. 1913 (19) as (1) i 1934 135–56 (20) *Inscrs. du Pont* (21) MER 1918–19 xxxvii 33–8 (22) *Antiochos d'Athènes* (23) *Recherches sur le symbolisme fun. des Rom.* (24) AC 1935 iv 5 ff (25) *Recherches sur le Manichéisme* (26) DS *sv Zodiacus* 1059 (27) *Bull. Inst. hist. belge de Rome* 1935 xv 119–31 (28) *After Life* (29) *Mem. Acad. Inscr.* 1913 xii 2 474 (30) *Mus. Belge* 1910 xiv 55–60 (31) CRAI 11 Sept. 1942 (32) *Bull Ac. roy. de Belge Cl. Lettres* 1903 554–74 (33) *Mél. Glotz* i 157–64 (34) *Syria* 1928 ix 101 ff (35) *Etudes syriennes.* Cuntz, O., *Stromateis* 1909. Curtius, L., *R.Mitt* i 1935 348–53. Czwalina, A., *Arithmetik d. Diophant. aus Alex.* 1952.

Dahlmann, RE Suppl. 6, 1935 1255 ff. Daiches, S., *Bab. Oil-Magic in the Talmud.* Darmstadt (1) *De Nechepsonis-Pet. isag. questiones* 1916 (2) *Quaestiones apotelesmaticae* 1916. Delambre, *Hist. de l'Astron. anc.* 1817. Delatte, A. (1) *Etude sur la litt. pythag.*, publ. *Binl. d. Hautes Etudes* Paris 1915 (2) *Mél.* H. Grégoire 1949 145–77 (3) *Herbarium* 1961 (4) with Derchain, *Les Intailles mag. gr.–eg.* 1964 (5) *Bull. Cl. Lettres, Ac. roy. Belge* 5th s. 1923 ix 58–76 (6) *La Vie de Pythag.* 1922. Delatte, L., *Une Office byz. d'Exorcisme* 1957. Delcourt, M., *Hermaphorodite* (Eng. version) 1961. Deonna, W., (1) with M. Renard, *Croyances et Supersitions de Table* 1961 (2) *Mercure et le Scorpion* 1959. Derchain, P., (1) as Nougayrol (1) 147–55 (2) *Pap. Salt 825*, 1965. Derichs, W., *Herakles Vorbild des Herrschers in d. Ant.* 1950. Detienne, M., *La notion de Daimon chez les Pythag.* 1963. Diehl, E., *Proklos, in Plat. Tim. comm.* 1906. Diels, H., (1) *Frag. d. Vorsokr.* (2) *Doxogr. gr.* 1879 (*placita*) (3) *Antike Teknik* (3rd ed. 1924) (4) *Archiv f. Gesch. d. Philos.* ii. Dicks, D. R. (1) JHS 1966 26–40 (2) CQ 1959 294–309 (3) *Geog. Frags. of Hipparch*, 1960 (4) *Early Gr. Astron. to Aristotle* 1970 (5) *Hermes* 1963 xci 67 f. Dieterich, K. (1) *Abraxas* (2) *Angelos.* Dieudonne, *Mél. Numismat.* 1909 i 1–9. Direnne, E., *Les Procés d'Impiété.* Dobrovolsky, (1) *Astron. News Letter* ciii 1959 (2) *Bull. Soc. fr. de Num.* Jan. 1962 115. Dobschütz, *Christian Life in Prim. Church.* Dodds, E. R., *The Greeks and the Irrational* 1959. Domaszewski, A. v., (1) *Archiv f. epigr. Mitt.* 1892 xv 182–93 (2) xvii 1 1894 34 (3) *Ber. Ak. Heidel.* 1916 7 & 1920 13. Dombart, T. (1) RE ii *Reihe* 2 1923 1578–86 (2) *Das Palat. Septizonium* 1922. Doresse, J., *The Secret Books of the Egyptian Gnostics* 1960. Dornseiff, F., *Das Alphabet in Mystik u. Magie* (*Stoicheia* 7) 2nd ed. 1925. Dörrie, H., *Der Königskult d. Antiochos in Komm.* 1964 (fasc. 60, *Abh. Ak. Wiss. Gött.*). Drachmann, A. G., *Centaurus* 1950 i 117–31. Dragendorff, H., with E. Kruger, *Das Grabmal von Igel* 1924. Drecker, J., *Die Theorie d. Sonnenuhren* 1925. Dreyer, J. L. E., (1) *Hist. of Planetary Systems* 1906 (2) reprinted as *Hist. of Astron.* 1953. Drower, E. S., *The Book of the Zodiac* (Mandaian) 1949. Duhem, P. (1) *Systéme du Monde* 1913 (2) ii 1914. Dümmler, *Akademica.*

Eberling, E., (1) *Briefe aus Uruk* (2) *Tod u. Leiben* i 1931. Eecke, P., *Diophante d'Alex.* 1926. Eilers, W., JNES 1948 vii 106–110. Eisler, R. (1) *The Royal Art of Astrology* 1946 (2) *Weltenmantel und Himmelszelt* 1910 (3) *Chemikerzeitung* 1925 no 83 (4) *Rev. de Synth. hist.* xli 1925. Eitrem, *Symb. Osl.* 2928 vii 53 ff. Engelbrecht, A., *Hephaistion von Theben* 1887. Enking, R., *Mitt deut. arch. Inst. Rom.*, *Abt.* lxvi 65–96. Erichsen, C., *Abh. Mainz* 1956 2. Erman, A., (1) *Zaubersprüche f. Kind u. Mutter, Berl. Pap.* 3027, 1901 (2) *Lit. of Anc. Eg.* (Blackman) 1927.

Falkenstein, A. von, as Nougayrol (1) 45–68. Farringdon, B. (1) *Greek Science* 1949 (2) *Faith of Epicurus* 1967. Faulker, R. O., *The Anc. Eg. Pyr. Texts* 1969. Ferrero, L., *Storia del Pitagorismo nel mondo rom.* 1955. Festugière, A., (1) *La Révélation d' Hermés* T. (2) *Rev. de Philol.* 1947 lxxiii (3) *Hermes Trismégiste* (4) *Mél. Cumont* 1936 85–1000. Finet, A., as in Nougayrol (1) 97–93. Fossey, C., *Textes assyr. et bab. rel. à la divination* 1905. Fotheringham, J. K., (1) *Quellen u. Stud. B* ii 1939 39 (2) *Observations* no 703 (1932) 338 (3) JHS 1919 (4) *ib.* 1925 (5) *Monthly Notices R. Astr. Soc.* 1924 lxxxiv 383 (6) AJA xxi 55 ff. Foucher, L., *La maison de la Procession Dionysiac à el Jem* 1963. Frank, E., *Plato u. sie sogennanten Pythagoraeer* 1923. Frankfort, H., (1) *Mem. 39 Eg. Explor. Soc.* 1933 (2) *Before Philosophy* 1949. Frits, K. v., RE xix 2351–66. Furlani, J., *Aeg.* July 1929 25 ff.

Gadd, C. J., (1) as in Nougayrol (1) (2) *Ideas of Divine Rule in Anc. East* (3) in Wolley *Alalakh.* Gagé, J., (1) *Basileia* 1968 (2) *Bull. Fac. Lettres Strasb.*

1954 xxxiii no 3 151–68 (3) *ib.* Dec. 1952 (4) *R. Hist. et Philol. Relig.* 1933 (5) *ib.* 1954 342–72 (6) *Mél. Cumont* i 1936 151–87 (7) RA 1930 xxxii 19 ff. Gandz, S., *Procs. Am. Acad. Jewish Research* 1949 xviii 213–54. Garnett, with Downing, *J. Philol.* 1894 xxiii 238–40. Geffcken, (1) *Hermes* 1914 xlix 321–51 (2) RE 1927 xiii 1777–85. Gercke, A. (1) *J. f. kl. Philol. Suppl.* 14 1885 (2) RE i 1894 1435–5 no 94. Gerstingen, *Sitz. Ak. Wiss. Wien, P.–H. Kl.*, 1928 208. Getty, R. J., (1) CQ 1941 xxxv 17–22 (2) TAPA 1960 xci 1960 310–23. Ghalioungui, P., *Magic and Medical Science in anc. Eg.* 1963. Gillings, R. J., *The Math. Teacher* 1962 lv 61–9. Ginzel, F. K., *HB math. u. techn. Chronologie* ii 1911. Gisinger, F., *Stoicheia* 1927 viii 107 ff. Glueck, N., *Deities and Dolphins* 1966. Goetze, A., (1) JCS 1957 xi 111 (2) xvi 1962 28 (3) *Kleinasien,* 2nd ed. 1957 (4) *Bab. Omen Texts* 1947 (5) JCS i 203–66 (6) JAOS lix 12. Gossmann, *Planetarium Bab.* (Deimel, *Sumer. Lex.* iv) 1950. Grabar, A., *L'Emp. dans l'Art byz.* Graeven, H., *RMitt* 1913 xxviii 271 ff. Graindor, *Byzantion* iv 469. Graubard, M., *Astrology and Alchemy* 2953. Grenier, A., (1) *Les relig. étrusque et rom.* 1948 (2) Lat. v 297. Gressmann, H., (1) *Die hellenist. Gestirnrelig : Der alte Orient* 1925 (2) *Alt or. Texte.* Griffith, F. L. (1) *Z. f. aeg. Spr.* 1900 xxxviii 81–5 (2) *Hieratic Pap. from Kahun & Gurob* 1898. Griffiths, J. G., (1) *The Origins of Osiris* 1966 (2) *Conflict of Horus & Seth* 1960. Grube, G. M. A., *Plato's Thought* 1935. Gundel, H. G., *Weltbild u. Astrol. in d. gr. Zauberpap.* 1968. Gundel, W., (1) RE 1922 xi 1143–93 (2) *ib.* 2 *Reihe* vi 1 1936 581–4 no 7 (3) *Abh. Bayer Ak. Wiss (p.–h.)* 1936 xii (4) *Dekan u. Dekansternbilder* 1936 (5) *J. d. Charackterologie* iv 1927 (6) RE v 2 1934 1132–4 (7) *Sterne u. Sternbilder im Glauben d. Alt.* 1922 (8) *De Stellarum Appellatione* 1907 (9) *Astrologumena,* with H. G. Gundel in Sudhoff, *Archiv, viert. f. Gesch. d. Med. etc. Beiheft* 6 (10) *Neue Texte des H.T.* 1936 (11) RE ii *Reihe* 5 *halb* 1927 348 (12) *Bursians J.* 1934. Guthrie, W. K. C., *Aristotle on the Heavens* 1945.

Haas, L., (1) *Programm d. Gymn. Burghausen* 1883 (2) *Ueber d. Schriften d. Sextus Empir.* 1883. Hahn, L., *De Censorini Fontibus* 1905. Halkin, L., *Rev. belge Philol. et Hist.* 1932 121–30. Hallock, R. T., JNES 1950 237–52. Hanfmann, G. M. A., (1) *The Seasons Sarcoph. in Dumbarton Oaks* 1951 (2) *Roman Art* 1964. Harder, F. (*Astrognost. Bemerkungen*) *Progr.* 1893. Harper, R. F., *Assyt. & Bab. Letters.* Harris, J. R., *Annotations of Cod. Bezae* 1901. Hartenstein, C., *Z. f. Philos.* 1938 xciv 217 ff. Hartman, L. F. JNES 1962 xxi 25–37. Hartner, W., JNES 1965 xxiv 1–16. Harward, J., *Epinomis of Plato.* Haussoulier, B., (1) *Rev. de Philol.* xxxv 1909 (2) REG 1919 xxxii 256 f (3) *Klio* 1909 ix 352 ff. Heath, T., (1) *Aristarchus of Samos* 1913 (2) *Manual of Gr. Mathematics.* Heeg, J., (1) *Hermes* 1910 lv 315 f (2) *Die angeblichen orphischen Erga kai Hemerai* 1907. Heidel, A., (1) AJP 1940 lxi 1–33 (2) *The Bab. Genesis* 1951 (3) JNES 1948 vii 98–105. Helm, R., *Philol.* Suppl. 21. Hertz, M., *De Nig. stud. et op.* 1845. Herz, N., *Gesch. d. Bahnbestimmung v. Planeten u. Kometen.* Herzog-Hauser, G., RE 2 *Reihe* vii 2 (1943) 1643 ff. Hilka, A., *Fest. Jahrh. kgl. Univ. zu Breslau* 1911 197. Hirschfeld, O., *Sitz. kgl. Ak. Wiss. Berlin (p.–h.)* (Jul. 1891) 1–35. Hogarth, *Carchemish.* Holtzappel, L., *Klio* xii. Hombert, P., (1) with C. Préaux, CE 1945 xx 139–46 (2) AC 1946 xiv 319–29. Homo, L., *Essai sur la règne de l'emp. Aurélien* 1904. Honigman, E., (1) *Hermes* 1924 lix 477 f (2) *Isis* 1950 xli 30 f (3) *Die Sieben Klimata* 1929 (4) RE Suppl. 4 1924 980. Hopfner, (1) *Klotho* v 1938 (2) RE *lithika* 749, 43 ff (3) *Gr.-aeg. Offenbarungzauber* ii 1924. Horna, *Anz. Wien Ak. Wiss.* 1929 xix 257. Housman, A. E., (1) *J. Class. Philol.* xxii 257–63 (2) CQ 1913 vii 109–114. Huelsen, C., (1) *Das Septizon. in Röm.* (2) *Z. f. Gesch. Archit.* v 1 1912. Hughes, G. R., JNES 1951 x 256 ff. Humann, with Puchstein, *Reisen in Kleinasien u. Nordsyrien* 1890 232–530. Hussey, M. I., JCS 1948 ii 21–32. Huxley, G. I., (1)

Interaction of Gr. & Bab. astron. 1964 (2) *Gr., R. and Byz. Studies* 1963 iv 83–96.

Ideler, *Phys. et med. min.* Ingham, M. F., *JEA* 1969 36–40.

Jacobsen, T., (1) in Frankfort (2); (2) *JNES* 1943 ii 159–72. Jaeger, W., *Aristoteles* 1923. Jahn, C. von, *Philol.* lii 18 ff. Jalabert & Mouterde, *Inscrs. gr. et lat. de la Syrie* (Comm. et Cyrrh.) 1929. Jastrow, M., (1) *Stud. in Hist. of Relig.* to C. H. Toy 1912 143–68 (2) *Z. f. Ass.* 1906 xx 105–29 (3) *Am. J. of Sem. Lang.* 1907 xxiii 95–115 (4) *Z. f. Ass.* 1908 xxi 27–82 (5) *Procs. roy. Soc. of Med.* March 1914 109–76 (6) *R. d'Ass.* 1910 vii 163 ff (7) *Relig. Bab.* 2nd ed. Jeremias, *HB d. altor. Geisteskultur.* Jessen, *RE* viii 62 ff. Jouguet, P., *J. d. Savants* 1926 6–8.

Kaibel, G., *Hermes* xxix 82–123. Keil, J., *Forchs. in Ephesos* iii 1923 127 ff nos. 41–2. Kerenyi, K., (1) *Archiv f. Relig.* 1923–4 xxii 245–56 (2) *Die gr.-orient. Romanlit.* 1927. Kern, O., (1) *Orphic. frag.* 1922 (2) *De Orphei . . . Theogoniis* 1888. Kerschensteiner, J., *Platon u. d. Orient* 1945. Kind, *RE* xix 1928 1, 110 f–2. King, L. W., *J. of Manchester Or. Soc.* 1911 95–8. Kirk, G. S. and J. E. Raven, *Presocratic Philosophers* 1957. Kirchner, J., *RE* xx 1 1941 75. Klauber, E. G., *Polit.-relig. Texte aus d. Sargoniderzeit* 1913. Klein, K., *Quaest. Nigidianae* 1861. Klein, J., *Gr. Math. Thought & the Origin of Algebra* 1968. Koldewey, R., *Das wiedererstehende Bab.* 3rd ed. 1914. Kornemann, E., *Die Alexandergesch. d. K.Ptol. v. Aeg.* 1935. Körte, *Archiv* x 25. Koster, J. W., (1) *Mnemos.* Suppl, 3 1951 59 ff (2) *Le Mythe de Platon.* Krall and Ginzel, *SB Ak. Wiss. Wien Math.-Nat. Cl.* lxxxviii 2 1883 655. Kramer, S. N., *JAOS* lxiii 1943 192–4. Krappe, A. H., *AJP* 1927 xlviii 559–66. Kroll, J., *Hermes* 1915 1 127–43. Kroll, W., (1) with Skutsch, ed. Firm. Mat. *Mathesis* 1897, 1912 (2) *Anthologiae* Vett. Val. 1908 (3) v 2 CCAG (3a) *ib.* vi (4) *Hermes* 1924 lix 474–7 (5) *RE* 2 *Reine* iv 1 1931 563 (6) *RE* Suppl. 5 1931 (7) xiv 1 1928 1102 no 2 (8) Suppl. 4 1924 32 no 68 (9) *NJ f.d.kl. Alt.* 1907 vii 559–83 (10) *RE* xi 1921 1634 no 16 (11) Suppl. 6 1935 1 f (12) xvii 1 1936 210–12 no 3 (13) 2 *Reihe* vi 1 1936 1288 no 9 (14) *Klio* 1923 xviii 213–25 (15) *Die Kosmologie d. Plinius* (16) *RE* xx 1 75 (17) *Philol.* 1898 lvii 123–33 (18) *RE* Suppl. 3 1918 412–14 (19) CCAG v 2 143 ff (20) *Philol.* lxiii 1904 135–8 (21) *RE* 1919 x 15 no 8 (22) *ib.* 15–17 no 9 (23) *RE* iii 1899 2045 (24) x 1919 15 ff (25) xxxiii 208 f (26) ix 802–4. Krumbholtz, *RhM* xli 324 ff. Kubitschek, W. K., *Grundriss d. ant. Zeitrechnung* 1928. Kuebler, *RE* xiv 1 1928 542 ff. Kugler, F. (1) *Sternkunde u. Sterndienst in Bab.* ii 1924. (2) *Die bab. Mondrechnung* 1900 (3) *Ergänzungen.*

Labriolle, P. de, *La Réaction paienne* 1950. Laessoe, J., *People of Anc. Assyria* 1963. Lambert, *JCS* 1962 xvi 59–77. Landsberger, B., *Ankara Fakültesi Dergisi* 1945 iii 150–9. Laqueur, R. E., xix 1 1928 1060–1101 no 1. Laroche, E., (1) *Rev. de Philol.* 1946 lxxiii 118–23 (2) *Rev. hittite et assyr.* 1952 xii 19–48 (3) *Rev. Ass.* 1958 lii 150–63. Lattimore, R., *Themes in Gr. and Latin Epitaphs* 1962. Lefebure, G. (1) *ASAE* xx (2) *Le Tombeau de Petosiris* i 1924. Lehmann, K., *Art Bull.* 1945 xxvii. Lenzen, V. F., *The Triumph of Dionysos on Textiles of Late Anc. Eg.* 1960. Levi, A., *La patera d'argento di Parabiago* 1935. Lewy, H., *JAOS* 1949 lxix 11. Lexa, F., *La Magie dans l'anc. Eg.* 1925. Lindsay, J. (1) *Origins of Alchemy* 1970 (2) *Leisure and Pleasure in R. Eg.* 1965 (3) *Men and Gods on the R. Nile* 1968 (4) *Cleopatra* 1971 (5) *Clashing Rocks* 1965 (6) *Byzantium into Europe* 1952 (7) *Short Hist. of Culture.* Loercher, A. *De Comp. et Fonte Libri Cic. qui est de Fato* 1907. Ludwich, A., *Philol.* 1904 lxiii 116–34. Luckenbill, J. D., *Anc. Records of Ass. and Bab.* ii 1927.

Maas, E. (1) *Aratea* (2) *Comm. in Arat. rel.* (3) *Comm. in Arati et Eudoxi Phain.* (4) *Die Tagesgoetter* 1902 (5) *Gnomon* 1929 50 (6) *Byz. Zeit.* 1934 76. McLean, C. V., *Astrol. and its Rel. to the OT* 1929. Macmullen, R. (1) *Enemies of the R. Order* 1967 (2) *Soldier and Civilian in the Later R. Emp.* 1963. Martin, H., *Ann. di Sc. Math. e Fis. di Tortolini* 1857 viii. Mates, B., *Stoic Logic* 1953. Matz, F., *Ak. Wiss. Mainz, Abh. Geistes & Sozialwiss. Kl.* 1952 no 10. Méautis, G., *Recherches sur le Pythag.* 1922. Meissner, B., (1) *Klio* 1925 xix 432–4 (2) *Bab. u. Assyr.* ii 1925 (3) *Bab.-Assyr. Lit.* 1927. Merlan, P., in *Camb. Hist. Later Gr. & Med. Philos.* 1967. Merlat, P., (1) *Repert. Inscrs. et Mons. Fig. du culte de Jup. Dolich.* 1951 (2) *Jup. Dol.* 1960. Merx, A., *Florilegium M. de Vogüé* 1909 427–44. Mesnil du Buisson, R. du, *Etudes sure les Dieux phénic. hérités par l'Emp. rom.* 1970. Mette, H. J., (1) *Sphairopoiia* 1936 (2) RE xvii 2 1937 2249–51. Mirmont, H. de la Ville de, *L'Astrologie chez les Gallo-Rom.* Mogenet, J., (1) *L'Intro. à l'Almagest* 1956 (2) *Autolykos, De Sphaera* etc. 1950. Monnerer de Villard, *Le Leggende orient. sui Magi evangelici* 1952. Moraux, P., *Alexandre d'Aphrodis.* 1924. Morenz, S. with D. Mueller, *Abh. Sächs. Ak. Wiss. zu Leipzig* (*p.–h.*) lii 1 1960. Mouterde, R., (1) CRAI 1956 45–8 (2) *Bull. Mus. Beyrouth* 1956 xiii 7–21. Mueller, F., *Stilist. Undersuch. d. Epinomis* 1927. Muenzer, F., RM 1914 lxix 625–9.

Neugebauer, O., (1) *The Exact Sciences in Antiquity* 1951 (2) *Vorgreich. Math.* 1934 (3) JNES 1942 xxv 396–403 (4) *Acta Or.* 1938 xvii 169–95 (5) in *Vistas in Astron.* ed. A. Beer i 47–51 (6) with H. O. Lange *Pap. Carlsberg* 1 1940 (7) TAPA 1942 xxxii 209 ff (8) with Knudtzon *Bull. Soc. roy. Lettres Lund* 1946–7 77 ff (9) *Stud. presented to H. Goldman* 1956 292–5 (10) JCS 1953 vii 100–3 (11) *Kgl. Danske Vid.* 1938 f 178 (12) *Isis* 1949 xl 240–56 (13) *Astron. Pap. aus Wien. Samml.* 1962 (14) JEA 1968 with Parkes liv 231–5 (15) with Turner. *Bull. Rylands Lib.* 32 (1) Sept. 1949 (16) *Isis* xxxvii 1947 38–41 (17) *Astron. Cuneiform Texts* 1955 (18) *Procs. Am. Philos. Soc.* 1963 cvii 333 f (19) with H. B. van Hoesen *Gr. Horoscopes* 1959 (20) *Eg. Astron. Texts,* with Parker i 1960 (21) with Volten, *Quellen* etc. *Gesch. d. Math. Astron. u. Phys., Abt B Studien* 4 1938 383–406 (22) JAOS 1943 lxiii 115–27 (23) *ib.* 1950 1–7 (24) JCS 1948 209–22 (25) with Sachs, *Archiv f. Orientforsch.* 1952 xvi 65 f (26) as (21) iii 1936 274. Nilsson, M. P., (1) *Hist. Notes & Papers* xviii 1943 (2) *Primitive Time-Reckoning* 1920 (3) RE 2 Reihe 1 1914 1643 ff (4) HTR 1940 xxxiii 1–8. Norden, *Agnostos Theos* 2nd ed. Nourrisson, *Essai sur Alex. d'Aphrod.* 1870. Nougayrol, J., (1) in *La Divination en Mesopot.* 1966 (xiv *Rencontres Assyr. Internat. Strasb.* 1965) (2) *Rev. Assyr.* xl 73–6 (3) *La Divination,* ed. A. Caquot & M. Leibovici 1968 (4) CRAI 16 Dec. 1955 509–19 (5) *Ann. Hautes-Et.* 5th s. 1944–5 30 ff. Nyberg. H. S., *Journ. Asiat.* 1931 ccxix 1–124, 193–244.

Oder, in Susemihl *Gesch. d. Alex. Lit.* Oefele, von, HERE xii 1921. Olivieri, *Ps.-Erathosthenis Catast.* Olmstead, A. T., (1) JAOS 1926 xlvi 87 (2) *Hist. of Persian Empire* 1959. Oppenheim, A. L., (1) *Letters from Mesopotamia* 1967 (2) *Anc. Mesop.* 1964 (3) as Nougayrol (1) 35–43 (4) *Der Tell Halaf* (5) *The Interpretation of Dreams in Anc. Near East.* Oppolzer, T. R. von, *Canon of Eclipses* 1962. Orange, H. P. l', *Apotheosis in Anc. Portraiture.* Otto, W., (1) *Priester u. Tempel im hellenist. Aeg.* 1905 (2) RE 1912 vii 12–42.

Pallottino, M., (1) *Etruscans* 1955 (2) *Arti Figurative* 1946 149 ff. Pannekoek, A., *Hist. of Astron.* 1961. Parker, H. M. D., *The R. Legions* 1928. Parker, R. A., (1) with W. H. Dubberstein *Bab. Chronology 626 B.C.–A.D. 45,* 1942 (2) *Eg. Calendar* (3) JEA 1957 xliii 86–100 (4) *A Saite Oracle Pap. from Thebes* 1962 (5) *A Vienna Demotic Pap.* 1959. Pascal, C. B., *Cults of Cisalpine Gaul*

1964. Pavlu, J., (1) *Comm. Vindob.* 1936 ii 29–55 (2) *Phil. Woch.* 1936 667–71 (3) 1937 988–92 (4) *Wien. St.* 1937 lv 55–68 (5) *ib.* 1938 27–44. Peek, *Mitt. d. Inst. f. aeg. Alt.* 1934 v 96 f. Perkins, Warde, R. *West and Parthian East.* Petersen, E., *RMitt.* 1910 56 ff. Pfeiffer, E., *Stud. z. ant. Sternglauben* 1916. Pfister, F., *Pflanzenaberglaube* in RE 1454. Phloratos, C. S., *Hē Prophēteiē tou P. Nig. Fig.* 1958. Picard, C. G., *Mon. Piot* 1962 77–94. Picard-Schmitter, M. T., *Mon. Piot* lii 1962 27–75. Piccaluga, G., *Lykaon* 1968. Pieper (1) *Orient. Literaturzeitung* 1927 (2) RE 1925 xvi 2 2160–7. Pietschmann-Pagel, *HB d. Gesch. d. Medizin.* Piganiol, A., *Mél. G. Glotz.* Pingree, D., *Isis* 1963 liv 232. Pitra. *Analecta sacra et classica.* Places, E. des, (1) AC 1942 xi 97–102 (2) *Mél. Cumont* 1936 129–42. Pogo, A., (1) *Isis* xvii (2) *ib.* xviii 1932 (3) *Osiris* i 1936 (4) *Isis* xiv 1930. Pohlenz, M., (1) *Nach. v.d. Gesell. Wiss. Gott.* (*p.h.*) NF *Fachgruppe* (Alt.) ii 1938 (2) RE xviii 2, 2 1949 418–440 no 5. Pope, A. V., *Archaeology* 1957 x 123 f. Porter, B., with R. Moss, *Topical Bibliog. of Anc. Eg, hierogl. texts* vi 1939. Post, L. A., *Cl. Weekly* 1932 xv 109. Pottier, *Mél. Boissier* 405 ff. Pradel, F., *Relig. Versuche* etc. iii 2 1907 8 ff. Preaux, J., *Lat.* 1967 1009–14. Preisendanz, K., RE xviii 2, 1 (1942) 1610–42. Premeı-stein, A. v., *Philol.* 1894; ii 400–15. Price, D. J. de Solla, (1) *Scince since Babylon* 1961 (2) with J. Needhamn *Heavenly Clockwork* 1960.

Raeder, H., *Platonis Epinomis* 1938. Read, F. W., *Proc. Soc. Bibl. Arch.* xxxviii 1916. Reece, B. R., *AJ Philol.* xc 1 no 357 1969 72–4. Rémondon, R., CE 1964 no 77–8 126–46. Rehm, A., (1) *Abh. Bayer Ak* (*p.h.*) 1919 xix 22 f (2) RE 1909 65 f (3) RE xviii 2, 3 1949 1295–1366 (4) RE 2 *Reihe* iii 1929 1154 (5) *Mythograph. Untersuch. ueber Sternsagen* 1896 (6) RE vii 1666 f (7) *Parapegmastudien* (*Abh. Bayer*) 1941. Reinach, T., REG 1890 362–79. Reitzenstein, R., (1) *Hellenist. Mysterienrelig.* 3rd ed. 1927 (2) *Poimandres* 1904. Reymond, E. A. E., *The Myth. Origins of the Eg. Temple* 1969. Riess, E., (1) *Cl. Weekly* xxvii 10, Dec. 1933 73–8 (2) RE ii 1896 1802 ff (3) *Nechesonis et Pet. frag., Philol. Suppl. Bd.* vi 1 1892 327 ff (4) as (3), (5) RE i 1894 2494 no 68 (6) *ib.* 2422 no 24. Ritterling, RE 1925 xxiv 1421. Robbins, R. E., (1) *J. Class. Philol.* 1927 xxii 1927 1–45 (2) Ptol. *Tetrabiblos,* Loeb. Robert, L., *Etudes epigr. et philol.* 1938. Robin, L., *La morale ant.* 1938. Roehig, A., *De Nig. Fig.* 1887. Rogers, R. S., (1) *Criminal Trials . . . under Tiberius* 1935 (2) *J. Cl. Philol.* xxi 1931 203 f (3) CW 1946–7 xxxix 53 f (4) TAPA lxxxii 1951 196–9 (5) lxxxiii 1952 279 ff. Rose, H. J., intro. and notes, Loeb *Nonnos.* Rostovtzeff, M., JEA 1926 xii 24–9. Rusch, A., *Mitt. d. Vorderasiat.-aeg. Gesell.* 1922 1 xxvii 5 ff.

Sachs, A. J., (1) JCS 1947 i 219–40 (2) vi 1952 151–6 (3) *ib.* 49–75 (4) vi 1952 105–14 (5) ii 1948 280 (6) vi 146–50. St. Giet, le Chanoine, *L'Apocalypse et l'Hist.* 1957. Salmasius, *De Annis Climactericis* 1648. Santillana, G. de, *Isis* 1949 xxxiii 248–62. Sarton, G., (1) *Intro. to the Hist. of Sc.* i 1927 (2). *Isis* 1952 xliii no 131 57 f. Schäfer, H., ZAS 1907 lxiv 132 f. Schanz, M., RH 1899 liv 23 ff. Scharff, A., *Hist. Zeit.* 1939 clxi 3–32. Schaumberger, J., *Sternkunde u. Sterndienst in Bab.* (*Erg.* iii. pl. 7 no 14). Schiaparelli, *I Primordi ed i Progressi dell'Astron. presso i Bab.* (*Scientia, div. di Sc.* iii Bologna) 1908. Schissel, *Phil. Woch.* 1929 1073. Schlachter, A., (1) *Stoicheia* 1927 viii 1–118 (2) *Globus.* Schmekel, A., *De Ovid. Pythag. Doctrinae Adumbratione.* Schmid, W., (1) RE vi 1900 2078–84 (2) Suppl. 6 1935 65–70. Schnabel, P., (1) *Berossus* 1923 (2) ZA 1926 iii 1 ff. Schott, A., (1) *Z.d. deut Morgen. Gesell.* 1934 lxxxviii (2) *Quellen u. Stud. Gesch. Math.* B4. Schrader, H., *Warburg Vörtrage* 1928 viii 99 ff. Schwabe, J., *Archetyp u. Tierkreis* 1951. Schwartz, E., (1) RE iii 1899 309 no 4 (2) iii 1894 1025–7 no 7. Scott, J. F., *Hist. of Maths. from Antiquity* 1958. Scott, K., *The Imperial Cult under the Flavians* 1936. Seyrig, H., (1)

Syria 1950 xx 189 ff (2) 1933 xiv 254. Simon, M., *Hercule et le Christianisme* 1955. Smith, E. Baldwin, *Archit. Symbolism of Imp. Rome & Middle Ages* 1956. Smith, S., AAA (Liverpool) xi 107–14. Snyder, W. F., JRS 1936 12–18. Sollberger, E., *Archiv f. Orient.* xvi 1953 230. Solmsen, F., TAPA 1942 lxxii 192–213. Spiegelberg (1) *Sitz. Ak. Heidel* no 3 1922 1 ff (2) *Aeg. Zeit Bd.* 48 146 (3) *Or. Lit.-Zeitung* 1902 v 6–9 (4) *ib.* 223–5. Stahl, W. H., TAPA lxxiii 1942 232–58. Stapleton, H. E., *Ambix* 1957 vi 1–9. Stegemann, V., *Astrologie u. Universal Gesch.* 1930. Stein, A., (1) RE 1949 xviii 2, 2 303 no 6 (2) RE ii *Reihe* 2 1923 1248 no 29 f (3) PIR ii, 2nd. ed. 1936 (4) *ib.* i 2nd ed. 1933 (5) *Aeg.* 1933 xiii 126–36, 331 f (6) RE 1919 1083 no 144 (7) *ib.* 159–63 no 159 (8) RE i 1894 135. Steinmetz, P., *Hermes* xciv 1966 450–82. Stemplinger, *Ant. u mod. Volksmedizin.* Stern, M., (1) *Calendrier de 354* (2) *J. des Sav.* Jan.–March 1965 117–31. Straaten, M. van, *Panétius* 1946. Strachan-Davidson, *Problems of R. Criminal Law.* Sudhoff (1) *A. f. d. Gesch. d. Naturwiss.* 1909 xi 471 ff (2) *Iatromathvornehmlich* 1902. Suter, *Die Math. u. Astronamen d. Araber* 1900. Suys, E., *Vie de Petosiris.* Swoboda, A., ed. of Nig. Fig. frags. 1889.

Tallqvist, K., *Akkad. Götterepitheta* 1938. Tannery, P., (1) *Recherches sur l'hist. de l'astron.* 1893 (2) *Notices et Extracts de MSS* 1886 (3) *Mém. scientifiques.* Tavenner, E., *Studies in Magic from Latin Lit.* 1916. Taylor, A. E., (1) *Proc Br. Ac,* xv 1929 (2) *Comm. on Plato's Timaeus* 1928. Thausing, G., *Die Auferstehungsgedanke in aeg. relig. Texten.* Theile, W., (1) *Schr. d. Konigsb. Gel. Ges.* 1942 1 xviii (2 *Ant. Himmselsbilder* (3) *Gnomon* 1931 vii 337–55. Thievens, A., *Astrol. in Mesopot. Culture* 1935. Thomas, I., *Selections illustr. Hist. of Greek Maths.* Thomson, G., (1) *The First Philosophers* 1955 (2) JHS 1943. Thompson, R. C., (1) *Proc. Soc. Bibl. Arch.* 1912 xxxiv 227–33 (2) *Reports of Magicians and Astrologers of Nineveh & Bab.* 1900. Thorndyke, L., (1) *J. C. Philol.* 1913 viii 415–35 (2) with Kibre *Cat. of Incipits* 1937 (3) *Hist. of Magic and Exper. Sc.* i (4) CP 1913 viii 415–35. Toscanne, *R. d'Ass.* xiv 1917. Toutain, J., *Les cults paiens dans l'emp. rom.* Turcan. R., (1) *Lat.* 1968 392–405 (2) *Les sarcoph. rom. à rep. dionys.* 1966 (3) *Lat.* 1964 42–35. Turner, E. G., see Neugebauer (15).

Ungnad, A., (1) *Arch. f. Orientsf.* xiv 251 (2) *Subartu* 1936. Usener, H., (1) RM 1905 lx 465–91 (2) *Kl. Schriften* 1914.

Valette, P., *De Oenomao Cynico* 1908. Vermaseren, H. J., (1) *Mithras the Secret God* 1963 (2) with C. C. van Essen. *Excavs. in Mithr. of Church of Santa Prisca* 1965 (3) *Legend of Attis in Gr. & R. Art* 1966. Veyne, P., *Lat.* 1964 xxiii 802–6. Virolleaud, C., (1) *Babyloniaca* 1907 i 192 (2) *Ann. Univ. de Paris* 1933 408 ff (3) *La Légende phén. de Daniel* (4) *L'Astrol. Chald.* 1908–12. Visscher, F. de, *Mél. Piganiol* 1966 761. Vogt. J., *Die alex. Muenzen* i 1924. Voigt, W. V., *Philol.* 1899 lviii 170–204. Vollgraff, W., *R. de Philol.* 1902 xvi 195 ff. Vreese, J. de, *Petron. 39 u.d. Astrologie* 1927.

Waerden, van den, (1) *Proc. Kon. Ned. Ak. v. Wetensch.* 1947 536 ff, 782 ff (2) JNES 1949 viii 6–26 (3) *ib.* 1951 x 20–34 (4) AfO 1953 xvi 216 ff (5) with Pritchett BCH 1961 42–4 (6) AfO 1963 xx 98 (7) *Jaarboek Ex Or. Lux* 1948 x 424 (8) JHS 1960 (9) *Die Anfange d. Astron.* 1965. Wageningen, v., RE xiv 1 1928 1118–33 no 6. Wainwright, G. A., (1) *Sky-Religion in Egypt* 1938 (2) *Griffiths Studies* 375. Walcot, P., *Hesiod and the Near East* 1966. Walden, J. W. H., *The Universities of anc. Greece* 1909. Wasserstein, A., JHS 1955 114–16. Waterman, L., *Roy. Corr. of the Assyr. Emp.* 4 vols. 1930–6. Webb, E. J., (1) JHS 1921 70 (2) 1928 54 (3) *Names of Stars* 1952. Weidner, E. F., (1) AfO 1942 xiv 172–95 & 308–18 (Enuma-Anu-Enlil) (2) 1954 xvii 71–89

(3) *Am. J. Sem. L.* 1924 xl 188–208 (4) AfO xvi (5) *Babyloniaca* 1912 vi 130 ff (6) *Alter u. Bedeutung d. Bab. Astron.* 1914. Weinreich, (1) *Die Trug d' Nektanebos* 1911 (2) *Ant. Heilungswunder* 1909. Weinstock, S., (1) JRS 1946 xxvi 101 ff (2) CP 1958 liii 91–9 (3) JRS 1946 xxxvi 101–29. Wellmann, M., (1) RE 1905 v 773–6 no 45 (2) *Hermes* 1919 liv. Wendland, P., *Philos. Schrift ueber d. Vorsehung* 1892. Weninger, L., *NJ f.d. kl. Alt.* 1971 xxxix 238 ff. Wessely, C., *Denk. Ak. Wiss. Wien* (p.-h.) xlii 2 1893. West, M. L., (1) CQ xiii 1963 154–6 (2) xvii 1967 1–15. Wiegand, *Forsch. in Ephesus.* Wilamowitz-Moellendorf, U. v., *Reden u. Vortraege* 1925. Wilpert, P., *Hermes* 1940 lxxv 4 369–96. Winlock, H. E., *Proc. Am. Philos. Soc.* 1940 lxxxiii 447–64. Wissowa, RE 1899 iii 1908–10 no 7. Wreszinski, *Schr. d. Koenigsb. gelehrten Gesell.* 1927 iv 2. Wuilleumier, P., (1) MER 1929 184–209 (2) RA 1932 xxxv. Wynghene, H. de, *Uebersicht ueber d. Keilschrift-Lit.* iii 1932 44 ff.

Yates, F. A., *The Art of Memory* 1969.

Zabkar, L. V., *A Study of the Ba Concept in anc. Eg. Texts* 1968. Zafiropulo, J., *Anaxagore* 1948. Zeller, E., (1) *Hermes* 1876 xi 430–3 (2) *Phil. d. Griech.* 4th ed. 1903 (3) 5th ed. 1923. Ziegler, K., (1) RE xviii 2, 1 1942 1400–4 (2) RM 1913 lxviii 336 ff (3) JJKA 1913 xvi 528 ff.

Index

I Gods and Heroes
(see also god-names as planets)

II Rulers

IV Persons
(including Authors and Astrologers)

V General

INDEX